SEARCHI?

The Biography of an Enigma

Born in Ireland in 1879, W.P.M. Kennedy was a distinguished Canadian academic and the leading Canadian constitutional law scholar for much of the twentieth century. Despite his trailblazing career, Kennedy has been a largely mysterious figure. Now, weaving together a number of key events and drawing on Kennedy's personal letters, Martin L. Friedland presents a lively biography of the man. *Searching for W.P.M. Kennedy* discusses Kennedy's contributions as a legal and interdisciplinary scholar and his work at the University of Toronto, where he founded the Faculty of Law. The book also details Kennedy's intriguing personal life, presenting stories about Kennedy's family and important friends, such as Prime Minister Mackenzie King.

Kennedy earned a reputation in some circles for being something of a scoundrel, and Friedland does not shy away from addressing Kennedy's exaggerated involvement in drafting the Irish constitution, his relationships with female students, or his constant quest for recognition. Throughout the biography, Friedland interjects his own personal narratives surrounding his interactions with the Kennedy family, including how he came to acquire the private letters noted in the book. The result is a highly readable biography of an important figure in the history of Canadian intellectual life.

MARTIN L. FRIEDLAND is a professor emeritus in the Faculty of Law at the University of Toronto.

MARTIN L. FRIEDLAND

Searching for W.P.M. Kennedy

The Biography of an Enigma

UNIVERSITY OF TORONTO PRESS
Toronto   Buffalo   London

© University of Toronto Press 2020
Toronto Buffalo London
utorontopress.com
Printed in Canada

ISBN 978-1-4875-0634-6 (cloth)   ISBN 978-1-4875-3392-2 (EPUB)
ISBN 978-1-4875-2525-5 (paper)   ISBN 978-1-4875-3391-5 (PDF)

Library and Archives Canada Cataloguing in Publication

Title: Searching for W.P.M. Kennedy : the biography of
an enigma / Martin L. Friedland
Names: Friedland, Martin L., author.
Identifiers: Canadiana (print) 2020015849X | Canadiana (ebook) 20200158503 |
ISBN 9781487506346 (cloth) | ISBN 9781487525255 (paper) |
ISBN 9781487533922 (EPUB) | ISBN 9781487533915 (PDF)
Subjects: LCSH: Kennedy, W. P. M. (William Paul McClure), 1879–1963. |
LCSH: Law teachers – Canada – Biography. | LCSH: Historians – Canada –
Biography. | LCSH: Deans (Education) – Canada – Biography. |
LCGFT: Biographies.
Classification: LCC KE416.K45 F75 2020 |
LCC KF345.Z9 K45 F75 2020 kfmod | DDC 340.92 – dc23

This book has been published with the help of a grant from the Federation
for the Humanities and Social Sciences, through the Awards to Scholarly
Publications Program, using funds provided by the Social Sciences and
Humanities Research Council of Canada.

University of Toronto Press acknowledges the financial assistance to its
publishing program of the Canada Council for the Arts and the Ontario Arts
Council, an agency of the Government of Ontario.

Canada Council   Conseil des Arts
for the Arts   du Canada

ONTARIO ARTS COUNCIL
CONSEIL DES ARTS DE L'ONTARIO
an Ontario government agency
un organisme du gouvernement de l'Ontario

Funded by the   Financé par le
Government   gouvernement
of Canada   du Canada

Canada

MIX
Paper from
responsible sources
FSC® C016245

Contents

Preface

Several years ago – out of the blue – one of the editors of Oxford University Press Canada sent me an email,[1] asking if I would write the introduction for the republication of W.P.M. Kennedy's groundbreaking study *The Constitution of Canada*, first published in 1922.[2] 'Is this something you might be interested in doing?' the editor asked. I wrote back the same day: 'I am not known as a constitutional law scholar, but I am interested in Kennedy and in Canadian intellectual history. I will get back to you.' Shortly after that, I agreed to write the introduction.

I had a number of interests in Kennedy. He was the first dean of law at the University of Toronto. In 1972, I became the school's fourth dean. As the founder of the law school, Kennedy now holds an exalted – though somewhat obscure – position in the history of the faculty. Studying his career, I believed, would give us a better understanding of the origins and the development of the Faculty of Law and of legal education in Canada.

I was also interested in Kennedy, whom I had never met, because, from my previous research,[3] I had found him to be one of the university's most distinguished, engaging, and enigmatic personalities. His book *The Constitution of*

* I am grateful for the assistance I received on this project from a number of excellent summer research assistants: Stephen Aylward, Keith Garrett, Benjamin Mayer-Goodman, Jenny Mao, Gordon Vance, and Iain Wilson. I was also assisted by many expert readers who saved me from errors and helped shape the manuscript into what I hope is a more readable book. Those who read individual sections or chapters are thanked in the appropriate endnotes. Persons who went over the entire manuscript and to whom I am indebted are Yasmin Dawood, Peter Hogg, Ian Kyer, Patricia McMahon, Christopher Moore, Jim Phillips, Alexander Pless, R.C.B. Risk, Kent Roach, Peter Russell, David Schneiderman, Robert Sharpe, and Lorne Sossin – a who's who of Canadian constitutional and legal history scholars. My wife, Judy Friedland, read an earlier draft and, as always, helped me guide the book to a safe landing. Archivists and librarians throughout the world graciously helped me find research material. I particularly want to thank Harold Averill and his fellow archivists at the University of Toronto Archives and Sufei Xu and her fellow librarians at the law school's Bora Laskin Law Library. As in the past – a period of over fifty years – it was a pleasure working with the University of Toronto Press.

Canada is still fairly well known to students of the Canadian constitution. By the end of the 1920s, Kennedy had written ten books. He was also a sparkling teacher. J.J. Robinette, one of Canada's greatest lawyers, who was taught by Kennedy in the 1920s, recalled that 'Kennedy was one of those brilliant Irishmen who could dazzle you ... a performer as much as a teacher.'[4] University of Toronto president Claude Bissell, who was a student in the 1930s, did not attend Kennedy's lectures, but recalled that his classmates were enthusiastic about Kennedy, of 'whose powers of memory and exposition students spoke with awe.'[5] Future judge Sydney Harris recalled his seminars in the mid-1930s: 'He was a great teacher ... oh, very eccentric ... He had his study on the second floor of the building in which we were ... and there was a couch in the room, and he would sleep on the couch between classes, and he would wake up and lecture to the class without getting up from the couch; most of his lectures were given while he was lying down.'[6] He was often referred to as a 'character'[7] and described himself as 'the last remaining character' in the university.[8]

I had yet another link to W.P.M. Kennedy. In 1983, my wife and I bought the Kennedy family cottage, located north of Huntsville and just west of Algonquin Park, where Kennedy and his wife Pauline – like many academics in those years – spent almost four months each summer, until several years before he died in 1963.[9] He had purchased the cottage on Beaver Lake in 1940, and each summer had his correspondence redirected to the post office in the nearby town of Kearney. He loved the cottage and is buried, alongside his wife, in an Anglican cemetery in the neighbouring town of Emsdale. The cottage came with a collection of his books and two trunks full of letters and documents, which he had accumulated over the summers but did not feel it necessary to take back to the city. I subsequently donated the documents in the trunks that were relevant to Dean Kennedy to the University of Toronto Archives.

One of the most important events in the history of the University of Toronto law school took place at that cottage.[10] Kennedy, a non-lawyer, who had, it seems, never taken a formal course in any legal subject, started the undergraduate 'Honour Law' program between the wars. Graduates received a BA degree from the university but were given no credit by the Law Society of Upper Canada, which operated Osgoode Hall Law School, the only professional law school in the province. Cecil Augustus Wright – usually referred to as 'Caesar' Wright – was a professor at Osgoode and was unhappy with the way legal education was being delivered there. He thought of Osgoode as a 'trade school.'

In 1945, Wright and his good friend and fellow lawyer Sidney Smith, who had just become the president of the University of Toronto, developed a plan to transfer professional legal education from Osgoode Hall to the University of Toronto. One aspect of the plan was that Bora Laskin, the future chief justice of Canada, would leave the University of Toronto, where he had been a student and a professor, and join Osgoode Hall Law School. Then, at an appropriate time, Wright, Laskin, and others, such as John Willis, would leave Osgoode and start a professional law school at the University of Toronto, with Wright as the dean.

The scheme required Kennedy's blessing – or at least his acquiescence. Laskin was one of Kennedy's favourite colleagues. So, one summer day in mid-July 1945, after Caesar Wright had discussed the plan with Laskin[11] at Wright's Magnetawan cottage, Wright and Laskin went to see Kennedy at his cottage on the lake near Kearney. Wright and Kennedy walked along a well-groomed waterside trail, with Laskin walking slightly behind. Laskin left the University of Toronto and went to Osgoode that year. In 1949, as anticipated, Wright, Willis, and Laskin left Osgoode and founded the so-called 'modern law school' at the University of Toronto. The Law Society, however, did not give up its monopoly on legal education. Graduates of the University of Toronto had to spend an extra year at Osgoode until 1957, when the Law Society recognized the University of Toronto law school and other law schools in Ontario were created.[12] Like Kennedy, I keep that path along the lakeshore of our cottage well groomed, and may someday put up a plaque in honour of the event that took place there.

When Kennedy's son Frere sold us the cottage, he knew – but never mentioned – that there was a large collection of letters in some of the trunks. I learned that the cottage was for sale towards the end of the winter of 1983. A notice for the property had been placed in the mailboxes of the law faculty, stating that the family would be happy if the property stayed in the academic community. The property, known by the Kennedys as 'Narrow Waters,' consisted of over 150 acres on a widening of the Magnetawan River. My wife and I went up north to look at the property. There was a heavy layer of snow on the ground. The price was low by later standards, but there had been no buyers because that was the period of very high interest rates and a glut of properties were for sale. We put in a somewhat lower offer, and Frere accepted it. I think he wanted us to have the property, which he believed we would use in much the same way as his family had used it. We have. That first summer I went through the papers in the trunks and kept those related to W.P.M., but destroyed most of those relating to his children. I felt I did not have a right to keep their papers, some of which dealt with personal issues. At the time, I had not considered writing a biography of Dean Kennedy.

When Frere Kennedy visited Narrow Waters the following year, he suggested that perhaps I should consider writing a biography of his father. Again, the papers in the trunk were never mentioned. I said I would think about it. Other projects, however, intervened. Moreover, apart from the papers in the cottage that I had saved, there appeared to be few other papers in existence, making the writing of a biography difficult. Kennedy had destroyed most of his personal papers in Toronto shortly before he retired. The prospect of a biography therefore had little appeal to me at that time. Further, Professor R.C.B. Risk, in his study of Canadian legal thought, had written a brilliant article on Kennedy, published in 1998 and appropriately entitled 'The Many Minds of W.P.M. Kennedy.'[13] It would, I thought, have to stand as the biography of Kennedy.

Writing the introduction to the republication of *The Constitution of Canada*, published in 2014, however, made me reconsider my view about writing a full biography. Kennedy seemed even more interesting than I had thought when I wrote the University of Toronto history. New material kept coming to light. With a bit more digging, I was able to find out much more about Kennedy's early years. There were whole areas that I had barely discussed in the earlier introduction, such as his supposed role in drafting the Irish constitution of 1922, his involvement in ending appeals to the Privy Council, and his participation in both the 1938 Rowell-Sirois Report on the Canadian constitution and several important 1950 federal-provincial conferences. There were also subjects that I had not even mentioned in my introduction. A plagiarism suit against H.G. Wells and the Macmillan Company that ended up in the UK Privy Council was one such event. I had read Brian McKillop's book *The Spinster and the Prophet*, dealing with this lawsuit that Florence Deeks brought against H.G. Wells, but had completely forgotten that Kennedy had played a role in that case.[14] Writing a full biography would enable me to describe the life of a fascinating character.

A biography could also let me discuss the growth of the University of Toronto into Canada's leading university. The year that Kennedy published his major book, *The Constitution of Canada*, was an important year in the history of the university. In early 1922, two important events took place at the University of Toronto: the discovery of insulin and the creation of the School of Graduate Studies. The former established Toronto's international reputation, and many would argue that the combination of the two was the turning point in Toronto becoming the leading university in Canada.[15]

A Kennedy biography would also allow me to expand on what I had said about the development of the law school and the many significant players who were there as students or faculty members, or both. So, it would be both a biography of a person and a biography of an institution. It would also shed light on the development of legal scholarship in Canada and the history of ideas, particularly with respect to constitutional law.

Still, I was wavering. Would there really be enough new material to justify an entire book? I continued to search for material on Kennedy while pursuing another interest: 'truth in the criminal justice system' – mainly centring on proof beyond a reasonable doubt and other standards of proof. I published a couple of articles on the issue of 'truth' and was hard at work looking at fact-finding in law and science in the seventeenth century, with particular emphasis on Lord Chancellor Francis Bacon, known for his interest in both law and science.[16] Thousands of scholars had, however, thought and written about Bacon. Only one or two had written anything about Kennedy. Moreover, I was getting bogged down in studying Bacon and wondered whether I could contribute anything original.

At about that point, I got an email from Barbara Laskin, Bora and Peggy Laskin's daughter. I had asked her to 'jot down some notes' about the Kennedys, telling her: 'Your memories would be important if I do more with the project.' She replied:[17]

> As I mentioned, I was invited to have tea on several occasions, with several of my girlfriends. We would go on Friday afternoon and would be greeted at the door by Mrs. Kennedy. She would read poetry to us in the sitting room – usually something by Pauline Johnson, of whom she was very fond. We sometimes played hide-and-seek – the house lent itself to that, as it was one of those dark, narrow Victorian buildings, with oak paneling and heavy blue velvet draperies between the hallway and the sitting room. Then we would take tea in the dining room – with a plate of homemade cookies prepared by her maid. I would be invited to stay on after my friends left and, as a special treat (!), to go upstairs to see 'the Dean' – she never called him anything else, that I can recall! I would knock very gingerly at the door and would be summoned into the room … I would then sit at his feet while he read excerpts of Shakespeare … There was a kind of hush around the Dean – she clearly revered him and elevated him to a kind of god-like status. I can remember that she kept a brass bell on the newel post at the bottom of the stairs, and used it to summon him to meals. Otherwise, he was not to be disturbed.

After reading this vivid portrait, I decided to abandon Bacon and concentrate on Kennedy. Hence, this book.

One similarity between a study of Bacon and writing a biography is that each raises the question of the search for truth. What is the standard of proof for scientific facts, for legal decisions in civil and criminal trials, and for facts in biographies? Biographers are not limited by the legal rules of evidence, such as the exclusion of hearsay and the rule against using self-serving evidence. Perhaps that is a later project to be undertaken. In the meantime, this book is my search for the truth about the life of W.P.M. Kennedy.

The search requires a discussion in various sections of how I went about finding – or not finding – the source material. Confirming Kennedy's involvement in a particular project normally does not require an extended discussion of how one found the material, but confirming a lack of involvement in a project that Kennedy claimed to have been involved in, but was not – such as his role in helping draft the Irish constitution of 1922 – is trickier and requires more investigation and comment. It is harder to prove a negative than a positive.

I also appear from time to time as a character in the book because of my connection to Kennedy and the law school.[18] The result is a more personal approach
to the presentation of the life of Kennedy than some readers may expect.

~

Kennedy himself was interested in biography. The first biography he wrote was
of a sixteenth-century Anglican bishop, *Archbishop Parker*, which he published
in 1908. In the book's preface, he stated:[19]

> The method which I have tried to follow in this book is twofold. First, an effort
> has been made to work through the various manuscript and printed sources of the
> period, and to approach the subject as it were first hand. Thus I have tried to arrive
> at accurate facts. Second, I have endeavored to eliminate prejudice and to deal
> fairly with all parties. I have, as it were, attempted to throw myself back into the
> period, and to look out on the complicated problems with Parker's eyes.

I have tried to do the same in this book – to 'arrive at accurate facts' and 'to
throw myself back into the period, and to look out on the complicated problems with [Kennedy's] eyes.'

Kennedy considered a large number of Canadian biographies in a review he
wrote for the American journal *The Bookman* in 1919. He called biography[20]
'one of the most fascinating literary forms.' As he explained: 'It shares the movement of the drama, the historical interest of the epic, the seductiveness of the
novel ... From its pages we catch something of that inspiration which belongs
to any phase of human activity, and from which none of us are alienated, to
which none of us are strangers.'

Kennedy also had views on what makes a great biographer. 'A great biographer,' he wrote, 'is no mere chronicler moving in the arid world of facts ... He
is no mere editor arranging the years as a tale that is told. He is all these, but he
is something more. He must possess that historical insight which sees behind
the rounded fact and can trace causes upon causes. He must record activities in
vital and interpretative relationship with the spirit of the age.'

A tall order. This story of W.P.M. Kennedy, I hope, also 'sees behind the
rounded fact,' traces 'causes upon causes,' and comes close to 'the seductiveness
of the novel.'

In 1926, Kennedy wrote a political biography, *Lord Elgin*,[21] about a particularly important governor general of Canada in the 1840s, who brought responsible government to Canada. The book was published by Oxford, and a 1948
UNESCO survey listed it as one of the 100 best Canadian books.[22] Kennedy
wrote in the preface: 'This book has been written in the midst of many other
engagements. I venture to hope, however, that it will present a general sketch of

Lord Elgin's career sufficiently adequate in outline and sufficiently intimate in detail to bring into relief the principles and accomplishments of his life.' I'll take that as my minimum objective – 'to bring into relief the principles and accomplishments of [Kennedy's] life.' But I hope this book goes further and shows the drama of his life as well.

This book is the first biography I have written, although my memoir, *My Life in Crime and Other Academic Adventures*,[23] published in 2007, is, of course, similar to a biography. I have also used a narrative form for other projects, starting with an article in 1981 about a criminal code produced for the British Colonial Office by R.S. Wright, later a High Court judge in England. I found in that case that, by telling a story of his code, I could shed light on the development of the criminal law. I concluded by stating: 'Then, as now, a combination of politics, personalities and pressure groups affected the outcome. The crucial events seem, in retrospect, largely unplotted and accidental.'[24] The same is true in this book.

Timeline

1879 – W.P.M. Kennedy born in Ireland.

1889 – Faculty of Law established at the University of Toronto; shuts down several years later.

1900 – Kennedy graduates from Trinity College Dublin.

1913 – Kennedy comes to St. Francis Xavier College, Nova Scotia.

1914 – Starts teaching at St. Michael's College, University of Toronto.

1915 – Marries Teresa Johnson.

1916 – Starts teaching English at University College and constitutional history in the Department of History, in addition to teaching at St. Michael's College.

1919 – Teresa (Johnson) Kennedy dies.

1920 – Marries Pauline Simpson.

1922 – Moves to the Department of Political Economy at the University of Toronto.

1922 – Publishes *The Constitution of Canada*.

1926 – Starts four-year Honour Law program in the Department of Political Economy.

1929 – Revised Honour Law program developed as a separate division in the Department of Political Economy.

1930 – Law school moves from Cumberland House to 43 St. George Street and in 1935 to 45 St. George Street.

1932 – Canon Henry Cody appointed president of the University of Toronto.

1935 – Kennedy establishes the *University of Toronto Law Journal*.

1937 – Honour Law becomes a separate department in the Faculty of Arts and Science.

1941 – Law becomes a separate division of the university, officially named the School of Law.

1942 – DJur doctoral degree established (becomes SJD degree in 1983).

1943 – Kennedy's title changed to dean.

1943 – Five-year LLB degree established (becomes three-year degree in 1949); renamed JD in 2001.

1945 – Sidney Smith becomes president of the University of Toronto.

1949 – Caesar Wright appointed dean of law and Kennedy retires.

1953 – Law moves to Cumberland House on St. George Street.

1956 – Law moves to the Glendon estate in North Toronto.

1957 – Law program recognized by the Law Society of Upper Canada.

1962 – Law moves to Flavelle House, its present home, on the main university campus.

1963 – W.P.M. Kennedy dies.

SEARCHING FOR W.P.M. KENNEDY

1

Coming to America

On Saturday, 30 March 1912, W.P.M. Kennedy boarded the steamship HMS *Caronia* in Liverpool, bound for New York City.[1] The thirty-three-year-old Kennedy was on his way – second class – to teach at a Catholic high school in Cuba.[2] It is likely that no one was there to see him off. He was estranged from his family, who lived in Glasgow, where his father was a Presbyterian minister. Kennedy's change to the Church of England sometime during his high school or university years must have been a blow to his father, and his later conversion to Catholicism would have driven a further wedge between him and his family.

The coal-burning *Caronia* was one of the Cunard Line's newest ships, having made its maiden voyage in 1905. The brochure for the trip suggests a level of luxury for its over 300 passengers, with – according to the brochure – 'an orchestra of highly trained musicians.' Judging by the passenger list, this vessel was not a ship for immigrants from Eastern Europe escaping to the New World. Nor was it close to the opulence of the White Star Line's newest vessel, the *Titanic*, with its over 1,300 passengers and 900 crew members.

There is, however, a connection between the two ships. The *Caronia* – and no doubt Kennedy – saw icebergs on the voyage to New York. The *Caronia's* captain, J.C. Barr, is today remembered because on the return trip to England he sent a wire on Sunday morning, 14 April, to the captain of the *Titanic*, which a few days earlier had set sail on its ill-fated voyage from Southampton to New York, warning him: 'West-bound steamers report bergs, growlers and field ice.' This wire was the first such warning received by the *Titanic*. There would be others. Shortly before midnight of that same day, 14 April, the *Titanic* struck an iceberg and sank early the next morning.[3] Kennedy had avoided disaster on his trip to America – one more example, as we will see throughout this book, of Kennedy's ability to land on his feet.

The *Caronia* arrived safely at the Cunard docks at West 14th Street in Lower Manhattan. Unfortunately, we know nothing about Kennedy's impression of New York City, with its striking skyline, including the almost completed

sixty-storey Woolworth Building. He did not spend much time in New York
before taking another steamer to Havana. By April, he was teaching in Cuba.
But his stay there was also short. He left Cuba in early September and returned
to the United Kingdom, again via New York City.[4]

The Catholic secondary school, referred to as the 'English College,' located in
a suburb of Havana, was apparently associated with the University of Havana.[5]
English was becoming a more important language after Spain had ceded control of Cuba to the United States following the Spanish-American War of 1898.
Before leaving Cuba, Kennedy got letters of reference from the school. The prefect of studies wrote: 'Mr. W.M. Kennedy has lectured in this College since April
of this year in English Literature and Modern History, and during that period
he shewed himself an efficient and successful member of our staff ... In addition to being an excellent teacher, Mr. Kennedy proved himself to be a thorough disciplinarian, and in point of conduct he was always most exemplary.'[6]

According to the prefect, the reason Kennedy left 'was owing to the climate
being unsuitable.' Temperatures in Havana in June average over 80 degrees
Fahrenheit (27 degrees Celsius). Kennedy, as we will see, had a frail disposition.
But it is likely that, more than the temperature being too hot for Kennedy, there
was the possibility of a civil war. Afro-Cubans rose up in the eastern section of
the country in May and June 1912, demanding equality. Over 5,000 protesters
were killed. In June – the month after Kennedy arrived – the United States sent
1,500 marines to protect US estates and mines in the eastern part of the country. The director of the school pointed out that Kennedy 'is now leaving of his
own accord' and added: 'During the time he has been here, he has shown that
he is an earnest and painstaking teacher and he certainly obtained very good
results from his students.'[7]

St. Francis Xavier College

Kennedy – now in Ireland – searched for another teaching position without
success. In March 1913, Reverend Joseph Darlington, the dean of studies and
professor of English at University College Dublin, a Catholic university, heard
that St. Francis Xavier College (StFX) in Canada was looking for staff. StFX is
in the town of Antigonish, Nova Scotia, just west of the southern part of Cape
Breton Island. Darlington wrote to James Tompkins, the vice rector of StFX,
stating:[8] 'Fr. McNeil S.J. has just told me you seek Tutors. I send you the address
of a brilliant [Trinity College Dublin] man who has been teaching since his
Degree: he has very good testimonials. He recently became a Catholic Convert
and is anxious to go to Canada.'

Father Neil McNeil was the Catholic archbishop of Toronto, who had earlier
been the rector of St. Francis Xavier College and continued to take an interest
in the college.[9]

St. Francis Xavier College, Antigonish, Nova Scotia

For some time, Tompkins had sought to improve the academic standing of the StFX staff,[10] having complained that 'there is no such thing as Catholic Higher Education in the country.' In a letter to Archbishop McNeil in 1912, he explained: 'The policy of getting our professors educated in the most celebrated universities of Europe and America will soon have us supplied with men whose standing cannot be disputed and whose names will be an advertisement for us all over the country.'[11]

Kennedy was at the time living as a guest at Mount Melleray Abbey, a Cistercian monastery in Waterford County in the south of Ireland. He sent his reference letters, including those from the Cuban college, to Vice Rector Tompkins. Most of the references were from Kennedy's own teachers during his time at Trinity College Dublin from 1896 to 1900 and were dated 1900 or 1901. One such letter was from the eminent Shakespearean scholar Edward Dowden, who wrote:[12]

Mr. W.W. Kennedy has terminated a distinguished undergraduate course in Trinity College, Dublin, by winning at his B.A. degree examination in honours, a Senior Moderatorship and Gold Medal in Modern Literature (English and French) [other awards are then listed] ... Such distinctions imply diligence in study as well as ability. I have known Mr. Kennedy not only as a member of my class in English Literature, but in other ways independent of my University duties. He has a zealous and active interest in Literary Subjects; he has been a wide-ranging reader in both English and French Literatures; and he possesses, I think, an aptitude for literary research.

Kennedy cabled the vice rector of StFX on 4 April 1913 stating: 'Darlington advises cable immediately if you want me and when other appointments offering cable passage money.'[13] Whether there were other offers is not known. Likely not. The college offered $1,000 a year plus room and board. On 23 April, Kennedy wrote to Tomkins to say: 'I beg to accept the appointment and to assure you that I shall do my utmost to carry out to your satisfaction the duties of the College.'[14]

Because of the high demand for passage to Canada through Halifax and Quebec, Kennedy had to come through New York. 'I find I shall want a few days in New York,' Kennedy wrote on arrival in New York, 'to look up some Jesuit friends and to buy some things.'[15] As it turned out, he also had to spend a few extra days in New York recovering from the trip. He cabled Tomkins for more money and later wrote on 24 May:[16] 'Thank you so much for the $100 which I got all right after a rather amusing process of proving who I was! I'm off today and I'm real glad to get out of this as the city is packed with tourists for some national festival and everything is at famine prices. I expect to get to you sometime in the middle of the week. I'm coming via Montreal as Cooks advised it saves changes and hotels.'

St. Francis Xavier, named after a sixteenth-century Jesuit missionary to the Far East, had been established on Cape Breton Island in 1853 to train priests for the large number of Catholic Highland Scots who had emigrated to eastern Nova Scotia in the late eighteenth and early nineteenth centuries. The college moved to Antigonish on the mainland in 1855. One of the principal reasons for emigration from Scotland was, as the historian of the college states, because of the 'persecution of Catholics, commonly led by rabid anti-Catholic Presbyterian ministers.' Scottish Catholics composed a majority of the population of eastern Nova Scotia, and there were relatively few priests for this growing population.[17]

Kennedy appeared to be a great success at StFX. Shortly after he arrived, the Toronto *Globe* contained a brief news item on his appointment – perhaps prepared by Archbishop McNeil – under the heading 'A Historian for St. Francis Xavier,'[18] stating in part:

The University of St. Francis Xavier's College, Antigonish, Nova Scotia, is about to add to its staff several distinguished professors, graduates of Oxford, Cambridge and Dublin. One of these has just arrived at Antigonish – Mr. W.P.M. Kennedy, M.A., professor of modern history and English literature. Mr. Kennedy had a brilliant career at Trinity College, Dublin, where he graduated in 1900 with highest honors, gold medal and exhibition. He was a pupil of the late Prof. Dowden.'

The student newspaper, the *Xaverian*, contained a glowing report, stating that 'Mr. Kennedy has won nothing but golden opinions from his students.' Kennedy told the newspaper that he 'studied history under ... the late Prof Stubbs, Oxford.'[19] Did he, in fact, study under the well-known William Stubbs after graduating from Trinity College Dublin in 1900? If so, it could not have been for long, because Stubbs became ill in November 1900 and died in April 1901.[20]

Kennedy became active in the life of the college, academically and socially. He even composed the first college song in 1913. Its chorus went as follows:[21]

> Xavier's, look not backwards. The future is thy goal.
> A new world lies before thee. Strong in its fierce young soul!
> Xavier's, thy quest is onward. Mid Empire newly born.
> Tis thine to move a people's heart, To greet a nation's morn!

Vice Rector Tompkins noted in a letter to the former president of Mount Allison College in New Brunswick that the professor of philosophy at StFX and Professor Kennedy 'are hard at work on a 600 page History of the Catholic Church in Nova Scotia.' Tompkins mentioned with pride in the same letter that 'Professor Kennedy has two books in the press and received the other day another order by cable from Constable of London.'[22]

Two months later, Kennedy was no longer at StFX. What had happened? On 18 May 1914, the rector of the college, Dr. H.P. MacPherson, wrote to a prominent alumnus in Boston, shortly after the closing exercises:[23] 'Our man Kennedy is gone. In spite of his learning he fizzled to nothing in the end. There is a loose screw in his mechanism. Should he show up around Cambridge [Massachusetts] you had better not notice him.'

Vice Rector Tompkins also wrote to his cousin, a graduate of StFX, then doing postgraduate work in Europe:[24]

> I must confess I am getting somewhat skeptical about the training of Oxford, etc. for a man who enters life in this country. They certainly throw a lot of debris on the world, incorrigible, self-centred, useless and insolent. We have had a sad case to deal with ourselves this year. I hope to the Lord that your training will not have rendered you useless when you come up against life in this country.

Tomkins went on:

> The Rector has written you about getting a good graduate in Modern History. I hope you will be able to do something for us ... For Heaven's sake try and get us a decent sober man with a level head. We are willing to pay him a good salary. Men on the other side write testimonials with an extraordinary disregard for facts. The matter of this letter is private and I don't want this repeated. Keep your

eye on Kennedy. He might possibly look you up. Keep clear of him … I wish you would try and find out through the Jesuits who this W.M. Kennedy is. What are his antecedents? You had better do it in a quiet way. I understand he was once a Jesuit novice. He says he studied History at Oxford for a time.

Moving to Toronto

Neither the letter from the rector nor the one from the vice rector indicates where Kennedy was heading. The vice rector appeared to believe that Kennedy would be returning to England. In fact, despite what had occurred in Nova Scotia, in the early summer of 1914 Kennedy had been offered a position at St. Michael's College at the University of Toronto. Archbishop McNeil again came to Kennedy's aid. Father Edmund McCorkell, who taught with Kennedy at St. Michael's and later became the president of St. Michael's, stated in an oral interview in 1974:[25] 'I don't know what happened down there [at StFX] … but McNeil, the Archbishop, who was influential down there … got him to come up here and got Father Carr to take him on the Staff.'

As a former rector of StFX who kept in close touch with the college, McNeil would have been aware of Kennedy's situation. Archbishop McNeil was interested in building up the academic strength of St. Michael's, as was Father Henry Carr, who would become the president of St. Michael's in 1915 and had been the driving force several years earlier in getting the University of Toronto to accept St. Michael's as one of the university's arts colleges, comparable to University, Victoria, and Trinity Colleges.[26]

It is now clear that Kennedy was forced to leave StFX because of a romantic entanglement with one of his students, Sara Josephine Cameron. One of three female students in a class of sixteen who graduated in 1916,[27] Sara lived at Mount St. Bernard, a women's institution, which was – Sara had written in an article on women and education – 'the first Convent School in America to secure affiliation and equal privileges with a Catholic University.'[28] She would have been in her second year when Kennedy taught there. Sara was not, however, just any student. She was the grandniece of the bishop of Antigonish, John Cameron, who had died in 1910. Her grandfather was Bishop Cameron's brother.[29]

While he was at StFX, Kennedy finished and published a book, *Parish Life under Queen Elizabeth*,[30] based on material he had brought with him to Nova Scotia. The title page states that he is a 'Professor of Modern History in the University of St. Francis Xavier's College, Antigonish, Nova Scotia.' There is a dedication page, which states: 'To S.J.C. October 12, 1913.' It is logical to conclude that the book is dedicated to Sara Josephine Cameron. There was obviously some sort of close relationship between the two or the dedication would not have been made. What type of relationship is not known, although it was clearly a serious one.

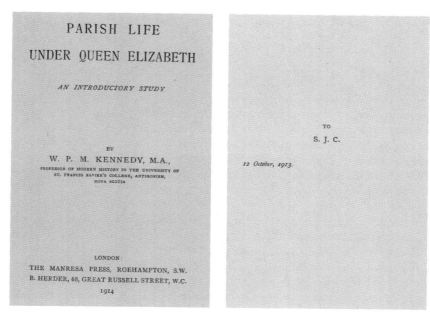

PARISH LIFE

UNDER QUEEN ELIZABETH

AN INTRODUCTORY STUDY

BY

W. P. M. KENNEDY, M.A.,
PROFESSOR OF MODERN HISTORY IN THE UNIVERSITY OF
ST. FRANCIS XAVIER'S COLLEGE, ANTIGONISH,
NOVA SCOTIA

LONDON :
THE MANRESA PRESS, ROEHAMPTON, S.W.
B. HERDER, 68, GREAT RUSSELL STREET, W.C.
1914

TO

S. J. C.

12 October, 1913.

Dedication and title page for *Parish Life under Queen Elizabeth* by
W.P.M. Kennedy, 1914

Kennedy's eldest child, Gilbert Kennedy, a law professor who later became
the deputy minister of justice in British Columbia, gave an oral interview in
1983 in which he states that in 1968 he met a priest, Father J.A. McLellan, who
had been in Sara Cameron's year in 1913–14. The priest asked Gilbert whether
his father had married Sara.[31] This revelation came as a surprise to Gilbert. It
was the first that he or his siblings knew of any such relationship.

Sara was part of a large family. Her father was a farmer in Antigonish County.
There were at least a dozen siblings, all of whom are now dead. She was the second oldest, and she died in 1990.[32] Born in 1893, she would have been about
twenty years old when Kennedy, who was then thirty-four, knew her. I spoke
to a number of Sara's nieces and nephews, who knew about the relationship,
claiming that her father put a stop to it.[33] One said that Kennedy was about to
propose and give her a ring. Another said that he actually gave her a ring. One
nephew said that Sara swore to her father on his deathbed that she would not
marry Kennedy. One relative said that the objection was because of religion.
Another said that it was because he was an Englishman. In any event, the family story is reasonably consistent with what the priest in British Columbia told
Gilbert Kennedy.

It is not difficult to understand why Kennedy would have been attracted to Sara. She was extremely bright. She graduated in 1916 at the top of the class, both male and female, with the highest standings in English literature, French, and history[34] – all subjects that interested Kennedy. She was interested in ideas. The college paper, the *Xaverian*, and the women's convent paper, *The Memorare*,[35] of which she had been an editor, published a number of articles she wrote that fit in well with Kennedy's interests, including one on the future of the British Empire, another on Francis Bacon, and still another on 'conversation.'[36] Her essay 'The Stage, the Press and the Pulpit, Their Comparative Influence' won first prize in the college's annual essay competition. *The Memorare* stated on her graduation:[37] 'We know little of Sara's juvenile career, but her college record was a brilliant one. Throughout her Arts Course her name usually topped the lists and in the senior year she led the whole University class.' The article goes on to say: 'We hoped to see her take up a post-graduate course for which she was so well qualified, but the beginning of the term found her engaged in the work of teaching. It is her intention to seek, like so many of our girls, her fortune in the Canadian West.'

In fact, Sara went west in 1920. She taught in non-Catholic schools in Battleford and Glaslyn, Saskatchewan. In 1936, she became an instructor at the government-run Saskatchewan Correspondence School in Regina, retiring in 1959.[38] Ship records show that she spent parts of two summers in Scotland and England in the early 1920s. She died in 1990 at the age of ninety-six. Her gravestone simply says: 'In loving memory of Sara Josephine, 1893–1990. Forever in our hearts.'[39]

I have been unable to find out anything more about Sara through her church, her retirement home, or the Regina University's Women's Club, of which she was a member. Her relatives remember her various visits to Antigonish. She was very strict, a nephew stated. A niece said that she died with a broken hip, after standing on a chair. She never married.

The official historian of St. Francis Xavier, Professor James Cameron – no relative of Sara – mentions in a footnote in his book on the university, *For the People: A History of St Francis Xavier University*, that Kennedy left in a cloud, but does not mention the Sara Cameron affair.[40] The noted historian P.B. Waite, however, states in his biography of Larry MacKenzie, who taught with Kennedy at Toronto:[41] 'The little college in the little town could not contain Kennedy. He was too hot to handle; if the girls in the St. Bernard residence were not scandalized, the Roman Catholic authorities of the college were. He was unloaded onto St. Michael's College.'

One interesting follow-up exchange of correspondence between Kennedy and St. Francis Xavier occurred in January 1915, six months after Kennedy left StFX,

Sara Josephine Cameron's gravestone, Regina, Saskatchewan

when he was at St. Michael's College. He wrote to the rector of StFX, wishing him a 'very happy and prosperous New Year' and stating: 'I shall always look back on the many happy days there and I shall ever be ready to help you in any way that I can.' Kennedy also wanted to let him know 'that I am getting on very well indeed, although my health is far from good.' The real reason for writing, however, was to ask for an honorary doctorate:[42]

> I write to ask you if St. F.X. could see its way to confer on me causa honoris an LL.D. for my work on Tudor History. There would be no necessity for any publicity at Commencements. It could be conferred at a special faculty meeting in absentia of course. I would deem it a sincere honour and it would help me here and Catholic Education. His Grace the Archbishop [of Toronto] will visit Washington in February and will propose me there for an honorary D. Lit. I would be most grateful if you considered this letter a formal application, and if you can see your way to do me this honour, I should be glad if it could be done at once for the new University Calendar which goes to press on February 1st.

Rector MacPherson replied, stating that he was 'very glad to learn that you are getting along well' and 'regret[s] to learn that your health is not as good as it might be.' On the issue of the honorary LL.D., the rector wrote: 'I have discussed with some members of the Faculty your application for the degree of LL.D., and from the views they expressed I am led to believe that a resolution in favor of granting you an LL.D. would not carry at a Faculty meeting.'[43]

So, who was this popular but unwanted teacher, this failed applicant? Who was W.P.M. Kennedy?

2

Earlier Years

Who Was W.P.M. Kennedy?

Kennedy's early years seem shrouded in a cloud, even his name. Readers may have noticed in the previous chapter that he was sometimes known as W.P.M. Kennedy, sometimes as W.W. Kennedy, and sometimes as W.M. Kennedy. Which is correct?

When I was preparing the introduction for the republication of his *Constitution of Canada*, I could not at first find W.P.M. Kennedy on any of the websites commonly used to search for ancestors. Moreover, the archivist at Trinity College Dublin could not find him in the college records.[1] She wondered whether William Waugh McClure Kennedy could be the person I was looking for. He was.

Sometime after leaving Trinity College Dublin, Kennedy started to substitute the given name 'Paul' for the name 'Waugh.' When or why is not clear. Professor Dowden, as we saw, had used the initials 'W.W.' in his reference letter of 1901. In his first book, *Archbishop Parker*, published in 1908, Kennedy used the initials 'W.M.'[2] But in a volume of poetry, which I found in his library at the cottage, he had written on the inside cover, 'W.P.M. Kennedy, Paris, Xmas 1904.'[3] So, the change was likely a gradual process. By the time he came to Canada, he was consistently using the initials 'W.P.M.'

Where was he born? In Kennedy's various who's who entries, he did not include his place of birth. When he died in 1963, a tribute prepared for the University of Toronto Senate by his friend and former colleague Bora Laskin said that he was born in Shankill Parish, County Dublin, a suburb of Dublin, Ireland,[4] as did another tribute – prepared by his friend, political scientist Alexander Brady – for the Royal Society of Canada.[5] The *Canadian Encyclopedia* also uses that birthplace. To add to the complication, Kennedy put 'Lurgan, Rutland, England,' a village near Peterborough, England, on his marriage certificate in 1920, suggesting that he had told his future in-laws and perhaps even his wife that he was born in England.[6] R.C.B. Risk simply says that Kennedy was born in Northern Ireland.[7]

William Waugh McClure Kennedy was born in Lurgan, County Armagh, Northern Ireland.[8] Northern Ireland was called 'Ulster' in those years. He was born on 8 January 1879 at 'The Manse,' the residence of his parents provided by and close to the church where his father was the Presbyterian minister. A document registered ten days later shows that the midwife was Agnes Sloan of Lurgan. The only place I found where Kennedy noted that he was born in Lurgan, Northern Ireland, was in the passenger list on his first trip to New York in 1912.[9]

Kennedy was the second of ten children, all born in Lurgan. An older sister had been born three years earlier but died in 1883. Seven girls were then born. Kennedy was the only male child for a number of years – with seven sisters. Being an only son growing up with seven sisters must have played a role in his development, but I have not been able to contact any of his siblings or their children. The last sibling, born in 1898 when Kennedy was at university, was also a male.

Lurgan is a city about 20 miles (30 kilometres) southwest of Belfast, with a population today of over 20,000.[10] When Kennedy was born, the population was about 10,000. Much of the economy during the nineteenth century centred on the linen trade. But the industry became less important over time, particularly in more recent times when foreign manufacturers replaced UK producers.

The Manse was in a section of Lurgan in Northern Ireland called Shankill Parish. It is clear that Kennedy wanted others to believe that he was born in Shankill, Dublin, and not in Shankill, Northern Ireland. Why? The likely explanation is that he did not want people to know that he had been born a Presbyterian and that his father was a Presbyterian minister. Kennedy came to Canada as a Catholic and did not want to be identified with the Protestants in Northern Ireland, who frequently clashed with Catholics. As we will see, some of his own ancestors were active on the Protestant side in these clashes.

Ancestors

Kennedy's father, Charles William Kennedy, was the minister at the Second Presbyterian Church on Hill Street in Lurgan, Northern Ireland.[11] The church had been completed in 1862, and Reverend Kennedy added a still-standing tower in 1890. He had been born in County Tyrone, adjoining Armagh County, in 1854; attended Magee College in Londonderry, Northern Ireland, which had opened in 1865, primarily as a theological college; then attended the English Presbyterian College in London; and obtained his pulpit in Lurgan in 1875.[12] The following year, he married Selina Waugh McClure, a year younger than him, who was from Lurgan. A number of her ancestors had also been Presbyterian ministers in Ireland.

W.P.M. Kennedy's father, Charles
William Kennedy

W.P.M. Kennedy's maternal grandfather was William Waugh McClure, born in 1817, who ran a number of businesses in Lurgan, including coal and timber and a wholesale and retail grocery business.[13] He was later appointed a justice of the peace, a relatively prestigious honour, and was also a coroner. I have not discovered why W.P.M. Kennedy objected to the 'Waugh' name. Selina's maternal grandmother had been born a Waugh.

Kennedy's paternal grandfather, John Sinclair Kennedy, also became a justice of the peace.[14] So with coroners and justices of the peace in the family, the law was not foreign to Kennedy as he was growing up. Moreover, the earlier career of his paternal grandfather had been in law enforcement, having worked for Inland Revenue as a 'riding officer' or, as they were called, 'ride officers,' who protected the revenue by preventing smuggling and detecting illegal distilleries.

I have been able to trace Kennedy's ancestors back to his great-grandfather Charles Kennedy, born in Dunboe, Northern Ireland, in 1781 and ordained as a Presbyterian minister in 1801 in Maghera, which is located in the very north of Ireland. His predecessor as minister had left for America because of preaching revolution against the British.[15] Kennedy's great-grandfather was said to be 'distinguished as a preacher by his dignified and graceful delivery.'[16] Overall, he

Second Presbyterian Church, Lurgan, Northern Ireland

was considered a success, increasing the membership in the congregation. But he had his own run-ins with the law.

There was growing enmity between Protestants and Catholics in the early 1800s. The historian of the Presbyterian Church in Maghera in Northern Ireland stated: 'The alliance with the Roman Catholics in 1798 had now been forgotten and in its place had come the rivalry between the orange and green.'[17] The orange were, of course, 'Orangemen' – Protestants named after Protestant King William of Orange, who became king in 1689. The green were Catholics, sometimes referred to as Ribbonmen because of the green ribbons they wore.

This hostility manifested itself in an incident involving Kennedy's great-grandfather, Charles Kennedy, in June 1813 in Maghera, after a Protestant fair. It was often at or after such fairs that riots took place. The Protestants, a report of the incident states, 'were attacked by a large body of [Catholic] men, who lay in wait for them near the house of the Reverend Charles Kennedy, a Presbyterian minister.' The report goes on to state that the Protestants 'were overpowered, and some of them disarmed, they fled for refuge to Mr. Kennedy's house.'[18] Kennedy's house was then seriously damaged. Such events were not uncommon. One scholar has written:[19] 'With party feelings up, sectarian clashes disrupted local fairs all across Ulster between 1812 and 1815.'

There was another serious riot involving Catholics and Protestants in Maghera in 1823, which again involved Kennedy's great-grandfather, Charles Kennedy.[20] Reverend Kennedy and others were charged with 'aiding and assisting' two murders, again in June, following a fair. The trial took place the following year. One report states, in part: 'A few minutes after nine, his Lordship, Mr. Justice Vandeleur, entered the Court. The Galleries were crowded to excess. The Rev. Mr. Kennedy was allowed a seat below the deck, beside his Counsel.' The main Crown witness testified that 'there was a riot between six and seven in the evening, in the streets, between two parties,' Protestants and Catholics. The Protestants took shelter in a nearby home. The Catholics 'attacked the house with stones.' The Protestants fired back, and two men were killed. The report concludes: 'His lordship charged the Jury, who, after half an hour's consultation returned a verdict – Not Guilty.'

Further charges were then brought against both sides for 'riotously assembling at Maghera on the 12th day of June last.' However, after the combatants had spent a night in jail, the charges were withdrawn by the representative of the Crown, who stated that 'he had been informed this morning, and he felt great pleasure in making the communication, that the prisoners, of both the parties, to be tried … had, in the prison, shaken hands and were mutually willing, for the future to abstain from all display of party feeling, and to live in good fellowship and neighborhood, and hoped the Court would allow them to return home without being brought to trial.'[21] The report of the case concludes: 'In the evening the individuals of the two parties [Orangemen and Ribbonmen] joined together in harmonious circles, and, over the social glass, forgave and forgot their former animosities.'

Similar events continued in Northern Ireland until the very serious 'troubles' in more recent times. There were seven such incidents involving the deaths in or around Lurgan of two or more persons from 1972 on.[22] No doubt, a number of such incidents occurred while W.P.M. Kennedy was growing up.[23]

As suggested earlier, this religious conflict – particularly having his great-grandfather charged with the murder of a Catholic – was likely the reason that W.P.M. Kennedy tried not only to distance himself but to completely disassociate

himself from Northern Ireland Protestants and his anti-Catholic ancestors, and
wanted the world to believe that he was born in Dublin, or in England.

Around 1900, Kennedy's father, Reverend Charles William Kennedy, moved
to Glasgow, Scotland, with his family to take a position as the minister of a large
parish church.[24] W.P.M. Kennedy did not go with the family. He remained in
Dublin. He was not listed as a member of the household in any census or other
lists of those living in the house in Glasgow, not far from the church. W.P.M.
never visited his family in Glasgow. Kennedy made his only trip back to the
United Kingdom in 1926, but, according to his family, did not visit Glasgow.

Kennedy's father died in March 1927. The *Aberdeen Press and Journal*
noted:[25] 'The death of the Reverend Charles William Kennedy, L.A., occurred
at his residence, Cambuslang. He ... was for 27 years minister of Dalmarnock
Parish Church, Glasgow, being senior minister of the Glasgow Presbytery.'[26]

Although I did not try to trace the Kennedy family further back than his
great-grandfather Kennedy, I suspect that the Kennedys were part of the large
group of Scots who came to Ireland in the early seventeenth century, following
the accession of Protestant King James VI of Scotland to the English throne,
when he became James I of England. The ancestry of W.P.M.'s mother, Selina
Waugh McClure, can, in fact, be traced back to this period, when James I of
England brought Protestant settlers from Scotland to Northern Ireland following the forfeiture of a half million acres of land by rebellious Catholic earls. A
descendant of one of these settlers, a history of the McClure family records,
was 'the late William Waugh McClure, Justice of the Peace, Windsor Terrace,
Lurgan, Ireland' – Kennedy's maternal grandfather.[27]

In 1942, in the first issue of the University of Toronto's *School of Law Review*,
there is an article entitled 'Dr. W.P.M. Kennedy' in which the author – no doubt
after an interview with Kennedy – describes Kennedy's background:[28]

> Dr. William Paul McClure Kennedy was born in Ireland in the year 1881 [it was, in
> fact, 1879] of parents, both of whom were descendants of ancient and noble fami-
> lies. In fact, both the Kennedys and the McClures played very prominent roles in
> the great Jacobite-Cromwellian struggle in the seventeenth century. But while the
> Kennedy's were faithful disciples of the Stuarts [Catholics], the McClures espoused
> the opposite cause.

How the Kennedys went from faithful Catholics to anti-Catholic Presbyterians
is not known.

Schooling

Kennedy's schooling is also a mystery. In his who's who entries, which he would
have prepared, he stated: 'Educated: private tuition; Paris; Vienna; Berlin;
Trinity College Dublin.'[29] One pictures Kennedy being sent to various private

schools on the continent before going to Trinity College Dublin. The biographical sketch of Kennedy in the student law review in 1942 states: 'Having received private tuition until the age of fifteen, he commenced his university career at Trinity College, Dublin.'[30]

In fact, as far as can be determined, all Kennedy's schooling before he went to Trinity College Dublin was in Lurgan, Northern Ireland. Again, he seems to have wanted to hide the fact that he grew up in Northern Ireland and went to a Protestant school. Instead, he gave himself a more interesting, international non-Protestant background.

Kennedy's father, the Reverend C.W. Kennedy, was the patron of a primary school on Hill Street in Lurgan, near the church. It is highly likely that W.P.M. would have attended that school.[31] He next attended Lurgan Ladies' High School on High Street in Lurgan, run by a Mrs. Graham, according to the historian of the Lurgan school system.[32] The fact that Kennedy attended a school for women and that he had seven sisters and no brothers living at home with him may well – as suggested earlier – have affected his life, his rebellion against his family, and his own story about his early education.

Why did Kennedy attend the girls' school? He was there until 1892 and yet could have been at Lurgan College during some of those years.[33] As it turned out, W.P.M. Kennedy – perhaps through his own persistence – switched to Lurgan College in 1892, which he attended from age thirteen to seventeen.[34]

Lurgan College had been founded in 1873, following a bequest from the owner of a brewery.[35] The will specified that 'no person being in Holy Orders, or a minister of any religious denomination shall at any time interfere in the management of the said school, or be appointed to serve as master' and that no religious instruction was to take place during school hours. The school opened in 1873, and in 1875 W.T. Kirkpatrick was appointed headmaster.[36] Enrolment rose to seventy students by 1880. Kirkpatrick is best known as the tutor, following his retirement in 1899, of C.S. Lewis, the famous writer and Anglican theologian, whose father had attended Lurgan College in 1879.[37]

Trinity College Dublin

In 1896, Kennedy entered Trinity College Dublin (TCD), an Anglican institution. He graduated in 1900 from the four-year honours program, having been taken off the rolls from June 1897 to September 1898 for non-payment of fees.[38] It is unclear from the record what he did in that year. Perhaps that is when he travelled to Paris, Vienna, and Berlin, and perhaps he was given credit for that year by TCD because he graduated in 1900. I could not find any records showing what he did in 1897–98. The honours course was a more difficult course than that undertaken by students for the pass degree. Pass degree students would have taken mathematics, mathematical physics, astronomy, experimental and natural sciences, logic, ethics, English composition, Greek,

Great Library, Trinity College
Dublin

Latin, French, and German. Honours students would have taken, in addition, modern history, modern literature, and other subjects.[39]

Kennedy graduated with honours, was a Senior Moderator, won the Gold Medal in Modern Literature, and received a £25 prize, worth over £300 today.[40] In his final year, he won the English Prose Prize for his essay 'The Literary Relations of France and England during the Eighteenth Century.' In 1897, he won the New Shakespeare Society Prize, having studied Shakespeare under Edward Dowden, who, as we have seen, would write a reference for him in 1901. Nobel-laureate William Butler Yeats, Ireland's most famous poet, had studied under Dowden at TCD before Kennedy arrived.[41] Yeats wanted to succeed Dowden, but was unsuccessful. Yeats describes his view of Dowden, a friend of his father, in a memoir written in 1916: 'Dowden was wise in his encouragement, never overpraising and never unsympathetic.' Kennedy had a lifelong interest in Shakespeare.

I suspect that John Pentland Mahaffy,[42] Kennedy's initial tutor at TCD, was probably the most important influence on Kennedy in a number of respects.[43] Mahaffy, the professor of ancient history, was a great conversationalist, having written a book on the subject, *The Principles of the Art of Conversation*.[44] His most famous student, Oscar Wilde, had described him[45] as 'a delightful talker,

Kennedy's tutor, John
Pentland Mahaffy, in
the 1890s

too, a really great talker in a certain way – an artist in vivid words and eloquent
pauses.' Wilde knew Mahaffy well, having travelled to Italy with him in 1873
and Greece in 1874.

Half a century later, students would say the same about Kennedy as a 'talker.'
Throughout his career, Kennedy was known as a stimulating and sparkling
teacher. J.J. Robinette recalled that 'Kennedy ... could dazzle you ... a performer as much as a teacher.'[46] Ontario Court of Appeal justice Sydney Robins,
who attended the School of Law in the early 1940s and was the president of the
Law Club in his final year, wrote about 'Doc Kennedy,' as the students called
him:[47]

His lectures to the small classes then at the school were given in his office, a
rather large room on the second floor at 45 St. George Street. Every lecture was
indeed a performance. He would speak while sometimes standing, sometimes
sitting, sometimes walking around the room, and sometimes lying down on his

psychiatrist-style couch. His lectures went beyond the law. He spoke also of history, politics, current events and the many prominent people he claimed to know and who had, or so he told us, sought his advice. He was certainly one of the most charismatic lecturers I ever had – always interesting, often funny, the words flowed effortlessly.

Another aspect of Mahaffy's character, which Kennedy emulated throughout his life, as we will see, was Mahaffy's ability to make friends with people in high positions.

But it was in Mahaffy's approach to scholarship where we see the greatest potential influence. His biographers, classicists at TCD like Mahaffy, could appreciate his approach to scholarship.[48] Mahaffy is perhaps best known for his work on the Flinders Petrie Ancient Egyptian Papyri. This material was the subject of several books Mahaffy published in the early 1890s. His biographers explain: 'There have been good papyrologists before him – better, indeed, in technique and care – but none of those who had worked on literary papyri previously had been capable of doing what Mahaffy did in bringing out the full social and cultural significance of such material.' One can say the same about Kennedy's book *The Constitution of Canada*, published in 1922.

Kennedy may also have been influenced by Mahaffy's dislike of nationalism, which he dealt with in his analysis of the Greek city states. Mahaffy believed, according to his biographers, that larger groupings of nations were better than small individual states. Mahaffy noted that[49] 'the world was, always had been, and always would be, better off without small, independent nationalistic states.' From his early days as a scholar, his biographers state, Mahaffy had 'preferred the large Hellenistic kingdom to the smaller city-states of classical Greece.' Kennedy's approach was similar. He opposed nationalism and supported larger groupings, in particular, the British Empire.

Kennedy entered Trinity College Dublin at the very time that one of its most famous graduates, Oscar Wilde, had just been convicted of gross indecency and sentenced to two years hard labour.[50] The conviction was in May 1895. Kennedy's future colleague in the School of Law, Eugene LaBrie, recalls Kennedy telling him that he had attended Wilde's trial. Whether he did, we will never know. Wilde was released from Reading Gaol in 1897 and went to France, where he died in November 1900. There would obviously have been considerable talk in the college about the case among the students. Would Mahaffy have discussed it in or out of class with Kennedy? Mahaffy and Wilde were very close. Wilde helped Mahaffy with one of his books, *Social Life in Greece*,[51] a book in which Mahaffy commented on homosexuality among Greek men – the first such scholarly discussion in English. These passages were removed for the second edition.

Mahaffy, however, did not support the petition to the Home Secretary for a clemency for Wilde in November 1895 and is reported as stating when he first heard of the accusation that he hoped he would never hear Wilde's name again.[52] His biographers report that he later commented: 'We no longer speak of Mr. Oscar Wilde ... the one blot on my tutorship.'

In 1919, five years after Mahaffy became the head of Trinity College Dublin, college records show that Kennedy received a doctor of letters from TCD.[53] As in Oxford and Cambridge, this degree is given to graduates of the university on the basis of significant published work. A notice in the *Globe*[54] in March 1919 stated: 'His doctorate is granted for his contributions to historical literature and to historical research.' Only one or two such degrees were given out each year by TCD in those years. As with St. Francis Xavier College, it is likely that Kennedy made the same request to TCD, either directly or indirectly. As the head of the college at the time, Mahaffy would have been involved in the decision to grant the honour, although there are no archival records of it. Nor are there records of the citation, if any. Kennedy did not go to Ireland to receive the degree.

3

After Trinity College Dublin

What did Kennedy do after he graduated from Trinity College Dublin? Again, it is not clear. It seems likely that he went to Oxford. Perhaps Mahaffy said to Kennedy what he had said to Wilde:[1] 'Go to Oxford, my dear Oscar; we are all much too clever for you over here.'

As noted earlier, Kennedy claimed that he studied with the historian William Stubbs at Oxford. In 1913, the student newspaper at St. Francis Xavier interviewed Kennedy and reported that he 'studied history under ... the late Professor Stubbs, Oxford.'[2] But, as already mentioned, Stubbs, at the time the Anglican bishop of Oxford, became ill in the fall of 1900 and died in April 1901. The editor of a book of his letters, published in 1903, writes: 'But the Bishop rallied. In 1900 he took a summer holiday. In the autumn he was again ill, and [his] letters tell of the growing illness.'[3] How long Kennedy stayed at Oxford, assuming he remained for a period of time, is not known.

Kennedy never claimed in print that he had a degree from Oxford, but he also never corrected the annual University of Toronto calendar, which each year – from the 1916–17 calendar until his death in 1963 – listed 'M.A. Dublin, Oxon' after his name,[4] giving the reader the impression that he had a degree from Oxford. My correspondence with Oxford University archivists, however, makes it clear that Kennedy never had an Oxford degree. In spite of that assurance, I asked them to again double check their records. An archivist once more reviewed their records and concluded: 'We can find no record, therefore, that Kennedy was a member of the University or obtained the degree of MA at Oxford.'[5]

Oxford, however, permits graduates of Trinity College Dublin, Cambridge, and certain other universities, who are at Oxford studying for a further degree, to obtain an Oxford BA by what is called 'incorporation,'[6] but there is also no evidence that this process was used. Foremost, it required the payment of fees, and Kennedy likely had little or no money in those years. Perhaps Kennedy, who more than likely spent some time at Oxford after he graduated from Trinity

College, justified in his own mind not correcting the record because he *could* have received an Oxford BA if he had become a registered student at Oxford.

We know from the copies of Kennedy's letters sent to St. Francis Xavier that in 1900 and 1901 he was applying for teaching positions throughout the United Kingdom – without success.[7] One application was to be an examiner in English at Glasgow University in the fall of 1901. His parents and siblings were by then in Glasgow, which suggests that there may have been the possibility of reconciliation with his family, but, as far as we know, it did not occur.

Most likely, Kennedy was in Dublin during those early years, because he was elected to the position of honorary librarian for 1901–02 in the Trinity College Dublin Philosophical Society, an important student society of which he would probably have been a member during his undergraduate years.[8] He was active in the society after graduation. In March 1901, for example, he presented a paper to the society on 'Anglo-Irish Poetry.'[9] The society is said to be 'the oldest student society' in the world, having been founded in 1683.[10] Its members included William B. Yeats, Bram Stoker, and Oscar Wilde. In the 1920s, Kennedy was part of a similar society at the University of Toronto, the Historical Club, where students presented and debated papers but were not the senior officers of the club. Kennedy himself was the president of the Historical Club for a number of years in the 1920s.[11]

A year after graduation, Kennedy took a position as tutor to a young ward of an Irish physician, Dr. Richard Atkinson Hayes. Hayes wrote a reference letter in March 1912 to assist Kennedy in getting a position, a copy of which ended up in the St. Francis Xavier files. Dr. Hayes, a respected physician, stated:[12] 'In August 1901 I engaged Mr. W.M. Kennedy with the approval of the then Lord Chancellor of Ireland, to act as Tutor and Companion to a young ward of mine, and he so acted until December 1903.' During that period, Dr. Hayes went on, Kennedy 'discharged his duties, which were often of an arduous nature, to my satisfaction, showing tact and judgment in the management of his pupil whom he also taught and encouraged in the practice of various sports – riding, shooting etc.' He then noted Kennedy's travels: 'Mr. Kennedy also accompanied my ward and his aunt on a long tour through Europe, the Near East, Egypt, the Holy Land etc. making all arrangements in a business-like and efficient manner.'

This period was an important one in Kennedy's life, yet we know almost nothing about it. In his various who's who entries, Kennedy does not mention the Middle East, but a student interviewer for the University of Toronto *School of Law Review* in 1942 reported that 'his legal interest has taken him to diverse corners of the globe – Egypt, the Soudan, Palestine, Syria, South Africa, and Australia.'[13] I have found no evidence, however, that he ever went to South Africa or Australia. Perhaps Kennedy's words were misinterpreted by the interviewer. His son, Gilbert Kennedy, was vague about his father's early travels in his oral history, stating simply: 'He travelled a lot, he travelled most of the world I understand.'[14]

I have not, unfortunately, been able to find out the name of the ward or his aunt. Did the ward or his aunt leave a memoir or letters about their travels? The lord chancellor of Ireland's Chancery records relating to wardships were unfortunately destroyed in a fire during the 1922 Irish Civil War. An Irish legal historian, who has worked in the Irish archives on Chancery records, sent me an email explaining: 'Wardship was indeed within the common law jurisdiction of the Irish lord chancellor. As far as I know records from 1901 would have been in the public records office which was then part of the Four Courts building. These were almost entirely destroyed in the fire in 1922 during the civil war.'[15]

So, the treasure trove of documents that I keep searching for has again eluded me. For the record, I have checked Dr. Hayes's will to see if he mentioned his ward; examined census and other records to find out who was living in his house over the years; and checked what is available showing Kennedy's foreign travel – without finding any indication who the ward might have been.

Mirfield Monastery

In September 1903, Kennedy was invited to spend a month in the House of the Resurrection in Mirfield, West Yorkshire, England.[16] The house had been acquired the previous year by an Anglican religious group, the Community of the Resurrection, which had started several years earlier at Oxford. The community can be traced to the well-known Oxford Movement, whose members wanted to bring the Anglican Church closer to Catholicism and also to help the working class. The community moved from Oxford to the industrial north to be closer to working people. The house, according to one memoir, was 'surrounded by ample and beautiful grounds' and 'sufficiently withdrawn to ensure quiet, and yet had excellent communications to facilitate the work undertaken by the brethren.' Mirfield was connected to the canal system and at a junction of two railways. The community is still active.[17] Its current website states that 'the founding brethren were Christian Socialists challenged by the poverty of the working classes.'

How long did Kennedy stay in Mirfield? The community archivist, Brother Steven Hawes, one of several dozen members of the Anglican community in Mirfield today, searched their records and replied that 'Mr. W.M. Kennedy did spend time at the House of the Resurrection, Mirfield, in 1903 and between 1906 and 1908. He may have also stayed in 1904–05 as well, although there is no record of his stay during that period. I don't know where he went after he left us.'[18] Kennedy appears to have had some health issues while he was at Mirfield. One of the entries in the register, dated 13 April 1907, states: 'Resolved that Mr. Kennedy should be invited to stay with us till July in the hope that he may be fit to return to work in October.'[19] It is not clear what these health concerns entailed. It could have been mental health issues, as Kennedy was considering changing his religious faith from Anglican to Roman Catholic.

House of the Resurrection, Mirfield, West Yorkshire, England

The head of the community was Father Walter Howard Frere, a Cambridge graduate, whose grandfather had been the master of Downing College.[20] Frere, who later became the bishop of Truro in Cornwall, was an important figure in Kennedy's life – sufficiently so that Kennedy named one of his sons 'Frere.' Kennedy dedicated his first book, *The Interpretation of the Bishops*,[21] published in 1908, to Walter Howard Frere, as he did for another study of ecclesiastical matters, published in 1924.[22] In 1921, Frere came to Toronto to lecture at Convocation Hall and Trinity College and no doubt spent time with Kennedy, discussing the latter project.[23]

My wife and I visited the Community of the Resurrection in Mirfield in April 2018. We stayed overnight, attended the evening Mass, walked through the beautiful grounds, had dinner, and – while observing complete silence – had breakfast with the members of the community. It was a unique experience

Bishop Walter Howard Frere

for us and even more moving knowing that Kennedy had spent a number of years – perhaps troubled years – there. Kennedy's son Frere, an Anglican priest, kept in touch with the community and spent some time there when he visited the United Kingdom in the 1980s.

When Kennedy first came to Mirfield, Father Walter Frere was then completing a book on Tudor history, *The English Church in the Reigns of Elizabeth and James I*, part of a series for the general reader on the development of the Anglican Church.[24] A contemporary of Father Frere wrote that Frere showed 'a steadfast adherence to the Catholic Faith, an unshaken loyalty to the English Church, a devotion to learning, a sensitiveness to social injustice, and a zealous solicitude for individual souls.'[25] Frere wanted the Anglican Church to keep the Catholic service, but not the link with Rome. There are Walter Frere papers at the University of York Archives in Northern England, but, unfortunately, there are no letters to or from Kennedy in that collection or at Mirfield.[26]

Kennedy worked on and off with Father Frere over the next half-dozen years on one specific aspect of Tudor ecclesiastical history, which resulted in a three-volume set of books entitled *Visitation Articles and Injunctions of the Period of the Reformation*, published by Longmans, Green and Company in 1910.[27] 'Visitations' were investigations ordered by bishops into ecclesiastical practices in their area of jurisdiction. 'Injunctions' were the orders that were issued following the investigations. As Frere and Kennedy say in the first sentence of the preface to volume one: 'There is no set of documents that gives such a vivid picture of the religious changes of the sixteenth century in England as these that belong to ecclesiastical visitation. In them the alterations may be followed year by year and even at times month by month, with an amount of detail which is enough to be illuminating and not enough to be burdensome.'[28] It therefore provides a picture of how Church doctrine was actually practised at that time.

The three volumes that Frere and Kennedy produced in 1910 were well received. The *English Historical Review* noted that it is a 'valuable collection of documents includ[ing] a number which are printed for the first time ... The notes are admirable.'[29] The reviewer, E.W. Watson, who later became the Regius Professor of Ecclesiastical History at Oxford, went on to say that the 'elaborate introduction is of the greatest value ... No such survey has hitherto been attempted ... a pioneer work.' Recent assessments are equally strong. A 2011 contribution to a book on Walter Frere states: 'Frere and Kennedy's joint effort ... is a landmark work in the field, a monumental achievement by any scholarly standard, collating information from a formidable number of sources ... [I]t changed the direction of later scholarship, forcing historians to examine what bishops actually *did* in their dioceses, once installed.'[30]

There is no doubt that Kennedy's work with Frere influenced his own later scholarship in a number of ways. As we will see, one of Kennedy's major contributions to legal scholarship was his collections of original documents on constitutional issues. He was interested in what those carrying out policy actually did. This approach to scholarship was particularly true in later years in the area of administrative law, where he was interested in studying various administrative schemes, such as taxation, labour law, and bankruptcy.

The influence of the Community of the Resurrection, which had a special interest in the labour movement, may also help account for Kennedy's later interest in industrial relations. During Kennedy's time at Mirfield there were several organized conferences between church and labour.[31]

Kennedy's study of Tudor ecclesiastical history may also have influenced his work in another way: whatever he later studied would have seemed less complicated and almost straightforward compared to the complexity of Tudor ecclesiastical history. Some events are, of course, well known: in the first half of the sixteenth century, Henry VIII's many wives, the annulment of his marriage to Catherine of Aragon, his divorce, marriage to Anne Boleyn and her execution, the closing down of monasteries, and the break with Rome. And, towards the end of the century, we know about Queen Elizabeth's defeat of the Spanish Armada in 1588.

In between and less well known are the reigns of Edward VI, who followed Henry VIII's ecclesiastical policies, and then Queen Mary Tudor, a Roman Catholic, who did not. The Church had to shift ground with each political change. What prayer book would be used? What language would be used in the prayer book? How would a church be decorated? What type of music could be played? Could ministers marry? Could one kneel? Could there be a screen in the middle of the church? What was the true meaning of Communion?

One of the most complex issues, to give a specific example, is that of so-called 'reservation,' that is, whether the Sacrament for the Communion – the consecrated bread and wine – can be 'reserved' by priests for later use by the sick and dying outside the church.[32] This rule changed from sovereign to sovereign. King Edward said it could not be so used. Queen Mary, a Catholic, said it could. It is not clear what the rule was in the Elizabethan years. Both Walter Frere and Kennedy wrote extensively on that particular issue. Kennedy devotes a thirty-five-page chapter in a book of essays he published in 1916 to that very question.[33]

Archbishop Parker

While Kennedy was at Mirfield, he also worked on a book about Archbishop Parker, the archbishop of Canterbury during most of Queen Elizabeth's reign.[34] Parker was a major actor in the various events discussed in the three *Visitation Articles and Injunctions* volumes about to be published by Frere and Kennedy. In the preface to *Archbishop Parker*, published in 1908, Kennedy thanks Walter Frere: 'I would express my sincerest thanks to Mr. Frere for guidance, supervision and note books, and for much patience with my inexperience.'[35]

The Parker book was part of a series published by Pitman and Sons, 'Makers of National History,' edited by Professor W.H. Hutton of St. John's College, Oxford.[36] In an introductory note to the volume, Hutton writes: 'It is intended in this series to commemorate important men whose share in the making of national history seems to need a more complete record than it has yet received.'

Whether Kennedy spent much time at St. John's College is not known. The college has no record of him, and Kennedy does not thank the college in his preface. He simply says:[37] 'Finally, I would like to thank Mr. Hutton, the general editor of the series, for expert criticism and kind suggestions.' He does, however, thank the Reverend E. Rhys Jones 'for much help and hospitality.' Rev. Rhys Jones was the minister at St. Luke's Vicarage, midway between London and Brighton, which indicates that Kennedy spent time there.

Parker was not, in fact, Kennedy's first book. Earlier that year he published a short book, *The 'Interpretation' of the Bishops and their Influence on Elizabethan Policy*, containing copies of three important documents with which Parker had been involved, and which had never before been properly edited.[38] They were preceded by an eighteen-page introductory essay. Again, he thanks Rev. E. Rhys Jones, 'beneath whose hospitable roof this little book was largely written.' Kennedy dedicates this book to Walter Howard Frere. The *English Historical Review* noted the publication with a short review, stating that the documents had 'never before been edited critically or even published *in extenso*.'[39]

Kennedy is still a good Anglican in the Parker book. He is sympathetic to Parker, a married priest, who found a 'via media' between the Roman Catholics and the Puritans. Kennedy writes in the preface:[40] 'Parker's primacy was perhaps the most important in the history of the English Church ... It required tact and wisdom to steer between these extremes and at the same time to preserve the catholicity of the Church.'

The book was generally well received. The *Guardian* reviewer wrote: 'Exceedingly well conceived, clearly expressed, and compiled with great care.'[41] The academically important *English Historical Review* was less kind.[42] Professor A.F. Pollard of London University conceded that Kennedy's 'ecclesiological labours on the period have fitted him to deal with some aspects of the subject,' but goes on to point out some omissions such as Archbishop Parker's literary work, Kennedy's failure to refer to legal historian Frederic Maitland's work ('with whose work Mr. Kennedy does not seem to be acquainted'), and some anachronisms.[43] Nevertheless, Kennedy now had to his credit a lengthy review in the *English Historical Review*, such that, in a later review in the same journal in 1917 of another Kennedy book, *Studies in Tudor History*, the reviewer could state: 'Mr. Kennedy has already achieved distinction with his *Life of Archbishop Parker*.'[44]

Conversion to Roman Catholicism and *Parish Life under Queen Elizabeth*

Sometime after 1908 Kennedy converted to Roman Catholicism. There is no clear indication when it was, why it was, or how it took place. It would likely have been between 1908 and 1912, when he was applying to teach at a Catholic boys' school. It seems probable that his conversion took place while working with Frere on the three-volume *Visitation Articles and Injunctions*, published in 1910. In Father Frere's preface, dated October 1910, he stated:[45] 'Mr. W.M. Kennedy worked at the whole in the earlier stages of preparation, and was responsible for seeing the greater part of the earlier set of documents through the press; but when that volume was printed off he was unable to give further help.'

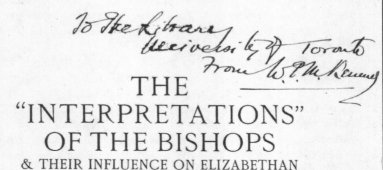

THE
"INTERPRETATIONS"
OF THE BISHOPS
& THEIR INFLUENCE ON ELIZABETHAN
EPISCOPAL POLICY

(With an Appendix of the Original Documents)

BY

W. M. KENNEDY

(e William Paul McLure Kennedy)

LONGMANS, GREEN & CO
39 PATERNOSTER ROW, LONDON
NEW YORK, BOMBAY AND CALCUTTA
1908

142319
21/4/17

Title page of *The 'Interpretations' of the Bishops* by W.M. Kennedy, 1908

It seems likely that Kennedy 'was unable to give further help' with the final volume because he had converted to Roman Catholicism and may not have been particularly welcome at the Community of the Resurrection, an Anglican community. Frere's brother did the extensive index for all three volumes. Such conversions were not exceptional. A number of important Catholic theologians, such as Cardinals Newman and Manning, had been involved in the Oxford Movement in the nineteenth century and had converted from Anglicanism to Catholicism. Many would say that it was probably easier to move from being a High Anglican to a Roman Catholic than from being a Presbyterian to an Anglican.

It is also likely that Kennedy's conversion coincided with his consistent adoption in his books of the name 'Paul.' In the *Archbishop Parker* book of 1908, he is W.M. Kennedy. He had already dropped 'Waugh.' In *Parish Life*, published in 1914, he is W.P.M. Kennedy.[46]

Kennedy's next book, *Parish Life under Queen Elizabeth*, was completed in 1914, while Kennedy was at St. Francis Xavier College.[47] It was published in England by the Catholic Library. (This book was the one dedicated to 'S.J.C.,' Sara Josephine Cameron.) Kennedy explains his object in publishing the book, stating: 'My object in this little book is to present a broad picture of Elizabethan life ... The book is intended for the general reader, who may wish to know something of how the Elizabethan Reformation affected the everyday life of the people.'[48] An unnamed reviewer in the *Globe* gave the book a good review, noting that 'Prof. Kennedy's work shows a good deal of research and care, and he brings to his task evidently a mind not only historically well equipped, but the historical instinct that ever goes with the judicial statement of facts.'[49]

In both *Archbishop Parker* and *Parish Life*, Kennedy claims to be seeking the truth. He states in the preface to *Archbishop Parker* that 'an effort has been made to work through the various manuscript and printed sources of the period, and to approach the subject as it were first hand. Thus I have tried to arrive at accurate facts.'[50] In *Parker* he writes as an Anglican, while *Parish Life*, dealing with roughly the same material, was written as a Catholic. One can see in the two books a difference in Kennedy's treatment of the various groups – so much for objective truth in scholarship.

In *Parish Life*, Archbishop Parker is still a somewhat admirable person. How could Kennedy say otherwise, having earlier published a positive assessment of Parker? A present-day Tudor scholar, John Craig, notes that, in *Parish Life*, 'apart from a grudging sympathy for Matthew Parker, Kennedy struggled to find anything good to say about his subject.'[51] Parker, according to Kennedy, was still 'a man of gentle temper, wide scholarship and far from ambitious,'[52] but he persecuted Catholics. 'He poured scorn and contumely on the Popes,' wrote Kennedy. 'He suppressed Catholicism firmly if more gently than his brethren.

He had no belief in the Mass, the Real Presence, Invocation of Saints, Purgatory. He gave no quarter to the traditional piety of Catholics.'

Moreover, Kennedy suggested, all the other bishops in England were worse, and Parker 'stands out in Elizabeth's reign as perhaps the only sincere bishop of his time.' The good guys are no longer those seeking a via media, but, rather, 'the strong men in reality were the conscientious Puritans and Catholics, who had the courage to refuse a position which gradually made itself secure.' Religious life was better before the Reformation, Kennedy concludes: 'The parish priests of Catholic England were worthy men and certainly they believed and taught the Catholic Faith, and carried out the duties of their sacred office with zeal and conviction, before decay set in with newer forces and newer ideas.' Elizabethan clergy, by contrast, showed 'little conviction, little zeal except in repressing Catholicism.' Professor Craig refers to such statements as 'confessional statements,' that is, 'holding to a confession of faith in the sense that a Catholic historian writes Catholic history and a Lutheran historian writes Lutheran history.'[53]

Needless to say, the Catholic journals liked the book. The reviewer for the Jesuit magazine *The Irish Monthly* gave it good review and assumed that Kennedy was a priest.[54] He wrote: 'There was room for the brief, clear and interesting work on this period of religious transition, which Father Kennedy ... has given us in his recent volume on the subject, one to which he has devoted careful study for many years.' He ends his review by stating: 'All this and more the author proves by copious references to contemporary Protestant documents, and few will venture to dissent from his conclusions.' A reviewer in another Catholic publication, *The Dublin Review*, published in London, reviewing the Catholic Library series, states: 'Then we have a first-rate piece of original work in the volume on *Parish Life under Elizabeth* by Professor W.P.M. Kennedy. One hardly expects in a series of this kind to find so genuinely important a contribution to historical knowledge ... [N]o future study of the Elizabethan settlement in religion can afford to neglect this unpretending little volume.'[55] The reviewer notes that 'the author in his Anglican days wrote a Life of Archbishop Parker' and adds that 'it is interesting to note, he still commends Parker as "by far the most conscientious man in ecclesiastical life during Elizabeth's reign."' The reviewer for the *English Historical Review*,[56] an Anglican, noted in a short review, however, that Kennedy has written 'a candid and bright little book ... an excellent, if prejudiced book.'

Other Books and Articles on Church History

Kennedy published a number of articles in the *English Historical Review* (*EHR*)[57] during this period and after he came to Canada, which will not be discussed here, except to note that in 1917 Kennedy published in the *EHR* a long list of visitation articles and injunctions prepared after the death of Archbishop Parker.[58] Kennedy states: 'Pending the preparation of a later series, it may be convenient to print a provisional list of materials for the years 1576–1603.' A three-volume set of these documents, prepared by Kennedy, was, indeed, published in 1924. These volumes, like his very first book, were dedicated to Walter Howard Frere.

In 1917, Longmans, Green and Company reissued the three-volume *Visitation Articles and Injunctions*.[59] This time, Kennedy was named as a co-author of all three books, not just 'with the assistance of' in the second volume. Each volume states: 'Edited, with Introduction and Notes, by W.H. Frere, M.A., and W.P.M. Kennedy, M.A.' The three volumes are otherwise the same as the 1910 volumes, including Frere's preface.

The last book to be examined in this chapter is *Studies in Tudor History*, published by Constable in London in 1916. By that time, Kennedy was a professor of English literature and history at St. Michael's College at the University of Toronto, but the book was mainly written while he was in England. Kennedy describes the book in his preface: 'My object in publishing this collection of studies in Tudor history is to present to the general student and reader some material connected with subjects which must be treated very briefly in the general histories of the period.'[60]

The book was dedicated to Professor A.F. Pollard of the University of London 'as a token of friendship and regard.'[61] A copy of a letter from Pollard to Kennedy in the St. Francis Xavier files states: 'I send you herewith the photograph for which you made a gratifying request. I am also pleased that you should dedicate your new volume to me, if you think it of any advantage.'[62]

Kennedy also thanks Walter Frere, stating: 'If I have succeeded at all in acquiring a contemporary outlook on Tudor history, it is due to the ideals which he laid before me many years ago. I would ask him, then, to accept my sincerest thanks for kindnesses which survive in spite of changes.' Those 'changes' refer to Kennedy's conversion to Roman Catholicism.

A Catholic reviewer in the quarterly journal *Studies: An Irish Quarterly Review*, published by Irish Jesuits, liked the book, stating:[63] 'The writer of these Studies has already secured a favourable reception for two previous works: *The Life of Dr. Parker* and *Parish Life under Queen Elizabeth*. The book before us is noticeable for the same quality which has given popularity to its predecessors.' He ends his review by applauding Kennedy's books and stating: 'May their success encourage the author to give us more of the same workmanship.'[64]

The Harvard historian Roger B. Merriman, however, was critical, particularly because of the absence of notes by Kennedy about his sources. Writing in the *American Historical Review*, Merriman states: 'There are a number of statements scattered through his pages which will make his readers "sit up"; some on account of their naïveté, others because of their wide departures from hitherto accepted views ... We look eagerly for the authority on which Mr. Kennedy rests his case; but none appears.'[65]

The title page of the book now lists after Kennedy's MA the letters 'F.R.Hist.S.' – Fellow of the Royal Historical Society, a prestigious society founded in 1868, which still exists.[66] The executive secretary of the society replied to my request for information by stating:[67] 'The only reference I can find is to a P.M. Kennedy, who was elected to the Society's Fellowship in 1914 and was "removed from the Rolls" in November 1920 ... I can't be any more specific about why his Fellowship ceased at this point – possibly he resigned it – but the old Minute books are not specific.' I suspect that Kennedy resigned for financial reasons. There was an annual fee for membership, and, as we will see in a later chapter, this period was a difficult time for Kennedy.

With this record of scholarship, it is understandable why Kennedy was considered a valuable asset at St. Michael's College at the University of Toronto.

4

St. Michael's College

We do not know the precise date that Kennedy left St. Francis Xavier College in Nova Scotia or arrived in Toronto to teach English literature at St. Michael's College. His son, Gilbert Kennedy, states in his oral interview that it would have been in the late summer of 1914, noting that 'in the summer of 1914 he canoed with a friend in the Hudson Bay area and when they came out in middle September couldn't believe it when they were told there was a war on in Europe.'[1]

We know that Kennedy was back in Toronto by mid-September because he wrote to the archbishop of Toronto, Neil McNeil, on 16 September that he was 'getting [his] work into shape for St. Michael's on the 29th.'[2] From the tone of the letter, Kennedy was on good terms with the archbishop, recommending a former student from Ramsgate, England, who wanted to become a priest in Canada and asking whether the archbishop had seen the review of his recent book, *Parish Life*, in the Catholic journal *The Record*.[3] About the war he wrote: 'I hope our Protestant brethren are edified by the general culture etc. evinced by Germany in this war. Poor little Catholic Belgium.'

Kennedy rented a room in an apartment block called the Lipton (since torn down to erect legislative office buildings) on the south side of Wellesley Street, between Bay Street and Queen's Park Crescent, across the road from his new teaching home, St. Michael's College. His salary for the year 1914–15 was $1,500, which may have included his moving expenses, and was $2,000 for each of the years 1915–16 and 1916–17.[4] All other full-time members of St. Michael's College were priests, who did not receive a salary.[5]

St. Michael's College, which had been founded by the French Basilians in 1852, became affiliated with the University of Toronto in 1881.[6] Affiliation, which had been rejected by the university in earlier years – in part because of prejudice against Catholics – had been promoted by the head of the college, Father John Teefy, who had graduated from University College, the university's non-denominational college, ten years earlier. Teefy had high ambitions for St. Michael's College. He wanted to create 'a great Catholic university bearing

St. Michael's College and St. Basil's Church, about 1870

the same relation to modern times that the University of Salamanca did to medieval.'[7]

In 1910, St. Michael's College had become fully recognized by the University of Toronto on the same basis as the other denominational arts colleges, Victoria and Trinity. Before 1910, University of Toronto courses had been taken by St. Michael's students through University College. Only nine students received BAs between 1881 and 1910.[8] After 1910, the number of undergraduate students at St. Michael's started to increase. In Kennedy's first year at St Michael's, there were 116 arts students.

The college yearbook for 1914–15 welcomed Kennedy, pointing out that the increase in students and new courses necessitated an increase in the college staff and stating:[9]

A valuable addition was made to the staff this year in the person of Mr. W. P. Kennedy, M.A., F.R.Hist.S., the Professor of English. Mr. Kennedy has received a thorough post-graduate course in European Universities. He is an author of acknowledged repute and a contributor to several of the leading literary reviews. As a reviewer of his latest work puts it, 'St. Michael's is to be congratulated on having secured the services of such an eminent scholar.'

The head of the college during Kennedy's first few years was Father Robert McBrady. Raised in a small town in Ontario, he had been educated in France. He had taught for over fifty years – teaching every subject at one time or another

Father Henry Carr, the superior of
St. Michael's College, 1915–25

except music. His obituary notice stated:[10] 'His greatest achievement, according to his own estimation, was that he said his prayers and did his work.' It seems unlikely that he played a significant role in bringing Kennedy to St. Michael's. Archbishop McNeil and Father Henry Carr would have been the key persons in doing so.

Scholarly Issues

McBrady's successor, Father Henry Carr, took over in 1915 and would have seen eye to eye with Kennedy on scholarly issues.[11] A graduate in Honours Classics from University College in 1903, Carr had been the driving force in bringing St. Michael's into the University of Toronto on equal terms with the other colleges. And, like Father Teefy, he had high ambitions for St. Michael's. Father Carr believed that in 'a comparatively short time' St. Michael's College could be made 'the greatest Catholic education centre in the world.'[12] St. Michael's did, in fact, develop into a major Catholic educational centre with the establishment of the Institute of Mediaeval Studies in 1929, renamed the Pontifical Institute of Mediaeval Studies in 1939.[13]

No doubt, Carr strongly supported a request that Kennedy made to the University of Toronto president, Robert Falconer, in the summer of 1915 to provide special funds to establish a mediaeval history library at the university.[14] Such a library was needed, Kennedy informed Falconer, because the English publisher Constable and Sons had asked him to write a major book, to be called 'The Spirit of the Middle Ages in England.' In mid-August, W.M. Meredith, the head of Constable, had written to Kennedy:[15]

> An urgent letter has been forwarded to me from the office to my holiday residence from Dr. Firth, Regius Professor of History at Oxford, asking us to approach you immediately with the view of your writing for us a volume of 200,000 words to be called The Spirit of the Middle Ages in England. I hasten to ask you if you could see your way clear to undertake such a book. You will understand that we want a work the product of original research among the [manuscripts] and documents, and Dr. Firth is confident that you can carry out our idea successfully.

Firth, a distinguished historian who specialized in Cromwell, had been the president of the Royal Historical Society in 1914, when Kennedy was elected to its membership.[16] Meredith knew Kennedy because Constable was in the process of publishing Kennedy's *Studies in Tudor History*. Meredith continued: 'We shall allow you nearly two years to carry it out, and from the pleasure with which I read the proofs of your Studies in Tudor History, I am confident that you could write us an excellent book.'

But Kennedy was an expert on the sixteenth century, not the Middle Ages. That later period was not, however, offered to him. Meredith explained: 'We would have offered you The Spirit of the XVI Century, only you once told me that you felt written out on that period.'

Kennedy would be expanding into a new period, a move that would enhance his reputation as an English historian. The problem was that he required copies of a large number of original manuscripts. Meredith had stated that it was to be 'the product of original research' among the manuscripts and documents. The documents he would have taken with him from England were from a later period. He thus approached President Falconer for help.

Falconer replied:[17] 'I am very much interested in your letter and I congratulate you on the offer which Messrs. Constable have made to you, and I sincerely hope that you may be able to carry it through. However, I do not see how it is possible for us to facilitate the matter in the way that you propose. We have reduced the outlay for books for the ensuing year very materially, and I am sure that the Librarian would not be able to find $1500 for the special department of Mediaeval History.' It was wartime. Falconer suggested that Kennedy might find donors who could purchase valuable editions and present them to St. Michael's or another library in Toronto.

Kennedy was clearly interested in doing the project. The financial terms proposed by Meredith were excellent. 'We offer you £200 pounds on publication

President Robert Falconer of the
University of Toronto, 1910

[over $35,000 in Canadian dollars today] and 12½% royalty on each copy sold.'[18] Kennedy needed money. Documents in the St. Michael's Archdiocese files show that Kennedy owed over $700 to the Catholic Church, consisting of a loan of $600 given to him shortly after he arrived at St. Francis Xavier College for rent in Antigonish and other expenses.[19] It was still unpaid.

Another term would have been particularly attractive to Kennedy. Meredith states: 'I may add in confidence that I am led to believe that an honorary Lit.D. from Oxford is attached to the successful carrying out of the project along the lines on which Dr. Firth and our house have agreed.' As we know, Kennedy was very anxious to receive an honorary doctorate. He would not receive his doctorate from Trinity College Dublin, based upon published work, until 1919, four years later.

Kennedy turned to Archbishop McNeil. At the end of September 1915,[20] Kennedy proposed that he 'would hand over at once all [his] historical library' in exchange for $1,500 and the extinguishment of the existing debt, although the latter arrangement is not clear from the records. There is no reply from McNeil in the diocese records. (McNeil tended not to keep copies of letters he sent.) The arrangement proposed by Kennedy did not go through, and in July 1918 Kennedy is again offering to sell a large portion of his library to the Church through the archbishop.[21]

In the end, Constable and Sons did not go ahead with the project. Perhaps if Kennedy had agreed to contribute his volume, the series might have been undertaken. So, if the money had been found and the mediaeval library at the University of Toronto had gone ahead, Kennedy would probably have undertaken the project and may not have entered the field of Canadian constitutional history. He would likely have become one of the world's great mediaeval scholars. Such are the twists and turns of most lives, but particularly that of W.P.M. Kennedy.

Although this attempt to build up the collection of mediaeval manuscripts in the university failed, it foreshadowed later developments and may even have played some role in laying the groundwork for what later became the world-famous Pontifical Institute for Mediaeval Studies.[22]

Kennedy may also have played a role in bringing the internationally renowned Sir Bertram Windle to St. Michael's College in 1919.[23] There is no direct evidence of this conjecture, but it is likely that they knew each other personally or by reputation. Windle was a then well-known medical doctor, anthropologist, and Catholic writer. Like Kennedy, although about twenty years his senior, Windle had attended Trinity College Dublin and later, like Kennedy, converted from being an Anglican to a Roman Catholic. Moreover, again like Kennedy, he was the honorary librarian of Trinity College Dublin's University Philosophical Society. And, in 1916, both Kennedy and Windle had one of their books reviewed in the very same issue of the Jesuit publication *Studies: An Irish Quarterly Review*.[24] Windle was the first major senior Catholic scholar to join St. Michael's College. Several years later, French philosophers Étienne Gilson and Jacques Maritain came to St. Michael's.

Involvement in College and University Life

There is no doubt that Kennedy was well liked by faculty and students at St. Michael's. Father Edmund McCorkell,[25] who arrived at St. Michael's College in 1917 to teach English after receiving an MA in English from the Catholic University of America in Washington, DC, gave an oral interview in the mid-1970s. In response to a question about Kennedy, McCorkell said:[26]

> Well, I got to know him very well because he was head of the Department of English ... He really was a very effective teacher, very brilliant, and he was quite a tonic here, and gave the place in the way of scholarship and general interest in these things ... He made an impression on the students and I liked him personally a lot and I think we all did. We felt that he did us a lot of good at a time we needed it ... He really was quite a success right from the start. I think he did the place a lot of good.

McCorkell added a caveat, however: 'It was hard to discover his true background. He boasted about so many things that they figured that he had to have lived a hundred years to do all the things that he said he did.'

Several items gleaned from the yearbooks and other sources indicate Kennedy's involvement in college life.[27] Within weeks after arriving at the college, he was one of the judges of a debate between students at St. Michael's and Osgoode Hall Law School on the topic of whether the vote should be extended to women. St. Michael's students argued the affirmative. The college yearbook states:[28] 'On the return of the judges all awaited breathlessly for the words of weal or woe to come from the lips of Prof. Kennedy, who had ascended the platform. He announced that St. Michael's had won, and for almost five minutes the walls of the assembly hall resounded with the exultant shouts of the boys of the double blue.'

In the 1916 yearbook, there is a list of a number of songs and other items.[29] One of these is listed simply as '"The Little Old Ford Rambled Right Along" Prof. Kennedy.' This song was number three on the US music charts in 1915. It was likely sung by Kennedy at a student event. It is a light-hearted song (available on YouTube), one of its verses – perhaps a bit racy for St. Michael's at the time – being:

> And the little old Ford it rambled right along,
> And the little old Ford it rambled right along,
> Now cut that out you naughty tease,
> 'Tis a left hand driver and a right hand squeeze!

Another indication of Kennedy's involvement in the college was the eulogy he delivered in 1916 when Sister Mary Austin died from a complication following surgery for appendicitis.[30] It is also an early demonstration of Kennedy's support for women in higher education. Sister Mary Austin had graduated with a BA from St. Michael's in 1912 with first-class honours and was one of the members of the teaching staff at St. Joseph's College, the Catholic college for women at the university. Kennedy wrote a moving tribute, stating that she was one of Canada's finest scholars, possessing 'rare judgment, continual study of student psychology ... The University has lost not only one of its most brilliant graduates but a teacher of the highest order and for myself, I have lost not a mere colleague, but a guide and counselor who never once misdirected me.'

Kennedy was also involved in the wider university community. He was in demand as a speaker. He gave a talk, for example, on Joseph Conrad to the Toronto branch of the English Association, meeting at Victoria College in 1917,[31] and he spoke to Le Club Politique, meeting in 1918 in the university library, on 'the share the University student should and will take in the political life of the country.'[32]

Kennedy was particularly popular with women's organizations. In 1917, he gave a talk to the Canadian Businesswomen's Club, reported in the *Globe*, making 'a strong appeal to the business women of Toronto to stand together and organize for the making of the new Canada.'[33] Kennedy stated: 'Organized effort without the vote is worth nothing. You have as much right to carry the burden of the nation as the men … Women have hopes and dreams and vision. We want this vision in national life.'

The University College Women's Literary Society presented a series of lectures by university professors on 'modern authors' during the 1917–18 year.[34] The entry in *Torontonensis* states that 'the executive thought the addresses would be even more inspiring if the professors chose the men in whom they were most interested.' All the speakers, except Kennedy, chose male authors – Joseph Conrad, J.M. Synge, George Meredith, and others. Not Kennedy. He chose to talk about Mrs. Alice Meynell, a contemporary English novelist and poet and an early supporter of D.H. Lawrence. The series was probably organized because the English department did not teach modern literature. In a letter to the *Globe* in 1920, Kennedy explained why modern authors were not studied:[35]

> It is emphatically necessary that undergraduates be given the best standards in literature and that they should acquire some background of criticism in order to form literary judgments … We exclude, for the present at least, from the undergraduate courses, such writers as Hardy, James, Meredith, Shaw and many others because we feel that our primary duty is to give that background of standards in English literature which will provide the student with some criterion of appreciation.

He also expressed strong views on the lecture method of teaching. Kennedy, as we know, was highly regarded as a lecturer. In 1917, he wrote about the subject in a letter to the *Varsity*, stating that while he 'valued most highly the tutorial system, lectures had a real and important place in education … Lectures can be stimulating, suggestive and beneficial, and I would be extremely sorry to see the day when lectures should be eliminated as your editorial suggests.'[36]

Like others in the university, Kennedy expressed strong views about the war and the sacrifices that had to be made. President Robert Falconer's opening address to the students in the fall of 1914 had described the conflict in moral terms.[37] 'This is the greatest of moral struggles,' he said. 'Are there to be democracies … or will force tower arrogantly above freedom and enslave intellect?' Classes were later cancelled to allow students to hear an appeal from Falconer to join the Canadian Officers Training Corps. Over 1,200 male students had joined the active force by the end of the 1916 academic year. By the end of the war, the number of casualties was enormous. Over 6,000 persons connected with the university – graduate, undergraduate, and staff – served in the active service. About 10 per cent of that number – more than 600 – died.[38]

In March 1915, Father Carr, the head of St. Michael's, addressed a recruitment meeting at the college:[39] 'We are at war. Our Government has with unprecedented unanimity taken this momentous step. Our duty as Catholic citizens is simple, clear and distinct. We must obey without questioning … As you know, the University authorities are straining every nerve to lead the country with its support. How could we hold up our heads if a finger could be pointed at St. Michael's?' He ended his speech by stating: 'I may say that seven priests of this house have offered their service, and add in conclusion that it will be the great disappointment of my life if it is not given to me to do my bit on the battlefield.'

Kennedy was equally forceful in a piece he wrote for the 1916 St. Michael's yearbook, stressing the need for self-sacrifice:[40]

> A soldier, then, sums up for us, inadequately it is true, our idea of self-sacrifice. He fights for others whom he knows not, for a land which perhaps is mentally indistinct to him. He takes his most valued possession – his life – and he offers it almost blindly to be used for some end for which, ordinarily speaking, it was never intended. Thus he takes his place in the realms of the heroic and is numbered with the Christ Himself … The basis of all things is self-sacrifice … Are we going to take out into the world the soldierly virtues? Or are we going to take out into the world the characteristics of cadly cowardice?

The war ended on Armistice Day, 11 November 1918. The Treaty of Versailles was signed on 28 June 1919. Was Kennedy involved in the peace process? About ten years after the end of the war, there is a press clipping about Kennedy being unable to accept an invitation to visit the University of Bratislava in Slovakia. The clipping states, among other facts, that Kennedy was an advisor to UK Prime Minister Lloyd George during the peace process:[41] 'On the Practical side he was a constitutional advisor for Lloyd George at the Versailles Peace Conference and one of the group of men who drew up the present constitution of the Irish Free State.' His involvement in drafting the Irish constitution will be dealt with in a later chapter. This clipping is the only reference that I have seen about his possible involvement in the Versailles conference. I have not seen any document stating that Kennedy was in any way connected with the peace process. There are no letters to or from Kennedy in the Lloyd George papers. Nor are there Kennedy letters in Prime Minister Borden's papers during this period – Borden was in Europe from November 1918 to May 1919.[42] It is, of course, possible and perhaps not unlikely that Kennedy expressed his views to a participant and that the letter did not end up in an archive. Certainly, he was not in Europe in those years. He never claimed in his own writing that he was involved in the peace process.

Teresa Johnson

On 14 December 1915 Kennedy married Teresa May Johnson in St. Basil's Church on the St. Michael's campus,[43] the oldest building at the University of Toronto still standing in its original location.

The wedding was performed by Kennedy's academic colleague, Father Michael Ryan.[44] Both Kennedy and Teresa stated on the marriage certificate that they were Roman Catholic and that he was thirty-three and she twenty-four. He was actually thirty-six. She entered on the form under 'occupation' the word 'Lady.' In fact, she worked for the English publisher J.M. Dent and Sons, which had opened an office in Toronto on Melinda Street in 1913. No doubt some of Kennedy's fellow St. Michael's colleagues were at the wedding, as well as employees from the Toronto office of J.M. Dent and Sons. Unfortunately, I have not found a single picture of Teresa, let alone a picture of her at the wedding.

What is known of Teresa Kennedy comes from her son Gilbert Kennedy's oral interview.[45] Gilbert stated that his mother, her brother, and their mother went out from England to California in about 1914 'to embark upon a venture which they had been told about.' Gilbert states:

> It turned out not to be much of a venture and grandmother and Dick returned to England, but mother decided that she wasn't doing that. She was going to Toronto to stay with this friend who had stayed at their place in England, Helen Kirkwood. And also apparently being an English scholar got herself a job at J.M. Dent's. When Dad moved to Toronto in '14 as an English scholar it was obvious that somehow or other he would run into her, and they met. I don't know the rest of the details.

Gilbert's spouse, Betty, told me that she believed the marriage took place because Teresa was pregnant, but I have seen no evidence of that.[46] Their first child, Gilbert, was born well over a year later.

I have not been able to discover the details of the California adventure, and I do not know why Teresa's father did not join them. Teresa's marriage certificate notes that her father, Richard Johnson, 'gentleman,' was still alive at the time. Nor have I been able to trace Teresa's relatives in the United Kingdom or elsewhere. According to Gilbert, his maternal grandparents lived in the town of Teddington, outside London, very close to Henry VIII's Hampton Court Palace.[47] Gilbert's maternal grandmother's family – their name was Davison – had come from Jersey in the Channel Islands.

Kennedy and his new bride moved into a suite in a private house at 10 Oriole Gardens, close to Upper Canada College.[48] Kennedy's health was not good during this period. He received a letter from President Falconer in June 1916, thanking him for sending his recently published book, *Studies in Tudor History*.

Falconer stated:[49] 'We should have been glad to have you take part in the work of the Summer Session, but I hope that though you have been prevented from this by ill-health the rest will soon restore you to health.' This letter is the first of a large number of letters between Kennedy and Falconer that refer to Kennedy's health.

During the summer of 1916, the Kennedys rented a cottage on Lake Muskoka, south of Port Carling. Kennedy invited Archbishop McNeil to spend some time with them in July.[50] The archbishop did not reply. Kennedy wrote again on 9 July, stating: 'I wrote to you on behalf of my wife some weeks ago, asking if you would come to stay with us between the 8th and the 31st of July. As I have received no reply, I fear that my letter must have been overlooked or has gone astray.' He renewed the invitation and set out detailed directions on which train to take and when, and ended by saying: 'We do hope you will come. We shall find it a real pleasure to have you.' There is no indication in the archbishop's records as to whether he came. I assume that he did not.

Their first child, Gilbert, was born at the summer cottage they rented in Muskoka in June 1917.[51] Teresa likely stopped working long before the baby was due and would not have worked outside their home after they returned to Toronto from Muskoka. The couple's second child, Beatrice Desiree, was born in October 1918, a little over a year later. Sometime during this period the Kennedys moved to an apartment closer to the university – the Althelma Apartments at the corner of Grosvenor Street and Surrey Place, later torn down to build Women's College Hospital.[52]

Money was a serious problem for Kennedy during this time. St. Michael's College was under financial pressure, and Father Carr was known for offering very modest salaries. Kennedy's total pay was $2,000 a year, worth about $30,000 today.[53]

To supplement his St. Michael's income, Kennedy started to teach in the University College English department as well as in the university's history department.[54] Some subjects, such as English, were college subjects and some university subjects. Modern history was a university subject, and the university paid for the teaching. English was a college subject, which the college paid for. The division between college and university subjects came about when Victoria College federated with the University of Toronto in the 1880s. A measure of expediency played a role in the division of subject matter. Victoria College, for example, did not have a professor of political economy, and so it went to the university. President Daniel Wilson wanted his subject of modern history to be a university subject, and his wish was accommodated. English literature, however, remained a college subject.[55] Each college had its own separate English department.

With the enlisting of many staff members, the head of University College's English department, W.J. Alexander, needed teaching help and hired Kennedy

George Wrong, appointed professor of
history in 1894

to teach a number of courses as a 'substitute lecturer.' Alexander wrote to Falconer, stating that Kennedy 'has been unusually successful in increasing the interest and stimulating the intellectual activities of the students.'[56] In addition, the chair of the university history department, George Wrong, wanted to reclaim jurisdiction over constitutional history, which was then being taught by Henry Lefroy in the Department of Political Economy.[57] In 1917–18, Kennedy taught constitutional history courses in the Department of History, one in Canadian and two in English constitutional history.[58]

As his correspondence with President Falconer shows, Kennedy was eager to obtain a permanent position in the history department, as well as continuing a limited involvement at St. Michael's.[59] At one point, Wrong had told Kennedy that he would become an assistant professor, but that position went to another lecturer in the department, Ralph Hodder Williams. Falconer wrote to Kennedy in June 1918, stating: 'Professor Hodder Williams has been made an Assistant Professor in the Department this year and Professor Wrong thought it was well to defer any action with regard to yourself until later.'

Kennedy complained to Falconer about his lack of a secure position and having to teach nineteen hours a week to barely get by financially. He was teaching English literature as a professor at St. Michael's College, modern history as a lecturer in the history department at the university, and English as a 'substitute lecturer' in W.J. Alexander's English department at University College.

His main interest, he told Falconer, was constitutional history, stating that English 'is a minor subject with me.' He wanted to drop teaching English at University College, but to continue teaching in the Department of History and at St. Michael's. Kennedy went on to say:[60]

> I was to some degree disappointed that I did not get promotion in History last year. Although there was no promise of this, yet I hoped that my position would be made secure, which it is not at present in the University. I find too that this scattering of interest in three departments is more than I can manage – both physically and intellectually. The ... work in three departments leaves me worn out each day, not to speak of the actual burden of class work, which ... now amounts to 19 hours a week.

Kennedy's health was an issue. The acting chair of history wrote to Falconer about Kennedy giving extra lectures to returned veterans in constitutional history. They could not be given in the summer, the acting chair said, because Kennedy had been 'advised by his doctor that he must undertake no work during the summer.' The special course, to be given in the winter of 1919, was to consist of thirty lectures at $10 a lecture, for a total of $300. Kennedy needed the money.[61]

The following year, both Falconer and Wrong agreed that Kennedy should become an assistant professor in the history department. 'Mr. Kennedy is doing excellent work,' Wrong wrote to Falconer, 'and I understand that he is to get the rank of Assistant Professor.'[62]

Kennedy was eventually appointed an assistant professor in the history department for the academic year 1919–20, receiving $2,200 while also continuing to teach English at St. Michael's College at $1,000 a year. On 15 November 1918, a few days after Armistice Day, Kennedy wrote to Falconer, thanking him for arranging for a permanent position.[63] 'I want to put on record my sincerest thanks for the kindness with which you put through my proposals with regard to my position here. It has taken off a great load of anxiety and has given me a definite answer to other calls from England for my services.'

Spanish Flu

On Sunday, 13 April 1919, Kennedy's wife, Teresa, died at the age of twenty-six from the Spanish flu.[64] Fifty thousand Canadians died of the flu – often an agonizing death – and a disproportionate number of them were women in their twenties.[65] Teresa's death certificate shows that, as was common in the case of the Spanish flu, she died of pneumonia, having had influenza for only

Yonge Street Gate of Mount Pleasant Cemetery

twenty-four hours.[66] Kennedy's two young children, both under two years old, were also infected. A week after his wife's death, Kennedy wrote to the chair of political economy, James Mavor, thanking him for his sympathy and adding:[67] 'Yes – we are fighting night and day for the lives of my two kiddies, Gilbert and Beatrice. Poor things they are still in danger – and we can only face each hour like flint.'

Teresa was buried at Mount Pleasant Cemetery.[68] Falconer arranged for Kennedy to receive $1,000 for funeral and other expenses,[69] although the actual amount turned out to be about half that amount.[70] Kennedy considered it a loan.[71] The children recovered. Teresa's friend, Helen Kirkwood, with whom Teresa stayed when she first came to Toronto, initially helped Kennedy look after the children.[72] Gilbert's wife, Betty, thought that the influenza affected her husband's health.[73] He later lost his spleen and suffered from epilepsy. Beatrice was later institutionalized because of mental illness.

Wrong wrote to Falconer in early May 1919, after hearing about 'a dreadful tragedy,' and suggested to Falconer that, if possible, Kennedy receive an increase in his salary.[74] That summer, Kennedy went with his two children and a nanny back to his cottage in Muskoka, during which time he was placed under a doctor's care. 'Insomnia plays hard with me and arterial trouble is threatening,' Kennedy wrote to Falconer.[75]

Later that month, Professor George Brett told Falconer that Kennedy did not think he would be able to teach in the next academic year.[76] George Brett, the distinguished chair of philosophy, had a cottage close to the one Kennedy was renting on Lake Muskoka and kept Falconer informed about Kennedy's progress. On top of his wife's death, there was a fire at Kennedy's cottage, and, according to Brett, 'some affair in England greatly upset him.' Kennedy, Brett wrote, became 'temporarily unhinged – not to say deranged.' (It is worth noting that Brett's field was psychology, and he published the final book in his famous trilogy, *A History of Psychology*, shortly thereafter.)[77] Brett thought that perhaps Kennedy should take a year's leave in England, with some pay, and leave his children with his mother-in-law in England.

By the end of the summer, however, Kennedy had recovered. 'The doctor's report,' he told Falconer, 'is very favourable and he thinks there is good improvement ... I have no wish personally to get leave of absence if it can possibly be avoided ... I am cheered up by the doctor's latest, as the whole future of the kiddies depends on my health.'[78]

5

Turning to the Canadian Constitution

In 1917 – or somewhat before then – Kennedy turned his attention to the Canadian constitution. Kennedy's interest in Tudor constitutional history was a natural entry into Canadian constitutional issues. His knowledge of church politics in the Tudor era gave him a good understanding of the various forces and interests that brought about change in society. His colleague at the University of Toronto, political scientist Alexander Brady, later wrote a memorial tribute in the *Proceedings and Transactions of the Royal Society of Canada*, 1964, stating that Kennedy's 'earlier explorations in ecclesiastical law and institutions exhibited the special bent of his mind, which in Canada found in the constitution a new and fascinating theme.'[1] But it was more than that, as R.C.B. Risk rightly observes.[2] Kennedy saw similarities between England under the Tudors and the constitutional development of Canada. The dominant objective of the Tudors, Risk argued, 'was to make England a unified nation, under the control of the state,' and Kennedy's 'story of Canada's nationhood paralleled the story of the emergence of the English nation state under the Tudors.'

Constitutional history would also provide a steady source of income. As we have seen, Kennedy was at that time supplementing his income by teaching three constitutional history courses in the history department.[3] George Wrong, the chair of history, likely encouraged Kennedy to teach and work on Canadian issues. Wrong had been telling President Falconer for years that constitutional history belonged in the history department, not in political economy, where it was then being taught. Wrong had written forcefully to Falconer in 1911: 'I should like you to put on record my strong dissent from any thought of again separating History and Constitutional History.'[4]

The year 1917 was the fiftieth anniversary of the British North America Act, and this fact alone would have stimulated interest in the constitution. Four lectures were delivered to large crowds in Convocation Hall in March 1917 by Falconer, Wrong, and others,[5] and were later published for the University of Toronto by Oxford University Press under the title *The Federation of Canada*

1867–1917.[6] A prefatory note to the volume states: 'Even though the thought of Canada is almost wholly occupied with the great war which is desolating the world, it would have involved the neglect of a patriotic duty to fail in commemorating so notable an anniversary as that of the fiftieth year of the federal union of the Canadian provinces.' There is no indication that Kennedy was considered as one of the lecturers. He was at that time not known as a Canadian constitutional scholar. That would soon change.

A.H.F. Lefroy

No one would have a greater influence on Kennedy's academic life at the University of Toronto than Augustus Henry Frazer (A.H.F.) Lefroy of the political economy department.[7] He had been appointed as professor of Roman law in 1899 and had been teaching constitutional law for a number of years. Politician and lawyer David Mills, the professor of constitutional and international law, had taught the subject until 1900, when he was replaced on a part-time basis by an Osgoode Hall Law School professor, James McGregor Young.[8] Mills had been appointed the minister of justice in Laurier's government in 1897 and obviously had his hands full.[9] Lefroy eventually took over the teaching of constitutional law from Young.

Lefroy was an English-trained lawyer – Oxford and the Inns of Court – who came to Canada to practise law in 1878, the year before Kennedy was born. He continued to practise while he taught at the university.[10] He was born in 1852 and, as we will see later, was, in fact, born in Toronto. Lefroy's office was in University College, where Kennedy taught English literature. It was natural for them to meet. They both had affection for the British Empire and an interest in constitutional history. Lefroy was directly descended from Henry VII and so would have had some interest in Tudor politics.[11] Both spoke out strongly and publicly for giving women the vote.[12] Lefroy was married with three sons. All three served in the military in the Great War. His youngest, Fraser Keith Lefroy, died on 7 April 1917 from wounds incurred at Vimy Ridge. Lefroy dedicated his last book, *A Short Treatise on Canadian Constitutional Law*, published in 1918, to his son.[13] Lefroy was sixty-five years old at the time. His son was twenty-three.

Kennedy worked closely with Lefroy for three years before his sudden death in 1919.[14] It was reported that he died 'after an illness of a few days brought about by a fainting attack.'[15] Kennedy had actively assisted Lefroy in the publication of Lefroy's text, *A Short Treatise*. In the preface to Kennedy's later major work, *The Constitution of Canada*, published in 1922, Kennedy states:[16]

> For three years before his death he and I worked through carefully the cases in constitutional law while preparing his *Short Treatise on Canadian Constitutional*

A.H.F. Lefroy

Sopwith Camel aircraft in front of University College in 1918

Law for publication. We discussed their bearing and importance, and in determining the form of his work we mutually agreed on many phrases and generalizations.
Almost naturally I have fallen back on these, and I acknowledge my obligations
elsewhere. I cannot, however, let this book go to the press without a recognition of
Professor Lefroy's insight into Canadian federalism, and of a friendship which was
so courteously willing to guide me in a new and difficult field.

Kennedy also acknowledged his indebtedness in obituaries in the *Varsity*[17]
and the *Canadian Law Times*.[18] He and Lefroy obviously got along well. In the
Canadian Law Times, Kennedy noted: 'As a personality, Lefroy was a man of
distinct charm ... [F]ewer memories of him will survive more fragrant than
his buoyant happy vitality.' Kennedy stated in the *Varsity* that 'in the Faculty
Union among his younger colleagues, he spent some of his happiest hours.' Like
Kennedy himself, Lefroy was 'widely read in modern history, in modern literature and in philosophy.' Lefroy, Kennedy stated, had a 'philosophy of law, which
looked behind the rounded case, the tabulated facts, the traditional forms, the
organized statute to principles, to causes, to the human forces at work behind
them all ... His positions were arrived at by incessant workings out of materials

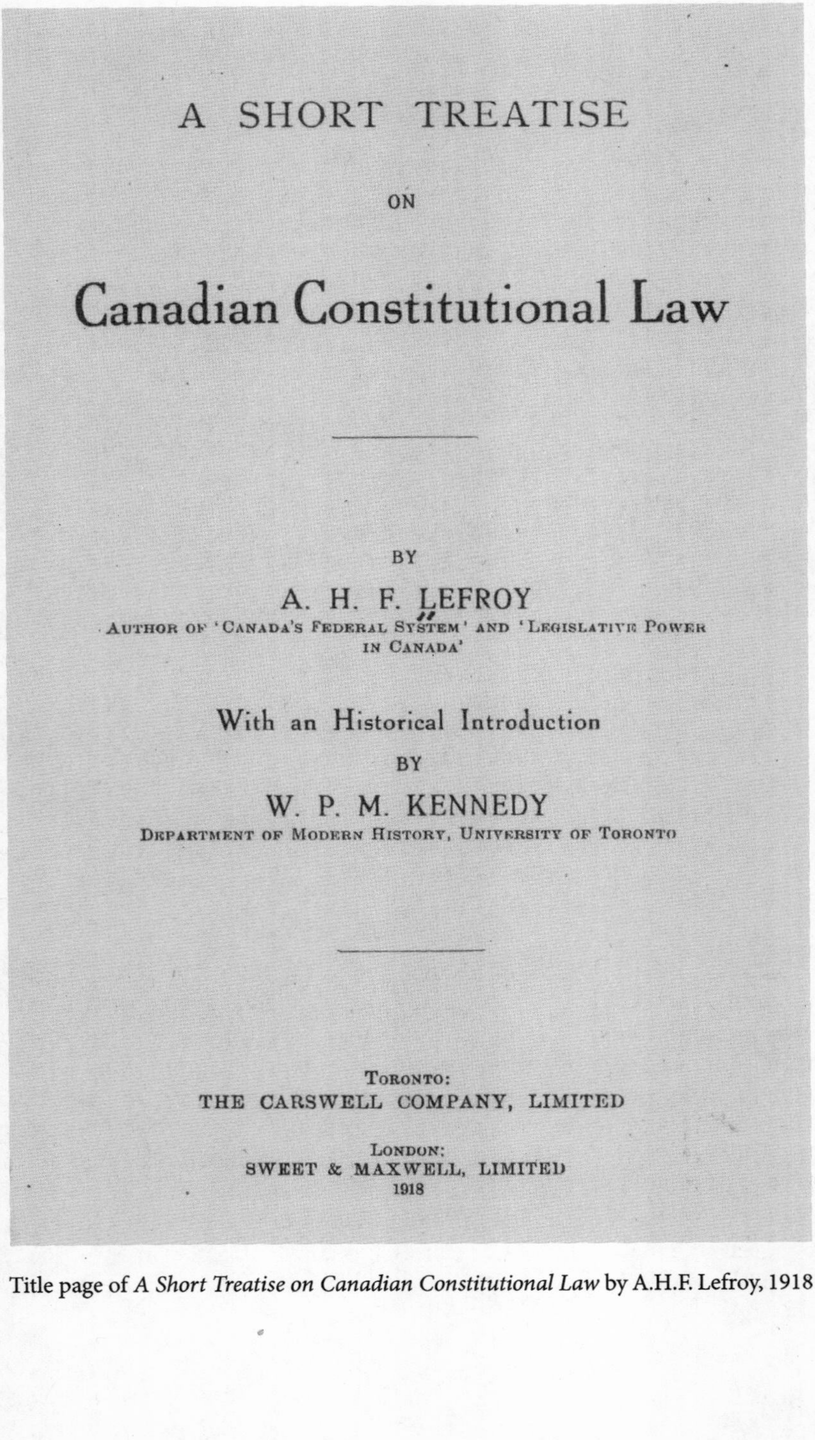

A SHORT TREATISE

ON

Canadian Constitutional Law

BY

A. H. F. LEFROY

AUTHOR OF 'CANADA'S FEDERAL SYSTEM' AND 'LEGISLATIVE POWER
IN CANADA'

With an Historical Introduction

BY

W. P. M. KENNEDY

DEPARTMENT OF MODERN HISTORY, UNIVERSITY OF TORONTO

TORONTO:
THE CARSWELL COMPANY, LIMITED

LONDON:
SWEET & MAXWELL, LIMITED
1918

Title page of *A Short Treatise on Canadian Constitutional Law* by A.H.F. Lefroy, 1918 for himself. He was a legal scientist.' This perspective would continue to be Kennedy's approach to scholarship.

Those three years working with Lefroy constituted Kennedy's entire legal education. It must have been a remarkable experience. He had a first-class teacher. R.C.B. Risk's assessment of Lefroy in the *Dictionary of Canadian Biography* is that Lefroy was 'the leading common-law scholar in Canada in the late 19th and early 20th centuries.'[19] Lefroy's major work was *The Law of Legislative Power in Canada*, published in 1897.[20] He published several other books and over thirty articles, including papers in the *Harvard Law Review*, the *Yale Law Journal*, and a large number of articles in the major English law journal, the *Law Quarterly Review*.

Kennedy had high praise for Lefroy's scholarship. He wrote in the *Varsity* that Lefroy 'poured into [his books] a legal knowledge which no one of his predecessors or contemporaries possessed. His position as an authority was recognized throughout the world, and he was in regular consultation with all the experts in his special subject.'[21] In another publication, Kennedy observed that Lefroy discovered 'the rationale of the Canadian constitution in its combination of federalism with what he [Lefroy] considered the freedom it provided for its own development in accordance with the growth of a young nation.'[22] As a result, Kennedy went on to say, Lefroy 'regarded as of slight applicability American federal jurisprudence.' Like Lefroy, Kennedy also rarely engaged in a detailed analysis of the American constitution. It is interesting to note that had David Mills – who had taught constitutional law before Lefroy – been Kennedy's mentor, Kennedy's scholarship may well have paid closer attention to American scholarship and decisions. Mills had received his LLB from the University of Michigan, and half of Mills's constitutional course had dealt with the American constitution.[23] The result might well have been that – through Kennedy's influence on such major figures as Bora Laskin – somewhat greater attention would have been paid to American constitutional law cases, which are now rarely cited by Canadian courts.

Lefroy's views on provincial powers also influenced Kennedy's early views on the division of powers under the British North American (BNA) Act. Kennedy wrote that Lefroy believed that the BNA Act 'must be interpreted liberally and the powers of the federal and provincial legislatures must each be considered plenary within its scope. Thus he really emphasized the powers of the provinces.'[24]

Like Kennedy, Lefroy had a high regard for Britain and the British Empire. According to R.C.B. Risk,[25] 'he had an unbounded loyalty to Britain and British models, which pervaded his constitutional scholarship as well. All his examples were English cases, and virtually all the references to secondary literature were to English legal scholarship or to continental writing about Roman law.'

Canada, Lefroy believed, would play an important role in the British Empire. He states in the preface to *A Short Treatise*:[26] 'The greatest pessimist ... cannot any longer doubt the glorious future which lies before the British Empire when, with the favour of Heaven, the allied nations have victoriously completed the present titanic struggle ... nor the place which this Dominion is destined to hold within it.'

The BNA Act, Lefroy argued, was a fine document. He states:[27] 'That Act, it may surely be said, is the most successful piece of constitutional legislation which has ever emanated from the Parliament at Westminster ... [T]he more thought and labour one expends on the Constitution of Canada under our Federation Act, the greater grows one's admiration for the wisdom and pre-science of those to whose constructive genius it is due.' It would, he believed, be a model for other countries.

Lefroy – and Kennedy in the first edition of his text on the Canadian con-stitution – rarely criticized Privy Council decisions. The Privy Council, Lefroy wrote, had 'done splendid work upon the interpretation and development of our constitutional system.'[28] When Lefroy did criticize a Privy Council judg-ment in the *Law Quarterly Review* in 1913, he said that never before had he 'seen the smallest loophole for criticism or for doubt as to the correctness of any one of [them] before this last Judgment.'[29]

A Short Treatise on Canadian Constitutional Law

What Kennedy added to Lefroy's *A Short Treatise* was a historical perspective. Lefroy had not looked at the history of the British North America Act in his earlier books. Kennedy wrote a thirty-five-page historical introduction to the book. About this historical material, Lefroy states in his preface:[30] 'I have had the good fortune to enlist the services of Professor W.P.M. Kennedy, of the Uni-versity of Toronto, in contributing an Historical Introduction which I feel sure will be found to add very materially to the interest and value of the book.'

Kennedy looked at what had led to the introduction of the BNA Act of 1867, stating:[31] 'Responsible federal government in Canada is an evolution through a hundred years of anxious questionings, of difficult and complicated situations, of wisdom and folly, of insight and blindness, of despair and faith ... Almost every step towards Canadian Confederation was taken in the light of past expe-rience in constitution making in Canada.'

Kennedy sets out his approach, similar to his approach in earlier books, in writing about that evolution:

It is not a mere retelling of a story. It is an attempt to interpret a development. It is not a mere summary of facts. It is an attempt to find in facts the complex characters and diverse conditions out of which they grew. It is an attempt to ani-mate documents and manuscripts – petitions, letters, ordinances, dispatches, Acts of Parliament – with something of the vital energy which once called them into being; to see the history with contemporary eyes; to reconstruct contemporary standards and ideals; to judge objectively the storm and stress of the human will, and in all the difficult process to give a true and adequate, but above all a living setting to Canadian Confederation.

Kennedy's writing on the Canadian constitution was similar to his earlier work on Tudor politics. Both attempt to 'animate documents and manuscripts.'

Lefroy's *A Short Treatise* was well received. An American reviewer in the *American Political Science Review* stated:[32] 'Mr. Lefroy's more exhaustive work on the constitutional jurisprudence of Canada is well known to special students of this subject, but the present volume will serve a very useful purpose in making accessible to Americans the outlines of a system which affords many interesting contrasts with their own ... Professor Kennedy's introduction is a noteworthy feature of the book. It is admirable both in its proportions and in the good judgment with which controversial historical questions are handled.' The *Harvard Law Review* noted that Mr. Lefroy 'gives us an admirable summary of the main legal hypotheses of Canadian federalism and ... Professor Kennedy of Toronto contributes a useful historical introduction in which Canadian constitutionalism prior to 1867 is discussed.'[33] The *Canadian Law Times*'s reviewer praised the book and noted that 'Professor Kennedy shows a truer sense of proportion than most writers on the subject.'[34] Finally, the *English Historical Review* stated:[35] 'Mr. Kennedy is to be congratulated on the success he has achieved in giving life and meaning to the dry bones of the past; and his attitude is, throughout, impartial and wide minded.'

Kennedy was also influenced by Lefroy's views on legal education. Lefroy had written an article in 1901 in the *University of Toronto Monthly*,[36] entitled 'A University Training as a Preparation for the Legal Profession.' One can see similarities between these views and Kennedy's later approach to legal education. Lefroy argued for the inclusion in legal education of jurisprudence, comparative law, constitutional law, international law, and legal history. He asked whether the study of these subjects is 'likely to conduce to [the law student] attaining a yet higher degree of success in his profession than he otherwise would have done.' Lefroy's answer:[37]

In my opinion it is as clear as the sun at noonday that they must and will do so. From the moment he commences his career those studies will heighten the interest of his work, and so lessen its burden. From the first day they will give him a better grasp on every text-book and on every case he reads ... They may not suffice to make a man a successful lawyer, but they will make a great lawyer greater.

Perhaps it was because of Lefroy's liberal views on legal education that the conservative benchers of the Law Society selected John Falconbridge in 1913 to be the principal of Osgoode Hall Law School rather than Lefroy, who was also a candidate for principal.[38]

Lefroy's Background

Because of Lefroy's importance in Kennedy's career, I will say more about Lefroy's background. He came from a particularly successful family.[39] His father, John Henry Lefroy, came to Canada from the United Kingdom in 1842 to head up the Dominion Observatory. The reader probably has a vague recollection of having heard the name Lefroy before. It may be because a mountain in the Rockies is named Mount Lefroy and because there is a painting by Lawren Harris of Mount Lefroy, which sold for $1.6 million in 2006, a then record for a Lawren Harris painting.[40] A painting of Lefroy's father, by Paul Kane, was sold for about $5 million in 2002 and donated to the Art Gallery of Ontario – establishing a record at the time as the highest price paid for a Canadian painting.[41]

Another relative was A.H.F. Lefroy's cousin, Thomas Lefroy, who had been the chief justice of Ireland from 1852 to 1866.[42] According to Toronto lawyer John Honsberger, whose law firm had occupied the same premises on Bond Street as Lefroy, Lefroy kept a portrait of his cousin, the chief justice, in his law office.[43] As another interesting aside, Tom Lefroy is perhaps best remembered today as Jane Austen's 'only known love interest who … shaped Jane's outlook on love and life.'[44] In one letter, dated 16 January 1796, Jane Austen writes:[45] 'At length the day is come on which I am to flirt my last with Tom Lefroy, and when you receive this it will be over. My tears flow as I write at the melancholy idea.'

Lefroy's mother's family had an equally distinguished background.[46] Emily Merry Lefroy, his mother, was the daughter of John Beverley Robinson, the chief justice of Upper Canada (later Canada West) from 1829 to 1862. He was one of the central figures in what is known as the 'family compact,' which controlled the governance of Upper Canada.

It is not at all surprising that Lefroy settled in Canada. He had been born in Toronto. His mother's family, the Robinsons, lived in Toronto, and his brother, a military man, had returned to Canada the year before A.H.F. Lefroy did.

Documents of the Canadian Constitution

While working with Lefroy on *A Short Treatise*, Kennedy was preparing a book for the Canadian division of Oxford University Press, reprinting primary Canadian constitutional documents: *Documents of the Canadian Constitution 1759–1915*.[47] The preface is dated 1 February 1918, five months before Lefroy's preface to *A Short Treatise*.[48] 'My primary object in publishing this collection of documents,' Kennedy wrote in the preface, 'has been to provide students of Canadian Constitutional development in the University of Toronto,

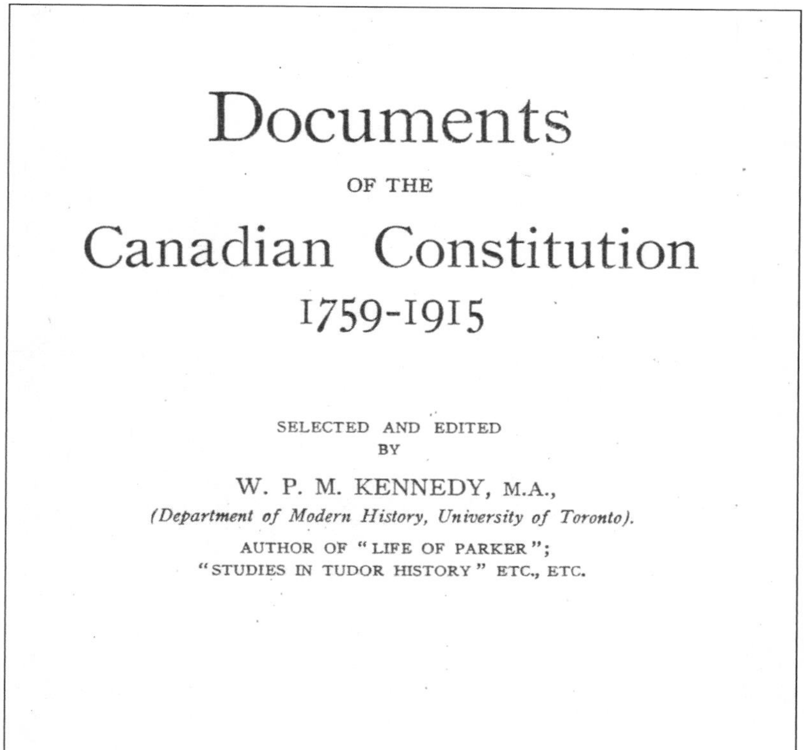

Documents

OF THE

Canadian Constitution
1759-1915

SELECTED AND EDITED
BY

W. P. M. KENNEDY, M.A.,
(Department of Modern History, University of Toronto).

AUTHOR OF "LIFE OF PARKER";
"STUDIES IN TUDOR HISTORY" ETC., ETC.

TORONTO
OXFORD UNIVERSITY PRESS
AND AT
LONDON, NEW YORK, MELBOURNE, BOMBAY
AND MADRAS
MCMXVIII

Title page of *Documents of the Canadian Constitution, 1759–1915*
by W.P.M. Kennedy, 1918

with a handy and convenient volume.' It was difficult at the time for students and others to find copies of these primary sources. Kennedy's entire career as a scholar since graduating from Trinity College Dublin centred on the effective use of primary documents.

Kennedy must have felt the need for such a volume in his teaching. Other collections were out of print or unsuitable. Lefroy had a volume of materials, but it was limited to case law.[49] Kennedy wanted a single volume, he explained in the preface, 'in which acts of parliament, ordinances, proclamations and such dry-as-dust material would be vitalized by being brought into touch with letters, speeches and contemporary illustrations.' He 'tried to include no document which has not proved its value in actual teaching.'

Documents of the Canadian Constitution was a great success and, along with his introduction to the later *A Short Treatise*, established his reputation as a serious scholar of constitutional law. The reviews were again excellent. The *Globe* stated:[50] 'Prof. Kennedy has placed students of Canadian history under a deep obligation.' The *Canadian Law Times* – probably written by Lefroy, its editor – said:[51] 'Professor Kennedy makes this development unfold itself with dramatic interest. No other volume in existence provides such an adequate collection of material for its study.' An English academic, who had published one of the out-of-date competing texts, noted in the *English Historical Review* Kennedy's 'service to students of Canadian history' and commented that, although the notes are very brief, they are 'always illuminating and to the point.'[52]

Kennedy dedicated the book to George Wrong:[53] 'To G.M. Wrong, Professor of Modern History in the University of Toronto as a token of friendship and esteem.' The preface concludes with the sentence: 'The dedication feebly acknowledges a friendship which lies deeper than common work in a common subject would suggest.' For reasons that will later become clear, the dedication and the last sentence were removed from the second and larger edition of the book, published by Oxford in 1930.[54]

It would not be such clear sailing in the coming years.

6

Pauline Simpson

In early May 1920, a little over a year after the death of Kennedy's first wife, an announcement appeared in the *Globe* newspaper:[1] 'Mrs. J.B. Simpson, 78 Fairholt Rd., Hamilton, begs to announce the engagement of her only daughter, Pauline, to Prof. W.P.M. Kennedy, M.A., Litt.D., University of Toronto. The marriage will take place very quietly late in June.' In fact, the marriage took place early in June – on 8 June at the bride's home in Hamilton. He was forty-one and she twenty-five. The marriage certificate had said[2] that the couple intended the marriage to take place in Toronto, but a later notice in the *Globe* said that the marriage had taken place at 78 Fairholt Road in Hamilton.[3]

Pauline Simpson was a student at University College. She had graduated from Hamilton Collegiate in 1915 and entered the home economics course at the university.[4] She did not graduate[5] in 1919, as anticipated, and instead became a special student in arts in the 1919–20 academic year.[6] She never did graduate. Anticipating graduation, her picture had been in the 1919 *Torontonensis* yearbook.[7] The entry starts with a poem: 'She has wit and song and sense/ Mirth and sport and eloquence' and then goes on: 'Pauline knows how to think, but, better still, she knows how to laugh and is a jolly companion. Steady enough to hold the position of Head of Queen's Hall, we prophecy even greater honours after college. Her fellow Hamiltonians hope these will not carry her far from home.' Queen's Hall, at the southeast corner of Queen's Park Crescent and since torn down, was at the time the only University College women's residence.[8] She had also been on the executive of the Women's Undergraduate Association of University College.[9]

According to Gilbert Kennedy, Pauline was one of Kennedy's students.[10] As we saw in an earlier chapter, this liaison was not his first relationship with a student. Gilbert states in his oral interview: 'He remarried in 1921 and this time a student in one of his English classes, Pauline Simpson.' The existing records do not show who Pauline's teachers were. Note that Gilbert said they were married in 1921, not 1920. Others have since used 1921 as the date of the marriage. This

SIMPSON, PAULINE.

"She has wit and song and sense
Mirth and sport and eloquence."

Pauline Simpson's entry in the 1919 *Torontonensis*

date is obviously what Gilbert's parents had told him. In fact, Gilbert did not know about his father's first marriage or that Pauline was not his birth mother until he was in his teenage years.[11] He states: 'When I was somewhat older, in my teens, both Bea [his younger sister] and I were advised by my stepmother that she was only my stepmother ... It made no difference, we continued on as one family unit. Matter of fact in some ways cemented it more.'

The application for the marriage license – sworn on 3 May 1920 – states that Kennedy was a Roman Catholic and Pauline was an Anglican.[12] There are some clear errors in the application. Kennedy's mother is not listed as Selina McClure Kennedy, as it should have stated, but rather as Ena McCullough Kennedy. And Kennedy states that he was born in Lurgan, England, rather than Lurgan, Ireland. This error was likely an attempt by Kennedy to deceive the Simpsons into thinking he was English, not Irish.

Pauline had four older brothers. Her father, who had been a conductor with the Grand Trunk Railway, died from inhaling coal fumes in the St. Clair tunnel in 1904.[13] The train had accidentally split apart while carrying coal under the St. Clair River from Port Huron, Michigan, to Sarnia, on the Canadian side. Six persons died in that tragic event. Pauline's father was in the caboose when his

Pauline Simpson's family

body was discovered.[14] Mrs. Jane Simpson then raised the five children on her own, at first in Sarnia and then in Hamilton, with, I assume, a small company pension and, according to one relative, some help from the Masonic Order.[15] All Pauline's brothers are now dead, and only two of their children are still alive, each of whom I spoke with. One nephew described his grandmother, Pauline's mother, as a person with 'a lot of guts.'[16] Her children were very successful: an industrial executive, a banker, a doctor, a lawyer, and, as we will see later in the case of Pauline, an important leader in many charitable organizations.

My conclusion from these discussions? Pauline's siblings viewed Kennedy as a rather odd character and were not pleased that Kennedy was Catholic and substantially older than Pauline or that she never finished her degree. She stayed home and looked after the children – with the help of a middle-aged Irish housekeeper[17] – at 110 Quebec Avenue, just north of High Park in the west end of Toronto, which they had acquired in 1921.[18] Behind Kennedy's back, they would sometimes refer to him as 'Mac,' presumably because of the name 'McClure,' or as 'Cooey,' because when he came into his home he would call out to Pauline with the birdcall 'Cooey.'[19] Pauline's nephew, now retired lawyer

George Simpson, the son of Pauline's youngest brother, described Kennedy as an 'odd duck' and referred to the 'strange relationship between Kennedy and the Simpsons.'[20] There was, he said, 'no great love lost' between Kennedy and his brothers-in-law.

The families were not close, although several of the grand nieces and nephews were married by Kennedy's son, Reverend Frere Kennedy. George Simpson had met Kennedy only a few times, but his older brother, also a lawyer, often dined with the Kennedys and sometimes stayed at the Kennedy home while attending his last year of Osgoode Hall Law School in the late 1940s. Like others I have talked with, George described Kennedy's habit of abruptly leaving for his study as soon as he finished the meal.[21] George's wife described Pauline as a 'dear lady.'

There is undoubtedly more to the story, because a number of the persons I communicated with, including Pauline's nephew George, pointed out to me that Pauline's eldest brother, John, an executive of Imperial Oil, did not attend the wedding because he got married in Ottawa on the very same day, 8 June 1920, that Pauline married Kennedy in Hamilton.[22] The brother's wedding certificate – he was thirty-eight and his bride thirty-seven – confirms that it was so.[23] Kennedy's wedding certificate shows that Pauline's mother was a witness at the Kennedy wedding in Hamilton.[24] To state the obvious, it is strange that the brother and sister could not coordinate the dates of the two weddings. Pauline's mother had to choose between the marriage of her eldest son and her only daughter, her baby, Pauline. Frere told me that Pauline's mother got along well with Kennedy.

Why was Kennedy's wedding held on 8 June, when Pauline's mother had put in the *Globe* that it would be in late June? Is it possible that Pauline was thought to be pregnant, and so the wedding was moved forward and took place in Hamilton, rather than Toronto? No child was born in the year after the wedding. But, as we will see later, the marriage upset a number of persons in the university. George Simpson told me that his aunt's generation never talked about such matters.[25] He also told me that 'there was something in the family he doesn't know anything about.' My chat with Pauline's niece, Jane Spears, the daughter of another brother, now in her nineties but still very sharp, more or less confirmed what George Simpson told me – that there is more to the story.

Two years after his marriage, Kennedy stated in a letter to the distinguished political science professor Berriedale Keith of Edinburgh University, without elaboration:[26] 'I've got into a hole with a graduate student here.' He was, no doubt, referring to his relationship with Pauline Simpson. There is no evidence that I have seen to suggest any involvement with another student after he married Pauline. The words 'got into a hole' suggest that there is, indeed, more to the story. It is not the language one would use if it had been a normal romance, even with one of his students.

Whatever the circumstances were, George Wrong would likely have disapproved. Five years after Kennedy's marriage, Lester B. (Mike) Pearson, then a lecturer in the history department, also married one of his students, but Wrong was not aware of the relationship. Historian John English wrote in his biography of Pearson that Pearson's colleagues, and especially Wrong, were apparently unaware of the developing romance.[27] Professor English states: 'The secret, as usual, was poorly kept, although Mike's colleagues apparently did not know. Not even Methodist self-righteousness could have excused Mike's serious dalliance with one of his students in the eyes of George Wrong. Fortunately, they were able to avoid his stern gaze.' Pearson and Wrong remained on good terms. Pearson also had a good rapport with Kennedy, who later suggested Pearson should apply to the Department of External Affairs and not stay in the academic world, where he would have to compete with the likes of Donald Creighton.[28]

Professor George Wrong

George Wrong, the chair of the history department, had a serious falling out with Kennedy in 1920. Wrong obviously disapproved of Kennedy's relationship with a student. Father McCorkell, Kennedy's colleague at St. Michael's College, later stated in an oral interview:[29] 'I think their quarrel was basically over this student that Kennedy married ... I don't know the whole story at all.' Vincent Bladen of the political economy department was equally vague in his memoirs, stating:[30] '[Kennedy] had some sort of conflict with Wrong.' Wrong had been a supporter of Kennedy before the announcement of his marriage to Pauline, arranging to assist him financially after his first wife died and telling President Falconer that 'Mr. Kennedy is doing excellent work.'[31] After the marriage to Pauline, Wrong wanted to get rid of Kennedy. There are no letters in the Wrong papers in the University of Toronto Archives that spell out his specific concern about Kennedy's conduct. There are many letters in the archives from Wrong to his wife Sofia over the years because he travelled extensively, but he was in Toronto in 1920 and so, unfortunately, there are no letters from him to his wife for that year, when more comments on the matter might have been written.

George Wrong graduated with a degree in theology from the University of Toronto's Anglican theological college, Wycliffe, in 1883, became an Anglican priest in 1886, and had taught church history at Wycliffe since his graduation. When the professor of modern history at the University of Toronto, Daniel Wilson, died in 1892, Wrong applied for the position. He was at first appointed as a lecturer and two years later, in 1894, was appointed as the chair of history. That appointment resulted in a major strike by University College students in 1895 – a strike led by future prime minister William Lyon Mackenzie King – the only significant strike in the university's history.[32]

George Wrong, circa 1925

The immediate cause of the strike was the dismissal by the government of the popular University College professor of Latin, William Dale, for publicly criticizing Wrong's appointment to the chair of history. Dale and others alleged that there were more qualified candidates and that the reason Wrong was appointed by the government of Ontario – in those years the government made the appointments to the University of Toronto – was because Wrong's father-in-law was Edward Blake, the chancellor of the university, who had been the premier of Ontario and the leader of the Liberal Party of Canada. The premier of Ontario was a Liberal, Oliver Mowat. The minister of education had been against Wrong's appointment, but was overruled.

Blake may, indeed, have played a role in the appointment by praising his son-in-law's qualifications for the job to government officials, while saying that he must keep out of the controversy. Another result of the appointment is that the issue played a role a number of years later in transferring the power of appointing professors from the government to the university. Wrong's appointment, however, turned out to be a good choice.[33] During his thirty-five-year career at the university, he was successful in building a strong history department and promoting the study of Canadian history. He was the founding editor of the *Canadian Historical Review* and the creator of the Champlain Society.

Others in the Department of History, including Wrong's son Hume (later a senior official in External Affairs), were hostile to Kennedy and at various times tried to block his advancement, in part because of what Hume Wrong referred to in a letter to his father several years later as the 'cause célèbre', which most likely refers to the circumstances surrounding his relationship with Pauline Simpson.[34]

It is possible that Wrong and Kennedy did not get along because they both came from modest backgrounds and both were upwardly mobile. We'll see evidence of this social climbing in the case of Kennedy in later chapters. Wrong gave the impression that he was part of the social elite. He took snuff and had a love affair with Oxford. Yet, he came from rather humble origins. As Christopher Moore has written, 'his parents and grandparents had been not-very-successful farmers in hardscrabble Elgin County, Ontario. His own college degree was from a low-church theological school, and he was never more than a summer visitor at his beloved Oxford.'[35]

Termination?

George Wrong must have told Kennedy that his position would be terminated, because a few weeks after his wedding Kennedy wrote from Nova Scotia – probably on his honeymoon – to the chair of political economy, James Mavor, informing Mavor that he was resigning from the University of Toronto in June of the following year. Kennedy asked Mavor to support his application to Dalhousie University, where the chair of history was vacant, as well as his applications to positions in the archives in Ottawa and Toronto.[36] 'I am quite downhearted,' Kennedy wrote to Mavor, 'but G.M. W[rong] has played a curious game to which there is neither Alpha nor Omega,' the first and last letters of the Greek alphabet – that is, from beginning to end.

Kennedy asked President Falconer to intervene in the dispute with George Wrong, but, on 29 November 1920, Kennedy wrote Falconer:[37] 'On reflection it will be far better not to mention any personal differences between me & Mr. Wrong ... I don't want ... to wash dirty linen, and above all, I do not wish to complicate a situation which will, someday & somehow straighten itself.' It did not straighten itself. On 25 November 1920, Wrong wrote to President Falconer asking that 'official notice should be given to Prof. Kennedy that his appointment terminates at the close of the present academic year.'[38]

The termination did not go through that year, but there was obviously no future for Kennedy in the history department. There are a number of letters in the Falconer papers showing Falconer writing on Kennedy's behalf in 1921 and 1922 to a number of colleges in England for a chair in English or modern history, including supporting Kennedy's applications for the chair of English language and literature at the recently established Royal Air Force College in England.[39] No offers were apparently forthcoming.

One possibility had been as head of the history department at McGill. In May 1921, Principal Arthur Currie of McGill had written to Falconer asking his opinion of Kennedy as the head of history.[40] Falconer had a high regard for Kennedy and gave a glowing recommendation, stating:[41]

> Professor W.P.M. Kennedy, who is on our staff in History, is a very brilliant man. He undoubtedly is one of the best scholars among the History men in Canada, having done particularly good work before he came to Canada on the Elizabethan period for which, I understand, he was given his Doctor of Letters at Trinity College, Dublin. He also got out about two years ago a valuable book of documents on Canadian history. I judge also that he is an interesting teacher. He is certainly a very interesting conversationalist, and has many of the characteristics of the Irish, although he is only partly of Irish descent. He has had a hard time here having lost his wife with the flu and being left with two small children. However, he has since married again and seems to me to have settled down to his more normal condition.

No mention was made by Falconer of the so-called 'cause célèbre.' Kennedy obviously was not offered the position.

Political economy then came to the rescue. In 1922, at age forty-three, Kennedy transferred from the Department of History to the Department of Political Economy, where Robert MacIver was the acting head and would the following year become the head of the department.[42] Kennedy would be a lecturer on federal institutions, and his total salary from political economy would be $2,000.[43] Kennedy, who continued to teach in the history department, was demoted by Wrong to 'special lecturer.'[44] Kennedy had wanted to maintain the rank of assistant professor, but Wrong refused his request, although the rank was later restored. Kennedy had earlier given up his academic position at St. Michael's College. Reversing the usual pattern, Kennedy had gone from assistant professor to lecturer in a few short years.

The withdrawal from St. Michael's was because Kennedy had ceased being a Roman Catholic and, in fact, ceased to be religious at all. Father McCorkell stated that even when he was at St. Michael's his religion was not clear,[45] and his

Robert MacIver, head of the Department of Political Economy, 1922–27

son Gilbert states in his oral interview that his father was not a church-goer.[46] In a letter to President Falconer in March 1922, Kennedy wrote:[47] 'I write to ask you to change my religious affiliations to "Church of England" on the records of the President's Office.' In a private exchange six years later with John Defoe, the influential editor of what later became the *Winnipeg Free Press*, Kennedy stressed that he was an agnostic. The newspaper had said in print that he was a Roman Catholic, and Kennedy wrote privately to Defoe to say:[48] 'I am not a R[oman] Catholic, nor an Anglo-Catholic and if I go to church at all I go to Dr. H.J. Cody's. Every atom of my convictions is against obscurantism … wherever found.' Kennedy had been quoted in the *Free Press* in connection with the issue of the disestablishment of the Church of England. He was, he explained to Defoe, against disestablishment – a divisive issue in England at the time – not on religious grounds, but because it would weaken the monarchy by removing the direct link with God in the consecration of a monarch in the coronation ceremony. 'Monarchy,' Kennedy believed, 'is our symbol of "unity."'[49]

Kennedy was grateful to MacIver. As Vincent Bladen later wrote,[50] 'MacIver bailed him out by appointing him as a Special Lecturer in Mediaeval Economics and in Federal Institutions.' Kennedy dedicated his 1922 book, *The Constitution of Canada*, to MacIver and also stated in the preface:[51] 'To Professor R.M. MacIver, University of Toronto, I am under the greatest obligations, and in the dedication I attempt not merely to acknowledge these, but to record a friendship which lies deeper than a common interest in history would suggest.' Given that MacIver is not otherwise mentioned in the book, it is obvious that personal reasons lay behind the dedication.

MacIver and Kennedy had much in common. They came to the University of Toronto at about the same time. MacIver had been teaching at the University of Aberdeen. Both had cottages on Lake Muskoka, as it seems did many members of the faculty. They also had similar interests in the development of national states.[52] MacIver likely supported Kennedy in the so-called 'cause célèbre' and assisted in his transition from history to political science. MacIver had had his own problems in the early 1920s when a member of the board of governors, Colonel Reuben Wells Leonard, wanted MacIver fired because of MacIver's ultra-socialistic teachings and his pro-labour book, *Labour in the Changing World*, published in 1919. MacIver's academic chair, Colonel Leonard said, should be renamed the 'Chair of Political Anarchy and Social Chaos.'[53] Falconer and others came to MacIver's defence. Whether Kennedy was involved is not known. In a speech at a special meeting in Convocation Hall, Falconer said that a professor should be able 'to pursue and expound his investigations without being compelled to justify himself to those who differ from him.'[54] MacIver left Toronto in 1927 for a distinguished career as a sociologist at Columbia University. Many years later, he wrote in his memoirs about 'the somewhat erratic but distinguished W.P.M. Kennedy.'[55]

A Productive Scholar

Kennedy was a very productive scholar in the early years of the 1920s. The next chapter will be devoted to his magnum opus – the book that cemented his reputation – *The Constitution of Canada*. There were also a large number of his book reviews in the new *Canadian Historical Review* and a number of articles in that journal and elsewhere on constitutional issues.

But Kennedy's growing interest in Canadian constitutional history had not entirely replaced his interest in the Tudor period. He published, in 1924, a

Alcuin Club Collections

XXVI

Elizabethan Episcopal Administration

An Essay in Sociology and Politics

By

W. P. M. Kennedy, M.A., Litt.D.

Trinity College, Dublin
Assistant Professor of Modern History and Special Lecturer in Federal
Institutions in the University of Toronto

Volume I

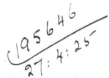

A. R. MOWBRAY & CO. Ltd.

London : 28 Margaret Street, Oxford Circus, W.1

Oxford : 9 High Street

Milwaukee, U.S.A. : The Morehouse Publishing Co.

1924

Printed in Great Britain

Title page of *Elizabethan Episcopal Administration: An Essay in Sociology and Politics*, vol. 1, by W.P.M. Kennedy, 1924 major three-volume study in Tudor ecclesiastical history: *Elizabethan Episcopal Administration*, dealing with visitations and injunctions.[56] Visitations, it will be recalled, were investigations ordered by bishops into ecclesiastical practices in the area under their jurisdiction. Injunctions were the orders that were issued following the investigations. The Crown, as the head of the Church of England, played a major role in the process of the administration of the visitations and the resulting orders. The second and third volumes of the book consist of copies of the primary documents. Volume one is Kennedy's two-hundred-page analysis of the documents.

Kennedy had always intended to continue his work in this field, as he had indicated in an article in the *English Historical Review*, published in 1917, where he had written:[57] 'The three volumes of Visitation Articles and Injunctions, 1536–75, which Dr. Frere and I published in 1910 ended with the death of Archbishop Parker. Pending the preparation of a later series, it may be convenient to print a provisional list of materials for the years 1576–1603.' The article is then followed by a three-page list of documents. When published, the later series would complete the presentation and study of all the relevant documents on visitations during Elizabeth I's reign.

However, Kennedy was having difficulty completing the task. Kennedy likely had brought with him from the United Kingdom copies of documents from archives and registries that were not available in print. The University of Toronto library and other libraries in Canada did not have the resources to purchase the books he needed. Those funds, however, eventually became available after the war through the dean of arts and science, Professor A.T. DeLury. Kennedy thanks in the preface 'my friend and colleague Professor A.T. DeLury ... for his kindness in being the means through which material aid was available to complete the necessary research.'[58] It did not hurt Kennedy's plea for funds that DeLury had had his own conflict with Wrong – DeLury had been one of the leaders in attacking Wrong's appointment as the professor of history in 1895.[59]

Not surprisingly, the book is dedicated to Walter Howard Frere, his mentor at Mirfield Monastery. Kennedy states:[60] 'In the dedication ... I acknowledge not only my greatest helper, but my greatest friend. Dr. Frere and I worked together for many years in Tudor history, and I am glad to think that he has been able to read this book in manuscript and to help it through the press. I should like to ask him to accept it as a tribute to a friendship which, since my university days, has known neither deviation nor shadow caused by turning.' Again, the 'turning' was a reference to Kennedy becoming a Catholic sometime before the Great War.

The subtitle of the book is 'An Essay in Sociology and Politics.' It deals with ecclesiastical matters, but is not confessional writing where events are told from the perspective of a particular religion, as his earlier books were. By now, Kennedy was an agnostic. 'I have no controversial purposes to serve,' he states in the

preface, dated 1 March 1923. 'I have tried to write as objectively as possible …
That the sphere should chance to be ecclesiastical is immaterial.'[61] The book is
a sociological study, enabling him to study society by the use of primary documents – his principal contribution to scholarship.

Kennedy goes on to say in the preface:[62] 'Small though the book is, as it has
grown I have found myself entering into the daily life of a people. I have seen
the clash of interests, the struggle of wills, the fermenting of political, ecclesiastical, religious propaganda, the gradual development of accepted positions – all
the storm and stress of not a few Elizabethan activities.' The articles and injunctions, Kennedy states, 'were intimately related to everyday life.'[63] Moreover,
Kennedy, for the first time in one of his books, used statistical tables, stating
in the preface:[64] 'I hope my readers will not be repelled by them … Statistics
are too often looked on as one of the historian's many valleys of dry bones; but
a little imagination can give them a fascinating sociological life.' In later years,
Kennedy continued his interest in 'everyday life' through his study of administrative tribunals and family law that looked at issues involving daily life.

Kennedy explained that the idea for this approach came from Dr. J.N. Figgis,
whom he had known from the House of the Resurrection in Mirfield.[65] Figgis
was an ordained priest who had received a doctorate from Cambridge under
the important historian Lord Acton. Figgis is remembered as part of a group
of British legal theorists, often referred to as pluralists, who included Harold
Laski and F.W. Maitland. They examined the sovereign power, suggesting that
it should not be limited to the state but, in the words of the *Oxford Dictionary of
Sociology*, should 'in addition be distributed amongst the self-governing associations of civil society.'[66] Kennedy's friend Robert MacIver, the chair of political
economy at the University of Toronto, to whom he dedicated his book on the
constitution of Canada, was a proponent of this approach and no doubt played
a significant role in convincing Kennedy to adopt a sociological viewpoint. Surprisingly, MacIver is not thanked in *Elizabethan Episcopal Administration*.

The concept of sovereignty, to which Kennedy would later return, was, in
Kennedy's view, at the heart of the break with Rome in the sixteenth century.
England had gone from 'the mediaeval theory of two sovereign spheres – spiri-
tual and temporal' to a single sovereign sphere where the state controls both.[67]
In later chapters, we will see Kennedy arguing that sovereignty can be distrib-
uted or subdivided by giving a measure of sovereign power over Canada to the
United Kingdom through the British Commonwealth. In breaking with Rome,
Kennedy states, 'the choice for England was not between [P]rotestantism and
Roman Catholicism, but between her own national life and authority and a
religious system which claimed a kind of universal political jurisdiction.'[68]

The book was well received and is still cited. It was Kennedy's last scholarly
work on Tudor history. In 1925, he announced in the *English Historical Review*
that he was not going to carry the work past Elizabeth's reign because of the

'pressure of other work.'[69] He then sets out a list of documents after 1603, 'with the hope that [the work] might be completed by some other worker, or at least that it will show the way to useful materials for social history.' The following year, 1926, he set out a list of documents prior to the reign of Elizabeth, stating:[70] 'The following notes represent the beginnings of research which I cannot now hope to finish. They are published in the hope that they may be of use to some other worker in Tudor history.' Kennedy's future scholarship would concentrate on the Canadian constitution.

7

The Constitution of Canada and Beyond

Kennedy's 1922 text, *The Constitution of Canada*, was built on his book of primary documents on the Canadian constitution and his historical introduction to Lefroy's *A Short Treatise on Canadian Constitutional Law*. It also reflected a number of ideas that Kennedy had been writing about in various journals prior to the book's publication.

He wrote in the UK periodical *The New Statesman* in 1919, for example, about Canada's place in the British Empire.[1] 'The Empire,' he stated, 'is worth preserving as a force to maintain justice and right in the world.' Canada has control over its internal affairs, he argued, but 'with all of Canada's freedom, with all her growing consciousness of nationality, there is still wanting that crown of nationality – effective control of foreign policy.' Many different ideas were being tossed around, such as an Empire Parliament, an Empire House of Lords, or an Empire Cabinet. Kennedy himself had suggested a scheme during the war:[2] 'Some months before the arrangements for an Imperial War Cabinet were made [in 1917], I suggested publicly that each Canadian Cabinet should have a Canadian Foreign Minister who would be *ipso facto* a member of the British Cabinet, and share the foreign policy of that Cabinet on Canada's behalf.' 'For Canada,' he argued, 'she must complete her Canadianism ... Time alone can give Canada an effective voice in foreign policy, and an effective voice in determining her foreign relations.' 'Just as I believe a super-world State may finally come,' he argued – before the founding of the League of Nations – 'so I believe there will be a super-State – called the British Commonwealth.'[3] But, he concluded, 'We must wait.'

In 1921, Kennedy wrote in the *British Contemporary Review* that, although Canada's Conservative prime minister, Sir Robert Borden, wanted change, 'the question of reconstruction of Imperial relations practically disappeared in Dominion political circles since Premier [Arthur] Meighen succeeded Sir Robert Borden.'[4] 'There really appears to be no general desire for change ... The Province of Quebec would be a solid group against it ... Quebec is satisfied with the contract arrived at in 1867, and she is not ready to risk her privileges, as she fears she might be compelled to do, in a wider grouping, a newer synthesis of Empire ... As far as Canada is concerned, all that seems clear at present is that the Empire is to be a voluntary league of autonomous nations, rather than a confederation of States with a confederate Constitution.'

Note that he refers to a 'confederate Constitution.' He made much of the distinction between a federation and a confederation. Both words were used in the debates leading to Confederation, but Kennedy wanted to limit the word 'confederation' to groupings of countries, such as the Austro-Hungarian Empire. In a 1921 article 'The Nature of Canadian Federalism' in the recently established *Canadian Historical Review*, he states that 'Canada is a federation.'[5] His plea never caught on, which is why we recently celebrated the 150th anniversary of 'Confederation' and not of 'Federation.' The twenty-page article, with an additional eight pages, was republished later that year as a short book by the University of Toronto Press, under the same title.[6]

Another article in the *Canadian Historical Review* in 1921 was entitled 'Nationalism and Self Determination.'[7] It criticized those, such as Woodrow Wilson, who advocated a separate political existence or self-determination on the basis of nationality. Kennedy believed[8] that nationalism is 'almost uniformly related to a fatherland; and it is of such consuming force that men will gladly die to preserve it.' There are also, he wrote, logistical problems.[9] If a plebiscite referendum is to be held to decide on sovereignty, how do you determine 'the precise area of the plebiscite?' How do you protect the inevitable 'small, a hopelessly small, minority of one nationality ... in a state entirely dominated by another nationality?' Populations move. Do you 'revise boundaries for each nation-state on some regular basis, such as the decennial census?' 'The idea that national and political lines must coincide – is not only impracticable,' Kennedy stated, 'but fundamentally unsound ... It is more likely to turn the world into a slaughter-house than into a paradise ... The nation which coincides with the state is too liable to become intolerant, to make nationalism the basis of the state; but the state in which there is a variety of national feeling is forced to learn in the school of experience lessons which will prove useful in world issues.'

All of these ideas are reflected in *The Constitution of Canada*.

A Major Text

It seemed natural for Kennedy to write a major text on the constitution of Canada for Oxford University Press. He had already published his book of documents on the constitution with Oxford.[10] There is a substantial file in the Oxford University Press Archives concerning the second edition of *The Constitution of Canada*, which came out in 1938, but relatively little on the first edition of 1922. The Oxford archivist explained that this gap in the records was 'due to the earlier publication being handled by our London office, which shed a great deal of material during war-time evacuation and later weeding of its files.'[11] There can be little doubt that the London file would have been an interesting and thick file. The very small file on the first edition in the Canadian branch contains the surprising fact that the contract executed by Kennedy in October 1918 was to produce a book jointly with University of Toronto historian and librarian W. Stewart Wallace to be entitled *The Development of Canadian Government*.[12] Royalties were to be 20 per cent after the first 2,500 copies.[13]

In October 1921, however, Wallace withdrew from any connection with the book.[14] Perhaps he felt he had his hands full, having just been appointed the assistant librarian at the University of Toronto, soon to become the head librarian, and had also taken on the editorship of the recently established *Canadian Historical Review*. Perhaps Wallace's close working relationship with George Wrong played a role in his withdrawal. And maybe Wallace had his eye on another book, *A First Book of Canadian History*, which he published in 1928 and which sold over half a million copies.[15] Kennedy simply mentions in the preface to his 1922 book that 'Mr. W.S. Wallace has given me, especially in the earlier chapters, the benefit of his knowledge of Canadian history.'[16]

Reception

Kennedy's 1922 book was a great achievement. It was particularly remarkable considering all the turmoil in his life in the years leading up to its publication and the new courses he was preparing in those years. It received many excellent reviews. These were collected in a one-page sheet prepared by Wm. Tyrrell and Company, booksellers and engravers at 8 King Street West,[17] Toronto, who were selling the book for $5.00 plus 20 cents for shipping.[18] The advertisement started with an endorsement from Viscount Richard Haldane, a past and future lord chancellor of England, who said it was 'a remarkable volume,' as well as a quote from a member and future chair of the university's board of governors, the Reverend Henry Cody, later the president of the University of Toronto, who said that the book was 'a national service to Canada and the Empire.'[19] These endorsements were followed by excerpts from twenty-three reviews. The book was favourably reviewed in the major English papers and journals. The *Times* called it 'a work of great accuracy and conspicuous fairness'; the *Observer*, 'alive, human, dramatic'; the *Law Quarterly Review*, 'an admirable and most readable book'; and *The New Statesman*, 'a book which will rank high in the literature of political science.'

Canadian reviews in papers and journals were equally positive. The *Canadian Historical Review* said that it was 'a theme worthy of a Macaulay'; and

THE CONSTITUTION OF CANADA

An Introduction to its Development and Law

BY

W. P. M. KENNEDY, M.A., LITT.D.

TRINITY COLLEGE, DUBLIN
ASSISTANT PROFESSOR OF MODERN HISTORY IN THE UNIVERSITY OF TORONTO

HUMPHREY MILFORD

OXFORD UNIVERSITY PRESS

LONDON   EDINBURGH   GLASGOW   COPENHAGEN
NEW YORK TORONTO MELBOURNE CAPE TOWN
BOMBAY   CALCUTTA   MADRAS   SHANGHAI

1922

Title page of *The Constitution of Canada: An Introduction to Its Development and Law*
by W.P.M. Kennedy, 1922

Advertisement by booksellers and engravers, Wm. Tyrrell and Company

Saturday Night said it was 'brilliant ... a monumental work.' No doubt, Kennedy was particularly pleased with the review by an unattributed reviewer in the Toronto *Star Weekly*, which compared his book to the discovery of insulin.[20] 'The sun of insulin is in the ascendancy,' the reviewer stated dramatically, 'but even its world rays cannot obscure other university stars of the first magnitude. One of the brightest of these is W.P.M. Kennedy, associate professor of modern history. His latest work, "The Constitution of Canada," is said to be in its way quite as epoch making as insulin.' The *Star Weekly* reported that the book had sold 3,000 to 4,000 copies in less than six months.[21] In the United States, the *Christian Science Monitor* called it 'masterly,' while in the *New Republic*, Harold Laski wrote: 'To say that Dr. Kennedy has written a valuable book is to do him less than justice; he has written what is likely long to remain the standard introduction to the study of the Canadian constitution.'[22]

The *Star Weekly* characterization may have been an exaggeration, but the book was indeed a major triumph and was responsible for establishing Kennedy's reputation as a major constitutional scholar. Political scientist Alan Cairns states that Kennedy was 'the most influential constitutional analyst of the period from the early twenties to the middle forties.'[23] Kennedy was

Canon Henry Cody, chairman of the University of Toronto Board of Governors

obviously pleased with the reception of his book. He kept Falconer informed of his scholarly work, writing:[24] 'The *Constitution* goes well. I had charming letters about it from [constitutional law scholar] Berriedale Keith of Edinburgh & from [Rodolphe] Lemieux the speaker [of the Canadian House of Commons]. [Ernest] Lapointe quoted it in the house.' Kennedy added a P.S. to the letter: 'Arthur Meighen wrote me a nice letter about an article of mine on Canada and the Imperial Conference.' Kennedy did not hide his light under a bushel, to use a biblical expression that Kennedy might have used.

Kennedy may have been a self-promotor and name-dropper, but I do not doubt that he actually corresponded with the persons whose names he was dropping. The prime ministers' papers in Library and Archives Canada, for example, show items relating to W.P.M. Kennedy in the papers of Robert Borden, Arthur Meighen, William Lyon Mackenzie King, and Richard Bennett. There are letters in these collections concerning gifts by Kennedy of books and articles, invitations to visit the university to address students, discussions of various public policy matters, and other items. By far the most entries are in the William Lyon Mackenzie King papers, where there are about seventy items listed, including letters relating to election results in 1926, 1930, and 1935.[25]

The correspondence appears to indicate that Kennedy was a Liberal supporter. 'A thousand congratulations,' he wrote to Mackenzie King at midnight on election day, 14 September 1926.[26] 'I could not do much publicly, but you may have recognized some of my handiwork in speeches and the press.' Kennedy seemed to have had a friendly although somewhat peripheral relationship with Mackenzie King. It is possible that King knew about and sympathized with Kennedy's troubles with George Wrong. As discussed in the previous chapter, King had had his own run-in with Wrong over twenty years earlier. It was the appointment of Wrong – the university chancellor Edward Blake's son-in-law – as the professor of history in 1894 that caused King to lead the famous student strike in 1895.[27]

The previously mentioned 1923 letter to Falconer shows that Kennedy had plans for follow-up volumes to his book on the constitution. Kennedy wrote:[28] 'I've been collecting material for the second vol. of my *Constitution*, on "The Government of Canada" which the Oxford Press have ordered. It may be two and will take me a year or two.' A similar plan was revealed to Berriedale Keith later that year:[29] 'I hope to add two vols. to the *Constitution of Canada*.' However, Kennedy's career path suddenly changed. At the end of the 1922 academic year, he was no longer, as the book states, an 'assistant professor of modern history in the University of Toronto.'[30] He was a special lecturer in the Department of Political Economy as well as in the Department of History.[31] The two further proposed volumes were never prepared.

Aim of the Book

Kennedy's book *The Constitution of Canada* traces the development of Canada from the earliest days of the French explorers until the date of publication. The comprehensive scope of the book is evident from an examination of the twenty-five chapter headings. All the important familiar events are discussed: the Royal Proclamation of 1763, the Quebec Act of 1774, the Constitution Act of 1791, Lord Durham's Report of 1840, the granting of responsible government in 1848, the British North America Act 1867, and later events up to and including 1922. The study, Kennedy states in the preface, is 'an evolutionary account of the various movements and stages which have issued into the organized political life of the Canada of to-day.'[32] 'It is well worth studying,' Kennedy writes, 'as a recent example of the process of nation-making.'[33]

> To understand [this nation-building] it is necessary to keep the social background always in view, to show how, under the special conditions of a new land, the conjuncture of groups detached from older countries, particularly England and France, the insistent near influence of a great neighbouring country already ahead in economic development, and the later influx of more heterogeneous elements from many lands ... have worked in the end to a certain unity and a sure nationhood.

This sociological approach is the same as he had used for his studies of Tudor ecclesiastical history. The aim, he states, 'is to trace the stream of development. The mere retelling of a well-known story lies more or less outside its purpose. It is rather an attempt to find in the facts the complex characters and diverse conditions out of which they grew; to seek the causes which gave energy and purpose to the constitutional evolution; to animate dead documents with something of the vital energy which called them into being.'[34]

Kennedy succeeds admirably in presenting this historical and, indeed, sociological view of the development of Canada. Unexpected events occur, but everything leads towards the present, with Canada as a nation within the British Empire. The book is written with a dramatic, engaging style, which is not surprising, given that Kennedy had won the prize in English prose at Trinity College Dublin. Here, for example, is how he describes the setting for the historic Quebec Conference of 1864, which led to the 'federation' of 1867.[35] 'On October 10, 1864,' he writes, 'there assembled at Quebec one of the most epoch-making conferences in history.' He continues:

> It is impossible to reconstruct those pregnant days without emotion. Outside, the most ghastly civil war in history was desolating a kindred race, and Sherman was on the move, leaving destruction and ruin in his wake. Inside, broken little provinces had toiled for a long colonial night and caught apparently nothing. Sectionalism was a recent sore. Party politics then as now were unstable. Jealousies, but recently shed, might easily be reassumed. Suspicion, publicly cast out, lay watching in the secret recesses of every heart. Every step forward meant a backward look to see how others viewed it.

In the preface, Kennedy states that the book had two aims. One was to study Canada 'as a recent example of the process of nation-making,' but a second aim was to use Canada 'as a most significant illustration of that real and yet not absolute sovereignty which defies the older theories of government and thereby leads us to a truer conception of the state.'[36]

Kennedy attacked the so-called Austinian doctrine of sovereignty, a now-discredited doctrine that had been developed by legal philosopher John Austin in the nineteenth century, which makes statehood conditional on full and absolute sovereignty. 'As the law of nations now stands,' Kennedy wrote, 'Canada is not a sovereign state ... Canada's position in the League of Nations is due to its position in the empire.'[37] It 'cannot negotiate directly with a foreign country in the political or any other important sphere.' Canada had signed the Treaty of Versailles officially ending the First World War acting on the advice of the British secretary of state for foreign affairs.

Canada's status, Kennedy argues, should be recognized by the law of nations. The future of the British Empire required it. Such an approach, as we saw earlier, de-emphasizes nationalism. Nationalism, he argued, causes wars. In historian Carl Berger's words, Kennedy 'was skeptical of post-war efforts to redraw the map of Europe so as to reflect the claims to political nationhood of all groups possessing sufficient cohesiveness to be regarded as nationalities. Doubting not only the practicality of applying such a doctrine to a continent having an estimated sixty-eight nationalities, Kennedy in addition charged that modern nationalism and the striving for absolute sovereignty was a retrogressive and dangerous force.'[38]

Groupings of nations, Kennedy argued, is better:[39] 'While the civilized world is groping for the solution of the problem [absolute sovereignty] thus created, the British Empire is at least [suggesting] the form which that solution must take.'[40]

Kennedy continued with this important theme over the years. 'Having cast down the Austinian idol,' he stated in 1924, 'let us grind it to powder.'[41] And, in a speech on Irish politics in Convocation Hall that same year, he stated that 'sovereignty is that pestilential legal fiction which has drenched this poor world in oceans of blood.'[42] He did not comment further on the danger of nationalism in the second edition in 1938. The growing threat of war caused by nationalism spoke for itself.

Over the years, Kennedy's views on the division of powers, however, would change dramatically. There is a marked contrast between the first and second edition with respect to his view of the Privy Council and its interpretation of the division of powers. In the first edition, he has few complaints about the Privy Council and is optimistic about how the court interpreted the distribution of power in the British North America Act. He stated:[43] 'Room was thus left for constitutional progress and for the development of a theory of constitutional law related as far as possible to the social and political growth of the people.' The Privy Council decisions, even those favouring provincial rights, 'have humanized the British North America Act. They have given it the elasticity of life.'[44]

Kennedy accepted without criticism Lord Watson's provincial rights view, set out in the 1892 *Maritime Bank* case, that 'the object of the Act was neither

to weld the provinces into one, nor to subordinate provincial governments to
a central authority, but to create a federal government in which they should all
be represented, entrusted with the exclusive administration of affairs in which
they had a common interest, each province retaining its independence and
autonomy.'[45] 'Lord Watson's conception,' Kennedy states, 'has been acted on to
such an extent that to abandon it would upset much of the structure of the
constitution.'[46]

There is no demand by Kennedy in the first edition to abolish appeals to the
Privy Council, although he writes of 'a future when Canada might reasonably
hope normally to make its own supreme court supreme in reality.'[47] And there
is no discussion of an amending formula.

In November 1921, the Privy Council released its judgment in the *Board of
Commerce* case, dealing with a 1919 federal Act controlling prices.[48] In a judgment delivered by Viscount Haldane, the court held the legislation invalid, stating that, under the 'peace, order and good government' clause, the legislation
would only be constitutional 'under necessity in highly exceptional circumstances.'[49] The decision was not published in the official law reports until 1922
and was probably on board a ship heading for Canada when Kennedy completed the proofs of his book. As all students of constitutional law learn, this
case led to the *Snider* case in 1925, where Haldane limited the 'peace, order and
good government' clause to 'extraordinary peril to the national life of Canada,
as a whole.'[50]

In the second edition of *The Constitution of Canada*, as we will see, Kennedy
strongly criticizes these decisions.

There are a number of important constitutional issues that Kennedy did not
mention in either edition. He did not, for example, mention the possibility of
a bill of rights. Nor did he have much to say about Aboriginal treaties or other
Aboriginal issues.[51] And there are relatively few discussions of the American
constitution, except to point out that the BNA Act was a reaction to the 'great
source of weakness' in the American system, that is, the power of the states.[52]

Nor does he discuss any reform of the Senate. The lack of senate reform was
the only major criticism of Kennedy's first edition that Harold Laski made in
his *New Republic* review:[53] 'Dr. Kennedy's program does not include any full
discussion of what may be termed the dynamics of the Canadian constitution.
It would be interesting to know whether the Dominion Senate is really necessary now; it has been, clearly enough, the outstanding institutional failure.'

There is also no mention in either edition of the possibility of a province uni-
laterally seceding from the federation. Kennedy would clearly have said it was
not possible, because he states that 'Canada's severance from the empire could
only take place by imperial and not by federal legislation.'[54]

We will return to Kennedy's changing views on the Canadian constitution in
later chapters.

8

Deeks v. H.G. Wells

In June 1923, Florence Deeks came to see W.P.M. Kennedy at his office in the cloisters of University College. Would Professor Kennedy, she asked, assist her in revising a book she was writing, 'The Highway of History?'[1] Kennedy agreed to do so, and thereby he became part of a long continuing legal saga which lasted eighteen years and ended up before the Judicial Committee of the Privy Council in England.

The story is a complex one, told brilliantly by historian Brian McKillop in *The Spinster and the Prophet: Florence Deeks, H.G. Wells, and the Mystery of the Purloined Past*, published in 2000. It is an important story in connection with Kennedy's life and career, however, because it affected Kennedy's reputation in some circles – and still does.

Florence Deeks was a student at the University of Toronto in the 1890s, but never graduated.[2] In about 1914, supported by her wealthy brother – who had made his money through railway engineering – she started researching and writing a manuscript, which she was going to call 'The Web of the World's Romance.'[3] It would – in her words – document 'man's struggle for social values including women's share in that struggle.' The Judicial Committee of the Privy Council, who later dealt with her case, described it this way: the manuscript 'involved the whole history of the world from its very beginning to the present day, with the special object of emphasizing the important part that women had played in the social development of the world.'[4] She did her research in the Toronto Public Reference Library on College Street, now the University of Toronto bookstore.[5]

Deeks completed her 185,000-word manuscript in 1918 and in July of that year took it to Macmillan Canada, then on Bond Street, just north of St. Michael's Hospital.[6] She had just turned fifty-four. She had previously left a copy of the manuscript with J.M. Dent and Sons, where Kennedy's late wife Teresa had worked.[7] The company declined to publish the manuscript.[8]

Florence Deeks (left) with her sister in London in the early 1930s to argue
her appeal to the Privy Council

Having kept the manuscript for over six months, Macmillan also turned it
down and suggested that Deeks try her hand at a different book. The plan of
her manuscript, she was told, was 'impractical.'[9] In 1920, however, Deeks discovered that the great author H.G. Wells had published a best-selling book, *The
Outline of History*, with Macmillan. It contained over 400,000 words and well
over 1,000 pages.[10] The book would make Wells rich. He received a royalty of 20
per cent on the advertised retail price,[11] and over two million copies were sold
in the United States and England alone. The book is said to have become at the
time 'the most popular work in the world by a living author.'[12]

Wells's book, Florence Deeks believed, plagiarized her manuscript. Wells
must have read her book, she concluded. The themes were the same. The contribution of women was also a feature of the Wells book. There were, she found,
factual errors she had made that were repeated in the Wells book.[13] Some of
the pages in her returned manuscript were well thumbed.[14] And how, she wondered, could Wells have written a 400,000-word book in just two years?[15]

With her wealthy brother's support, she engaged one of Canada's pre-eminent
lawyers, Norman Tilley.[16] There was no rush to bring legal action, which did

H.G. Wells, author of *The
Outline of History*

not need to be commenced until 1925. A number of experts, including George
Brett, the head of philosophy at the university, and Catholic scholar Bertram
Windle of St. Michael's College – names that the reader will remember from
earlier chapters – supported her position.[17]

Kennedy's Involvement

In the meantime, Florence Deeks continued work on a somewhat different version of her book, which she entitled 'The Highway of History,' and at this point
she came to see W.P.M. Kennedy. Whether Kennedy knew her through his late
wife's association with J.M. Dent and Sons or through others in the history
department is not known, but it is likely that he would have been aware that
the book she had been working on for years had been turned down by several
publishers, including Dent and Sons, and that important persons in the university with whom Kennedy was close thought that H.G. Wells had used her
ideas. Deeks would almost certainly have known about Kennedy because of his

Faculty offices in the University College cloisters

support for women's issues and his visibility at the university and in the wider community.

Kennedy was definitely interested in undertaking the work. As we know, he needed money in these years, particularly because he had recently purchased a modest home at 110 Quebec Avenue, just north of High Park, into which he and Pauline and their two children had moved in 1921. In a handwritten memorandum to her legal counsel before the trial, Deeks outlined her relationship with Kennedy:[18]

By 1923 the case seemed to be rather well worked up but as nothing further of any importance was done and I was anxious to complete my book I began the last revisions in June (1923) with the help of Prof W.P.M. Kennedy ... Because of his great interest in the book he had repeatedly offered to help me through with it to the end. He would not only write the preface and help get a publisher but he would help through to publication by reading galley proofs, etc. – help, he said, which he had never before given to anyone but which he was glad to give in this case because of his interest in the work.

Kennedy, she wrote, wanted secrecy: 'He enjoined secrecy with regard to his private help. He especially did not want Professor Wrong, the head of his department, or Sir Robert Falconer to know.' As we know, Kennedy's relationship with Wrong was rocky enough without giving Wrong additional ammunition. Kennedy started to work on the manuscript that summer at his rented summer cottage at Kincardine on Lake Huron. Deeks worked with Kennedy on and off over the next two years.

In her memorandum to her counsel, Deeks expressed her concern with Kennedy's bills. She wrote:

> Prof. Kennedy was very expensive and kept constantly charging higher and higher for his help. Several times I had to dispute his bills and make definite agreements with him concerning his charges – from which, however, he constantly deviated. This expense worried me but as my brother made no serious objection and the book seemed to be progressing favourably I kept on with the work.

And she expressed concern with his recommendations, stating:

> I got along rather fast, but more and more I was suspicious of the 'good faith' of Prof. Kennedy, not only with regard to his bills but also with regard to the help he was giving me. There were times when I believed he made alterations to injure rather than to improve my work. When at last he advised me to add ten, and more, chapters – which would keep me writing until the case was outlawed [that is, barred by a statute of limitations] I was much puzzled.

Deeks believed that Kennedy had a personal connection with Macmillan. 'Prof. Kennedy and Prof. Stewart Wallace, the university librarian,' she wrote, 'were completely "tied up" with the Macmillan Company. It was said – generally – that Prof. Kennedy, Prof. Wallace and Mr. Eayrs (President of the Macmillan Co. of Canada) were on especially good terms of friendship.'

She ended her relationship with Kennedy in early 1925 and turned to others in the history department, stating: 'After a few more circumstances my faith in Prof. Kennedy was so shaken that I cautiously withdrew from accepting any more help from him. I then received valuable assistance from Prof. Wrong and his son ... Murray Wrong of Oxford, Prof. Fay, Prof. Taylor and Prof. Flenley. I finished the work in June 1925.'

When the manuscript was finally finished, Florence Deeks and her sister took copies to New York and left them with a number of major publishers. The book was rejected by all the publishers, in part because of other general histories that had already been published. An editor at Little, Brown and Company, the last publisher to respond, told her: 'Your book would be subject to comparison with

Wells' "Outline of History." For that reason I think you will have difficulty in securing a publisher at the present time.[19]

In October 1925, a writ was issued in Ontario for half a million dollars with Florence Deeks as the plaintiff against the defendants Macmillan and H.G. Wells. The writ was eventually served on the defendants in November 1927[20] and was heard by Ontario Supreme Court Justice William Raney,[21] without a jury, in a six-day trial in 1930.[22]

Florence Deeks's brother, George Deeks, was no longer willing to continue to support the lawsuit; as a consequence, Norman Tilley would no longer be representing her.[23] Her brother had lost a case in the Privy Council in 1916 and had to pay all the costs. He knew how expensive litigation could be. A noted Toronto lawyer, R.S. Robertson of the Fasken firm, later the chief justice of Ontario, took over the case.[24]

Counsel for Deeks introduced a number of experts, including George Brett, the head of philosophy at the University of Toronto, and William Irwin, a professor of Oriental studies at the university.[25] We do not know whether Kennedy believed it was plagiarism. Deeks never mentioned Kennedy's view, which suggests that he may have been doubtful about the merits of her case.

The defendants claimed that Deeks's manuscript was never sent to England and that Wells had never seen it. They were, however, worried. The lawsuit is not 'a bluff,' the head of the New York division wrote to the head of the Canadian division, stating that if 'you are thinking that the present move is a bluff I advise you to remove such an idea at once from your minds as these people are taking enormous pains in this matter.'[26] The defendants engaged their own experts. One of the defendants' experts was Frank Underhill of the history department.[27]

In his reasons for judgment, delivered on 27 September 1930, Justice Raney held against Deeks. Raney had no doubt about his decision. He said it was not necessary to hear final arguments by the defence. He referred to the 'fantastic hypotheses' of the plaintiff's lead expert, Professor Irwin, the professor of Oriental languages, who was supported by the plaintiff's other experts. Raney believed the defendants' evidence: 'Mr. Wells' evidence was a flat denial. He had never seen or heard of Miss Deeks' manuscript. The evidence of the witnesses called by the Macmillan Company satisfies me of the good faith of that company and that no improper use was made of Miss Deeks' manuscript.'[28]

'There is no doubt,' Raney stated, that Florence Deeks 'believed in the wickedness of the Macmillan company of Toronto and of Mr. Wells ... [A]s time passed it became an obsession.' He concluded his judgment by stating:[29] 'This action ought not to have been brought; having been brought, it ought to have been discontinued after the examinations for discovery, and certainly it ought not to have been brought to trial. As it is, I have no alternative but to give the defendants their costs.'

Kennedy's Name at the Trial

W.P.M. Kennedy's name came up only once in the trial, but in an important context. Counsel for Macmillan, R.D. Moorhead, asked Deeks at the very end of his cross-examination a final and important series of question:[30]

> Q: I think you told [counsel for another defendant] that you revised your book in 1920? – A. Yes.
> Q: I think you told him that you revised your book in 1923? – A. My final revision.
> Q: You did make [revisions] in 1925? – A. That took me from 1923 to 1925.
> [And then counsel asked the very final question in the cross-examinations.]
> Q: Now, just one more question, and I am through – for a time did you have an expert, Professor Kennedy, help you to revise, to a very considerable extent your whole work? – A. Yes in 1923 and 1925.

Kennedy's name had not come up in the examination for discovery of Deeks. Why was it asked? It appears to have been asked in order to get on the record Deeks's admission that Kennedy had worked on the subsequent manuscript in the event that the defendants wanted to bring forward evidence or suggest in closing argument a serious allegation they had been exploring.

The potential allegation was that Deeks's original manuscript, 'The Web of the World's Romance,' which had been turned down by Macmillan, had later been deliberately changed by Deeks and Kennedy to make it seem more like the Wells manuscript.

McKillop explores this question in some detail in his book. Macmillan knew that Kennedy had worked on a later version of Deeks's manuscript and started making enquiries. McKillop writes:[31]

> This trail of assumption inevitably led to the earlier involvement of W.P.M. Kennedy in the preparation of 'The Highway of History.' Could it be that, as Wells suggested, the entire exercise was some kind of elaborate smokescreen, a way of incorporating elements of *The Outline of History* into a second Deeks manuscript and then somehow slipping them into an altered version of 'The Web' as if to suggest they were Florence Deeks's original thoughts?

Two years earlier, Wells had written to Macmillan putting forward this very scenario: 'Our case will be that the Web has been rewritten to substantiate this claim since the appearance of the Outline.'[32]

In 1927, Macmillan began investigating Kennedy's involvement in the case. They spoke with Professor Robert MacIver, who had recently moved from the University of Toronto to Columbia University.[33] MacIver, it will be recalled, was the person who had brought Kennedy into the Department of Political

Economy in 1922, after George Wrong had, in effect, fired him. MacIver had also given advice to Deeks on her lawsuit, recommending she drop the case.

After a discussion with Macmillan in New York in September 1927, MacIver prepared a short confidential memorandum – a little over one page long – for Macmillan about what George Wrong had told him in 1925 about Kennedy's involvement with Florence Deeks. Wrong had informed MacIver that Deeks had told him[34]

> that Professor Kennedy had undertaken the revision of the manuscript, that he had charged her very considerable sums for this work, and that in addition Miss Deeks had visited Professor Kennedy at his summer cottage at Kincardine, Ontario, during the process of revision. Professor Wrong informed me that Professor Kennedy had originally demanded the sum of $100 per chapter, which Miss Deeks professed to be quite willing to pay, that afterwards he had made several additional charges on various grounds, and that the total sum he received for these revisions was in the neighborhood of $15,000.

MacIver goes on to state: 'This information was later confirmed to me by Miss Deeks, though not with any financial details, at an interview which I had with her in May, 1927.' MacIver also notes: 'At the time of our interview Professor Wrong informed me that he had just received from Miss Deeks herself the statement of the expenditures which she had incurred to Professor Kennedy.'

Fifteen thousand dollars was an enormous sum – over $200,000 today – about five times Kennedy's annual salary.[35] The head of Macmillan's New York office took the issue of this alleged payment very seriously, writing to the head of the Toronto office:[36]

> In view of Professor MacIver's statement to us yesterday to the effect that Miss Deeks employed Professor Kennedy of Toronto to revise her MS ... and paid him large sums of money for such revision the Deeks' suit, to my mind, takes on a different complexion. Whereas formerly it seemed a perfectly honest and innocent suit it now apparently becomes a plot to rob this and the other companies attacked in the suit not only of their money but of their good name.

There are no records in the Deeks papers of what the total amount was. And Kennedy left no records about his involvement in the case. The case is not mentioned in Gilbert Kennedy's long oral history. The $15,000 figure is hearsay upon hearsay upon hearsay. The higher the figure, the more suspicious the conduct. As McKillop puts it:[37] 'Not stated in MacIver's memorandum, but clearly implied, was the notion that Kennedy would only have charged such an exorbitant amount if he had been involved in something of great risk to himself and his career. Had the mercurial Irishman become a party to plagiarism?'

77 Spadina Road, as it appears today

We do not know what Kennedy actually contributed to Deeks's manuscript or what he received for his work, although we can be sure that it was a substantial sum and would be sufficient to allow him to move in 1925 from his modest home on Quebec Avenue, near High Park, to his fine home at 77 Spadina Road, for which he paid exactly $15,000 in early 1925 – $8,000 in cash and a mortgage of $7,000.[38]

In the end, no evidence was introduced by the defendants that Florence Deeks's original manuscript had or might have been changed. It is highly likely that no such evidence was found. Even if the defendants had some evidence, it was a dangerous tactic to introduce the evidence unless it was more or less conclusive. In any event, the defendants were confident of winning the case. They were not even called on to give a closing argument. We do not know whether they would have suggested the possibility that the manuscript might have been changed if they had given closing addresses.

McKillop suggests that, by introducing the fact that Deeks was revising the work with Kennedy's help, counsel for the defendants 'had introduced doubt and confusion over whether "The Web" had remained unrevised after Ms. Deeks had seen *The Outline*.'[39] 'The implication was clear,' McKillop goes on to say. 'She had used Wells's book to improve her own.'

Did MacIver believe that Kennedy was involved in wrongdoing? MacIver does not mention the Deeks case in his memoirs, but speaks well of Kennedy, stating: 'Another of a group of really good men was the Englishman Vincent Bladen, and from the History Department we acquired our professor of constitutional law, the somewhat erratic but distinguished W.P.M. Kennedy. I became quite proud of our department.'[40] This wording is not language he would have used about someone whom he thought participated in fraudulent conduct. Wrong had also told President Falconer about the payment,[41] but it did not seem to have affected Falconer's good relationship with Kennedy.

I do not believe that Kennedy was involved in any fraudulent conduct, although he certainly would have regarded Florence Deeks, with her brother's deep pockets, as a good way to improve his standard of living – as did many of the other University of Toronto professors involved in the case, including George Wrong. McKillop writes:[42] 'The defendants gleaned nothing further about the relationship between "The Web" and "The Highway of History" before the trial took place.' It should also be noted that Macmillan New York, who were the ones exploring the issue of fraud, published a book by Kennedy in 1932, so they apparently did not hold any such alleged conduct against him.[43]

Kennedy's alleged conduct would have fortified George Wrong's view that Kennedy was an undesirable person. He continued to badmouth Kennedy in his correspondence with President Falconer. In a note to Falconer in the summer of 1926, he added to comments he had made about Kennedy over the phone, stating:[44]

> I think that I ought to add one thing to what I have said about K. Some years ago when I had to make up my mind about him, I consulted Brett who had much to do with him and is a psychologist. He said that his peculiarity would probably intensify as he grew older and considered him as distinctly abnormal ... I see now increased signs of his lack of sane mentality. His megalomania has increased. He calls himself the official advisor of the Irish State and says that all the Canadian provinces go to him for counsel.

Appeals

Florence Deeks appealed to the Ontario Court of Appeal,[45] representing herself.[46] The court unanimously dismissed the appeal in August 1931,[47] but gave her leave to appeal directly to the Privy Council, bypassing the Supreme Court of Canada, as was permissible at the time. The record book for the Privy Council appeal consisted of over 500 pages.

She appeared without counsel before the Privy Council, which allowed her to proceed, even though the Privy Council's usual practice was not to hear appeals when there were concurrent findings of fact in the courts below. There was some hope for her when their Lordships raised questions about the fact that Macmillan Canada had recorded on its log that Deeks's manuscript had been returned to her in February 1919, when other evidence indicated that it was not returned until April 1919. Lord Atkin asked:[48] 'How do you account for the falsity of the Macmillan Record Book?' In the end, the Privy Council held in her favour on this factual issue – that the manuscript was not returned until April 1919. Nevertheless, counsel for the defendants were able to suggest that perhaps the confusion came about because she had retrieved and then tampered with the manuscript to make it seem more like the Wells book.[49] So, the issue of fraudulent conduct was introduced in the Privy Council.

The hearing lasted three days. Lord Atkin gave the judgment for the three-member Privy Council, delivered on 3 November 1932. After stating that 'Miss Deeks has argued the case with great candour and with great force,' he went on:[50]

> Their Lordships ... are quite convinced that the case made ... is quite insufficient to displace the conviction that is derived from the direct evidence that there was in this case no copying in fact ... The result is this: that in the opinion of their Lordships not only did Miss Deeks fail to make out her case, but that it was definitely established that the manuscript in this case did not leave Canada and that Mr. Wells did not have any access to it and did not use it at all in the preparation of his work.

A rehearing by a five-member panel of the Privy Council produced a similar result, as did a later petition to King George V.[51]

Two weeks after the Privy Council decision, on 18 November 1932, Florence Deeks took her further revised manuscript, 'The Highway of History,' to the London office of J.M. Dent and Sons. Within a week she received a rejection letter, stating, in part:[52] 'The great objection to the publication of this manuscript is that it covers the same ground as Mr. H.G. Wells' book, and his book has now been on the market for some time in both a long and shortened form, and it is really established ... Finally, it would be really impossible to compete now with Mr. Wells' book in the matter of price.'

Lord J.R. Atkin chaired the panel of
the Judicial Committee of the Privy
Council hearing the Deeks appeal

In the preface to the unpublished manuscript, dated October 1934, deposited
in the extensive Deeks papers in the Toronto Reference Library, Deeks thanks
a number of persons at the University of Toronto for their help. She does not
mention Kennedy.

Florence Deeks died in 1959 at the age of ninety-four and is buried in Mount
Pleasant Cemetery.[53]

Plagiarism?

McKillop wonders whether the decision in the case was the right one. He
states:[54] 'Historical records now available provide a far more comprehensive
body of evidence than that heard in the courts.' He sets out a possible scenario
whereby the manuscript could have been sent to England and seen by Wells.
In this scenario, a Macmillan editor in New York sends the manuscript to a
Macmillan science editor in London, knowing that it would then likely get into
Wells's hands.

I will not comment on that reasonable speculation. I have not spent five years
studying the case, as McKillop did. Nor have I studied Wells's archival records
in England and elsewhere.

If I had to make a decision, however, I would – with some hesitation – likely agree with the Privy Council. It is, of course, *possible* that Wells had used Deeks's manuscript, but that is not the question. It was up to the plaintiff to show that it was *probable* that he had done so – the standard of proof in civil cases – not that it was *possible*. On the other hand, if the case was not a plagiarism case, but a case about whether Wells saw the manuscript and used her ideas, I think I would have found on a balance of probabilities in favour of Deeks, assuming that stealing ideas can be the basis for finding the defendant liable, which is doubtful in these circumstances.

A recent book by Ruth Panofsky, *The Literary Legacy of the Macmillan Company of Canada*, briefly examines the Deeks/Wells case. She does not disagree with McKillop's conclusion, maintaining that 'Deeks may have been the victim of a justice system that favoured prominent writers and their publishers over unknown spinsters who aspired to authorship.'[55] She stresses one important fact: the head of Macmillan's Canadian branch was not truthful ('he did not hesitate to perjure himself') in his evidence at the trial when he denied knowing anything about the discharge of his predecessor, who had been the head of the Canadian branch when the Macmillan Company had custody of Florence Deeks's manuscript.[56]

The head of Macmillan Canada had been forced to resign because he was improperly carrying on other unrelated business at the Macmillan office. His successor was asked by Deeks's counsel about the company's former head:[57]

Q: He was discharged from Macmillans? – A. Yes.
Q: At about what time? – A. February of 1921.
Q: And there had been irregularities there on his part? – A. I understand so.
Q: You were there? – A. Yes, I was there. I understand so.
Q: Perhaps you know more about that? – A. No, I do not.

Both McKillop and Panofsky note that the then current head of the Toronto office being examined, Hugh Eayrs, did in fact know more about it. The former head had not given evidence. He was in Kingston Penitentiary at the time of the trial on an unrelated matter. The Toronto *Mail and Empire* commented 'that the officials of the Macmillan Company were not above reproach when the President went to the penitentiary and if he would do that he would surely steal a manuscript.'[58]

So, my conclusion is that it is possible, but not probable on a balance of probability, that Wells plagiarized Florence Deeks's manuscript; that it is probable that he used her ideas; but that it is not close to probable that Deeks and Kennedy fraudulently changed her manuscript to appear more like Wells's book.

9

The Irish Constitution

Kennedy's youngest child, Shelagh Lindsey, read the introduction I had prepared for the republication of Kennedy's book *The Constitution of Canada*. She liked what I had written, saying that she thought I had captured her father's life and character well. She had, however, one complaint: I did not say anything about her father's work on the Irish constitution.[1]

She was right. I barely mentioned his contribution to Irish politics. I was not sure what to say. How much was he involved in the drafting of the 1922 Constitution of the Irish Free State? I could avoid that discussion in the earlier introduction, but I cannot avoid it in this biography.

Kennedy certainly claimed that he was involved in the drafting of the constitution. In a 1934 review, published in the *American Bar Association Journal*, of the book *The Constitution of the Irish Free State* by Leo Kohn, Kennedy finishes with the following words:[2] 'As the present reviewer helped to draft the constitution, and as he knows intimately, if in eternal confidences, much of its creation, and as he saw it moulded standing outside the passion and the controversy, he has a special interest in Dr. Kohn's book.' In his Goldwin Smith Lectures at Cornell University in 1927, Kennedy devoted the second of his two lectures to the Irish Free State. The text of that lecture, entitled 'The Working Constitution of the Irish Free State,' has not survived, but there are press reports of the event in the *Cornell Daily*. In the publicity leading up to the lecture, Kennedy is described as having been 'constitutional advisor to the Irish Free State, and an important figure in the drawing up of the Irish constitution.'[3] According to the press report after his lecture, one would conclude that Kennedy was a central figure in the drafting of the constitution and, indeed, may even have been in Ireland at the time, which he was not. The press report later stated:[4] 'More than 300 people were present. As constitutional advisor to the Free State, Professor Kennedy was one of those instrumental in the drafting of both the Bill of Rights and the constitution itself, and he presented to his audience yesterday the intentions which the framers of the documents sought to put in effect, and the varying conflicts, which beset their path.'

Hugh Kennedy, later the chief
justice of Ireland

Was Kennedy intimately involved in the drafting of the constitution? His nemesis, George Wrong, did not think so. As we have seen, he complained to President Falconer in a letter in the summer of 1926 that Kennedy's 'megalomania has increased. He calls himself the official advisor of the Irish State.'[5] I will explore the question in some detail. The issue is important in understanding Kennedy's life, and it is not easy to prove a negative.

The many published accounts of the drafting of the Irish constitution do not mention W.P.M. Kennedy. They do, of course, mention Hugh Kennedy, later the chief justice of Ireland, who was the attorney general and legal advisor to the 1922 committee, simply called the 'Constitution Committee,' as well as a member of that committee. The book on the Irish constitution by Leo Kohn[6] that Kennedy reviewed in 1934 does not mention him in its 423 pages, nor do the many memoirs I have looked at by participants in the establishment of the Irish Free State. Chief Justice Hugh Kennedy gave a talk to the Canadian Bar Association[7] in 1928 on the drafting of the constitution and does not mention Kennedy. University of Toronto historian Donald McDougall prepared a paper on the drafting of the constitution for the 1939 volume in honour of George Wrong and does not mention Kennedy,[8] even though Kennedy took part in the celebration and published a paper in that volume.

Two extensive studies were published in 1970 on the Constitution of the Irish Free State, following the release by the British government of documents relating to the drafting of the constitution. One multipart study[9] was by Canadian scholar Donald Akenson and a colleague, J.F. Fallin, in the journal *Eire-Ireland*. There are many references to Hugh Kennedy, but none to W.P.M. Kennedy. The same is true of another multipart study[10] in the *Irish Jurist* in 1970.

The Irish Constitution Committee, 1922, with Darrell Figgis, fourth from the left, and
Hugh Kennedy, third from the right; Michael Collins, the chair, is not in the picture

Irish Politics

I cannot provide here a detailed description of the establishment of the Irish
Free State. It is a complex story. In a nutshell, after rebellion and civil war, the
Constitution of the Irish Free State entered into force on 6 December 1922.[11]

The committee tasked to draft the constitution had been set up by the Provisional Government in January 1922. It was chaired by Michael Collins, the
chair of the Provisional Government, who was later assassinated, with Darrell Figgis as the vice-chair. Figgis became the acting chair because of Collins's
many other responsibilities. Hugh Kennedy, the attorney general, was a key
member of the committee. He was strongly in favour of modelling the Irish
constitution on Canada. As one Irish scholar, who has studied the life of Hugh
Kennedy,[12] put it: 'In the language of the Treaty, Ireland was to have the constitutional status of Canada, and the law, practice and constitutional usage which
governed the relationship of the British Crown and Parliament to Canada were,
at the insistence of the Irish negotiators, to govern their relationship with the
Free State also.' There were a number of specific references to Canada in both
the treaty and the constitution.[13]

On a number of occasions, W.P.M. Kennedy stated that he had worked with
Vice-Chair Darrell Figgis. The entry for Kennedy in the 1935 *British Who's
Who*,[14] prepared by Kennedy, stated, for example: 'Adviser to the late Darrell
Figgis in drafting Constitution of Irish Free State, 1922.' The current British
Who Was Who reads:[15] 'Legal Adviser to Committee which drafted the Consti-
tution of the IFS.'[16]

There is no evidence that Darrell Figgis and W.P.M. Kennedy had known
each other in England where each lived for over a decade. In 1913, Kennedy

Darrell Figgis, vice-chair of the
Irish Constitution Committee

went to Cuba, and Figgis returned to Ireland, where he became a gun runner for the Irish rebels and was subsequently interned by the British.[17] He committed suicide in 1925. Like Kennedy, he did not leave the bulk of his papers to the archives, as many of his colleagues did. His death would therefore have made it difficult for anyone to refute Kennedy's claim about his involvement through Figgis in drafting the Irish constitution.

Irish Archival Papers

I have not gone through the extensive collection of archival papers relating to the drafting of the Irish constitution. There are a number of different drafts and versions of the constitution, the final version of which was approved by the Provisional Government on 25 October 1922 and by the House of Lords in the United Kingdom on 5 December 1922. The archives at University College Dublin hold the very extensive Hugh Kennedy papers, where the finding aid alone is over 400 pages long. There is no mention by Figgis of W.P.M. Kennedy in the finding aid, although there is some routine correspondence related to requesting some of Kennedy's publications.[18]

I did not personally go through the Hugh Kennedy papers, having instead relied on the expertise of persons who have gone through the documents for their own scholarly work. The archival records from the Irish side were released sometime after 1970. There are at least two recent PhD dissertations on the drafting of the Irish constitution. The more recent one is by Dr. Laura Cahillane, a lecturer in law at the University of Limerick, whose PhD dissertation, 'The Genesis, Drafting and Legacy of the Irish Free State Constitution,' was completed in 2011.[19] I contacted her, setting out the claim by Kennedy in his review of the book by Leo Kohn and asking her whether she had come across W.P.M. Kennedy in her research. She replied: 'I am surprised to see that quotation from Kennedy's review of Kohn's book because I have not seen any evidence linking Kennedy with the 1922 Constitution – of course that is not to say that that evidence does not exist.'[20]

She suggested that I contact Thomas Mohr of University College Dublin, who had completed his PhD dissertation,[21] 'The Irish Free State and the Legal Implications of Dominion Status,' in 2007 and has since then published extensively on this period of Irish history. Professor Mohr also has an interest in Canadian constitutional law. I subsequently met with Professor Mohr when he gave a talk at the University of Toronto law school. His reply to my questions was as follows:

> Yes, I am familiar with the man himself and am interested in the questions that you raise. First, I can tell you that WPM Kennedy had no official role in drafting the Constitution of the Irish Free State. He was just one of many external figures with whom members of the committee drafting the Irish Constitution were in correspondence. The committee asked for some of his publications and Kennedy obliged them. He never had any official position as an external advisor.[22]

In follow-up emails, Professor Mohr stated[23] that as part of his research he had looked through the surviving papers of Darrell Figgis in the National Archives of Ireland, but, he added, 'my notes do not mention any correspondence with Kennedy, which would definitely have been of interest to me.' Mohr further stated: 'One thing my notes have revealed is that Figgis was interested in inviting a number of prominent Canadians of Irish descent over to Dublin to give advice to the Irish Constitution Committee. Kennedy might have fallen into this category but he was not one of the persons specifically named. Figgis only named Charles Murphy and Charles Doherty.' Both were Canadian politicians.[24]

During the drafting process, Figgis and his staff were also producing a collection of 'Select Constitutions of the World,' which was completed in September 1922 and published later that year.[25] Nineteen constitutions are included, one of them being the British North America Act. The Canadian constitution is preceded by a historical introduction, perhaps drawn in part from W.P.M. Kennedy's historical introduction to Lefroy's *A Short Treatise on Canadian Constitutional Law* and Kennedy's book *Documents on the Canadian Constitution*, both of which the committee had. A number of people are thanked in the preface to the book on the nineteen constitutions, but W.P.M. Kennedy is not one of them. Kennedy's major book on the constitution of Canada had already been published but may not have been available to Figgis when he and his assistants were working on *Select Constitutions*.[26] Similarly, Kennedy's book was likely not used by the Constitution Committee, whose final draft was approved by the Provisional Government in October 1922.[27] Professor Mohr also states:[28] 'I can tell you that W.P.M. Kennedy was not mentioned or cited in the debates of the Irish Constituent Assembly. Other authorities with whom Figgis and others corresponded were, however, cited such as A.B. Keith and H. Duncan Hall, but not Kennedy.'[29]

In late 1922, Figgis published a book, *The Irish Constitution Explained*.[30] Canada is mentioned sixteen times in that book, compared to Australia and South Africa, which are mentioned seven and two times, respectively. W.P.M. Kennedy is not mentioned in the book. The *Toronto Telegram* stated,[31] without elaboration, in March 1924 – at the time that Kennedy was about to deliver a major address in Convocation Hall on the Irish constitution – that 'Prof. Kennedy has been asked to prepare four studies, dealing with the custom and practice of the Canadian Constitution, which are a fundamental part of the Free State's policy.' Could these have been comments that Figgis wanted for further work he was planning?

Kennedy's Books

One book that the Constitution Committee did not initially have was Kennedy's book *The Nature of Canadian Federalism*, published by the University of Toronto Press in 1921. This book was, as mentioned in an earlier chapter, a slightly expanded version of an article with the same title that he had published in the *Canadian Historical Review* earlier that year. The committee wrote to the University of Toronto Press in early 1922 asking for three copies of the book. The press sent complimentary copies of the book and, no doubt with Kennedy's enthusiastic approval, played up the request in various ways. The *Globe* had a brief notice,[32] under the heading 'Canada Is Model for Dail Eireann [the Irish Legislature],' stating: 'Evidently Dail Eireann hopes to benefit in the formation of the new Irish Free State by references to methods of self-government in this country.' The *Varsity* had a two-column story[33] on Kennedy and his book under the heading 'Irish Free State Writes for Book,' stating that the book 'is to be used, doubtless, as an aid in drawing up the Constitution of the Irish Free State.' The news about the request for the book was the first public statement that I have come across concerning Kennedy's involvement with the Irish constitution.

Persons would, of course, see references in the press to Hugh Kennedy, and some might assume that this individual was W.P.M. Kennedy. There is no evidence that Kennedy initially exaggerated in print his connection with the drafting of the constitution. In 1923, for example, he published a thoughtful journal article in *The North American Review*,[34] 'Significance of the Irish Free State,' where he offered high praise for the new state and its constitution. He stated: 'The creation of the Irish Free State is one of the most significant facts in modern history – significant for the British Empire, for political science and for the world at large.' Moreover, Kennedy wrote, the Irish Free State, unlike Canada, can amend its own constitution. He applauded the independence that Ireland received and hoped that it paved the way to greater independence for Canada, stating: 'The Irish Free State receives the status of Canada. We may now reverse it and say that Canada receives the status of the Irish Free State.'[35]

The one fault that Kennedy found in the Irish constitution is that it retained appeals to the Privy Council. 'Irish Free Staters,' he predicted correctly, 'will not long allow their lawsuits to receive final decision in London ... Where the treaty is in question, a panel of British and Irish judges must be set up.'[36]

He praised the fact that Ireland stayed within the Commonwealth. He ends his paper: 'As it stands, it is a noble document, based on the people, reflecting their hopes and aspirations, and giving us, in these latter days when at times the lamp of faith burns dim, a hope and an inspiration that in the iron bands of liberty the Commonwealth of British Nations may achieve high and glorious purpose, that sovereignty may take on its real and true meaning, and that in interdependence and union the political groups of the world may find the guarantee of realizing the highest and noblest in their peculiar community organizations.'[37]

Nowhere in that 1923 paper does he even hint that he played a role in the drafting of the Irish constitution.

Convocation Hall Lecture

The following year, however, the University of Toronto Alumni Association invited Kennedy to present a lecture on the Irish Free State to be delivered in Convocation Hall on 5 March 1924. It was a great success. The *Toronto Daily Star* reported:[38] 'It was an address in which Prof. Kennedy's learning and his brilliance mingled with his eloquence, an address which will give a better understanding of the newest member of the British Commonwealth of Nations to not only the large audience in Convocation Hall, but also to those who heard the lecture broadcast by radio by the Star's station CFCA.'

The lecture was closely based[39] on Kennedy's 1923 paper. His involvement in advising the Irish government came up only once, when he was criticizing appeals to the Privy Council from Ireland. He states: 'I have suggested to Darrell Figgis and to President Cosgrave a valid change [in the Constitution] in the following words.' He then sets out the scheme that he had proposed in his 1923 article, that is, no appeals in civil, criminal, or even constitutional cases and an

Convocation Hall in the 1920s

appeal to a panel of English and Irish judges when the Anglo-Irish Treaty was called into question. It is likely that he had sent a copy of his earlier paper to President Cosgrave and Darrell Figgis.

The presentation was, understandably, more dramatic than the earlier article. It contained poetry and provocative ideas, delivered in his distinctive Irish accent. The *Toronto Daily Star* described it this way:[40] 'Professor Kennedy, in his gown, which to a colorblind eye is of purple and gold, and radiating from Convocation Hall, rather grieves some of the faculty scattered among the audience. He displays enthusiasm – real enthusiasm. He's forty-three and if he had come from Oxford he ought to know better than to raise his voice and elevate his language over what has happened in Ireland – or anywhere. But his alma mater is in Dublin.' Reading the lecture gives one an understanding of why Kennedy was regarded as one of the university's best lecturers.

His admiration of the British Commonwealth is evident throughout. He states: 'Fortunately, in this case – and as I believe rightly – the Irish Free State, while receiving full recognition, decided to accept the status of the Dominion of Canada in lieu of independence ... Her adherence to the British Commonwealth brings her out of misty obscurantism into contact with the most vital forces in modern history. For I believe in the British Commonwealth – believe in it, because it stands for political realism. It is the crowning witness to the fact that all life is interdependent.'

W.P.M. Kennedy in the *Toronto Daily Star*,
7 March 1924

He again speaks out against the traditional versions of sovereignty, 'the pestilential legal fiction which has drenched this poor world in oceans of blood.'[41]

He paints pictures with his words. As in a later 1927 lecture at Cornell, he ends his lecture with a portrait of President Cosgrave taking his seat in 1923 at the League of Nations in Geneva. Kennedy eloquently states:[42]

The scene shifts to the Hall of the League of Nations on September 10, 1923. The President of the League has introduced a new delegate. THERE HE STANDS. His hair prematurely grey. His cheeks sunk with suffering. His eyes deep with sorrow. His shoulders bent with burdens. Ringing cheers greet him. They grow in volume and sound. Now they sink to the deep undertone of joy – now they swell to the wild crescendo of enthusiasm. THERE HE STANDS. Across the retina of his mind rushes – in broken pictures – his own history, that of his race and people. He does not hear the cheers: his own heart is speaking to him. It tells him of passion and love, of hatred and amity, of disappointment and hope. Into those crowded moments are crushed the minglings of the centuries. THERE HE STANDS. The head falls: the tears fill his eye: the shoulders deepen in their curve: the tongue is parched and dry. Still they cheer until the glad welcome at last dies down to a magnificent and eloquent silence. He sees a prison-cell. He hears taunt of 'rebel,' and then – as though caught by magic he seems to hear the old hillside command 'Attention' take on a newer meaning. The heels come together as of yore: the head is erect: the shoulders square: the eyes flash with glory: the tongue is moist to utterance. His lips move – President William Cosgrave speaks: – 'In the name of God. To this Assembly of the League of Nations health and life greetings. I come for the Irish Free State to hush forever the battle-hymn of hate' – to hush forever the battle-hymn of hate.

Then, after a few closing sentences, he says: 'Ladies and gentlemen, I should like to leave it at that.'

Later Issues

Almost a year later, Kennedy without doubt contributed to an issue that had been smouldering between the United Kingdom and the Irish Free State. Ireland had joined the League of Nations in 1923, the first dominion to do so. Canada did not join until the following year. Members of the League, under article 18 of the Covenant, were obliged to register any treaties with the League, and in July 1924 the Irish Free State registered the Anglo-Irish Treaty. The British, however, took the position that treaties between members of the Commonwealth did not come under article 18. In December 1924, Kennedy sent a letter, which may have been gratuitous, to Ireland's prime minister Cosgrave and the minister of justice Desmond Fitzgerald commenting on the process. It seems that Kennedy wanted greater coordination between Canada and Ireland because both had a common interest in moving towards greater independence. In April 1925, Fitzgerald thanks Kennedy for his 'prompt interest in this matter.'[43]

Fitzgerald explained to Kennedy[44] that the Irish Free State 'joined the League accepting the Covenant and registered the Treaty as bound to do under Article 18.' Fitzgerald also noted 'for your strictly private information that the British Government, while still maintaining their own opinion on the matter don't intend to pursue the matter any further.' He closes with the statement: 'I don't know whether you will agree with my point of view in this. I shall at all times appreciate very highly your observations on this or on any other matters.' Kennedy's involvement with this issue is confirmed by correspondence he had with Prime Minister Mackenzie King in February 1924, in which he asked Mackenzie King for Canada's position on the issue, stating: 'I am being consulted and I must have some idea of the attitude of the Canadian government ... Can the Free State appeal to the League under it? I am being pressed on this question very hard.'[45] Kennedy's question certainly shows involvement with at least this one issue.

My Conclusion

What was Kennedy's involvement in the drafting of the Constitution of the Irish Free State? My conclusion is that he carefully studied the issues and followed the events, and made at least some contribution to the drafting of the constitution and its later interpretation in that his books were used by the drafters, and, on a number of occasions, he offered advice to the Irish government. It is likely that there are other examples of similar involvements in various Irish government files,[46] but it is clear that he never had an *official* position or made a substantial contribution in the drafting of the Irish constitution or in its interpretation. He exaggerated his role, and, after Darrell Figgis died in 1925, Kennedy's claim of intimate involvement in the Irish constitution became even more exaggerated. Indeed, he later may have come to believe that he was one of the key figures in the drafting the Irish constitution.

10

Productive Years

Kennedy's scholarly output in the 1920s was staggering. His 1922 book, *The Constitution of Canada*, continued to garner high praise. Two years later, as described previously, his last book on Tudor politics, a major three-volume study in ecclesiastical history, *Elizabethan Episcopal Administration*, was published. It is not surprising that President Falconer and others at the University of Toronto valued his contribution to the reputation of the university.

There was a renaissance at the university in 1922, with the discovery of insulin and the creation of the School of Graduate Studies. Kennedy was part of that renaissance and was able to contribute to the graduate program.[1] Relatively few PhDs were awarded in those years in the social sciences. From 1915 until 1939, for example, only about ten PhDs were awarded in political economy. Kennedy was one of the few persons in the Departments of History or Political Economy with a doctorate, albeit one based on previously published work.

He was also an important figure in the University of Toronto Senate and in advising President Falconer on some tricky issues of governance, such as whether the faculty could bypass the senate and go directly to the board of governors – Kennedy said yes – and whether the faculty could bypass the board and go directly to the government – Kennedy said no.[2] He was also involved with Hart House, serving as a member – and one year as chair – of the Hart House Billiard Committee. According to his son Gilbert's oral interview, he was 'a champion English billiard player.'[3] There was a billiard room in the basement of Hart House in the place now occupied by the Arbour Room. Kennedy also frequented the Faculty Club, which was then in the upper gallery of Hart House, overlooking the Great Hall, and is now a celebrated restaurant.

The Annals of the American Academy of Political and Social Science

In 1923, Kennedy edited an issue[4] devoted to Canada of the prestigious journal *The Annals of the American Academy of Political and Social Science*, the

Kennedy reading a copy of *The Annals of the American
Academy of Political and Social Science*, 1923

organ of the American Academy of Political and Social Science. Founded
in 1889 and based at the University of Pennsylvania, the *Annals* came out
with a special issue six times a year – and still does. Leading scholars contributed and still contribute to the journal. This editorship was certainly a
coup for Kennedy personally and added to the reputation of the University
of Toronto.

Over forty persons published articles in the issue Kennedy edited – academics,
politicians, civil servants, businessmen, and others – on a wide range of issues.
The politicians included Independent Labour Party member J.S. Woodsworth,
writing on 'Political Developments within the Labour Movement in Canada,'
and Conservative Sir Thomas White, who had been the federal minister of
finance from 1911–19, writing about 'The War Finance of Canada.' Kennedy
organized the volume, chose the contributors, and wrote the preface as well as

Sir Edmund Walker, chancellor of the
University of Toronto

the 'Select Bibliography of Social and Economic Conditions in Canada.' It was
a multidisciplinary volume.

In his preface, Kennedy stated his objective:[5] 'Recent years have intensified
and developed the organized social and industrial life of Canada, and, with that
development, problems – some of an international nature, some peculiar to the
Dominion – have forced themselves to the front and demanded consideration.
An effort is made in this volume to present facts and trends as to these modern
Canadian activities by writers most familiar with the various fields.' It is not
known how it came about that Kennedy was asked to organize the issue. Was
it his idea? Or was he invited to do it? Most likely it was the latter. There are no
surviving *Annals* archival papers to answer that question.

The majority of the academics were from the University of Toronto, including psychologist George Brett, the vice-chair of graduate studies, who wrote on
higher education; economic historian C.R. Fay of political economy, who wrote
on agricultural cooperation in the Canadian West; and R.M. MacIver, soon to
be the chair of political economy, who wrote on arbitration and conciliation in
Canada.

Another author closely associated with the University of Toronto was Sir
Edmund Walker, an important person in the history of the university, who
served as chairman of the university's board of governors from 1910 until
1923. In 1923, Walker became the chancellor of the University of Toronto, and
Kennedy sent him a note of congratulations commenting that 'it is a partial

recognition of all that you have done for us to which time alone will bring full appreciation.'[6] Walker had been the president of the Bank of Commerce. His article was on 'Canadian Banking.' He died the following year, and Kennedy wrote the biographical entry on him for the British *Dictionary of National Biography (DNB)*. The entry in the *DNB* shows Walker's importance in the development of the Canadian banking system – which still exists today. 'Not only was the growth of the Bank of Commerce due in great part to Walker's skill and personality,' Kennedy wrote, 'but the Canadian banking system as a whole owes its present form largely to his efforts. He was a lifelong advocate of the branch-banking system, and always strenuously opposed attempts to change the Canadian branch system to the system of local banks which prevails in the United States.'[7]

The first section on Canada's population begins with an article entitled 'The Growth of Population in Canada,' contributed by R.H. Coats, the Dominion statistician. One can see the growth in cities, particularly Toronto, whose population in 1921 was about half a million. Half the population growth in Ontario since the 1911 census was in Toronto. Coats does not speculate on Canada's future population, then close to nine million.[8] The last article in the population section was by the controversial civil servant and poet Duncan Campbell Scott, the deputy superintendent-general of Indian affairs. Scott does not mention 'residential schools,' but writes: 'It will be gathered from this sketch that the policy is to protect the Indian, to guard his identity as a race and at the same time to apply methods which will destroy that identity and lead eventually to his disappearance as a separate division of the population.'[9] This article certainly indicates the thinking of the time. Kennedy himself said very little about Indigenous peoples in his own writings.

Kennedy was careful to say that the opinions presented are the responsibility of the authors, stating: 'I have made it clear to each writer that the responsibility is a personal one, and as a consequence I have deliberately made no attempt to correct the material in any of the manuscripts or to suggest the inclusion or exclusion of any particular judgments or opinions.'[10]

The position of women is not discussed in detail in the collection. Only one woman contributed to the collection of over forty articles. Marion Findlay, from the Ontario Department of Labour, wrote on 'Protection of Workers in Industry' and dealt with the Mothers' Allowance Acts, designed to help mothers in need in some provinces, which gave special protection to employed women. Findlay wrote: 'As the amount of protection afforded by means of collective bargaining to women and young persons, who need it most, is almost negligible, it is natural that the tendency of protective labour legislation in Canada, as in other countries, should be to apply in a greater measure to them.'[11] An article on divorce in Canada also discusses the difficulties women face in dissolving a marriage.[12]

The editing of this volume stamped Kennedy as a promoter of interdisciplinary studies. It also allowed him to establish personal contacts with a large number of influential persons in Canada.

The Cambridge History of the British Empire

In September 1925, an announcement about Kennedy appeared in the Canadian newspapers. Under the heading 'Toronto Professor Given Heavy Task,' the *Globe* reported:[13] 'Tribute is paid to the literary standing of Prof. W.P.M. Kennedy and the modern history department at the University of Toronto, in the former's appointment, announced yesterday, as editor of the Canadian book of the eight-volume history of the British Empire, being produced under the aegis of Cambridge University.' The article went on to say:[14] 'Prof. Kennedy will supervise this 1,000-page volume, the fourth in the set, which will recount the history of British North America from 1663 to 1919. Canadian scholars and public men will be asked to write sections of it, and it is hoped that the work will be completed in time for the sixtieth anniversary of confederation, in 1927, although the whole history will not be ready until 1930.'

As it turned out, the Canadian volume was not published until 1930,[15] and the final volume on South Africa not until 1936. In their preface to the volume on Canada and Newfoundland, the general editors of the series thanked Kennedy 'for valuable advice and assistance at every stage both in the planning and execution of the volume.'[16] They also thanked President Falconer, chairman of the board, Rev. Dr. H.J. Cody, and Professor Harold Innis 'for generous assistance and counsel.' Neither Cody nor Innis contributed a chapter, but Falconer had two chapters.[17]

As with the *Annals*, distinguished academics and others contributed to the collection. Dominion archivists G. Lanctôt and Adam Shortt prepared chapters, and Chief Archivist A.G. Doughty did the seventy-five page bibliography. Also participating were such important figures as O.D. Skelton, later the deputy minister of foreign affairs, and Newton Rowell, who would go on to be the chief justice of Ontario and the initial chair of the Rowell-Sirois Committee on Dominion-Provincial Relations.

Historians from across Canada were selected – from Laval, McGill, and the University of Montreal in Quebec; from the University of Toronto, Queen's, and McMaster in Ontario; and from the universities of Alberta and Saskatchewan in the west. The largest group of historians came from the University of Toronto. Stewart Wallace contributed three of the thirty-three articles in the collection; Chester Martin, who had taken over from George Wrong as the chair of history in 1927 and who Kennedy considered 'the outstanding historian in Canada at the present day,'[18] contributed two articles; and Toronto political economists, Alexander Brady, A.J. Glazebrook, and W.T. Jackman, each wrote an article.

THE
CAMBRIDGE HISTORY
OF THE
BRITISH EMPIRE

General Editors

J. HOLLAND ROSE, M.A., LITT.D.
*Vere Harmsworth Professor of Naval History in the University
of Cambridge; Fellow of Christ's College, Cambridge*

A. P. NEWTON, M.A., D.LIT.
*Rhodes Professor of Imperial History in the University
of London; Fellow of King's College, London*

E. A. BENIANS, M.A.
*Fellow and Senior Tutor of St John's
College, Cambridge*

Advisor for the Dominion of Canada

W. P. M. KENNEDY, M.A., LITT.D.
Professor of Law in the University of Toronto

VOLUME VI

CANADA
and
NEWFOUNDLAND

CAMBRIDGE
AT THE UNIVERSITY PRESS
1930

Title page of *The Cambridge History of the British Empire*, vol. VI, *Canada
and Newfoundland*, edited by W.P.M. Kennedy, 1930

The Cambridge book on Canada proceeded chronologically. The first article was by University of Toronto geologist Arthur Coleman,[19] who started with the geological formation of Canada, continued through the ice age, and ended the chapter with – as in the *Annals* – an unflattering portrait of Indigenous peoples. The final chapter on cultural development was by President Falconer. The last few sentences state:[20] 'She [Canada] is set in the midst of the modern world with her gates open on the East to Europe, on the South to the United States, and on the Pacific to the Orient. Through her universities also the ideas of world-wide culture are being sown upon receptive soil. The probability, however, is that her civilisation will remain predominantly of the Anglo-Saxon type which she has inherited, but that it will slowly adjust itself to the forces of the world in which she is placed, yet distinguishable withal from that of her neighbour.' Was he right? In part, yes, except that the multicultural nature of Canadian society was not anticipated, nor was the growing recognition of the importance, and neglect, of the Indigenous peoples.

Canada is seen as a success by the general editors, who state in the preface to the volume on Canada:[21] 'Almost alone among great nation-builders, the Fathers of Confederation shed no blood, squandered no resources and bequeathed to the future no heritage of hate, but rather pointed mankind forward to an era of wider unions and more assured peace and prosperity … Resulting largely from the bold progressiveness of Canadian statesmen, they have gone far towards transforming the British Empire into a British Commonwealth of Nations.'

Kennedy contributed one article, 'The Constitution and Its Working, 1867–1921,' and took the same approach as in many of his other writings. He uses carefully constructed images. In his first paragraph he states:[22] 'The British North America Acts are something like an institutional loom, in which for sixty years has been woven and rewoven a tapestry of law, custom, convention and tradition, as each generation has imaged the pattern and tried to express it in the web of constitutional life.' The final paragraph of his paper has two evocative images.[23] One is an image of Canadians being cautious in their politics: 'It is indeed true that Canadians walk oftenest by the still waters and along the quiet paths of tradition and that their historical origins do not favour creative politics.' The other image is of a balance or gyroscope: 'Under [the British North America Acts], with a thousand traditions working through them, Canada has succeeded in establishing an equitable balance of exceedingly delicate centrifugal and centripetal forces.'

Kennedy made some predictions in his article with respect to the power to amend the constitution. He turned out to be right, again using the metaphor of centrifugal and centripetal forces, stating:[24]

Much discussion has taken place in Canada whether some plan could not be evolved by which Canada could obtain constituent [that is, amending] powers.

Nothing, however, has emerged. Quebec stands fairly solid for the *status quo* ...
There is indeed a growing demand for change; but it is well to remember that the
Confederation is the child of serious and honourable obligations and that it has
taken many years so to balance delicate and dangerous centrifugal and centripetal
forces as to produce a corporate consciousness and the sense of nationhood. Sober
realism seems to say that the granting of full constituent powers at present to the
Dominion would be an exceedingly precarious experiment ... Constituent powers
will undoubtedly come one day: but it is likely they will come guarded by a 'bill of
rights' – covering clauses as in the Australian Commonwealth Act – beyond the
legislative competence of the Dominion.

Kennedy's view that Quebec stood for the status quo was confirmed at the cel-
ebrations commemorating sixty years of Confederation at the University of
Toronto in 1927, when the first speaker at Convocation Hall, Premier Louis-
Alexandre Taschereau of Quebec, stated:[25] 'Every Canadian must understand
that sixty years ago we formed not a homogeneous country but a confederation
of different provinces for certain purposes, with the distinct understanding that
each of these provinces should retain certain things ... Traditions, creed, laws,
national aspirations, language and a heritage were abandoned by none of the
contracting parties ... To live and endure the spirit as well as the letter of the
Confederation must be respected.'

The Cambridge book, like the *Annals*, again brought Kennedy into close
touch with many influential persons. Surviving correspondence shows an
increasing number of social engagements. As we know, in 1925 the Kennedys moved into a larger and finer house at 77 Spadina Road, where they
started to entertain more. In addition, Kennedy had become a member of
the elite Historical Club, which George Wrong had established in 1904.[26] The
club was open to any senior male student in any faculty along with a select
group of faculty members, and the members debated current issues every two
weeks at the homes of significant public figures. In the 1925–26 academic
year, Kennedy was the honorary president, and Lester Pearson was the lead
faculty member. Meetings were held at the residences of Canon Cody, Vincent Massey, and Sir William Mulock – to pick three well-known persons –
as well as at the homes of George Wrong and W.P.M. Kennedy. The debate
at Kennedy's home was on the subject 'Resolved that a grave danger to the
British Commonwealth of Nations lies in the anomalies of its foreign policy.'
Future lawyer J.J. Robinette argued for the affirmative. Two weeks later at Sir
Joseph Flavelle's mansion – part of today's law school – J.M. Tory, the younger
brother of the founder of the Torys law firm, argued for the negative on a
motion whether the Canadian National Railway (CNR) should be merged
with the Canadian Pacific Railway (CPR).

Alexander Brady,
professor of political
science

Trip to the United Kingdom

In the spring of 1926, in the early stages of organizing the volume for Cambridge University Press, Kennedy went to England to talk with the general editors and others about the project. His main contact was J. Holland Rose, the professor of naval history in Cambridge, who would contribute a chapter in the volume on the conflicts in North America in the early years between Britain and France. Kennedy was accompanied on the trip by Alexander Brady, who would write a chapter on the history of industrial development in Canada since Confederation.

Kennedy's trip to London was noted in the Toronto papers.[27] The *Toronto Daily Star* stated in mid-May 1926: 'Professor W.P.M. Kennedy, of the department of history of the University of Toronto, will leave for England May 22 in connection with the Cambridge History of the British Empire with which he is associated as editor. He will also represent the University of Toronto at the Anglo-American history conference in London in the month of July.'

The London conference had been organized by Professor A.F. Pollard of the University of London,[28] who had been one of Kennedy's mentors in London before Kennedy came to Canada and to whom Kennedy had dedicated one of his books on Tudor history. There is no indication that either Kennedy or Brady presented a formal paper or the extent to which they participated in the proceedings or took part in the many social events. This meeting was the second Anglo-American Historical Conference, following an initial one five years earlier. It was an important event, with major political figures, such as Prime Minister Stanley Baldwin, taking part. Did Kennedy attend the so-called soiree for the delegates at the home of Viscountess Astor or the organized visit to Lambeth Palace where the archbishop of Canterbury entertained the delegates?

Perhaps not, because Kennedy had to return to Canada for health reasons midway through the conference. He became ill while staying with Professor Rose in Cambridge and had to come back to Canada in mid-July 1926. The *Toronto Daily Star* wrote:[29] 'Professor W.P.M. Kennedy ... has taken ill and on medical advice returned home to Toronto to undergo [an] operation.' Kennedy wrote to President Falconer on 2 August from the Chateau Laurier in Ottawa:[30]

> I had booked to sail on Aug. 6 but came home a fortnight or so earlier ... I got laid low at Cambridge with severe inflammation of the gall bladder. It cleared up a little, but caught me again at Dublin and on medical advice – confirmed by a cable from my own physician – I came home in the middle of July. An operation won't be necessary – at least not immediately and I've been allowed after a fortnight in bed to come here [Ottawa] and go home each week end.

He added that he 'got the History well under way at Cambridge, London, Oxford and Dublin so that my two months in England fulfilled its main function.' He has been busy in Ottawa, he told Falconer, consulting with various potential authors. 'I have acres of work to do here [Ottawa] for the History and to carry on here at Rose's request, consultations over it with McArthur, Doughty, Lanctôt, Trotter, Burt, etc. So I've my hands full.'

Their correspondence over the years often refers to Kennedy's health problems. Falconer always seemed to take them seriously, never dismissing them as the complaints of a hypochondriac. As early as 1916, the subject of Kennedy's health had come up in their correspondence.[31] In August 1923, Kennedy complained about a recurrence of his 'old intestinal troubles' and a sprained ankle.[32] In April of 1924, Falconer writes:[33] 'I am very sorry for the reason that kept you from the dinner on Saturday night. I hope, however, that by this time your ear is quite better and you are out again.'

The complaints continued over the years. In October 1927, for example, Falconer ends a letter stating:[34] 'I hope your eyes are better.' At times, Kennedy's illnesses could be very debilitating. In February 1930, Falconer writes:[35] 'I am sorry to know that you have been laid aside and are in such bad shape. However, rest, I hope, may restore you, and certainly you should not take on any extra duties in the meantime but go slowly.' The following week, Kennedy ends a letter, stating:[36] 'I am able to do a certain amount of my work ... I have to go to bed every afternoon, at half-past one, in a darkened room, and am allowed to see no one. I get down to the University every morning, for my Undergraduate work, and on Friday afternoons and Saturday morning, for my Graduate work. I am sorry to say that I am not pulling up as the Doctor hoped, and the insomnia is still severe.' The extent of the correspondence on health matters between Kennedy and Falconer may well have set a University of Toronto record for such correspondence between a president and a faculty member. The only challenger might be, as we will see, the correspondence on health-related matters between Kennedy and Falconer's successor, President Cody.

The volume on Canada was published by Cambridge in 1930 to good reviews. Falconer wrote to Kennedy:[37] 'Thank you for the copy of press notices as to the Cambridge History. It must be gratifying to you and to Professor Rose to have this happy issue out [after] all your troubles that hung over this volume so long.'

Various Invitations

After his 1926 trip to the United Kingdom, Kennedy never returned to England or, as far as I can determine, travelled outside of North America. There was the occasional trip to the United States and to Ottawa and Quebec, but I have not come across records of any other travel. Kennedy's daughter-in-law Betty Kennedy says he never visited Gilbert in British Columbia, except for a visit shortly after he retired.[38]

As noted earlier, Kennedy delivered well-received lectures at Cornell University in 1927 on 'The Working Constitutions of the Oldest and Newest British Dominions.' The Canadian papers announced this 'signal honour,' the *Mail and Empire* stating:[39] 'This is probably the first time that a Canadian has been honored in this way.' The lectures were named after the wealthy Canadian historian and journalist Goldwin Smith, who had been a member of the important Commission on the University of Toronto, established in 1906, and had then become a member of the board of governors.[40] When he died in 1910, Smith left the enormous sum of $700,000 – about equal to the entire university budget that year[41] – to Cornell University, where he had been a professor for several years in the 1860s, rather than to the University of Toronto, because he was angry that the Ontario government had imposed a death duty tax.[42]

An invitation to lecture at Bratislava University in Slovakia in 1928 was turned down by Kennedy, a newspaper report stated, because of the unfortunate circumstance that another member of the political economy department was on leave that year and Kennedy could not leave the university.[43] Whether he otherwise would have gone is doubtful, particularly for reasons of health.

The press reported another invitation in 1927 – to be a member of a royal commission on India. The Canadian Press report, under the heading 'Offer from India Declined by Toronto Professor,' stated:[44]

> Strong pressure has been brought to bear to secure Prof. W.P.M. Kennedy, of Toronto University, as a member of the proposed Royal Commission on the revision of the Courts of India. Sir R.V. Reddie, former member of the Madras Government announced that Prof. Kennedy's appointment as an expert on Imperial constitutional law would carry with it the approval of all constitutionalists in India. Unfortunately, however, Prof. Kennedy, because of the condition of his eyes, will, at present, be unable to accept the appointment.

As with the Irish constitution, there is no evidence that Kennedy was ever invited to be involved with such a committee, although one cannot be sure. A number of important commissions or committees were operating in India about that time.[45] One was the Simon Commission, composed of British parliamentarians. The other was the Butler Committee. There was also a non-governmental committee consisting of Hindus, with future prime minister Jawaharlal Nehru as its chair, and a similar non-governmental committee composed of Muslims. There was, the India Office informed me, no commission on the revision of the courts at that time. The most likely body was the three-person Butler Committee, established by the British government to investigate and clarify the relationship between Great Britain and the Indian princes. The chairman was Sir Spencer Harcourt Butler, a career senior administrator in India. One of its members was the renowned legal historian W.S. Holdsworth. Kennedy could have been a valuable member. Perhaps Holdsworth sounded him out on the possibility.

Note also that the newspaper report just mentioned refers to Sir R.V. Reddie. My best guess is that this person was, in fact, a South Asian, Sir C.R. Reddy, who had been on an Indian government scholarship to Cambridge in the early years of the century and was the founder and head of an important university in Madras.[46] He might well have known of Kennedy's work on Canadian constitutional law and perhaps known Kennedy. The letter that Kennedy received may well have been from Reddy, urging Kennedy to permit his name to be put forward for a place on the Butler Committee.

The curator of the post-1858 India Office records searched its records and answered my query about whether Kennedy was asked to be a member:[47] 'As you say, the Simon Commission consisted of MPs, so I had a bit of a search for the Butler Committee.' The document relating to the Indian States Committee, he wrote, 'did have some correspondence regarding who should serve on the Committee, but Kennedy's name does not appear.'

Kennedy had other links with India. Gilbert Kennedy mentioned in his oral interview that his father 'had a wide field of correspondents ... some of whom he had never met ... For example, one of them was Sir C.P. Ramaswami,'[48] who might also have been urging Kennedy's appointment to the Butler Committee. He was a lawyer and from 1931 was a law member of the Executive Council of the Governor of India.[49] His correspondence with Kennedy apparently did not survive in Canada or India.

Toronto Bankers' Educational Association

During this period, Kennedy was giving lectures to the Toronto Bankers' Educational Association, organized by the extension department at the university.[50] Lectures were given by members of regular departments, as in the University of Michigan, rather than through a separate department with its own faculty, as in the University of Wisconsin. Adult education was strongly supported by Falconer and MacIver and others in the university. The Workers Educational Association (WEA) started giving lectures to workers just after the war. Falconer wrote to Kennedy in June 1918, saying:[51] 'I should have written to you about the WEA but it was only a few days ago that final arrangements were made in so far indeed as they are final. I think they are hoping that you will take a class in Constitutional History or possibly Political Theory.' Kennedy did not teach for the WEA that first year. The following year his wife died. In 1919, the Toronto Bankers' Association made arrangements for the university to give courses. We know that Kennedy gave a course to the Bankers' Association in the years 1926–27 and 1927–28 on 'Modern Government and Public Finance.' Whether he taught for the WEA or the Bankers' Association before that is not clear. He no doubt preferred teaching for the 'bankers' because they paid $400 a course, whereas the 'workers' paid between $100 and $200.[52]

A typed draft of Kennedy's lectures, now in the University of Toronto Archives, was found in a trunk at our cottage that had once been owned by the Kennedys.[53] The lectures were taken down – perhaps in shorthand – and then typed by H.H. Loosemore,[54] a retired banker, who had been the manager of a number of branches of the Bank of Commerce. The draft would obviously have been done with the consent and perhaps the encouragement of Kennedy. Perhaps Kennedy thought there would later be an interest in publishing the material, but I have found no evidence that the manuscript was ever submitted to a publisher. There is evidence that during this period he was attempting to organize under his editorship 'a new National History of Canada in several volumes,' but without success.[55] Perhaps these lectures were to be part of that series.

The lectures are valuable because they shed light on Kennedy's ideas on many subjects, such as the constitution, appeals to the Privy Council, Crown .attorneys, separate schools, Irish politics, and many other issues. On the drafting of a constitution, for example, Kennedy remarked: 'Anyone can write a Constitution. [I] will write one any time for $100!! But will the Constitution which anybody writes <u>Work</u>? Must be from life and soul of the People.' On appeals to the Privy Council, he said: 'Strongly opposed to appeals. Reflects on the judiciary. Without controversy, the Australian bar is the greatest in the Empire, because there has been thrown on them the tremendous responsibility of final decision.'[56] On criminal law prosecutors, he pointed out: 'Public prosecutor in the United States is National Hero – up to him to get a conviction. Crown Attorney on the other hand does not matter if he gets a conviction or not – wants to see justice done.' On separate schools, he commented: 'Does not believe in Separate Schools. Our Schools should be the clearing-house of the nation, where all the children of the nation should meet.' On justice, he said: 'Most wonderful thing that the British system has been preserved in Canada ... Nearest approach I know to actual objectivity.'

All in all, with his health issues, heavy teaching, public lectures, raising a family of four children, involvement in University of Toronto politics, and continuing controversy with George Wrong, it is a wonder that he was able to research and publish as much as he did. In the next chapter we look at several other publications not yet mentioned.

11

Lord Elgin and More

In the summer of 1926, Kennedy's 275-page book, *Lord Elgin*, was published by Oxford University Press. As stated in the preface, the book was included in a list created for UNESCO in 1948 of the hundred best Canadian books.[1] Lord Elgin had been the governor general of Canada between the years 1847 and 1854 and, because of his actions bringing about responsible government, was an important figure on Canada's path towards self-government. He introduced the practice of taking as constitutional advisors leaders of the party that commanded the confidence of the elected assembly – the key to responsible government. Elgin is also important in the history of the University of Toronto because he signed a controversial bill in 1850, creating the secular University of Toronto out of the Anglican King's College. Kennedy sent a personal copy of the book to Robert Falconer, the president of the University of Toronto, who replied in late August: 'I read your "Elgin" with a great deal of pleasure. I should think it was very well done. One can easily see that "Elgin" is one of your heroes.'[2]

Kennedy also sent a copy – dated 17 August 1926 – to Viscount Richard Haldane, a member of the House of Lords and a former lord chancellor. I know that he sent a copy to Haldane, because a few years back I ordered a used copy of *Lord Elgin* from an English bookseller and – to my surprise – it contained the following handwritten inscription:

> The Right Hon Viscount Haldane
> With the author's compliments and sincerest thanks.
> W.P.M. Kennedy
> August 17, 1926

We do not know why Kennedy is offering his 'sincerest thanks.' Perhaps it is because Haldane had met with him, possibly in Haldane's office, while Kennedy was in London attending the Anglo-American history conference. There

THE MAKERS OF CANADA SERIES

Anniversary Edition

LORD ELGIN

BY

W. P. M. KENNEDY

Illustrated under the direction of A. G. Doughty, C.M.G., Litt.D.
Deputy Minister, Public Archives of Canada

LONDON AND TORONTO
OXFORD UNIVERSITY PRESS
1926

Title page of *Lord Elgin* by W.P.M. Kennedy, 1926

The Right Hon Viscount Haldane
with the author's compliments
& sincerest thanks

W.P.M. Kennedy,
August 17, 1926.

Handwritten inscription to Viscount Richard Haldane by
W.P.M. Kennedy in a copy of *Lord Elgin*

had been a general invitation from the Privy Council office to the delegates to attend sessions of the Privy Council. On the other hand, it is possible that Haldane and Kennedy had been friends, as Kennedy states in a tribute to Haldane in the *Canadian Bar Review* (*CBR*) after Haldane died in 1928.

Kennedy wrote in the *CBR* about what a great man Haldane was.[3] 'Talk to him of theoretical or applied economics,' Kennedy wrote, 'and he moved with skilled familiarity on the mountains of theory or along the mundane valleys of finance, international trade, capital and labour … We marveled at the width of his horizons … His appreciation of the creative in human life was as great as his appreciation of the noblest ideals of law. To know him intimately was a liberal education … There was then in the make-up of Lord Haldane's personality all those qualities which make a great gentleman and a great friend.' Kennedy then says that 'one example will suffice.' That example, Kennedy states, was that 'in the course of our regular correspondence' Haldane gave a detailed reply to a 'small point in constitutional law.' This letter appears to be the only piece of correspondence between them that has survived in the Haldane papers.

The letter, however, does not seem to indicate more than a casual relationship. The letter is dated 24 July 1923, and it obviously came in response to a letter from Kennedy – not in the Haldane archives – asking a question about the

Viscount Richard Haldane

Bonanza Creek case, a 1916 Privy Council case on which Haldane sat. (The case decided, not surprisingly, that an Ontario company created by letters patent could constitutionally acquire mining rights outside the province.) Haldane's letter is signed 'Yours very truly' and simply sets out some legal issues that the Privy Council had considered. Haldane writes: 'I am writing from memory, but that was the conclusion to which our researches led us.'[4] Kennedy, however, exaggerated Haldane's response, stating in his *CBR* tribute that 'I got back a long discussion of it which he had amplified by work in the libraries.'[5]

Kennedy would frequently refer to his close friendship with Haldane – after Haldane died. He referred to Haldane, as previously noted, as 'my great friend' in the *CBR* memorial tribute. In an article in a South African law journal in 1934, he referred to Haldane as 'my lifelong friend.'[6] And he sometimes referred to Haldane's help 'in the actual drafting of the course' in law at the University of Toronto. He did so in an article in 1933 in the British *Journal of the Society of Public Teachers of Law*[7] and also in the mid-1940s in a memo to Sidney Smith,[8] who had just taken over as the president of the University of Toronto. Indeed, in the memo to Smith, Kennedy went further and also gave credit to Lord Atkin, saying that he met the two men in 1925 and made plans with them for the teaching of law as a social science. Kennedy was not in England in 1925, so he must have meant 1926, the only time he returned to England.[9]

But maybe he did know Haldane well. It is hard to know. Kennedy wrote to Larry MacKenzie in August 1928, when MacKenzie was still in Geneva about to depart for his new position at the University of Toronto:[10] 'It was sad about Haldane. I had a letter from his death bed – a mere scrawl – and one from his sister. I've lost the oldest friend I've had. He knew me from my earliest days and his loyalty and devotion and adaptability to positions were wonderful – a great man and a wonderful person to work with.'

So, what is the truth? We know that there was some relationship between them, and I have no doubt that Kennedy sent a number of students and colleagues to visit Haldane when they visited England, as Kennedy claimed in the *CBR* article. But a close friendship? The real relationship is probably somewhere between being a casual correspondent and a strong friendship. If so, once again we find some exaggeration of the truth.

Lord Elgin

Kennedy's *Lord Elgin* was part of the 'Makers of Canada' series, a twelve-volume set of books, published by Oxford University Press in 1926 and edited by the principal of Upper Canada College, W.L. Grant. Kennedy states in the preface that 'without [Grant's] encouragement I should never have had the courage to undertake the book or to complete it.'[11] Oxford had purchased the rights to material originally published in twenty volumes earlier in the century

Governor General Lord Elgin

(from 1904 on) by the Toronto publisher George M. Morang. Some volumes were dropped by Oxford, and some were published by authors other than the original authors. There had been an earlier volume on Lord Elgin, which was rejected for the new Oxford edition. Principal Grant states in the preface to the new series:[12] 'Our view of Lord Elgin has been so vitally altered by [scholars] that Sir John Bourinot's volume has been replaced by one from the pen of Professor Kennedy.'

We know how busy Kennedy was on other projects during this period. He acknowledges this in his preface:[13] 'This book has been written in the midst of many other engagements ... I am quite conscious of many limitations and I only allowed the book to go to press as a Pisgah view of an historical land flowing with milk and honey.' Naturally, I had to look up the word 'Pisgah' and discovered – as the reader probably already knows – that it was another name for Mount Nebo in Jordan, from which Moses looked on the land of Israel. With his background in ecclesiastical history, Kennedy often used biblical references.[14]

Kennedy describes in dramatic detail Lord Elgin's deliberations in 1849 on whether to sign the contentious Rebellion Losses Bill, which compensated persons whose property had been damaged in the 1838 rebellion in Lower Canada – including compensating those who had *supported* the rebellion. 'Promising channels of approach brought him [Elgin] up against steep cliffs of impossibilities,' Kennedy wrote in his characteristic style. He went on: 'The conclusions of the night prove the delusive phantoms of the morning.'[15] The *Globe* reviewer noted that Lord Elgin's action in signing that bill was 'another step taken in the developing of Canadian government leading later to the broader union.'[16]

William Lyon Mackenzie

Another volume that had been dropped from the earlier series was one on William Lyon Mackenzie, the leader of the rebellion in Upper Canada in 1838 and the grandfather of Prime Minister William Lyon Mackenzie King. The book had been prepared for the 1906 series by George Lindsey,[17] who had condensed an earlier history of Mackenzie, published in 1862, written by Lindsey's father, William Lyon Mackenzie's son-in-law. Needless to say, it was a very favourable one-sided view of Mackenzie.

Instead of a new single volume on Mackenzie, Principal Grant decided that Mackenzie would be added to a volume that had been written for the earlier series by McGill political economist Stephen Leacock,[18] which contained descriptions of other important figures, including Robert Baldwin, Louis-Hippolyte LaFontaine, and Francis Hincks. The new volume for Oxford would be entitled *Mackenzie, Baldwin, LaFontaine, and Hincks*. Leacock would still be credited as the author.

The new section on Mackenzie would, however, be written by Kennedy and added to the Leacock book, which Kennedy would revise. In his preface, Kennedy thanks 'Professor Leacock for his courteous permission to deal as I wished with his work and for his kindness during the process of revision' and notes that he has 'endeavoured as far as possible to preserve the spirit and form of the original work.'[19] Principal Grant referred in his general introduction to the series to 'Professor W.P.M. Kennedy of the University of Toronto, the eloquent and scholarly author of "*The Constitutional History of Canada.*"' Grant went on to say: 'Mackenzie was an important and a vivid figure in the early history of Upper Canada. Eyes still flash and foreheads redden as men discuss whether at the great crisis [of 1837] he was rebel or patriot.'[20]

There is a fascinating back story to the earlier volume that had been prepared by George Lindsey and is relevant to understanding the relationship between W.P.M. Kennedy and William Lyon Mackenzie King. The Lindsey book had

William Lyon Mackenzie King, prime minister, in front of a picture of
his late mother, with whom he communicated

Rebel William Lyon Mackenzie

been a last-minute substitution for a volume on Mackenzie, written by historian William Dawson LeSueur, which had been rejected by the publisher, Morang. Once again, as with the *Deeks* case, Canadian historian Brian McKillop has brought this story to life. The book by LeSueur on Mackenzie was eventually published in 1979, with a scholarly introduction by McKillop.[21]

McKillop does not mention Kennedy by name in his introduction. He lists the few books written about Mackenzie and simply states:[22] 'Another ... was novelesque in form and substance. Admirable in the way it evoked the details and atmosphere of Mackenzie's age, it was less a full-scale biography than it was an attempt to use the fictional form to portray Mackenzie's part in the coming and course of the Upper Canadian rebellion of 1837.' McKillop was referring to Kennedy's book. Not an unfair assessment. The book is, indeed, more novelesque than any other Kennedy book.

In brief, here is the background story. LeSueur's book presented a biography of Mackenzie, the rebel, that was totally unacceptable to supporters of the Liberal Party and particularly to Mackenzie's grandson, William Lyon Mackenzie King, the future prime minister of Canada. King was at the time the deputy minister of labour in the Laurier government and had serious political ambitions. He wanted his grandfather to be seen as an important person in the development of responsible government in Canada. He and other relatives had provided family records to assist LeSueur in writing the biography. LeSueur knew that King 'actively opposed him as the biographer of his grandfather and was lobbying to this effect,'[23] but Morang convinced King that LeSueur would be a good choice.

Mackenzie King hated the eventual manuscript. His diary entry for 28 April 1908 states[24] that it was 'a vile production ... [I]t begins by saying Canada wd. have been better off without Mackenzie, and is full of all the unkind things that could be said ... [I]t wd. serve as a campaign document for the Tories.' Morang turned down the book.

LeSueur had argued that Mackenzie had slowed down the move towards responsible government, stating: 'As to his influence on the political development of Canada, very different views have been expressed; but the best opinion of today ... [is] that it was retardatory rather than otherwise.' LeSueur concludes his book by stating that because of Mackenzie's actions, Upper Canada 'was most needlessly dragged out of a course of steady and peaceful, if not very rapid, constitutional development.'[25]

There is no doubt that Mackenzie King played a major role in having the book rejected.[26] Mackenzie King was so upset that he pressured Morang to reject the manuscript. LeSueur wanted to get the manuscript back from Morang in order to publish it with another publisher, but Morang refused to return it, even though LeSueur had already returned the $500 he had been paid. A lawsuit was brought by LeSueur, and the case ended up in the Supreme Court of Canada, which held in 1911 in favour of LeSueur. It was well known throughout the case that William Lyon Mackenzie King was behind the refusal to return the manuscript.[27]

That was not the end of the story, because Mackenzie King then brought a successful injunction preventing LeSueur from using any of the material that the Mackenzie family had provided to LeSueur. I will not go into the various subsequent lawsuits. Mackenzie King testified in one of them. A 1911 entry in King's diary[28] states that the LeSueur biography was a 'conspiracy ... to have Mackenzie written down instead of up.' King obviously had strong feelings about his grandfather's role in bringing about responsible government.

Prime Minister Mackenzie King

Kennedy's portrait of Mackenzie no doubt pleased King, although it is not a particularly flattering picture of the man. Mackenzie possessed, according to Kennedy,[29] 'the defects of his virtues. He had all the fine qualities of his race – its perseverance, its tenacity, its imagination, its zeal, its uncanny energy; but unfortunately he had too large a share of its defects. He was vain and uncompromising. His perseverance and tenacity lacked that sobriety of purpose which dignifies reform movements and rescues them from the violence of uncharted agitation.'

Whatever Mackenzie's personal defects, the important conclusion that Kennedy reached was one that King would have liked. Mackenzie had not 'retarded' responsible government. Rather, Mackenzie's actions had contributed to its attainment. Kennedy concludes the book in his typical dramatic manner by describing Mackenzie's final days in Toronto:[30] 'The old man is gathered to the land he loved as its political achievement acquires strength under the healing influences of responsible government. As Mackenzie passes out of Canadian history it is not too much to say that he gave to Canada a love foolish but strong, tragic but deathless, and that the promise of [confederation] was in a great measure the offspring of 1837.'

Mackenzie King must have been grateful for these words. There is no direct evidence that Mackenzie King played a role in the selection of Kennedy to write the short biography of Mackenzie, but it is unlikely that King was not involved.

Kennedy had started corresponding with King in 1923, but there appears to be no mention of the Mackenzie biography in the King papers. Perhaps the discussion was over the telephone or in person. They could have met through the warden of Hart House, Burgon Bickersteth, who was very close to Mackenzie King.[31] King had been to Hart House on several occasions before February 1927, the year that King was the principal speaker in a celebrated Hart House debate on the topic of greater independence for the dominions.[32] King, who had recently returned from the 1926 Imperial Conference, which produced an important step towards full nationhood, strongly supported greater independence. The house divided 408 to 125 in King's favour. Kennedy, who was active in Hart House affairs, was likely at that debate.[33]

Quid Pro Quo

Was there a quid quo pro for Kennedy's positive treatment of King's grandfather? In a letter marked 'Confidential' to Mackenzie King on 20 May,[34] as Kennedy was leaving for London, he thanked King for providing 'your most generous letters of introduction' for persons in the United Kingdom. He then tells King 'in confidence' that in July it would be 'officially announced … that I have been offered and accepted the new chair of Political Institutions in the Faculty of Politics and Law here at U of T.' That announcement will be discussed in the next chapter. It is the next part of the letter that is relevant here. Kennedy states: 'I hope some day you will remember that matter of an honorary degree which you promised to me as soon as your public engagements would allow.'

The honorary degree was to be from Harvard University. King replied on 22 May 1926,[35] congratulating Kennedy on his new chair: 'I was delighted to

learn from your letter received yesterday of the acceptance of the new chair
of Political Institutions in the Faculty of Politics at the University of Toronto.
May I extend to you my hearty congratulations and best of wishes.' King then
turned to the honorary degree, stating: 'Though I have not written you of the
matter, I did communicate some little time ago with one or two of my friends at
Harvard University concerning the recognition which I hope may be extended
by Harvard to yourself.'

The Mackenzie King papers then show that on the very same day King sent
a letter to Canadian-born William B. Munro, a professor in Harvard's Department of Government, stating:[36] 'Some time when you are considering Honorary Degrees at Harvard might I suggest your giving thought to Professor W.P.M.
Kennedy, of Toronto University, with whose works on constitutional history
you will be more than familiar. Kennedy's work is increasing in appreciation in
all parts of the British Empire and, I hope, in the United States as well.' Munro
replied saying:[37] 'It would be very appropriate to have Kennedy on our list of
honorary graduates, for he has done excellent work.' It is not known whether
Professor Munro passed on the request to Harvard, but an honorary degree was
not awarded to Kennedy. A Harvard archivist wrote to me stating:[38] 'A review of
the honorary degree records for the years 1926–1935 did not find any mention
of the possibility of an honorary degree for Kennedy.'

Other King Correspondence

There is an extensive body of correspondence in the Mackenzie King papers –
about seventy letters – between Kennedy and Mackenzie King over the years.[39]
The King/Kennedy letters cover the period from February 1924 to May 1948. I
will deal with some of the early letters in this section.

It is interesting to observe that, unlike most cases where Kennedy plays up
and perhaps exaggerates his relationship with important figures, in the case of
Mackenzie King he appears publicly to play down his relationship.

The correspondence covers a wide group of subjects. The first letter in the
collection is dated February 1924 and suggests a relatively close relationship
between the two. It starts by saying:[40] 'My dear Premier, I write to you on some
matters which have been in my mind.' This letter is likely not the first time they
exchanged views. Each subject discussed suggests wider issues. 'How did Newfoundland in 1917,' Kennedy asks, 'apply the Act of 1911 [preventing the British House of Lords from dealing with money matters] to its second chamber?'
'It may be well to look at this,' Kennedy suggests, adding: 'I think you have an
opportunity next session to deal with the Senate. It is long overdue.' Kennedy is
obviously promoting senate reform.

In another brief comment in the same letter, as we saw in the chapter on the
Irish constitution, Kennedy asks King for the 'official opinion on the registration

of the Irish Treaty at the League.' Kennedy states: 'I want this definitely and am prepared to wait a few days for it. I am being consulted and I must have some idea of the attitude of the Canadian government.' There is an odd demanding tone to this request. The request, however, confirms that Kennedy played at least some role in interpreting the Irish constitution.

The letter was not, however, answered by King. On 13 January 1925, almost a year later, Kennedy writes again, saying:[41] 'I am anxiously waiting for the promised answer to my last letter.' A further question is asked about the League of Nations. Kennedy states: 'Have you noticed that Chamberlain [the British prime minister] at his first Session of the Council of the League saluted it "on the part of the British Empire" and that at the Second Session he said he spoke "in the name of six governments."' Kennedy then asks: 'Who are the <u>six</u>? Was he authorized to do so? Did Canada authorize him?' In another letter, two weeks later, Kennedy writes:[42] 'I have been waiting for the promised reply to my two questions which you promised to discuss with Mr. Lapointe: (a) Canada's attitude to the registration of the Irish Treaty (b) Canada's attitude to Mr. Chamberlain's claim at the League of Nations, to speak "in the name of six nations."'

Kennedy then adds another question, relating to a recent speech by British prime minister Stanley Baldwin, who was reported to have said that '"The Empire Delegation" to the League of Nations must try in future to arrive at a uniform policy before the meetings, as it is dangerous to the unity of the Empire to have diversity of opinion.' Kennedy then asks: 'I should like to know the interpretation which you place on these words. It seems to me that Baldwin has no idea of our separate status in the League, and this talk of speaking for six nations and of Empire Delegations is quite contrary to the claims made by the leaders of all political parties in Canada … [W]e simply cannot afford to let these things go unchallenged. I have written to you personally about these matters, and I sincerely hope that I can get from you some authoritative reply.'

King replies in some detail and ends by stating:[43] 'I shall be obliged if you will regard any comments I have made as confidential. You will of course recognize that any statement that may appear advisable for me to make on these questions should be made in Parliament. I have appreciated your trenchant comments, and shall be glad to hear from you again at any time.' It is not clear why King felt it necessary to respond to Kennedy's questions. Perhaps it was simply that King was trying to keep on the good side of one of his apparent supporters.

The correspondence clearly shows that Kennedy supported King at this time. 'A thousand congratulations,' he wrote to King at midnight of election day, 14 September 1926.[44] 'It's going to be a great victory.' Letters were sent by Kennedy following elections in 1930, which King lost, and 1935, which he won. Following the 1935 victory, Kennedy wrote:[45] 'You will remember that in July 1930, I wrote you saying that the party of reform could never be defeated in reality.

Yesterday that came true. I write you a personal letter of sincerest personal congratulations and good wishes.'

Whether Kennedy continued to quietly support the Liberals is not clear. His son Gilbert states in his oral interview that his father was not a supporter of any one party. Gilbert stated:[46] 'No party affiliation that I know of. Well I know there weren't. As far as Dad was concerned sometimes he would hope that one party would get in, sometimes he would hope that another party would get in, it would depend on the situation; it would depend on who was in, how long they had been in, who the leader of the other party was, and so on.' It should also be noted that in 1932 Kennedy dedicated a book to the Conservative prime minister Richard Bennett, but that did not indicate political support of the party. He simply wrote: 'To Richard Bedford Bennett in friendship and esteem.'[47]

The year 1926 was a particularly important year in Canadian constitutional politics because it was the year of the King-Byng dispute. The issue was whether Governor General Byng was obliged to accept Prime Minister King's request that Parliament be prorogued by the governor general and an election held. King did not have a majority in the House of Commons and wanted to avoid censure by Parliament over a scandal in the customs department. Byng, however, refused the request for prorogation and on 28 June 1926 invited Arthur Meighen to form the government. It became a major controversy and is still debated.

Kennedy was in England at the time of the King-Byng affair. 'I've been driven crazy over the constitutional issue here by the papers,' Kennedy wrote to President Falconer on 2 August 1926,[48] and went on to state that he had issued the following release to the Associated Press: 'Professor Kennedy has a stringent rule to grant no interview or to write on any matters in party politics. He cannot see his way, in the present case, to break this rule.'

In England, it was clear that the king was bound by the prime minister's advice. King George VI had taken Prime Minister Ramsay Macdonald's advice in 1924 to prorogue Parliament. Kennedy, however, quietly supported Byng, taking the position that uniformity in the British Empire was not necessary. Canada could differ from the British practice. The British Empire does not and should not always speak with one voice, Kennedy argued. Canada could establish its own separate status in the community of nations.

Kennedy set out his views on this issue in the British journal *Contemporary Review* in the fall of 1926.[49] 'It is for Canada,' he wrote, 'as for every other nation, to control and create its status. Whether, then, Lord Byng acted as he should have done is beside the question. Under our interpretation of "equality of status" there was no obligation on him to follow British precedents.' He had sent a draft of the article to King for his 'confidential perusal,' adding: 'It is along such lines, I venture to think, that the Imperial Conference ought to be guided.'[50]

King was about to go to the important Imperial Conference in London. On 9 October 1926, King replied:[51] 'I have in the press of affairs during the past fortnight [following his election victory] only had time to go through it hurriedly but I shall take the first opportunity during the voyage to read it with care.' King had read enough, however, to state: 'I think I should agree with your main thesis that equality of states does not necessarily mean identity of precedent and practice.' He then adds: 'It does not necessarily follow, however, that those who during the recent campaign emphasized British precedent were on the wrong track. It must be remembered that they were answering opponents who put forward the view that there must of necessity be a distinction between the powers of the Sovereign in the Mother Country and of his representative in a Dominion. Our Liberal friends, so far as I have observed, were insisting that identity of practice was permissible rather than that it must always be followed.'

The November 1926 conference was important because it led to the Balfour Report, dealing with the independence of the dominions. It declared all the dominions to be 'autonomous Communities within the British Empire, equal in status, in no way subordinate one to another in any aspect of their domestic or external affairs, though united by a common allegiance to the Crown, and freely associated as members of the British Commonwealth of Nations.'[52] Kennedy's views, particularly those expressed in the *Contemporary Review*, probably indirectly influenced the Balfour Report, which O.D. Skelton, the deputy minister who accompanied King to the conference, privately referred to as 'really an epoch-making document, the most important pronouncement on the subject ever made, and 90% of it is in the right direction.'[53]

Family Planning

The correspondence with Mackenzie King reveals another interesting aspect of Kennedy's life, which I have not seen mentioned anywhere else, that is, Kennedy's apparent support of family planning. He wrote to King on 4 April 1924, complaining about Canadian customs officials barring family planning books by the English activist Marie Stopes from entering Canada. Kennedy's letter is not in the King files, but King's detailed response is. Kennedy, who had now abandoned Catholicism, had concluded that it was Roman Catholic pressure that caused the Department of Customs to act, but King states it was, in fact, Protestant pressure, particularly that of Reverend J.G. Shearer, the general secretary of the Social Service Council of Canada, who was a well-known moral crusader. King writes:[54] 'The point I would like particularly to bring to your attention, in view of the impression you apparently have that some Roman Catholic influence is at work, is that in this matter it has been Protestant influences and not Roman Catholic which are responsible for the course the Minister of Customs has found it necessary to take.'

Section 207(2) of the Criminal Code made it illegal to distribute birth control devices. This prohibition had been introduced into the Code in 1900 and
was not removed until 1969. The Code in the 1920s stated:[55] 'Every one is guilty
of an indictable offence and liable to two years' imprisonment who knowingly,
without lawful justification or excuse ... offers to sell, advertises, publishes an
advertisement of, or has for sale or disposal any means or instructions or any
medicine, drug or article intended or represented as a means of preventing conception.' The books by Marie Stopes advocated using condoms as a means of
family planning.

King included the custom inspector's report, which he asked Kennedy to
return. 'From Mr. Roe's report,' King states, 'you will see that he is of the opinion that two at least of the books mentioned are a violation of the Criminal
Code and should not therefore be permitted to be brought into the country or
offered for sale in Canada.' King went on to say: 'It may well be that the Criminal Code in the particular referred to goes too far, but until Parliament amends
the law you will, I am sure, be the first to recognize that the Ministers of the
Crown cannot do other than seek to uphold it.'[56] In fact, it is likely that King did
not think that the law went too far. He had in his youth been actively involved
in social purity movements.[57]

Kennedy replied to King,[58] pointing out that section 207 included the words
'without excuse' and asked: 'What do the words "without excuse" mean?' King
did not reply. The issue raised by Kennedy was dealt with for the first time
in a 1937 case, R. v. Palmer.[59] Miss Palmer was an employee of the Parents'
Information Bureau of Kitchener, who offered condoms and contraceptive jel-
lies for sale to married women in a poor part of Kitchener, Ontario. The trial
judge found that the public good was served by her acts, which were therefore
not 'without excuse,' and acquitted her. The Crown appealed, and Chief Justice
Newton Rowell held for the Ontario Court of Appeal that, because this case was
a Crown appeal and there was *some* evidence to support the finding by the trial
judge, the court would uphold the acquittal.

Kennedy also questioned whether the Code 'authorizes the Minister to "ban"
books.' Kennedy states, 'I have asked legal opinion on this and am open to
conviction. This section creates an offence, but under what law is a censorship
established to prevent the offense being committed? Your Sect. 207 states what
will happen in certain defined circumstances.' Again, King does not deal with
this argument. Kennedy ends by stating: 'I would respectfully point out that
there is trouble in the air over this matter.'[60]

This issue sheds further light on Kennedy's concern about women that we
saw earlier with respect to urging women to campaign for the right to vote. One
can also see it in his various attempts to obtain academic positions for some of
his female students. There are letters to Falconer and others trying to promote
women as lecturers in history and political economy. One of these persons, for

example, was Marjorie Reid, one of his students at the University of Toronto, who went on to study at Oxford. He wrote a number of letters on her behalf, without success, stating in a letter to the University of Wisconsin: 'As she is one of my old pupils who has had a distinguished course, I am only anxious that she be given a fair chance to develop her academic ability as a teacher.'[61] And, in a letter to the University of British Columbia urging her appointment, he stated that 'there is not much chance of promotion for a woman here.'[62] We will see in a later chapter that several years later he appointed a woman to a full-time position in the Honour Law program.

12

Starting a Law Program

For several decades, there had been a jurisdictional dispute at the University of Toronto between the Departments of History and Political Economy as to which department would teach constitutional history. In 1906 and again in 1910, the head of history, George Wrong, convinced the university that constitutional history properly belonged to history, not political economy.[1] But Kennedy was now in the political economy department and, despite having been booted out of history, was also still teaching constitutional history in that department. Wrong did not want any part of him. It was not just the 'cause célèbre' of Kennedy having had a romantic relationship with one of his students, but also Kennedy's alleged exaggeration of his involvement in world affairs and the rumoured exorbitant $15,000 fee that Wrong believed Kennedy had received from Florence Deeks for his work on her manuscript.

On 7 January 1926, Wrong wrote to President Falconer, stating that he and Robert MacIver, the head of political economy, had agreed that constitutional history belonged in the history department: 'It should now be made fully definite that Constitutional History is in the department of History and that the proposed arrangement should be made with this as a fixed policy. For myself I should wish to be relieved, when the arrangement is made, of any authority and responsibility in respect of Mr. Kennedy.' There would be, Wrong stated, a transition year, adding: 'I do not think there will be any difficulty in respect of this, but I should wish that the authority in respect of the doing of this work should be with Professor MacIver and not with me.'[2]

MacIver would in return get support from the university for creating a program in law within his department. There was a successful commerce program[3] in the political economy department; why not a law program? Falconer had always wanted a law program. Indeed, he wanted a law *school* in the university. In 1913, he had told the Ontario Bar Association:[4] 'We have lost a very great deal by the fact that we have no faculty of law ... [A]ll the maturity of

President Robert Falconer in his office in Simcoe Hall, 1929

intellectual thought that gathers around the faculty of law has been lost to the University of Toronto.'

Kennedy and MacIver had been having discussions on the possibility of a law program. If Kennedy could not teach constitutional history, what would he do? Moving to an academic position at another institution would have been difficult. He now had four young children. His youngest child, Shelagh, was born in early February 1926, about the time that Wrong and MacIver had agreed that political economy would no longer teach constitutional history.

One possibility for Kennedy, however, was to become the Dominion archivist. The position had been held since 1904 by Sir Arthur Doughty – the first Dominion archivist – and it was rumoured that he was about to become the chief archivist for the Hudson's Bay Company in Winnipeg. Kennedy was qualified for the position, having engaged in archival work for most of his career. He was respected by many of the key people in the archives in Ottawa. Kennedy was reasonably close with Doughty and may have had his support.

There were, however, persons who wanted to block Kennedy's appointment. They included members of the Wrong family. Hume Wrong, George Wrong's son, who was then in the University of Toronto history department, wrote to his father that Kennedy's appointment 'would be good for the University, but mighty bad for the Archives.'[5] But, in an added note, he wrote that he had just learned that Vincent Massey had said privately that Doughty might stay on. Doughty did remain, after receiving an 'increased salary' arranged by Prime Minister Mackenzie King.[6] Doughty was valuable to King and closely involved with King's day-to-day activities. He did not retire until 1935.[7]

Gathering Staff

So, law it would be. Prospects of developing an effective law program, headed by Kennedy, looked good. A very able academic, James Forrester Davison, had joined the political economy department in the fall of 1924 to teach Roman law and other subjects.[8] Davison had graduated in 1923 from Dalhousie Law School, standing second in his class, and went on to complete the newly established Master of Laws degree at Harvard in 1923–24. Dalhousie Law School had been established in 1883 and in the early 1920s had a first-rate faculty, consisting of Dean Donald MacRae, who later became the dean of Osgoode Hall Law School; John Read, who became the dean after MacRae and would later become a member of the International Court of Justice; and Sidney Smith,[9] who would become the dean at Dalhousie after Read and much later the president of the University of Toronto.

Davison taught for a few years at Toronto and then returned to do a doctorate at Harvard under Felix Frankfurter. He did not return to Toronto, taking a position as a professor of law at George Washington University in Washington, DC. Louis Brandeis, a member of the United States Supreme Court, played a role in that appointment. A letter from Brandeis to Frankfurter in 1929 states:[10] 'We like your Davison much. Hope he will take the job here, if you can spare him.' A few years later, Davison published a casebook with Frankfurter on administrative law – one of the earliest books in the new field of administrative law.

Davison worked closely with Kennedy in developing the law program at the University of Toronto. He described the new course in a letter in July 1926 to his friend Larry MacKenzie, who had been his classmate at the Dalhousie Law School and would join him at the University of Toronto in the fall of that year:[11] 'We started consideration of the changed course last November and by Xmas had a new course worked out, which consolidated the various courses.' At that point, he and Kennedy were the only full-time teachers in the program. Davison told MacKenzie: 'Until this year the course in Politics and Law has, for the law, been given by Kennedy, two part time lecturers Clute and Foster and myself.' He didn't think much of the part-timers, describing them in a letter to MacKenzie[12] the previous year as 'quite awful.'

He was more ambivalent about Kennedy,[13] writing:

As for the man himself he is twice as wild as H.L. Stewart [a controversial professor of philosophy at Dalhousie, who had been hired from the University of Belfast]

Norman ('Larry') MacKenzie in 1943 as president
of the University of New Brunswick

and supremely unreliable except on paper. He is also exceedingly brilliant on the whole. His additional vice is constant intrigue for self-advancement. This year through the Board of Governors and over the heads of MacIver and the President he has achieved a full professorship in Federal Institutions, and his expenses for a trip to Europe. This is not the end of his ambitions but it is expected that he will remain quiet for a year or two.

Davison played a key role in persuading his good friend, Norman ('Larry') MacKenzie to come to the University of Toronto. In his letter to MacKenzie[14] about the need to replace the part-timers with a full-time position, he stated: 'Everyone agrees but they know of no one available and I kept repeating as I have now for a year that I know of a person namely N.A.M. MacKenzie ... Will you tell me whether you would consider coming next session and what you would expect?'

MacKenzie, who had served in the Great War for which he was awarded a Military Cross, stood third in the Dalhousie graduating class.[15] He, like Davison, went on to Harvard to complete an LLM. They roomed together at Harvard. MacKenzie worked there with Manley O. Hudson, the distinguished professor of international law, and Hudson assisted MacKenzie in furthering his career at Cambridge University and later at the International Labour Office in Geneva. Hudson wrote in a letter of recommendation:[16] He 'shows a capacity for research and investigation that is unusual. He has an industrious disposition and an investigative mind and gives promise of rare scholarship.' Falconer made an offer to MacKenzie in May 1926 at a salary of $3,600,[17] just under what he was making in Geneva. He was then aged thirty-two. MacKenzie, like Kennedy, was a very productive scholar, publishing regularly in the *Canadian Bar Review*, the *American Journal of International Law*, and the *British Yearbook of International Law*.

Falconer's letter, offering the position to MacKenzie, expressed optimism about the future of the law program:[18]

> We have ... come to the point of strengthening this department in order that larger opportunities may be given to those who are to take Political Science on the law side for an honour course leading to the Bachelor of Arts degree ... I have no doubt that the opening here is one of the best in Canada and I should hope that in time there will be closer relations with the Osgoode Hall Law School, so that in this largest English-speaking province of the Dominion we may have in a few years a centre of legal education which will be worthy of the country.

MacKenzie came to Toronto for the fall term of 1926. He and Davison overlapped. We know they overlapped because one day that fall, MacKenzie recalled,[19] President Falconer called both of them into his office and said: 'Don't let Kennedy push you around. If he tries it you come to me.' MacKenzie later explained the remark as Nova Scotians 'sticking together.' One can picture the animated discussions that Kennedy would have had with MacKenzie and Davison, both of whom, like Kennedy, were interested in public policy and public law, which eventually resulted in a new Honour Law program in law at the University of Toronto.

Kennedy and MacKenzie had a very close relationship. In a note to Falconer in 1931, Kennedy described MacKenzie as a 'loyal, loveable and generous colleague.'[20] They worked together until 1940, when MacKenzie left to become the president of the University of New Brunswick (UNB). Kennedy wrote a congratulatory note, saying:[21] 'You have been with me so long and so happily.' MacKenzie later left UNB in 1944 to become the president of the University of British Columbia. Professor P.B. Waite published a fine biography of MacKenzie in 1985, *Lord of Point Grey: Larry MacKenzie of UBC*.[22] MacKenzie cooperated fully in the biography. He was obviously fond of Kennedy, but he recognized some of Kennedy's imperfections. Waite writes: 'Kennedy was, according to Larry, a "real bastard,"[23] whom you couldn't trust an inch, nor believe a word he said, but whenever he set pen to paper he was magnificent.'

MacKenzie taught a range of subjects[24] apart from his specialty, international law. In 1928–29, Kennedy asked him to teach sociological jurisprudence for which he would be paid an extra $800 above his $3,600 salary. He advised MacKenzie: 'You can begin with the analytical and historical jurists, Bentham, Austin, Maine & Co, à la Vinogradoff, & go on to the immensely important moderns, linking economic and social thought with law.'

Developing the Program

Kennedy's official academic title changed in the spring of 1926. He was forty-seven years old. It was not, as he had told Prime Minister Mackenzie King, a 'new chair of Political Institutions in the Faculty of Politics and Law here at U of T.' There was, of course, no such faculty. The program was still simply a division of political economy. And the eventual title for Kennedy's position was worked out several months later as 'Professor of Law and Political Institutions.'[25]

MacIver left for Columbia University the following year, and E.J. Urwick became the head of the Department of Political Economy.[26] Urwick, a sixty-year-old Englishman, had come to Canada after retiring from his position as professor of social philosophy at the University of London. He was an ambitious administrator. Under his guidance, political economy at the University of Toronto would become the largest academic department in the university, covering such subjects as political science, economics, commerce, sociology, and law, and forcing a move from Baldwin House (now called Cumberland House) on St. George Street in 1933 to larger quarters in the McMaster Building on Bloor Street, where the department remained until Sidney Smith Hall was built in the early 1960s.[27] (This building was the original home of McMaster University, which moved to Hamilton, Ontario, in 1930.) In October 1927, Urwick confirmed the arrangement with Wrong, writing to President Falconer: 'I should ... make it clear that Constitutional History is not in question, as we fully understand that this subject belongs to the Department of Modern History.'[28] But he also confirmed that it was their understanding that the Department of Political Economy included 'Political Institutions and Law.'

It may be that Kennedy had other ambitions during this period. According to Harold Innis in a letter to Falconer a few years later, Kennedy had had his eye on becoming head of the political economy department, thinking that Urwick was to be chair for only one year. Urwick's continued role as head of the department was, said Innis, a disappointment to Kennedy and, according to Innis, helped explain the background to the troubles in political economy in those years. Innis, who later became chair of the department, wrote:[29]

> The various strong contestants were anxious to improve their relative positions against the appointment of Prof. Urwick's successor. The rumor that Prof. Urwick was appointed for only one year was largely responsible for the tremendous energy which Prof. Kennedy displayed last year. He spent his energies and of course ended in failure except that he succeeded in gaining control of a substantial part of the course over which he exercises complete jurisdiction.

If Kennedy had become chair of political economy, would he have continued his quest to develop a major law program under his personal guidance?

E.J. Urwick, the head of
political economy, 1927–37

The exact shape of the law program in these early years is unclear. It seems to
have changed from year to year. Basically, it involved the first two years in non-
law subjects and then two final years of legal subjects. The program resulted in a
BA in Politics and Law. About ten persons graduated with that degree each year
in 1928, 1929, and 1930. After a further year of study, a student could also receive
an LLB from the University of Toronto. Few students at that time went on to the
LLB – only a couple a year. Those who did go on often took the year-long course
while attending the law school operated by the legal profession at Osgoode Hall.
No credit for these University of Toronto degrees was given by Osgoode.

One person who claimed to have received an LLB was Kennedy himself. In
the 1929–30 university calendar, the degree of LLB first appeared after Kennedy's
name and was there every subsequent year, as well as in various *Who's Who in
Canada* volumes.[30] I have not, however, found any evidence in the records of convocation or the senate that Kennedy was ever awarded an LLB, even an honorary
one. When Bora Laskin and Caesar Wright presented a lengthy memorial address
to the senate after Kennedy died, there was no mention of Kennedy's LLB.[31]

Earlier Law Programs at the University

It may be useful at this stage to provide a brief overview of the previous teaching of law at the University of Toronto.[32] There had been a Faculty of Law at
King's College, which had been founded in 1827. The chair of law was given on

a part-time basis to William Hume Blake, the father of the later politician and chancellor of the University of Toronto, Edward Blake.[33]

King's College became the secular University of Toronto in 1850. A new University of Toronto Act was enacted in 1853. A very significant feature of the 1853 Act was the elimination of both the Faculties of Medicine and Law. Although the university would continue to examine and grant degrees in these fields, it would not offer any instruction. One reason for the elimination of these faculties was because Edgerton Ryerson, the superintendent of education, recommended that both law and medicine should be run by private institutions, perhaps housed on the university campus, with special grants from the government.

Over the years, there had been considerable dissatisfaction with the inadequate legal education offered by the Law Society of Upper Canada and the failure of the University of Toronto to offer instruction in law. American universities, such as Harvard, Columbia, and Michigan, had already established large, full-time, three-year postgraduate institutions. In 1883, Dalhousie established a law program, whereas the Law Society of Upper Canada simply offered a voluntary lecture program. Aspiring lawyers were expected to learn mostly by private study and apprenticeship with practising lawyers.[34]

In early June 1887, the registrar of the university sent a letter to the Law Society,[35] stating that 'at a meeting of the Senate of the University of Toronto, held May 27th, it was resolved that the Senate should invite the Law Society of Upper Canada to co-operate with it in considering the question of the establishment of a Teaching Faculty in law in the University.' The University of Toronto's vice-chancellor, William Mulock, had grand ambitions for the faculty. 'I see our way clearly,' he wrote the minister of education, George Ross, 'to the establishment at once of the best Law Faculty on this continent.'[36]

A joint committee was set up by the Law Society and the university senate, which reported in early 1888, recommending a four-year course leading to an LLB degree, to be run jointly by the Law Society and the University of Toronto. The university would be responsible for the first two years and the Law Society for the last two.

The Law Society set up a committee of 'benchers' (governors) to study the proposal and to get input from the other universities and the county law associations. Not surprisingly, the other universities did not like the concept. As the *Canada Law Journal*[37] stated, 'there is in the minds of some who discuss it a tinge of jealousy of Toronto University.' Principal George Grant of Queen's thought that the Law Society should in all cases require a university degree before studying law. Trinity College, which was not then part of the University of Toronto, was also worried about the effect of the scheme on its arts program. Many lawyers were unhappy about the possibility that the apprenticeship period, known as articling, would be shortened. Lawyers from outside Toronto did not want a school centred in Toronto that would deprive them of articling students – whether it was run by the University of Toronto or the Law Society.

A further committee was established by the benchers to study legal education, and this time the committee recommended that the Law Society 'reor-
ganize' its own school[38] and appoint a full-time president. 'It is not desirable,'
the committee stated, 'to enter into any arrangement with any University for
the education of students, nor to shorten in any way the period of study or
service of students.' In January 1889, the Law Society approved the committee's
report; a month later the new law school, Osgoode Hall Law School, was officially established. Students would spend three years articling and at the same
time attend lectures in the morning and late afternoons during the academic
year. Those without a university degree – about half had degrees – would spend
an extra two years articling. One change made by the benchers of the Law Society, however, was to substitute for the words 'it is not desirable,' the words 'it is
not expedient at present.'[39] The amendment passed by a single vote. The door,
therefore, was left slightly ajar.

On 10 January 1889, a week after the Law Society vote, an Order in Council
was approved by the province permitting the establishment of the new faculty
at the university and appointing two part-time professors. One was a judge,
William Proudfoot, who in the 1840s had articled for William Hume Blake,
the first professor of law in King's College, and who was about to retire from
the bench because of his poor hearing.[40] Proudfoot remained a professor until
1900. The second professor was David Mills, who had graduated from the University of Michigan Law School in 1867 and later became a federal cabinet minister. He lectured effectively in constitutional and international law, in spite of
the fact that he lived and practised in London, Ontario. In 1897, he became the
federal minister of justice and eventually resigned his professorship.

At the turn of the century, the government appointed two replacement part-
time professors. One was A.H.F. Lefroy, the Oxford-educated Canadian, whom
we encountered in an earlier chapter. Lefroy remained a professor until his
death in 1919, publishing four major books and over thirty substantial articles.
The second professor, James McGregor Young, was a Toronto graduate of 1884,
who also lectured at Osgoode Hall Law School. He resigned in 1913 to concentrate on the practice of law. The government had also appointed in 1889 a
number of honorary and unpaid lecturers who included Edward and Samuel
Blake, D'Alton McCarthy, Jr., and B.B. Osler, some of the very best lawyers in
Canada and the founders of some of Canada's major law firms. Unfortunately,
most of the lectures were never delivered and the scheme, which looked good
on paper, was abandoned after a few years.

The university law course attracted only a handful of LLB students each
year – graduates included Chief Justice Lyman Duff, Clara Brett Martin, the
first woman barrister in the British Empire, and future prime minister William Lyon Mackenzie King. Many arts students, however, such as later heads
of the Law Society of Upper Canada, J.J. Robinette and Brendan O'Brien,

Lyman Duff (left), a law graduate who later became the chief justice of Canada;
picture taken about the time he left a small-town practice in Fergus, Ontario,
for British Columbia. Clara Brett Martin (right), another early law graduate,
who became the first woman barrister in the British Empire

took individual law courses as part of their BAs. The LLB program, however,
could not compete with Osgoode Hall Law School, and the University of
Toronto therefore had a very small undergraduate program, in contrast to
the hundreds at Osgoode Hall. The university's LLB graduates still had to
spend three years at Osgoode. Over the years, individual instructors, often
lecturers at Osgoode Hall, would be hired to give specific courses on a part-
time basis.

The important Royal Commission on the University of Toronto of 1906 tried
to create a Faculty of Law at the university in conjunction with the Law Society
of Upper Canada, but, as in the past, the Law Society was unwilling to give up its
monopoly on legal education. There was continuing tension between those who
advocated the teaching of law as a science and those who advocated practical
on-the-job training. It was not until 1957 that the Law Society would give up its
monopoly on the training of aspiring lawyers in the province.

Honour Law Course

Kennedy and Urwick had further plans for their undergraduate Honour Law course. In December 1928, Kennedy wrote to Falconer: 'I left a copy of the new undergraduate Honour course in law for your information. The course has been carefully worked out by Professor Urwick, the head of the department, and myself.'[41] They wanted it to begin in September of 1929. 'Both of us are thoroughly convinced,' Kennedy wrote, 'that the present arrangement cannot go on.' The following day, Falconer replied, thanking Kennedy for the 'outline of the changes that you propose in the law section of the political science graduating course.' He added: 'The changes seem to be quite reasonable, and with your explanation I fully approve.'[42] The structure of the course would therefore change. In previous years, Kennedy explained to Falconer, the second year was devoted to economics, which was fine for the students who were going on to get their degree in economics, but not for those who chose law for their final two years. The second year would no longer concentrate on economics.

A serious problem, however, was that Davison, who was on leave completing his doctorate, was thinking of staying in the United States. The previous year, 1927, Kennedy had written to Falconer, saying: 'I trust it will be possible for you to promote Mr. J.F. Davison next session to Assistant-Professor of Roman Law and Jurisprudence ... [H]e has become one of the most valued and promising men. In addition his work and teaching have become a source of academic strength ...We should not now wish to lose Mr. Davison.'[43]

Kennedy later wrote a memo to Urwick and Falconer, dated January 1929, saying how big a loss Davison would be:[44] 'Mr. Davison lectures on our two great pivotal subjects, round which all else converges, or toward which all else moves – Roman Law and Jurisprudence ... Without a thoroughly competent man with experience we should now be like Hamlet without the prince ... As I see it, the loss of Mr. Davison will create a situation which must at once be faced if the honour course is to survive.' Falconer replied, saying he increased the offer to Davison by $500. Kennedy then reported: 'I have had a line from Davison who seems to be attracted by our new honour course in law. He is also anxious about some arrangement of courses within it, and I think we can arrive at something mutually beneficial.'[45]

Davison had, however, indicated that he was looking for a position in a professional Faculty of Law. 'My concern,' he had written to Kennedy, 'is chiefly with the possibility of a full course in Law in the University and the opportunity to teach practical and technical courses in the Common Law.'[46] Kennedy replied to Davison, stating: 'If you mean by the phrase "full law school course in the university" the development of a full Faculty of Law here, I must say candidly that I think, first, that it will never come except through a liaison with Osgoode Hall[47]... and secondly, I think that eventuality is as far off, if

Frederick C. Auld

not farther off than ever.' Kennedy then wrote to Falconer: 'I think it would be well, if I might suggest it, that you should make it clear to him that there is no immediate prospect of a separate Faculty of Law.'[48] Kennedy adds in his note to Falconer that, when a Faculty of Law comes to the university, 'it will doubtless come along some lines of union with Osgoode.'

As we know, Davison did not return. His replacement was Frederick C. Auld,[49] an Oxford-trained Canadian lawyer from Prince Edward Island, who had spent a number of years in practice. An Honour Law student in the 1930s, Sydney Hermant, described Auld as a 'wonderful, typical old school, absent-minded professor.'[50] He may have been knowledgeable about Roman law, but was not a very strong or productive scholar.[51] He spent most of his career as the editor of a commercial publication, the *Canadian Abridgment*, which summarized the case law for practitioners. It is still in print and, while useful for the practice of law, is not important for the development of the theory of law. One of its merits, however, was that it provided employment for out-of-work lawyers, for example – as we will see – Bora Laskin. Larry MacKenzie was happy with the appointment, writing in his memoirs: 'Much to my joy he took over Roman Law and Jurisprudence.'[52]

A highly qualified woman, Adelaide Macdonald, had been appointed as a lecturer in 1927, but left in 1930. She had graduated in 1922 with a BA from the University of Toronto in political economy – she was the class valedictorian – and received an MA in 1925. She then spent time at Urwick's former school, the London School of Sociology, and at Berlin University, although it does not appear that she received a degree from either institution. Kennedy was keen

Adelaide Macdonald Sinclair, sometime
during the Second World War

to have her on staff, in part because he was worried about his own health. He
wrote to Falconer in December 1927: 'I do not want an impasse[53] to happen,
such as does when a man falls ill and his courses drop; and Miss Macdonald will gradually understudy my fields in view of such a situation ... Miss M.
graduated in Politics and Law, and took first class honours in her law papers,
as elsewhere.' Falconer agreed: 'Professor Urwick has spoken to me in regard
to the ... change of title for Miss Macdonald.[54] I see no reason why [it] should
not be carried out at the time of the next consideration of our estimates.' She
taught six hours a week in the 1929–30 academic year, and Kennedy had made
plans for her to teach in the 1930–31 academic year, noting in a memo: 'Miss
Macdonald will take over Canadian Administrative Law[55] in 1930–31 and in
future, and will drop Political Theory.'

In 1930, Adelaide Macdonald married a successful lawyer, Donald B. Sinclair,
who had received his call in 1915. They moved into a fine home on Glenayr
Road[56] in Forest Hill Village. As the *Varsity* reported:[57] 'Unwilling to combine a
career and marriage she stopped teaching when she married.' Her husband died
in 1938, and she had a brilliant subsequent career as Adelaide Macdonald Sinclair, first with the Wartime Prices and Trades Board, then as the commander of
the Canadian Women's Royal Canadian Naval Service (WRCNS, known as the
'Wrens'), and finally, as the *New York Times*[58] stated in an obituary in 1982, as
'one of the highest ranking women at the United Nations,' the deputy executive
director for UNICEF programs from 1957 to 1967. For her wartime work, the

Jacob Finkelman, the first Jew
to be appointed to the full-time
professoriate at the University
of Toronto

University of Toronto awarded her an honorary doctorate in 1946. An intriguing question comes to mind: If she had remained single and continued teaching, would Jacob Finkelman, to whom we now turn, have been appointed at that time?

Jacob Finkelman,[59] who had graduated from the Honour Law program, was appointed a lecturer in 1930. Kennedy pressed Falconer to appoint him,[60] saying:

> He did extremely well with us and has swept Osgoode Hall with first of first class honours, and will be called to the bar in June ... Our opinion of him coincides with that of Dean Sidney Smith that he is a man of first class mind ... He is not much to look at; but he is humble, gentlemanly, scholarly and has a facility of putting clearly his ideas, and of grasping the limitation of a subject. We all think very highly of him here.

Kennedy noted that Finkelman 'is a Hebrew' and added: 'As far as I am concerned this is no objection.' Nor would it have been to Falconer, says his biographer James Greenlee,[61] remarking that Falconer 'was among the least anti-Semitic types of his generation.'[62] Before he was appointed, however, according to Finkelman's later recollection in an oral interview for the Osgoode Society,[63] he had to meet the head of political economy, E.J. Urwick, as well as the deans of arts and of the graduate school and Canon Cody, the chairman of the board. After his appointment, Larry MacKenzie asked Finkelman if he was 'surprised at the number of people you saw before you were appointed to the staff of the university.' 'No, I wasn't,' Finkelman replied. 'I assumed that an appointment to the staff of the university is a very important thing and that you would have to go through seeing, being interviewed by various people.' 'Nonsense,' said MacKenzie. 'Kennedy wanted to make sure that anyone who had anything to do with your appointment knew that you were Jewish ... [so] that when he recommended promotion, you would get the promotion and there would be no difficulty about that.' In 1934, Finkelman was promoted to assistant professor, without difficulty. Finkelman was the first Jewish person appointed to a full-time position at the University of Toronto.[64]

Kennedy was concerned about his own health during this period.[65] 'I am snatching a moment when the Doctor has allowed me out for an hour,' he told Falconer, 'to write to you about the junior appointment in Law.' He was also worried about the growth in the number of students, stating: 'The situation is that there are thirty-four hours a week Undergraduate work; that we have two Ph.D. candidates in Law; four M.A. candidates in law; and five other candidates for M.A. in Law about to register. Indeed I am told that the entire graduating class last year in Law (B.A. 1929) is registering for the M.A. except two.'

Finkelman was born in Russia[66] in 1907 and came with his parents, who were tailors, to Hamilton because his mother's brother lived there. He was about one year old when he arrived. In a disarming oral interview for the Osgoode Society, he told the interviewer that he did not know the town he was from – 'it was one of those towns in Russia.' He also did not know his age when he came. When asked for his full name, he replied: 'I just have the one name, Jacob Finkelman.' Did his father do well in business? 'No, he was getting by. He was getting by.' 'Was it expected that you go to university?' 'Well, it was assumed that I would go to university, because I had polio when I was three years old, and my right arm is wasted, and to earn a living I had to have something that had an intellectual quality, so it was assumed that I would go to the university.' There was no university in Hamilton at the time, and so Finkelman enrolled in the political science course at the University of Toronto, with a concentration on law, eventually getting a BA, an MA, and an LLB, and being called to the bar with the silver medal.

Finkelman thought of teaching and applied for a Harvard Fellowship, which he was awarded. Before he left for Harvard, Kennedy told him that there was the possibility of a position in Alberta. Would he be interested, Kennedy asked? Then Larry MacKenzie called Finkelman to tell him that the position was really in Toronto. Finkelman was hired, but not to teach labour law, for which he was later known. In the end, he never went to Harvard. And he got into labour law by accident. While articling with a Hamilton lawyer, he had done research on an organized labour case involving criminal conspiracy and then wrote his LLB thesis on the topic. After he was hired as a lecturer, Kennedy helped him revise the thesis, and it was published under their joint names, Kennedy and Finkelman, by the University of Toronto Press as *The Right to Trade*. Finkelman states in his oral interview:[67]

> Apparently it went over very well. And then I think it was about 1932 he came into my office one day and he said, 'you are teaching a course in labour law.' I said, 'what do I know about labour law?' Well, he said, 'you have got the basic cases for the Right to Trade, and you can make up a course on labour law' ... I was the first professor in a law school in Canada who taught labour law.

Like MacKenzie, Finkelman was very close to Kennedy.[68] 'What was Kennedy like?' he was asked by the interviewer. Finkelman replied: 'It is hard to describe him. He was a wild man, he was an Irish man, he was a very wild man in many ways. But he was very, very good, very good. I enjoyed my association with him.'

Several years later, Finkelman, with the permission of the university, accepted a position for a year as the registrar of a new labour court, composed of Ontario Supreme Court judges, to administer the Collective Bargaining Act. He then returned to the university. In 1944, he became chair of the new Labour Board, a position he held until 1967, and for part of that time he taught administrative law at the university. He was later appointed the chair of the federal Public Service Staff Relations Board in Ottawa.

So, by the early 1930s, there were four persons working full-time in the law program: W.P.M. Kennedy, Larry MacKenzie, Frederick Auld, and Jacob Finkelman.

13

Creating a Law School

When Bora Laskin, later the chief justice of Canada, entered the Honour Law program in September 1930, there were, as we have seen, four full-time faculty members. Kennedy was the head of the program, which was still nominally in the Department of Political Economy, but as a separate administrative unit with its own budget. The next senior person was Larry MacKenzie, then Frederick Auld, and finally Jacob Finkelman, who started teaching the year Laskin arrived.

The law school was at that time located at 43 St. George Street, an old house on the east side of the street, north of College Street and just north of the elegant Baldwin House (now called Cumberland House), where law had earlier been located along with other departments and where it would return sometime after Caesar Wright arrived in 1949.[1]

What was life like at 43 St. George Street? Fortunately, the Osgoode Society and other organizations conducted a number of oral interviews with persons who attended Kennedy's law school in the early 1930s. Following are some comments by three distinguished judges who were at the law school in those years: Bora Laskin[2], who started his BA in law in 1930; G. Arthur Martin,[3] who started in 1931; and William ('Bill') Howland,[4] who started in 1932. This sample is not, of course, representative of the classes in those years, which would have included students who failed, students who switched from the honours course to a general BA, and those who were not as academically minded as these three. They may not have been so enthused about the law school.

Bora Laskin came into the second year of the course, because at that time persons with five years of high school could do the four-year Honour Law program in three years.[5] He grew up in Fort William, now Thunder Bay, at the head of the Great Lakes. His father, a merchant, had come to Canada from Russia in 1906 to escape persecution of Jews, later bringing over his fiancée, whom he married in Winnipeg when she arrived in Canada. They later moved to Fort William. Bora was born in 1912, the eldest of three brothers. Philip

45 St. George Street, the home of the law school from 1935 to 1953

Girard, Laskin's biographer, recounts in his book, *Bora Laskin: Bringing Law to Life*,[6] Laskin's academic bent as shown by a description of his bar mitzvah in Fort William in 1925. The Winnipeg Yiddish newspaper described the event as follows: The young Laskin 'recited the *maftir* very well. Then he delivered a forty-five minute sermon in Hebrew which greatly impressed the congregation.' Later, the paper went on to say, he 'played "Hatikvah" on the violin accompanied by his younger brother.'[7] He was a great success in high school as an athlete and academically, becoming the class valedictorian. He chose to attend the University of Toronto, rather than the much closer University of Manitoba, stating in a later interview that he 'was attracted by the programme of the newly established department of law under W.P.M. Kennedy.'[8]

Laskin remembers sitting on hard wooden kitchen chairs and writing on his knees. There were no desks and no library in the building. Classes were held at the law school in the mornings. His best friend in the class was another Jewish student from a small town, Abraham Acker,[9] who would later be the gold medalist at Osgoode Hall Law School. About thirty students started the BA program in law, and around half of them graduated with that degree. Some dropouts had transferred to the three-year general program. The relatively small number of students from the Honour Law course later took a disproportionate share of the Osgoode medals. Kyer and Bickenbach, in their book *The Fiercest Debate*, compiled convincing statistics on the success of the Honour Law students, stating:[10] 'Between 1930 and 1943, 169 of the 213 graduates of the University of Toronto honours law course went on to Osgoode Hall ... Of the Osgoode Hall students who failed during this period, only a little over

Bora Laskin at his graduation from Osgoode Hall Law School, 1936

1 per cent were Kennedy's graduates; of those who graduated with honours, one-third were from Kennedy's school.'

Laskin comments about his four law teachers at the University of Toronto:

> All four of these teachers in Toronto gave you a feeling that Law was something more than a narrow discipline. I knew something about Holmes and Brandeis and Cardozo long ahead of anything that people who didn't take the law program did, or indeed ... so far as people at Osgoode Hall were concerned because the interest in law as a social science, and indeed as a humanity, was aroused in me by the teachers at the University of Toronto.[11]

There were also the non-legal subjects. Laskin states:

> I took history – I remember taking lectures I think from Glazebrook, if not also from Underhill. There was a programme in political theory. I remember Alex Brady with great affection as giving that program. There was a course in philosophy [given by] G.S. Brett ... who was then head of the department of philosophy, and who was very much interested in legal philosophy and indeed he fashioned a special course for the law students in philosophy so that we could be oriented towards legal philosophy rather than to deal with matters of logic and other aspects of philosophy ... There was no jurisprudence taught at Osgoode Hall Law School.[12]

G. Arthur Martin,[13] one of the finest criminal lawyers in Canada in any time period and later a judge of the Ontario Court of Appeal, was equally complimentary about the program. Like Laskin, he had grown up in a small town in Ontario, Huntsville, where his father was a doctor. The course, he recalled, started with about twenty students and had about fourteen at the end of the second year. Why did he enter the Honour Law course, he was asked? His reply:

> I looked at the curriculum and it was a very interesting course. You took some non-legal subjects, for instance, philosophy was a compulsory course through the whole four years. In first year, in addition to philosophy we took economics, ancient history, French; we took English legal history, a study of the English legal system generally, contracts; I think torts was a second year subject, criminal law, and Canadian constitutional history, English constitutional law in third year. And in the fourth year the emphasis was on comparative constitutional law, public international law, conflict of laws, jurisprudence, Roman law, I think Roman law was a second year course ... I think it was a magnificently structured course as a pre-law school course ... I found the four years at university highly stimulating and the head of the course was the late Dr. W.P.M. Kennedy who was an authority on Canadian constitutional history and he was an inspiring teacher. And I thoroughly enjoyed my four years.[14]

G. Arthur Martin at his graduation from Osgoode Hall Law School, 1938

Martin was asked about Kennedy's method of teaching:

> We had very small classes, sometimes the class would only be 12 or 14, and he
> would sit on his couch, and sometimes we would group around him, sometimes
> he would even lie down and he would fire questions at you, or he would give you
> a little introductory talk. Then my recollection is, we were given topics which we
> were to go and work out. I suppose someone might be given constitutional law,
> habeas corpus, and you would come, not the next day, but the next week probably,
> and read the paper to the class that you had prepared ... Then it would be criti-
> cised by the Dean, questions would be asked. That was his method. Other courses
> not quite that way. Contracts and torts were taught from a case book.[15]

His conclusion:

> It was a marvellous course. As you can see the entire focus wasn't on law, because
> we did have other subjects which we carried through the whole four years, like
> philosophy, political science. But the courses in contracts and torts were really part
> of the preparation for the course on jurisprudence in the final year.[16]

Martin later graduated from Osgoode Hall Law School in 1938 with the gold
medal.

William Howland,[17] later the chief justice of Ontario – he had been the chief
justice of the moot court – echoed the views of Laskin and Martin. He was from
Toronto and, like Martin, his father was a doctor. He recalls that there were
about twenty-five in the class. He stated in his oral interview:

> It was an excellent course and as I have said since then, the four years of phi-
> losophy one had in that course ... one year on logic and three years on Plato and
> the modern philosophies were the things that probably really taught me how to
> think. And the history and the political science and the jurisprudence, it wasn't a
> trade course in the sense that ... you know one tends to have that thrown at the
> education system that why would you take law in university? Well, it was a pretty
> liberal ... general liberal education ... I had a high regard for that course.[18]

Like Laskin, Howland also completed his University of Toronto LLB while
he was at Osgoode Hall Law School. He graduated as the silver medalist at
Osgoode Hall Law School in 1939.

As to Kennedy, Howland states:

> Well, Dr. Kennedy was an amazing character and he was an Irishman and there
> was a good deal of blarney with him but he had written a history ... he had writ-
> ten a tome on constitutional law and he was a very colourful lecturer and a very

William Howland at his graduation from Osgoode Hall Law School, 1939

colourful figure. So that nobody would ever forget William Paul McClure Kennedy. And he was, as I say, a character in some ways, because I remember later on, Arthur Macdonald, who was a lawyer in practice and taught at Osgoode, went up to have dinner with the Kennedys on one occasion and afterwards ... Dr. Kennedy called down to his wife as he left them to go upstairs, 'Don't be any longer, dear, than you absolutely have to.' He wasn't being rude but that was part of his character.[19]

Holmesian Philosophy

Laskin mentioned exposure to Oliver Wendell Holmes in his oral interview. It is not surprising that the law school was dominated by Holmesian ideas, including those of his disciples, such as Dean Roscoe Pound and Benjamin Cardozo.[20] Holmes's philosophy was the gospel at Harvard in those years, and the two key legal academics working with Kennedy at the University of Toronto in the 1920s were Larry MacKenzie and Forrester Davison, both of whom had completed their master of law degree at Harvard.

Holmes's philosophy – sometimes referred to as sociological jurisprudence or social engineering or realism or pragmatism – continued to be the philosophy of the University of Toronto law school in later years and when I was a student in the 1950s. In a paper that I prepared in a tribute to my classmate Harry Arthurs, later the dean of Osgoode and then president of York University, I traced the influences in Harry's (and my) life:[21]

> As I now look back on our law school days, we were all Holmesians, although most of us would not, perhaps, have known it at the time. That was the dominant philosophy at the University of Toronto Law School in those years. Our professors – particularly Laskin – spouted Holmes's well-known statements from his scholarly writing, such as: 'the felt necessities of the time'; 'The prophecies of what the courts will do in fact, and nothing more pretentious, are what I mean by the law'; 'the black-letter man may be the man of the present, but the man of the future is the man of statistics and the master of economics'; and 'the life of the law has not been logic: it has been experience.' And we were familiar with quotations from some of Holmes's judgments, such as: 'The common law is not a brooding omnipresence in the sky'; 'judges do and must legislate, but they can do so only interstitially; they are confined from molar to molecular motions'; and 'the best test of truth is the power of thought to get itself accepted in the competition of the market.'

Laskin absorbed this philosophy at the University of Toronto law school and later at Harvard, and passed it on through his own teaching. This philosophy was also that of Felix Frankfurter, who was influential in the thinking of Forrester Davison. Davison in turn helped Kennedy work out the Honour Law

Justice Oliver Wendell Holmes of the US Supreme Court in 1930

program in the mid-1920s. Kennedy apparently corresponded with Frank-furter, because Davison wrote to Larry MacKenzie in 1930:[22] 'WPMK had a wonderful start in correspondence with FF but I fear the latter found himself unable to cope with such a frequent and voluminous correspondent.' Unfortu-nately, none of this correspondence appears to have survived. Davison went on to say that 'FF was very pleased however with the review K wrote of Frankfurter and Landis's book "The Business of the Supreme Court."' Kennedy had written in the *English Historical Review*:[23] 'Professor Frankfurter and Professor Landis bring to their work juristic learning and experience, and they have written a book in which exact scholarship and wide research are combined with a fine sense of legal and historical atmosphere and a thorough appreciation of the influence of social and economic forces on judicial interpretation.'

Kennedy had written shortly before Laskin entered law school that law should 'serve social ends' and legislation should be preceded by 'a carefully sifted examination of social facts.'[24] We have seen in earlier chapters Kennedy's inter-est in social facts. His study of Elizabethan politics was a study of social facts. His final ecclesiastical study, *Elizabethan Episcopal Administration*, published in 1924, was subtitled 'An Essay in Sociology and Politics.' As noted earlier, he used statistical tables in that book, stating in the preface: 'A little imagination can give them a fascinating sociological life.'[25] In 1923, again as we have seen, Kennedy edited an issue of the prestigious *Annals of the American Academy of Political and Social Science* devoted to understanding Canadian society. It is full of facts. In the preface he states: 'An effort is made in this volume to present facts and trends as to these modern Canadian activities by writers most familiar with the various fields.'[26] In many ways his major historical text, *The Constitution of Canada*, published in 1922, was a sociological study. It is not surprising that Harold Laski, who supported a sociological approach to the law, wrote a favourable review of the book in the *New Republic*[27] and also wrote to Holmes commending Kennedy's book. In his review, Laski stated: 'Nor is his work useful to lawyers only. Students of political science will be grateful for an admirable analysis of a unique and supremely interesting type of federalism.' In his letter to Holmes,[28] Laski commented: 'Kennedy's *Canadian Constitution* I do hope you will get and read; I thought it quite excellent and it throws a flood of light on your own constitution. It's the kind of historical analysis I have prayed for of the American without being able to find, and I learned a very great deal from it.'

Kennedy often used the phrase 'sociological jurisprudence.' In looking for a replacement for Davison, he told MacKenzie: 'We want someone who has an interest in sociological jurisprudence and can read German and French.'[29] He later wrote to MacKenzie: 'I should be personally obliged if you worked along lines of letting the students merely read some books on the analytical and historical jurists, and throwing your weight on the philosophical and sociological jurists. This will help to continue the Harvard tradition here.'[30]

Kennedy outlined his approach in a number of journal articles. He explained the purpose of the Honour Law program in the British *Journal of the Society of Public Teachers of Law* in 1933, stating: 'Its raison d'être is the study of law as a social science, a process of social engineering, in which the knowledge of practical work ... is deepened by an educational purpose, by an inquiry into the social worth of legal doctrines, and above all, by a critical attempt to find out if law in its various aspects is in reality serving the ends of society.'[31] The following year, he wrote in the *South African Law Times*: 'We are concerned ... to create a body of citizens endowed with an insight into law as the basic social science, and capable of making ... it the finest of all instruments in the service of mankind.'[32] The approach is spelled out in a series of lectures that Kennedy gave in 1931 at Lafayette College in Pennsylvania, stating:[33] 'The works of Dean Pound and of Judge Cardozo are read and studied with us, not merely because of their learning and brilliant suggestiveness, but because they contain the promise of legal progress amid the complex social problems of present-day life.'

Kennedy's philosophy is also set out in detail in an article in the *Scots Law Times* of 1937 under the title 'A Project of Legal Education.'[34] He writes: 'The great general principle behind our work is the conviction that law is one of the greatest of university subjects, not merely as a magnificent discipline, but as the fundamental social science on which every aspect of our civilisations must inevitably rest ... Law is not a mere trade or a learned profession – it is the great living palpitating social force which conditions all life – moral, intellectual, cultural, economic ... We aim, as Mr. Justice Holmes has said, to seek "accurately measured social desires" rather than the "revolting" and barren perpetuation of "tradition."'

The approach can be called 'sociological jurisprudence' or 'realism' or 'pragmatism.' Holmes – and by extension, Kennedy – was a pragmatist or, as Cheryl Misak, a philosopher who has studied the pragmatists, has stated, Holmes was at least a 'fellow traveler' of the pragmatists.[35] He was one of the founding members of the Metaphysical Club at Harvard, out of which the pragmatists emerged. They included such important names as Charles Peirce, William James, and John Dewey. 'Law for Holmes,' Misak writes, 'grows in a fallible way, where doubt, conflict and disputes about what the law is are resolved under the force of experience.'[36] Roscoe Pound,[37] a follower of Holmes, had put it this way in 1908: 'The sociological movement in jurisprudence is a movement for pragmatism as a philosophy of law; for the adjustment of principles and doctrines to the human conditions they are to govern rather than to assumed first principles; for putting the human factor in the central place and relegating logic to its true position as an instrument.' As previously noted, Kennedy specifically told MacKenzie that he wanted his students to 'continue the Harvard tradition here.'[38]

Caesar Wright's legal philosophy[39] was similar to Kennedy's. He had completed his doctorate at Harvard in 1927, after topping his class and receiving the gold medal both at Osgoode Hall Law School and earlier in history and political economy at the University of Western Ontario. One of his mentors at Harvard was Dean Roscoe Pound, a Holmes disciple. Kennedy invited Wright to be one of the first speakers at the University of Toronto Law Club,[40] which had been newly established by the students. The lecture took place in the Junior Common Room of University College in January 1931 and was published the following year[41] in the *Canadian Bar Review*. Wright told the students: 'Today our concern is not so much with what law is, but why it is and what it is for ... [L]aw is to-day not being studied as a dissociated group of rules of absolute validity, but as one of several means of ordering social conduct.' The principal example he gave was the new administrative tribunals.

Kennedy and Wright therefore saw eye to eye on legal philosophy – both could be labelled realists or pragmatists. But their relationship was somewhat rocky. In part, this friction was due to minor irritants, discussed by Kyer and Bickenbach.

Cecil Augustus Wright, usually referred to as Caesar Wright, 1923

Wright, for example, was upset that Jacob Finkelman was using material from Wright's casebook on contracts without acknowledgement and in 1933 had the dean of Osgoode, John Falconbridge, send a strongly worded letter of complaint to Finkelman, with copies to Kennedy and the chair of the Law Society's Legal Education Committee.[42]

Another incident that same year[43] showed a testy relationship between Wright and Kennedy. Kennedy had had Larry MacKenzie write to Dean Sidney Smith of Dalhousie with a request for a one-year credit for a student who had been through the Honour Law program at the University of Toronto. MacKenzie had included in the letter Kennedy's previously mentioned article about the Honour Law course published in the British *Journal of the Society of Public Teachers of Law*. Dean Smith shared the correspondence with his friend Caesar Wright (they had taught together at Osgoode for several years), making fun of Kennedy's assertion in the article that Haldane had 'lent his constructive skill in the actual drafting of the courses.' Wright and Smith were against giving any credit to Kennedy's graduates. Indeed, Wright even took the position that graduates of Kennedy's course should not be eligible for postgraduate work at Osgoode. Wright wrote to Smith, stating: 'As a matter of fact, it has always been my contention, and I have tried to get the Dean here to take some action on it, that K's course should not even entitle a man seeking entrance here to admittance as a graduate student.' Wright did not trust Kennedy. He was concerned that Kennedy would eventually succeed in getting recognition of his program. In his letter to Smith, Wright stated: 'I feel quite sure that it will not be long before K. obtains his Law School. The Dean [Falconbridge] does not or says he does not believe it. K. is a clever man.'

Kennedy and Wright's principal difference was whether non-legal subjects should be integrated with legal subjects or whether the legal course should come only after undergraduate study, as at Harvard. In his letter to Smith, Wright went on to say: 'I think you know my own personal views regarding University Law Schools. I am quite convinced a University is the proper place. I am equally sure that its place should be *after* and not concurrent with an Arts course.'

'In retrospect,' writes Philip Girard[44] in his biography of Bora Laskin, 'the differences between the two men seem slight enough that one is compelled to ask why they could not have compromised on a scheme to present to the benchers. A five-year university degree with a predominance of arts course in the early years and law courses in the later years would seem to have been an obvious solution, and is the principal mode of legal education in Australia today.' Their personalities, however, made it difficult for them to compromise, for example, by permitting previous university training in another field as a substitute for the five-year course. But, as Girard goes on to say: 'Both had elevated notions of their own importance, demanded absolute loyalty from their own acolytes, and liked to run their own show.'

The Law Society of Upper Canada

As shown in the previous chapter, there had been a long history of conflict between the University of Toronto and the Law Society of Upper Canada. It continued through the 1920s and 1930s. In 1924, the University of Toronto Senate had passed a motion[45] that university representatives meet with the Law

John D. Falconbridge, dean of
Osgoode Hall Law School, 1923–48

Society benchers to discuss setting up a law faculty at the university. Subsequently, a joint Law Society/University of Toronto committee was established to work out a scheme. The result was a proposal for students in the law and politics stream leading to a BA to take half of their final year courses at Osgoode and, upon receiving their BA, could enter second year at Osgoode. The Law Society's Legal Education Committee, however, rejected the proposal. It did not like the fact that the students would have one less year of articling. Other universities objected that the arrangement favoured the University of Toronto. And it is likely that Kennedy was against it, because it contemplated a three-year BA, rather than a four-year Honours BA.

The result was that the University of Toronto, as discussed earlier, went ahead with its four-year Honour Law program in 1926. It also resulted in a senate committee – named the Board of Legal Studies[46] – to oversee law studies at the university. The first chair was the chancellor of University of Toronto's Trinity College, who died in 1927 and was replaced by the head of the Legal Education Committee of the Law Society of Upper Canada, M.H. Ludwig. Kennedy was a member of that senate committee. By the end of the 1927–28 academic year, the dean of Osgoode Hall Law School, John Falconbridge, had become chair.

Falconbridge stepped down as chair[47] in 1930 over the issue of whether the university should be able to award a master's degree in law – an LLM – for those with an LLB. It would require a year of advanced legal study and a thesis that would make 'a contribution to legal scholarship and learning.' The degree would be under the jurisdiction of the School of Graduate Studies. Falconbridge sent a long memo outlining his concerns with the proposal. He wanted 'some responsible body of lawyers to share the control' of the degree, and, in the absence of any other such body, it should be the Board of Legal Studies. Falconbridge also wanted the possible subject areas to be cut down.

As proposed, the subject areas covered the whole field of law. 'To a board of lawyers,' Falconbridge argued, 'this seemed rather an excessive burden to be assumed by the staff in law, consisting of three members.' 'With the greatest diffidence,' Falconbridge stated, 'I venture to question the adequacy of a staff of three men, engaged in undergraduate instruction, to direct and supervise graduate work in all the special fields of law mentioned in [Kennedy's] report.' Falconbridge noted that 'neither Dalhousie Law School nor Osgoode Hall Law School is yet prepared to encourage and undertake graduate courses, although each of these schools has a larger staff in law than that of the University of Toronto.' It should, he suggested, be an MA, not an LLM, adding: 'The proposal would seem in effect be to establish a school of graduate studies in law without any corresponding school of undergraduate studies in law.'

Falconbridge resigned as chair in order to present his own views to the university senate. The staff of the law program met and reduced the range of courses to seven fields:[48] constitutional law, international law, Roman law, British administrative law, jurisprudence, history of English law, and comparative law. The senate did not approve the degree. However, MAs and PhDs would continue to be offered through the graduate school. In Kennedy's article in the 1933 *Journal of the Society of Public Teachers of Law*, he noted that there were sixteen students reading for the master's degree.[49] An LLM was not offered until 1938,[50] the year after law officially separated from political economy. In 1942, the year after law separated from the Faculty of Arts and Science, the degree of DJur (doctor of jurisprudence)[51] – similar to a PhD – was introduced. (This degree is not to be confused with the present JD degree, which was introduced in 2001.)

In the spring of 1932, the question of the university and legal education in Ontario once again came to the fore.[52] The benchers of the Law Society changed their minds about requiring two years of university as a prerequisite for admission to Osgoode Hall Law School, a requirement that had been established in 1927. A high school education would once again be enough. In the fall of 1932, Ludwig, chair of the Law Society's Legal Education Committee, asked the Osgoode students for their opinion on the lower standards. A student committee was established, which disapproved of the change, noting that at present about 90 per cent of students were university graduates.

One student, Donald Carrick,[53] was particularly vocal about the Law Society's approach to legal education. He had a BA in English and history from the University of Toronto and an LLB from Harvard Law School, but was given no credit for his LLB when he entered Osgoode in 1931. He was well known to the public because he had been the intercollegiate heavyweight boxing champion and had represented Canada in the 1928 Olympics. He wrote a scathing article in the Osgoode student paper, *Obiter Dicta*, under the heading 'Wasting Three Years at Osgoode.'[54] Law Society members, he wrote, 'worship at the shrine of the practical' and 'keep Osgoode Hall a trade school where we memorize a lot of rules of thumb to throw out on examination papers.' The theory is, he concluded, 'that by keeping a man at the office long enough to prevent him learning anything at the law school, and by keeping him at the law school long enough to prevent him from learning anything at the office, you turn out a duly qualified practitioner.' Needless to say, the article attracted considerable attention.

On 15 June 1933, a Special Committee of the Legal Education Committee[55] was created to 'investigate the subject of Legal Education in all its aspects and report their conclusions and recommendations.' Their report was adopted by the benchers of the Law Society on 21 February 1935. It had been signed on 14 February – not the Valentine's Day present that the progressives such as Wright, Falconbridge, and Kennedy were hoping for.

The report argued against requiring a university education, stating: 'The emphasis laid upon the importance of a university degree has to some extent obscured the advantages which students may and ought to derive from five years' experience in actual practice in an office.'[56] The concentration on office work was accentuated. Osgoode students would spend all day at the office with lectures at 9 in the morning and at 4:40 in the afternoon. There would be one year full-time at Osgoode, then two years of articles, then two years of school. There would still be only three full-time instructors.

The adoption of the report set back the cause of legal education in Ontario for many years and in the meantime hindered the development of legal education at the University of Toronto. The *Canadian Bar Review*,[57] edited by Caesar Wright, published the report of the 1935 Special Education Committee in its June 1935 issue, having previously published the critical report by the committee of Osgoode students.[58] A number of prominent legal figures commented negatively about the report in the June issue.[59] Kennedy was not one of them, and, as far as I can determine from newspapers and other documents, he did not comment publicly about the report.

In 1937, Caesar Wright published an article in the *Canadian Bar Review*, critical of the benchers' position.[60] He sent a copy to Kennedy,[61] stating: 'Feeling energetic over the week-end, I wrote an article on Legal Reform and the Profession, in which I make some very uncomplimentary remarks about the attitude of the profession in establishing proper law faculties, etc.' The article was clearly aimed at his employer, the Law Society of Upper Canada, but he never actually referred to the Law Society. He concentrated on law reform. He concluded the article: 'We have law schools and faculties, but are they, to any extent, encouraged, staffed or endowed with a view to doing more than teaching the mechanics of the profession?'

We do not, unfortunately, have Kennedy's reply. Wright had a long quotation in his article from a piece that had been published earlier that year by Kennedy in the *Scots Law Times*.[62] The quote is introduced by Wright's statement: 'A Canadian writer [Kennedy] has admirably summed up the requirements of this broader conception [of law].' Law, Wright argued, should not be 'merely a depositary of a historical knowledge of the law in ancient times and a school for propounding the law as it stands today.'[63] The quote by Kennedy starts with a quotation from Holmes: 'For "the man of science in the law is not merely a bookworm."' It then goes on to state: 'He sees the past of law, and, in so far as he has insight, he sees growth in response to social demand. The common law owes its life to experience. On the other hand, he learns to see the present – its problems, its difficulties, its castings off – and he is always asking how far it is responsible for social conditions, how far it can be beneficial.' So once again, Kennedy and Wright are in agreement on the concept of law, and once again Holmes is a central figure for each of them.

One result of the strong position taken by the Law Society is that Kennedy forged ahead with his plans to expand the law program at the University of Toronto. The next important step was to formally separate law from the Department of Political Economy. In 1937, law became a completely separate department[64] in the Faculty of Arts and Science.

∼

Before I conclude this chapter, I owe it to the reader to discuss briefly a further question: What happened to Holmesian philosophy? It seems that few people in Canadian law schools discuss Holmes today. A survey published in 1995[65] of law schools in England, Australia, and Canada showed that Holmes was not even on the list of the forty or so legal philosophers mentioned by those responding to the survey, although, to be fair, his disciple Pound was.

This book is not the place for a detailed analysis of why Holmes has been neglected, but one important reason[66] for his neglect is that Holmes – in my view wrongly – was considered by many as a legal positivist, whose views could lead to fascism. One article published in 1945, for example, was entitled 'Hobbes, Holmes, and Hitler.' And the Harvard legal scholar, Lon Fuller,[67] wrote in 1958: 'During the last half century in this country no issue of legal philosophy has caused more spilling of ink and adrenalin than the assertion that there are "totalitarian" implications in the views of Oliver Wendell Holmes.'[68]

My reading of Holmes, however, shows that Holmes did not want a complete separation of law and morals, but rather, as one recent biographer states,[69] Holmes 'replaces the question of *whether* law is separate from morals by the inquiry of *how* the two may be understood to interact.' In his important lecture 'The Path of the Law,'[70] published in the *Harvard Law Review* in 1897, Holmes states that morality plays a role in developing the law: 'The law is the witness and external deposit of our moral life. Its history is the history of the moral development of the race.'

It is possible that Holmes may have a resurrection. Justice Richard Posner, a former noted academic, concluded his foreword to a collection of papers celebrating the centennial of 'The Path of the Law' in 1997 by stating that, after reflection, 'we see what a previous generation saw – that Holmes was the greatest legal thinker and greatest judge in our history.'[71] He also points out that it is hard to classify Holmes, stating that 'there is unending debate over whether Holmes is better described as a formalist or a realist, a pragmatist or a logical positivist, a liberal or a reactionary, a Puritan or a Social Darwinist.'

After reading the Holmes-Pollock letters,[72] Dean W.P.M. Kennedy concluded in a review in 1942[73] that Holmes does not belong in 'any clear-cut school of legal thought.' The same might be said for Kennedy himself. He would not have objected, however, to being called a Holmesian.

14

More Projects

Throughout the 1930s, Kennedy kept up a steady stream of projects and publications. We look at three specific projects in this chapter. They show how involved he was in the first half of the 1930s in Canadian history and the political life of Canada. In a subsequent chapter, we concentrate on a number of publications that furthered scholarship in Canada, such as the *University of Toronto Law Journal*; following that chapter, we discuss projects and publications involving the Canadian constitution, including the second edition of his major work, *The Constitution of Canada*, and his work for the Rowell-Sirois Royal Commission on Dominion-Provincial Relations.

Laws of Quebec

In 1931, Kennedy published a book, printed in French and English, entitled *Reports on the Laws of Quebec, 1767–1770*.[1] It sounds like a dull subject, but it dealt with a crucial event in Canada's history, that is, the decision by the British to use French civil law in Quebec along with English criminal law. Of particular significance was Governor Guy Carleton's important report, which had recommended that French civil law be reintroduced in Quebec.

The book's co-author was Gustave Lanctôt of the Public Archives of Canada, who had earlier contributed to two of Kennedy's collected works. The book was published as Publication No. 12 of the Archives of Canada series of publications.

Lanctôt was a Québécois[2] who had attended the University of Montreal, was a Rhodes Scholar at Oxford, and joined the Public Archives in 1912. After serving as part of the Canadian overseas military force, he received a DLitt from the Sorbonne and, much later, became Canada's chief archivist, after Arthur Doughty retired in 1935. Kennedy, it will be recalled, had had his eye on that position many years earlier. Lanctôt had a distinguished career, becoming the president of the Royal Society. He was given the Governor General's Award for French non-fiction – for his *Histoire du Canada* – and became an Officer of the

Publications of the Public Archives of Canada
No. 12

REPORTS ON

THE LAWS OF QUEBEC

1767-1770

EDITED
WITH AN INTRODUCTION AND NOTES

BY

W. P. M. KENNEDY
Professor of Law in the University of Toronto

AND

GUSTAVE LANCTOT, D.Litt. (Paris)
PUBLIC ARCHIVES

PUBLISHED UNDER THE DIRECTION OF THE DOMINION ARCHIVIST

OTTAWA
F. A. ACLAND
PRINTER TO THE KING'S MOST EXCELLENT MAJESTY
1931

Title page of *Reports on the Laws of Quebec, 1767–1770* edited by
W.P.M. Kennedy and Gustave Lanctôt, 1931

Order of Canada in 1967, the first year that the medals were awarded. His family later made history – or at least the news – when his Order of Canada medal was put up for auction on eBay but was later removed because such an auction was against eBay rules.[3]

Lanctôt was not originally a co-author of the *Reports on the Laws of Quebec*, but had been serving as the book's editor for the Public Archives, the publisher of the book. On 17 March 1930, Lanctôt sent a note to Kennedy:[4] 'Dear Mr. Kennedy, I had no idea, when I undertook to edit your report on the Laws of Quebec, there would be so much work involved. I believe there will be close to 200 foot-notes. In consequence, Dr. Doughty and I have thought that we would change the title page to the one I am enclosing ... which I hope will be agreeable to you.' Lanctôt was added as the second author. There is no response from Kennedy in the Lanctôt papers. I assume that Kennedy could not object to what appeared to be more than simply a suggestion.

The book was well received. The reviewer in the *Canadian Historical Review* commented on 'the usefulness of a book which all students of the period will find of great value,'[5] and an American reviewer in a historical journal, now the *Journal of American History*, stated: 'Students interested in Canadian legal and constitutional history will welcome the publication of *Reports on the Laws of Quebec*.'[6] The *Journal of Comparative Legislation and International Law* noted: 'Professor W.P.M. Kennedy's energy has restored to us the long-lost text of the report made by the Governor of Quebec and the Chief Justice in September 1769 on the legal system in Quebec ... A full index and careful notes add to the completeness and value of the publication.'[7]

The review in what would become the *Journal of American History* states: 'Two of the "reports" (those by Carleton and Hey [William Hey, the chief justice of Quebec]) edited here have been noted as "missing" for about one hundred and fifty years. As a matter of fact the originals are still missing. Official "duplicates bound up for the King's own use," however, were discovered in 1924 by Professor Kennedy among the royal manuscripts in the British Museum and are here printed for the first time.'[8] Previous to that, only the broad strokes of the reports were known.

Kennedy did not have a copy of Carleton's report when he published his 1922 book, *The Constitution of Canada*, but subsequently made further attempts to find it. He notes in the preface[9] to the book on the laws of Quebec – a preface signed by Kennedy alone – that although the reports could not be found in the Privy Council papers in the Public Records Office (PRO), there was a reference to duplicate copies that were 'bound up for the King's own use.' Kennedy states: 'This record interested me and suggested that the King's official set might be found among the Royal or King's manuscripts in the British Museum [not the PRO]. Here I traced them in 1924 without much trouble ... From this source I had transcripts made – which I have presented to the Canadian Archives – of the long lost reports of Carleton and Hey, and they are here printed for the first time.'[10]

An Archives of Canada employee who worked out of the PRO in London wrote to Lanctôt congratulating him and Kennedy on the book, stating: 'It is fortunate that Professor Kennedy found these papers and I am still unable to discover how we came to overlook them ... I myself ... went through this collection which had already been examined by [another archivist], but how I came to miss this volume as well I cannot really imagine. In any event Professor Kennedy must have been pleased to find these papers for which we had looked here in the P.R.O. for so many years in vain.'[11] They missed them, of course, because they were looking in the wrong collection in the wrong building.

Now for some background on the issue and why the finding of the Carleton report was an important discovery. Under the Treaty of Paris of 1763 – after France had been defeated by the British in the Seven Years' War that ended in 1760 – France surrendered its lands in North America to Great Britain. Following the Treaty of Paris, the British government enacted the Royal Proclamation of 1763, which decreed that the courts in Quebec were to decide 'all Causes, as well Criminal as Civil, according to Law and Equity, and as near as may be agreeable to the Laws of England.'[12]

After considerable agitation from the former French citizens in Quebec, the British government took steps to reconsider whether the colony should be under English or French law. The thirteen American colonies were, of course, under English law. The governor of Quebec, Guy Carleton, along with the chief justice and the attorney general of Quebec, were to advise the British government on what should be done. In brief, both the chief justice and the attorney general took the position that British civil and criminal law should continue to apply. The chief justice emphasized the assimilation of French-Canadian society into the rest of the North American colonies. He favoured 'means of Assimilating the Canadians to English Sentiments and Manners ... rather than to return back to the whole of their ancient Constitution and Law, which would fix them in Habits averse to any Change.'[13]

Carleton's report, however, argued persuasively that a conquering nation had to be gracious and generous about the laws and customs of the occupied territory. 'It cannot but be very obvious,' Carleton wrote, 'that in whatever light that Ordinance [imposing English civil law] is considered ... it is as impossible, as it would be injurious, to carry the Plan into execution.' He later spoke of 'the impossibility of abrogating at once the Laws of a Country well cultivated and long settled, and substituting others in their stead ... We apprehend the measure [imposing English civil law] to be exceedingly Dangerous, and such as might put the Country itself in Hazard, without a very strong Military Force to support it.'[14]

'At the same Time,' he went on, 'to restore and establish the whole of the [French] Canadian Laws, without introducing any part of the Law and Constitution of England would likewise be subject to many Objections, Your Majesty's ancient Subjects resident here seem entitled to certain Benefits and personal Rights derived from the British Constitution.' He therefore recommended that 'the Criminal Laws of England ... and the Act of Habeas Corpus are what in the Course of this Report We shall presume principally to Recommend.'[15]

The Quebec Act of 1774[16] followed Carleton's recommendations. Section 8 of the Act specifically provided that 'Property and Civil Rights' should be under the 'Laws of Canada,' that is, under French law. The later British North American Act of 1867 similarly provided that 'Property and Civil Rights' would come under the jurisdiction of the provinces. Criminal law and procedure would, however, come under federal jurisdiction. As Oliver Mowat, later the premier of Ontario, stated in arguing for criminal law and procedure to be under federal jurisdiction, unlike in the United States: 'It would weld us into a nation.'[17]

There has been considerable debate among politicians and historians for over 250 years as to whether it was wise to enact the Quebec Act. Did it harm Canada? Did it contribute to the American Revolution? What effect did it have on the governance of other territories in the British Empire? And many other important questions.

But, for over 150 years, while opinions were being formed on the Quebec Act, the actual arguments of its key advocate, Guy Carleton, were not part of the debate. The book by A.G. Bradley on Carleton,[18] *Sir Guy Carleton (Lord Dorchester)*, for example, in the previously discussed 1906 series on the 'Makers of Canada,' was written without access to the report, as was its reissue,[19] entitled *Lord Dorchester*, in the 1926 Oxford series. That reissue had an introduction by a distinguished historian, A.L. Burt, who argued against the wisdom of the Quebec Act.

Who knows what conclusions these writers would have drawn if they had been able to read Carleton's persuasive report. And who knows what Burt might have concluded in a subsequent scholarly book,[20] *The Old Province of Quebec*, published in 1933, with only one reference to the Kennedy and Lanctôt book, if Burt had not already committed himself to an anti-Carleton position in 1926.

The Law of Nationality

Another important document in a different subject area for which Kennedy can claim credit deals with the law of nationality. In early 1930, the federal government issued a sixty-five-page report on the law of nationality prepared by Kennedy. The full title of the document,[21] marked 'Confidential' but made public in 1931, is 'Report Submitted to the Honourable the Secretary of State for Canada on Some Problems in the Law of Nationality by W.P.M. Kennedy.' The report had been asked for and received by Prime Minister Mackenzie King and his secretary of state, Fernand Rinfret – a Montreal lawyer and brother of Chief Justice Thibaudeau Rinfret – but King lost the election in July 1930,

<u>CONFIDENTIAL</u>

REPORT

SUBMITTED TO

THE HONOURABLE THE SECRETARY OF STATE FOR CANADA ON SOME PROBLEMS IN THE LAW OF NATIONALITY

By

W. P. M. KENNEDY

OTTAWA
F. A. ACLAND
PRINTER TO THE KING'S MOST EXCELLENT MAJESTY
1930

Title page of the *Report Submitted to the Honourable the Secretary of State for Canada on Some Problems in the Law of Nationality* by W.P.M. Kennedy, 1930 and the task of dealing with the issue of nationality fell to the Conservative prime minister, R.B. Bennett, and his secretary of state, C.H. Cahan. (Cahan was a Montreal lawyer who had run unsuccessfully against Bennett in 1927 for the leadership of the Conservative Party.) In 1931, legislation along the lines of Kennedy's report was introduced in the House of Commons by the Bennett government, received second reading, but was then withdrawn. It was not until 1946 that a new Citizenship Act was passed by the Liberal government of Mackenzie King.

Here is how Kennedy described his involvement in the issue in his *British Who's Who* entry in 1935:[22] 'Member of and Draughtsman to the Committee of the Government of Canada on the Law of Nationality, 1928–29 (thanked by the Government of Canada for his services); appointed by the Government of Canada to prepare a confidential report on the Workings of the Law of Nationality, 1930.' This entry is not an exaggerated claim. The committee mentioned is, no doubt, the Interdepartmental Government Committee, involving the Departments of the Secretary of State, External Affairs, and Immigration.

The law of nationality in that period was extremely complex, and it can only be touched on here. R.B. Bennett told the House in 1929,[23] when in opposition: 'This is one of the most difficult of all matters that we could undertake to deal with.' Senior government official O.D Skelton of the Department of Foreign Affairs stated that same year in a private memorandum:[24] 'The subject is one in which much confusion and ambiguity exist, and further consideration will be required.' It is not surprising, therefore, that the government wanted a thorough study of the subject and turned to W.P.M. Kennedy.

There are many important issues involved in the subject of nationality or citizenship, some of which are still relevant today, such as obtaining and losing citizenship; dual citizenship; birthright citizenship; effect of marriage on citizenship; and many more. Nationality was particularly important in the 1930s with the rise of fascist states that claimed criminal jurisdiction over their nationals, wherever the crime was committed.[25]

The question of the effect of marriage on the citizenship of women was also of particular interest at the time. Canada's first female member of Parliament (MP), Agnes Macphail, had a strong interest in the topic, stating: "There are many Canadian women who resent the injustice which women who are British subjects, but married to aliens, suffer in regard to naturalization ... [I]t certainly is insulting to women to assume that their allegiance can be transferred without their own consent ... I appeal to the members of this House in the name of the womanhood of this country to see that this injustice is removed and that women have the same right of citizenship accorded to men."[26] At the time, under Canadian law, women in Canada and the majority of other countries would automatically take the nationality of their husbands when they married and would lose their nationality if the husband became a 'foreign national.'

Kennedy's report outlines some of the difficulties that could arise, particularly because, in the case of the United States, a woman who married an American did not automatically become an American citizen. Here is one of a number of examples given by Kennedy in the report: 'X, a Canadian national and a subject of His Majesty, &c., marries Y, a citizen of the United States, in Canada and continues to reside there. Y returns to the United States, never returns, deserts her. She now becomes a public charge in Canada, which she has never left in her whole life. She is stateless.'[27]

The law, he pointed out, was introduced in the nineteenth century, adding: 'There is nothing sacrosanct about the law as it now stands. Indeed the rule of law "that the wife of a British subject shall be deemed to be a British subject, and the wife of an alien shall be deemed to be an alien" [the then Canadian law] is comparatively new.'[28] The law with respect to women varied from country to country. 'In no field, possibly, of the law of nationality do so many divergences exist,'[29] Kennedy stated in his report. Kennedy did extensive research on the question of women and nationality. He wrote in the report:

> The writer has attempted with the generous assistance of Professor Manley Hudson … and of confidential assistance from officials at Washington, D.C., to examine the nationality laws of possibly almost every country in the world. All this information the writer has available for the Secretary of State at any time he may require some point elucidated. To include it in this Report is unnecessary, although its acquisition by the author was a necessary duty in compiling his work.[30]

I was not able to determine how much time he spent on the report and what remuneration he received.

The subject of nationality or citizenship had previously come up in the Imperial Conference of 1926 and again at an Imperial Conference in 1929. It had also come up internationally. The League of Nations was interested in the topic and held a conference in The Hague in March and April 1930 to formulate accepted rules of international law on nationality and other topics. The conference's main achievement was the conclusion of the first international convention on the conflict of nationality laws.

Kennedy had asked Mackenzie King to appoint him as a delegate to that conference. It was an odd request. The entire letter, dated 2 February 1930, reads as follows:[31]

> My dear Prime Minister,
> I am writing to you personally and direct. I wonder if you have made your choice for Canadian representatives at the Hague Conference on the Codification of International Law, which I believe will be about March – if not, I should deem it

an honour to be considered as I have given my life to this work. It is very improbable that I would be able to go, but an invitation from the Prime Minister of Canada to his alma mater in this connection would be a most grateful compliment and I assure you would be highly appreciated by all classes in Ontario. With kindest regards.

Ever yours,
W.P.M. Kennedy

King put his own note, dated 13 February 1930, at the top of Kennedy's note, asking an aide to reply that such an appointment was not possible and adding that Kennedy 'has a weakness for recognition.'

Cahan's 1931 bill,[32] 'An Act to Define Canadian Nationals and to Provide for Loss or Renunciation of Canadian Nationality,' adopted in principle Kennedy's report, which had included a draft Act. It dealt with the issue of women and citizenship. And it adopted Kennedy's view that we should use the term 'nationality' rather than 'citizenship.' 'Nationality,' Kennedy argued, had been used in several earlier Canadian statutes and in the Treaty of Versailles after the First World War. Moreover, the word 'citizen' suggests to many a republic not a monarchy, as in the United States, where the designation is citizen. The term 'citizen,' Kennedy wrote, would 'indicate no subjection to the Crown.' 'British subject' would also not be good because it would indicate too close an identification with the British and 'would not be a solution likely to gain general acceptance.'[33] Using the term 'nationality' would avoid these problems.

Cahan acknowledged Kennedy's work when introducing the legislation on 14 April 1931:[34]

Upon assuming the duties of Secretary of State I found that investigations had been made with respect to the application of the existing statute by the permanent officials of the State Department and the permanent officials of the Department of External Affairs. I found that during the regime of the previous government the then Prime Minister, the right hon. the leader of the opposition (Mr. Mackenzie King) had procured from Professor W.P.M. Kennedy of Toronto university a very lengthy study of the essentials of Canadian nationality. With the assistance of the permanent officials of the State Department and of the Department of External Affairs I have drafted this bill in order to express in appropriate terms for legislative enactment what I believe to be the essential qualification for Canadian nationality.

The bill was supported by the Liberals, now in opposition. The former secretary of state, Fernand Rinfret, stated on second reading in late May 1931:[35] 'I hold in my hand a report on this very problem which was made to the Secretary of State by a learned professor in Toronto. I do not intend to quote very extensively from this report, but a passing allusion to it may clarify the situation ... The term Canadian national ... satisfies both, the idea of Canadian national autonomy and Canada's essential position in relation to the crown and the empire ... We agree with the principle of the bill, affecting as it does a matter upon which the late administration had been working for some time.'

The bill was, however, withdrawn on 14 July 1931. There were details in the bill that the three main departments interested in the subject – the secretaries of state, external affairs, and immigration – could not agree upon.[36] Moreover, as Cahan told the House, the minister of immigration was preoccupied chairing the special committee investigating the politically charged Beauharnois Affair, involving alleged payoffs to Liberal politicians for approving the construction of a hydroelectric project on the St. Lawrence River.[37]

In addition, there was opposition from British Columbia about children of Asian workers in Canada becoming Canadian nationals. MP Thomas Reid from British Columbia argued on second reading in May that the bill should be amended. He stated: 'I think this is one of the most important bills which has ever come before this house.' In a lengthy diatribe, Reid noted:

> I contend that the provisions of this bill should be changed to such an extent as not to extend this right [of nationality] to any child of alien parentage born within His Majesty's dominions or on board a British ship, unless the parents of such child are fit and proper persons, both physically and morally, to become naturalized citizens of this country ... On the Pacific coast we are faced with a race problem ... Steps should be taken immediately to conserve our heritage for our own people.[38]

Cahan acknowledged that there was concern, 'especially from the province of British Columbia, on the ground that under its terms one of the Japanese or Chinese race who was born in British Columbia would thereby become a Canadian national.'[39] He assured the House that 'this bill makes no change whatever in the existing law.' Kennedy had not recommended or even discussed any change in the law in his report.

Cahan later told the House: 'I regret that we will be unable to proceed ... I think that the underlying principles of that bill meet with the general approval of this house.'[40]

The legislation was withdrawn, but a second bill dealing specifically with women and nationality, which had been introduced in January 1931, along the lines recommended by Kennedy, was enacted by Parliament. It had followed the recommendations of the conference at The Hague of 1930 and the Imperial Conference of 1929. Cahan wrote to Bennett in June 1931,[41] saying that Canada should go ahead with the legislation on women even though Britain was not at the time ready to proceed. '[T]he British Government,' Cahan wrote, 'is not now willing to carry out the resolutions of the last Imperial Conference, which authorize this proposed legislation. It seems to me that Canada, which now has many hundreds of women, who are without nationality by reason of their marriage to American citizens, should not delay dealing with the matter.' The legislation was brought into operation in 1932.

In November 1934, Kennedy wrote to Cahan urging the reintroduction of the earlier bill on nationalism, stating: 'I venture to hope that you will make an opportunity to reintroduce your Nationals' Bill at the coming session. Last night I was at a company of young lawyers of the party and they urged me most strongly once more with great respect to bring this matter to your attention ... There are a great number of our young lawyers also interested in it and they hope that a measure largely uncontentious should not be held up for administrative reasons.'[42] Note that Kennedy, chameleon-like, seems to be suggesting to Cahan that, like Cahan, he is a Conservative Party supporter, by using such language as 'the party' and 'our young lawyers.'

Cahan passed on Kennedy's letter to Prime Minister Bennett concerning the nationality bill, which, Cahan said, 'I introduced to the Commons in 1931 and then subsequently withdrew pursuant to your personal instructions.' Cahan noted that he had recently learned that 'this matter had been removed from my personal jurisdiction.' Cahan interpreted his removal 'as a clear intimation of your lack of confidence in the ability and efficiency with which this Department should be administered, an intimation which should, in ordinary course, call for my resignation as Secretary of State; but, in view of pending political complications and the expediency of maintaining a united front to the radical tendencies of these times, I have hesitated to adopt that course.'[43] I take this explanation to mean that there was an election in the offing.

In a note in 1935 in the first volume of his new *University of Toronto Law Journal*, Kennedy referred to the possibility of reintroducing the legislation.[44] Kennedy wrote: 'Pressure of national affairs, as well as administration details, prevented the progress of the measure ... but we understand that it will be reintroduced this session.' It was not reintroduced, and in October 1935 Mackenzie King replaced Bennett as prime minister. King did not reintroduce the legislation either.

In 1946, however, the Liberal secretary of state in King's government, Paul Martin, who had been one of Kennedy's students at the University of Toronto in the 1920s (although not in the Honour Law program), introduced the Canadian Citizenship Act. It was enacted as an amendment to the British North America Act, without seeking or obtaining the approval of the provinces, which the BNA Act permitted in certain cases. Martin told the House[45] that the purpose of the bill was similar to the 1931 Conservative bill, 'not in the details of the present bill, but following its main principle.' Kennedy was only mentioned a few times in the debates. The legislation, however, used the designation 'citizenship' and not 'nationality,' which Kennedy had recommended. The legislation continued to prohibit dual citizenship, which was later permitted by legislation in the multicultural 1970s. In his memoirs,[46] Paul Martin talked about Lester Pearson bringing in a new Canadian flag. Martin wrote that Pearson 'rightly believed that the moment had arrived to fashion a flag that would give Canadians a feeling of pride, as well as a distinct identity. It was the same impulse that had driven me to introduce the Citizenship Act in 1947.' A similar feeling of pride in his new country must have driven Kennedy to seek the enactment of the earlier nationality bill.

Comparative Law

The final area that will be considered in this chapter is Kennedy's work on comparative law. Kennedy's interest in comparative law led to an interesting, but difficult, assignment, which caused him to clash with a number of important Canadian academic lawyers – in particular, Deans John Falconbridge of Osgoode Hall Law School and Sidney Smith of Dalhousie Law School. The story sheds light on how Kennedy was regarded by some of the key players in legal education in Canada at the time – people who would later play a role in reshaping Kennedy's law school.

In late 1931, Kennedy became a member and secretary[47] of a committee of distinguished Canadian lawyers, judges, and academics charged with organizing reports on Canadian law for an International Congress of Comparative Law that was to be held the following summer at The Hague in the Netherlands. Each country was asked to prepare reports on twenty possible topics.

I was not aware of Kennedy's role in the congress until, while doing research for the present book, I stumbled on a thick file in the McGill Archives of papers of C.S. LeMesurier, the then acting dean of the McGill Law School. (Dean Percy Corbett was on a medical leave.)

There were a number of academics on the committee, including Sidney Smith, John Falconbridge, and Cecil Wright, all teaching at Osgoode Hall Law School, and Kennedy's colleagues, Larry MacKenzie and F.C. Auld. There were also a number of judges and several important lawyers, such as Newton Rowell from Toronto and Louis St. Laurent, a future Canadian prime minister, from Quebec City. Justice Lyman Poore Duff of the Supreme Court of Canada was the chairman of the committee, but was not an effective leader, because at that very time he had also taken on the chairmanship of an important and onerous royal commission, the Transportation Commission, which was 'to Inquire into Railways and Transportation in Canada.'[48]

Duff had been reluctant to take on the royal commission because of his ill health. Indeed, he was in the hospital when he was appointed to the commission in November 1931. Not only did he continue to sit in the Supreme Court of Canada over the next year, but he and his fellow royal commissioners on transportation travelled back and forth across the country throughout the year. He was again hospitalized in May and June of 1932, according to his biographer, because of his drinking. He obviously had very little time or energy to devote to the Comparative Law Committee and did not attend the congress at The Hague in the summer of 1932. His commission reported on 21 September 1932, shortly after the congress concluded. He then had what Prime Minister R.B. Bennett described as a 'complete nervous breakdown.'[49]

Why Duff accepted the appointment to chair the Comparative Law Committee is uncertain. Perhaps it was because the chair of the English committee was Viscount Sankey, the lord chancellor of England, and Duff considered himself to be Sankey's equivalent. He had, however, been passed over as chief justice by Mackenzie King in 1924, in part because of his drinking, but still had ambitions of becoming chief justice of Canada. As it turned out, he stopped drinking and in March 1933 was selected by R.B. Bennett to be the chief justice of Canada.

Did Kennedy play a role in Duff's selection as the head of the Canadian Comparative Law Committee? The secretary general of the academy in Berlin had written to Kennedy and others about helping to organize the committee. Duff was a graduate of the Faculty of Law at the University of Toronto before the faculty was disbanded, earning his LLB in 1889, and it would be surprising if Kennedy had not established some connection with Duff, particularly because Duff had received an honorary doctorate from the University of Toronto in 1922. Kennedy thought highly of Duff. James Snell and Frederick Vaughan stated in their history of the Supreme Court that, at the time of Duff's appointment, Kennedy 'judged him to have the best legal mind in the modern history of Canada.'[50] Kennedy wrote to Duff on his retirement in January 1944, indicating some familiarity: 'At the end of your long and magnificent career, I send you my very best wishes for a happy retirement and my deepest appreciation of what you have done in your high office for the development and progress of law.'[51]

The congress was being held under the auspices of the International Academy of Comparative Law, founded after the First World War in 1924. Leading American academics would be involved in the congress. They included Dean John Wigmore of Northwestern University, the author of *Wigmore on Evidence*, who headed the American Bar Association Committee on the congress, and Dean Roscoe Pound of Harvard, who had written an article the previous year on the revival of comparative law and later would become president of the academy. Wigmore took an active role in encouraging widespread participation from the United States and Canada. This event was the first such international congress on comparative law, which continues to take place today every four years. Kennedy would be interacting with many important world figures. It was, Wigmore pointed out, 'the first time, since the St. Louis Louisiana Purchase Exposition of 1904, of holding a World Congress of Lawyers.'[52] One can see why Kennedy wanted to participate.

Kennedy had been interested in comparative law and had been a member of the British Institute of International and Comparative Law and a contributor to its *Journal of Comparative Legislation and International Law*. So, it was appropriate for Wigmore and the secretary general of the congress, Elemer Balogh, who had founded the organization, to turn to Kennedy to participate in organizing a national committee for Canada. In turn, Kennedy sought and received the assistance of the Canadian Bar Association. It was a difficult task, much like herding cats, and, as we have seen, Duff was not available to help with the herding. A Canadian Bar Association representative on the national committee, O.M. Biggar, wrote to LeMesurier about the selection of members of the committee, stating: 'Its complete organization must, I suppose, be delayed until Mr. Justice Duff has dealt with the railway problem. That he should have become engrossed in it at this time is rather unfortunate owing to the shortness of the time available for the preparation of reports.'[53]

By mid-December 1931, very little had been done by the Canadian committee, except to select most of the members of the committee. That had not been easy. A report about the committee had appeared in the *Canadian Bar Review*:[54] 'We have received a programme of the Conference of Comparative Law to be held under the auspices of the International Academy of Comparative Law ... The Chairman of the Committee is the Right Honourable Mr. Justice Duff of the Supreme Court of Canada, and Professor W.P.M. Kennedy, M.A., LL.B., Litt.D., Professor of Law in the University of Toronto, is acting as secretary.'

Falconbridge had earlier complained to Kennedy that a number of scholars had been omitted from the committee. He wrote:[55] 'Why is Sidney Smith not mentioned among those who have been asked to join the committee? ... It seems to be objectionable to omit the Dean of the Dalhousie Law School from the list of invited guests, and not to give him at least the opportunity to decline to act. And why is Clyde Auld not a member of the committee? He is peculiarly qualified with regard to Comparative Law.' It is likely that Auld was not insulted by the omission, but it is equally likely that Smith might hold a grudge for being publicly overlooked by Kennedy.

Kennedy had his own complaint.[56] The *Canadian Bar Review* notice, Kennedy wrote, had mentioned that he was the secretary of the committee, but did not mention that he was also a member. Others rightly complained that Laval and the University of Montreal had been left out and the Western universities were not represented. A judge on the national committee wrote to the secretary general[57] about Kennedy. 'It is unfortunate,' he wrote, 'that Professor Kennedy waited so long before publishing the list of questions you had sent him, and also that he did not communicate with the Western Universities or the French Universities of the Province of Quebec.' There were a lot of egos to be stroked. Eventually, a representative committee was developed.

Kennedy defended his conduct,[58] writing to LeMesurier in January 1932: 'I quite agree with you about the shortness of the time. This is not my fault. I placed the entire matter in the hands of the Canadian Bar Association in February 1931.'

According to the organizers in Berlin, reports were needed from national committees on twenty topics. Reports were to be somewhere between 500 and 5,000 words – not a very precise direction. It was also not clear whether the congress wanted comparative reports or reports about the individual nation's laws on the topic. Kennedy thought that only national reports were expected. There was not, Kennedy wrote, the expertise on foreign law to offer a comparative perspective.[59] But what was expected was not clear until early 1932. Material did not come from Berlin until the New Year. A Quebec judge who was on the national committee assured LeMesurier in mid-January that 'the questionnaire which you received a proof of is practically all the information Professor Kennedy has received.'[60]

From what I can determine from the LeMesurier file, Kennedy did his best to determine who should do what reports and how the reports should be developed. He sounded out Dean Falconbridge and together they concluded that Falconbridge, Donald MacRae, John Robinette, and Cecil Wright, all of Osgoode, would do reports. Wright's report was on marriage law, and Kennedy's was on administrative law. Jacob Finkelman and Larry MacKenzie also prepared reports. Kennedy sought the assistance of LeMesurier in finding Quebec lawyers to do reports. He wrote to LeMesurier:[61] 'I am sorry to worry you so much but the whole matter is initially confused and it has been impossible to iron it out.'

The trouble came with the participation of Dalhousie. Kennedy sent a memo suggesting what reports the Dalhousie faculty should contribute. This communication got Smith annoyed. He wrote to LeMesurier on 26 January 1932:

> I share John D's [Falconbridge's] wrath with respect to Kennedy in some measure. About ten days ago I received a letter from Kennedy telling me that both Osgoode and Toronto had picked certain topics upon which they were to prepare reports for the National Academy of Comparative Law, and that he was assigning to McGill and Dalhousie certain topics in the residue. Knowing Kennedy as I do, I have a definite feeling that the scheme is one for his own aggrandizement.[62]

Falconbridge agreed with Smith, writing to LeMesurier in mid-January:[63] 'Things are getting into rather a snarl chiefly I think owing to Kennedy's peculiarities.' Later, in February 1932, he wrote to Balogh:

> As you may have conjectured from your correspondence with different people here, there was a good deal of friction here, which delayed the formation of a

committee until it was almost too late to do anything. Professor Kennedy is a man of great ability and industry, but he has a way of conducting himself which irritates a good many people. He succeeded in antagonizing the staff of Dalhousie Law School, at Halifax, to such an extent that they refused to contribute any reports, setting up as an excuse that they were asked too late for them to do anything.[64]

Falconbridge defended his own conduct as a member of the national committee in a letter to Sidney Smith,[65] stating: 'I did not think (though I ought to have thought) that Kennedy would proceed to "assign" reports to people without asking for their consent.'

As stated earlier, Duff did not go to the congress in early August 1932. Neither did Kennedy, nor, as far as I can determine, did any Canadian academic. Falconbridge would have liked to have gone, but explained to the secretary general, Elemer Balogh: 'As to my attending the Congress, I am afraid that there is little chance of any subvention which might enable me to go to Europe this year. As you say, the general reporters obviously ought to be present at the Congress in order to lead the discussion, but it is not so important that the contributors of national or regional reports should be present. I think that the general reporter in my own subject will have no difficulty in understanding my point of view and will not need any explanation from me.'[66]

The congress was, it seems, a great success. The *Tulane Law Review* stated:[67] 'The International Congress of Comparative Law ... can well be regarded as the most significant international gathering of lawyers ever held. Thirty-one nations, represented by three hundred and fifty delegates, participated in this international manifestation of effort toward legal cooperation.'

Justice E. Fabre Surveyer of the Quebec Superior Court was one of only two Canadians to attend the conference, though Canadians had been responsible for fifteen reports. He wrote in the *Fortnightly Law Journal*:[68] 'Canada ... may well be proud of those who, not only without remuneration, but without hope of notoriety which may inspire writers from countries with a larger population, have laboured to put the name of Canada lawyers before the jurists assembled at The Hague.'

In early January 1933, no formal report concerning the conference had appeared. The secretary general, Professor Dr. Elemer Balogh, wrote to those who had contributed reports, stating:[69] 'The Academy would have wished to arrange for the printing of these reports forthwith in its volumes of the Congress.' He then added: 'Owing to the present crisis, the printer is not yet in a position to undertake the publication of this work in extenso.' The crisis was, of course, Hitler's rise to power. Hitler had received the highest number of votes and seats in the German federal elections in November 1932, was demanding to be the Reich chancellor, and was appointed by Hindenburg as chancellor at the end of January 1933. The Reichstag fire would occur the following month.

Balogh was a Hungarian Jew and knew he had to get out of Germany. He had travelled to North America just after the congress, in the fall of 1932, on a lecture tour – including lectures at McGill and the University of Toronto – seeking a permanent position in North America. It did not come, although he eventually received a position in South Africa.

There is an exchange of correspondence in the LeMesurier file between the principal of McGill, Arthur Currie, and Law Dean Percy Corbett. The Carnegie Foundation had established a fund to finance the employment of German professors who could no longer teach in Germany. Their salaries would be paid for two years, but the foundation required that a university applying for funds had to show that there was 'a reasonable possibility of providing a permanent position for the scholar.'[70] Currie asked whether there was anyone that Corbett wished to hire under the scheme and suggested that perhaps Balogh would be suitable. Corbett responded that Balogh 'is tremendously learned, but he lectured here last October and I believe that all my colleagues would agree that we couldn't do with [Balogh] at any price … [H]e is conceited, inconsiderate and generally impossible as an individual. He went on from us to Toronto, spreading devastation.'[71] Currie responded: 'To my mind, a few good Scotsmen in American Universities would give more lasting benefits to these institutions than many times their number of German Jews.'[72]

There is no other record of what happened when Balogh came to the University of Toronto to lecture. There was little possibility of bringing him there under the Carnegie plan. The biographer of President Cody states: 'As the university had no money for new appointments, only one or two were accepted … When Harold Laski, the famous British economist, recommended a refugee professor to the Law Faculty, Cody explained that there were no funds for an eventual appointment.'[73] Paul Stortz, the most recent scholar to study these appointments,[74] identifies about twenty refugee professors and lecturers at the University of Toronto, at least half of whom were Jewish. These included Heinrich J.U. Rubin, who taught comparative law. It is worth noting that Cody was not, according to his biographer D.C. Masters, anti-Semitic: 'Cody's record in regard to the appointment of refugee academics reflected his relations with the Jewish community in general. He appreciated them.' Masters goes on to say: 'Cody went beyond the courtesies of his relations with the rich. He defended Jewish academics against the prejudices of some critics of the university.'[75] I have been unable to discover anything about Balogh's career in South Africa.

15

Running a Law School

Canon Henry Cody

Canon Henry Cody, the chairman of the board of governors since 1923, took over from Robert Falconer[1] as president of the university on 1 July 1932. Falconer had been in poor health. In June 1930, he had learned of a severe heart disorder and later suffered a mild heart attack, but he wanted to stay in office a full twenty-five years before retiring.

Kennedy was very close to Cody, just as he had been to Falconer. He wrote to Cody[2] after the announcement of his appointment, saying: 'I considered myself very fortunate that, when an old friend is passing out, I should find another old friend taking on his duties.' When Cody had first made it known that he was prepared to take on the task, Kennedy wrote to him[3] that the news 'brought me the greatest joy' and went on to state: 'I do not know anyone alive who can carry out the work that lies before you so well. Indeed, I want to be quite frank with you and to tell you that I had more or less decided to go the United States if certain rumours about the presidency had come true.'

The other candidates being considered[4] were R.C. Wallace, who was then president of the University of Alberta, later becoming principal of Queen's University, and Vincent Massey, who was then the ambassador to Washington and was actively seeking the position. Neither was interviewed by the board. There is no indication that Kennedy ever had dealings with Wallace. Was it Vincent Massey whom Kennedy feared might take over? Massey had taught in the history department until 1919, was a close friend of George Wrong, and may well have shared Wrong's view of Kennedy. Moreover, he had wanted Kennedy's colleague, Larry MacKenzie, to be his assistant as ambassador in Washington in the 1920s, but MacKenzie chose to remain with Kennedy at the university. Massey then chose Wrong's son, Hume, who we know shared his father's views about Kennedy. The almost complete absence of the Massey name in the chapters thus far in this book, in contrast to the many other well-known

Canon Henry Cody (left) with Premier George Henry after the announcement
of Cody's appointment as president in October 1931

University of Toronto persons mentioned, perhaps speaks volumes about their
relationship.

The university community was generally pleased with the appointment.[5] A
graduate of Wycliffe College in theology in 1893, Cody had been a member of
the important Royal Commission on the University of Toronto, which reported
in 1906, and had been the minister of the large St. Paul's Anglican Church on
Bloor Street East since 1899, having served as a curate there since his graduation.

Kennedy had written to Cody, telling him that '90% of the staff would welcome you as Sir Robert's successor more than any man alive.'[6] But there was less
enthusiasm in some quarters. Historian Frank Underhill, for example, about
whom we will hear much in a later chapter, had expressed to a friend his concerns, stating: 'If he does get the job I expect that those of us who are connected
with the [Canadian] Forum [magazine] will have to watch our step.'[7]

Kennedy and Cody, who was a noted public speaker, had known each other
for well over a decade. Kennedy's second wife, Pauline, had first met Cody in
1918, she reminded him in a December 1932 letter, stating: 'Fourteen years
ago at Old Queen's Hall I met you and that evening as I watched and listened

to you, life took on a broader meaning.'[8] Queen's Hall was, it will be recalled, the women's residence where Pauline was the student head of the residence. Pauline became a loyal participant in St. Paul's church. Is it possible that Cody played a role in calming the waters in the Kennedy/Wrong affair?

There is correspondence between Cody and Kennedy going back to 1922, when Kennedy gave Cody the potentially explosive information that, in Kennedy's view, pre-Confederation legislation guaranteeing Catholic schools did not carry over into Confederation.[9] I have not seen any further correspondence on this matter. A few years later, Kennedy offered advice to Canon Cody when Cody, as an Anglican minister, was asked to address the League of Nations in Geneva. Kennedy stated: 'Like the great Christian ideals of the church [the League] requires "cooperative grace," and like them it bears fruit only in the sincerity of that cooperation ... This is our N. American gift to civilization – as an old mystic said: "There's a dearer way to the heart of God than a spear" – and I think we've found it in the will to peace.'[10] As with President Falconer, the correspondence between Kennedy and Cody over many years shows that they were genuinely close friends.

Kennedy had also been friendly with Cody's son, Maurice.[11] Maurice had graduated in modern history in 1921 and from Osgoode Hall Law School in 1924, and had a brilliant career ahead of him, but tragically drowned in the summer of 1927 while on a fishing trip. Kennedy was at the time at a cottage on Kingsmere Lake, near Ottawa, and Mackenzie King, whose summer home was on the same lake, came across the lake to give Kennedy the news. Kennedy later played a role in establishing the Maurice Cody Memorial Scholarship in Modern History at the university.

Cody's early years as president were difficult years.[12] The Great Depression seriously affected the university. Provincial grants were reduced from $2 million in 1930 to $1.2 million in 1934. There were no federal grants in those years. At the same time, student tuition fees increased, putting a strain on the students. The development of new programs was affected. The only major new building on the campus was the addition to the Royal Ontario Museum on Queen's Park, which opened in 1933. The building had been approved before the Depression started, so it was allowed to proceed as a make-work project. To increase the number of jobs, no machinery was permitted, only pickaxes, shovels, and horse-drawn wagons.

Faculty salaries were frozen. Kennedy told Cody about how difficult it was to get by financially and wrote to him in early September 1932, saying: 'I do appreciate your generous offer of help and I trust everything in your hands.'[13] That quote can be found in D.C. Masters's fine biography of Cody. But there is more to the story, which may not have been important in writing the life of Cody, but which I believe is relevant to understand Kennedy's life and the problems he faced.

Kennedy was in serious debt. On 9 September 1932, on his return from his cottage, he wrote a letter to Cody, from which the above quote is drawn. He adds, in part:[14]

> I cannot refrain from writing at once to thank you for your kindness to me today, and for the hope which you gave me. The pressing need is to get $3000 to satisfy urgent claims, then to get rid of loans on my [insurance] policies and the chattel mortgage and the bank loan before they fall due in another round of interest by November ($7,300). The $3,000 would simply close the telephone two or three or four times a day and pressing letters. I don't want to get into the money lenders loans … to 14% and 20% … You can realize perhaps how I shall want to hear from you, for I can't put off these things more than the end of the month or so.

Cody must have then sent some used clothing to the Kennedys, because on 2 December 1932 Pauline Kennedy writes to Cody:[15] 'This beautiful December morning my health is rapidly returning to me. A few moments ago, I learned that not one alteration, in the garments, is necessary, you will be interested to know and also that the lovely black fur-trimmed coat … fits me perfectly.' Cody's wife had died a few months earlier.

Two weeks later, W.P.M. Kennedy writes: 'Thank you deeply for your further letter of Dec. 17, with enclosure. We have now practically wiped out those private debts which were so intolerable both in themselves and psychologically. You cannot tell – and never will understand in this world – what I owe to you.' Kennedy then adds: 'Would you care to drop in for informal Xmas dinner at 6 pm – or after? My wife would welcome you and so would the children and myself.'[16] The enclosure was most likely a cheque for $3,000. We do not know whether Cody came for Christmas dinner.

Four years later, financial problems again arose. Pauline Kennedy wrote to Cody in March 1936. She had met with him the previous Friday night. She told him: 'I intend to carry out your last [conversation] with me on Friday evening … Our overhead expenses have been too great and with great pain in our hearts and peace in our souls my husband and I decided to cancel the insurance. It has been done and now we shall undertake to work out our problems without adding debt upon debt and forever trying to pay off the oldest debt.'[17] I assume that this insurance was a 'whole life' insurance policy on Kennedy's life, which provided, unlike term insurance, a sum of money to the insured person if the policy was cancelled.

That was not the end of Kennedy's financial problems. A year later, Kennedy asks Cody if he could use his influence to increase the editorial fee for the new *University of Toronto Law Journal* from $400 a year to $500. In that letter of January 1937, Kennedy offers a strong clue as to why he has been in serious debt, apart from his lifestyle. He opens the letter by stating: 'As you know the doctor is back into our home once more and I must do my utmost to earn all that I can.'[18]

The medical bills over the years must have been staggering. There was, of course, no public health insurance and no university-sponsored private insurance. Many letters – perhaps every fifth letter to or from Falconer and Cody – say something about Kennedy's health or that of Pauline and the children. All of the children, particularly Gilbert and Beatrice, who appeared to continue to suffer from the effect of the Spanish flu they had contracted in 1919, were, it seems, frequently ill. Pauline, for example, had an unspecified operation in 1926, which Kennedy described to Cody as being more serious than they had hoped it would be.[19]

Kennedy was very frequently under a doctor's care. In February 1930, as we saw earlier, he wrote to Falconer: 'I have to go to bed every afternoon, at half-past one, in a darkened room, and am allowed to see no one ... I am sorry to say that I am not pulling up as the Doctor hoped, and the insomnia is still severe.'[20] This situation continued through the 1930s. In August 1932, for example, Kennedy wrote to Cody: 'I wd. have acknowledged your letter earlier, but I am laid up with severe rheumatism and trouble in both ears and have not been up.'[21] And a typical note from Cody to Kennedy in August 1934: 'I am sorry to hear what you tell me about your son, Gilbert, and about your own health.'[22] And one from Cody to Kennedy in June 1936: 'I hope that you are all happily settled down at your summer place, and that the complete rest will give you restoration of health by the autumn.'[23]

Day-to-Day Tasks

In spite of his health and financial problems, Kennedy continued his involvement with university-wide issues. Over the years, he had advised President Falconer on a range of issues, such as amendments to the University Act in 1926 and revision of the statutes of the University of Toronto Senate in 1928. Kennedy remained active in the senate and its various committees during Cody's tenure, particularly the Board of Legal Studies Committee. In 1932, for example, he was asked by President Falconer to be a member of the senate's committee to interview the board of governors. He was also appointed a member of a committee tasked with revising the calendar of the School of Graduate Studies in 1936 and became a member of the Workers Education Association Committee in 1940, to give other examples.

Kennedy also had to run a law school. The number of students – undergraduate and graduate – kept increasing. Not only was there an increase in the 1930s in the Honour Law program and in courses open to other arts students, but the law school was increasingly responsible for teaching in other departments and faculties, such as a commercial law course in both the Departments of Commerce and Finance, and in the Faculty of Engineering.

And a law school required a law library. Students had been using the legislative library in Queen's Park, but this practice was stopped by the legislative librarian, and so in 1929 we find Kennedy writing to Cody, as chair of the board of governors, asking for a special grant of $1,500 for law reports 'to make our library in the University even possess the appearance of usefulness in Law.'[24] In 1936, we see another request to Cody, this time as president, for a special grant of $460 to purchase a complete set of criminal reports that had come available – no doubt because of the Depression – at 'less than one-half the published price.'[25]

A law school also requires space for faculty and seminar rooms. The law school had moved from Baldwin House to a house at 43 St. George Street and then a few years later to a somewhat larger house immediately north of that, 45 St. George Street.[26]

Kennedy was able to obtain a number of prizes for student achievements. In 1929, for example, Newton Rowell and his wife donated a prize in memory of their son,[27] Langford Rowell, to be awarded to the student obtaining the highest standing in the second year of the Honour Law course – today awarded to the student standing first in the first year of the JD course. (The degree was formerly known as an LLB – bachelor of laws – but since 2001 is called a JD – juris doctor, a graduate degree.) In 1934, the MacMurchy Gold Medal in Law was established – Kennedy donated $15 – for the highest standing in the final year of the course, established in memory of a member of the board of governors and solicitor for the Canadian Pacific Railway, Angus MacMurchy K.C., a good friend of Kennedy[28] and of the law school.[29] That medal is now awarded to the student with the highest overall ranking in the JD course.

Kennedy had several years earlier attempted to have a gold medal in politics and law named after his friend Sir John Willison, the biographer of Wilfrid Laurier and the Canadian correspondent of the *London Times*, who had recently died. President Falconer, however, told Kennedy that he had spoken to Henry Cody, the chair of the board, and 'several points have come up in connection with it that seem to require more consideration.'[30] As it turned out, the medal was not named after Willison. Some years later, however, Willison's widow donated the funds to name the medal after her brother, Angus MacMurchy, who died in 1932. There is obviously more to the story.

And, of course, Kennedy was responsible for the courses being offered in the Honour Law program. These changed from year to year, often depending on staffing issues and changes in the nature of the program. In 1935, for example, we see correspondence between Kennedy and Urwick[31] on whether economics should continue to be offered to first-year law students. Urwick, the head of economics, thought it should not and wanted to stop offering to law students the course then being jointly given by economist Vincent Bladen and political scientist C.B. Macpherson, an 'Introduction to Economics and

C.B. Macpherson,
Department of Political
Economy

Political Science.' But Kennedy wanted it, stating:[32] 'I believe it would be most unfortunate for our students to lose all connection with Economics as a subject in First Year. The connection for the Law students in First Year is almost immemorial and I do not wish it lightly to be broken.' And then he adds in his note to Urwick – to illustrate the point made earlier about his and his family's health – 'I should be glad if you and Innis could lunch with me some day next week at the Faculty Union. I have not been very well and Gilbert has been sick.'

Macpherson continued to teach a political theory course to third-year law students. One exchange in the law school correspondence between Macpherson and Kennedy in 1937 shows the range of theorists discussed in the course:[33] Bentham, Mill, Machiavelli, Bodin, Grotius, Hobbes, and Locke. Kennedy agreed with Macpherson's plan and added: 'Please do not burden the reading any more than you can help as I find the students have all their work cut out for them in Third Year.'[34]

New subjects were introduced, such as administrative law. Another was criminology. Kenneth Gray, who was both a psychiatrist and a lawyer, was appointed – without remuneration – a lecturer in medical jurisprudence and for many years taught a course at the law school in the medical aspects of criminal insanity.[35]

With this range of subjects, it is understandable why many excellent students applied for the Honour Law course and why many went on to fulfilling careers in the law and other fields. The law school files contain a number of letters with respect to students applying for postgraduate scholarships. In those days, there were very few available. The Rhodes Scholarship to Oxford was particularly attractive. Kennedy wrote long detailed letters supporting a number of his former students. A surprising number of the applications were successful. Some of these names will appear in the next section on hiring.

Professor of Law

When Cody was about to take office as president, Kennedy sent him a long letter 'to put on record certain things for the files of the Department,' outlining what he hoped to achieve in the coming years, an agenda which came to pass.[36] He also wanted, of course, to get Cody's support.

Kennedy's first request was 'to have my title changed from "Professor of Law and Political Institutions" to "Professor of Law."' 'I desire the title changed to "Professor of Law,"' Kennedy went on, 'as I want this title preserved solely for the person in charge of Law work both now and in the future. As I explained [in a meeting the day before] the words "and Political Institutions" were used in the past for the purpose of rescuing "Political Institutions" from the aggressions of other departments [that is, history]. I have never taught Political Institutions. I am not competent to teach them, and the field is entirely in the hands of Professor Brady and his assistants.' Kennedy signed that letter as 'Professor of Law,' as he normally did.[37] The change was made official by the board of governors the following year, 1933.

Kennedy also asked for an allocation of $250 for secretarial work, the same allocation as for the past year.[38] Cody granted this request by allowing Kennedy to continue to use the secretarial services of Alison Ewart, MA,[39] the person who had been the secretary he shared the previous year with the Department of History and who had just become the new head of all the University of Toronto Press's publications and journals, including the new 'legal studies' series of books, which will be discussed in the next chapter. She remained head of University of Toronto Press publications until 1945, without, I assume, continuing as Kennedy's secretary, but one never knows.

Another request was for Professor Larry MacKenzie to be promoted to 'Professor of Public and Private International Law.' Again, this action was carried out the following year.[40] The final request was for the appointment of 'another lecturer.' 'The need of a new lecturer is more than urgent,' Kennedy wrote to Cody, 'but on your suggestion, we shall struggle on under grave difficulties this session.'[41]

New Appointment

There were, as we have seen, only four faculty members in 1932: Kennedy, MacKenzie, Auld, and Finkelman. Kennedy was keeping his eye on a number of potential junior appointments. He was interested, for example, in Kenneth Morden, one of his former students, who had won the University of Toronto and Osgoode Hall gold medals and had been called to the bar in 1931. Kennedy wrote to him in June 1931 about his standing at Osgoode: 'I had always believed that you would come out on top ... I do not know what you intend to do; but I should like if you called in to see me before I leave for the summer on June 23rd. I am in my office every morning between ten and twelve.'[42] Morden was then practising at McCarthy and McCarthy, and there is no indication whether there was any follow-up. He, like his son, John Morden, another University of Toronto law graduate, became a justice of the Ontario Court of Appeal.

Another graduate that Kennedy was keeping his eye on was J.L. Stewart, who, in Kennedy's words, 'gained a brilliant first class with first class in all his papers' in third year and had also been the president of the Law Club.[43] Stewart was awarded a Rhodes Scholarship, starting in September 1932 after his third year, taking his LLB at Oxford. As it turned out, he joined Fraser and Beatty and never sought an academic career. He was later the legal advisor to the important Carter Committee on Taxation.

But the graduate Kennedy particularly wanted for an appointment was Francis Vallat, who went to Cambridge University in the fall of 1932. He had led the class in his graduating year, and Kennedy had written to Cambridge: 'I have no hesitation in saying that, if his promise is only half fulfilled, he will have a future of the greatest distinction.'[44] Vallat worked at Cambridge with international lawyer A.D. McNair, who later became the president of the International Court at The Hague. Kennedy wrote to Vallat in May 1934, saying that President Cody would be visiting Cambridge and would like to meet him:[45]

> In the future some time there is just a possibility that I may get you on the staff here. So then, if you see Dr. Cody, do not tell him that you are interested in International Law as that would finish any chance you have got. You would be needed for the Common Law and for History of English Law. Now remember, I am making no promises and all this is extremely vague. I am just trying to see how the land lies, and not a little will depend on the impression which you make on him if he sees you.

In March 1935, Kennedy wrote Cody, urging him to appoint Vallat to the law school. Vallat had by then received a Cambridge LLB and had recently been called to the English bar, both with great distinction.[46] Cody agreed with the appointment, but the final decision was up to the board. The board delayed a decision, likely for economic reasons, and in the meantime Vallat took a position at the University of Bristol.[47]

Another candidate suddenly appeared. Kennedy wrote to his contact in Cambridge,[48] E.R. Wade, the constitutional law scholar, expressing his disappointment in Vallat's decision, but noted: 'I have appointed a Saskatchewan Rhodes Scholar who had a brilliant career at Oxford – and comes with the most cordial approval and praise from [C.K.] Allen and A.G. [Arthur Goodhart].' Vallat remained in England and achieved the success that Kennedy had predicted. His obituary in *The Independent* in 2008 stated that Sir Francis Vallat 'was an international lawyer of stature who straddled the worlds of government service, of academe, and of private practice with great aplomb over more than half a century.'[49] He had been a professor of international law at the University of London and a senior advisor to the foreign office. Vallat wrote about Kennedy, stating:[50]

> W.P.M. Kennedy was a great character. Both as a writer and a teacher he was forceful, clear and inspiring. I owe a great deal of such success as I have had with law to his insistence on hard work as the basis of progress in a legal career. I remember very well sitting in one of his classes in the early stages of our course. We were a pretty bright class but this meant nothing to W.P.M. He thought we were bone lazy and told us that we were so dull that he could hear the rust in our brains scraping as we tried to think. This seemed pretty harsh at the time but in the end it produced a keenness of a sense of the need for hard work which otherwise might never have developed.

The new appointment was Russell Hopkins, who only stayed at the University of Toronto law school for a year. He was poached by Dean F.C. Cronkite of the University of Saskatchewan, where Hopkins had been a student before going to Oxford. Professor J.A. Corry of Saskatchewan had recently taken a position in the political science department at Queen's University, and his position was offered to Hopkins.[51] It would be a permanent position at a salary more than double the $1,500 he was receiving from Toronto. Kennedy told Cody he was sorry Hopkins was leaving: 'We lose him with great regret.'[52] Cody responded that it was 'natural for him to take the professorship in his old University.'[53] Kennedy offered Dean Cronkite some advice:[54] 'You must keep him tuned up to scholarship and productive work. He ought to publish his Oxford doctorate.' Hopkins never did publish his dissertation. He later became Law Clerk and

The Honour Law class of 1936. Two students are at either end of the first row and the
rest behind the faculty. The five faculty members in the front row are, from left to right,
Larry MacKenzie, Fred Auld, W.P.M. Kennedy, Jacob Finkelman, and Russell Hopkins;
William Howland appears behind Kennedy and Finkelman

Parliamentary Counsel to the Canadian Senate and wrote a number of books
on the parliamentary process.

Who would replace Hopkins? Larry MacKenzie recommended another
Rhodes Scholar from the West, James Coyne, later the controversial governor
of the Bank of Canada.[55] Kennedy, however, had had enough of Rhodes Scholars from the West, stating: 'I am "off" Rhodes Scholars for a while, especially
westerners.'[56] Fred Auld suggested Bora Laskin: 'It seems to me, all things considered that Laskin is familiar more than any candidate whose name presents
itself with our work and our ideals; and his enthusiasm and loyalty, with his
capacity for hard work, make his claims as a candidate exceedingly weighty. For
that reason, I earnestly recommend his choice.'[57]

Laskin, however, was about to go to Harvard to enter the LLM program.
Kennedy had written to Dean Roscoe Pound recommending him: 'I think I
can assure you that he will be a great credit to your graduate school and will
do admirable work.'[58] He had also written to Felix Frankfurter to help get a

scholarship for Laskin: 'I am extremely anxious to obtain a Fellowship at Harvard Law School next session for a young student of mine who is exceptionally able.'[59] No doubt Kennedy thought of how unfair it had been to lure Finkelman into teaching in 1932, thus losing forever his year of graduate work at Harvard.

Another candidate was available, J.M. Gage, who had been in practice in Hamilton for the past four years. He had topped his class in politics and law at the law school, winning the gold medal. He then won the gold medal at Osgoode and received his LLB and MA from the University of Toronto. 'If this fails or falls through,' Kennedy wrote to Finkelman, 'I intend to approach Laskin.'[60] Gage was willing to come for $1,500, which had been Hopkins's salary, even though it was less than he was then making.[61] Cody approved of the appointment, telling Kennedy: 'You seem to have gotten a good man in Mr. Gage.'[62] All this correspondence takes place with Kennedy up at his cottage at Otter Lake. Once again, we see Kennedy telling Cody about his health: 'I am much better. I am still very thin and have had headaches all summer, but I feel less tired. Mrs. K. has had annoying rheumatism, or something, for some weeks.'[63]

Kennedy wrote to Gage just before his appointment by the board, advising him to take scholarly work seriously. 'The teaching is important indeed,' Kennedy wrote, 'and the general advancement of our purposes; but most important is scholarship and productive work. The life is a happy and creative one and has compensations which are inestimable.'[64] By Christmas, however, it was obvious that Gage was unhappy as a law teacher and wanted to return to the practice of law.[65]

Who would now replace Gage? Kennedy turned to one of Laskin's classmates, Moffatt Hancock, who had just completed his doctorate at the University of Michigan under the well-known conflict of law scholar, H.E. Yntema. Hancock had been one of two students in his class in the Honour Law program to graduate with first-class standing – despite his deteriorating eye condition. In December 1936, Kennedy invited Hancock to come and see him, stating: 'Is it possible that you will be in Toronto during the Christmas holidays? If so, I should like to see you on a matter of some importance. It may be that something will turn in your way ... Of course, I am making no promise of any sort.'[66] Kennedy then wrote to Cody, and the board approved. Hancock stayed at the University of Toronto for ten years and was to become one of the pre-eminent conflict of law scholars in North America at Dalhousie and then at Stanford.

There were now five strong professors in the law school.

The Law Club

As we saw in the previous chapter, Kennedy was highly regarded by his students. One particularly important institution that he established with the help of his students was the Law Club. But even with their help, the club took a

Moffatt Hancock, appointed
in 1937

significant amount of Kennedy's time and effort to organize. It did, however, bring a large measure of prestige to the law school and helped establish the reputation of the school. In the 1930s, perhaps a quarter of all the correspondence in the law school files relates to the Law Club. Every invitation for an outside speaker on the campus had to be approved by the president of the university. Every payment of a fee or expenses had to be approved by the board.

There were at least four meetings each year attended by law students, law graduates, and others. Guest speakers were brought in for the meetings and a banquet held at the end of each academic year. The Law Club became an important institution in the university and the legal profession. Judges and other members of the profession were invited to attend. Often the speaker was a significant American law professor, such as Dean Roscoe Pound of Harvard or Professor Manley Hudson of Harvard. Sometimes it was a leading lawyer, such as J.J. Robinette or Joseph Sedgwick.

The club first had to be approved by the president and the university's primary disciplinary body, the Caput (Latin for 'head'), made up of the heads of faculties and other senior officials in the university. In November 1930, Kennedy asked President Falconer to request the Caput to approve 'the Constitution of the new Law Club' and to approve the proposed speakers for the 1930–31 academic year.[67] The opening meeting was to be in December 1930 with, as speaker, Charles Morse, the editor of the *Canadian Bar Review* and registrar of the Exchequer Court of Canada, the predecessor of the Federal Court of Canada. He would speak about the 'Profession of Law.' Caesar Wright of Osgoode would give the January 1931 lecture, discussed earlier, on 'Present Tendencies in Law.' In February, it would be a senior counsel, Norman Walker, K.C., on 'The Preparation of a Case for Trial,' and finally, in March, the Hon. Newton Rowell would give the address at the final banquet on 'The Judicial Committee of the Privy Council and the Interpretation of the Canadian Constitution.'

Kennedy had invited Newton Rowell to be the honorary president of the Law Club, with Kennedy serving as the honorary vice-president. 'The object of the Club,' Kennedy told Rowell, 'is not social but scholarly.'[68] Many of the talks given at the Law Club were later published as articles.

Rowell was one of Canada's leading litigators and a founder of the firm now called McMillan LPP. He had been active in both Ontario and federal politics, and had been a Canadian delegate to the League of Nations. He often appeared in the Privy Council. Kennedy helped him with some of his cases, likely including the *Edwards* case – usually referred to as the 'Persons Case' – which Rowell won, resulting in the possibility of appointing women to the Senate of Canada. In February 1929, Kennedy wrote to Falconer, stating in passing: 'Last night I was doing some work with Mr. Rowell on some cases which he has in hand.'[69] In 1936, Rowell became the chief justice of Ontario and in 1937 was appointed as the chairman of the Royal Commission on Dominion-Provincial Relations, to be discussed in the next chapter.

Rowell, a member of the university's board of governors, was a strong supporter of the law school. The Rowell Room in Flavelle House at the law school is named after him. That support continued in successive generations. A recent major addition to the law school is named after Rowell's grandson, Hal Jackman. Kennedy wrote the obituary notice for the Royal Society after Rowell died in 1941, pointing out Rowell's close involvement with the law school: 'Few knew too of his loyalty and devotion to the School of Law of the University of Toronto which he lived to see develop into one of the great university law schools of the world.'[70]

The Law Club's first dinner was to have been held at the recently opened Royal York Hotel, but, as it turned out, took place at the Ontario Club, a private club then located on Wellington Street, where Commerce Court now stands.[71] The Law Club built upon rather than established the tradition of guest lecturers and fancy dinners. There is, for example, extensive documentation of a visit by Arthur Goodhart, an American academic, who was then teaching at Cambridge and was the editor of the leading English law journal, the *Law Quarterly Review*. He was a visitor at Yale in 1929, and Kennedy arranged for him to give two lectures at the University of Toronto, one on 'Present Day Development

Newton Rowell, later the chief justice of Ontario, in 1930

in English Jurisprudence' and another on 'General Strikes, Trade Unions and the Law'.[72] Kennedy hosted dinners for Goodhart at the Faculty Union in Hart House on Saturday night – dinner jacket required – and at lunch and supper on Sunday at Kennedy's home at 77 Spadina Road.[73]

The 1938 Banquet

The most famous annual banquet was in 1938, on the hundredth anniversary of Lord Durham's report. The dinner was at the Great Hall of Hart House on 8 March 1938. Kennedy gave the toast to Lord Durham, and Viscount Tweedsmuir, the governor general, replied. The surprisingly interesting correspondence in the law school files devoted to these events illustrates the energy that Kennedy expended on them.

Others had been asked to give the toast, but had declined. Kennedy had previously invited Prime Minister Mackenzie King to give the toast with Tweedsmuir replying, but King replied that the House would be in session and he could not risk being away from Ottawa, stating that there is 'every reason to believe that questions of first importance will be arising from day to day in the course of the approaching session.' He added, however: 'I shall be pleased to support the invitation you have extended to His Excellency.'[74]

Mackenzie King was not the first to be invited to give the toast. R.B. Bennett, the leader of the opposition, was. 'My first inclination would be to accept,' Bennett had replied. But the banquet was a year away, and Bennett said that he could not make plans that far in advance.[75] He later declined the invitation, no doubt because he was thinking of retiring from Canadian politics and leaving Canada to live in England. Bennett had previously given a talk to the Law Club in 1934, delivered on condition that no reporters be present.[76]

So, Kennedy himself gave the toast. The governor general's staff were hesitant to commit the governor general so far in advance, but eventually said yes – if the banquet could be held on 8 March 1938, when the governor general would be in Toronto to attend an event organized by the Toronto Skating Club. Another stipulation was that he would have to leave Hart House at 9 p.m. to get to the skating event on time.[77] When inviting the governor general, Kennedy had expressed the view that Durham's report was 'the most important event in the history of Canada and the modern British Empire.' The governor general would speak to the memory of Lord Durham. Two hundred people would probably attend.[78]

In his toast, Kennedy dramatically described the scene[79] when Lord Durham arrived in Canada – a country 'where hands were still ready for the sword and pike, where fingers still itched for the trigger.' He had been 'sent not merely to diagnose the causes of the recent troubles but find, if possible, a permanent cure.' Durham's solution was responsible government: 'Representative government,' said Kennedy, 'based on however wide a franchise, was the negation of autonomy, so long as executive power resided in a Governor responsible to the Cabinet at Westminster and not to a cabinet responsible to the local House of Assembly.' Kennedy ignored discussion of Durham's proposal for assimilating French Canada into English Canada.[80]

Kennedy took note of the dangerous times – it was 1938 – that the world faced a hundred years later: 'Tonight, we celebrate Lord Durham's memory at a moment when European civilization is in possible danger, when the peace-structure so hopefully reared at Geneva is perhaps in the process of disintegration; when ugly volcanic rumblings from the East perhaps presage tremendous significances.' He ended his speech with the following words: 'I give you the toast to the memory of Lord Durham.'

The governor general, Lord Tweedsmuir, replied:[81] 'The work he accomplished was greater than the man ... The foundation stone of his structure was the gift of responsible government, and that endures.'

It was clearly a memorable evening. The speeches were printed in the *University of Toronto Monthly*. Justice Sydney Harris, who was at the banquet when he was a student, remembers 'the occasion well – especially the sweepstakes on the length of President Cody's remarks! which preceded our "Wild Irish Rose" rendition to the Dean.'[82]

Kennedy's son Gilbert also recalls that famous dinner in his oral interview.[83] He goes on to state: 'Other speakers at these annual dinners included Samuel Williston of contracts fame; Jackson – a Justice of the Supreme Court of the United States; Sir Owen Dixon, Chief Justice of Australia.'

The law school now had its own home with five professors and a growing number of students. It had responsibility for its own budget and, on 1 July 1937, became a separate department in the Faculty of Arts and Science. It would no longer be part of the Department of Political Economy. It was known for its strong teaching. We turn now to Kennedy's promotion of scholarship in the 1930s.

16

Encouraging Scholarship

Kennedy clearly valued scholarship. In the last chapter, we saw his advice to Dean Cronkite of Saskatchewan about Russell Hopkins: 'You must keep him tuned up to scholarship and productive work.' And we saw Kennedy's advice to Hopkins's replacement, J.M. Gage: 'The <u>teaching</u> is <u>important</u> indeed and the general advancement of our purposes; but most important is scholarship and productive work.'[1] Kennedy had given similar advice to J.F. Davison when Davison decided to remain at Harvard to work with Frankfurter: 'I would like to suggest that the beginnings which you are now making with Dr. Frankfurter be carried on. There is no greater danger than sitting down as a professor, and merely doing one's job, without adding to scholarship.'[2] Throughout the 1930s, Kennedy took active steps to encourage scholarship.

Kennedy himself was immersed in scholarly endeavours. Among the honours that came his way in the 1930s because of his own scholarship were membership in the Royal Society of Canada and the sought-after honorary doctorate, an LLD, from the University of Montreal.[3]

He was inducted, along with President Cody, as a fellow of the Royal Society at its annual meeting at McMaster University in Hamilton in 1935. The nomination was put forward by former president Robert Falconer, who had been the president of the Royal Society in 1931–32; by noted scholar Harold Innis, who had just been inducted; and by W.S. Wallace, the university librarian and then secretary of the Royal Society's Social Science Academy. It would have been hard for the society to have turned Kennedy down. It is not known whether he was nominated in previous years. Could his membership have been opposed by George Wrong, who had been a member since 1908? Certainly, he could influence the vote, but it does not appear that a member of the society had a veto (or blackball) on the election of a proposed member either for the Royal Society of Canada or the Royal Society of London.[4]

Kennedy's honorary degree from the University of Montreal on 26 May 1939 resulted from a nomination by the dean of the Faculty of Law, Justice Philippe

W.P.M. Kennedy in 1939, about to receive an honorary doctorate from the University of Montreal. Note the word 'laundry' in the background

Demers. Gustave Lanctôt, the chief archivist of Canada, with whom Kennedy had published the historical work on the laws of Quebec, received a similar degree at the same convocation. Kennedy's citation reads as follows:[5]

> Professeur de droit à l'Université de Toronto, auteur d'un grand nombre d'ouvrages remarquables de droit constitutionel et de droit comparé, chargé de recherches et de travaux importants par le gouvernement du Canada, Monsieur Kennedy jouit d'une réputation internationale qui a porté plusieurs Etats étrangers à rechercher ses conseils.

Later that summer, Kennedy was asked by the University of Montreal to supply a picture of himself. The request was repeated in October. Kennedy's response was that he had replied to the earlier request:[6] 'I at once wrote and told you that I had not the kind of photograph you requested – indeed that I had no photograph at all. I could not see my way in the middle of the summer to come down to Toronto and get the special kind of photograph taken which you requested. First of all it would have cost me a good deal of unnecessary expense and, secondly, I could not feel justified in going to this. Meanwhile I may say that I am none too well and I cannot go down town for this purpose, while I do not feel in the least justified in doing so while Canada is at war.' There are surprisingly few pictures of Kennedy. He may have been egocentric, but he did not appear to be particularly vain.

We also have his son Gilbert's recollections about the Montreal event. In his oral interview, Gilbert stated:[7] 'I did attend the honorary degree given to him by the University of Montreal in 1939, at a time when the University of Montreal was in downtown Montreal and didn't have a large enough convocation hall of its own, and the faculty procession proceeded through downtown Montreal to a local theatre, which they hired for the day. My picture of Dad in that procession has a store sign immediately above him advertising laundry.'

University of Toronto Press

In 1931, Kennedy started a series of legal publications with the University of Toronto Press. The first book in the series was *The Law of the Taxing Power in Canada*, written with Dalton Wells, a University of Toronto graduate from 1922, who later also received an MA from the university. Kennedy's name came first. In 1946, at age forty-five, Wells was appointed to the Supreme Court of Ontario, later becoming the chief justice of the High Court of Ontario.

The book was likely based on Wells's MA thesis, although the thesis is not mentioned in the book's preface. The 157-page book was well received. Professor Berriedale Keith of Edinburgh noted in the British *Journal of Comparative Legislation and International Law*: 'To Professor Kennedy ... and Mr. D.C. Wells, of Osgoode Hall, Toronto, we owe an interesting discussion of the law affecting the power to tax in Canada, which will serve excellently all those who desire

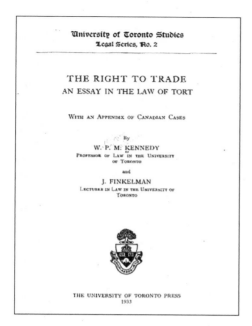

Title page of *The Right to Trade: An Essay in the Law of Tort* by W.P.M. Kennedy and J. Finkelman, 1933

to obtain a sound grounding in the fundamental issues of a difficult question.'[8] The editor of the *Canadian Bar Review*, Charles Morse, wrote in the *Canadian Historical Review*: 'By his share in the authorship of the book in hand Professor Kennedy has made another useful contribution to the growing library of works interpretive of the constitution of Canada.'[9] The book was dedicated to Newton Rowell, the honorary president of the Law Club and with whom Kennedy had worked on a number of constitutional cases: 'In the dedication we would record not only an old and valued personal friendship, but also a recognized authority in Canadian constitutional law.'[10]

Two years later, in 1933, Kennedy published a book with Jacob Finkelman, *The Right to Trade: An Essay in the Law of Tort* – again Kennedy's name came first. The *Cambridge Law Journal* called it 'a most commendable little book, dealing in a stimulating and suggestive manner with a difficult topic which has not hitherto received the attention which it deserves.'[11] Berriedale Keith in the *Journal of Comparative Legislation and International Law* gave another flattering review: 'A most interesting effort to deal with the vexed question of the law of England regarding the existence and extent of the right to trade.'[12] During his articling with Joseph Sweet of Hamilton – later a county court judge – Finkelman had done research on conspiracy cases against trade unions. When he returned to teach at the university, he wrote his master's thesis on these cases.

According to Finkelman's oral interview, Kennedy 'decided that it ... was good enough to get published. So he sat down with me and we revised it, and we put out a study called the Right to Trade.' As we have seen, that led to Finkelman teaching a course in labour law.[13]

The next study was to be on the Ontario Municipal Board. Bora Laskin was completing his LLM at Harvard on that tribunal. In February 1937, he wrote to Finkelman: 'I am beginning to drive myself in completing my study of the Municipal Board as I realize the magnitude of undertaking to make a decent survey of its varied activities.'[14] Finkelman wrote back: 'Have you thought of the possibility that we might revise your thesis and publish it in the [University of Toronto Studies, Legal Series]. Dr. Kennedy is looking for material.'[15] The Studies Committee of the University of Toronto Press recorded that $600 had been set aside for its publication by Finkelman and Laskin, but it was delayed from year to year.[16] 'Word had been received from Professor Kennedy,' the Studies Committee minutes record in March 1939, 'that Legal Study No. 3 on "Municipal Law" would not be ready until the early fall of 1939.'[17] Then, a few months later, it was reported: 'As unforeseen delays have occurred in the preparation of the manuscript for this Study, it has been necessary to postpone the printing until the beginning of the academic year 1940–41.'[18] In March 1940, the minutes note that 'no work will be commenced upon it this year.'[19] Then, in April 1942, the minutes state that letters were read from Professors Finkelman and Kennedy that the Municipal Board study would be replaced by a new study, 'Procedure Before Administrative Tribunals in Canada.'[20] Neither the 'Municipal Law' study, nor the 'Procedure Before Administrative Tribunals' study was ever published.

A third study, however, did appear in 1940. The minutes of the Studies Committee note: 'The Manager reported that Professor Kennedy had arranged for Mr. H.G. Fox to publish his Ph.D. thesis in amplified form as a textbook in the Legal Series. As the book, however, is being entirely paid for by Mr. Fox, no appropriation will be necessary from the Studies allocation.'[21]

In 1937, Harold Fox had applied to do a PhD in law. He had graduated from the University of Toronto with a BA in 1917 and an LLB in 1922, and then had made a name for himself as a practitioner in patents and trademark cases and as an author in these fields. In 1934, he won a major case in the Privy Council[22] for the person who had invented the zipper and was paid in company shares. He then became the general manager of the company, the Lightning Fastener Company, located in St. Catharines, Ontario. His PhD dissertation was published as a single-authored book in the legal studies series, *The Canadian Law of Trade Marks and Industrial Designs*, as was another book, *The Law of Copyright*. Kennedy and Auld are thanked 'for the assistance generously given.'[23] Each book has now gone through a number of editions, and the name Fox is still one of the most cited names in Canada in intellectual property. In 1940, Fox became counsel to McCarthy and McCarthy, having been recruited by the

Harold G. Fox, intellectual property scholar

losing counsel in the Zipper case. He also became a special lecturer in the subject at the University of Toronto School of Law.

Only one further study appeared in the Legal Series. In 1948, Eugene R. LaBrie and J.R. Westlake published *Deductions under the Income War Tax Act: A Return to Business Principles*. Westlake was one of LaBrie's students at the University of Toronto, who had come from Alberta to do graduate work at Toronto. In fact, he had been a classmate of LaBrie at the University of Alberta and then joined the military.[24] We will learn more about LaBrie in a later chapter. LaBrie had come from Alberta to do graduate work at Toronto in 1943 and was later hired on in the faculty in 1946 to replace Bora Laskin who had transferred to Osgoode Hall Law School. Coincidentally, while preparing this paragraph I got a call from LaBrie,[25] who had been my professor at law school and with whom I have kept in touch while writing this book, perhaps speaking to him about once a year. He was interested in my progress on the manuscript. LaBrie said he is still in good health at the age of ninety-seven and still working on his farm near Ajax, Ontario.

Professor Maxwell Cohen gave the book a sympathetic review in the *Canadian Journal of Economics and Political Science*. 'The study,' Cohen wrote, 'comes at a moment when interest in taxation problems has deepened and widened among professionals and laymen alike.'[26] This book was the last in the series. Later books, including LaBrie's doctoral dissertation, *The Meaning of Income in the Law of Income Tax*, published by the University of Toronto Press, were not part of any series.

There is no question that the University of Toronto Studies, Legal Series inspired McGill to create its own series. The task of organizing it was given to Professor Frank Scott, who wrote on 2 April 1937[27] to the Canadian legal publisher, Burroughs, who passed it on to Carswell's. Scott had written that they should take as their model the books that Kennedy had published. The first book in the new McGill series, published by Carswell's in 1938, was by George Nichols, the former editor of the *Canadian Bar Review*, on regulatory offences in Quebec.[28]

Graduate Programs

Kennedy also wanted to encourage scholarship through graduate work at the University of Toronto and elsewhere. Some, but not many, students who received a BA in the Honour Law program went on to do a postgraduate LLB at the university. The numbers were low, however, because the degree required the writing of a number of exams and the production of a thesis. Moreover, the exams and the preparation of the thesis came at the same time of the year as the Osgoode Hall Law School exams, and most students who were interested in the LLB degree were simultaneously students at Osgoode Hall. It was easier to do an MA degree through the School of Graduate Studies, and in some years around half a dozen to a dozen students graduated with an MA in law. Some students who were studying for an LLB had applied to have the University of Toronto exams switched to September, where there would be no conflict with Osgoode exams, but the requirement was not changed. Kennedy had written: 'We should try to do our best for these Osgoode men, in order to encourage the LL.B. work.'[29] But the University of Toronto registrar was not encouraging, stating: 'When a man does try to sit on two stools there is always the possibility of a collapse.'[30] There were also some students – perhaps two or three a year – who entered the regular PhD program in law, run by the graduate school.

An LLM had been established in 1903,[31] but nobody appeared to know what the requirements were. When a student applied for enrolment in the LLM program in 1929, Kennedy told the registrar that he had 'no precedent to work on' for such a degree.[32] In any event, graduate degrees were now handled by the School of Graduate Studies, which had been set up in 1922, and not by departments. As we saw in an earlier chapter, Kennedy wanted a new LLM that would be run through the graduate school, but it had been opposed by Dean Falconbridge of Osgoode Hall Law School. Such a degree was not established – or re-established – until 1938, when it could be awarded by the separate Department of Law. Very few students took that degree. It required a complete year of full-time work, writing a number of exams, ability in another language, and a thesis that made 'a contribution to legal scholarship and learning.'[33] And it first required an LLB or its equivalent. Again, it was easier to do a regular MA, where the residence requirements were not, it seems, as demanding. It was not until 1942 that the first person received an LLM. He was Wen-han Chin, from Chongqing, formerly Chungking, in southwest China.[34] He returned to China and worked in the Ministry of Foreign Affairs.

Kennedy had tried to establish a degree of doctor of civil law, awarded on the basis of previously published work produced after graduation and not a dissertation – similar to the doctoral degree that Kennedy had received in 1919 from Trinity College Dublin, but this proposal was not accepted by the senate. In 1942, provision was made for a doctor juris or DJur degree.[35] Several students received it, such as Morris Shumiatcher in 1945, who had graduated from the University of Saskatchewan, and Eugene LaBrie, also in 1945. The SJD (doctor of juridical science) degree took over from the DJur in 1983.

University of Toronto Law Journal

In 1935, the University of Toronto Press issued the first part of the first volume of the *University of Toronto Law Journal* (*UTLJ*). A second part came out in January 1936. Together, the volume, edited by Kennedy, amounted to over 450 pages. Kennedy wrote to President Cody in January 1936 when the second part appeared: 'I have much pleasure in sending you the final part of Vol 1 of the University of Toronto Law Journal with my best compliments and esteem. I hope, too, you will accept it as a small recognition of your great work of promoting scholarship and research.'[36]

Cody, as chairman of the University of Toronto Press's Printing and Publishing Committee, had supported the establishment of the *UTLJ*. It was the fourth journal published by the University of Toronto Press. The *Canadian Historical Review*, established in 1921 by George Wrong, was the first, followed by the *Canadian Journal of Economics and Political Science*, established in 1928 by E.J. Urwick, and then the *University of Toronto Quarterly*, a literary journal, the first issue of which came out in 1931.

The first volume of the *UTLJ* was a major accomplishment. Kennedy wrote to Cody on 18 April 1935: 'The April "Law Quarterly Review" has just come in, with a leading editorial notice of [the *UTLJ*] which is received [states the *LQR*] as "the most important contribution to the study of comparative law that has been made in recent years … a review of outstanding quality."'[37]

This achievement, Kennedy had pointed out in his foreword,[38] 'is the natural outcome of a new vigour in legal studies in the University of Toronto. Its appearance has been delayed in order that time might be given to watch the success or failure of the Honour School of Law and of graduate legal studies. After a period of years, it is evident that these developments are permanent.' The *UTLJ*, he wrote, would foster new scholarship: '[We] aim to produce a journal, learned and scientific, with high standards of scholarship and research which will be of

THE
UNIVERSITY OF TORONTO
LAW JOURNAL

EDITED BY
W. P. M. KENNEDY
Professor of Law in the University of Toronto

VOLUME I
1935-6

PUBLISHED BY
THE UNIVERSITY OF TORONTO PRESS

FOR SALE BY
THE CARSWELL COMPANY, TORONTO
THE LAW BOOK COMPANY OF AUSTRALASIA, SYDNEY

Title page of the first issue of the *University of Toronto Law Journal*, 1935 interest to teachers and students of law, to members of the profession, to jurists, and to men of affairs.' Kennedy went on to write:

> We venture specially to hope that we may be able to do something to encourage legal scholarship in Canada, to foster a knowledge of the comparative laws of the British Empire ... as expressions of organized community life, of ordered progress, and of social justice, and that we may also strengthen those ties of scholarship, learning, and personal friendships which happily bind the law schools and the law teachers in the universities of the United States with us their partners, in the heritage and traditions of the common law.

Fifty years later, law school professor R.C.B. Risk, then editor of the *UTLJ*, reviewed that first volume.[39] He concluded: 'It was a remarkable volume indeed: it was the beginning of the first scholarly legal journal in Canada; it contained articles that continue to be illuminating and stimulating; and it introduced into Canada ways of thinking about law that continue to be among the major elements of our thought.' Both Dick Risk and I know how important that first volume remained. As students at the law school in the 1950s, we still read some of the articles in that first volume, such as John Willis's article on administrative law and Caesar Wright's on the restatement of contracts and agency.

All the members of the faculty contributed to the volume, including Moffat Hancock, who would soon be joining the faculty, and J.F. Davison, who had previously been a faculty member. Kennedy himself made a large number of contributions. Deans John Falconbridge of Osgoode and Percy Corbett of McGill contributed, as did political scientists Keith Berriedale and J.A. Corry. There were over thirty books reviewed. Future leading members of the profession, such as J.J. Robinette and G. Arthur Martin, wrote notes on cases or reviewed books. Caesar Wright and Frank Scott contributed material. American scholars, such as Edwin Borchard, Philip Jessup, and Samuel Thorne, reviewed books, as did English scholars, such as William Holdsworth, Ivor Jennings, and E.C.S. Wade. Even Lord Macmillan of the House of Lords reviewed a book – on feudal law. The *UTLJ*'s contributors were a who's who of the common law world. And that was only the initial volume.

The *UTLJ* also explored various law reform endeavours. The first volume had articles on three reports of the American Law Institute – on contracts, agency, and conflicts of law. Kennedy wrote a note on the New York Law Revision Commission,[40] which had been established the previous year. The chair of that commission, Dean C.K. Burdick of Cornell, a Law Club banquet speaker, had discussed the work of the commission. 'The importance of this commission,' Kennedy wrote in the *UTLJ*, 'lies in the fact that it is not a commission appointed merely for the revision of the statutes, but is a permanent advisory body to the legislature to which it must report annually.' Kennedy makes a plea that 'its proceedings and accomplishments ought to be watched with serious concern ... The state of New York has set an example for law reform based on scientific observation, on expert research, on objectivity, on a comprehensive and modern view of the functions of law ... The law revision commission of the state of New York may well constitute an inspiration and a source of emulation.' A more modest Law Revision Committee, however, based on an English model, was established on a pro bono basis in 1941 by the government of Ontario to study questions that had been referred to it by the attorney general of Ontario. Kennedy appointed Fred Auld to be the University of Toronto School of Law's representative on the committee.[41] Kennedy would clearly have preferred the New York model.

In the same volume, Jacob Finkelman described the work being done in labour law at the law school through the Industrial Law Research Council.[42] 'There is probably no field of law where research is more necessary,' wrote Finkelman, 'than in industrial relations ... The law itself is confused, the judgments are conflicting, and the juristic principles seem to be out of tune with social life.' An Industrial Law Research Council was established with the cooperation of the Workers' Educational Association (WEA) of Ontario, in Finkelman's words, 'to examine industrial law as it is, how it works in practice, to consider and criticize such legislative proposals as are made for its amendment from time to time, and to issue periodical reports on the progress of the research of which several have already appeared.' Again, we see the necessity of learning how the law works in practice. Kennedy was the chair and Fred Auld, the vice-chair. Other members included Larry MacKenzie, Harold Innis, Cecil Wright, J.J. Robinette, Dana Porter, and the secretary of the WEA of Ontario, Drummond Wren. The council continued for a number of years. In 1941, Kennedy was the president, with Finkelman as the director of research and Bora Laskin as the assistant director of research.

Kennedy was, of course, delighted with the reception of that first volume. The minutes of the Executive Committee of the University of Toronto Press, with President Cody in the chair, record the following:[43] 'Two letters were then read from Professor Kennedy regarding the first number of The Law Journal. The first one stated that it was a great pleasure to have carried through the publication of the first number under happier circumstances than he had ever experienced and the belief that this co-operation will continue to function in the future.'

His second letter stated that he was under the impression that all editorial fees were temporarily suspended as from the 1934–35 session. 'Finding that these fees are still being paid to the editors of The Historical Review and The Quarterly, he respectfully submits that the Law Journal ought to be placed on the same footing and suggests $400 a volume.'

The journal had over 300 orders in its first year, including a bulk order from Carswell and Company, which handled distribution. The Depression would, of course, have affected sales. It certainly affected costs. The minutes of 1938 state, for example: 'In connection with the four periodicals it was decided to invite each of the editors to meet with the Committee and to ask them, in view of the necessity for economies and elimination of excess deficits, to offer suggestions as to ways and means of reducing expenditures.'[44] Kennedy had wanted the *UTLJ* to publish two volumes a year. A compromise was reached, the minutes state: 'In view of the suggestion of the editor it was decided to recommend that the Law Journal remain for the time being an annual publication and that in compensation for cancellation of the bi-annual offer the number of pages in each issue be increased by 70, making a total of 320 pages per year'[45] for the *UTLJ*. That was still about the size of the journal in 1958 when I graduated from the law school. It did not publish two volumes a year until 1967. It subsequently increased in size over the years, with over 600 pages in volume 66 in 2016. It finally published three volumes a year in 2017.

The *University of Toronto Law Journal* today is similar in its approach to the law to the *UTLJ* established by Kennedy. Its current website states:[46]

> The University of Toronto Law Journal has taken a broad and visionary approach to legal scholarship since its beginnings in 1935. Its first editor, Professor WPM Kennedy, hoped that the Journal would foster a knowledge of law 'as expressions of organized human life, of ordered progress, and of social justice.' The University of Toronto Law Journal has since established itself as a leading journal for theoretical, interdisciplinary, comparative and other conceptually oriented inquiries into law and law reform. The Journal regularly publishes articles that study law from such perspectives as legal philosophy, law and economics, legal history, criminology, law and literature, and feminist analysis.

Kennedy would be pleased.

17

Rethinking Canadian Constitutional Law

Kennedy was the leading Canadian constitutional scholar in the interwar years in both scholarly output and reputation. Public law scholar E.C.S. Wade of Cambridge University wrote in the *University of Toronto Quarterly* in 1935 that Kennedy is 'the leading authority upon the constitutional law and history of the Dominion of Canada.'[1] Similarly, Chief Justice Newton Rowell, as the chair of what later became the Rowell-Sirois Commission, recommended in 1937 that Kennedy be asked to do a constitutional study for the commission, stating that Kennedy is 'the acknowledged expert in this field.'[2] And political scientist Alan Cairns, as noted earlier, stated in 1971 that Kennedy was 'the most influential constitutional analyst of the period from the early twenties to the middle forties.'[3]

Kennedy's early books on the constitution, in the words of Columbia University historian J.B. Brebner, 'gave constitutional history a brilliant, new, flying start.'[4] The pace of Kennedy's scholarly works continued in the 1930s, although his views changed. Over the decades since the first edition of his *Constitution of Canada* text in 1922, Kennedy went from being an admirer of the Judicial Committee of the Privy Council's interpretation of the British North America Act to a harsh critic.

In 1930, he published a 'revised and enlarged' edition of his book of documents on the Canadian constitution, *Statutes, Treaties and Documents of the Canadian Constitution*, first published in 1918. He greatly reduced the documents for the period from 1791 to 1840 because, as he stated in the preface,[5] they were increasingly available from other sources, and he also wanted to make room for more documents since 1867. In addition to older friends that he had thanked in the first edition, he adds, in particular, historian Frank Underhill and law scholar Larry MacKenzie. He also thanks his wife, Pauline, for seeing the book through the press and doing the index.

The first edition, it will be recalled, had been dedicated to George Wrong. The second edition was dedicated to the memory of two former students whose careers 'were cut off at the beginnings of brilliant promise': Maurice Cody, son of the chairman of the university's board of governors, Canon Henry Cody; and Dent McCrea, a graduate of Loyola University of Montreal, who had been doing graduate work at the University of Toronto when he died suddenly. George Wrong is not mentioned in the new preface. It should be added that, at the end of the decade, Kennedy contributed a chapter to a book of essays[6] in honour of Wrong's eightieth birthday and managed to write the chapter, 'The Terms of the British North America Act,' without citing or mentioning Wrong.

In 1932, Kennedy published a series of lectures[7] – the Kirby Lectures – that he had delivered in 1931 at highly regarded Lafayette College in Pennsylvania. Dalhousie political scientist Robert A. MacKay, later a member of the Rowell-Sirois Commission, praised the book in the *Canadian Historical Review* as 'an important contribution to the philosophy of the constitution' and commented on 'the brilliance of style and intuition ... [and] wealth of scholarship and patient research which characterize Professor Kennedy's work.'[8]

Kennedy offers a relatively simple theory of the state and of the law. 'The state, the political organization, is a function of society – it is not society itself.'[9] He goes on to say that the state is 'established by society as a means to achieve certain purposes ... to carry out certain social ends.'[10] As to law, 'the state is a great social engineer and its laws are its means to its ends ... socially created rules of social engineering.'[11] Again, we see the Holmesian concept of 'social engineering.' And, once again, we see Kennedy not disputing statements that he is a lawyer. The Lafayette College paper noted that Kennedy is 'a member of the Canadian bar' and 'will draw from his long experience in the Canadian Courts.'[12]

At this stage, Kennedy is still somewhat moderate in his criticism of the Privy Council, stating: 'I am personally inclined to think that at present provincial rights are too strongly entrenched behind judicial decisions and public opinion to allow any rapid and effective method of constitutional change in the near future.' But then he notes that 'we are beginning in constitutional law methods of consultation between the federal and provincial governments which will, in the long run, serve us better than law.'[13] He is moving slowly towards a greater centralization of state power.

There is probably no single event to explain the shift, although it likely started with the Privy Council case of *Snider* in 1925, where the 'peace, order, and good government' clause was limited to 'extraordinary peril to the national life of Canada, as a whole.'[14] Kennedy wanted a strong central government, stating in his lecture that the drafters of the BNA Act had tried to avoid, in the words of John A. Macdonald, 'that great source of weakness which had been the cause' of the civil war in the United States, that is, strong local state power. The courts, he said, 'have reversed the whole scheme of 1867.' The 'Great Depression' had already begun and – Kennedy went on – the 'rigidity of our constitutional law

W.P.M. Kennedy, on the occasion of the Lafayette College Kirby Lectures, 1931

is causing us many difficulties and these are beginning to be seriously felt with the increasing complexities of social and economic conditions.'[15] He was, as we have seen, personally facing economic hardship.

The Kirby Lectures – Kirby had founded the 'Five and Dime' stores – drew on Kennedy's earlier Cornell lectures – the Goldwin Smith Lectures – delivered in 1928 and published by Cornell in 1930.

Two years later – in 1934 – Oxford University Press published his *Essays in Constitutional Law*, which contained seven of Kennedy's previously published essays, including the article 'The Nature of Canadian Federalism,' published as a book in 1921 by the University of Toronto Press. Also included was a major address on the constitutional law of the British Empire that he had delivered to the Canadian Bar Association in 1929. The Canadian Bar Association's invitation – Kennedy wrote to Cody in 1929 – was 'the greatest honour I have ever received.'[16] There was also an article on the Statute of Westminster that had earlier been published in the British journal, the *Law Quarterly Review* (*LQR*). When Arthur Goodhart, the *LQR* editor, had visited Toronto in the late 1920s, he had said that one of the reasons he wanted to come to Toronto was to persuade Kennedy to contribute an article to his influential journal. The collection of Kennedy's essays was dedicated to Prime Minister R.B. Bennett 'in friendship and esteem'[17] – once again publicly declaring his friendship with an important public figure. And once again, Kennedy's wife saw the book through the press and compiled the index.

Again, the reviews and later comments were excellent. Professor E.C.S. Wade of Cambridge used the word 'brilliant' twice in his review.[18] American political scientist Edward Corwin later referred to Kennedy's ideas on federalism as 'illuminating.'[19] Justice William Riddell's review in the *Canadian Bar Review* noted: 'The whole work is to be recommended to all who wish to understand the present Constitution of Canada and the new British Empire.'[20] Riddell and others picked up on Kennedy's point that, in both Canada and the United States, 'the most cherished aims of the founders have been nullified' by the courts. In Canada, the federal power had been weakened in spite of the intention of the founders to make it strong; in the United States, the federal power had been strengthened in spite of the intention of the founders to protect state rights.

Even though there was understandably some repetition of ideas from one series of lectures to another, Kennedy's output was staggering.[21] In addition to the works already discussed, he also contributed a major article in the mid-1930s on Canadian constitutional law to *The Encyclopedia of Canada*, edited by the university librarian W. Stewart Wallace. Donald Creighton singled out Kennedy's article for praise in his review of the *Encyclopedia* in the *Canadian Historical Review*.[22] The *Encyclopedia* also brought in extra income, but not much.[23] Kennedy was paid half a cent a word, amounting to the grand total for Kennedy of $20 for 4,000 words, but not insignificant in the Depression years.

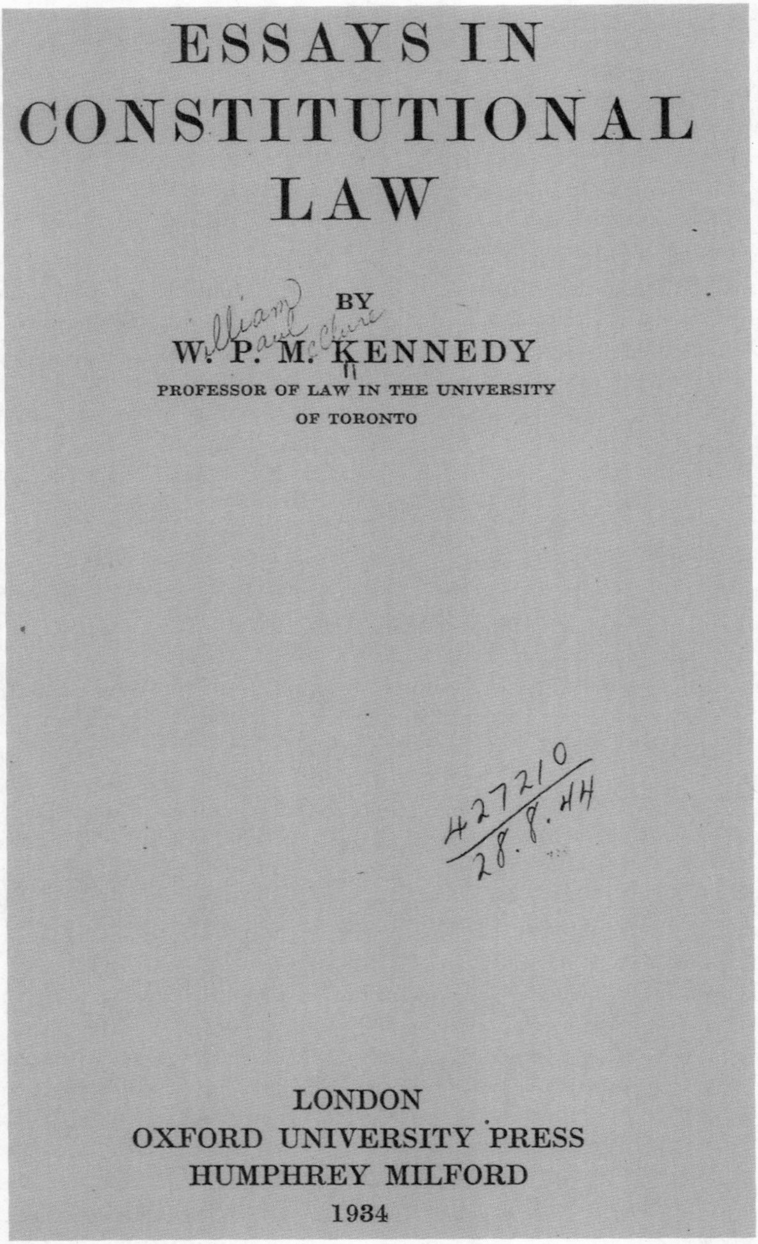

ESSAYS IN
CONSTITUTIONAL
LAW

BY

W. P. M. KENNEDY

PROFESSOR OF LAW IN THE UNIVERSITY

OF TORONTO

LONDON

OXFORD UNIVERSITY PRESS

HUMPHREY MILFORD

1934

Title page of *Essays in Constitutional Law* by W.P.M. Kennedy, 1934

It would be worth close to $300 today. Most of Kennedy's colleagues contributed articles.

Kennedy also published a number of articles analysing the constitutional law of Australia and a major book on the constitution of South Africa, *The Law and Custom of the South African Constitution*, co-authored with South African lawyer H.J. Schlosberg and published in 1935 by Oxford University Press. Kennedy had been interested in South Africa since the Boer War, he wrote to General Jan Smuts, sometime prime minister of South Africa: 'My interest in South Africa goes back to those tragic days of war when my people were there as foes. There is something sublime in the fact that I am now writing to you in friendship and in profound esteem.'[24] He obviously also had correspondence with Prime Minister Hertzog, because the book is dedicated to Hertzog 'by kind permission.'

In his memoirs, Schlosberg tells of being about to complete a book on the law of evidence when 'a letter arrived from Professor W.P.M. Kennedy of Toronto University asking me to write what [Kennedy] hoped would be a standard work on the Law of the South African Constitution. There was no full, up-to-date book on the subject.' Schlosberg goes on: 'I replied that I did not feel qualified to undertake such a colossal task, and at the end of a lot of hard work might fail to find a publisher. [Kennedy] promised to lend his name to mine on the title page, and said that he would revise everything I wrote and submit the manuscript to the Oxford University Press with every prospect of publication.'[25]

After five years of hard work, Schlosberg produced a lengthy manuscript,[26] which Kennedy revised, and which was, indeed, published by Oxford – with Kennedy's name coming first. The book was over 600 pages long. It also had excellent reviews. E.C.S. Wade's review noted that the part of the book dealing with what Wade called 'the government of the natives' is among the most valuable features of the book. Wade wrote: 'The Canadian professor can view the ever-present problem of a European minority, ruling a land where the native population outnumbers the white man by five to one, more dispassionately than the least biased of local authors ... In the result, criticism of administration of native affairs is not spared.'[27]

Kennedy did not – as far as I can determine – write about the governance of Indigenous peoples in Canada. Few academics did. He had only one index entry under the word 'Indian' in his book on the constitution of Canada – a passing reference to the Election Act. Even in the section of the book where he discusses the Royal Proclamation of 1763, following the Seven Years' War, the Proclamation's final paragraphs, which deal with 'Lands of the Indians,' are not mentioned, although there is a reference to the 'complex Indian problem.'[28] Indigenous persons were barely mentioned in the British North America Act or in later comments on the Act until the 1960s. Peter Russell wrote in his recent book on the Canadian constitution, *Canada's Odyssey*: 'The idea of involving them in the construction of a new political community never occurred to Confederation's architects,' except to give jurisdiction over Indigenous people to

THE
LAW AND CUSTOM
OF THE
SOUTH AFRICAN
CONSTITUTION

A TREATISE ON THE
CONSTITUTIONAL AND ADMINISTRATIVE
LAW OF THE UNION OF SOUTH AFRICA,
THE MANDATED TERRITORY OF SOUTH-
WEST AFRICA, AND THE SOUTH AFRICAN
CROWN TERRITORIES

BY

W. P. M. KENNEDY
PROFESSOR OF LAW IN THE UNIVERSITY
OF TORONTO

AND

H. J. SCHLOSBERG
OF GRAY'S INN, BARRISTER-AT-LAW;
LATE OF THE TRANSVAAL BAR
SOLICITOR OF THE SUPREME COURT OF SOUTH AFRICA

LONDON
OXFORD UNIVERSITY PRESS
HUMPHREY MILFORD
1935

Title page of *The Law and Custom of the South African Constitution* by
W.P.M. Kennedy and H.J. Schlosberg, 1935

the federal government.[29] The book on South Africa therefore gives us a clue about what might have been Kennedy's ideas on Indigenous matters in Canada, although there is no direct comparison with Canada in the South Africa book and no indication whether Kennedy had a hand in writing this material. Nor is it known whether Kennedy himself held these views.

Part seven of the South Africa book contains a section entitled 'The Government of the Natives.' Kennedy and Schlosberg conclude: 'The representation of native opinion in the government of the country is entirely inadequate ... The affairs of the natives in matters of local government, where that has been allowed them, have been conducted so well that a little more may be done in the way of having a non-European native commission ... [They are] without any direct representation in the government of the Union.'[30]

Schlosberg, using a different name, H.J. May, produced further editions of the text, entitled *The South African Constitution*, but without Kennedy's involvement. A third edition[31] was brought out by Juta and Company, South Africa, in 1955. Kennedy is not mentioned in that volume, perhaps suggesting that Schlosberg thought he had been taken advantage of by Kennedy.

Division of Power and the Amending Formula

Kennedy wrote on so many constitutional issues that a book – even a series of books – could be written on the subject of Kennedy and the constitution. I will therefore be highly selective and deal mainly with several central issues such as the division of legislative power, appeals to the Privy Council, and the amending power.[32]

In January 1935, the Conservative government under R.B. Bennett set up a Special Committee on the Amendment of the British North America Act. The Orders of Reference were passed on 28 January 1935:

> *Resolved,* – That, in the opinion of this House, a special committee should be set up to study and report on the best method by which the British North America Act may be amended so that while safeguarding the existing rights of racial and religious minorities and legitimate provincial claims to autonomy, the Dominion Government may be given adequate power to deal effectively with urgent economic problems which are essentially national in scope.[33]

The government was concerned that the courts would not uphold the constitutional validity of the Canadian 'New Deal' legislation, which was needed to deal with the Depression. A particularly strong twelve-person House of Commons committee[34] was established, which included Hugh Guthrie, the Conservative minister of justice, and Ernest Lapointe, the past Liberal minister of justice, who would again become the minister of justice after Mackenzie King won the election in the fall of 1935. Another member was the former Liberal and now independent member Henri Bourassa, the founder of *Le Devoir*. Still another was J.S. Woodsworth, one of the founders of the Co-operative Commonwealth Federation (CCF) party. The chair of the Special Committee was F.W. Turnbull, a relatively unknown Conservative lawyer from Regina.

The committee invited seven persons to address them. From the civil service were W.S. Edwards, the deputy minister of justice, and O.D. Skelton, the under-secretary of state for external affairs, and two clerks of the House of Commons, Arthur Beauchesne and M. Ollivier. There was one political science profes-sor, N. McL. Rogers of Queen's, and two law professors, Frank Scott of McGill and W.P.M. Kennedy of Toronto. The provinces did not participate. They had wanted a Dominion-Provincial Conference.

Kennedy and Scott gave evidence on Tuesday, 26 March 1935, and the com-mittee issued its report on 19 June 1935. It unanimously recommended that a 'Dominion-Provincial Conference be held as early as possible in the pres-ent year to study the subject matter of the resolution.' The committee there-fore refrained, in its words, 'from recommending any form of procedure for amendment so as to leave the proposed conference entirely free in its study of the question, except that the committee is definitely of the opinion that minor-ity rights agreed upon and granted under the provisions of the British North America Act should not be interfered with.'[35]

The Liberals won the election in the fall of 1935, and a Dominion-Provincial Conference was held in December. Mackenzie King presented a proposed amending formula – two-thirds of the provinces representing at least 55 per cent of the population, with unanimity for certain fundamental matters. This proposal was not accepted by the provinces. As a result, in 1937 King set up the Rowell Commission, whose work – and Kennedy's involvement in it – will be discussed at the end of this chapter.

Kennedy had presented a number of proposals to the 1935 Special Commit-tee. In his evidence, he discussed his own proposed amending formula, which required approval by both Houses of Parliament and two-thirds of the prov-inces. He did not require a percentage of the population, as Mackenzie King later proposed, stating that 'if you get a resolution passed by both houses of parliament – and if you have two-thirds of the provinces agreeing, I think it will pretty well represent Canadian opinion.' Some provisions in Kennedy's scheme, such as 'the Quebec Civil Code, education, marriage,' and other matters would require unanimity. Still other enumerated sections could be changed without any provincial consent, such as unemployment insurance, which the prov-inces wanted to be under federal jurisdiction. He presented a draft Act to the committee, saying that it was 'very roughly done, which I drew up last night.' Kennedy was opposed to referenda, telling the committee: 'I am very strongly opposed – I cannot say it too emphatically – to referenda.'[36]

On a strict legal basis, Kennedy said, there is no necessity for Parliament to consult the provinces on any proposed amendment. 'I think the parliament of Canada,' Kennedy stated, 'can present any address to the parliament of the United Kingdom.' Lapointe interjected: 'You would not advise this parliament to do so.' Kennedy: 'I do not think it would be a very wise thing.'[37]

Kennedy expressed views on a number of other issues, such as the right of a province to secede from the confederation. He was asked by a member, Peter Veniot, the first Acadian premier of New Brunswick and later the postmaster general under Mackenzie King: 'Under the present Act has not a province the right to secede?' Kennedy answered: 'No, sir, not without the permission of the parliament of the United Kingdom.'[38] He had earlier expressed similar views in *The Cambridge History of the British Empire*, stating: 'It need hardly be added that no province has the constitutional right of secession from the confederation.'[39]

As we know, Kennedy held a strong view on appeals to the Privy Council, telling the Special Committee: 'If we in Canada are not capable of interpreting our own constitution we should not have a legislature at all. If we are given the power to make laws, we surely should have the power to interpret them.' He then commented on the beneficial effect of having the final appeal in one's own country as was done in Australia, stating: 'I have read, I think, every judgment that has ever been delivered by the high court of Australia, and the strength of insight, the judicial capacity, the quality of their jurisprudence is magnificent, because from the day they started out they felt they had to build their own house.'[40] At that point, he was cut off by the chair: 'Are you not getting outside the scope of our reference?' Kennedy admitted that he was. Nevertheless, members of the committee, particularly Ernest Lapointe, wanted to hear more from Kennedy on abolishing Privy Council appeals. The chair's solution was to go into private session, which would then not appear on the record. As we will later see, Lapointe also had strong feelings on the need to abolish such appeals.[41]

Kennedy did not recommend a Dominion-Provincial Conference. Rather, he suggested a royal commission. The Special Committee noted in its brief report that 'Dr. Kennedy, Professor of Law at Toronto University, suggested that a Royal Commission should be appointed to study the workings of the Act, with a view to recommending a rearrangement of powers if thought necessary.'[42] Kennedy told the Special Committee: 'I believe that a commission formed of judges and men of independence, men commanding public respect, to go around the country and take evidence as to how the B.N.A Act is actually working would get somewhere; because the problem of the British North America Act is an economic problem, it is a social problem and it is a financial problem and it is emphatically necessary that we should find out how it all works.'[43] The Liberal government took up his suggestion in 1937, after the failure of the Dominion-Provincial Conference in late 1935, resulting in the Rowell-Sirois Commission, in which Kennedy was a consultant. Did he have his eye on this possibility in making his recommendations?

Second Edition of *The Constitution of Canada*

The second edition of Kennedy's *The Constitution of Canada,* entitled *The Constitution of Canada, 1534–1937: An Introduction to Its Development, Law and Custom*, was published in 1938. It was dedicated to his wife and four children. The original text was not changed, but four new chapters were added in part two of the book. This addition, Kennedy explained in the preface, 'covers the years 1922 to 1937.' It is, he concedes, not a complete survey. 'In recent years,' he stated, 'much new light has been thrown on this period in scholarly treatises and research.' He is only offering a picture of the 'essential elements ... [of] the constitution ... [as] to write of it in every aspect of its development would take up many volumes.' 'It is impossible for several reasons to cover this period in elaborate detail,' he stated. One of those reasons was that 'we do not as yet possess all the material, which some time will be available to help in filling in personal knowledge, for anything like a balanced and definitive study.' Moreover, he noted, 'I have enjoyed the friendship and confidences of Canadian statesmen of all parties and it is obvious that any expression of my knowledge must be governed by the courtesy due to this fact.'[44]

The four additional chapters of the second edition cover the 'essential elements' of the Canadian constitution. The first of these chapters deals with administrative law and reprints almost word for word an article he published in 1934 in the British *Juridical Review*,[45] 'Aspects of Administrative Law in Canada,' a subject that is rightly, but not normally covered in a book on constitutional law. He noted the increased use of delegation to ministers and other bodies and looks at ways of controlling its misuse. The new chapter in the second edition of his book on the constitution is entitled 'Tendencies in Canadian Administration.' Kennedy and others at the law school, such as MacKenzie, Finkelman, and later, Laskin, were showing great interest in administrative law. One difference between the 1934 article and the chapter in the second edition was the dropping of any discussion of Chief Justice Hewart's strong attack against delegated legislation in England made in his book *The New Despotism*, published in 1929. In exchange for dropping Hewart, Kennedy added references to John Willis, an Englishman then teaching at Dalhousie, who had worked with Felix Frankfurter at Harvard and had recently published a text, *Parliamentary Powers of English Government Departments*.[46] Willis was a critic of Hewart. Kennedy's new chapter and several other chapters in the second edition, wrote political scientist Edward Corwin in the *Canadian Historical*

THE CONSTITUTION
OF CANADA
1534–1937

AN INTRODUCTION TO
ITS DEVELOPMENT LAW AND
CUSTOM

By

W. P. M. KENNEDY

PROFESSOR OF LAW IN THE UNIVERSITY OF
TORONTO

SECOND EDITION

OXFORD UNIVERSITY PRESS
LONDON NEW YORK TORONTO

Title page of the second edition of *The Constitution of Canada: 1534–1937* by W.P.M. Kennedy, 1938

Review, were 'outstanding for purposes of comparison with American ideas and institutions.'[47]

The other three chapters of the second edition are not as easily traced, but all come from Kennedy's earlier writings. 'Aspects of Constitutional Law and Custom' starts with a discussion of nationality, which drew on Kennedy's 1930 report to the government, *The Law of Nationality in Canada*,[48] as well as other writings on the topic. He then examined legislative powers and the interpretation of the BNA Act as a statute of the Parliament of the United Kingdom and not as a constitution, the result of which, Kennedy wrote, has unfortunately 'divorced it from history and from the intention of those who in truth framed it, with the result that the centrifugal forces in Canadian national life have been strengthened.'[49] Again, he uses the image of centrifugal and centripetal forces.

Kennedy's views on what he considered to be a mistaken interpretation of the BNA Act by the Privy Council are picked up later in the decade in the O'Connor Report, prepared by the parliamentary counsel to the Senate, William O'Connor, who, at the request of the speaker of the Senate, had been asked to examine the legislative powers of the federal government that the drafters of the BNA Act had intended and the powers as later interpreted by the Privy Council. In a note in April 1939 to former prime minister Arthur Meighen, who was then a member of the Senate, Kennedy wrote: 'I have just finished a careful reading of Mr. O'Connor's Report and I venture to think that it is one of the most important criticisms of the law which has appeared in Canada ... Is there any hope of getting any legislation introduced in the Senate along the lines of which I write? Is there no man in Canada who will give us a lead along these lines? If there is, I think he would rally the people behind him.'[50] Meighen did not take up Kennedy's challenge.

Legislative history was, according to the then current method of statutory construction, not relevant. There had been some hope of a different approach following Lord Chancellor John Sankey's decision in the well-known Persons Case, released in 1929, which decided, contrary to the unanimous decision of the Supreme Court of Canada, that women were 'persons' and so could be senators under the relevant provisions of the BNA Act. This case was the one where the 'living tree doctrine' – now widely used to interpret the Charter of Rights and Freedoms – was first enunciated. But the Sankey court in the same case also held that the doctrine did not apply to the division of powers. Kennedy criticized this aspect of the decision in a 1930 article in the *Canadian Bar Review*. Not surprisingly, he applauded the actual decision holding in favour of women being appointed to the Senate in one of his Lafayette College lectures, stating: 'At rare moments, when there is a problem which does not arouse strong federal and provincial passions, the courts will apply a broad principle of "public policy," as when, in 1929, they decided that the word "person" in the constitution included women for purposes of appointment to the senate – a decision completely out of harmony with the principles of interpretation that are usually followed.'[51]

There is some evidence,[52] as we have seen, that Kennedy assisted Newton Rowell, counsel for the women in the case, by helping to prepare the arguments for the Supreme Court and the Privy Council. As we have seen, he was very close to Rowell – through the Law Club, as his editor for the book on Canada in the Cambridge British Empire series, and socially. Rowell received the sum of $10,000 for his appearance in the Privy Council, the same amount that he was paid annually when he later became the chief justice of Ontario.[53] It is not known whether Kennedy received any compensation for the assistance he gave to Rowell. It is likely that he did.

Kennedy notes, of course, in the second edition of *The Constitution of Canada* that the Privy Council 'decided that the phrase "qualified persons" in the British North America Act included women for purposes of appointment to the senate. The vast importance of the judgment,' Kennedy goes on to say, 'lies in the enunciation of a completely new principle of interpretation … that the British North America Act planted in Canada, a living tree capable of growth and expansion within its natural limits, and that the provisions of the Act should not be cut down by a narrow and technical construction, but should be given a large and liberal interpretation.'[54]

Kennedy had been following the issue for a decade. In the first edition of his book on the Canadian constitution, he had managed to slip in a footnote after the book was completed, mentioning a document dated three days after the date of Kennedy's preface, stating, without further comment: 'An official opinion of the federal minister of justice has laid it down that no woman senators can be created without an amendment of the B.N.A Act, 1867.'[55]

Kennedy noted in the second edition that Lord Sankey, 'having gone so far … proceeded to point out that this new doctrine had no application to the sections governing the distribution of legislative power.'[56] Sankey later reiterated the living tree doctrine without this limitation, but Kennedy was not convinced that it would be followed by the Privy Council in later cases, stating: 'We have no assurances that it will uniformly prevail.'[57] His prediction proved to be correct because, after the supplementary chapter was ready for publication, the Privy Council delivered its judgments in the New Deal cases, which reverted to the narrow statutory interpretation approach. The living tree seemed to have perished, only to be revived many decades later by the Supreme Court of Canada as the correct method of interpreting the British North America Act and the Charter of Rights and Freedoms.

Instead of rewriting these supplementary chapters for the new edition, Kennedy added an appendix entitled 'The Canadian "New Deal."' He also added an appendix concerning the abdication of Edward VIII, which had recently taken place. Kennedy was at his cottage on Otter Lake in Muskoka and relied

on Jacob Finkelman to send him material on the New Deal cases as well as on
the discussions in the Canadian House of Commons. He wrote to Finkelman
on 16 June 1937: 'I've got to add an appendix to the new edition of my Constitution of Canada. I can do it here, but I need you to send me [various docu-
ments] ... Look up and be sure to get me the debates complete.'[58] On 27 June,
he wrote again to Finkelman: 'Please don't send any more Hansards bound or
unbound. I have got quite enough. Once I got started, I got the abdication quite
well enough, without getting lost in the minutiae of constitutional pedantry –
that's all my book needed.'[59]

In case after case, the Privy Council held in the New Deal cases that the
federal government could not enact social and economic legislation, such as
establishing marketing boards and establishing a scheme of unemployment
insurance. Kennedy had predicted this ruling and wrote in appendix one in
the second edition of *The Constitution of Canada*: 'The judgments make it clear
that the hope which some citizens drew from the *Edwards* case that the judicial
committee might be disposed to treat the Act as a "constitution," are vain, in
spite of the unqualified use which Lord Sankey made of that conception in a
later case.'[60]

He concludes the appendix by stating: 'In the far-off days of 1864–7 the men
who made the dominion deliberately looked forward to a time when its citizens
would forget that they were upper or lower Canadians, Nova Scotians, New
Brunswickers and so on, and would become Canadians. The problems of the
British North America Act and of its interpretation would seem to await solution in the realization of that vision.'[61]

Kennedy's solution to what he considered a misinterpretation of the division
of powers was outlined in another of the supplementary chapters, 'The Statute
of Westminster,' where he sets out in greater detail the scheme of amending the
British North America Act, which he had proposed to the Special Parliamentary Committee in 1935, discussed earlier. In the new chapter, he wrote:

> The truth is that we have outgrown the British North America Act. Canada is
> attempting to-day to carry on the highly complex life of a modern state under a
> constitution drawn up for a primitive community, scarcely emerging from pioneer
> agricultural conditions.[62]

The new British North America Act, he argued, 'should be re-enacted in
Canada as part of Canadian law.' Further, he stressed, 'all appeals to the judicial
committee should be abolished – a power clearly belonging to-day to Canada
and its provinces. This ... proposal is of fundamental importance if our constitution is to be truly Canadian.'[63]

The federal government, Kennedy argued in the second edition, was meant
to have the residuary power that would allow it to pass laws 'of national

importance.'[64] This interpretation was John A. Macdonald's view and also the view of the colonial secretary, Lord Carnarvon. Carnarvon had stated:[65] 'The real object which we have in view is to give to the central government those high functions and almost sovereign powers by which general principles and uniformity of legislation may be secured in those questions that are of common import to all the provinces.'

Viscount Haldane had, however, in a judgment in the Privy Council, limited the 'peace, order, and good government' section, in Kennedy's words in the second edition, to 'cases arising out of some extraordinary national peril.'[66] Thus, says Kennedy, 'the residuum of powers would appear to have passed largely to the provinces under their exclusive authority over "property and civil rights."'[67] The problem was created, he states in the second edition, because the Privy Council interpreted the BNA Act as a statute and not as a constitution. Legislative history was, according to the techniques of statutory interpretation used at the time, not relevant.

In a strong critique in the *Canadian Bar Review* in 1937, Kennedy wrote in his typical dramatic style: 'The federal "general power" is gone with the winds. It can be relied on at the best when the nation is intoxicated with alcohol, at worst when the nation is intoxicated with war; but in times of sober poverty, sober financial chaos, sober unemployment, sober exploitation, it cannot be used.' 'The time has come,' Kennedy went on to say in the *CBR* article, 'to abandon tinkering with or twisting the British North America Act.' 'We must,' he went on, 'seek machinery to do in Canada certain things: (i) to repeal the B.N.A. Act *in toto*; (ii) to rewrite completely the constitution; (iii) to provide reasonable and sane and workable constituent machinery; (iv) to abolish all appeals to the Judicial Committee. I submit that every one of these things is necessary; and above all we must get rid of all the past decisions of the Judicial Committee, for they will hang round the necks of the judiciary, if appeals are abolished.'[68]

Appeals to the Privy Council

A few months after November 1937 – the date stated in the preface for the second edition of *The Constitution of Canada* – Kennedy became involved in an attempt to abolish appeals to the Privy Council. In January 1938, the former Conservative minister of justice, C.H. Cahan, now in opposition, with whom Kennedy had worked on the question of nationality in the early part of the decade, wrote to Kennedy to seek his help on a private member's bill that Cahan was about to introduce. Cahan wrote: 'I enclose the first draft of such a bill. Will you, please, do me the favour to examine its terms and suggest any improvements which may occur to you?'[69] There are over twenty letters to and from Kennedy in the Cahan files in Library and Archives Canada for the years 1938–39 relating to this issue. Kennedy agreed to help and replied: 'It is high time that the matter was debated in relation to a definite bill ... So I hope that you will proceed at all cost. In this connection I think you might have support, unofficially at any rate, of Mr. Lapointe [the then Liberal minister of justice.]'[70] The bill, Bill 19, as originally drafted, dealt directly with the question of appeals to the Privy Council.

Kennedy helped arrange for Prime Minister Mackenzie King and his minister of justice, Ernest Lapointe, to be onside and to allow the private member's bill to proceed. Kennedy wrote to Cahan in mid-March 1938: 'I may tell you that I entered into personal correspondence with the Prime Minister and Mr. Lapointe and I do not think it will be anyone's fault if opportunity is not given to you to discuss your bill.'[71] The following month, Kennedy wrote: 'I think I told you that I wrote personally to the Prime Minister and to Mr. Lapointe asking for the widest facilities for debate and they replied that they would be delighted to do everything in their power to assist you.'[72]

Kennedy advised Cahan on the content of a possible second reading speech in the House of Commons. One of Kennedy's letters contains a six-page handwritten argument, including suggestions that Cahan should quote from an address to the *Cercle Universitaire* at Montreal in 1932 by Ernest Lapointe and a Canadian Bar Association speech by Louis St. Laurent in 1931.[73] Both were, of course, well-known Liberals. Lapointe had stated: 'I cannot find a single reason to justify Canada's being the only country in the world of her rank, her population and intellectual development to confess her inability to settle her own judicial conflicts.'

There were, however, a number of unclear constitutional issues to be determined, in particular whether the federal government had the legislative power under the BNA Act to bar appeals to the Privy Council from provincial courts, not just from the Supreme Court of Canada. And there had been a Privy Council decision in 1926 that prevented Canada from abolishing appeals to the Privy Council in criminal cases.[74] Since then, the Statute of Westminster had been enacted for the British Empire in 1931, and in 1933 Canada had legislatively ended appeals to the Privy Council in criminal cases, which had been upheld by the Privy Council in 1935.[75] But non-criminal appeals from provincial courts continued to be a troubling question.

Mackenzie King was, it seems, cautious about the politics of proceeding. The press was divided on the wisdom of Cahan's bill. The *Toronto Daily Star*, for example, wanted appeals abolished, but the *Globe and Mail* wanted 'fuller use' of 'the Empire's ability and genius.'[76] A new bill was prepared by Cahan in early 1939, with Kennedy's support, amending the Supreme Court Act. It was cleverly structured. It did not directly abolish appeals to the Privy Council. Instead, it dealt with the Supreme Court of Canada. The federal government had clear constitutional authority under section 101 of the BNA Act to legislate on matters involving the Supreme Court. The key section of the proposed bill was section 54(3), which stated: 'The judgment of the Court shall in all cases be final and conclusive.'[77] The government would therefore be *indirectly* abolishing appeals to the Privy Council.

The government then took over the bill. Cahan wrote to Kennedy in April 1939: 'I have discussed Bill number 9 with Mr. Lapointe, the Minister of Justice, and he has promised that when I move the second reading of the bill on Friday evening next, he will announce that the government has decided to refer the bill to the Supreme Court of Canada and thence to the Judicial Committee, for an opinion as to whether the terms of the bill are within the legislative jurisdiction of parliament.'[78]

In late April 1939, a reference was directed by the federal government to the Supreme Court of Canada, which in early 1941 upheld the bill's validity by a majority of four to two. Ontario and several other provinces appealed to the Privy Council, but that hearing was delayed because of the war and was not heard until 1947. The Privy Council agreed with Chief Justice Duff in the Supreme Court of Canada that section 101 of the BNA Act gives the federal government 'all ancillary powers necessary to enable Parliament to attain its objects fully and completely. So read it imports authority to establish a court having supreme and final appellate jurisdiction in Canada.' The Privy Council went even further, stating: 'In the opinion of their Lordships the same considerations lead to the conclusion that the court so established must have not only "final" or "ultimate" but also exclusive appellate jurisdiction,' thus permitting the elimination of appeals to the Privy Council from provincial courts.[79]

The Liberals, who were still in power – now under Louis St. Laurent – enacted the new Supreme Court of Canada Act in 1949, which abolished all appeals to the Privy Council and at the same time raised the number of judges on the Supreme Court to nine, three of whom had to be from Quebec and trained in the civil law.[80]

So, Kennedy played an important role in the story of the abolition of appeals to the Privy Council – not a widely known feather in Kennedy's cap.

Rowell-Sirois Report

Kennedy was also involved in the Rowell-Sirois Commission, which reported in May 1940 and which he had recommended be established in his evidence to the Special House Committee in 1935. His work, however, proved to be far less effective here than in many of his other projects.

The Royal Commission on Dominion-Provincial Relations had been established in August 1937 by the federal Liberal government of Mackenzie King. It had been asked 'to consider and report upon the facts disclosed by their investigations; and to express what in their opinion ... will best effect a balanced relationship between the financial powers and the obligations and functions of

each governing body, and conduce to a more efficient, independent and eco-
nomical discharge of governmental responsibilities in Canada.'[81] Its chair was
the chief justice of Ontario, Newton Rowell. But Joseph Sirois, a notary public
from Quebec and a professor of constitutional and administrative law at Laval,
replaced him as chair in 1938 after Rowell became incapacitated. Hence, two
persons were named as the chairs of the final report.

In its report, the commission stated that 'the research program of the Commission was the most comprehensive ever undertaken in Canada in a public
inquiry.'[82] Alexander Brady went even further in his review of the report in the
Canadian Historical Review, stating: 'It is one of the most comprehensive public inquiries undertaken in the modern British Empire.'[83] In the short run, the
report brought about a constitutional amendment (section 91.2A), transferring
unemployment insurance from the provinces to the federal government. In the
longer run, it brought about a sharing of corporate and personal income tax
and succession duties between the federal government and the provinces as
well as the ability of the provinces to raise funds by indirect taxation, such as
the sales tax.

Kennedy was asked by Rowell to do a background report for the commission on a number of other federal constitutions. The invitation to do so was
on 8 November 1937, the very month that Kennedy dated his preface to the
second edition of his text on the constitution of Canada. He was now free to
take on other and paid assignments. Rowell wrote: 'Our object in having this
study made is to see if the constitutions and experience of other federations
would throw light on some of the problems the Commission is called upon to
consider.'[84] Rowell went on to say that there had been references to the American constitution in the discussions leading to Confederation: 'Undoubtedly the
Fathers of Confederation profited by this study of the constitution and of the
experience of the United States. It may be that a further study of the United
States constitution, in the light of the experience of the past seventy years, as
well as the study of the other constitutions mentioned in the memorandum,
will be helpful to us in the work the commission is called upon to do.'[85]

On the same day, Rowell wrote to a member of the commission, R.A.
MacKay: 'Mr. Skelton [Alexander Skelton, the secretary of the commission and
the son of O.D. Skelton] and I thought that ... the best thing to do was to ask
Professor Kennedy (who is the acknowledged expert in the field) to undertake
the study, which he has agreed to do.'[86]

The Rowell-Sirois files in Library and Archives Canada contain four preliminary reports and four final reports by Kennedy on four federal countries:
the United States, Australia, Switzerland, and Argentina. The undated – but
likely early May 1938 – final reporting letter by Kennedy to Rowell stated: 'In
pursuance of your directions, in writing and in interviews, I have made an

examination of the distribution of legislative powers in the United States, in Australia, in Switzerland and in Argentina ... As requested, I have been more detailed in connection with the United States.'[87] He was asked to examine the constitutions of these counties with special reference to taxation, welfare legislation, labour legislation, the treaty-making power, and the residuary power. The final report on the United States consisted of ninety-eight typed pages and the one on Australia seventy-six pages, with shorter documents on Switzerland and Argentina.

His reports were not, however, cited or mentioned in the Rowell-Sirois Report, nor in the list of studies that were included as appendices to the report, or even listed as 'mimeographed studies' in the report. There is a list of these mimeographed studies in Alexander Brady's nine-page review of the Rowell-Sirois Report in the *Canadian Historical Review*,[88] and Kennedy's studies are again not mentioned. Each of Kennedy's studies was put on 'stencils,' and so all of them were likely distributed to the commissioners, but probably no further. He is, however, listed – along with dozens of other researchers – in the introduction to the report.

I agree with Professor R.C.B. Risk's assessment of Kennedy's reports: 'All were descriptive of structure and doctrine, with very little reflection and commentary.'[89] It certainly required a lot of digging by Kennedy, particularly with respect to Switzerland and Argentina. Perhaps if Rowell had continued to chair the commission, the studies would have played a larger role in the deliberations and in the commission's final report. Rowell was particularly interested in constitutional law. Commissioner MacKay, professor of political science at Dalhousie, later stated in a personal memoir that 'Justice Rowell was in on the early discussions, but his interests at this stage were mainly centred on constitutional matters rather than on economics and finance ... I have often speculated what would have been the nature of the report had the original personnel continued.'[90]

It is also possible that the commissioners were annoyed with the bills that Kennedy was submitting every month. He was to be paid $20 a day 'for time actually engaged on the work, being on the same basis as the economists have been engaged.'[91] Kennedy was to have started his work on the project on Monday, 8 November 1937. There is a note in the government file from the assistant to the secretary saying that Kennedy had telephoned to Ottawa to say that he had in fact commenced work on Saturday, 6 November, two days earlier.[92] Every month a statement would come from Kennedy, outlining the days worked. He worked every day in that month, November, including all weekends, for a total of twenty-six days.[93] He sent a note to Secretary Skelton during the month that the work 'is much vaster than I thought. However, I shall see to it that you have the complete report by May 1st. I have so arranged my time that I can give eight or nine hours every day, including Sundays, to the work, in order to have it finished in time.'[94] He also mentioned that he was including a small amount for taxis 'as I am suffering from a slight heart affection, and cannot walk very much.'[95]

For the month of December, Kennedy claimed to have worked every day including Christmas day, for a total of thirty-one days.[96] In January 1938, he only worked thirty out of thirty-one days.[97] And so on. The total amount claimed was $3,460 for the days spent on the work between November 1937 and early May 1938 – substantially more than the amount he was getting paid by the university during that time period. In his request for the final payment, he writes on 5 May 1938: 'I shall be glad if you will let me have my cheque at your earliest convenience, as I am somewhat worn out and want to get a little change if possible.'[98]

These charges undoubtedly raised a few eyebrows at the commission. Did he really work all these days, considering he was also running a law school? There was perhaps a stronger reaction when Kennedy wrote Skelton complaining in a long letter that the commission had deducted $9 in taxi expenses from Kennedy's March bill, stating: 'It is annoying that you should have been compelled to take the action which you have done.' Kennedy then threatened to take up the matter with Mackenzie King and Ernest Lapointe, with whom, he said, he was 'in personal correspondence over some legal matters.'[99] Skelton sent back a two-page letter politely explaining that these were Department of Finance rules and that it would require a Treasury Board minute to reverse the practice that barred travelling expenses within the researcher's home city. 'I suggested the deletion of the $9.00 item from your account,' Skelton wrote. 'I assumed that in view of the relative insignificance of the amount that you would prefer this course.'[100] These financial matters may well have played a role in the decision by Skelton and some members of the commission not to publish Kennedy's work and for the commission not to cite his reports.

By this point, Kennedy's champion, Chief Justice Rowell, was no longer active in the work of the commission. As the Dictionary of Canadian Biography states: 'The commission was in Toronto when, on 7 May 1938 [two days after Kennedy had submitted his final bill], Rowell suffered a heart attack, followed by a stroke that robbed him of speech. In November his resignations from the commission and from his position as chief justice were accepted, and Sirois took over as chairman.'[101]

Rowell died in 1942. President Cody asked Kennedy to write the obituary for the Royal Society of Canada. 'In 1936,' Kennedy wrote, 'he became the Chief Justice of Ontario. He interrupted his judicial life to assume the Chairmanship of the Royal Commission on Dominion-Provincial Relations. Stricken down in the midst of this great work, he never recovered.'[102] Kennedy was anxious, he told Cody, to keep in the obituary the reference to the School of Law: 'I am specially anxious that reference should be made, as I have done, to the School of Law in which his interests and devotion were centred.'[103]

This analysis of Kennedy's involvement in constitutional law ends with an excerpt from an article by Kennedy published in 1940 in the St. Louis–based *Washington University Law Quarterly*, entitled 'The Judicial Process and Canadian Legislative Powers.' It sums up this chapter and Kennedy's views during the 1930s. He wrote:

> We can easily see from this survey how hampered and tied the federal legislature has become, how narrowed are its powers, how circumscribed its authority – and all this quite unnecessarily so ... Canada is unable to meet services which are in truth national – old age pensions, minimum-wage laws, hours of labour, unemployment insurance, in a word all the vast demands of social legislation – but which, by unfortunate and unaccountable interpretation of the British North America Act are given to the provinces ... accentuated by the Privy Council decisions – and with the clear terms of the Act so obscured and twisted and misquoted in favour of the provinces, we have reached a position in which federalism ... becomes a source of national weakness. Provincial rights have become national wrongs.[104]

Kennedy then says: 'Of the future, I cannot write here.' I must admit that I assumed that Kennedy continued to hold these views, just as Laskin did when he taught me in the 1950s and which he continued to hold when he was on the Supreme Court of Canada. Laskin held these centralist views to such an extent as a judge that Justice Brian Dickson accused Laskin in one 1983 case of 'blind centralism.'[105]

What of Kennedy's future views? It turns out that Kennedy's views changed, according to his son Gilbert Kennedy, who was a professor of constitutional law at the University of British Columbia (UBC) Law School and later the deputy minister of justice in British Columbia. They changed in part because of the Rowell-Sirois Commission and the subsequent granting of taxing powers to the federal government. We will see in a later chapter that Kennedy also played a role as an advisor to the government of Ontario in three important federal-provincial conferences in 1950, the last of which dealt with the taxing and spending power. As has been noted by others, these conferences had 'a strongly centralizing effect' on the levers of power.[106] In his oral interview in 1983, Gilbert Kennedy notes that, in his early years, he accepted his father's views of the misinterpretation of the BNA Act by the Privy Council. He goes on to say that his father felt that 'the Privy Council beginning with Lord Watson had misinterpreted the BNA Act in favour of the provinces rather than Ottawa.' Gilbert then started teaching constitutional law at UBC and 'began to feel that despite the Privy Council mistakes – so called – maybe they were right.'

Gilbert then discusses his father's changed views: 'And I was amazed on my return to Toronto on a visit to Dad [after his retirement] on my way for a trip to Ottawa – I would sometimes stop off in Toronto overnight – and Dad said something about how the federal government's use of the taxing power had changed the whole balance of legislative power and we went on to discuss this and it was obvious that his views had changed very materially from his earlier writings – most of his earlier writings should be amended accordingly.' Gilbert was not the only one who heard of W.P.M.'s changed views, he said: 'I know that Bora Laskin has, as a regular visitor at the house. I know that Charlie Bourne [a law professor at UBC who had been in the Honour Law program] has because Charlie told me about it and was so surprised. And yet, not everyone realizes that Dad changed his mind because he didn't publish his changes.'[107]

18

The War Years

King George VI and Queen Elizabeth visited Canada in May and June 1939. This visit was the first ever visit to Canada by a reigning sovereign. On Monday, 22 May they visited Toronto, toured the university campus, and had a state lunch in the Great Hall of Hart House. They then attended the Queen's Plate and later opened the Queen Elizabeth Way.

One and a half million people saw the royal couple in Toronto. A special twelve-car train, painted blue and gold, carried the royal couple around the country. The library on the train included W.P.M. Kennedy's *The Constitution of Canada.*[1]

Four hundred persons attended the non-alcoholic lunch at Hart House, including Mackenzie King and President Cody. Professor and Mrs. Kennedy were not invited. Neither were deans or principals. Nor, initially, were members of the board of governors, apart from the chairman of the board. It was – the premier's office said – an Ontario government event, not a university event.[2] Were the Kennedys – strong monarchists – in the crowd of over 10,000 persons gathered in front of Hart House to see the royal couple?[3] Or were they perhaps in the throngs on Avenue Road, near the Kennedys' home on Spadina Road, when the royal procession went north on Avenue Road following a visit to the Legislative Assembly Building? We know that the Kennedys were not yet at the cottage because, as we saw in an earlier chapter, Kennedy was to receive an honorary doctorate from the University of Montreal on 26 May 1939, four days later.

Refugees

On 27 May 1939, the day after Kennedy received his honorary degree from the University of Montreal, the ocean liner *St. Louis*, carrying over 900 European Jews who were trying to escape from the Nazis, arrived in Cuba.[4] These were desperate times for those on board. Germany had been given the

King George VI and Queen Elizabeth leaving Hart House, 22 May 1939.
Some members of the Hart House staff are on the right

German-speaking part of Czechoslovakia earlier that academic year at a conference in Munich, and *Kristallnacht* had occurred in November 1938. On 22 May 1939, the day the royal couple visited the university, Germany and Italy had entered into an alliance.

The visas of all but a few of those on board the *St. Louis* were declared invalid, and the ship left Havana on 2 June 1939. The United States refused entry, as did Canada. Prime Minister Mackenzie King had left the decision to his director of immigration, F.C. Blair, who said 'the line must be drawn somewhere.' None of the passengers qualified for admission to Canada, and the ship returned to Europe. About a third of the passengers did not survive the Holocaust. Canada recently apologized for its role in denying entry to Canada.

A telegram with forty-one signatures of persons connected with the University of Toronto, spearheaded by George Wrong, was sent to Prime Minister Mackenzie King on 7 June 1939: 'We, the undersigned Christian citizens of Canada, respectfully suggest that ... you forthwith offer to the 907 homeless exiles on board ... sanctuary in Canada.'[5] Many prominent academics, such as former president Robert Falconer and the principal of University College, Malcolm Wallace, signed, as did a number of clerics. Kennedy did not. It is not known whether he was asked by Wrong to do so. Perhaps not. He would likely have already left for Muskoka. It is very likely that he would have signed, if asked to do so, considering his lack of anti-Semitism and, as we will see, his willingness to assist so-called 'enemy aliens' to enrol in the law school.

According to historian Paul Stortz, who has studied refugee professors at the University of Toronto, 'U of T president Henry Cody was a strong Jewish ally and under his leadership, the university helped focus attention on the plight of European Jews, took in Jewish students and hired a number of displaced academics.'[6]

As we saw earlier, between 1935 and 1945 the university hired twenty refugee European lecturers and professors, at least half of whom were Jewish.[7] Some came with Carnegie Foundation money, which required that the university to which they were attached had guaranteed that their salaries would be paid after the Carnegie money ended. Another group, the Canadian Society for the Protection of Science and Learning, was organized in April 1939 by librarian Stewart Wallace and was supported by Kennedy. The society was run through the Royal Society of Canada and helped secure positions for five of the twenty persons hired by the University of Toronto. Physics, chemistry, mathematics, and fine arts were among the departments that were able to take advantage of these programs.

Law did not. When Harold Laski from the London School of Economics wrote to Kennedy about a refugee professor from the University of Vienna, Kennedy replied, after consulting Cody, that there were no funds for an appointment.[8] A recommendation to Kennedy by Edwin Borchard of Yale about a German law professor had the same result.[9]

In at least one case, Kennedy had a run-in with the notorious F.C. Blair – of 'None Is Too Many' notoriety[10] – the head of the immigration branch in Ottawa. Kennedy wanted to appoint a Dr. H.J.U. Rubin, a Jewish legal scholar from the University of Vienna, as a Special Lecturer in Comparative Law, without remuneration. Rubin had been admitted to Canada as a 'visitor.' Kennedy assured Cody in a letter dated 27 October 1938 that Mr. Rubin 'has a brilliant record at Vienna … and it is distinctly understood that his appointment involves the University in no expense.'[11] In an earlier letter, Kennedy had asked Cody: 'Under the circumstances can we pay him anything?'[12] Cody said he could not. The board approved the appointment. This case was one of the twenty referred to earlier.

Kennedy must then have heard that Blair had become interested in the case and wrote to Blair: 'Mr. Rubin did not apply to me for work here. His name came to me quite apart from him from another source and I was delighted to invite him as a distinguished lawyer to lecture in an honorary capacity.'[13] Blair wrote back to Kennedy saying that he had been concerned because he had been informed by an unnamed 'gentleman from Toronto' 'that Dr. Rubin applied to the University and was engaged by them to lecture on International Law.' 'We

Frank Underhill, in uniform during the First World War

naturally reached the conclusion,' Blair wrote, 'that, following Dr. Rubin's tem- porary entry to Canada for a specific purpose, with regard to which he testified under oath, he applied for a position with the University.'[14] I have not been able to discover what subsequently happened to Dr. Rubin.

Academic Freedom

The approaching war affected attitudes towards academic freedom.[15] On 13 April 1939, an outraged board of governors dealt with provocative remarks made by history professor Frank Underhill, who had stated with respect to Canada's involvement in a future war: 'We must therefore make it clear to the world, and especially to Great Britain, that the poppies blooming in Flanders fields have no further interest for us.'[16] On the same day, the Ontario Legislative Assembly discussed the issue, led by the leader of the opposition and future premier George Drew. Premier Mitchell Hepburn ended the debate saying that if the university did not discipline Underhill, the government would.[17]

A close examination of issues involving Underhill and academic freedom is important in the present manuscript because of Kennedy's involvement in those issues and the conclusion drawn by several distinguished academics concerning Kennedy's alleged lack of support for Underhill, which may have affected and may continue to affect Kennedy's overall reputation.

On 19 April 1939 the dean of arts and science, Sam Beatty, along with Ches- ter Martin, the head of history, Harold Innis, the head of political economy, and W.P.M. Kennedy appeared before the board arguing that the matter should be handled internally by a committee of academics. The remarks in question, they noted, were made four years earlier at an academic-style conference at Lake Couchiching in Muskoka. Cody, with the support of the professors, recommended that the board 'take no further action at present.'[18] Kennedy was clearly supporting Underhill at this time.

The board and the Ontario government had dealt with a number of ear- lier instances of allegedly improper statements by Underhill, a University of Toronto graduate who had been teaching at the University of Saskatchewan when he was hired to teach in the University of Toronto's history department in 1927. One incident in 1927 involved alleged statements by Underhill that the British were 'as much if not more to blame for the war than the Germans.'[19]

A further incident occurred in January 1931, the year before Falconer left the presidency, when sixty-eight University of Toronto professors sent a public let- ter to the press, protesting against the action of the Toronto police commission in preventing a group called the Fellowship of Reconciliation from holding a public meeting.[20] The letter had been drafted by Underhill and classicist Eric Havelock, and was signed by other leading members of the academic com- munity. Kennedy and Finkelman did not sign the letter, although Auld and MacKenzie did. Some members of the board of governors were incensed with the actions of the professors and asked Falconer to meet with a group of them to warn them of the danger to the university if they got involved in public con- troversies. Falconer reported to Cody that the six signatories he met with had undertaken 'to use their influence with the members of their staff to refrain from further discussions on this or other political matters.'[21]

A few months later, in the spring of 1931, Underhill wrote an article in the British *New Statesman and Nation* criticizing Prime Minister R.B. Bennett's handling of imperial relations. Falconer again wrote to Underhill, cautioning him that such writing 'endangers the autonomy of the University.'[22] Underhill responded that many professors had engaged in such public discussions in the past and specifically mentioned George Wrong, W.P.M. Kennedy, and the new head of history, Chester Martin. 'In the light of all these cases,' Underhill wrote, 'I still fail to see what is so particularly reprehensible in my own conduct.' Moreover, he argued, 'if professors at Toronto must keep their mouths shut in order to preserve the autonomy of the University, then that autonomy is already lost.'[23] Falconer did not change his mind, stating: 'Your letter leaves me still of the same opinion as to the inexpediency of professors in the University of Toronto taking part in political journalism, by which I mean discussing current politics in such a way as to bring party criticism upon the writer.'[24]

Kennedy's views concerning *public* comments on party politics would have been consistent with Falconer's. It was not comment on public affairs that Fal- coner was concerned with, but comment on party politics. In a letter to Under- hill in September 1931, Falconer stated that he has in the past had 'to defend the professors in their right to teach their subjects with complete freedom ... But for a professor, whose salary and positions are maintained by the goodwill of the people as a whole, to enter into party-politics, is in my judgment not only inexpedient but dangerous to the well-being of the University ... [That] a professor like most other people should have strong party convictions is only natural ... [but] he should I believe restrain himself from taking part publicly in party matters.'[25] He compared academics to judges. Kennedy would have agreed. As we saw in an earlier chapter, Kennedy refused to comment to the press on the King-Byng affair involving the controversial dissolution of Parliament in 1926. In 1934, he emphasized the limited role of an academic in his response to an invitation by Ontario Attorney General Arthur Roebuck for Kennedy to be a member of an Ontario committee 'appointed in connection with the forthcoming Conference concerning the proposed revision of the B.N.A. Act.' 'It is, therefore, a great pleasure to me,' Kennedy replied, 'to be of any help to you in this capacity [that is, to give expert advice], where necessarily I cannot have, and do not desire to have, any say in those matters of policy or in the presentation of an argument, responsibility for which must always exclusively belong to the Government which honours me in using my services.'[26] Kennedy's views on what is, and what is not, a 'matter of policy,' however, is never spelled out.

No doubt, the real concern of the board was that Underhill was a founding member of the left-wing CCF party and publicly supported the party. Underhill and others were forced by the university to resign their executive positions in the CCF clubs with which they were associated. Cody did not want professors publicly discussing controversial topics. Cody himself, however, often openly discussed such subjects. In the summer of 1933, for example, he had been in Italy, from where he returned praising aspects of Mussolini's regime.[27]

We now arrive at the 'Flanders field' statement, where, as stated earlier, the board took no action at its April 1939 meeting on the advice of Cody, supported by Kennedy and others. There was strong support for Cody by faculty and students. The statement was made by Underhill at a conference at Lake Couchiching south of Muskoka four years earlier and had not created any controversy at the time. Moreover, Underhill expressed regret, saying: 'I now see that this sentence of mine about Flanders poppies ... [was] phrased in such a way as to be offensive to a good many people, and I regret very much having expressed myself in this way.'[28] No action was taken by the board.

But times were different in the summer of 1940 when Underhill, again at a conference at Lake Couchiching, made what was considered a controversial statement. Now it was the desperate summer of 1940. France had fallen. England might be invaded. The Battle of Britain in the air was about to begin. Underhill stated what was obvious to everyone at the conference: Canada now had 'two loyalties, the old one to the British connection ... and the new one to North America involving common action with the States ... We can no longer put all our eggs in the British basket.'[29] At the 12 September 1940 board meeting, the governors unanimously wanted Underhill fired. Some prominent citizens, such as the former prime minister Arthur Meighen, even wanted him interned.[30] Underhill admitted that he was not seriously misquoted. He had indeed used the phrase 'put all our eggs in the British basket.' He had concluded his remarks by stating: 'The nineteenth century world under British economic leadership and kept peaceful by British sea-power has passed forever ... All these conditions are going to make the big power next door to us relatively much more important to us when we consider our security in an uneasy world.'[31]

There were a number of further board meetings on the 'two loyalties' statement. At a later meeting in September, the university solicitor, Hamilton Cassels, advised the board that the evidence did not support dismissal for cause. Cody was wavering on what to do. At a board meeting on 19 December 1940, Cody reversed his earlier position and concluded that 'viewing his record as a whole, I believe it is in the best interest of the University that his services be dispensed with.' Underhill's statements, Cody said, 'have been discussed by the Board of Governors on seven separate occasions ... There is always the fear that he will again make some statement in such a form that public indignation will be aroused and further injury done to the good name and usefulness of the university.'[32] A delegation of the board came to seek Underhill's resignation, but Underhill refused to resign.

On 7 January 1941, Cody met with about two dozen senior academic administrators, the leading humanities and social science professors in the university. Kennedy was, of course, included. Cody took notes at that meeting. A number of academic writers over the years have examined those notes and concluded that Kennedy did *not* support Underhill remaining in the university. This meeting therefore plays an important role in determining Kennedy's reputation, because it is likely the overwhelming opinion of the academic community today is that Underhill was harshly dealt with by the board. Michiel Horn, in his book on academic freedom in Canada, to pick one example, stated: 'Only W.P.M. Kennedy of the department of Law, who said that the "basis of academic freedom was common sense," seemed to support Cody's stand.'[33] Philip Girard, Laskin's biographer, to take another example, stated: 'Most of the professoriate supported Underhill, but W.P.M. Kennedy did not. Arguing that "common sense is the basis of freedom," Kennedy found Underhill singularly deficient in that commodity.'[34] R.D. Francis, Underhill's biographer, also concluded that Kennedy 'supported President Cody.'[35] D.C. Masters, Cody's biographer, did not, however, take a position on whether Kennedy supported Underhill, but simply stated that 'Professor W.P.M. Kennedy argued that "common sense is the basis of freedom" and that it had not been shown by Underhill.'[36]

Here is all that Cody wrote relating to Kennedy's remarks: 'Prof. Kennedy – "common sense is basis of academic freedom" – Will be trouble in U. of T.'[37] I have not found any other contemporary statement relating to that meeting. I do not doubt that Kennedy said what Cody recorded, but what is its meaning?

W.P.M. Kennedy in his office, date uncertain

Both sentences seem sensible. Virtually every faculty member said that Under-hill's remarks were unfortunate in the circumstances of the time and that there would be trouble in the university whatever the board decided.

I believe that Kennedy would likely have urged Cody not to support the fir-ing of Underhill but might possibly have added – like the next speaker – that he would support whatever the president decided.

Kennedy and Underhill were friends, and Kennedy had a high regard for Underhill's intellect. Although he had not supported Underhill's appointment to the history department in 1927 because he felt that Underhill was not interested in history, Kennedy wanted him at the university. He had warned Cody – at the time the chair of the board – that Underhill 'has absolutely no interest in history ... He is "bored" with Canadian History ... I'd love to see him here, especially in Philosophy, as I have a great regard for him as man and scholar.'[38] He clearly supported Underhill in 1939. Moreover, Kennedy was knowledgeable about American-Canadian relations and would have appreciated the correctness of Underhill's observations about the 'two loyalties.'

One new perspective that can be added to the debate comes from Kennedy's son Gilbert, who stated in his oral interview in 1983:

> Like all universities, Toronto had a Board of Governors ... Sometimes they'd want to interfere with the continuing appointment of a faculty member because of his political leanings, something that the President couldn't stand. And my father was called in by the President [Cody] to defend on two occasions two faculty members, one was Underhill for his C.C.F. leanings ... the other was a Philosophy professor at Trinity College [George Grube] who had run as a C.C.F. school board trustee, unsuccessfully. [Board member Herbert] Bruce thought that all of these, both of these people, should be disposed of. Unsuccessfully. And that's the kind of thing that Dad had a reputation for around the University. He was helpful, he could be a help in doing that kind of job.[39]

Herbert Bruce, surgeon and former lieutenant governor of Ontario, was an active member of the board who often attacked President Cody's actions and was one of the movers of the motion to fire Underhill in 1941. Gilbert had graduated from his father's law school in 1940 and was close to his father. If Kennedy senior had been in favour of firing Underhill, his son would surely have known. Further, Underhill sent a note to Larry MacKenzie in September 1940 discussing his position in the university, and there is no mention that Kennedy was supporting his dismissal.[40]

As it turned out, Underhill was not dismissed, even though the motion to do so was passed by the board (7 to 4) at its June 1941 meeting. Dismissal required the consent of the president, and Cody would now not give his consent. Underhill went off to the United States for the next academic year with a Guggenheim Fellowship.[41]

What likely caused Cody to change his mind was pressure that had been put on him by the Department of External Affairs. Hugh Keenleyside, a senior civil servant in the department, who was then a member of the Canadian section of the recently established Permanent Joint Board on Defence and to whom Underhill had written about the affair, sent a telegram to Cody, dated 9 January 1941, stating, in part:

> I suggest that every possible step be taken to postpone action until present international crisis is ended. Proposed action against a man widely known in United States as exponent of idea of continental cooperation might have most serious

repercussions in that country where it would dismay and disappoint our friends encourage and strengthen the hands of those who are critical of 'British Imperialism,' provide ammunition for isolationist leaders and all totalitarian groups and do cause of Canada and Empire great harm.[42]

Keenleyside was an important figure in Canada–US relations, acting as a go-between for Mackenzie King, Franklin Roosevelt, and the American secretary of state, Cordell Hull. He had been a friend of Frank Underhill since spending a year in Toronto before joining the foreign service.[43]

Cody read Keenleyside's telegram to the board at their meeting on 9 January 1941. The board also heard from Cody that Premier Hepburn was worried.[44] The board postponed making a decision on whether to fire Underhill until their June meeting.

This information from Keenleyside and perhaps communication from Mackenzie King and/or O.D. Skelton, the undersecretary of state, would have influenced Cody's ultimate decision not to support removal. Cody closely followed American foreign policy.[45] I would not be surprised to learn that W.P.M. Kennedy played some role in the intervention by Keenleyside and Skelton. He knew both of them reasonably well. Indeed, Kennedy had written an introduction to Keenleyside's 400-page scholarly manuscript published by Knopf in 1929, entitled *Canada and the United States: Some Aspects of their Historical Relations*.[46] How Kennedy came to be asked to write the introduction is not clear. My guess is that the publisher suggested it because of Kennedy's reputation in the United States. Or it could have been Kennedy himself who suggested it. Keenleyside spent a year in Toronto with a publishing firm and had considerable contact during that time with faculty from the university. The reviewer in the *Canadian Historical Review* commends both Keenleyside and Kennedy, stating: 'The general characterization of Mr. Keenleyside's labours in Professor Kennedy's brief and thoughtful introduction, few will challenge. It is impartial, but fearless, and ... there is evidence throughout of exhaustive research and a strong desire to be fair.'[47]

Wartime Campus

Canada had entered the war on 10 September 1939. 'Last year we began the year under the shadow of a threatening war,' President Cody told the incoming class. 'For the time the cloud was lifted, a respite was given. Today the storm has broken upon us.'[48] In early September – a week after Britain had declared war – Cody was anxious for Canada to join her, stating that 'our gratitude to the Motherland from whom we sprang demands it.'[49] As described at the beginning of this chapter, the strong attachment to Great Britain had been evident a few months earlier during the visit of the royal couple to Canada.

Students in uniform in the Hart House library, 1942

Whereas the students had been under great pressure to enlist during the First World War, this time they were not immediately urged to enlist. The chief of defence staff, General A.G.L. McNaughton, had told the universities that the students could 'serve the country in a most valuable way by continuing their university training until graduation.'

Some activities were curtailed because of the war. Intercollegiate athletic schedules were cancelled, though exhibition games took place. Interfaculty competitions, however, increased during this period. Hart House reluctantly suspended its debates, and the number of dances was reduced. The sombre tone of the campus resembled that during the First World War.[50]

The number of students and alumni who died in the Second World War totalled 557, somewhat fewer than the number who died in the First World War. Their names are listed on the memorial tablet under Soldiers' Tower. The number who served in the forces was substantially higher – more than 10,000, compared to about 6,000 in the Great War. Well over half those who died had served in the Royal Canadian Air Force (RCAF).[51]

As the war continued, the campus took on the appearance of a military camp. Many students were in uniform, and special courses were given for military personnel and others. In the summer of 1941, for example, 500 members of the RCAF, many of whom lived and ate in Hart House, were given a three-month training course as radar technicians.[52] Overall enrolment at the university went down slightly, from 8,000 in 1938–39 to under 7,000 in 1943–44, and then rose with the return of the first group of veterans. Enrolment in engineering increased, while that in the Faculty of Arts – law's home until 1941 – decreased.

Canada's wartime experience drew it closer to the United States. Frank Underhill turned out to be right. Canada would no longer be putting all her 'eggs in the British basket.' Canada was now tied militarily to the United States. It purchased large quantities of military equipment from American suppliers, thus departing from the British imperial principle of similarity of equipment. Moreover, American research and manufacturing had for the most part taken over the development of advanced weapons and equipment. Canadian universities would contribute to their development, though not to the same extent as American universities, where 'the war brought about fundamental changes in the relationship between science and government.'[53] Finally, the link with British universities continued to weaken because of the close contacts made during the war between Canadian and American scientists. Indeed, the rapid and extensive shift in emphasis on all fronts from Britain to the United States probably surprised even Underhill.[54]

19

The Changing Law School

The student-run *School of Law Review* published a list – in its December 1944 issue – of law students and recent law graduates who were on active service. There were eighty-five names on the list, which the *Law Review* acknowledged was 'incomplete.' Each of the 1939 and 1940 graduating classes contained fourteen names of persons on active service – a significant proportion of the members of those classes. The list did not, however, contain the names of persons who had died on active service. In that same 1944 issue, recent deaths were noted of five Honour Law graduates.[1] Six deaths were listed in the *Law Review* issue of April 1945.[2]

J.K. Macalister

One student from the class of 1937 listed as on active service was Sergeant J.K. Macalister. Macalister's tragic story[3] was not widely known – in spite of his brilliant record – until recent years. I did not know it until I started writing the history of the University of Toronto. It is a moving story that tells us much about the role of chance in most careers, in this case Macalister's and Bora Laskin's careers.

W.P.M. Kennedy had had his eye on Ken Macalister since he entered the law school in 1933. Macalister had a superlative academic record – better than any previous University of Toronto law student and possibly better than any law student since then. Kennedy wrote in 1936 in a letter recommending him for a Rhodes Scholarship that Macalister, who was then in his final year of the Honour Law course, had stood first with first-class honours in his first three years. 'This record,' Kennedy went on to say, 'is unique from two points of view: (i) not only was he first of firsts in the honours of each year, but he obtained first of first class honours in <u>each subject</u> in <u>each</u> year; (ii) he obtained <u>every</u> prize and scholarship available [Kennedy's underlining]. This is an academic record which is unequaled ... I have no hesitation in saying that he has the finest mind

J.K. Macalister, a Rhodes Scholar,
was executed by the Nazis at
Buchenwald in 1944

which I have met with for many years.'[4] Kennedy had kept in touch with him over the years as a possible future faculty member.

Macalister also stood first in his final year of the Honour Law program, received a first at Oxford as a Rhodes Scholar, and then the highest standing in the English bar exams. He tried to join the Canadian Army while in England but was rejected because of his poor eyesight. He then tried to join the French Army (he had married a French woman) and then the British Army, but was again unsuccessful.

In May 1940 – out of the blue – Macalister found himself in the running for a position at the University of Toronto law school. Professor Larry MacKenzie had been asked by the University of New Brunswick if he would allow his name to be considered for president of that university. MacKenzie discussed the question with Kennedy and President Cody and others, and in June decided to let his name stand. The interview was held at the Royal York Hotel in Toronto in mid-July, and MacKenzie was selected. In August 1940, the New Brunswick government approved the appointment. MacKenzie would receive $6,000 a year and a president's house. He was at the time receiving about $4,000 from the University of Toronto. Gilbert Kennedy recalls driving MacKenzie up to the cottage to inform his father of the formal appointment. MacKenzie wrote to Kennedy: 'It is with a great deal of regret that I leave Toronto.'[5] And Kennedy replied: 'You have been with me so long and so happily.'[6] Kennedy, of course, now had to find someone to teach MacKenzie's courses, starting in September.

Macalister was not alone in being considered for MacKenzie's position. The other person was Bora Laskin. On 11 August 1940, Kennedy told Cody that he advised MacKenzie to accept the New Brunswick offer, stating: 'It is an office from which he can do great work.' He then added: 'I have Laskin in mind as junior appointment.'[7] Laskin was available. He had been turned down for a position with the Department of Justice in Ottawa in January 1940 and was still working on the *Canadian Abridgment*, edited by Fred Auld. The possibility of an appointment was, no doubt, discussed with Laskin. Someone from the Department of External Affairs must also have heard of the possibility of MacKenzie leaving, and in August contacted Kennedy and President Cody, offering his services. Kennedy wrote to Cody: 'I would be most grateful if you gave him [the person from External Affairs] no encouragement ... My mind turns to a junior appointment ... I shall see you on September 10. I have fully discussed the situation with my colleagues.'[8]

Macalister's name was not specifically mentioned in that letter as a possibility, which seems odd. One possible explanation is that Cody had just dealt with the Underhill 'Flanders field' controversy, and Kennedy would have known that Macalister had also been involved in the League against War and Fascism, which was, according to the RCMP commissioner, 'used more and more by the Communist Party of Canada as a cloak for their actions.'[9]

MacKenzie favoured appointing Macalister. He knew Macalister well and had also written a very strong letter on his behalf for the Rhodes Scholarship, stating that Macalister was 'probably the best student' he had worked with at the University of Toronto.[10] MacKenzie was also concerned about the optics of appointing another Jewish professor to a very small department. 'You and I know,' he wrote to Finkelman, 'that even in Canada anti-Semitism is a threat that has to be kept in mind and in check.'[11]

It is not exactly clear how the events unfolded over the summer. Kennedy was up at the cottage; Cody was out of the country; and, as historian Jonathan Vance shows in his fine book on Macalister and Frank Pickersgill, *Unlikely Soldiers*, Macalister's tutor at Oxford, C.K. Allen, played a role in the drama. Here is what I think likely took place. Kennedy must have written to Macalister in June to sound him out on a possible appointment. Macalister wrote back on 22 June, saying, 'I have been trying for two months to get into the British Army ... I have an interview in London on July 1 as the final hope. If I am not accepted then I suppose the only thing to do then will be to go home ... I'd like to teach for a while or get some government work.'[12] This reply indicates that a formal offer likely had not yet been made by Kennedy.

Macalister was unsure what to do. He was without funds and was waiting to hear from the British Army. In July, he was interviewed and accepted into what was called the Field Security Police, a body connected with the ultra-secret spy agency, the Special Operations Executive (SOE), although its connection was, of course, not publicly known at the time. At the end of August, he was still waiting to be called up. He wrote to MacKenzie: 'I am still here after three months trying to get into the British Army. They are willing to take me "some time" but don't care if I starve in the meantime. I think if nothing happens by the end of this month, I shall get a passage home.'[13] Jonathan Vance describes what then took place:

> In mid-September 1940, things came to a head. Two letters reached Ken at his Oxford lodgings: one was the expected call-up notice from the Field Security Police; the other was from his University of Toronto professor N.A. MacKenzie, offering him a lectureship in law. With only a few hours to decide, Ken opted to present himself [for duty] at Winchester and be attested into the Field Security Police.

The following day, as Vance records, Macalister received two more messages:

> a cable from MacKenzie, who was about to leave Toronto to take up the presidency of the University of New Brunswick, asking for an immediate response to his offer; and an airmail letter from [Macalister's mother], who claimed that her heart was weak and might not be able to withstand the knowledge that her only son was on active service. She begged him not to enlist, and to return to Canada instead.[14]

Macalister tried to get a release from the army but was unsuccessful. If he left the country, he would be classed as a deserter. On 16 September 1940, Macalister sent a wire to Kennedy stating:[15] 'IN ARMY SINCE YESTERDAY SORRY MANY THANKS – MACALISTER.' The next day, the position was offered to Bora Laskin, who accepted the offer.

Macalister became a SOE agent, and in 1943 he and Frank Pickersgill – a Toronto MA in classics and a brother of the future cabinet minister Jack Pickersgill – were parachuted behind enemy lines in France to act as secret agents. They were captured, tortured, and executed at Buchenwald concentration camp on 14 September 1944, just a year later.

Kennedy wrote to Cody on 19 September 1940: 'Following our conversations, I beg to recommend that Mr. Bora Laskin, B.A. (Law); M.A., LL.B. (Toronto); LL.M. (Cum magna laude, Harvard) be appointed <u>Lecturer in Law</u>, for the session 1940–41, at the salary of $1800 ... I beg to thank you for your kind consideration and I trust that I have not taken up too much of your time.'[16] One wonders what they discussed in their 'conversations.'

Cody was obviously concerned about Laskin's political views because he asked Kennedy to make thorough inquiries into Laskin's background. Kennedy wrote to Cody on 21 September 1940:

> I made all the private inquiries possible before my recommendation went to you, about his political opinions and affiliations ... I have asked Laskin to

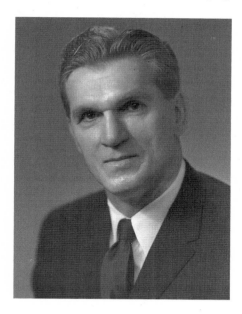

Bora Laskin, around 1960

declare unequivocally that he has no connexion – public or private, expressly or implicitly – with organized or unorganized Communism, Fascism or any subversive movement; and he has <u>categorically made</u> such declaration and repeated it in the presence of a witness. I have told him – as indeed I tell all those whom I recommend to you for appointment – that his duties are to teach law, not to make any public statements – oral or written – on political or public questions.[17]

The Underhill affair cast its long shadow over the hiring of Bora Laskin.

The School of Law

The formal structure of the law school changed during the war years. Law would no longer be part of the Faculty of Arts and Science, but would be a separate division of the university. Perhaps to emphasize its separate existence and to follow the usage of the prestigious American law schools, such as the Harvard Law School, its name was officially changed to the 'School of Law.' In April 1941, the University of Toronto Senate passed a statute:[18] 'That the Faculty of Law of the University of Toronto, at present in existence, be known henceforth as the School of Law of the University of Toronto.' There would be a Council of the School of Law, with the chair appointed by the president. The teaching faculty of the school would 'include the teaching members of the Department of Law in the Faculty of Arts for the time being.' The statute would come into effect on 1 July 1941. Kennedy sent a letter to Cody that month on behalf of himself and his colleagues, 'convey[ing] to you personally and to the Board of Governors our sincerest thanks for the courtesy and co-operation in connection with the School of Law.'[19]

Kennedy would now be known as 'Chairman of the Faculty of the School of Law.' Laskin would become 'Secretary of the Faculty Council of the School of Law.' Laskin had taken over this position from Finkelman and would, as with Finkelman, be heavily relied on by Kennedy, who wrote to Cody in October 1941: 'I could not possibly work without Mr. Laskin's assistance.'[20] Kennedy found, however, that he was having a problem explaining his title outside the university. When he was asked later that year by Attorney General Gordon Conant to serve as a member of a newly established attorney general's Law Revision Committee or to designate another member of the faculty, Kennedy chose Fred Auld, but had to carefully explain how to describe Auld's position on the committee. He wrote the attorney general that he would 'be particularly grateful if the announcement of Professor Auld's appointment appeared in the following form:[21] "Professor F.C. Auld, M.A., B.C.L., Professor of Law in the School of Law, University of Toronto (designated by Dr. W.P.M. Kennedy, Chairman of the Faculty of the School of Law, University of Toronto)."'

No doubt, in part to make his awkward title more manageable, but also to increase Kennedy's status within and outside the university, his title was changed to dean in 1943. Kennedy might have been a dean, but was he the dean of the School of Law or of the Faculty of Law? The status of the law school was not entirely clear, and so, when Caesar Wright became dean in 1949, he obtained clarification from the senate that it was legally a Faculty of Law not a School of Law. Both terms, however, continued to be used interchangeably, and in Kennedy's years as dean, the program was usually referred to as the Honour Law program or course.

As to the newly established committee on law revision, Kennedy had been advocating for a law revision committee for several years, but was not particularly happy with the structure of this one, which was similar to the British lord chancellor's Law Revision Committee. The members were not paid, and they could only study topics that were referred to the committee by the attorney general. Kennedy had wanted a more permanent body, such as the New York Law Revision Committee, which could choose the subjects it examined and would give its members an honorarium. If the Ontario committee had come with an honorarium, one suspects that Kennedy would have accepted membership on the committee.

Kennedy continued to be short of money and continued to have health problems. One sees references in these years to Kennedy's physical health throughout his correspondence, such as in a letter from Cody to Kennedy in January 1941: 'Take care of your health and go to bed as early as you can';[22] or a letter in

June 1942 from the head of the Council of Legal Education in England: 'I am so sorry to learn that you have been ill and in the hands of doctors and dentists';[23] or a letter from Kennedy to Sir Owen Dixon of Australia in March 1943: 'I have been ill with the prevailing influenza';[24] or to Laskin in August 1943: 'I have been going very quietly and taking some care as I have not been my best self all summer.'[25]

Laskin handled many of the routine details of administering the School of Law, particularly over the four to five months each summer that Kennedy spent up north. Here is a typical set of instructions from Kennedy to Laskin in August 1943, similar to the instructions he would earlier have given to Finkelman:

> It will be necessary for someone to be in the School of Law every day from September 9 or so on as I or Finkelman was, since you will have to see inquirers and guide them into law. In fact our first year depends on this. Put up a notice at once headed Interviews with Students and give date and times and room, and state that all students considering the study of law may have an interview.[26]

Laskin obviously did a good job in persuading students to enter the Honour Law course, because the first-year class for 1943–44 was the biggest class on record.[27] There were fifty-one Honour Law students in first year, seven of whom were women, and eleven students from the West Indies. By contrast, in 1941–42 there had been only thirty-four students in first year, of whom four were women.[28]

The war brought a number of personnel changes in the School of Law. Some of those teaching in the program, such as Ken Gray from psychiatry and C.B. Macpherson from political economy, left to join the military or the government. Most students entered the Canadian Officers Training Corps. A law student wrote in the student paper: 'Most of us are taking military training this year – and this means girls too.'[29] In 1942, twenty-one Honour Law students took part in the call for help with the fall harvest.[30]

Kennedy and others ran the various programs at the School of Law. The Industrial Law Research Council continued,[31] with its office at the law school. Kennedy was the president, Finkelman the director of research, and Laskin the assistant director. Similarly, the law school maintained its work with the Workers Education Association.[32] In May 1940, Kennedy was appointed to a joint committee of members of the university and the WEA to act as a liaison between the Department of Extension and the WEA on educational matters.[33]

It was a busy time for Kennedy, administratively. There were letters to write about former students who wanted to be considered for officer training or to join a special unit. In March 1943, for example, Kennedy wrote to a major, saying that Barry Shapiro, then at the law firm Luxenberg and Levinter – and much later a Superior Court judge – who had graduated with high honours in 1938, wished to be an officer in the signals corps. Kennedy wrote: 'His reputation is spotless ... He has an excellently trained mind, with a sense of values and has a good capacity for sizing up a situation.'[34] Moreover a law library had to be run. Kennedy, it seems, approved the books for the library.[35] 'There is a new book on tort which seems to be pretty good,' Finkelman wrote to Kennedy in 1941, 'and I think we ought to have it for the Library – "Treatise on the Law of Torts" by W.L. Prosser.' Further, every year Kennedy continued to edit a volume of the *University of Toronto Law Journal*. And there were the usual committees of the senate and other university bodies on which Kennedy took part.

The reputation of the School of Law kept growing. Former president Falconer sent a letter in February 1942, telling Kennedy that he had 'worked up a Law School in the University which has surpassed any hopes I had of a faculty such as we should have got if "Osgoode" had come into the University.'[36] In 1943, the School of Law changed its curriculum to provide for a five-year program, leading to an LLB at the end of the fifth year. By the year 1947–48, this five-year combined program had over 200 registered students.[37] Still, no credit for any of the University of Toronto law courses was given by Osgoode Hall Law School.

The activities of the Law Club[38] continued – even intensified – through the war years. Towards the end of each year there continued to be a final ban-quet, with important speakers, which added to the reputation of the School of Law, both within and outside of Canada. Dean Roscoe Pound of Harvard was the speaker in 1939 in Burwash Hall at Victoria College, and Professor H.E. Yntema of the University of Michigan spoke at the banquet in the Great Hall, Hart House, in 1940. A Supreme Court of Ontario judge, Fred Barlow, sent a note to Kennedy complimenting him on his remarks at that banquet and asked for a copy of his speech. Kennedy's reply is instructive on how he pre-pared his remarks for such occasions: 'As regards my address it was practically extempore. I had a few ideas in my head and I never prepare a speech in detail or deliver it from notes.'[39] This description must be accurate, because I rarely saw in any files I examined – unlike in the Caesar Wright files – written notes for such informal talks. Formal lectures, such as the Cornell lectures, would, however, be written in advance. A number of his students adopted Kennedy's technique. I know that Charles Dubin, with whom I articled, did.

Although the Law Club was run by the students, all the correspondence – and there were usually more than a dozen letters for each banquet speaker – was handled by Kennedy. As in previous years, the Law Club had other speakers to address the students during the year. In the first term of 1943, for example, talks were given by the attorney general of Ontario, Leslie Blackwell, defence lawyer G. Arthur Martin, and Jacob Finkelman. The invitations would appear to have been extended directly by the students as there is no correspondence relating to them in the law school files.

The British High Commissioner, Sir Gerald Campbell, was to be the banquet speaker in 1941, but his appearance had to be cancelled because he had just been made the ambassador to the United States. Kennedy had heard rumours of the appointment and wrote: 'I would still hope that you could run up [from Washington] for the meeting.'[40] Campbell replied: 'I should not dare to make any such commitment since I have no idea what my duties will demand for me.'[41] Kennedy then persuaded W.F. Chipman, a Montreal lawyer who taught civil law at McGill, to fill in as the speaker.

The following year, Harvard law professor Samuel Williston, the contracts scholar, agreed to come, even though, Williston wrote, 'I have a very low opinion of myself as an occasional speaker.'[42] The United States then entered the war, and Kennedy wrote to Williston: 'Strange things have happened since you promised to come to us, and now we shall welcome you as a brother in arms in this terrific struggle.'[43] Kennedy later wrote: 'You have forged another link between us and Harvard.'[44] Williston replied that he was telling all his colleagues of the 'good work that you are doing ... and the fine spirit of aiming at the best that I found in your Faculty.'[45] In 1943, Sir Owen Dixon, an important Australian jurist who was at the time the Australian ambassador to the United States, was invited to give the address. Dixon replied: 'I look forward with great pleasure to meeting you. It is hardly necessary to tell you how familiar your name is to lawyers in Australia.'[46] The event was a great success. In a letter of thanks, Kennedy remarked – and one believes it was reciprocated: 'We have laid the foundations of a long and lasting friendship.'[47] In 1944, the New Zealand ambassador to the United States, Walter Nash, who was charged with implementing the New Zealand Social Security Plan, gave the address, and in 1945 the American ambassador to Canada, Ray Atherton, was the speaker at the Royal York Hotel. Links with these speakers continued to enhance the university's international reputation.

Kennedy had some difficulty securing a speaker for the 1946 banquet. He first invited the new president of the university, Sidney Smith, who declined because of overwork, stating: 'I have been hardly able to think.' Kennedy had suggested he talk about legal education, but Smith said that even if he were able to come, 'I have in mind that I should not deal in public with legal education. Many of the sentences that I would invoke would be scrutinized by those whose interests are inimical to the development that you and I have close to heart.'[48] The head of the Wartime Prices and Trade Board, banker Donald Gordon, with whom Kennedy's wife, Pauline, had been working during the war, was next asked, but declined because of his work.[49] For similar reasons, criminal lawyer and later chief justice of Canada, John Cartwright, also declined.[50] Finally, the chief justice of Ontario, R.S. Robertson, who had become the honorary president of the Law Club after Newton Rowell died, filled in as the speaker. But, in the end, illness prevented him from coming, and his colleague Justice Robert Laidlaw spoke.[51]

The students started a law review in the academic year 1941–42. Kennedy had to obtain Cody's approval. Kennedy wrote: 'With your permission the students of the School of Law wish to issue, two or three times a session, a small mimeographed pamphlet, domestic to the School of Law, called the School of Law Review.'[52] Cody approved. The following year the review was printed, rather than mimeographed. It contained some serious articles, some humorous pieces, and mostly human-interest stories centred on the law school. Volume 1 of the printed version[53] started with an article by Charles F. Scott – later a senior partner with Gowlings in Ottawa – on social security, 'The [British] Beveridge Plan in Canada.' There was also a humorous article in that issue by Sandford World, whose wit later became well known to the Toronto legal community. Here are World's comments on Laskin: 'We like Mr. Laskin – in fact, there is little in life more enjoyable than baskin' in the rays of Laskin; but we wish he would stop giving us so many cases.'[54] Volume 2, to pick another year,[55] has a lead article by Professor Larry MacKenzie on the 'Wartime Information Board' and an article on Professor Auld by a West Indian student, Gloria Carpenter, who will be discussed later. She writes: 'All in all, Mr. Auld is the most approachable of a very approachable staff; a man of quiet manner but of definite opinions, a delightful conversationalist, and a charming gentleman, with a delightful sense of humour.'[56] The journal, renamed the *Faculty of Law Review*, became a serious academic law journal in 1949. It is today Canada's oldest student-edited law review and, according to its website, 'it is also the only journal of its kind in Canada edited entirely by students and devoted solely to contributions from students.'[57]

The Students

The most visible change in the School of Law student body during the war was the number of black students from the West Indies. Joan Hodgson, who entered first year in 1942–43, recalled in an oral interview[58] coming into her first class in late September and discovering that about one-third of the class of about twenty-five students were black. The only black persons she had previously met, she said, were train porters. She went on: 'I had a father who treated everyone with great respect, and the train porters were treated that way. So I walked in, and I thought, "well, that's interesting," and we all became great friends.'

Because of the war, West Indian students, who would normally have done their legal training in England, could not, without considerable danger, go there. Two West Indian students entered the first-year Honour Law program for the 1941–42 academic year: Charles Bourne, who was white, from Barbados; and Gloria Carpenter, who was black, from Jamaica. Bourne had already

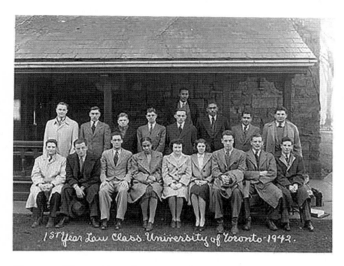

First-year Honour Law class, 1942. The women in the first row are,
from left to right, Eugenia Charles, Thelma Kerr Thompson, and
Joan Morris Hodgson

been accepted at an Oxford college but wrote to Kennedy saying that he could not go over owing to the war.[59] He had an excellent high school record from a college in Barbados. 'We must stretch every point to take in this man,'[60] Kennedy wrote to Finkelman from the cottage. The university registrar allowed Bourne to enter the first year, even though he did not have the required third language, apparently a requirement for entry. Bourne had asked for an estimate of the cost of attending, and Finkelman replied: 'The fees for the first year would amount to approximately Two Hundred Dollars and I believe that you could live quite comfortably in Toronto for about Four Hundred Dollars for the school year. Some students have been able to live on less. Of course this does not take into account the cost of clothes.'[61] It would, at the time, take four years for an Honours BA and two more years for an LLB. A few years later, one could complete both degrees in five years.

Bourne was at the time articling with a firm of solicitors in Barbados.[62] He never returned to Barbados to practise law. He had an excellent record at the School of Law – standing first in all four years and serving as the president of the Law Club and chief justice of the moot court – and Kennedy encouraged him to do graduate work in England at Cambridge, where after one year he received an LLM. He then accepted an appointment to teach in Saskatchewan, later moving to the University of British Columbia where he had a stellar career in international law. Along the way, he received an earned doctorate in 1970 from the University of Toronto School of Law. An article about Bourne in the *Canadian Yearbook of International Law* states that Bourne 'has provided intellectual and moral leadership in the teaching and practice of international law in Canada and changed perceptions inside and outside the country on the future development of the international law of water resources.'[63]

Gloria Carpenter came to the law school from Jamaica. Her qualifications to enter the Honours BA course were 'better than our honour matric,'[64] Finkelman wrote to Kennedy. She was the first woman of colour to graduate from the University of Toronto School of Law. She had good marks and was the editor of the 1944–45 edition of the student law review, where she featured an article by Norman Manley, who would become the first prime minister of Jamaica, on 'The New Constitution of Jamaica.'[65] After graduation she attended Girton College, Cambridge, and was awarded a first class in her LLB in 1946. Prior to then, female students graduating from Cambridge only received a diploma – unlike at Oxford where degrees were first granted to women in 1921. Some Cambridge websites say that she was 'probably the first black woman at the University of Cambridge.'[66] She returned to the West Indies with her husband and was a part-time lecturer in the Faculty of Social Sciences at the new University of the West Indies in Jamaica, writing about family law and various social issues. She also 'played an integral role in the establishment in 1973 of the Faculty of Law at the University of [the] West Indies,'[67] as will be discussed later.

Both Bourne and Carpenter became students of the English Middle Temple at the end of their first year in Toronto, without actually going to London. Kennedy had worked out an arrangement with the Council of Legal Education in England to permit students studying at the University of Toronto to qualify for part of their English law studies and for other students to write English bar exams in Toronto. The following year, 1942–43, there were more students from the West Indies, encouraged to attend by a memorandum sent by Kennedy to all the attorneys-general in the West Indies and advertisements placed in various newspapers in the West Indies.[68]

Gilbert Kennedy taught that second class and recalls his father's interest in students from the West Indies: 'We had many of these students up to the house. Dad liked to get them up to the house, get them talking. They were older, more mature; they were students who wanted to become barristers as opposed to solicitors.'[69] A West Indian student, Eric C. Tomlinson, said in a letter to the editor in the first printed issue of the *School of Law Review*: 'The West Indian Law Students are ... here because the University of Toronto is at present a centre for the English Bar Examinations and those using the opportunity are, and will ever be grateful to the individuals who made it possible, and still more grateful for the opportunity to study law under such capable guidance and in such cheerful and congenial an atmosphere.'[70] Laskin wrote to Kennedy in the summer of 1943: 'I gather from remarks dropped by some of our present West Indian students that they have given us very good publicity. From what I can learn, they all enjoyed their year with us.'[71] Kennedy wrote back: 'I am glad that B.W.I. students are responding. I think we shall not lose that connection after the war.'[72] As it turned out, it was more or less lost after the war.

The students from the West Indies had a major impact on the future of the West Indies.[73] Eugenia Charles became the prime minister of Dominica. Noor Hassanali, an Indo-Trinidadian, who left after first year to continue his studies in England, became the president of Trinidad and Tobago. Eugene Dupuch, who received his LLB in 1947, became a 'famed politician and lawyer' and had one of the three law schools in the British West Indies named after him.[74] He had been a member of Parliament from Crooked Island in the Bahamas. Gilbert Kennedy recalls that Dupuch 'sent us – because he was in regular correspondence with us – he sent us a newspaper with the headline "Dupuch Wins Crooked Island Election."'[75] A number of graduates later became judges: Louis Fox became a member of the Jamaica Court of Appeal; and Telford Georges, a gold medalist who had been president of the Law Club, became chief judge of three Commonwealth countries in turn, Tanzania, Zimbabwe, and the Bahamas.

The student body at the School of Law during the war years was relatively diverse. In addition to the West Indies students, there were a number of Chinese students from mainland China, who came to do master's degrees in law. Mr. Du-pei Han spent two years at the law school and received his MA in law on the topic 'Substance and Procedure in Anglo-American Conflict of Laws.'[76] Another student from China, Wen-han Chin, as mentioned in an earlier chapter, received an LLM the following year.[77] Kennedy had a particular interest in Chinese studies at the University of Toronto, supported the establishment of the university's School of Chinese Studies, and was a member of the senate's Committee on Chinese Studies.

A Japanese Canadian, George Tamaki, received an LLM in 1945, writing a thesis on nationality under Bora Laskin's supervision.[78] Although born in Canada and a graduate of the University of British Columbia, he had been removed from the West Coast because of the war – he was not interned – and graduated with a law degree at the top of his class from Dalhousie University. He applied to do an LLM at the University of Toronto, but the board's policy in 1942 was not to accept Japanese students. The policy changed the following year, and Kennedy accepted Tamaki as a graduate student, writing to a professor at Dalhousie: 'We shall do our best for T., and I shall take a personal interest in him.' There were two conditions, imposed by the board of governors: that Tamaki be a British subject, which he was, being born in Canada; and that he was 'not under R.C.M.P. suspicion,'[79] which he wasn't. Tamaki became one of Canada's leading tax practitioners and ended up as a partner in Stikeman Elliott.

There were other graduate students at the School of Law in those years. They included Morris Shumiatcher, a law graduate from the University of Alberta, and Eugene LaBrie, who is discussed in a later chapter. Shumiatcher came as the first Newton Rowell Fellow, a three-year scholarship worth $500 a year, established in 1942 after the death of Chief Justice Rowell 'for graduate legal studies in the School of Law.'[80] The public documents say that it was given 'by an anonymous donor,' but the correspondence makes it clear that it was given by Mr. J.E. Atkinson, the president of the *Toronto Daily Star*.[81] Shumiatcher first completed an LLM and then started a doctoral dissertation on 'The Farmer's Creditors Arrangement Act: A Study in Canadian Administrative Law.'[82] The degree was granted in 1945, having been interrupted by Shumiatcher's military service. He went on to be a leading counsel in Saskatchewan. As senior legal counsel in Tommy Douglas's provincial government, he was responsible for drafting the 1947 Saskatchewan Bill of Rights, the first such document in the British Commonwealth.

Kennedy wanted to further develop the graduate program. In December 1945, he wrote to Dean George Curtis of the UBC Law School, saying: 'You will be glad to know that we have become a real centre for [graduate] work in Canada and that we have already graduated in these degrees several students. At present we have ten or twelve of them. Your school would, of course, come under our regulations in this respect, and we shall be glad to welcome your graduates for post-graduate work here.'[83]

'Enemy Aliens'

Another group of students who attended the University of Toronto because of the war were persons who had been sent from England to Canada as 'enemy aliens.'[84] These 'accidental immigrants' had been rounded up after the start of the war and interned in England. Over 2,500 men were sent to internment camps in Canada. For the year 1942–43, a group of sixteen internees and two Japanese Canadians from western Canada wanted to study at a Canadian university. Cody was enthusiastically in favour of admitting them, but the board of governors was opposed. The board finally backed down in late 1942, after the minister of defence gave a way out by stating that the released internees could take military training. A large number of these students attended the University of Toronto and later had extraordinary careers. One of them, Walter Kohn, won a Nobel Prize in chemistry; another was the philosopher and student of the Holocaust Emil Fackenheim; still another was Josef Kates, who helped build Canada's first electronic computer.

The School of Law took in at least three of these students who later had important careers. One was Carl Morawetz, who became 'the undisputed dean of the bankruptcy bar in Ontario, perhaps in Canada.'[85] His son, Geoffrey

Carl Morawetz, shortly after arriving
in Canada as an 'enemy alien'

Morawetz, now chief justice of the Superior Court of Ontario, specializing in bankruptcy and commercial disputes, remembers his father 'fondly speaking' of Dean Kennedy.[86] His father had received his law degree from the University of Vienna, left Austria for England because he was Jewish, and was admitted by Kennedy into the LLB program for the academic year 1942–43, graduating in late 1943. In an issue of the student law review, he compared studying law in Vienna and in Canada: 'I feel quite certain that the most excellent student at Vienna did not receive as much co-operation or "special tuition" as does a student here. It is really amazing to find members of the staff here so unselfishly devoting precious time to help an interested student.'[87]

The Law Society of Upper Canada would not allow Morawetz to article because he was still considered an enemy alien. Kennedy and Professor Auld, however, devised a scheme to allow him to article in Prince Edward Island (PEI), where Auld had grown up and still maintained a close connection. The Law Society of Prince Edward Island cooperated enthusiastically,[88] arranging articles in late 1944, while permitting Morawetz to continue with his legal studies in Toronto. Morawetz completed an LLM and a DJur degree at the University of Toronto, and was admitted to the Prince Edward Island Bar. He was accompanied at the ceremony by Auld, who was already a member of the PEI Bar. Morawetz addressed the bar of the province at the opening of the court on the proposed new Income Tax Act.

Another student was Eric Koch, from Frankfurt, Germany, who came with his family to England as a refugee in 1935 and studied at Cranbrook School in Kent. 'I went to Cambridge in the fall of 1937 [to study law],' he wrote in 2016, 'and was interned on May 12, 1940, three weeks before my final exams. The University gave students in my situation their degrees – on the basis of an *aegrotat*.'[89] The internment took place just after the Nazis invaded the Low Countries. Koch graduated from the University of Toronto with an LLB in 1943. Like Morawetz, he wrote an article for the student paper, comparing Cambridge and Toronto, stating: 'At Cambridge, the relationship between professors and students is not as close as here.'[90] In a memoir,[91] he stated that he would have gone on to attend Osgoode Hall Law School and to article to get his call to the bar, but Osgoode was not open to 'enemy aliens.' So, like Laskin and others had done before him, he earned a living by spending a year and a half summarizing legal decisions for Auld's *Canadian Abridgment* at, he recalls, 50 cents a case – no matter how complex the case was. In 1944 he joined the Canadian Broadcasting Corporation (CBC) – at first in 'The Voice of Canada,' broadcasting to Germany. He had been in the Canadian Officers' Training Corps while a student and later tried to join the Canadian military, but was turned down because of his feet. He stayed as a producer at the CBC, developing a large number of radio and television programs. He wrote over ten books. (I attended the launch for his second last book in 2016.) He lived in a retirement home on Avenue Road and died in 2018 at the age of ninety-eight.[92]

Peter and Ivy

A third 'enemy alien' who studied at the School of Law in those years was Peter Fuld. His story combined with the story of a West Indies student, Ivy Lawrence, could be the subject of a movie or a television series.[93] Fuld was the son of a wealthy Jewish telephone manufacturer in Frankfurt, Germany, who died in 1932 when Fuld was eleven years old. He lived with his non-Jewish mother in Frankfurt and, because he was half-Jewish, left Germany for England in 1939. His mother remained in Germany. His father's property was confiscated by the Nazis. Peter was interned in England as an enemy alien and sent to Canada, where the Birks family of Montreal (the jewellers) became involved in his case and arranged for him to attend the University of Toronto. Fuld entered the Sociology and Philosophy (Soc. and Phil.) Honour course in September 1941, but switched to the second year of the School of Law course in September 1942.

Ivy Lawrence was also entering the second year of the law program that year. She was born in Montreal of Trinidadian parents and had graduated with a BA

Peter Fuld and Ivy Lawrence, who fell in love while
students in the Honour Law Program

from McGill, where she was the president of the Women's Debating Union and
the first woman to be awarded the McGill Debating Key. She was given a year's
credit and a scholarship by the School of Law. Her law school classmate Joan
Hodgson described Ivy as 'one of the most beautiful women I have known.'[94]

Peter and Ivy fell in love. Joan Hodgson remembers seeing them walking
through the campus hand in hand. Both Peter and Ivy graduated with LLBs
from Toronto in 1945 and went to England to see Peter's mother, who had
moved to London. Mrs. Fuld refused to give her consent to the marriage and
threatened to kill herself if they got married. They continued to see each other
and continued to look at possible houses to live in after they got married.

They never married. Each married someone else – in each case there were
several marriages. Ivy was called to the bar in England in 1947 and went to
Trinidad in 1948, where she was involved in adult education. In the meantime,
Peter had regained his father's manufacturing business in Germany and became
very wealthy. In 1960, he was diagnosed with brain cancer and died in Frankfurt in 1962 at age forty-one, leaving an estate of about six million pounds. Ivy
had married a diplomat in 1959 and was living in Jamaica.

Peter Fuld's will left his mother one-third of the residuary estate, and Ivy was
to receive 15 per cent of the remaining two-thirds. The will and various codicils
to the will were contested by Fuld's mother and others. There was a ninety-one
day trial in London in 1965 before Justice Leslie Scarman, later Lord Scarman,
involving nineteen trial lawyers, which set a record for the longest and costli-
est trial over an estate up to then in British history. The legal issue for Scarman was where Fuld was domiciled, a legal term about where his true ultimate

intended home was. This detail would affect the law that was to be applied to determining the validity of the will. Scarman concluded his domicile was Germany. Scarman, known as one of England's finest judges who would become the first chair of the English Law Commission, went into the facts in some detail. For example, the fact that Peter and Ivy fell in love was not drawn by me from some tabloid newspaper, but from Scarman himself, who wrote: 'He fell in love with Ivy Maynier (then Ivy Lawrence), whom he first met as a fellow-student in October, 1942; they were in love by the spring of 1943.'[95] At another point, he found as a fact that as late as 1950 they were still thinking of getting married, stating: 'In 1950 Ivy Maynier visited Europe. She went on a holiday in Germany with Peter ... At this time he was thinking seriously of marrying Ivy, and they went house-hunting in London.'[96] But his mother continued to object.

The will was upheld by Scarman.[97] It was worth, in Scarman's estimation, 'some £6 million.' That sum would be worth over 100 million pounds today. Ivy's share would therefore be, in today's value, over ten million pounds. The will specified that Ivy was to use two-thirds of her share 'to the furtherance of the teaching of law in the West Indies.'[98] The establishment of the Norman Manley School of Law in Jamaica in 1973 was the direct result of this bequest. Ivy joined the administrative staff of the university.

The story does not end there. Ivy died in 1999 and left $600,000 to the Faculty of Law at the University of Toronto to be 'awarded to students from underrepresented minority groups who demonstrate financial need.' This sum was matched by the university to create a $1.2 million endowment for the Ivy Maynier Bursary.[99]

20

The Cottage

In 1940, Kennedy purchased a large block of land – 150 acres – on the Magnetawan River, near the picturesque town of Kearney, north of Huntsville and just west of Algonquin Park. It became a significant part of his life in the 1940s and 50s. Every summer, the Kennedy family – like many other University of Toronto families – escaped the summer heat by heading north.

It may seem unusual to devote a whole chapter to 'the cottage' in a biography, but it was a very important part of Kennedy's life. He usually went up to the cottage in mid-May and did not return until mid-September. Perhaps a third of his life in Canada was spent at a cottage. It also demonstrates his work ethic – as a gardener, which did not differ in effort and devotion from his activities as a scholar.

Northern Ontario was the principal destination for the University of Toronto professoriate. As we saw in an earlier chapter,[1] Caesar Wright had a cottage in Parry Sound and Sidney Smith a cottage in Muskoka. There was – and still is – a large contingent of University of Toronto families at the 1,600 acre Madawaska Club at Go Home Bay on Georgian Bay, established around the turn of the last century and composed mainly of scientists. The original intention had been to establish the club in Algonquin Park on the Madawaska River – hence the name – but that did not work out because the logging companies operating in the park opposed it. In 1898, faculty members established the club and, with government support, a research station at Go Home Bay.[2]

In his early years at the university, Kennedy and his first wife had spent at least one summer in Quebec, on the north shore of the St. Lawrence River, downriver from Quebec City. Perhaps George Wrong, with whom he was friendly in those years and who had a summer residence at the English-speaking enclave of Murray Bay, had encouraged him to summer in Quebec.

In later years, the Kennedys had rented a cottage on Lake Muskoka. Their eldest child, Gilbert, was born in Muskoka in the summer of 1917. W.P.M. returned to Lake Muskoka in the summer of 1919 – after his first wife died – with his two children, Gilbert and Beatrice. Later, he and Pauline and their

W.P.M. and Pauline Kennedy, sitting on the
running board of their car, 1934

growing family continued to spend their summers in Muskoka, Haliburton, or
Lake Huron, apart from the summer of 1926, when Kennedy returned to the
United Kingdom, and 1927, which they spent on Kingsmere Lake in the Gatin-
eaus, near Prime Minister Mackenzie King's summer residence, while Kennedy
worked in Ottawa. The family later rented a cottage on Mary Lake and then on
Otter Lake in Muskoka, south of Huntsville. Kennedy's son Frere recalls that
there was a nine-hole golf course at Otter Lake and that his father was a good
golfer. He also recalls that they had a cat at Otter Lake, but did not have cats or
dogs at any other cottage or at home.[3]

According to Frere, Kennedy heard about a cottage for sale near the small
town of Kearney, just west of Algonquin Park. Kennedy learned about the cottage from the owner's son, who worked in the superintendent's office at the
university. He and Pauline purchased the property as joint tenants for $2,500 –
consisting of $1,000 cash and a mortgage of $1,500. The mortgage was at 5
per cent and required yearly payments of $250. The substantial payment he
received in the late 1930s from his work on the Rowell-Sirois Report no doubt
made such a purchase feasible.

The property consisted of about 150 acres of forest with almost a mile of
shoreline on both the Magnetawan River and Beaver Lake, a mile-wide circular-
shaped widening of the river.[4] As stated earlier, this property is now owned by
my wife and me, having been purchased from Frere Kennedy in 1983.

Kennedy in front of the Narrow Waters gate

Frere kept a diary, which we found in one of the trunks at the cottage, of events at the property between 1940 and 1945.[5] The first three entries are as follows:

1940

May 11 – Dad, Mother, Mr. Finkelman and Frere drive up to Kearney and see the place for the first time, are shown about by old Mr. Robert Shortreed, and drive home that afternoon.

May 23 – Dad, Mother, and Gilbert make first official visit to "Narrow Waters"; it rains most of the time, dishwashing and housecleaning are in vogue, and car gets up the hill with difficulty and Sam's help.

May 30 – The three pioneers depart, having ordered the lumber for the Children's Cottage.

Jacob Finkelman had come up, according to Frere's later recollection, to draft the offer of purchase and sale. Sam was the handyman. Robert Shortreed's decision to sell the property may have been because his wife was ill at the time. She died in December 1940. Other members of the Shortreed family had four contiguous cottages on a much larger lake, Sand Lake, that fed into Beaver Lake and so had no need for the cottage.[6]

Kennedy named the property 'Narrow Waters,' after a sixteenth-century castle on a river in Northern Ireland. Frere told me that his father's very first memory in his life was of this castle. We still have the Narrow Waters sign used by the Kennedys, and we often refer to the property as Narrow Waters. In 1881, the property had originally been granted by the Crown without charge to the Sims family, who developed the land as a farm.[7] A section of the land adjoining the concession road was cleared. Several large stone cairns are still standing a few hundred yards from the concession road. There is nothing to indicate where the farmhouse was located on the property. It was likely close to the public road. There are the remains of a large shed near one of the cairns, which was likely used by the Sims family for the storage of crops.

As with many persons who came to farm in the area, the Sims family found that the financial reward for their back-breaking effort was disappointing. The rock-laden soil was of poor quality. The timber on the property would have provided a decent income, but, by the turn of the century, most of the trees of commercial value had been removed, floated downriver to Kearney in the spring or transported by horses over the ice in the winter. Understandably, the Sims family left for a free land grant in the west just after the turn of the century. Mr. Sims's son returned to visit the property one summer about forty years later. The Kennedys commemorated that visit with a carved inscription on a very large shelf fungus – over 14 inches (36 centimetres) wide – they had found on a dead tree on the property. The inscriptions include the signatures of W.P.M. and Pauline and their four children. The fungus is now prominently displayed in the cottage, as it was in Kennedy's time. The carved inscription, dated 11 September 1944, reads: 'Mr. Albert Sims, son of the pioneer of our property, visits our place for the first time since he left with his father for the West in 1901.' The fungus is decorated with pictures of a bear, a person paddling a canoe, and a vegetable garden, with individual pictures of tomatoes, a cabbage, and a cucumber. According to Frere, his father was an 'exceptionally good' canoeist and, as we will see further on, was devoted to his vegetable and flower gardens.

The property had been purchased before the Great War by the Shortreeds, a family from Guelph, Ontario, who used it as a summer cottage. Some of the furnishings – still in the cottage – came from Guelph. There is, for example, an upright piano in the cottage manufactured by Bell Pianos of Guelph. None of the Kennedys played the piano. We have never had it tuned, but it still sounds in tune. A former neighbour of ours in Kearney, the composer John Weinzweig, visited the cottage a number of years ago, played the piano, and commented that it was still in surprisingly good shape. Weinzweig was, however, known for his atonal compositions.

Sometime before the First World War, the Shortreeds built a wooden cottage, about 20 by 30 feet (6 by 9 metres) in size and 60 feet (18 metres) from the lake. A road allowance of 60 feet (18 metres) prevented it from being built any closer. There is a steep hill down to the cottage from a high ridge running

The main cabin, the children's sleeping cabin, and the barn during
Kennedy's years at the cottage

the length of the property, and the Shortreeds and Kennedys would have had
some difficulty getting their cars up and down that hill. The Shortreeds had also
built the frame for a small canvas-covered sleeping cabin. One of the Kennedys'
first tasks after purchasing the property was to order wood to turn that frame
into a small sleeping cabin for their four children. The Shortreeds had also built
another, but smaller, cottage about 500 feet (152 metres) north of the main cottage, where W.P.M. and Pauline slept. They also built a boat house, which is no
longer standing but was there in Kennedy's time, as well as a storage structure
built at the bottom of the road, which we call the 'barn' but the Kennedys called
the 'OPM.' I was puzzled when I read the initials OPM in the diaries, but Frere
later explained that the acronym stood for 'office of production management,'
an office created by President Franklin Roosevelt. This term was apt for the
Kennedy operations, as we will see.

The probable reason that the Shortreeds had purchased the land in this area
was because Mr. Shortreed's brother was the owner and operator of a timber
mill in Kearney. He had purchased the mill in 1908 and owned it until the 1930s,
when it was sold. It was still operating in the 1960s. The wood for the cottage –
still in excellent condition over 100 years later – would likely have come from
that mill. Journalist Roy MacGregor, who has researched the Shortreed Lumber
Company for his book on Tom Thompson, states that the company dealt in

'various hardwoods, pine, hemlock, tan bark for the Huntsville tannery, cedar shingles, posts and poles and pulpwood.'[8]

In earlier years, Kearney had been an important centre for the lumber trade. There was a large supply of white pine and other species in the surrounding forests. The town had several factories, milling the lumber and manufacturing furniture. As a result, there was a large collection of lumbermen, who cut the trees, brought them to the mills, squared the logs, and sent them by rail to Ottawa. The logs were then floated down the Ottawa River to Montreal and shipped to the eastern United States and Europe. The white pines on the property would probably have been cut in the 1890s. The early logging was restricted for economic reasons to the stands of massive white pine and later the hemlocks, whose bark was used for leather tanning.[9] There are now only two old growth white pines on the property, probably not cut because they were in awkward locations and were not as straight as was required.

Kearney was also an important location because a railway had been constructed by lumber baron J.R. Booth in the 1890s, running from Georgian Bay to the Ottawa River and cutting through Algonquin Park.[10] Square-cut logs and other wood products could now be shipped by rail to Georgian Bay to the west and to Ottawa to the east. Logging was big business and the town was thriving.[11] The railway tracks were located about half a mile from the Kennedy property. Frere says that he cannot recall hearing the train whistle at the cottage. Freight and passenger trains operated through Kearney during Kennedy's time, but later ceased operating, and the rails were removed in the late 1950s.

The number of physically able workers in Kearney was so large that the town was able to field strong baseball teams. In 1903, 1904, and 1905, the relatively small town of Kearney – indeed it was not large enough to officially be called a town until 1908 – won the provincial men's baseball championship.[12]

The railway would also handle passenger traffic, and the Kennedys' visitors and family members usually came by train. There was at least one train in each direction every day – and so one could take the Grand Trunk train from Toronto to the town of Scotia Junction, north of Huntsville, and then transfer to the Booth Railway, whose trains ran in an east-west direction through Scotia Junction and Kearney. Persons could also take the Grand Trunk train from Toronto to the nearby town of Emsdale and be picked up there.

The Kennedys would normally drive to the cottage. One of their first cars was a 1932 Chrysler 7, which they drove from Toronto, up Highway 11, through the centre of the towns of Barrie, Orillia, Gravenhurst, Bracebridge, and Huntsville, and then along the Old Muskoka Road north to Emsdale, often stopping for dinner at a resort called Green Acres between the small towns of Scotia and Emsdale. The road from Emsdale to Kearney was not paved until 1954. Today, Highway 11 bypasses all these towns. W.P.M. Kennedy was never the driver. He tried, but, according to Frere, never learned to drive. Pauline or one of the children would be the drivers. According to Frere, W.P.M. also did not manage the household funds. He left that to Pauline.

Winnie Trainor, the fiancée of Tom Thompson, the artist associated with what was later known as the Group of Seven, worked in the office of the Shortreed lumber mill.[13] Did she ever visit the Shortreed cottage? Perhaps. Did Tom Thompson, who died – mysteriously – in 1917? Perhaps not, because Winnie took the office position in Kearney after her fiancé was found dead in Canoe Lake. But her father, a lumberman, was likely friendly with the Shortreeds. Winnie and her family summered at their cottage on Canoe Lake, as did Tom Thompson. Both would have gone through Kearney by train on many occasions on their way to and from the park. I'd like to believe that Tom Thompson visited Narrow Waters. Unfortunately, we have not discovered a Tom Thompson sketch hidden under the old cottage.

Kennedy was remembered as a character by some of the older townsfolk, who had known him and with whom I spoke after we purchased the property in 1983. He certainly looked like an interesting character, judging by the picture we have of him at Narrow Waters, standing beside the bean stalks, with rubber boots, smoking his pipe. That appears to be Pauline behind him. The picture was taken by David Vanek, a faculty member in the 1940s, when he first visited Narrow Waters. Frere states that Kennedy always had a pipe and always smoked Macdonald's Cut Brier tobacco. When he went to England in the summer of 1926, Pauline mailed the tobacco to him from Canada. Kennedy was always clean shaven. Frere tells me that every morning at Narrow Waters he, Frere, would carry a pot of hot water up to Kennedy and Pauline's cottage to allow W.P.M. to shave before coming down to the main cabin.

The then mayor of the town, Harold Shaw, remembered Kennedy well; as did trapper, guide, and writer Ralph Bice, who was the mayor when Kennedy first came to the cottage; and as did Eric Sheehan, who replaced the cottage roof for Kennedy. Many years later, Eric's son, Vincent Sheehan, would replace that roof for the Friedland family. Both father and son were well-known trappers in the Kearney area. W.P.M., according to Frere, did not hunt or trap, although he and Pauline kept a gun at the cottage to control rodents and animals that interfered with their gardening. There were and still are several deer antlers on the wall of the old cottage, but whether they were put up by the Shortreeds or by the Kennedys is not known.

The documents left in the cottage show that for many years a Sam Wilton assisted the Kennedys in running the cottage. The Kennedys did not have electricity and so were required to have ice cut from the lake each winter and stored in the icehouse. Sam helped with that task. The storage structure or barn, as we call it, still contains equipment used for cutting ice, such as a one-handle large saw and heavy tongs for lifting ice. There were several iceboxes in the cottage when we bought it.

W.P.M. Kennedy at the cottage in 1947; photo taken by David Vanek

Beaver Lake was certainly a good lake for fishing and, again, according to Frere, W.P.M. would sometimes try his hand, as had the Shortreeds. We found a canvas-covered fly-fishing basket in the cottage. We also discovered on an inside wall several pencil-drawn outlines of fish. One showed a fish with the notation: '17 ½ inches 2 ⅛ lbs landed by Mrs. R. Shortreed May 27, 1918.' There are two other entries on the wall, indicating a fish of 4 pounds (1.8 kilograms) caught in 1924 and a trout caught in 1925.

Although the Kennedys did not have electricity, they had – at least in later years – propane tanks for cooking, for refrigeration, and for lights. And they had a battery-operated short-wave radio, which would provide them with the wartime news. The Kennedys had a well for drinking water on the upper part of the property that used gravity flow down to the cottage. They also had, at some later point, a gas pump that could draw water from the lake to a tank on the hill that could be used for washing and showering. They did not have indoor plumbing, however. There were two outhouses on the property, which we continued to use until we installed electricity and a septic system in the early 1990s.

They also did not have a telephone. The Kennedys would have to go into town to use the phone and to pick up mail. The town of Kearney had several general stores in those days, and the Kennedy family would get their provisions there. They would get their milk from a working farm, the O'Connor farm, adjoining the property, or from another farm, the Reid farm, on the far side of Beaver Lake. The red-roofed barn from the latter farm is still standing, but the property is now a summer residence.

After the cutting of the tall pines by the end of the century, maples took over most of the property. Frere cannot recall the family producing maple syrup, but someone – perhaps it was the Shortreeds – tapped the mature trees to make maple syrup. Some of the equipment used for producing maple syrup was left in the cottage.

About ten acres of land adjacent to the public road that the Sims family had used for farming were replanted by the Kennedys in the early 1940s with small red and Scotch pine saplings. The government supplied the saplings free of charge, and the Kennedys carefully planted them in rows.[14] The Kennedy pine forest, now part of a forest management agreement with the province, is over seventy-five years old.

The Kennedys constructed a small sleeping cabin for the four Kennedy children beside the main cottage. The main cottage was comprised of one large room and a front porch the width of the building. On the back of the main cottage, the Kennedys built a kitchen, with a wood burning stove, and a guest room.

Almost twenty years ago, we added a winterized structure, about the same size as the main cottage, and integrated it, structurally and aesthetically, with the old cottage, which we left untouched, except to remove the kitchen and the guest bedroom. Frere, Shelagh, and Beatrice visited the cottage in 2002 and were pleased with what we had done to match the old and the new cottages.

As part of the war effort, the Kennedys planted a large 'victory garden' on about two acres of land that the Sims had cleared many years earlier and also constructed a concrete cold cellar in the hill behind the main cottage to store the produce. Frere well remembered planting the pine saplings, tending the vegetables, and building the root cellar.

During the war years, Frere kept a record of what they did each day at the cottage. His handwritten notes were typed by him in 1945 in his spare time while in the army, camped at Ipperwash, Ontario. The typed document of over thirty pages shows the progress of the work on the cottage and the victory garden, and of the war. Here is a sampling of the almost daily entries:

1940

June 4 – Dad, Mother, Gilbert, Shelagh and Frere arrive for the summer and see a deer on their way into Kearney. [Beatrice, we will see in the next chapter, was confined in a mental hospital at the time.]

August 8 – Mr. Finkelman's first visit during which he sprains his ankle and takes snaps of Dad and Frere painting the kitchen.

August 24 – Mr. Finkelman up again and demonstrates how to catch fish by landing one from the wharf.

August 30 – Gilbert and Professor MacKenzie [Larry MacKenzie, president-elect of UNB] make a surprise visit, arriving in time for dinner.

September 8 – Dad, Mother and Frere leave ahead of schedule in a fine rain, phone '77' [Spadina Road] from Barrie and drive through a dense fog.

October 11 – Dad, Mother, Gilbert, Shelagh and Frere make the famous Thanksgiving visit to 'Narrow Waters.'

October 14 – We close the cottage and leave, rather cold.

1941

May 23 – Gilbert and Beatrice come up by train to Huntsville, Beatrice for her first view of the place.

May 24 – Beatrice digs the first tree-hole.

July 14 – Bora and Peggy Laskin arrive just as the Kitchen Pantry is being completed.

July 21 – New door by refrigerator is hung and Bora and Peggy leave.

August 1 – The Codys arrive with Dr. and Mrs. Coulton. [G.G. Coulton was a Cambridge mediaeval historian who spent the war years at the University of Toronto.]

August 14 – An otter or a weasel is seen on the tennis lawn. Doug Creighton arrives and the Ice House is begun.

August 15 – Mother and Gilbert take the Coultons to the Falconers.

August 26 – End of Doug Creighton's visit.

September 12 – Dad, Mother and Frere leave for Toronto.

1942

May 13 – Dad, Mother, Shelagh and Frere make 'Narrow Waters' in five hours, obeying the new speed limit.

May 18 – Dad and Frere battle a porcupine beneath the Visitors' Room in the wee hours of the morning. Mother shoots a groundhog with the rifle hip high.

May 20 – Mother and Frere get the 1,500 trees from Scotia.

May 21 – Garden all in.

June 7 – A severe frost kills the beans.

July 5 – Beatrice, Shelagh, Rachel [English girl spending the war years with the Kennedys] and Frere go to church in the row-boat and get doused coming home. [The diary never mentions Kennedy going to church.]

August 7 – Mr. Finkelman's three-day visit.

August 19 – Dr. Innis arrives and enjoys crosscutting.

August 30 – Dad and Frere take Mother on her first row down the Magnetawan to see the west side of the place.

September 7 – Harvesting completed and preserves to station.

September 8 – Rachel departs with 640 lbs. of preserves.

1943

May 20 – Thursday. At 4.20 on the morning after Churchill addressed Congress, Dad, mother and Frere prepare for the fourth war-time summer. An hour and twenty minutes later, there were happy good-byes to Gilbert Beatrice Shelagh and Hannah as we drive off in a heavy-laden car for eight-thirty breakfast at the Albion [hotel in Gravenhurst] and bumpy road from Gravenhurst on.

May 21 – Frere gets up at 7.45 and over the eight o'clock news hears of Admiral Yamamoto's death in action.

May 23 – 'We three' go for a happy walk and listen to Sir William Beveridge before retiring.

May 26 – Sam comes down and 900 hills (twenty rows) of potatoes go in.

May 27 – Dad Gilbert Sam and Frere put in more of the garden with lots of seed to spare! Extra turnip seeds are sown high speed just before dinner!

May 29 – One hundred Jack and one hundred Scotch pine go in today.

May 31 – Three hills of cucumber are put in outside the kitchen.

June 5 – Dad mows the road today and news of Churchill's return to England comes through. A cheery fire in the living room grate in the evening.

June 6 – Mother talks to Mrs. O'Connor of the glorious northern lights last night, and Dad oils the living room floor in the afternoon.

June 8 – Today is Dad's and Mother's twenty-third wedding day, and we row down the river to receive a long letter from Shelagh.

July 1 – Dominion Day. Dad and Shelagh pick 4½ quarts of strawberries. Later Sam and Shelagh hoe the potatoes and corn while Frere varnishes the mantelpiece and cupboard in Dad's and Mother's house.

July 10 – Frere arrives back from Dad's and Mother's house just in time to hear Mr. King announce that Canadian troops are now in action in Sicily.

July 22 – The three boys lengthen Lakeshore trail to Blueberry point … [This entry shows, as discussed in the preface, that the Lakeshore trail – which my family continues to carefully groom and still calls the Lakeshore trail – was completed before the day in 1945 that Caesar Wright and Bora Laskin came to tell Kennedy that Bora was seriously thinking of moving to Osgoode Hall Law School and walked along that trail.]

August 11 – Churchill puts in a busy day at Quebec. So do we at Narrow Waters by harvesting 22 quarts of carrots, 11 quarts of peas, 6 of rhubarb, 6 beans, 26 of beets and 18 of choke cherries! Mother has Shelagh, Rachel and Frere draped in produce for a picture, but alas no film!

The diary continues through the end of the summer of 1943 and the summer of 1944, but I think the reader has a good idea of the activities at Narrow Waters, and only the entries for June 1944 around the time of the invasion of Normandy will be set out:

1944

June 6 – The greatest military operation of all history, the invasion of the French coast, has begun. Dad paints the floors of the Children's Cottage, Visitors' Room and Kitchen. The rebroadcast of the King's message and the President's prayer come over well, and we go off to bed knowing that the first landings were successful.

June 7 – More turnips are planted and box of chocolates from Beatrice arrives for Dad and Mother. Raw, cold and 48 degrees.

June 8 – Dad's and Mother's Wedding Day and a special fire in the living room, with poached eggs for breakfast. A row of sunflowers is planted after we remove the 200th basket of stones from this strip. The invasion's success continues.

June 9 – There are radio requests for increased Victory gardens and Dad and Frere plant seven more rows of potatoes. It is the Third Canadian Division that is fighting in France.

The trunk also contained a diary prepared by W.P.M. for the summer of 1947, which will be mentioned again in a later chapter. Whether there were diaries for other summers is not known. There is no evidence that W.P.M. kept a diary of his life in Toronto. There is in W.P.M.'s diary for 1947 a meticulous attention to detail, not unlike Kennedy's scholarship. As we will see in that chapter, his scholarship slowed down after the war. In many respects – at least during the summer months – the cottage became a substitute for scholarship. One senses from reading Frere's outline of activities that this neglect of scholarship over the summers started during the war years.

After the war, the Kennedys continued to spend long summers at the cottage, usually from May to mid-September. During these postwar years, Eugene LaBrie was often the person getting the directives about the School of Law from the north. Although invited to the cottage, LaBrie never managed to get there. But faculty member David Vanek did and describes in some detail in his memoirs his visit in 1947.

Finkelman had warned Vanek what to expect, Vanek recounts in his memoirs: '[He] cautioned me that the Dean directed his family like a commander of a military establishment. An atmosphere of strict discipline prevailed. Activities were regulated for each segment of the day. Meals were frugal. "You will be hungry," he warned, "so take along some chocolate bars." There will be no snacks between meals and no food after dinner, which will be held early. After dinner, the Dean will turn on the radio for the news. When the news is over, he will examine his pocket watch and announce it is time for bed.'[15]

Vanek's wife decided not to join her husband, who felt obliged to go. The conditions were precisely what Finkelman predicted – the routine was regimented, and Vanek needed the chocolate bars. Vanek added several other features, such as Mrs. Kennedy picking him up from the train at a milk stand in open country, presumably at a crossroads north of Kearney on the railway line into Algonquin Park. When they got to the gate at the top of the hill above the cottage, Vanek relates, Pauline 'called in a loud, clear, soprano voice, "cooie." From the distance came back the answering call of the mate in a high pitched male voice, "cooie."' Vanek then describes seeing Kennedy in front of the cottage: 'We opened the gate, got back in the car, and Pauline drove down the lane. There, standing in the lane, we came upon William Paul McClure Kennedy, appearing as I had never before beheld him. He was clad in knee high boots, breeches, cowboy hat, and no shirt. With his thin frame, the sun outlined every rib of his body.' Vanek asked if he could take a picture.

Vanek also describes his walk with Kennedy through the forest, where important university figures had cut down trees. 'With considerable pride,' Vanek recalls, Kennedy 'pointed to a stump and, with relish, commented: "This one was cut down by Innis."'[16] There was always work to do. During the summer of 1947, the correspondence shows that the Kennedys installed a new gas water pump to bring up lake water, put a new roof on the barn, and painted the barn and the ice house. The correspondence relating to these projects shows a very close relationship between Kennedy and the local Kearney workers. They are addressed in the letters as 'My dear Friend.'[17]

21

The Family

One cannot know W.P.M. Kennedy without knowing his family, his relationships with his wife and each of his children, and their views of Kennedy. I believe this is true for any biography. In the present case, knowledge of his family provides additional evidence of the stress that Kennedy was under during many periods of his life. We will start with his spouse and then briefly discuss each of his children up to the period just before Kennedy retired. The stories of their lives and careers will be continued in the final chapter.

Pauline

Pauline was a homemaker who devoted herself to her husband and her four children, often entertained guests for dinner, handled the finances, and did all the driving until the children were able to do so. She was also very prominent in many charities and organizations. In 1939, she was elected the president of the Women's Canadian Club of Toronto, which she claimed in a speech was 'doubtless the most successful woman's club, numerically and educationally, in Canada.'[1] Like the men's Canadian Club, it brought in important speakers. Thérèse Casgrain, for example, a leader of the women's suffrage movement in Quebec, spoke to the club during Pauline's two-year presidency.[2]

In 1941, Pauline became the first chair of the Consumers Branch of the Toronto-area Wartime Prices and Trade Board, established immediately before the start of the war and designed 'to prevent the kind of inflationary spiral that had led the country into an economic depression and widespread social unrest,' which had taken place during and after the First World War.[3] In 1941, the banker Donald Gordon was selected by the government to build up a body of competent administrators, and Pauline was one of the unpaid administrators.[4] Press reports show that she often presided at meetings, travelled to other cities in Ontario to give talks, and gave advice to the public and others on a number of topics. The *Globe and Mail*, for example, reported in 1946: 'The last letter of

Pauline Kennedy in the late 1930s

Mrs. W.P.M. Kennedy, chairman of the Toronto Consumer Branch Committee of the Wartime Prices and Trade Board, to her liaison officers was full of
important information about food and asked for additions' to such practical
suggestions as 'Do *not* allow *one crumb* of bread to enter your garbage tin' and
'Plan your home garden now. Why not plant a few carrots in your flower bed?'[5]
It is therefore not surprising that the Kennedys grew many vegetable crops at
Narrow Waters.

When her work with the board ended in 1947, Pauline became one of the
founders and the first vice-president of the Canadian Association of Consumers, later renamed the Consumer's Association of Canada.[6] At first it was
a women's organization, but in 1961 it expanded the membership to include
men.[7]

In 1945, Pauline became the first chair of the Women's Advisory Council of
the Canadian Society for the Control of Cancer. The society had been founded
in 1938 and in 1946 changed its name to the Canadian Cancer Society.[8] Today
it is Canada's largest national cancer charity and the largest national charitable
funder of cancer research in Canada.[9] The *Globe and Mail* reported that, at
the first meeting of the Advisory Council at which Mrs. Kennedy presided,
pathologist William Boyd, the speaker, told the meeting held in Simpson's
Arcadian Court that 'education is one of the biggest factors in combatting the
menace.'[10] That message was often repeated by Mrs. Kennedy, such as in 1948
at a meeting at the Canadian Cancer Society's Ontario headquarters: 'First, we
must acquaint ourselves with the facts and danger signals. Then we must spread
our information around as widely as possible.' The *Globe and Mail* went on to
report: 'Mrs. Kennedy stressed the crying need for service to existing cancer
patients in the city, such as home visiting, baby-sitting, occupational therapy,
making cancer dressings, driving cancer patients and a dozen other things.'[11]
She was very good friends with Mrs. Ruth Frankel, one of the Cancer Society's leading figures and a prominent member of the Jewish community, who
sometimes sent her car to have Pauline picked up for meetings.[12] Ruth Frankel's
family owned Frankel Steel.

Here, then, is a talented and important woman about whom readers have
never heard, who made many important contributions to society, apart from
supporting W.P.M. Kennedy and their four children. In many respects she is as
deserving of a biography as her husband.

There were other outside activities. In 1943 Pauline was chair of the Toronto
Housing Registry Committee, which arranged for Toronto women to open
their homes to women workers from outside Toronto who came to work in
war plants.[13] The next year, there was a note in the *Varsity* asking that 'all girls
interested in tagging [collecting funds by selling tags] for the Women's College Hospital on Saturday October 21 please call Mrs. Kennedy.'[14] And, unlike
her husband, she was involved in St. Paul's Church, where Canon Cody had

been the minister. She was also an active supporter of the Anglican Order of St. John the Divine, the women's half of the men's Order of St. John the Evangelist, where Frere was a priest.[15]

Pauline would sometimes complain in her frequent correspondence with Frere about the burden of her schedule. In a note in March 1945, she wrote:[16]

Tomorrow at 10.30 I expect the five ladies who are on that Invitations Committee I chair and I wish they were not coming ... [I] could scream every time the telephone rings. For instance here is my day tomorrow:

10.30 to 12.30	5 women of committee
2 pm to 2.15	secretary of Cancer Society to discuss announcements of a meeting and for me to sign cheques
2.15 to 2.35	visit to W.P.T.B to sign letters
2. 45	tea time – Canadian Club – Dr. Sidney Smith to hear his speech on Canadianism the second time

No doubt, Kennedy encouraged and was proud of his wife's accomplishments.

Gilbert

Kennedy was also proud of his eldest child, Gilbert, who had graduated from the Honour Law program in 1939 with the MacMurchy Gold Medal.[17] He was homeschooled in his early years, and then attended Brown School on Avenue Road, just south of St. Clair Avenue, and the University of Toronto Schools (UTS).[18] At the University of Toronto, Gilbert had been the chief justice of the moot court program and participated in Hart House debates. He later graduated from Osgoode Hall Law School in 1942, one of only five students who graduated with honours. While attending Osgoode, he received an MA and LLB from the University of Toronto School of Law.[19]

Born in 1917, Gilbert almost died from the Spanish flu in 1919 – as we know, his birth mother died from it[20] – and likely, in part because of this, according to his wife, Betty Kennedy, he later had serious medical problems, such as having his spleen removed at the age of sixteen,[21] suffering from grand mal epilepsy, which first appeared in 1932,[22] and osteoporosis.[23] Because of his epilepsy, he never got his driver's license.[24] And because of his health, he was not a candidate for military service.

After getting his call to the bar, he practised as a partner with a senior Toronto lawyer, Arthur A. Macdonald,[25] while teaching part-time for five hours a week – criminal law and torts – at the University of Toronto School of Law at 8.30 every morning of the week.[26] In 1946 – to his father's apparent surprise – he decided to take a position at the newly established law school at the University

Gilbert Kennedy, graduating from the University of Toronto,
with his father in the University College quadrangle

of British Columbia (UBC). He was dining in Hart House, he states in his oral interview, and a group of university presidents passed by. Larry MacKenzie, the president of UBC, who knew him well, stepped out of line and said: 'Gilbert, I've started a new law school, would you like to come?' This conversation took place in early May or June 1946.[27] He started in September – the third person hired to teach at UBC Law School. George Curtis, the dean, had been hired the previous year.[28] W.P.M. Kennedy later wrote to Dean Vincent MacDonald: 'Gilbert went to the west of his own free will. I had no idea that he was entering the academic life until he had examined offers from the U.S.A. and Canadian schools, and he presented me with his decision.'[29]

Gilbert's lengthy oral interview sheds light on his father in a number of areas, some of which have been touched on earlier. When asked whether he attended Sunday school or was taken to church regularly, Gilbert replied: 'No, I did not attend Sunday school. I was not taken to church. My sister and I, that's Beatrice and I, did attend on our own St. Paul's Anglican Church on Bloor Street East ... I entered the world as a Roman Catholic and my Roman Catholic baptism was accepted by the Anglican church for my confirmation. My brother and I were confirmed at the same time, the only time that I saw Dad in church.'[30] Gilbert was asked by the interviewer 'about the influence on you of the values that you learned at home.' His answer: 'I suppose the first and most important thing that stands out in my mind is tolerance for others. Dad kept drumming that in casually but in many ways. For us there was no difference between a Jew and anybody else. Well we had one [Jacob Finkelman] eating with us regularly, and there were no problems.'[31]

There are seven complete pages in the oral interview devoted to stamp collecting, on which W.P.M. worked closely with Gilbert and Frere over many years.[32] W.P.M. and Gilbert continued to collect stamps into their retirement years. W.P.M. would have friends and colleagues save used stamps for him. There are a number of letters in the law school files and in the correspondence left at the cottage about stamps. W.P.M. seems to have been particularly interested in West Indian stamps. There are indications that it was a costly hobby.[33] Frere inherited his father's collection, which he kept at a bank for safekeeping. The collection, however, disappeared from the bank, and, according to Frere, a settlement with the bank for about $5,000 soon followed.[34] There were no comparable activities that W.P.M. engaged in with his daughters.

In 1948, Gilbert married Betty, a mathematician, who was also teaching at UBC. He had first met her in the spring of 1947 at a time when she was already engaged. She married her fiancé that summer, but, on a holiday trip in the mountains, a railway ferry hit the small boat that she and her husband and a friend were in, resulting in the death of everyone except Betty, who was able to swim to safety. About a year after they had first met, Gilbert took her to the

UBC Law Ball.[35] In May 1948, they visited the Kennedys in Toronto and then at the cottage.[36] They were married later that summer in a small church outside of Vancouver. Frere was the best man and his sister Shelagh was the maid of honour.[37] W.P.M. and Pauline did not attend.

At my request, Betty – in her words – 'put together in an unpolished document … recollections of the family.' She wrote:

> I found their family very different from anything I had met before – I think I was probably pretty naïve. All of the children had attended private schools, they had a live-in housekeeper. The focus of the family was the Dean. Nothing must disturb him. He spent the entire day on a chaise lounge in a big living area of the main cottage. He read a lot and loved to talk law with Gilbert … Pauline was not pleased with Gilbert's choice of a potential bride – she felt that it was [unsatisfactory] for him to marry a westerner (they were definitely different and did not have the same standards as her group of family and friends in Ontario) and even more damning, she did not think he should marry a widow. I rather liked the Dean, but found her difficult.[38]

In her recollections of the family, Betty went on to describe a later visit to the Kennedys in Toronto over Christmas 1952, when Gilbert was at Harvard and they lived in Boston:

> We stayed with them for several days. Again the whole focus of the family was keeping the Dean happy and 'quiet.' Meals were quite rigid in timing and certain subjects were to be avoided. I was told by [Gilbert] that there was a period where his father had drunk heavily and spent unwisely. I gather he had little money sense. We met none of their friends. I gathered from things Pauline said that even at this time the Dean was very demanding sexually, and apparently wanted intercourse almost every day. Frere's room was in the sunroom so that he had to go through his parents' bedroom to get out – most peculiar.[39]

In a telephone conversation I had with Shelagh, she made the same point about Frere's room and, by implication, the fact that he would necessarily hear what was taking place in the next room.[40] In my many conversations with Frere, understandably, the subject never came up, and I never asked him about it.

I am not sure how this information fits in with an understanding of W.P.M. Kennedy. Should I have included it? To leave out facts that both his daughter and daughter-in-law thought important in knowing Kennedy might give a misleading picture of Kennedy. We know that he was interested in the subject of sex. His first and second spouses may have been pregnant when he married them,[41] and he had to leave St. Francis Xavier College in 1914 because of a relationship with a student.[42] In February 1918, he gave a talk to a French club at the university, *Le Club Politique*, during which he included a discussion of prostitution. He is reported in the *Varsity* to have said: 'University men must stand for the highest moral purity, eliminate the phrase "fallen" and "bad" women from their vocabulary, must rather pity the women, and come down with a heavy hand on the men making the women such as they are ... In the reconstruction after the war, the home life should be one of the first things tended to. The home was a national necessity, but its great defect, rather its primal defect, had been and is, the lack of authority. Liberty has become license, children rule the home.'[43]

In later years, according to Eugene LaBrie, Kennedy became famous for two lectures. One was a recreation of the opening of the first Parliament in Niagara-on-the-Lake, Ontario, in 1792. The other lecture was entitled 'The Nude and the Naked.'[44] Joan Hodgson (née Morris), who entered the first year of the Honour Law course in 1942, described that lecture in a recent oral interview with the Osgoode Society. She said that in her final year Kennedy 'devoted one lecture in educating in sex, believe it or not, in your last year ... I don't think it was terribly technically specific, in scientific terms, but generally ... the association of males and females and how they should get along and how you should treat them, and this kind of thing.' Joan was asked by the interviewer what Kennedy's philosophy was. She replied: 'Oh, very broad minded, but just don't get physically involved unless you are really sure you like him.' She was asked: 'And what was your reaction to this conversation?' 'I just remember sitting there absolutely blank-faced trying not to show any expression.' 'Were you the only one in the room?' 'It was the whole class.'[45]

Joan Hodgson relates another curious story in her oral interview and in a telephone discussion I had with her. She refers to Kennedy as 'an absolutely mad Irishman' who 'made the law come alive.'[46] She graduated from the Honour Law course in 1946, the same year that Frere – who had returned to the School of Law after his military service – graduated with his LLB. Later, while attending Osgoode Hall Law School, she boarded in a home on Spadina Road, across the street from the Kennedys. She sometimes went to church with Pauline and her children and often had dinner at the Kennedys' home. She states in her oral interview: 'Dr. Kennedy was determined that I was going to marry [Frere].' She was invited to dinner one day and was told to 'please come 15 minutes earlier, the Dr. wants to speak to you.' She goes on: 'So I went up to his study, and he proceeded to tell me how fine a man his son ... was, but he needed a steadying hand of an intelligent woman.'[47] She had been to a couple of movies with Frere. She told the dean that she was fond of Frere, but that was about all. It is likely that Frere never knew about the proposal. I never discussed it with him.

Beatrice

Beatrice Kennedy, in contrast to Gilbert, had a sad life.[48] She was born in October 1918 and, like Gilbert, was close to death after getting the Spanish flu in 1919.[49] She had difficulty at school, changing from Huron Street Public School to Brown Public School, then to Bishop Strachan, a private girls' school, and finally to Harbord Collegiate, where she repeated her final year.[50] She was, however, able to enter the University of Toronto in September 1939 and take up residence at Trinity College's St. Hilda's on Devonshire Place. She rarely attended lectures, however, and left her first exam after half an hour.

Later that year she became suicidal and on 1 May 1940 was certified by her family physician under Ontario's mental health legislation. She was admitted to the Toronto Psychiatric Hospital (TPH) at Surrey Place, just north of College Street. With the help of Frere and the support of Betty, I was able to obtain Beatrice's psychiatric records from TPH, as well as her records from Whitby Psychiatric Hospital (now the Ontario Shores Centre for Mental Health Sciences), where Beatrice spent many years. A history of the treatment of mental illness in Canada could be written from those records. I will just touch on them here. The records show that in her late teens Beatrice wanted to end her life. She drove at high speeds on Bloor Street,[51] turned on the gas at home, and thought of using carbon monoxide in a closed garage and other ways for ending her life.[52]

The Toronto Psychiatric Hospital was opened in 1925, with Clarence Farrar, the chair of psychiatry at the university, as its medical director. He had graduated from Johns Hopkins University Medical School in 1900; spent two years studying in Heidelberg with Emil Kraepelin, Alois Alzheimer, and others; practised in the United States for several years; and then came to Canada in 1923 to be the medical director of Homewood Sanitarium in Guelph. From 1931 to 1965, he was the editor of the *American Journal of Psychiatry*.[53] With the support of the Rockefeller Foundation, a research unit was established at the Toronto Psychiatric Hospital in the late 1930s.[54] Dr. Mary Jackson, who graduated from the University of Toronto Medical School in 1929, was chief of staff at TPH. She was the first woman to receive such a senior position in the Faculty of Medicine at the university, later becoming the assistant director (medical) of the university's Clarke Institute of Psychiatry.[55] She was the one in charge of Beatrice's treatment, under the direct supervision of Farrar. Both were actively involved in the case.[56]

Kennedy and Farrar had had a professional relationship. Dr. Kenneth Gray, a member of Farrar's Department of Psychiatry, taught a course in the law school, and members of the law faculty gave seminars in the Department of Psychiatry.[57] Farrar was Kennedy's guest at the law banquet in 1942 and perhaps in other years.[58] Farrar had firm views on psychiatric treatment. He did not believe in psychoanalysis and initially such treatment was not offered to Beatrice. He considered heredity very important in determining mental illness and was very involved in the eugenics movement, successfully lobbying for eugenics legislation for Alberta (the Sexual Sterilization Act), but failed to get such an Act introduced in Ontario.[59] His diagnosis of Beatrice was schizophrenia.[60] Pauline told the doctors that one of Kennedy's sisters in Scotland had been mentally ill, but was never institutionalized.[61] The treatment Farrar proposed was insulin shock, which had been introduced in Canada in 1937 and had just started at the TPH in 1940–41.[62]

As we have seen, Kennedy had purchased the Narrow Waters property in the spring of 1940 and had gone up north in June 1940. Beatrice had been admitted on 1 May.[63] Kennedy wrote to President Cody from the cottage on 17 June 1940, stating: 'I miss Beatrice. We all do. The gap is wide; but here too we carry on. And our sorrow is small in the scales of a world in agony. If you see Beatrice or have any news let us know.'[64] In August 1940, he wrote again: 'We have no good news of Beatrice. There is no change and I have consented to insulin. We are reconciled and our sorrow is little indeed in this world's troubles.'[65]

Dr. Jackson's notes in the hospital records, shortly after Beatrice was admitted, state: 'When patient first came to the hospital she was extremely disturbed, obviously depressed at times and had many self-accusatory ideas, as well as those of persecutory nature ... Her whole thought centred about the present – how there was some plot to do harm to her family, that she was the cause of the world's disorder, that there was a disturbed state in the University as well as her family and that we in some way were implicated.'[66]

Beatrice received forty-eight insulin treatments from September to December 1940, resulting in sixteen comas. The treatments seemed to be working. The records note: 'Marked improvement'; and Farrar permitted Beatrice to go home for Christmas and return to see him at the end of the month. She was then discharged to her mother. Beatrice thought of going back to university in the fall.[67]

A social worker connected with the hospital thought Beatrice should get a position as a teller in a bank,[68] which she did, and worked at the Dominion Bank for the next two years,[69] receiving a promotion to a position related to foreign currency in the discount department.[70] She lived at St. Hilda's residence during the summer of 1941, while the family was up north.[71] Over the next few years, her condition deteriorated. She felt the bank was spying on her, had an outburst at the bank, and was let go. She returned to the Toronto Psychiatric Hospital in October 1943, was released, and later again readmitted and released. Dr. Farrar saw Beatrice on several occasions and maintained his diagnosis of schizophrenia, writing: 'diagnosis of schizo-affective condition would be in order. The personality inadequacy is apparent, however.'[72]

She returned again to the hospital in June 1944, concerned about plots against her and her family, and was discharged the end of August 1944.[73] Her parents were at the cottage at the time of admission.[74] There were no further

insulin shock treatments during this latter period, but four electroconvulsive
therapy (ECT) shock treatments were administered and 'intensive psychotherapy and occupational therapy.'[75] ECT had been added to the psychiatrists' arse-
nal at about that time.[76] Dr. Jackson writes: 'After four electroshock treatments,
the patient showed a remarkable improvement, was cheery, happy, active and
very cooperative.'[77] Dr. Farrar agreed, writing: 'After brief electric shock therapy marked change has been observed, beginning after first treatment. She is
cheerful, even euphoric, and very freely talkative.'[78] She went to the cottage with
Frere later that summer. She had lost a new job she had taken at Imperial Oil.

Throughout Beatrice's time at TPH, information was being collected on what
preceded her first admission. Her family doctor said that she was 'unnecessarily
shy and sensitive.' Dr. Jackson concluded that Kennedy 'tended to dominate the
home.' She also noted that W.P.M. was 'a genius with all the usual accompanying instability.' Dr. Jackson talked with Beatrice and recorded that 'there was
a marked idea of self-blame "that she had ruined the family" and something
dreadful was going to happen; that there was to be a big trial in Convocation
Hall at which time her father would lose his position.'[79] Beatrice talked about
trouble with the history department – events which had occurred more than
fifteen years earlier, when she was five or six years old.[80] Pauline told Dr. Jackson that Beatrice felt that she was the 'black sheep of the family' and that she
had disgraced the family at the bank and the university.[81]

Beatrice told the doctors that 'they could not have much social life at home
because of her father's peculiarities';[82] that 'she and her half-sister had clash-
ing temperaments';[83] that her father 'would come to see her if he were alive';[84]
that she always felt she was the dull one; that 'she wished someone would kill
her and that she wanted to die';[85] and that 'she does not understand why all
people do not want to kill themselves.'[86] She also told one of the psychiatrists
that something happened during the year 1938, which 'she does not intend to
discuss with anyone.'[87] The extensive file does not contain any further mention
about what might have occurred in 1938, and I have not seen any other reference to what may or may not have taken place.

Kennedy had a long interview with Farrar and told him that Beatrice was
'dull, and the basis for her sense of inferiority actually existed.' He said that Beatrice liked horseback riding, swimming, and was a good dancer. He also told
Farrar that, unlike in the past, she 'now seems to show considerable affection
for him, embracing him when they meet.'[88] One of the psychiatrists had noted
in the file that Beatrice 'was outside the circle of affection.'[89] Kennedy now felt,
Farrar records, that 'probably wrong attitudes were assumed towards her. There
was sometimes a tendency to badger her a little because of her inadequacy.'[90]

In November 1944, a serious incident occurred in the Kennedy home. Beatrice threatened members of the family with a knife. It is not clear what actually
occurred. The hospital records put it this way in various reports: 'threatened

Judy Friedland saying goodbye to Beatrice, who visited the cottage
with Frere and Shelagh in 1992

family with a knife';[91] 'tried to attack sister with a carving knife';[92] and 'murderous attack on some member of the family'.[93] Betty's view is that 'Gilbert was the one who stopped her from trying to knife Shelagh'.[94] Frere had a different recollection, saying that the 'plan was to kill her father ... to prevent him from affecting Shelagh, like father did to her'.[95] Both John and Barbara Laskin heard from their parents that the attack was against W.P.M.[96]

In any event, Beatrice was kept under close supervision at TPH until arrangements were made for her to be admitted to the Whitby Psychiatric Hospital, about 50 kilometres (30 miles) east of Toronto. She was admitted at the end of November 1944 and discharged in October 1961, as 'self-supporting'. The financial cost to the family, Kennedy wrote, was 'almost impossible to contemplate'.[97] The diagnosis continued to be schizophrenia. During the latter part of that period, she lived at a boarding house in Whitby and worked in the dining room at Whitby Ladies' College. Betty observed that, in her visits with the Kennedys, 'Beatrice was rarely ever mentioned'.[98] I went through hundreds of letters from Pauline and W.P.M. Kennedy to Frere that had been left at the cottage and found surprisingly few references to Beatrice. There were very few letters to or from Beatrice, compared to the other children. She occasionally visited her family at the cottage.[99]

Frere

After deciding that practising law was not for him, Frere Kennedy had a very satisfying career as an Anglican priest. He was born in 1923 – the first of Pauline's children – attended Huron Public School and, like Gilbert, the University of Toronto Schools.[100] He entered his father's Honour Law course in September 1941. He told me that he 'deeply respected' his father and regarded him as 'close to a genius,' but found him 'difficult to understand' and 'didn't get along well' with him. He also found that there were many changes in his father's moods. W.P.M. would 'hold forth at dinners,' but next morning 'be very glum.' Frere said, however, that he 'liked his mother ... She was kind and compassionate.'[101]

At university, Frere was active in the Glee Club, the *Faculty of Law Review*, and at Hart House.[102] He successfully completed his first two years but started having problems in his third year. W.P.M. wrote to President Cody in March 1944: 'We are very worried about Frere, who for another year is unable to continue his work.' Two months later, Kennedy wrote to Cody from the cottage: 'Frere is holding his own. Pauline came up today. She is poorly and needs great care and attention at this trying period.'[103] The trying period likely relates to Beatrice's hospitalization in TPH and Pauline's surgery. Frere would also have been affected by these events. He was very close to Beatrice, he says, both as a brother and later as a priest.

The fact that he had not enlisted may also have weighed heavily on him during the early years of the war. In early October 1944, he enlisted in the army and, after training in Canada, went overseas. On 21 October 1944, Kennedy wrote to Frere:[104]

> I am sure indeed that you will give the best that is in you and be a credit to the service and yourself and us. I live from day to day in the knowledge that you have done what is honorable and manly. I would not have had you do otherwise … You have given me more than any father could ask and I love you for it; for you have been the best of sons and – much more – a dear considerate, and cooperative friend.

The letters from W.P.M. to Frere show a closeness that is not found in the letters to the other children. After training in Canada, Frere left for England. Dean Kennedy and other members of the family wrote to Frere frequently while he was overseas. They numbered all the letters. There were over eighty letters in 1945. Many of them dealt with routine chores at the cottage and described the vegetable garden and the flowers. Here is one from W.P.M. dated 8 July 1945 – dramatically and in typical Kennedy style – describing the perennial bed:[105]

> Here are hundreds of pinks dancing in the west wind in the light of the sinking sun, 57 irises (flags) still left in their glory, 3 of the most perfect peonies you ever saw, and nearly 40 sprigs of perfect promise on the delphiniums, with several hollyhocks going to bloom and an inexplicable fox-glove growing with a phlox. The whole thing would delight you. Then we had glorious soft rain in the night and the morning glories, nasturtium, petunias, shooting up.

And there were comments about politics and world events. On 4 March 1945, for example, Kennedy writes: 'The war seems to be going splendidly as far as we can tell, and it looks as if the German push had really worked out for our advantage so that G[ermany] may not be able to hold out for the summer.'[106] In April 1945, Kennedy writes: 'We listen to the San Francisco broadcasts, and tonight we shall listen, at 7.30 p.m., to President Truman's radio address for the opening meeting of the Conference.'[107] The following month, 26 June 1945, Kennedy notes: 'The Great Charter [of the United Nations] is signed today – all that each of us can do is to hope that a creative meaning can be worked into it.'[108]

In May 1945, Frere wrote to his father that he is 'somewhere in Europe.' He had not seen front-line service. The European war was now over, and Frere had volunteered for service in the Pacific front and transferred to the 48th Highlanders. Frere told his father that he 'has no desire to remain in the army of occupation.' Kennedy replied in a touching note to Frere:

> Mother and I know that you give it your very best and wisest judgment. We would not be human – either of us – did we not feel something which every heart must

Frere Kennedy enlisted in the army in October 1944

feel about you going to face that cruel ordeal; but – and I want you to know this without <u>any reserve</u> or <u>equivocation</u> on our part – you have our <u>fullest support</u>. We know you <u>followed your conscience</u> and <u>duty</u>, and we are <u>just as proud of you as we can be</u>.[109]

In earlier correspondence, however, Kennedy had wanted Frere to come home and not volunteer for the Pacific, stating:[110] 'You've done your duty, there are <u>lots</u> in Canada to go to the Pacific. So hurry back to us; and won't we just be <u>glad</u> to see you!!!'

On 15 August, after the bombing of Hiroshima and Nagasaki, Japan surrendered. The war was over, and Frere, who had not yet left Canada for the Pacific front, could remain in Canada. Frere started back in the Honour Law program in September 1945, was given credit for a year as a veteran, and completed his BA and LLB through a combined program in the spring of 1946.[111] He then worked full-time with C.C.H. publishers, primarily as the editor of a loose-leaf reporter on labour law.[112] He did not attend Osgoode Hall Law School.[113]

Frere then went west and articled in British Columbia with T.G. Norris, who later became a justice on the British Columbia Court of Appeal. Frere's LLB from the University of Toronto was approved by the Law Society of British Columbia, and, after completing a number of practice courses, he was called to the British Columbia Bar in 1951.[114] He practised with Norris for a short period, but concluded he wanted to become a priest. Frere told me that he remembers going to St. Paul's Church with his mother when he was six or seven and thinking then that he might be a minister like Dr. Cody. His mother, he said, noticed him waving his hands like Dr. Cody did. He was, after all, named after an Anglican bishop, Walter Howard Frere.[115] Gilbert states in his oral interview: 'Not being really happy with practice – and I think having a hankering to do what he really wanted to do – and that was to go into the Church, headed East, stopped in Regina for a year to work with the Y.M.C.A., and – he was then at about the age of thirty – entered Lennoxville, Bishop's University, in the theological course.'[116]

Shelagh

Shelagh's life story is not easy to unravel. She was born in February 1926, three years after Frere was born.[117] She graduated from Harbord Collegiate in 1944 and entered the University of Toronto, taking a BA degree, majoring in philosophy.[118] She was, apparently, lively and outspoken. Frere recalls that she 'held forth on all her views' and 'had great capacity for making friends.' Frere and others say that she was very much like her father.[119] She was a good student and was very involved in a large number of extracurricular activities: She was the University College editor of the magazine *The Undergrad* and a reporter for the *Varsity*. She was also active in the Philosophical Society, the Modern Letters

Shelagh Kennedy Lindsey and her father at 77 Spadina Road on the day of
her wedding, 29 May 1948

Club, and the Student Christian Movement; and participated in the Japanese/ Canadian Committee that promoted human rights with respect to the deportation after the war of Japanese Canadians following the Supreme Court of Canada and Privy Council decisions upholding the government's decision to do so.[120]

At the end of May 1948, the year she graduated, she married a zoology student, Casimir Charles Lindsey, who was also graduating from the University of Toronto that year, having served overseas for several years in the Canadian Intelligence Corps. The wedding was in Toronto in the chapel at St. Paul's Church.[121] Casimir came from a distinguished family. His great-great-grandfather on his father's side was the rebel William Lyon Mackenzie; hence, he was a second cousin of Mackenzie King. He was also a second cousin of Dr. Norman Bethune on his father's side. His great-grandfather on his mother's side was Casimir Gzowski, the famous Canadian engineer who built railways and canals.[122] His father, a Lieutenant Colonel in the Canadian Army, was friendly with Prime Minister King and advised him on military matters.[123] Cas, as he was known, told me about W.P.M. Kennedy wanting Cas's father to use his influence to obtain a British birthday honour for Kennedy, but his father refused to do so.

Shelagh and Cas had known each other as students at the University of Toronto. W.P.M. wrote to Frere on 4 March 1945: 'Casimir Lindsey is here and is coming to lunch. He comes for a fortnight on March 12, en route to India. Shelagh and he have become engaged. He had a long private chat with me and he gave S. a most beautiful ring. His people are greatly pleased. I hope it will turn out well; but mother and I decidedly think that each must follow his or her own wisdom and make life for each.'[124] Gilbert wrote to Frere a few days later about the engagement, stating: 'She is still in the clouds and the talk of the campus ... She goes to Professors and begs extra time for essays and when they ask why, she takes off her glove and shows the alleged $600 ring.'[125]

After they graduated from the University of Toronto, the couple went to live in Vancouver, where Cas was doing an MA in biology, specializing in fish. They then went to Cambridge University, where he obtained a PhD, and returned to BC to teach at the University of British Columbia. Like many women at the time, Shelagh went where her husband's career took her. During that period, they spent a year in Singapore, and he travelled to many other countries in connection with his work.[126] From 1966 to 1979, Cas was a professor at the University of Manitoba. In a later chapter, Shelagh's interest in the work of Marshall McLuhan will be explored.

22
Sidney Smith Arrives

There were serious doubts in the minds of many as to whether President Henry Cody was the right person to oversee the anticipated number of students who would be attending the University of Toronto after the war. As predicted, enrolment in universities soared.[1] The federal government, reversing the position it had taken after the First World War, took responsibility for the post-secondary education of veterans. In 1945, enrolment at the University of Toronto was about 7,000 – the same as it had been at the beginning of the war. In 1946–47, however, it would more than double to over 17,000.[2] About half the students were veterans. Toronto took about a quarter of all of the veterans in Canada who went on to university.

The School of Law contributed to the increase in numbers for students in the Honour Law course and also for students in other faculties taking individual law courses offered through the law school. For 1935–36, there were a total of 472 students taking one or more courses; for 1943–44 there were 563; and for 1945–46, because of the returning veterans, there were over 850.

The Conservative premier George Drew, who had been elected in August 1943 and had clashed with Cody on a number of issues, was certainly one of those who had his doubts about Cody.[3] Even though Cody had turned seventy-five in 1943 and his health was deteriorating, he did not want to retire. The chairman of the board, Bruce Macdonald, told Cody that he 'must contemplate resignation.' Dr. Bruce and several other influential members of the board wanted Vincent Massey, then Canada's high commissioner in London, to succeed Cody as president.[4]

Cody had, however, thought up a plan that would prolong his presidency for at least a few more years. His scheme was first revealed to the board on 9 March 1944. University College needed a new principal. Cody proposed that Sidney Smith, the president of the University of Manitoba for the previous ten years, would be invited to become the new principal of the college, with the right to succeed Cody as president. In the meantime, the forty-seven-year-old Smith would be executive assistant to Cody.

President Cody (left) with Sidney Smith, principal of University College
and assistant to the president, in 1944 or 1945

In April, the board approved the plan. Smith was known to many influential persons in Ontario because he had taught at Osgoode Hall Law School from 1925 until 1929, when he returned to Dalhousie, his alma mater, to be the dean of law, later moving to Manitoba. He was highly regarded as a university president and had taken over the position of the head of the organization of Canadian universities from Cody. He was also a major figure in the Conservative Party, which would have appealed to Premier Drew and others. In 1957 he would leave the University of Toronto to become John Diefenbaker's secretary of state for external affairs.[5]

Smith accepted the proposal and took over as president on 1 July 1945 – sooner than Cody had hoped. Cody took over the vacant position as chancellor created by the death on 1 October 1944 of Sir William Mulock, the 100-year-old chancellor. Perhaps because of Mulock's age, Kennedy did not seem to have had much to do with him, but commented to the *Varsity*: 'In the life and experience of Sir William there is inspiration and example for every student of this university.'[6] Cody was acclaimed chancellor by the senate for a four-year term in November 1944.[7]

Kennedy wrote to Cody: 'Heartfelt congratulations. Smith will do splendidly, indeed, and the whole idea is admirable ... Please convey to him at once the assurance of my sincerest and good will and desire and promise to cooperate with him in every way in my power.'[8] At about the same time, Kennedy wrote to Smith congratulating him on his appointment: 'I offer you my heartiest and warmest welcome and the assurance of my generous cooperation. You are taking on one of the biggest jobs in Canada ... in your future succession to Cody – and I know that you're the man I always hoped for.'[9] Smith replied: 'I appreciate more than perhaps you could understand, your gracious assurance of co-operation.'[10] As we have seen, their relations over the years had not always been so friendly. During his first year at the university, Smith taught the property course in the Faculty of Law, and no doubt there were conversations about legal education between Kennedy and Smith before or after classes.[11]

Cody replied to Kennedy, who was then at the cottage: 'I am glad to know that you heartily approve. I had in mind all the while the still further strengthening of the Faculty of Law.'[12] And Kennedy noted in his response: 'We'll need all ... Smith's vision as I hear S[hirley] Denison has been appointed treasurer of the L[aw] S[ociety], so prospects are scarcely, to say the least, in propitious hands.'[13]

John Shirley Denison was an important figure in the debate on legal education in Ontario. He was a practitioner from Toronto, who had taught part-time at Osgoode Hall Law School from 1910 until the mid-1920s.[14] He had entered Osgoode Hall Law School directly from high school. In 1931 he became a bencher and was treasurer from 1944 to 1947. Many of the senior members of the profession had not gone to university.[15] Denison was a strong advocate of the articling system and consequently wanted to maintain the Law Society's 'strict and beneficial control' over its members.[16] Office training, he maintained, was the 'crying need' of legal education in the United States.

The faculty at Osgoode Hall Law School took the position that this view overemphasized office training and was designed for the economic advantage of members of the profession. A full-time law program, with a measure of articling after its completion, would be preferable. The dean of Osgoode Hall Law School, John Falconbridge, a soft-spoken respected scholar, had so argued for many years. The son of the chief justice of the High Court of Justice of Ontario, Falconbridge had attended the University of Toronto and then graduated from Osgoode. He started lecturing full-time at Osgoode in 1909, becoming dean in 1923, which office he held until 1948, when Caesar Wright became dean of the school.[17] Falconbridge's scholarship was noteworthy, writing in a variety of fields, including conflicts of laws. Some of his books, such as the *Law of Mortgages* and the *Law of Sales*, are still in print and still widely used.

Caesar Wright

If Kennedy was happy that Smith had returned to Ontario, Caesar Wright was ecstatic. He wired Smith: 'Allah be praised. Lassie come home. Never happier in my life. Love to Harriet. Caesar.'[18] Wright and Smith were close friends. Smith, a Dalhousie law graduate who had spent a year doing postgraduate work at Harvard, had joined Osgoode in 1925 and had taught Wright, who stood first in each year and graduated with the Law Society Gold Medal.[19] Wright had entered Osgoode after receiving the gold medal in political science and history from the University of Western Ontario.[20] The *Toronto Telegram* reported that Wright had a standing at Osgoode of 94.5 per cent, 'one of the highest in the history of the law school.'[21] The two full-time staff members at Osgoode, Falconbridge and MacRae, had written to Harvard law dean Roscoe Pound that in selecting Wright 'as our first representative to you we are naturally indicating a special confidence that he is possessed of ability and scholarship which will do us credit.'[22]

Wright did brilliantly in his one year at Harvard and accepted an offer to be the fourth full-time teacher at Osgoode, along with Falconbridge, former Dalhousie law dean Donald MacRae, and Smith. Wright had entered the Harvard LLM/SJD program, which required taking courses, writing final exams, and doing a number of papers, including a major paper, which Wright prepared for torts scholar Francis Bohlen on 'gross negligence.'[23] At the end of the year, the faculty assessed the performance of each graduate student. If the student passed 'with high rank,' the student would be awarded a master's degree, but if the student passed 'with distinguished excellence,' an SJD degree was awarded.[24] I always assumed Wright's doctorate was on the basis of a thesis, but, in fact, at Harvard neither the LLM nor the SJD in those years required a thesis.

Wright's paper for Bohlen was an impressive work. It was never published during Wright's lifetime, even though he had the opportunity to do so shortly before he began his teaching at Osgoode. Harvard law professor Henry Hart wrote to Wright a month before he graduated, saying: 'Dean Pound has suggested that it would be an exceedingly valuable thing for the Review to be able to publish an article by you.'[25] Why did Wright not submit the gross negligence article? No doubt, as often happens in such cases, the author became heavily involved in teaching and never found the time to revise the paper. Wright had three courses to prepare, commencing in September 1927: jurisprudence, wills and trusts, and agency and partnerships.[26] Torts was not one of his courses. And, as we will see, he also got caught up in the issue of legal education. His first major publication was the paper he delivered in 1931 to the University of Toronto Law Club on 'The Modern Approach to Law,' later published in the *Canadian Bar Review* under the title 'An Extra-Legal Approach to Law.'[27] Like Holmes and Pound – and Kennedy – it preached a 'pragmatic or utilitarian

Caesar Wright (left) and Sidney Smith in March 1948

approach' to law.[28] Still, the failure to publish his paper on gross negligence is a mystery. It is also possible, as sometimes happens to brilliant students, that his personal standards were so high that in his own mind he had not met those standards.

For a renowned academic, his lifetime publication record – particularly when compared to Kennedy's – was not impressive. It is true that as assistant editor and then editor of the *Canadian Bar Review* from 1935 to 1945 he wrote a large number of book reviews and comments on cases in the *CBR*, but he never undertook a major multidimensional project on torts or any other subject. The longest paper he prepared, it seems, was the gross negligence paper. That paper was found among his papers long after his death and published as an eighty-one-page article with 247 footnotes in the *University of Toronto Law Journal* in 1983, well over fifty years after it was written.[29] As Kyer and Bickenbach note, in that ten year period from 1935 to 1945 as editor of the *Canadian Bar Review*, 'he wrote nearly 90% of what he was to publish in his life: more than a thousand pages.'[30]

Moreover, in 1942, in addition to the *Canadian Bar Review*, Wright became editor of the *Dominion Law Reports* and the *Canadian Criminal Cases*, which he continued to edit throughout his career and which took a not insignificant amount of time and energy away from scholarly work.[31] I mention Wright's publication record because, as we will see, contrary to Kennedy's view of the role of an academic, there was a distinct lack of emphasis on legal scholarship by Caesar Wright during the period when he was dean of the University of Toronto law school from 1949 to 1967.[32] The reader may be surprised to learn that even Bora Laskin did not produce a scholarly book on constitutional law or any other subject. It was only *after* he became a judge in 1965 that Laskin produced his Hamlyn Lectures, *The British Tradition in Canadian Law*, in 1969.[33]

Wright and Smith had much in common. Both believed in a full-time law school, whether at the university or run jointly by the Law Society and the university. In 1929, Smith became dean at Dalhousie,[34] and Wright would keep him informed about developments in Ontario. In 1933, for example, Wright wrote to Smith, complaining about Kennedy's plans for a law school: 'I feel quite sure that it will not be long before K. obtains his Law School ... I think you know my own personal views regarding University Law Schools. I am quite convinced a University is the proper place. I am equally sure that its place should be after and not concurrent with an Arts course.'[35] I will not set out here in detail Wright's long fight with the benchers of the Law Society of Upper Canada, which has been fully documented in Kyer and Bickenbach's book, *The Fiercest Debate*.

Wright continued to write provocatively about legal education and law reform. In 1937, for example, he published an article in the *Canadian Bar Review* about the lack of interest by the profession in law reform.[36] He sent Kennedy a copy of the proposed article, in which he quoted extensively from one of Kennedy's own pieces. Wright's article was given prominence in the press. He wrote to his friend Sidney Smith, now in Manitoba: 'I have reason to believe the shot went home and I am looking forward with some pleasure to being on the carpet as having uttered "disloyal" comments concerning my employers ... Frankly, I should welcome a showdown, as I think it must come sooner or later and at the moment I am not particularly concerned with the outcome one way or another.'[37] He was, in those years, keeping half an eye open for other possible teaching possibilities. In 1938, he heard that a new law school might be opening in British Columbia. There was also talk of a position at the University of Western Ontario. At about the same time, he was making inquiries about a teaching position in the United States. He did not, however, follow through with any of these possibilities.

The Smith and Wright families were very close. They sometimes holidayed together. When Wright married in the summer of 1930, he and his wife, Marie, who had been one year behind Caesar at Western, honeymooned in Nova Scotia with the Smiths.[38] Shortly after Smith came to the University of Toronto, they vacationed in New York City together.[39] There can be little doubt that Smith and Wright often talked privately about legal education, discussions which were not recorded on paper.

There is some indication that Cody had approached Wright about leaving Osgoode for the University of Toronto in the academic year 1944–45, but nothing came of it.[40] Kennedy was prepared to give up the deanship. He told Smith in mid-July 1945: 'I want you at once to know that, if it is wise, if changes *come*, I am willing indeed to do only my teaching and writing and serve under anyone else as dean. I am alone interested in the School of Law and the administration is freely and gladly in your hands. I am not worrying.'[41]

Kennedy's health continued to be poor. In August 1943, for example – he was then sixty-four – he wrote to Cody: 'I tire easily and have had a bit of intestinal trouble and insomnia off and on all summer.'[42] A week later, Kennedy wrote: 'I am tied up today with severe lumbago.'[43] The following summer, he wrote to Fred Auld: 'I am tired and a bit worn with extra cares.'[44] In March 1946, he wrote to Dean Vincent MacDonald of Dalhousie University Law School: 'I am getting very tired and I should very much like to retire. I am utterly overwhelmed with outside professional work in addition to the daily task here; and I never seem to get clear of things.'[45] Eugene LaBrie, who was completing his doctorate and teaching at the School of Law in those years, was close to Kennedy and stressed in his various conversations with me that Kennedy wanted out and would make remarks such as 'so weary I cannot keep up any more' and 'I think I have to resign' – but Smith wanted him to stay until the timing was right.[46]

In any event, Smith was saying very little publicly in his first year at the University of Toronto as principal of University College. Wright noted in a letter to a Canadian Bar Association official in February 1945: 'I do not think Smith is, as yet, willing to put his foot into troubled waters.'[47] Smith, it seems, was careful to keep his options open in his first year at the university.

Resignations

The University of Toronto School of Law was weakened in the summer of 1945 by the departures of two important members of the staff: Moffatt Hancock and Bora Laskin. They had been classmates in the early 1930s and were good friends. In June 1945, Dalhousie law dean Vincent MacDonald offered a position to Hancock, following the resignation of a Dalhousie colleague late in the academic year. In a gracious note to Kennedy in late June, Hancock stressed that the financial offer was a strong factor in his decision: 'Yesterday I received an offer from Dalhousie of $4,000 a year with annual increases of $250 up to $5,000. So I accepted at once.'[48] He was only making $2,500 at Toronto. The uncertainty of the future of the law program at the University of Toronto may also have played a role in his decision.

At about the same time, Laskin received an offer from the Law Society to replace Donald MacRae of Osgoode, who had just retired. Again, the offer was significantly higher than Laskin was receiving at Toronto – $4,000 rather than $2,500. Laskin had married Peggy in 1938, and they had a son, John, in 1942. He later told Sidney Smith that money was not a factor, but one wonders. Eugene LaBrie thinks it was a major consideration.[49] When Laskin arrived at Osgoode, he discovered that Falconbridge had been authorized to go up to $5,000; Laskin then asked for and got an extra thousand dollars.[50] Laskin would also be able to work closely with Caesar Wright, with whom he had built a strong relationship while a student at Osgoode and later as the formally unrecognized assistant editor of the *Canadian Bar Review* when Wright took over the editorship from Charles Morse in 1936. Laskin was also an associate editor of the *Dominion Law Reports* and *Canadian Criminal Cases* under Wright. Both the review and the journals brought in extra income, but interfered with his scholarship. The extra income from Osgoode would allow him to cut down on this work.[51] In fact, he ceased his work for the *Canadian Bar Review* in 1945 after Wright ceased being its editor, but continued editing the law reports until he became a judge in 1965.[52]

Further, Laskin was, it seems, aware that his friend Moffatt Hancock was leaving and that it was uncertain how long Jacob Finkelman would continue teaching. Finkelman had told Wright shortly after the offer was made to Laskin: 'Unless there is a definite move for amalgamation within the next year with considerable hope of success, there is no use in my staying on at the University.'[53] That left only Kennedy, with whom Laskin was very close, and Fred Auld, who was almost a generation older than Laskin.

Osgoode would offer greater stimulation. Falconbridge was a strong academic with a good publication record. Further, the highly respected John Willis, who, like Laskin, was interested in administrative law, had recently joined the Osgoode faculty. Moreover, Laskin would be the first Jew to teach at Osgoode Hall Law School – an important first – and he would be closer to the profession. His friends were with the downtown bar – such persons as Eddie Goodman, Charles Dubin, and Sydney Robins – rather than in the university. And, as Laskin said to Smith, he wanted 'to cut his teeth on a new job.'[54] So it is understandable that the Osgoode offer was an attractive one.

Laskin talked it over with Finkelman. He also wanted to discuss it with Wright and Kennedy, who were both up at their cottages. Laskin first went to see Wright at his rented cottage on Lake Ahmic near the town of Magnetawan on Monday, 9 May and stayed two nights. On Wednesday, he and Wright went to see Kennedy at his cottage on Beaver Lake, near the town of Kearney. Laskin described that meeting to Ian Kyer in an interview in 1980: 'When they arrived, they walked with Kennedy along a winding path through the woods along the lakeshore. As the three of them walked along single file, with Kennedy leading the way with his walking-stick, Wright and Laskin began to explain why they thought Kennedy should approve Laskin's acceptance of the Osgoode Hall job.'[55]

Laskin 'raved about,' Wright later wrote to President Smith.[56] Kennedy and Smith did not want to lose Laskin. In a letter from Smith to Wright, dated 9 July 1945, Smith argued that Laskin should remain at the university and that Wright should join the faculty at Toronto as dean, which, as we have seen, would have met with Kennedy's approval.[57] Kennedy had also suggested that Laskin be made an associate professor and be given an $800 raise.[58]

Laskin arranged to see Smith at his cottage on Lake Muskoka the following day, Thursday, 12 July. Kennedy had prepared a private note for Smith, which Laskin was to hand to Smith when he arrived. In the letter, Kennedy urged Smith that 'the very highest offer possible be made to Laskin to retain him.' Nevertheless, he conceded that there might be something in the arguments that Caesar and Laskin were making. He would leave it to Smith's judgment, stating:

> Wright and [Laskin] both think that the offer is of some significance and may do much to help bring Osgoode and U of T together. From my point of view, my chief aim has been and will always be to improve and benefit legal education and scholarship and I feel that if Laskin's going would help that purpose, I shall be satisfied indeed. It may be that the time has come if he goes, for you to take such action as may bring matters to the point of discussion with the benchers.[59]

When Laskin arrived at Smith's cottage, he found that Smith had already left because of a break-in at his home in Toronto. Laskin left the sealed envelope at the cottage for Smith to see when he returned. As it turned out, Smith met with Laskin on Friday, 13 July in Toronto. Smith had not seen Kennedy's letter, but made an offer to Laskin that was higher than he was then receiving, but not close to the Law Society offer of $4,000. In the end, according to Laskin's note to Wright about the meeting, Smith did his best to persuade him to stay, but accepted Laskin's resignation and offered him good wishes for the future, hoping that Laskin would 'play a part in a finer and better and bigger scheme for legal education in Ontario.'[60] Smith also told Laskin that he was 'prepared to open up the legal education tangle, first, through the Board of Governors and then by approaching the Benchers.'[61]

Laskin cabled Kennedy that same day, saying he was accepting the Law Society's offer. Wright's plan had been outlined to Smith in a letter in July. At an opportune time, Wright wrote, he, Willis, and Laskin would move to the University of Toronto, stating: 'WPM, I am convinced, will go if I indicate that I will come up. I am not interested in the present setup. I am interested in a good professional school. I *will go* – provided there is hope – and enough money to live on – and I am sure I can take Laskin and Willis – both of whom should be there.'[62] That was the plan. It is not clear how much of it Laskin was aware of. He certainly knew that he would assist in bringing the two schools closer together.

How much more he knew is not known. Both Sydney Robins and Eugene LaBrie are certain he was not part of any conspiracy.[63]

Kennedy accepted Laskin's decision. They remained good friends. In Kennedy's correspondence with his son Frere, no hostility is displayed towards Laskin. Kennedy wrote to Frere in July 1945:[64]

> Well LaBrie has been appt. in Hancock's place and I am now considering what to do about Laskin, who after a long conversation with President Smith, has decided to leave for Osgoode. I expect [Finkelman] up later and will make no recommendation to the President until I see Finkelman.

Kennedy does not seem angry. Perhaps he knew through Finkelman that Laskin was thinking seriously of leaving. In that same letter, he tells Frere, in a matter of fact manner: 'Peggy comes next weekend.' Gilbert, who was working in Toronto at the time and teaching part-time at the School of Law, also mentions Hancock leaving, but says nothing about Laskin leaving.

After Laskin had decided to leave, Kennedy, as stated earlier, assured President Smith that he was willing to step down as dean.[65] Kennedy now had to hire two more faculty members before the new term started at the end of September. One of them was Eugene LaBrie, who had been a gold medalist from the University of Alberta and had come to Toronto to do graduate work in the early 1940s. As mentioned earlier, he was the first Newton Rowell Fellow at the law school.

LaBrie's father had come to Alberta from the Gaspe Peninsula, a LaBrie ancestor having come to New France as a soldier in the seventeenth century. LaBrie grew up on a farm and went to a one-room public school. His mother had been a schoolteacher in England. LaBrie completed an LLM on the subject of taxation in Alberta under the Social Credit government, was rejected by the military, and enrolled in the DJur program. He completed the course work in the spring of 1945, but, for financial reasons, could not return to complete his dissertation on 'The Meaning of Income in the Law of Income Tax.'[66] That summer, LaBrie was considering an offer to teach for the coming year at the University of Alberta when he received a telegram from Finkelman saying that Hancock and Laskin had resigned and offering LaBrie a full-time position at $2,400 a year. Labrie accepted and took over as secretary of the faculty, an official faculty position that Bora Laskin had filled before him. This position also enabled him to finish his doctorate, which was completed that year and later published by the University of Toronto Press. Laskin had started out as his supervisor, but, as the resident expert on taxation, LaBrie did not need supervision.[67] Other books on taxation followed, including *The Principles of Canadian Income Taxation.*

In 1945–46, with Laskin gone, LaBrie had been asked to teach constitutional law, but gave it up when Laskin returned in 1949. He also taught tax law, but had

Eugene LaBrie in the early 1950s

to give that up too with Willis's arrival the same year. Apart from Laskin, LaBrie was the only one of Kennedy's appointments remaining at the law school when I was a student in 1955. I had him for three courses: company law, tax law, and international law. We liked LaBrie as a teacher. He had a distinctive method of speech: 'He kept – or perhaps invented – his slow western drawl and his gentle sense of humour.'[68] In 1963, LaBrie left the University of Toronto and entered private practice in Toronto, but continued to teach for the next two years on a part-time basis every Friday in the new law course at the University of Western Ontario under Ivan Rand. LaBrie remembers visiting Kennedy in 1963 and telling him: 'The law school is assured of permanence. Your school is bound to survive. I'm leaving.'[69]

Another former Honour Law student, David Vanek – who had been two years behind Laskin in the law program and was also an honours student – was hired. He had a high regard for Kennedy. In his memoirs, he refers to Kennedy as an 'inspirational teacher.'[70] Vanek had been called to the bar in 1939, spent a number of years in intelligence during the war, and then had a brief period in practice. He was, however, well known to Fred Auld because Vanek had, like Laskin and others, been employed almost full-time while at Osgoode and during articling on Auld's *Canadian Abridgement*. In June 1946, he got a call from Finkelman, Vanek writes in his memoirs: 'He told me that Dean Kennedy was

David Vanek's call to the bar, 1939

contemplating offering me a position as a lecturer in the School of Law ... It was like throwing a lifeline to a drowning man. I lost no time in stating that I would be delighted to accept the appointment if offered to me.'[71] Vanek taught for the next four years, also earning an LLB while there. He taught for one year under Wright, but his appointment was not renewed. In 1968 he was appointed a provincial court judge, serving with distinction for the next twenty years.

Negotiations

As noted earlier, Smith told Laskin at their meeting at Simcoe Hall on Friday, 13 July that he was 'prepared to open up the legal education tangle, first, through the Board of Governors and then by approaching the Benchers.'[72] He had laid low on legal education in his first year at the university.

Premier Drew had strengthened the board of governors by appointing Eric Phillips as the chair of the board in 1944. Phillips, a graduate of the university's Faculty of Engineering, had won the Military Cross in the First World War for 'conspicuous gallantry.' He continued as chair of the board until he resigned in 1964. President Claude Bissell remarked on Phillips's reputation in the business world 'for brilliance and ruthlessness, a combination that carried him to the top,'[73] and noted that 'Phillips had a powerful and incisive mind ... [F]ew could resist the combination of toughness, intelligence and charm.'[74] Phillips was close to Premier Drew, and he and President Smith had an excellent working relationship. The vice-chair of the board was Henry Borden, a top lawyer and the head of the large law firm now called Borden Ladner Gervais. All three – Smith, Phillips, and Borden – had roots in the Maritimes. Smith and Borden had graduated from Dalhousie Law School. Borden went on to Oxford as a Rhodes Scholar.[75] The Smiths, Bordens, and Wrights were the best of friends.

In early October 1945, Smith started the ball rolling on the subject of legal education. He asked Kennedy to prepare a memo for the next meeting of the board, outlining the history of the law school. He wanted it, he said, 'as ammunition.'[76] Within two weeks, Kennedy sent a long detailed memo to Smith, giving the long history of law at the university, going back to King's College.[77] In December, the board passed the following resolution:

> Resolved that the Chairman appoint a special committee to consider legal education; to consult thereon with the Prime Minister and the Attorney General of the Province; to appoint representatives to confer with the cooperation between the Law Society of Upper Canada and University in the field of legal education; and to report to the Board of Governors.[78]

Smith wanted the school to be 'the outstanding law school in Canada and one of the leading law schools in North America'[79] He no doubt preferred a university-run law school, as at Dalhousie, where he had been the dean, but would also accept a law school jointly run by the University of Toronto and the Law Society, as in Manitoba. The key to getting the Law Society to engage in discussions was to involve the premier, George Drew, who would be able to put pressure on the benchers to participate in a joint committee. The implicit threat would be that the government could pass legislation on the issue.

Chairman Eric Phillips selected the members of the board who would serve on the committee. President Smith was to be the chair, with Phillips and Borden as members, along with Justice John Hope of the Superior Court and two lawyers who were University of Toronto graduates – although neither had been in the Honour Law program – Arthur Kelly, later on the Ontario Court of Appeal, and Beverley Matthews, a gold medalist from Osgoode and later a senior partner at McCarthy and McCarthy. Board member R.S. Robertson, the chief justice of Ontario, had been asked to serve, but declined because of other obligations. His place was taken by Matthews. Robertson was the honorary president of the Law Club and, with Kennedy's help, had received an honorary doctorate in 1943. But, as someone who did not go to university, he would likely have been less sympathetic to the idea of a full-time law school at the university than the others. He had written to Wright over the summer of 1945, stating: 'I think the Benchers would wisely think twice before abandoning control of legal education.'[80]

Smith informed Kennedy of the steps he had taken, and Kennedy replied on 18 December 1946: 'I think the action which you have taken is most wise in the circumstances, and I shall look forward with great hopes to something creative

Five treasurers of the Law Society of Upper Canada: from left to right,
Shirley Denison, R.S. Robertson, Cyril Carson, D'Alton Lally McCarthy,
and Gershom Mason, May 1950

arising out it.'[81] The committee moved slowly. In June 1946 they prepared a
draft letter for Drew to send to the Law Society, a version of which was then
sent by Premier Drew to both the university and the Law Society in October
1946. The letter stated, in part: 'In my official capacity and also as a member of
the Bar, it occurs to me that if there is to be a School of Law at the University of
Toronto it should perhaps assume a more important role than it has occupied
in the past. It seems possible that there is a duplication or perhaps lack of coordination between the two courses.' The letter went on to say:

> I understand that the Benchers of the Law Society have a Legal Education Com-
> mittee and there is a similar committee of the Board of Governors of the Univer-
> sity. May I suggest the advisability of a joint committee being set up with say five
> representatives from each of these committees under an independent chairman,
> whom they would appoint, and the joint committee consider the possibility of
> improving legal education under some plan of effective cooperation between the
> Law Society of Upper Canada and the University of Toronto.[82]

Anticipating a positive reaction from the Law Society, Smith asked Kennedy to update his memo.[83] There was, however, no response from the Law Society. In December 1946, Phillips re-sent Drew's letter, diplomatically suggesting that perhaps it had never been received by the Law Society. Finally, in mid-January 1947, the Law Society went along with Drew's suggestion and set up a Liaison Committee to meet with the university delegation.[84]

The Law Society Liaison Committee was composed of the treasurer, John Shirley Denison, who, as noted earlier, had gone directly from high school to Osgoode Hall Law School, as had two other benchers appointed to the committee, Cyril Carson, a future treasurer, and John Cartwright, a future chief justice of Canada. The other members were the chair of the Legal Education Committee, Gershom Mason, who would take over as treasurer in 1947, and the official guardian for children in Ontario, Percy Wilson, who was the chair of the Law Society's Special Committee that continued operating during this period.[85]

Failure of the Joint Committee

The ten-person Joint Committee – consisting of members of the University of Toronto's board of governors and benchers of the Law Society of Upper Canada – met on at least four occasions. All the meetings were in the elegant board of governors' room in Simcoe Hall, the main administrative centre of the university.[86] After the introductory meeting in early February 1947, President Smith telephoned Kennedy and gave a report of the meeting. Smith later followed up with a request for twelve copies of the School of Law calendar and various other documents.[87] Kennedy appeared optimistic. In early March, Kennedy wrote to Leonard Brockington, a well-known lawyer who was to be the guest speaker at the annual Law Club banquet later that month, explaining that he, Kennedy, was going to reply to the toast to the School of Law and that he would be careful to 'not stir any of the ancient fires' between the university and the Law Society. 'Indeed,' Kennedy went on to write, 'it is necessary to be somewhat careful in this connexion ... as I wish to tell you in the strictest confidence that there are hopes of reconstructing the Benchers School in cooperation with our Faculty. This cannot be referred to in public at the moment, but the atmosphere is very friendly and I am steering a very careful course.'[88] Later in March, Smith wrote to Kennedy asking for more information, such as whether an Honour Law degree from Toronto was recognized by the Inns of Court.[89] Kennedy assured him that the Toronto law degrees were recognized by the Inns in the same way as law degrees from Oxford and Cambridge were recognized.[90]

Kennedy more or less left the negotiations to Smith. Occasionally, Smith would make a public statement, such as a comment quoted in the *Globe and Mail* on 20 October 1948 that any new law school should be part of the university.[91] He referred to the Ontario system of legal training as 'ridiculous' and, comparing law with training for other professions, stated that 'legal education has made no progress at all … [T]he day of a specialized law school is over. I am convinced the law school should be part of the university.'

Denison, the Law Society treasurer and leader of the members of the Liaison Committee, sent the Joint Committee a memorandum which made it clear that the benchers believed concurrent office training was of great importance.[92] Chief Justice R.S. Robertson agreed to chair the Joint Committee. President Smith and Official Guardian Percy Wilson from the benchers' delegation met over the summer and hammered out a complicated compromise scheme in which the University of Toronto and the Law Society would have joint control over legal education.[93]

Further meetings of the Joint Committee were held in October and December 1947, but the Law Society representatives refused to take a firm stand.[94] In March 1948, the Smith/Wilson compromise proposal was, in effect, repudiated by the benchers of the Law Society, and the Joint Committee was quietly disbanded.[95] The Law Society's Special Committee on Legal Education, however, continued its deliberations. At the May meeting of Convocation, the Special Committee reported that the committee 'is of the opinion that a full-time Law School at this time is not practicable or desirable.'

23

Final Years as Dean

A School to Run

Meanwhile, Kennedy, who turned sixty-five in January 1945, had a law school to run. According to David Vanek, Kennedy was a good administrator and wrote in his memoirs: 'As chairman, Kennedy was business-like, precise and efficient.'[1] The number of students had increased significantly. In September 1945, there were fifty-two students registered for the final year of the LLB course, twenty of whom were ex-servicemen.[2] In the Honour Law course there were sixteen students in 1946, but in November 1948 there were eighty-one students, twenty-two of whom were veterans and fifty-nine civilians.[3] Veterans who had come into the Honour Law course with grade 13 were entitled to complete the course in three years rather than four.[4]

Staffing the courses was not easy, with Laskin and Hancock gone. There were five full-time professors: Kennedy, Auld, Finkelman, LaBrie, and Vanek. Finkelman, however, took a further leave of absence for the year 1945–46 when his appointment as chair of the Ontario Labour Relations Board was renewed. Other staff members were part-timers. They included Honour Law graduates, such as Charles Dubin and Lloyd Holden, later to be judges in the Ontario Court of Appeal. Dubin, for example, taught four hours a week in 1945–46 for $1,200, while practising with his former classmate Jack Kimber.[5] Kennedy's son Gilbert, as we have seen, also taught part-time for several years, while in private practice, before going to the University of British Columbia. Graduate students who also taught included C.W. Leviston, G.W. Reed, S.F. Sommerfeld, and J.R. Westlake. Kennedy, it seems, did not want to fill positions with permanent staff in case there was some form of merger of Osgoode Hall Law School and the University of Toronto School of Law.

As dean, Kennedy had to make recommendations on salaries – always a difficult but important part of a dean's work. It tends to set the tone of an institution.

W.P.M. Kennedy about to attend a convocation ceremony, date uncertain

An exchange with Fred Auld is instructive. Kennedy must have indicated to Auld in connection with his annual salary determination – the letter is not in the file – that Auld should limit his further involvement with the now completed *Canadian Abridgment* and not participate in the annual supplements, no doubt meant to encourage Auld to engage in more scholarly activities. Auld responded: 'Thanks very much for your letter in respect of salary increases. I propose to confine my outside activities, as regards the Canadian Abridgment, to advisory and supervisory work, as editor-in-chief ... This can be done without any curtailing or impairment of my university work. I think it would be unfortunate if my connection with this work, which meets with a gratifying measure of approval from the legal profession, should carry on with the omission of my name from the title-page.'[6] Auld never did become a productive scholar.

As dean, Kennedy was also involved in university affairs. He was, as dean, now a member of Caput, a body that handled disciplinary matters in the university. In 1948, for example, he was involved in a case of 'dishonest practices' and another with the copying and sale of student notes.[7] He was also a member of the committee responsible for the new Institute of Industrial Relations, headed by Vincent Bladen, and continued his involvement with the Workers Educational Association.[8]

There were also minor issues that required attention. One was complaints from his students that Osgoode Hall law students were using the University of Toronto law library and making it difficult for University of Toronto students.[9] Another was from the head of philosophy, Tom Goudge, father of the future Court of Appeal justice Stephen Goudge, complaining that fourth-year law students were being kept overtime at a law class on St. George Street and were always about ten minutes late for Goudge's philosophy class at University College.[10]

And Banquets to Organize

The Law Club, and particularly the club's annual banquet, continued to be important for the School of Law and for Kennedy, and continued to take a considerable amount of Kennedy's time and energy – at least judging by the extensive correspondence in the law school files. Organizing the 1946 spring banquet was probably relatively easy. The chief justice of Ontario, R.S. Robertson, who was also the honorary president of the Law Club, was the speaker at Cody Hall in St. Paul's Church on Bloor Street East.

By contrast, the 1947 banquet in honour of the sixtieth anniversary – the diamond anniversary – of the founding of the Faculty of Law in 1887 was a more complicated endeavour. It was held in the Crystal Ballroom of the King Edward Hotel, and the speaker was Leonard Brockington, the founding chair of the

Canadian Broadcasting Corporation and a respected senior lawyer who was counsel to what is now known as Gowlings. The president of the University of British Columbia, Larry MacKenzie, attended. Gilbert Kennedy, also at UBC, was unable to be there. Kennedy noted sadly to MacKenzie: 'We only wish that Gilbert was coming too, but I expect the expense and lectures rule this completely out of the question.'[11] The event was covered by the CBC, domestically and internationally. As Kennedy said he would, he stayed clear of the Osgoode/Toronto controversy. He did, however, discuss his approach to legal education, saying that the success of the law school was attributable 'to the fact of its modern approach to legal education as a scheme of human engineering and to the atmosphere of broad humane learning.'[12] Brockington wrote to Kennedy after the event: 'It was a great delight to me to notice the great esteem in which your eminent qualities of head and heart are held by all those who come within your pervading influence.'[13]

The 1948 banquet was planned to honour the one hundredth anniversary of responsible government in Canada and the Baldwin-LaFontaine ministry. It was held at the Fiesta Room of the Prince George Hotel – since torn down – at King and York Streets. A who's who of distinguished Canadians reluctantly turned down the invitation to speak. In the fall of 1947, Chief Justice Thibaudeau Rinfret, who had come close to being the speaker the previous year, was again asked to be the speaker. Kennedy wrote: 'I know that your coming would be a real asset to us as we want to make the celebration a symbol of the basic principles, not merely of responsible government, but of the essential union of French and Anglo-Saxons in the fundamentals of our statehood.'[14] Rinfret had to decline because of the pressure of work. We learn in the correspondence that Supreme Court of Canada justice Patrick Kerwin, who would succeed Rinfret as chief justice, had had a serious accident over the summer and had not heard any cases in the fall, resulting in Rinfret having to bear more of the load of writing judgments than usual.[15] We also learn that the governor general, Viscount Alexander of Tunis, was often not in Ottawa, requiring the chief justice to be in Ottawa to fill in as the royal representative.[16] Rinfret said that he could come if the event was at the end of March, but Kennedy pointed out that students were about to have exams then.[17]

The next person invited was Lester Pearson, the undersecretary of state for external affairs. Kennedy suggested that he might talk 'on the international situation from the Canadian point of view, and ... might work it in some way with the centenary of responsible government and the Baldwin-Lafontaine Ministry.' 'For old times' sake,' Kennedy pleaded, 'I trust that you will send me a favourable reply.'[18] It will be recalled that, in the 1920s, Kennedy had advised Pearson to go into external affairs and not try to compete with scholars like Donald Creighton in the history department. He had also written a strong letter of support on Pearson's behalf. Pearson replied that 'with the best will in the world it is not possible.'[19] He had, he said, already promised a number of speeches in February and March, and noted: 'I am afraid that I cannot very well undertake any more in the circumstances; otherwise people would think I have nothing to do in the Department of External Affairs.'

The new chancellor of the university, Vincent Massey, also said no. Kennedy had written to Massey, struggling to find a connection with responsible government: 'We propose, if possible, to make this annual banquet somewhat of a celebration of the centenary of responsible government ... As you have personally seen and taken part in so many of the developments since 1848, we venture to think that you would be a most welcome and admirable guest.'[20] It was late January, and the talk was about six weeks away. Understandably, Massey said no: 'To make an address on this occasion, of the kind which would be appropriate, would require very careful preparation, and as I look at my engagement book I can see how difficult it would be to find the time for it.'[21]

Fortunately, Chief Justice J.T. Thorson of the Exchequer Court of Canada accepted. The speech went well, and Thorson replied to Kennedy's thank-you letter: 'While I discovered that preparation for my remarks involved more work than I had anticipated I enjoyed meeting the students and members of the faculty ... You have done very remarkable work at the University of Toronto and it will miss you greatly when you retire.'[22]

Canadian Association of Law Teachers

Kennedy played a role in creating the Canadian Association of Law Teachers. In September 1947, Frank Scott of McGill, with the support of George Curtis of UBC, sent letters to the Canadian law deans seeking their views about creating an association of Canadian law schools.[23] The idea had been discussed by a number of law teachers at the annual meeting of the Canadian Bar Association in Ottawa earlier that month. Kennedy agreed that forming an association was a good idea and replied: 'I was very glad indeed to get your letter of September 19th for the simple reason that before the war I sounded out various people about an organization such as you have in mind and got very little support for it. However, I think the time is ripe for something of this nature and we shall be glad to give it all the support in our power.' But Kennedy had a number of concerns. One was that the organization should be an organization of teachers, not schools. The latter, Kennedy wisely wrote, 'would commit each school officially to the proposed activities and would lead to endless difficulties.' He had, he said, discussed the concept with the English legal historian William Holdsworth, who had advised him to call the organization the 'Canadian Association of Public Teachers of Law.' Kennedy also advised Scott that it was unwise to link it with the meetings of the Canadian Bar Association because attendance

Frank Scott, McGill Law
School, 1948

by law teachers would not be good. He suggested that the meeting should be at some central location, such as Montreal.

'I believe,' Kennedy went on to say, 'that we would do well to have it here [Toronto] and I could arrange for accommodations. Christmas would be the best time as then it will be possible to get rooms ... I shall be perfectly willing to help you and get the thing under way, as it is one of my dream children and I am more than ever convinced that the time is now riper than ever.'[24] Scott sent a copy of Kennedy's letter to Caesar Wright of Osgoode, who replied: 'In the main, I am in entire agreement with what Kennedy sets out and, as a matter of fact, I discussed the matter with him before he wrote it ... I certainly should be glad to attend.'[25] Vincent MacDonald of Dalhousie also agreed with Kennedy; writing to Kennedy in late 1947, he said: 'As I told Scott I agreed almost completely with your views as to [an] embryo association of Law Teachers and trust it will be delivered to the world in due time.'[26] The suggested meeting did not, however, take place that Christmas.

For the next couple of years, informal meetings took place in connection with the annual Canadian Bar Association (CBA) meetings. In 1948, sixteen law teachers, including Finkelman from Toronto and Laskin from Osgoode, met in August in Montreal.[27] Kennedy was as usual at the cottage, perhaps one of the reasons why he wanted the meeting held over the Christmas break. The following year, the meeting was in Banff just before the CBA meeting. As Kennedy had suggested, these were meetings of law teachers, not of law schools. Then, in 1950, a formal meeting of the Canadian Association of Law Teachers (CALT) was held in Kingston in connection with the annual meeting of the Congress of the Social Sciences and Humanities. From then on, the CALT has usually met annually in connection with the congress.[28]

Scholarly Activities

Kennedy continued to be heavily involved in scholarship. In the 1945–46 annual report to the president, Kennedy noted five scholarly publications by him, three in the *University of Toronto Law Journal*, one in the *Canadian Bar Review*, and another in the *Law Quarterly Review*.[29] This number would be a strong publication record for any academic, particularly a dean, in any time period, including today. No one else at the School of Law came close. Fred Auld had only one publication, which was the annual volume for 1945 of the *Canadian Abridgement* in which he prepared summaries for the titles 'taxation' to 'trials.' It is not surprising that Kennedy wanted Auld to stop or at least cut back his involvement with the *Abridgment*.

It appears that Kennedy was working on a major constitutional law text in those years. Dean Vincent MacDonald of Dalhousie Law School wrote to Kennedy in 1946 about the possibility of MacDonald doing a book on constitutional law, but said he had decided against it, having heard that Kennedy was working on just such a book. MacDonald wrote: 'What about your magnum opus on Constitutional Law? I have had thoughts of various works on that subject, in whole or in part, myself; but have been deterred by reason of your own announced intention to do likewise.'[30] Kennedy replied: 'About my book – those three volumes still lie unfinished although they have been planned and contracted for long years ago.'[31] I have, however, not seen any other reference to these books.[32] Kennedy then adds: 'I had a line from Stevens and Sons [a British Publisher] about a manual on Canadian Constitutional Law which I had to refuse. I told [George] Keeton, the editor, that my present contract would prohibit me from doing such a book. They offered a hundred pounds in advance of royalties on delivery of the manuscript.' Kennedy suggested to MacDonald that he might be interested, stating: 'I think you or Bora Laskin are the only people that I could recommend for such a book.'[33] Neither Laskin nor MacDonald did write such a text, although Laskin's constitutional law casebook contained many notes by Laskin. Indeed, it was not until Peter Hogg wrote his book *Constitutional Law of Canada* in 1977 that such a book appeared.

MacDonald did, however, write to Kennedy in 1947, saying that he was thinking of publishing a collection of his published and unpublished essays on constitutional law, as Kennedy had done ten years earlier, and wondered whether Kennedy could suggest a publisher.[34] MacDonald thought highly of Kennedy's scholarship. In an earlier letter, he noted that he had been preparing an article for the *Canadian Bar Review* 'in the course of which I have been struck anew with awe in the consideration of your enormous learning and facility in expression.'[35] Kennedy replied that the University of Toronto Press might be interested, stating: 'It might be that we could publish your constitutional articles as a volume in the University of Toronto Legal Studies,' and invited

Justice Vincent MacDonald in 1964

MacDonald to send the collection to him.[36] It does not appear that the manuscript was ever sent to Kennedy or was ever published.

In these later years at the university, Kennedy also offered advice to governments. In July 1947, for example, he was asked by the clerk of the Special Joint Committee of the Senate and House of Commons on Human Rights and Fundamental Freedoms for his views on 'the question of the power of the Parliament of Canada to enact a comprehensive bill of rights applicable to all of Canada.'[37] The Canadian Bar Association, John Diefenbaker, and others, such as Frank Scott of McGill, had been arguing for a bill of rights. Instead of replying to the committee, Kennedy wrote directly to Prime Minister Louis St. Laurent, with whom he had had previous dealings.

Kennedy wrote that he associated himself with the evidence of Frederick Varcoe, the deputy minister of justice, and argued: 'It is evident that a comprehensive bill of rights would mean, both for the federal parliament and provincial legislatures, a surrender of their supreme powers. In other words, we would be departing from the doctrine of legislative supremacy, for it is obvious that a bill of rights, if it is to have any meaning, must be beyond the everyday authority of the legislatures, and must be subject to change only by some method extra-legislative ... I do not think it would be possible to have a comprehensive bill of rights covering the whole of Canada. I submit that any bill of rights, however drawn up, must be divided into two parts – one dealing with federal subject matters and the other dealing with provincial subject matters.'[38]

The federal government accepted this argument, and when a bill of rights was enacted in 1960, it applied only to matters under federal jurisdiction. A relatively recent book, Christopher MacLennan's *Toward the Charter*, describes Kennedy's contribution to the issue, stating: 'The most influential and best-argued reply came from the dean of the University of Toronto's Faculty of Law, W.P.M. Kennedy, who upheld the government's reasoning that a bill of rights was a departure from the British tradition of parliamentary supremacy and beyond federal jurisdiction.'[39]

It was not until the Charter of Rights and Freedoms was enacted by the United Kingdom Parliament in 1982, at Canada's request, that Canada had a bill of rights that applied to both the federal and provincial governments. Would Kennedy have approved of the Canadian Charter? Perhaps. Many persons changed their views over the years on the value of a charter, and, as we saw earlier, Kennedy apparently changed his views on the division of powers. In 1947, however, Kennedy was against a bill of rights. He added the following to his letter to St. Laurent:

> Although it is not therefore the question submitted to me, I do not believe that a bill of rights is really necessary. I think that our 'freedoms' are well enough protected in the ordinary law and, if this is not so, it ought to be possible to change the law in the various jurisdictions to suit occasions. I would also like to submit that a bill of rights must, by its very nature, be drawn up in terms which are not terms of art. As a consequence, there would be interminable litigation and the interpretation of the terms would vary in a different manner with the changes of the judiciary. This is the experience of the United States.[40]

Kennedy was also busy editing the *University of Toronto Law Journal*. He did so until he retired, and Jacob Finkelman then succeeded him as editor. Many of the contributors were international scholars from a wide range of disciplines, and the articles continued to be influential. An article by New York University political scientist Clyde Eagleton, for example, entitled 'The Share of Canada in the Making of the United Nations,' was sufficiently important that the under-secretary of state for external affairs, Escott Reid, ordered 400 off-prints.[41]

The last issue of the *UTLJ* that Kennedy edited contains a note from Kennedy under the heading 'Ave Atque Vale' – 'Hail and Farewell.' He wrote: 'Since I founded the *University of Toronto Law Journal* in 1935, I have been responsible for the editorship of every issue. With this issue that responsibility ceases, as my retirement from the Faculty of the School of Law, on July 1, 1949, carries with it the completion of my editorial duties.' He was rightly proud of what he had accomplished and how the *UTLJ* fit in with his strong belief in full-time legal education in a university. He wrote:

> I do not retire without carrying with me many reasons for a modest pride. The *Journal* has been a living witness to full-time legal education with a full-time staff in a university faculty. I am more than ever convinced that any such education outside the intellectual activities of a university is, in the final analysis, barren and fruitless as it does not tend to produce that zeal for law as one of the most vital, indeed the most fundamental, sources of human progress whether municipally or internationally. The *Journal* stands as some small illustration of the validity of my life-long convictions in this connection.[42]

Before we return to the playing out of the Osgoode/University of Toronto controversy, we should again remind ourselves of how close Kennedy and Wright were on jurisprudential questions. Both revered Roscoe Pound, a disciple of Justice Holmes. Wright reviewed a book on jurisprudence for Kennedy's *UTLJ* in 1947, in which he stated:

> Some twenty years ago I was privileged to attend Professor Pound's famous course on jurisprudence at the Harvard law school. Like all others equally so privileged the impact of his overwhelming knowledge and the wide vistas which he then laid before persons who, like myself, had been trained in the black-letter analytical jargon of Austin [John Austin, the nineteenth century British legal philosopher] was an experience to which the much-abused adjective 'terrific' can do justice. There can be little doubt that Professor Pound's influence on juristic thought has been greater than any living English-speaking writer or thinker.[43]

At about the same time Kennedy reviewed a book of essays dedicated to Pound in the *University of Chicago Law Review*, stating:

> Pound stands in a class by himself. His scholarship is amazing ... Running through all this is his exposition of law as a scheme of social engineering ... He has ... disclose[d] how barren have been historical and analytical jurisprudences, whether as specifically taught, or as explicably or implicitly informing teaching

and practice. They tore the law away from life and society, fortified it as a mystic cult living on its own fat and deriving its ideals and philosophies from contemplating its own navel ... He was the first ... who successfully tried to persuade both faculties of law and the practicing lawyers to think of law not in terms of patterns of legal rules, but in terms of the ways of living of actual human beings.[44]

This review of essays in honour of Pound is also interesting because it mentions Kennedy's own legal education – which almost certainly was non-existent until he worked with Lefroy on constitutional law during the Great War. In the review, Kennedy writes: 'As I look back half a century ago to the beginnings of my own legal education and to law as I long knew it, it is nothing less than amazing to be brought up, dead on as it were, with the progress that has been made.' Perhaps he now actually believed he was trained as a lawyer at the turn of the century.

24

The Struggle Continues

Shortly after the University of Toronto/Law Society of Upper Canada Joint Committee disbanded in the spring of 1948, Dean John Falconbridge of Osgoode, who had been dean since 1925 and a faculty member since 1904, announced that he wished to step down as dean, but stay on as a faculty member, and recommended that Caesar Wright be his replacement. Wright had recently been appointed Osgoode's vice-dean. The benchers had little choice and appointed Wright dean as of 1 March 1948. Kennedy sent a note to Wright on behalf of his colleagues, saying they 'desire to convey to you our appreciation of your scholarship and work and our desire to cooperate with you in every way in our power.'[1] Wright replied, expressing his thanks and stating: 'I wish you would convey to your faculty my very sincere thanks and assure them of my very earnest desire to co-operate with them and with your School in every way in which it may lie within my power.'[2]

At this point of time, Wright and Kennedy seemed to have developed a respectful relationship. Certainly, Kennedy and Falconbridge got along well. In December 1947, Kennedy had sent Falconbridge a note about a book Falconbridge was reviewing for the *University of Toronto Law Journal*, and Kennedy added at the end: 'I send you the best season's greetings and my kindest regards. You and I have grown old together in our work, and it is a pleasure to look back on all these years of unbroken friendship.'[3]

The Law Society's Special Committee

The Law Society's Special Committee on Legal Education continued to deliberate. On 30 December 1948, the committee met to determine whether it should approve a three-year full-time program, as proposed by Dean Wright.[4] At the end of the meeting, the committee decided that there would be a majority report and two dissenting reports. The majority report, approved by four members of the Special Committee, was written by Hamilton Cassels of Blakes, the chair of the Law Society's Legal Education Committee.[5] They wanted to stick with the existing system of concurrent classes and articling, arguing that there was 'no fundamental difference in the situation' between now and when the report of the earlier Special Committee was released in 1935.[6] Cassels had been telling Convocation that law professors, including, of course, Caesar Wright, were 'notoriously prone to attack the existing order of things.'[7] The majority did concede, however, that training in law offices had to be improved. The principal recommendation of the majority was 'that a concurrent law school and practical training be continued and that no change be made in the present entrance requirement [that is, a minimum of high school graduation] or the length of service under articles prescribed for graduate or high school matriculation students.'[8]

In contrast, Percy Wilson, the official guardian, who had chaired the Special Committee and with whom John Cartwright concurred, agreed with Wright that a full-time law school should be established, saying: 'I favour a full time law school, or as close to such a system as financial and other conditions of the Law Society of Upper Canada will permit.' Office training during the year would not be abandoned, but would take place during the summers and for a year after completing law school.[9]

Another minority report was by Park Jamieson, a bencher from Sarnia, who wanted a full-time school on a five-year trial basis, with a four-year program consisting of two years full time at Osgoode, then office training – usually referred to as articling – for a full year, with a final year consisting of lectures and office training.[10] The third year of articling could therefore take place outside of Toronto, where it necessarily would continue under the system accepted by the majority. As we will see, this proposal turned out to be the system adopted by the Law Society from 1949 until 1957.

The benchers met in full Convocation on 20 January 1949. Hamilton Cassels moved that the majority report he had drafted be accepted, and it was approved with minor modifications. The full report was not, however, released to the press, but only a modified version of the majority report. This abridged version gave the impression that the Law Society was speaking with one voice, a voice favouring the status quo, whereas the committee had been split 4–3. Wright wrote to the dean of McGill, C.S. LeMesurier, that there was 'a policy of silence in an attempt to create an appearance of unanimity which is far from the truth.'[11] The three reports were not released to the press or the public or even to Dean Wright and his colleagues.[12]

Wright and other members of the Osgoode faculty read about the decision the following morning in the *Globe and Mail*. The headline was 'More Practical Training Decreed for Lawyers.'[13] Only a summary of the majority report had been released. The fact that there were dissents was not mentioned by the *Globe and Mail* in the discussion of the majority report. That morning, members of the faculty met in Dean Wright's office, and Wright said he was resigning. John

Willis, Bora Laskin, and Stanley Edwards also resigned. (Edwards, an Alberta graduate with a master's degree from Harvard, subsequently went into practice with the law firm Fraser Beatty.) Although Falconbridge agreed with his colleagues, he did not resign, having only a short period of time left before his retirement – and his pension. Many years later, John Willis said that they did not expect the benchers would accept their resignations. 'What we hoped and expected ... was that the resignations of all the full time teachers ... would force the Benchers to reverse their decree and we should stay at Osgoode.'[14] The resignations were not to take effect until the end of June.

Dean Wright made strong comments to the press, which no doubt stiffened the backs of the conservative benchers. He told the *Globe and Mail* on the day the report was released: 'Students working in offices all day just become parrots ... They can't explore a legal problem. They just accept it.' Wright also commented to the *Globe and Mail*: 'If medical education was controlled by the medical profession as law is by the legal profession, we would be back in the days of the leeches.'[15]

Kennedy, diplomatically, did not comment publicly on the resignations. The *Varsity* reported that 'Dean Kennedy of the School of Law yesterday refused to make a statement on the resignation, stating that there was no connection between the University Law School and Osgoode.'[16]

There was little sympathy for the Law Society in the press or by the public or by many practising lawyers. Historian Christopher Moore, who wrote the official history of the Law Society, *The Law Society of Upper Canada and Ontario's Lawyers 1797–1997*, stated that Wright's resignation was the 'first substantial, and greatest single, blow to the hegemony of the benchers over governance of the legal profession in Ontario ... [T]hey lost the unquestioning respect they had once enjoyed ... The almost sacrosanct authority of Osgoode Hall had at last been effectively questioned.'[17]

No doubt Caesar Wright and Sidney Smith were in close contact throughout this period. Many members of the Law Society and others believed that the whole plan had been engineered by Smith and Wright. Shortly after the resignations, Smith told Dean LeMesurier of McGill: 'For your ear, we are ready to take on our staff Wright, Laskin and Willis.'[18] Whether Laskin knew this is unclear. They would, of course, have known it was a possibility, and they were surely hoping that it would come about. Laskin recalled in an oral interview in 1977: 'As far as I was concerned, I didn't have a job. I didn't know where I was going to go. I suppose that I could have gone into practice.' He added: 'We started to look around and then Sidney Smith came to us, I think it was somewhere around the end of March.'[19]

The announcement that the three academics were coming to the University of Toronto was made by the university on 10 March 1949. Wright, Willis, and Laskin were happy to be at the university. Laskin's salary was a slight step up from what he was making at Osgoode, $6,650 instead of $6,500.[20] Smith wrote

Three law professors who left Osgoode Hall Law School and joined the Faculty
of Law at the University of Toronto: from left to right, John Willis, Bora Laskin,
and Caesar Wright, who became dean

to the Law Society treasurer, Gershom Mason, on 10 March, informing him
that Wright was to be the new dean of law at the University of Toronto and Willis and Laskin would be professors.[21] Wright wrote a gracious note to Mason,
saying: 'I know that the last two months have been distressing to you – they
certainly have been to me. By this note I merely wanted you to know that nothing in the recent controversy has in any way altered or changed my sincere
admiration – and, I hope friendship – for you personally.'[22]

Wright hoped that the Law Society would opt out of legal education and
restrict its role to ensuring professional competence and discipline. He wrote
to Roscoe Pound later that month: 'I am hoping that eventually in the not too
distant future the University and the Law Society will be able to work out some
mutually satisfactory arrangement whereby the Law Society still retains control
over discipline and admission to practice and the University provides the academic training in a full-time law school.'[23]

Kennedy left for the cottage in May and instructed Eugene LaBrie to hand
over Kennedy's keys to the law school to Wright.[24] LaBrie later noted that

Kennedy was genuinely pleased that Wright was succeeding him, stating that Kennedy was 'very enthusiastic' about the change and 'very pleased to hand [the School] over to Wright.'[25] On 29 May 1949, Kennedy sent a warm letter to Wright from Narrow Waters:

Just a line now that my work is done to give you a very warm and sincere welcome to a faculty which has been my life's work. I can think of no one whom I could desire more to be my successor and to play out my hand. If ever you want me you have only to ask me, in of course an entirely personal way between you and me. At any rate, I know you will never sell down the river to the 'barbarians' the heritage and goals of a real university legal education … You carry with you every unqualified atom of my sincerest good will; I can say no more than that had the selection been mine, I should have unequivocally asked you to be my successor. It is not often in life that one can hand over one's job as I now do to one in whom lies one's fullest confidence and admiration.[26]

On 25 May, Kennedy sent a gracious note to Sidney Smith, saying: 'I had hoped to see you before I came up here for a rest before leaving for B.C.' He went on:

I write to tell you, an official farewell, how deeply I have valued the opportunity to serve with you and I want to thank you for your consideration and patience and cooperation. I wish you continued success in your fine work, and I give to your care and keeping the Faculty of Law. I trust you not … to sell it down the river to Osgoode. There might be an occasion when a little cash from the Benchers might seem helpful, but the long distance view is the statesman's policy; and there is always a danger that a Faculty of Law is only a 'trade school' writ large, as is far too common in the U.S.A. to the everlasting detriment of those things in law which are more excellent. Even indirect indications of policy from Benchers is just a snare and a delusion.[27]

The letter asks Smith to 'please tear up this note, as it is not one I should care to have preserved among "presidential archives"!' The letter concludes with a biblical reference. He tells Smith: 'I trust, when your time comes to retire, that you will know, as I know, the great truth of the Prophet [Zachariah]: "At Eventime it shall be light."' He signs the letter 'very best love and wishes, yours affectionately, W.P.M.K.'

Osgoode Hall Law School

Before continuing with the story at the university, I will very briefly sketch out what subsequently happened at Osgoode Hall Law School.[28] The benchers did not, as Wright and others had hoped, throw in the towel. They reactivated the

Special Committee on Legal Education, which quickly changed course with what future treasurer John Arnup later described as a 'remarkable reversal of what the committee had recommended three months before.'[29] They now rejected the plan that had been proposed by the majority of the Special Committee and approved by Convocation – and had brought about the resignations.

They adopted – in time for the 1949–50 academic year – the scheme that had been put forward by bencher Park Jamieson in his minority report. There would be a four-year program for those with a university education, comprised of two years full-time at Osgoode, then a year of articling any place in Ontario, and finally a further year of articling and lectures at Osgoode Hall. Practice groups were started to improve the articling experience. The five-year program for those without a university degree was eliminated in 1952.[30] Moreover, the benchers continued with plans to build a new educational wing at the northeast corner of Osgoode Hall. Because of the returning veterans, there were 700 first-year students in 1946–47. Although the numbers then started to go down, they went up again after 1952, when it was predicted that the numbers would double before the 1960s.[31]

The Law Society also found a new dean for Osgoode. He was C.E. Smalley-Baker, who had a decent record as an administrator. A Maritimer who had received a law degree from Harvard in 1915, he was wounded while serving in France, became a Rhodes Scholar, was admitted to the bar in England, practised there for a number of years, and then helped found the Birmingham Law School, where he became the dean. The fifty-eight-year-old professor, however, had a drinking problem.[32] Nevertheless, he was a credible dean in those early years. He was able to attract a number of good academics, such as David Smout, who was also teaching at Birmingham, and Desmond Morton, a charismatic Irishman, who had graduated from Trinity College Dublin. In 1950, Allan Leal, a future dean, joined the faculty after completing an LLM at Harvard. He had earlier been selected as a Rhodes Scholar, but did not go to England because he had enrolled in the army.

It was, however, the part-timers who were the mainstay of the law program. The Law Society hired some superb adjunct lecturers, such as Charles Dubin, William Howland, G. Arthur Martin, Sydney Robins, and Walter Williston, all of whom were Honour Law graduates of the University of Toronto,[33] plus Brendan O'Brien, who had taken constitutional law from Kennedy at the university. Most continued to teach at Osgoode for a number of years.

In 1955, the Law Society changed its tune. It was now interested in sharing the delivery of legal education with the universities.[34] What caused the change of heart were the projections about the growth in numbers that would hit the universities and Osgoode Hall Law School the following decade. It appeared that about 1,500 persons would want to attend law school in Ontario.[35] Although Osgoode had recently constructed a new education wing, this building could not take all of the potential students. The legal profession did not want their fees increased or the Law Society to borrow funds – which they had not done for a century – to pay for another major addition to Osgoode. Moreover, there was no assurance that government funding of Osgoode students would continue.

Meanwhile, Queen's University wanted to establish a law school, but insisted on equality with Osgoode. It should not, Queen's argued, take longer to qualify for the bar by going to a university law school than by going to Osgoode. Wright worked closely with political scientist and lawyer Alec Corry of Queen's in the negotiations. The final details were worked out over two days in early 1957 by Corry and two benchers, Park Jamieson and John Arnup. Wright was not at those meetings. 'To be quite frank,' Principal W.A. Mackintosh of Queen's wrote to Sidney Smith, 'I do not think Caesar Wright would help at this stage.'[36] He might have upset the apple cart.

The solution that was adopted was to make the law schools, including Osgoode, a three-year course, followed by a year of articling and a six-month practical bar admission course. Wright was 'incredulous but ecstatic.'[37] The proposal was unanimously approved by the Law Society benchers on 15 February 1957 – a somewhat belated Valentine's Day present for those in the University of Toronto Faculty of Law (including the author) who would therefore save a year.[38] Queen's moved quickly and opened its law school for the following September. Ottawa opened a common law school in 1957 (it already had a civil law program), and Western did so in 1959, with former Supreme Court of Canada justice Ivan Rand as the dean.[39]

Osgoode Hall Law School, like the other university law schools, became a three-year program, followed by a year of articling and then a six-month bar admission course. Only University of Toronto graduates were in the first bar admission course. I was one of them. In the early 1960s, Osgoode dean Allan Leal hired a number of full-time academics, including the future Osgoode dean Harry Arthurs, future Superior Court judge Alan Linden, future Harvard law professor Paul Weiler, and me.

In early 1965, rumours were circulating that Osgoode Hall Law School was considering moving to York University in the north end of Toronto. Again, the Law Society had been motivated by numbers. There was a demand for law students and lawyers in Ontario. Osgoode would have to expand to construct a new addition, which it did not want to do. So an affiliation was worked out with York University.[40] Although happy teaching at Osgoode at its downtown location, I was not keen on a daily trek to Keele Street and Steeles Avenue. I decided to apply to move back to my alma mater, the University of Toronto.

As had taken place twenty years earlier, there were some discussions about a merger with the University of Toronto. Harry Arthurs, who was deeply involved in planning the move to York University, has written about the affiliation with York, stating: 'During this period, attempts were made to reconcile opposing points of view within the faculty [about the move]. Amongst the compromises considered were merger with the University of Toronto's Faculty of Law to produce a single large, semi-autonomous school in a downtown location, and survival as an independent law school, with a corporate existence separate from the Law Society.[41] At a faculty council meeting in April 1965, Wright and his colleagues unanimously turned down this option. (I had not yet joined the Faculty of Law.) Gerald Le Dain, a Quebec lawyer and academic and later a justice of the Supreme Court of Canada, was selected as dean of Osgoode Hall Law School. He was succeeded in 1972 by my fellow classmate, Harry Arthurs, who had received an LLM from Harvard and would later become the president of York University.

University of Toronto Faculty of Law

The new University of Toronto Faculty of Law[42] – established in 1949, with Wright as dean – did not at first thrive. It had some difficult years. Its three-year LLB degree was not recognized by the Law Society as equivalent to the Osgoode degree, and so University of Toronto graduates had to spend a year articling and then take the final year at Osgoode, which was made up of articling and classes. It therefore required an extra year if a student chose to study law at the University of Toronto. This requirement would not change, as we have seen, until 1957, when other universities were permitted to start law schools.

When Caesar Wright took over on 1 July 1949, he changed the nature of the law program. He introduced a three-year LLB program, which he had advocated when he was at Osgoode, and stopped enrolling students in the Honour Law course.[43] Of course, arrangements had to be made for students who were then in Kennedy's Honour Law and LLB courses to complete their degrees.[44] The calendar for the 1949–50 academic year had already been prepared. Wright's memo stated: 'The Four-Year Honour Course in Law, as outlined in the calendar of the School of Law and the Faculty of Arts for 1949–50 is discontinued, and no candidates will be accepted for admission to this course in the academic year 1949–50.'[45] Eugene LaBrie, the secretary of the faculty, was upset, later stating that this change was 'not so much a merger of Osgoode and Toronto as a hostile takeover of the latter.'[46] He called Wright at his cottage to complain and did not want to change the calendar as instructed by Wright. The calendar was changed.

The law school building at 45 St. George Street was also changed by Wright.[47] Kennedy had had rather modest furnishings. An appraisal for insurance purposes at the time stated an overall value of only about $1,000, which included all the furniture and shelving and some of the professor's books, although not Kennedy's library.[48] Wright removed the bookcases in Kennedy's office and reconfigured the space so that Wright's secretary, whom he had brought with him from Osgoode, Joyce McLennan, would have an office adjoining his. Kennedy's secretary had been on another floor.[49] Ms. McLennan – we always called her Joyce – was much beloved by faculty and students and, surprisingly according to today's law schools, was the *only* non-academic staff member in the faculty, apart from librarians, until 1972. She prepared the calendars and time-tables, and even produced a short history of law at the University of Toronto from its beginnings at King's College. Laskin took over Vanek's office – and his constitutional law course – and Vanek was housed in the former secretary's office.[50] An office was not set aside for Kennedy.[51]

The key issue for the new school was, as has been noted, recognition of its new LLB degree by the Law Society. Wright's memo in June 1949 stated: 'The University of Toronto has proposed to the Law Society of Upper Canada that its three-year course leading to the degree of Bachelor of Laws be accepted by the Law Society of Upper Canada as "at least equivalent to the first two years" during which students must give their full time to attendance at Osgoode Hall Law School under the four-year course provided for in the Law Society's new scheme of legal education.'[52]

The Law Society was quick to respond. At the end of June 1949, the Law Society set out a scheme for approval of a law degree from any Canadian law school and then, with particular reference to the University of Toronto, stated that 'it would be hoped that the curriculum and the teaching and the examinations set for the three years of the University of Toronto's proposed course leading to the degree of Bachelor of Laws would enable a student graduated from the course, subject to character qualifications, to be admitted without further examination to the third year of the Osgoode Hall Law School course.'[53] One can see why the university made the request for two years' recognition. Without some assurance from the Law Society, the existing rule provided *no* advanced standing, which would have made it difficult to attract any new LLB candidates for the course that was starting in September. Wright had been dealing with the benchers for over thirty years and no doubt thought that this concession was all that could be achieved at this time. He told Arthur Goodhart in mid-March, shortly after he came to the university, that he took on the job 'with a hope, and it is only a hope, at the moment, of receiving recognition from the Law Society for its LL.B. degree ... It may be that we will need enabling legislation to permit Toronto graduates to be called to the Bar after some period of apprenticeship.'[54]

Wright was able to assemble an excellent faculty. Almost all had American graduate degrees. Most had done graduate work at Harvard, such as Jim Milner from Dalhousie; Albert Abel, a graduate school friend of Laskin, who was teaching at West Virginia; and David Kilgour, an Osgoode medalist. In addition, there was Robert McKay, an Osgoode graduate, who had done his graduate work at Columbia; Abe Weston, an Oxford graduate, the only new hire with a degree from England; Edward McWhinney, an Australian who had done his

Baldwin House, now called Cumberland House; today the
International Student Centre

doctorate at Yale; and Wolfgang Friedmann, a senior distinguished German-trained international and comparative law scholar, then teaching at the University of London and the University of Melbourne.[55] David Vanek taught for one year under Wright, but was not kept on; Jacob Finkelman stayed for a few more years.[56] Eugene LaBrie and Bora Laskin were the only Kennedy appointments remaining as of the 1953–54 academic year. LaBrie would resign in 1963[57] and Laskin in 1965, when he was appointed to the Ontario Court of Appeal.

The first class of students under Dean Wright was admitted in September 1949 and spent three years at the law school, graduating with an LLB in June 1952.[58] The number of new students in the law faculty remained low for a number of years: only nineteen graduated in 1953, and a mere ten students graduated in 1954.[59] One University of Toronto board member wrote to Premier Frost, saying that something must be done because the faculty 'at present almost equals in number its students.'[60] The university had expected more students, and in the fall of 1953 the law school moved into larger quarters, from 45 to 43 St. George Street, its former home and originally the home of

University of Toronto law
students demonstrate in front
of Osgoode Hall in 1952

the architect of University College, Frederick Cumberland – at the time called
Baldwin House, but later named Cumberland House.[61] The quality of the faculty was not, however, enough to attract a respectable number of students. In
the fall of 1951, John Willis returned to Halifax, stating: 'Just two years after it
started as a professional school the School of Law is to all intents and purposes
dead.' Wright gave some thought to an offer to teach at the University of California, Los Angeles (UCLA).[62]

The Law Society ignored the university's request for full recognition of its
program. It took a year and a half for the treasurer of the Law Society, Cyril
Carson, to respond to a letter from Henry Borden, the chairman of the University of Toronto's Board of Governor's Legal Education Committee. Borden
was certainly not used to such treatment. Premier Leslie Frost, however, was
not prepared to help the university. Eric Phillips had a long discussion with
Frost on legal education and reported to Smith that 'he is definitely anti-Wright
and has the impression that you have been taken into camp by Caesar Wright
and have unwittingly become the vehicle to make articulate Caesar's hatred of
Osgoode.'[63] The University of Toronto Board of Governors was aware of the
strong feelings against Wright and removed him from the board's Legal Education Committee.

A peaceful demonstration by about forty-five law students in 1952 in front
of Osgoode Hall, asking for the elimination of the final year at Osgoode for
Toronto graduates, brought publicity, but no positive response from the Law
Society.[64] One unnamed demonstrator told the press that the present arrangement was 'giving Toronto lawyers the equivalent of slave labour.'[65] 'Surely the
practicing lawyers of Ontario,' responded Treasurer Cyril Carson, 'are best able
to judge the period required for service under articles before Call to the Bar.'[66]

Flavelle House, formerly the home of Joseph Flavelle. Seen here are
Governor General Lord Minto and Lady Minto arriving at the home
shortly after it was completed in 1903

Because an extra year was required if one attended the University of Toronto
Faculty of Law, most of the students who were drawn to the course were academically inclined. I entered the law school at Cumberland House in September 1955. We received a first-class legal education. The numbers continued to
rise because of the quality of the course. The law school outgrew its quarters
on St. George Street and moved into a grand house on the Glendon estate
on Bayview Avenue, in the northern part of Toronto. For most law students,
this arrangement was in some respects even better than being on the campus
because the law professors were to a considerable extent captive there and were
almost always available to the students. They ate lunch with the students in the
only lunchroom in the building. I seem to recall walking in the Don Valley
ravine talking law with Bora Laskin, but it may not be an accurate memory.[67]

In addition to the quality of the program, the fact that the university LLB was
fully recognized by the Law Society in 1957 resulted in enrolment at Toronto
rising significantly. In 1962, the law school moved to Flavelle House on the
University of Toronto downtown campus, and the number of law students at
the university rose to about 400.[68] The faculty had felt isolated at Glendon and

The official opening of Flavelle House, 22 November 1962: left to right,
Principal J.A. Corry of Queen's, Lord Patrick Devlin, Caesar Wright,
Chief Justice of Ontario J.C. McRuer, and Dean E.N. Griswold of Harvard

wanted to return to the main campus. President Claude Bissell supported the
move, telling Eric Phillips that 'it would give the Faculty a central position on
the campus.' 'Moreover,' he added, 'it has Caesar Wright's apparently enthusiastic support, which, as you realize, is no small matter.'[69] A library, designed by
Vincent Massey's son Hart Massey, with classrooms underneath, and a separate, but connected, moot court building were constructed. The Department
of History had previously occupied the building and was forced to move, a fact
not soon forgotten by its faculty members. The official opening, attended by
Lord Devlin of the British House of Lords, Harvard law dean Erwin Griswold,
and other dignitaries, was held on 22 November 1962.[70] Dean Kennedy was not
well enough to attend the opening.[71]

Wright resigned effective 30 June 1967. Not only was his health not good –
he was a heavy smoker – but he felt pressure to resign because a university
committee had recently brought in a report recommending that deans be limited to a seven-year initial appointment.[72] At that point, Wright had been dean

for eighteen years. According to then president Claude Bissell's diary, Wright seemed 'quite happy at the prospect of a sabbatical and a return as professor.'[73] He died suddenly on 24 April 1967 at the age of sixty-two, just two months before retiring.[74] Convocation Hall was packed for his funeral. The Law Society, which was to have given him an honorary degree later in the spring, noted that 'he has rightly been called the architect of legal education in Ontario.' The degree was awarded posthumously.[75]

Ronald St. John Macdonald, a Maritimer and a distinguished professor of international law who would later be a justice of the European Court of Human Rights in Strasbourg, was selected as dean. Like Kennedy, he strongly supported legal scholarship. In 1968 he established a committee on research which I chaired, with Ian Baxter, Jim Milner, and Stephen Waddams as members, all of whom supported more scholarly publication by faculty members. An earlier report, commissioned by Wright in 1966 on teaching and research, had played down the importance of published research, stating that reading and thinking for the purpose of teaching is research. The earlier report went on to say, however, that 'the Faculty should recognize that all members from time to time in their research will be led to inquire into matters that they should publish elsewhere than in the classroom' and research leading to publication 'should be encouraged and facilitated.'[76] Like Dean Kennedy, the later research committee was strongly in favour of published scholarly research.

For some time, the university had been concerned about what was happening at the Faculty of Law. In the summer of 1969, President Claude Bissell sent a dramatic memorandum to the teaching faculty and the legal members of the board, stating that 'the Faculty was falling behind in all of the basic areas that determine academic quality ... The question now before us is whether we want to retain a first class Faculty of Law, or whether we want to abandon the enterprise entirely.'[77]

In early 1972, I was selected as the fourth dean of law. At about the same time, my classmate and friend, Harry Arthurs, was appointed dean of Osgoode. Harry and I set up a number of cooperative programs, such as sharing library resources and making each school's small specialized courses available to both faculties, but at the same time we were each competing to improve the teaching, research, community involvement, and reputations of our schools.[78] In *The University of Toronto: A History*, published in 2002, I immodestly wrote:[79] 'Under Friedland's deanship, the faculty deliberately moved more directly into the University, by increasing the amount of interdisciplinary work and placing a greater emphasis on scholarship.' I then noted that a 'succession of future deans – Frank Iacobucci, Rob Prichard, Bob Sharpe, and Ron Daniels – would appear to have brought the school to the position dreamed of by Sidney Smith: "a Law School that would rank first in Canada and be among the leading schools of the North American continent."' That position has been solidified by later deans.

25

Retirement

Dean Kennedy retired on 30 June 1949. Six months earlier, he had celebrated his seventieth birthday at a small gathering at his home at 77 Spadina Road. The *Globe and Mail* commented on his retirement, stating that Kennedy 'leaves academic work after a career of the highest distinction. Generations of students remember him thankfully as a great teacher who joins wisdom, humour and kindliness to vast learning.'[1] He was the main speaker at the Law Club's annual banquet held on 17 March 1949 – St. Patrick's Day – in the elegant Crystal Ballroom of the King Edward Hotel. The letter of invitation stated: 'This year we will honour Dr. W.P.M. Kennedy, who is retiring from the post as Dean of the Law School at the end of this term after 35 years with the University … Dr. Kennedy will be our guest speaker, and there is little need to tell you that we expect a truly inspiring address.'[2]

The *Globe and Mail* reported the following day: 'Barristers, jurists and students crowded the room to pay tribute to Dean Kennedy … Through it all, he sat with his eyelids lowered, his mouth working sometimes. But when he stood to reply it was with the wry wit, the undimmed enthusiasm, the youthful idealism that made him famous.' His theme was not about legal education – a delicate subject, considering that the week before the university had announced that Caesar Wright and his two colleagues were coming to the law school, and it was unclear whether the Law Society would recognize the School of Law – but rather about 'mediocrity in education.' Kennedy urged the creation of some new institution between the university and high school. He would also like to see a reduction of lectures: 'I would like to see lectures reduced by two-thirds and the students placed under wise directors of studies.'[3] At the conclusion of the banquet, those attending sang 'My Wild Irish Rose.' Kennedy wept, as did many in the audience.[4]

The retirement date had been determined two years earlier. Towards the end of 1947, Kennedy had been offered a one-year fellowship at St. John's College, Cambridge, to be taken up in October 1949. The fellowship was for

'a distinguished and outstanding scholar from the Dominions.'[5] Kennedy
explained the invitation in response to a note of congratulations from his former student Charles Bourne, who had studied at St. John's and was now teaching at the University of Saskatchewan: 'St. John's College have appointed me to a
fellowship for a year. I shall have a suite of rooms and an adequate honorarium.
I shall have no lecturing to do. The idea is along the same lines as a fellowship
at All Souls, Oxford. I expect that Mrs. Kennedy will go with me, but we shall
not be going until perhaps late next year.'[6] And Kennedy replied to a letter of
congratulations from Dean Vincent MacDonald of Dalhousie, stating: 'When
I get there, it will be a rest.'[7] On 19 May 1948, the University of Toronto Board
of Governors sent Kennedy their congratulations on being selected for the 'first
invitation under a fellowship which will bring to Cambridge from time to time
"a distinguished and outstanding scholar from the Dominions."'[8] Sidney Smith
sent his congratulations, and Kennedy replied: 'In July, 1949, I lay down my
work after an unbroken thirty-five years; and it is a source of great pride to me
that, during all these years, the Presidents and Governors have been more than
kind and considerate.'[9]

As it turned out, Kennedy was not able to take up the fellowship. The correspondence on the fellowship is missing from the St. John's Archives, but the St.
John's Council minutes of 5 May 1949 simply state: 'The Master reported that
William Paul McClure Kennedy had written to inform him that owing to ill-
health he will be unable to fulfil the conditions subject to which he was elected
to a Fellowship ... for one year from 1st October 1949.'[10]

With a fixed retirement date, Kennedy started going through his personal
papers in early 1948. On 16 February 1948, he sent a letter to Mrs. Newton
Rowell: 'I have been going through crowds of old letters going back forty years
and I have been destroying those of no interest.' He then stated that he came
across replies to letters he had sent to some judges in England along with
his tribute to her husband that he did for the Royal Society of Canada. 'After
we lost Mr. Rowell,' Kennedy wrote, 'I sent my printed appreciation of him
which I also sent to you to my close friends, Lords Wright, Sankey, Macmillan and Simon, who were also friends of your dear husband. In my process of
destruction, I found their replies and I think you might care to keep them as
part of your family records.'[11] The 'destruction' took place at his office at the
law school. Gilbert was asked in his oral interview whether any of Kennedy's
papers survived. He replied: 'No, I am told – I was in British Columbia at the
time he retired – but I am told that he destroyed all his files before retiring –
just before retiring. He had boxes of them, file boxes of them, in his office
across the top of his long bookshelf.'[12] Kennedy's daughter Shelagh told me
that her father 'did not want a biography ... didn't want people to know what
he had done.'

Involvement in the Law School

Kennedy was only peripherally involved in Caesar Wright's Faculty of Law.[13] As we saw in the last chapter, he was not given an office. Nor was he given a course to teach. He had one graduate student in 1953, a British West Indies student who had just completed his LLB at the University of Toronto. The topic was on the proposed plans for a British West Indies federation.[14] He also gave four lectures on constitutional law in the spring of 1952 and 1953 'at Caesar's request' to the second-year class, for which he was paid $250 each year.[15] He noted in a letter to Frere in early 1952: 'I'll get $250 which is a terrific help towards [Beatrice's] apartment, which is a great burden to mother and me.'[16]

He certainly wanted to be more involved in the law school, writing to Dean Wright in November 1953: 'My troubles last winter arose mostly from having nothing to do. Sid [Smith] was in and he promised to talk to you when he could ... It's up to you! No legal obligation, but *moral* – far more demanding. I trust you will take this up with Bora and see if something can be done.'[17] Nothing further was done. He certainly did not lecture at any time to my class that entered in 1955. Wright's notes of his welcoming remarks to my class do not mention Kennedy, but simply say there was a 'reorganization in 1949.'[18]

It is not clear whether Kennedy attended the annual banquets, which continued over the years with special guest speakers. The banquets were less lavish than they had been in Kennedy's days, although the very early ones were black-tie events. Supreme Court of Canada justice Ivan Rand was the speaker at the 1950 banquet, held in the Oak Room of Union Station.[19] There is no indication in the records that Kennedy attended. Alec Corry, the new principal of Queen's, was the speaker in 1953, and again there is no indication that Kennedy was there.[20] As the second vice-president of the Student Law Society, I organized the banquet in 1957. My hazy recollection of the event is that very few outside guests were invited for the dinner at the Savarin Tavern on Bay Street, where noted litigator Joseph Sedgwick was the speaker. (Unlike my current interest in archival materials, I did not keep any records of my law school days, except for a copy of my criminal law notes.) Those attending were law students and faculty members. I think I would have remembered if Kennedy had been at that banquet. Wright kept copies of his introductory remarks for some of those banquets, and there is no mention of Kennedy being present.[21]

For the most part, Kennedy stayed out of the politics of legal education, although not completely. In a letter to Premier Leslie Frost in mid-January 1950 about other matters, Kennedy must have raised the subject with Frost, who replied: 'I shall be glad to have a chat with you some of these days concerning legal education. Have you discussed this with [Attorney General Dana] Porter? I think that he is very much interested in some of the difficulties which you have in mind.'[22] We do not know what those difficulties were, but it is more than likely that they involved recognition by the Law Society of the University of Toronto Faculty of Law.

Wright seems to have wanted Kennedy's ties to the law school cut. R.C.B. Risk states in his article on Kennedy: 'Within a few years [Wright] had erased whatever remained of Kennedy's vision and established his vision of a professional law school.'[23] Similarly, Philip Girard observes in his biography of Bora Laskin that 'once in power, Wright would do all he could to exclude Kennedy from the life of the law school and to erase and obscure his place in the collective memory of the institution.'[24] The Wright papers – mainly through correspondence with Gilbert Kennedy – show that Wright spoke to Kennedy from time to time, but indicate nothing about Kennedy's involvement with the Faculty of Law.

Wright did not introduce much in the way of curriculum reform. The courses offered at the school did not differ in any significant way from those at Osgoode Hall before 1949. 'Nor did Wright do much to encourage the academic, multidisciplinary, extralegal approach to law that he had at times vigorously advocated. In some respects Wright's school was less academic and less innovative in its curriculum than Kennedy's school had been in the 1930s and early 1940s, because Wright was at heart a practice-oriented teacher.'[25] Bora Laskin, who continued to visit Kennedy over the years, also ignored Kennedy – probably by oversight – in writing an article published in 1953 in the United Kingdom on law teaching in Canada, an omission that disturbed Kennedy's son Gilbert and Eugene LaBrie.[26]

Honours

The University of Toronto honoured Kennedy by awarding him an honorary doctor of laws in 1953. The convocation address was, however, delivered by another honorary graduate that day, Paul-Edouard Gagnon, a Catholic bishop from Quebec, who would later become a cardinal.[27] The citation for Kennedy, drafted by Sidney Smith, referred to Kennedy's Irish accent: 'During two-score years and more in Canada, the brilliance and eloquence of that tongue have been as durable as its brogue ... For him, the state under the Rule of Law must be the servant and not the master of the people. For him, Constitutional Law, in which he is an outstanding scholar and a distinguished adviser, is not a monument, but rather a growing tree.' Smith concluded:

Mr. Chancellor: In the name of the Senate I request you to confer the degree of Doctor of Laws, *honoris causa*, on William Paul McClure Kennedy, whose gift for friendship has made this University a finer place, whose wit and dialectic have made it a livelier place, whose scholarship has distinguished it, and whose vision, by improving legal education, has advanced the law itself.[28]

Kennedy, beside a military officer, in an academic procession in 1953, about
to receive an honorary doctorate from the University of Toronto. The mace
carrier leads the procession, followed by Chancellor Vincent Massey

After receiving the degree at the spring convocation, Kennedy went with Pauline to Narrow Waters. In a note, he thanked Smith for his generous remarks, to which Smith replied: 'It was a source of great personal joy to me to see the conferment of the highest accolade of the University on you last Friday … I was delighted to read that you stood the day well and that you are feeling better in that delightful spot.' Then Smith adds, intriguingly: 'Isn't that a splendid invitation that you have received from the United Nations! I do hope that you will be able to accept it.'[29] I have been unable to discover what the invitation was. Correspondence with the United Nations Archives has produced no clue. Whatever the invitation was, Kennedy obviously turned it down. Kennedy had previously turned down a request from UNESCO in 1948 to prepare a report

W.P.M. Kennedy and Pauline Kennedy seem content at
Narrow Waters, date unknown

for a project entitled "Methods in Political Science."[30] Strangely, Kennedy
replied: 'I am a lawyer and would not hold myself out in any way as competent
to write a paper for your learned organization.'[31] Once again, he seems to have
thought of himself as a full-fledged lawyer.

I was surprised to discover that when the law school returned to the University of Toronto campus in the early 1960s, Wright sought to have the moot
court named after Kennedy.[32] Like Dick Risk, I was not aware of this, and in my
time as a professor at the law school I never heard the name Kennedy associated
with the moot court or saw any sign or picture indicating that it was called the
Kennedy moot court. The Wright papers contain Smith's remarks at the opening ceremony on 22 November 1962. Wright made some generous comments
about Kennedy, stating: 'And this end result – with the feeling of permanence
and belonging that any home-building always brings – is in truth a tribute to
the untiring and inspired efforts of Dean W.P.M. Kennedy who for years kept
the light of legal education glowing in this University at a time when lesser
men might have quailed.'[33] There is no mention in these remarks of naming the
moot court after Kennedy.

That evening, however, there was a dinner honouring those receiving honorary degrees that day. After praising the honorary graduates as well as the former
chancellor of the university, Edward Blake, and his father, William Blake, the
first professor of law at the university when it was King's College, and suggesting that the new wing of the law school should be named 'Blake Hall,' Wright

suggested that the moot court should be named after Kennedy, stating: 'While engaged in praising great men, may I take this opportunity of expressing to you again my suggestion that our Moot Courtroom, to be built in the immediate future as part of the present law building should be known as the Kennedy Moot Courtroom in honour of its first Dean.'[34] Nothing came of this suggestion. It may be that the idea did not appeal to the board of governors. The Kennedy name was never attached to the room. Many years later, it was named the Rosalie Silberman Abella Moot Court Room.

There is, however, a medal named after Kennedy – the W.P.M. Kennedy Silver Medal for the second highest standing on graduation. For a number of years, there was also the W.P.M. Kennedy Award for outstanding law teaching in Canada, which had been established by the Samuel E. Weir Foundation. Weir, who died in the early 1980s, had been a bencher of the Law Society who took several courses at the University of Toronto School of Law towards an LLB. The president of the foundation was Eugene LaBrie, who had been Weir's lawyer and executor.[35] The memorial award is no longer given.[36]

Federal/Provincial Conferences

Shortly after Kennedy retired, he was invited by the premier of Ontario, Leslie Frost, to serve as an advisor to the Ontario government for three important federal-provincial conferences[37] that took place in 1950, the first and last in Ottawa and the second in Quebec City. Kennedy participated in all of them, accompanied by Pauline, staying at the Chateau Laurier in Ottawa and the Chateau Frontenac in Quebec City.[38]

On 14 September 1949, the federal prime minister, Louis St. Laurent, sent a letter to all ten premiers (Newfoundland had just joined Confederation), inviting them to a conference to discuss a process of amending the British North America Act. St. Laurent stated:

> For some time the government has been giving consideration to devising a satisfactory means of removing the necessity, on every occasion on which an amendment to the British North America Act is required, of going through the form of having the amendment made by the Parliament of the United Kingdom. It does not accord with the status of Canada as a fully autonomous nation that we should be obliged to have recourse to the Parliament of another country, however close our association with that country, to determine our own affairs.[39]

Kennedy had given thought to and written about this issue. He had given expert evidence on the matter in testimony before a Special House of Commons Committee in 1935 and discussed the issue in the second edition of his book on the constitution of Canada.[40]

Prime Minister St. Laurent opened the first conference in the House of Commons on 10 January 1950. Kennedy had been invited as one of the province of Ontario representatives, the only person who was part of the Ontario delegation and not a cabinet minister or a civil servant. St. Laurent's opening remarks stressed the importance of the meeting: 'It is our hope that this will prove to be an historic occasion. It is the first occasion since Confederation that a conference has met for the exclusive purpose of considering the constitution of our country.' A recently enacted constitutional amendment had given the federal government the power to enact legislation that related to federal powers, without having to ask the British Parliament to pass legislation and without the need to seek the approval of the provinces. Similarly, the provinces had been given power in the British North America Act to amend provincial constitutions.

'There is, however,' St. Laurent went on to say, 'no means whereby legislative authorities responsible to the people of Canada can make such amendments as may from time to time be required in the third area of the constitution, namely, the part of our constitution that is of concern to both federal and provincial authorities.' A method to do so, he argued, has to be found, and he ended his remarks by stating: 'Sooner or later this challenge will have to be met, because sooner or later the people of Canada are going to insist that somehow means shall be found by which complete jurisdiction over the constitution of Canada is established in Canada.'[41]

Premier Frost was the next speaker, setting out the history of the issue and agreeing with St. Laurent that a method should be found to amend the constitution in Canada. 'I shall not discuss this matter in detail at this time,' he stated, 'but it occurs to me that the method should be (a) elastic enough to meet the needs of a growing and developing nation; (b) difficult enough to discourage indiscriminate tampering with our constitution; and (c) rigid enough to provide ample safeguards to protect minorities and fundamentals and the federal system under which we have developed so satisfactorily during the last eighty-three years.'[42]

I cannot determine the extent to which Kennedy helped shape these remarks – the archival records do not shed light on this issue – but several brief passages in Frost's remarks dealing with the Statute of Westminster and the American system for amending its constitution, which Kennedy had discussed in his report for the Rowell-Sirois Report, suggest his input.

Shortly after the conclusion of the conference, Frost sent a letter to Kennedy, stating: 'I can assure you that it was a great help to have an old veteran like yourself taking part in the deliberations. I am sure that we made some progress.'[43]

The second conference, which Kennedy also attended as an advisor, was held in the legislative assembly chamber in Quebec City in September 1950,[44] at which a continuing committee of attorneys-general was set up to study various proposals for an amending procedure 'which, while having in view the

December 1950 Dominion-Provincial Conference in Ottawa. Prime Minister
Louis St. Laurent is in the centre, and Ontario Premier Leslie Frost is to his right

safeguarding of those basic rights, would assure adequate flexibility in the constitution.'[45] Frost sent a memo to Kennedy in advance of the meeting, enclosing a
memo which, Frost stated, 'is now being considered by the Attorney-General ...
I would like your views. What do you think? Is this the right method?' Unfortunately, I do not have Kennedy's response. The *Globe and Mail* reported at the
end of the second conference that 'substantial progress has been made toward
bringing to Canada full power to amend the Canadian constitutions.'[46]

A further conference was to be held in Ottawa after a federal-provincial fiscal conference. The fiscal conference, which started on 4 December 1950, was a
significant conference that played a major role in shaping the future of Canada.
The meeting, which Kennedy attended,[47] was originally scheduled for the fall
of 1950, but had to be postponed because a special session of Parliament had
been called because of the Korean War. The fiscal meeting filled the slot that had
been set aside for the third constitutional conference.[48] Frost's executive assistant wrote to Kennedy on 10 November 1950, saying, 'I presume that you have
already been advised by the Government that the Prime Minister would appreciate your going to Ottawa for the resumption of the Dominion-Provincial
Conference on December 4th.'[49]

The third meeting dealt with the issue of taxation, old age pensions, and
equalization.[50] These were issues that had interested Kennedy in the past. It will
be recalled that he wrote a book with Dalton Wells in the early 1930s, *The Law
of the Taxing Power in Canada*, and the Rowell-Sirois Report had dealt, in part,
with taxation and related matters. Kennedy wrote to Frere just before leaving
Toronto by train for Ottawa. He does not mention the issues to be debated, but
states: 'I got a new pair of shoes and a hearing aid.'[51] He described in some detail
his new hearing aid, which he said was 'excellent': 'It fits into a vest pocket and
has two magnificent controls – volume and tone – it's just like a very miniature

radio. I've really got almost accustomed to it and the improvement and convenience are excellent.'

At the conclusion of the conference, it was agreed in principle – with details to be later worked out – that the provinces and the federal government would share the distribution of what is called 'direct taxation' – income and corporate taxes as well as succession duties, which would be collected by the federal government.[52] (Under the British North America Act, both the federal government and the provinces had jurisdiction over direct taxation.[53]) During the war, however, the provinces had 'rented' their jurisdiction over direct taxation to Ottawa in exchange for a fixed annual payment.[54]

The participants at the federal-provincial conference also agreed that the provinces would be given power, which they did not then have under the BNA Act, to collect indirect taxes, such as retail sales taxes.[55] The provincial taxing power had been limited to 'direct taxation.'

Further, old age pensions were expanded. The means test for those seventy and older that had been established in 1927 would be abolished, and all citizens would receive $40 a month from the federal government. The scheme, to be worked out later with the provinces, would be funded through the income tax system. Ontario was the first to develop the scheme with Ottawa on a fifty-fifty basis. Kennedy must have been very pleased to now be receiving $40 a month for himself and the prospect of a further $40 for Pauline. A scheme for needs-based pensions for those between sixty-five and seventy was also agreed upon, with details to be later worked out.[56]

Finally, a scheme for payment of provinces based on need was established. Canada's system of equalization payments first established in the 1950s is recognized as an important contributor to Canadian society.[57]

It is hard to conceive of a fuller agenda for the conference and a more successful result. Kennedy participated in these important changes, although how much input he had is uncertain.

He wrote to Frere about the conference shortly after returning to Toronto on Friday afternoon, 8 December 1950, stating:[58] 'I was most tired all week as the conference was in camera dealing with concrete and abstruse financial proposals. Indeed I'm so tired I'm resting up over the weekend. I can tell you little except what has appeared in the papers: but it seems that two amendments to [the] B.N.A. Act are proposed for consideration and report (a) to give federal legislature control over old age pensions – especially perhaps to collect special taxes for them; (b) to give province power to levy some form of indirect taxes – e.g. a retail tax. There was substantial agreement on these and pending reports on them.'

As to amending the BNA Act, Kennedy wrote:

Mr. St. Laurent thought it wise to postpone the adjourned constitutional conference. He felt if we could get these two proposals settled and out of the way, the ground would be cleared for wider actions. Indeed, no one was sorry to get home as we were all worn out and the shadow of war and defense expenditures hung heavy over all these things and over the entire capital – to say nothing of the fact that federal ministers had to get ready to meet P.M. of U.K. [Clement Atlee came to Ottawa, as part of his visit to Washington, to discuss the war in Korea.]

Frost called an election in the fall of 1951. Kennedy wrote to him wishing him well, and Frost replied on 9 October 1951: 'I have endeavoured to bring to public life, particularly intergovernmental relations, a spirit of understanding and co-operation and I think it shows results in what we have been able to do.'[59] He won the election the next month with a resounding increase in seats.

Decline in Scholarly Writing

Kennedy engaged in very little scholarly writing after he retired. His son Gilbert states in his oral interview: 'We tried to persuade him to write, hoping it would be his memoirs but no, he read. And continued to read very actively all that time. It was difficult to keep him supplied with books.'[60]

W.P.M.'s last article, 'The Office of Governor General in Canada,' was published in the *Canadian Bar Review* in 1953. No doubt, he prepared it because of questions arising from the appointment of Vincent Massey in 1952 as the first Canadian-born governor general. All former governors general had been British subjects, not Canadian citizens. Kennedy pointed out that these former governors general were each given special letters patent by the reigning sovereign, but in 1947 – in preparation for a Canadian governor general and to indicate the independence of Canada – new and up-to-date letters patent were issued.[61] The intricacies of the subject are not easy to understand.[62] Kennedy's final article shows his wonderful grasp of the complexities of constitutional law and practice.

Kennedy's relationship with the *University of Toronto Law Journal* dramatically shows the decline of his involvement with the Faculty of Law. He edited the first issue of volume 8, published in 1949,[63] and contributed ten book reviews to the next volume, edited by Jacob Finkelman. He also wrote a short note on the new *Caribbean Law Journal* in which he pointed out that two of its three editors were graduates of his Honour Law program: Gloria Cumper (formerly Carpenter) and Louis Fox.[64] In the next volume of the *UTLJ*, he contributed five reviews and two short notes on matters involving royalty, one entitled 'Royal Style and Titles' and the other 'The Regency Acts,'[65] but nothing after that.

Kennedy continued, however, to take an interest in the *UTLJ* and would speak from time to time on the phone to the head of the University of Toronto Press (UTP), Marshall Jeanneret – a graduate of the Honour Law program.

Jeanneret described Kennedy in his memoirs, *God and Mammon: Universities as Publishers*, published in 1989:

> W.P.M. Kennedy ... helped to inspire Smith's lament that 'there are too few characters left on the campus.' In a lovably irresponsible way, there was no more colourful a personality on the faculty during my pre-war undergraduate days than 'W.P.M.K.' I never saw him after I returned to the Press in 1953 (he lived until 1963), but he telephoned me perhaps two or three times each year to ask about our progress on the current issue of the *Law Journal*, which he had founded, to confirm again the number of free copies he wanted to receive, and to make various publishing suggestions for the benefit of the university's scholarly-publishing arm generally. I always asked after his health and he always answered: 'Middlin', middlin'', and then would add: 'But no visitors! *No* visitors!'[66]

One of Kennedy's comments to Jeanneret resulted in a very significant change in the direction of the UTP, which has added considerably to the prestige of the press and therefore to the reputation of the university. Jeanneret wrote:

> During one of these telephone calls after I had been back at the Press for two or three years [that is, 1955 or 1956] Kennedy outlined his latest publishing inspiration. I can reconstruct his comments fairly accurately, having had frequent reason to recall them later. They went very much like this:
>
> 'Remember that 1959 is almost upon us, Marsh! It will be the Press's *great* opportunity to mark the anniversary with a proper edition of the Works.' I cautiously admitted I was mystified and asked him which anniversary he meant.
>
> 'Why, *On Liberty*, of course!' he fairly screamed into the phone. 'The centenary of the most important essay in the history of political science, Marsh! What is needed is a scholar's Mill! I am *amazed* you are not planning one!'[67]

This conversation led Jeanneret and UTP's chief editor Francess Halpenny to start the ball rolling for the production of the collected works of John Stuart Mill, under the direction of English scholar A.S.P. Woodhouse and his student John Robson, who had completed his PhD on Mill under Woodhouse.[68] This project was the first of many important collected works, which now include the collected works of Erasmus, Northrop Frye, Bernard Lonergan, and many others. Moreover, other major projects followed, such as the *Records of Early English Drama*, the *Dictionary of Old English*, and the *Dictionary of Canadian Biography*.[69] The strong scholarly reputation of the UTP owes much to Kennedy's suggestion to Jeanneret to produce Mill's collected works.

26

Final Days

Pauline

After her husband's retirement, Pauline Kennedy would occasionally join the Faculty of Law wives for tea. There is a copy of a note in a law school file to her, dated 2 November 1954, stating: 'It was good of you to be with us last Saturday at the School of Law tea, and I merely wanted to let you know how much we appreciated your assistance. An affair of this kind would not be complete without you and we are all very grateful for all that you have done for us.'[1] There is no indication who signed it, but it was likely from Dean Wright's wife, Marie.

Pauline continued her involvement in charitable work. In 1956, Pauline had her picture in the *Globe and Mail* for the start of the sale of daffodils to benefit the Canadian Cancer Society.[2] Kennedy wrote to Frere on 2 May 1956 at 8.30 p.m.: 'I am alone, except for Eva [a housekeeper], and so am answering. Mother has been out nearly all day. She left at 11 am for a welcome home for Mrs. Frankel, and got back in time for dinner. She left at 8 pm for another meeting and will not be in till I am in bed.'[3] This involvement in her outside activities obviously added to her husband's loneliness in his final years.

After her husband died in 1963, Pauline moved to the University Apartments at the southeast corner of St. George and Bloor Streets.[4] These apartments later became housing for graduate students, and still later were taken down to build a large residence for Woodsworth College.

Pauline died on 26 April 1966 at the age of seventy-one.[5] Unlike W.P.M. and Beatrice, she was not cremated and, after a service at St. Paul's Church, was buried in Emsdale, alongside her husband. She had a number of operations over the years, but it is not clear what they were for. In a letter from W.P.M. to Frere in August 1954, he says that Pauline is having 'the same old trouble with her insides'[6] and two years later refers to an operation she had.[7] W.P.M. did not have a will. The home and cottage, their main assets, had been in their joint names. Pauline's will, drafted by Anne Dubin, was dated 24 June 1965.[8] The estate was valued at $63,000, including the property at Beaver Lake that was valued at $20,000 and left to Frere. The family home at 77 Spadina Road, which Pauline sold when she moved, constituted the bulk of her estate. Beatrice was given a life interest in the estate, with power to encroach up to $1,000 a year. After Beatrice's death, the sum remaining would go equally to the surviving children and, in case of a deceased sibling, to that person's children.

There were a number of specific bequests in Pauline's will. Beatrice was left all Pauline's jewelry; Gilbert received a silver tray and tea service; Shelagh, a pair of silver candelabra; and Frere, some silver, a pastel by Canadian painter C.W. Jefferys, purchased by the Kennedys in the mid-1920s, and two candlesticks. Those candlesticks had been given to Dean Kennedy as a gift at a Law Club dinner in 1947 to celebrate the sixtieth anniversary of the founding of the Faculty of Law.[9] Frere, in turn, gave the candlesticks to me, in my capacity as dean, in the 1970s to give to the law school, and in particular to the student-run *Faculty of Law Review*. There was also a small sentimental gift to Barbara Laskin of a 'framed Little Indian Girl's head' and to Peggy Laskin, a painting by Franklin Carmichael and a pewter tea set, which Barbara says she now has and treasures.[10]

Kennedy's children continued to play a role in his life, even though for much of his retirement none of them lived in Toronto for significant periods of time. Their relationship with their father sheds further light on W.P.M.'s character.

Gilbert and Betty

In August 1949, shortly after he had retired, W.P.M. and Pauline travelled west to visit Gilbert and Betty in their new home in Vancouver. The four of them then travelled to the annual Canadian Bar Association meeting in Banff. Betty writes: 'While at Banff, Gilbert was due for some kind of award which was given at the banquet. He walked across the floor to receive it and had a seizure. Mrs. K hustled the Dean out of the room and pretended she did not know Gilbert. Others came to help me get him back to our room.'[11] Odd, but illustrative of Pauline's protective nature towards her husband.

Gilbert was a successful teacher and scholar, was active in the Canadian Bar Association, and, like his father, was sometimes critical of the judiciary.[12] In 1953, he received a fellowship to do a doctorate at Harvard on the law of adoption in Canada, which resulted in a number of publications on the subject.[13] Several years later, he and Betty adopted three girls in succession, ages seven, twelve, and eight.[14] Pauline, Betty told me, had been against adoption.[15] These were W.P.M. and Pauline's only grandchildren, and there are no great-grandchildren, so the Kennedy name – through W.P.M. – will not continue into the future.

In 1957, Gilbert and Betty moved to Victoria when Gilbert became the deputy attorney general of British Columbia, a position he held with distinction.

Betty taught mathematics at the University of Victoria, was involved in a number of charitable and other causes, and in 1988 received an honorary doctorate from the University of Victoria.[16] Gilbert retired in 1982 at the age of sixty-five and died in Victoria in 1999 at the age of eighty-two. He had been replaced as deputy minister in 1973 when Dave Barrett's New Democratic Party government defeated W.A.C. Bennett's Social Credit government.[17] Gilbert was not interested in being second in command, nor in being dean of the soon-to-be-opened University of Victoria Law School, for which he had been interviewed.[18] He was appointed by the new government to revise the statutes of British Columbia, a task which later became simply a consolidation of the statutes, a far less ambitious project.[19]

At the time of writing, Betty lived in a condo in Victoria, continued driving in her mid-nineties – she would drive to her cottage on Galiano Island – and had a perceptive intellect. The ten-acre cottage, with old growth redwoods on it, had been purchased in the early 1960s. Betty later donated it to the province to become a public park. The person who did the oral interview with Gilbert described Betty to me a few years ago as being 'active, precise and energetic both in mind and body.'[20] She died on 24 April 2019 at the age of ninety-six.[21]

Over the years, by chance, I had a number of pleasant interchanges with Gilbert when he was deputy attorney general. In 1965, he sent me a complimentary note on a report I did that year on legal aid in Ontario for the Joint Committee on Legal Aid. We first met in person in 1971–72 when the federal Law Reform Commission, on which I was a member, travelled to British Columbia to consult with the bar on our proposed program of work. I also received a lengthy note from Gilbert shortly after I became dean in 1972. He wrote, echoing his father's views on the role of academics: 'You will have a wonderful opportunity to do things as Dean at Toronto, maintaining, I hope, an opportunity for continued true research. But teaching and the effective working for a law school come first – or should come first, because I fear they are too often forgotten in the modern law teacher's scramble for paying jobs outside his regular professional role.' He also called for more research: 'It is from the law schools that we must hope to get ideas for, by way of illustration, a new system for the administration of justice.'[22] So Gilbert's views on the role of an academic were similar to those of his father.

Beatrice

Beatrice returned from living in Whitby to Toronto in the mid-1960s – her father had died in 1963 – and worked at Knox College at the university as a waitress.[23] In 1969, she and Frere went on a holiday to the United Kingdom and visited relatives in Scotland. On 19 June 1970, she returned to Whitby as an 'informal patient.' She had again been having 'auditory hallucinations and suicidal thoughts'. Again, she was given electroconvulsive therapy (ECT) treatments. A doctor at Whitby noted on the file that she has had psychotherapy, drug therapy, recreational therapy, and ECTs, and added: 'Her depression improved after a series of 6 ECT and she has not been bothered by suicidal thoughts since.'[24] She was finally discharged in February 1976.[25]

She returned to work at Knox College as a housekeeper and much later visited the cottage in June 1992 with Frere and Shelagh, which is when my wife and I met her. She moved into a retirement home in Etobicoke and died in her sleep in the summer of 2002. The funeral was in St. Paul's Church in Toronto, with Frere giving the eulogy.[26] Frere told me that he 'was very close to my sister, both as a brother and as a priest.'[27] She was cremated, and Shelagh and Frere lowered her ashes into the ground alongside their parents in St. Mark's Cemetery in Emsdale, Ontario.[28] Frere, Shelagh, the local priest, and a family friend were at the burial.

There is a small memorial stone on the ground for all three. Beatrice had accumulated some funds from her few years working in the early 1940s at about $15 a week at the Dominion Bank. She did not touch that sum and probably saved some of her pay from Knox College and from the life estate that Pauline had left to her; when she died, she left $60,000 each to Frere and Shelagh and money for Gilbert and Betty's three children.[29]

Frere

As we saw, Frere became an Anglican priest. He graduated from Bishop's College in June 1956 with a licentiate in sacred theology with first-class honours. Gilbert said in his oral interview: 'I don't know how strongly his desire was either made public or known to the rest of us seriously, until it happened ... He was just unsettled, he wasn't sure what he wanted to do. We knew that Mother wanted him to go there. Dad wasn't pushing anybody into anything unless he wanted to go there. Once the person made up their mind that's what they wanted to do, they got all the help that Dad could give.'[30]

W.P.M. had in fact strongly pushed Frere to go to Bishop's, once Frere had decided to become a priest. In a letter to Frere dated 13 May 1954, W.P.M. wrote:[31] 'I do hope you will go to Bishops.' That was changed to 'I do think you should go,' and a few lines later he wrote: 'This would be my dearest wish for you and I do hope that you will follow it.' In the next paragraph, he wrote: 'I do hope it will be Bishops College as that wd. just fill in my picture of happiness.' Kennedy ended the letter: 'And now, once more, every good wish and blessing on your decision; and don't forget Bishops College for my sake,' with 'my sake' underlined three times. Contrary to Gilbert's assertion, it seems that W.P.M. sometimes did put pressure on his children.

Frere Kennedy, with his sisters Beatrice (middle) and Shelagh,
with the Friedlands and their dog, Tippy

Frere at age ninety

Frere entered Holy Orders in September 1955. Kennedy wrote a note to him, stating:

My very dear son,
Just a line to wish you every real happiness in Holy Orders. I know you will have it, because I know all your actions are inspired by convictions of truth. I shall be thinking of you on Sept. 21.

Every good wish and all my love.
Dad[32]

Frere was an Anglican priest in Quebec, in Willowdale, Ontario, and at a retreat – the Order of St. John the Evangelist – in Bracebridge, Ontario, not far from the cottage in Kearney. He did not sell the cottage to us until the retreat closed down in the early 1980s. In 1969, when Frere and Beatrice went to the United Kingdom, Frere visited the monastery in Mirfield, England, where his father had lived for a number of years before the First World War. Frere continued to keep in touch with some of the priests there. Frere's life at the retreat in Bracebridge was not unlike the life at the Church of the Resurrection in Mirfield. He later moved to Ottawa and entered a retirement home, still later transferring to a nursing home. I visited him at both locations in Ottawa, corresponded regularly with him, and also had a number of discussions with him over the phone. He died a peaceful death on 10 April 2019 at the age of ninety-six.[33] His friend, Neil Stephens, a fellow priest, delivered the obituary. He was buried in early May 2019 at the family plot in Emsdale.

Shelagh and Cas

Shelagh and Cas returned to Vancouver from Winnipeg in 1979, when Cas was appointed the director of the Institute of Resource Ecology at UBC. He was a noted researcher, producing four books and over sixty papers, and became a fellow of the Royal Society of Canada in 1974.[34] After his retirement in 1988, he devoted himself to painting and was included in a number of juried shows.[35]

While living in Winnipeg, Shelagh completed a master's degree at Stanford University on Marshall McLuhan. She had taken courses with him at the University of Toronto and considered him a good friend. In 1980, she donated three boxes of material on McLuhan to the University of Manitoba Archives. There are also a number of letters from her in the McLuhan papers in the Library and Archives Canada in Ottawa. One of these letters to McLuhan, dated 18 September 1966, describes her likely thesis: 'There is a strong possibility that my thesis will be an attempt to define and test the concept of Low definition in relation to political figures largely based on some of the ideas you suggested about the Kennedy-Nixon debates. [This] summer I have been trying to isolate the various variables which may influence the presentation of political figures on Television.'[36]

Her thesis was never published, but she wrote at least half a dozen articles on semiotics – the theory of signs, a subject that interested McLuhan. While in Winnipeg, she taught part-time at the School of Architecture at the University of Manitoba, and when they returned to Vancouver, she was involved with the UBC School of Architecture. When she died in 2015, the flag at UBC was lowered in remembrance, and the UBC website stated that 'Adjunct Professor Shelagh Pauline Lindsey … worked at the School of Architecture from 1980 to 1995, lecturing and supervising graduate students on the behavioural basis of design.'[37]

Shelagh also knew Harold Innis, McLuhan's predecessor in the field of communications at the University of Toronto. Innis was a good friend of W.P.M.
Kennedy, and Pauline was friendly with Innis's wife, Mary Quale Innis. So
Shelagh would have known Harold Innis reasonably well. Some of her articles
discuss Innis and McLuhan together.[38] She was an active supporter of the Harold Innis Foundation in the 1970s, which Marshall McLuhan and Peter Russell helped to organize. Russell notes:[39] 'I saw a fair bit of her then and found
her to be very lively and a character like her father.' In 2007, she and Cas
moved from their home to a retirement residence. New homes were found
for their two 'beloved cats.' She continued her involvement with the Unitarian
Church.[40]

Shelagh called me in May 2014 after she had read my introduction to the
republication of Kennedy's book on the Canadian constitution, noting that it
'gave real insight into the man ... first time I understood my family ... filled in
some of the blanks ... never could tell whether things were true.' She said she
'didn't like her mother' and 'stuck with her father.'[41] By contrast, Cas told me
that 'she obeyed her father and tolerated his idiosyncrasies, but her feelings
towards her mother were warmer ... [S]he was never very happy about the
dean.'[42] Cas described Pauline as 'patient, loyal and long-suffering.'[43] Shelagh
and I talked for over an hour. She mentioned that she 'had somewhat the same
as Beatrice in the form of depression.'

I knew from conversations with her brother and sister-in-law that she was
being treated at the time. Shelagh told me that her doctor wanted to give her
electroconvulsive therapy every six weeks. That was the last time I spoke to her.
She died on 27 February 2015. Cas prepared a brief obituary for the papers,
which ended with the following comments: 'Her larger-than-life personality
suggested the influence of her Irish-born father Dean Kennedy. She was kind,
she was helpful, and she was not afraid to say what she thought. So she was
loved and respected by a great many friends. According to her wishes, crema-
tion has taken place, and there will be no funeral service.'[44]

W.P.M. Kennedy

W.P.M. Kennedy died on 12 August 1963 at the Toronto General Hospital at
the age of eighty-four.[45] I do not know the exact cause of death. Eugene LaBrie
saw him a few months before he died and says that Kennedy was suffering from
shingles and had failing eyesight.[46] His doctors, Dr. Wilson and Dr. Dafoe, the
brother of the famous Dr. Dafoe who treated the Dionne quintuplets, would
come to his home. He rarely went to doctors' offices.[47] As stated earlier, Kennedy did not attend the opening of the law school on the main campus in 1962
because of his health.[48] With all the health issues that Kennedy faced throughout his life, it is somewhat surprising that he lived to the age of eighty-four.

According to his son Frere, W.P.M. 'did not have a good retirement.'[49] He rarely came to the Faculty Union – except on Saturday mornings to read the British journals – and did not write. He read, to the extent that his eyesight permitted, and had relatively few visitors, apart from Bora Laskin, Jacob Finkelman, Eugene LaBrie, and a few others. Many of his good friends had already died. Robert Falconer died twenty years earlier, Canon Cody and Harold Innis about ten years earlier. Pauline continued to be heavily involved in charitable work. He certainly seemed to lead a lonely existence.

Caesar Wright would call him on his birthday. In January 1952, a note to Frere states that 'Caesar and his wife will be in for a late quiet supper,' a further indication that Kennedy and Wright got along reasonably well on a personal level.[50] Another letter to Frere in March 1953 again indicates a good personal relationship. Kennedy wrote to Frere: 'Cecil and Mrs. Wright sail for England on April 28 when he will lecture at Cambridge, Oxford and London. It is quite an honour and I feel that he will do a real good job and be a credit to Canada.'[51]

Kennedy appeared to discourage visitors, as we saw in his conversations with Marshall Jeanneret of the University of Toronto Press.[52] In his letters to Frere he would often say that his condition was 'middlin'' or 'middling.' In a letter in May 1954, for example, he writes; 'I keep middling and vary a lot.'[53] Two month later, he wrote: 'I feel middling. I had a poor day y'day with terrible heat.'[54] And the following month, he wrote: 'I'm just middling, but I still survive.'[55] He stopped going to the cottage in 1954.[56] By 1956, he was having trouble walking more than a short distance. He wrote to Frere in May 1956: 'I try to keep up a good heart, but I'm getting weaker and can with some difficulty get about as far as Bloor' – about a block away.[57] In July 1957, he tells Frere that he has not been out of the house for five days.[58]

He continued to be in need of money. His university pension, according to Shelagh, was only about $6,000, and the medical bills would have been high. Gilbert paid for the help the family needed.[59] W.P.M. wrote to Frere in 1953, saying that he was unable to afford to have their house painted.[60] In 1956, they rented their garage – for $10 a month.[61] LaBrie says Kennedy was poor.[62]

Pauline was particularly worried about their financial position. W.P.M. wrote to Frere in early 1951: 'I think she worries about the future quite a bit. For the present we are solvent, but she looks ahead I fear.'[63] In 1951, as we saw, Kennedy had been an advisor to the government of Ontario for a number of federal-provincial conferences, and no doubt it helped their solvency. But money was a constant problem. There were additional expenses, the correspondence indicates, such as paying for Beatrice's apartment and for the insurance on Frere's car while he was at Bishop's College.[64]

Kennedy was concerned about the cottage expenses, writing to Frere in 1954 asking if they should sell it. Kennedy was no longer able to go there. He wrote: 'Sam wrote to say that all is O.K. at N.W. I wish we knew what is best to do with

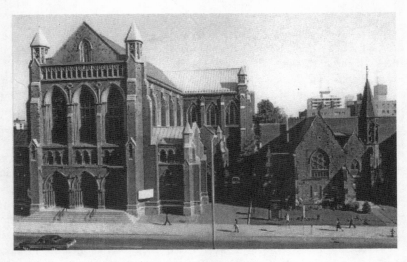

St. Paul's Anglican Church, Bloor Street East

St. Mark's Cemetery

it. We are, as I've told you paying out a lot on it for taxes, etc., but M[other] and G. and B., and C. and S. are all against selling it.'[65] Frere started renting it. W.P.M. told Frere in July 1957: 'At least we're more than covering expenses there.'[66]

Frere, who resided in Quebec in those years, came home to be with his father at the end. W.P.M. refused to have Frere or any other priest give him Communion. Frere says that he, Frere, made the sign of the cross with his right hand as W.P.M. died.

The funeral for W.P.M. was at 2 p.m. at St. Paul's Church.[67] Gilbert and Shelagh came in from the West. Finkelman, LaBrie, and Laskin were among the pallbearers.[68] He was cremated, and several years later his ashes were buried in St. Mark's Cemetery in Emsdale, Ontario, where Pauline had been buried.[69] In lieu of flowers, donations to the Canadian Cancer Society, one of Pauline's charities, were requested.[70] There is no headstone at the burial plot.

27

Summing Up

There was a lengthy obituary in the *Globe and Mail*[1] the day after Kennedy's death and a number of later tributes. His friend, political scientist Alexander Brady, wrote the obituary for the Royal Society of Canada in which he said that Kennedy 'never failed to inspire younger colleagues with an interest in research and writing.' He also mentioned his fame as a teacher:

> Dean Kennedy had the type of personality which creates academic legends. In the classroom especially his energy, imagination, wit, eloquence, and fiery zeal for his subject came into abundant play ... Academic colleagues are of course more difficult to impress than undergraduates, but few of his contemporaries in Toronto failed to recognize that in 'W.P.M.K.' they had in their midst a striking personality with more than ordinary gifts and abilities. As scholar, administrator, and teacher he made a mark on the university community of his day and on the study of Canada's constitution.

Eugene LaBrie, a former editor of the *University of Toronto Law Journal*, wrote in the *UTLJ* about Kennedy's contribution to the *Journal*: 'There are few worthwhile institutions that do not owe their origin to the vision, guidance and tireless efforts of some outstanding individual. This Journal is no exception.' LaBrie went on to say:

> [The Journal] is irredeemably in debt to William Paul McClure Kennedy, M.A., LL.B., Litt.D., LL.D., F.R.S.C., dean emeritus of the Faculty of Law, University of Toronto, who from his founding of the Journal in 1935 until his retirement in 1949, gave unsparingly of his ability, energy, and time to place this publication on a firm foundation as one of the leading scholarly publications on this continent. Dean Kennedy brought to this task an unusual and necessary combination of faculties of scholarship, expression, and administration.[2]

Finally, in the fall of 1963, Bora Laskin prepared and moved a tribute to Kennedy in the senate of the university, which was seconded by Dean Wright. Laskin went over Kennedy's scholarly career and noted his contribution to legal education:

> With faith and with resolution, he nurtured on this campus a socio-humanist philosophy of law; and ... he exercised his irresistible powers of persuasion to bring the University to establish in 1930 an active Department of Law in which this philosophy could be given concreteness ... History will document more than does this brief recital what unparalleled achievement was his in igniting the flame of systematic University legal studies in Ontario, which had sputtered out a half century before, and keeping it burning brightly for a generation, ready for his successor to carry to the mountain top.[3]

Readers will make their own overall assessment of Kennedy's legacy. Here are my thoughts. There is no doubt that he was a significant scholar, both in Tudor history and the law. His multidisciplinary approach to the law was unique in Canada at the time. His scholarly output was at least equal to major scholars at leading institutions today. The quality and breadth of his scholarship – from his Tudor ecclesiastic writing in his early years, to his classic text on Canadian constitutional law, to later books on various aspects of the law – is almost unparalleled. The establishment of the *University of Toronto Law Journal* is another lasting accomplishment.

Like many academics, his views on interpreting the constitution changed over the years. In the early 1920s, he approved the interpretation of the division of powers that had been developed by the Privy Council, resulting in the provinces having greater power than had been intended by the drafters of the constitution. Over the next several decades, he criticized that interpretation and wanted the federal government to have greater powers. Further, he became strongly in favour of Canada having the final court of appeal. A third change was in the 1940s and 50s, where he took the position – but not publicly – that the federal taxing and spending power righted the balance between the two levels of government.

He had been against a bill of rights in the 1950s, and one can only speculate on what he would have thought of the Charter of Rights and Freedoms, which now plays such a significant role in the development of the law. My guess is that he would initially have been against it, but would slowly have come to accept the importance of the Charter in the development of the law.

Through his scholarship and teaching, he had an effect on the development of the law in Canada, particularly constitutional law. He also encouraged the development of other areas of law, such as administrative law, labour law, and tax law. As someone not trained in the common law, he was understandingly more interested in constitutions and statutes than in judge-made law, such as contracts and torts.

Kennedy was an exciting, inspiring, and influential teacher. He founded the Honour Law program at the University of Toronto, which developed, under Kennedy, into a Department of Law and then into a separate School of Law. Moreover, his teaching and scholarship were done under difficult personal circumstances, considering his and his family's health, the threats to his position in the university, his personal financial difficulties, and problems within his family.

There is no doubt that he altered the facts about his early life. He probably started revising his background innocently. He did not want to be associated with Northern Ireland Protestantism, after rejecting his father's Presbyterian faith and later converting to Roman Catholicism. He needed to reinvent a new identity, particularly after he came to Canada as a Catholic in 1913. It was not difficult to do, and he found that he could get away with it.

Further, there is little doubt that he exaggerated his role in the drafting of the Irish constitution. It may have come about because others confused him with another Kennedy, Hugh Kennedy, who had been active in Irish politics. Kennedy did not, however, correct these misinterpretations. He did play some relatively minor role in Irish politics, and over time and over the years he may have started to half-believe what he was claiming and what others were writing about him. In later years, he did not exaggerate his involvement with a number of important government committees and commissions in Canada.

Again, one can fault him for claiming to be a lawyer and having an LLB. We do not know the full story. Perhaps President Falconer or the chair of the board of governors, Canon Cody, or future chief justice Newton Rowell suggested that, as head of the law program, he should start using the degree. Again, it seems he started to believe that he was trained as a lawyer. The claimed MA from Oxford is also troublesome. It is likely that he spent some time at Oxford after graduating from Trinity College Dublin, but how much is not clear. If he had actually been enrolled as a student at Oxford, he would have been entitled to claim an Oxford BA and then an MA, which is always subsequently granted, but he does not appear to have ever been officially on the Oxford records. As far as I can tell, he never put 'MA Oxon' after his name, although he did not correct the annual calendars that stated, under the heading 'education,' 'M.A. Dublin, Oxon,' which certainly suggested to readers that he had an Oxford degree. No doubt, he had been the one to initially supply this information.

There is also no doubt that he did considerable self-promotion, such as asking St. Francis Xavier to grant him an honorary LLD or asking Prime Minister Mackenzie King to recommend to Harvard that he receive an honorary degree, among other such requests.

Kennedy was a self-centred domineering egotist. He was always the centre of attention to whom everyone must cater and tiptoe around. Perhaps his children avoided his domination by leaving Toronto. Nevertheless, he appeared to have been a good husband and father. He was particularly devoted to Frere, was proud of Gilbert, and encouraged Shelagh. His relationship with Beatrice is uncertain. He admitted to the psychiatrists that he may have been too harsh on her, but whether that contributed to her mental condition is unclear.

Readers with expertise in mental illness will have their own views about Kennedy's possible personality disorders. I asked a distinguished psychiatrist, Mary Seeman, for her views about Kennedy's mental health.[4] She read the draft manuscript and tentatively concluded that 'he may have no psychiatric condition per se but a personality disorder characterized by self-aggrandizement and some measure of deceit.' Kennedy, she wrote, 'seems like an ebullient man of "striking" personality, given to self-promotion, domineering with family members and, at some points in life, abusing alcohol, overspending, showing signs of hypersexuality and coming across as a "Mad Irishman."' Kennedy's disorder, Dr. Seeman went on to say, 'sounds like hypomania, a not infrequent accompaniment of people who get a lot done, who don't need much sleep, who win over other people, inspire others and generally insist on things going their way.' Kennedy, Dr. Seeman observes, does not appear to have shown any signs of paranoia similar to those of his daughter Beatrice. As to depression, she writes: 'I was looking for evidence of possible periods of depression because you would expect this in someone who shows signs of mania. There are constant references to ill health (mostly unspecified) and insomnia and needing a rest. These could be depression – but the insomnia could also be due to hypomania. He could not have been so very productive and also be depressed for any great length of time.'

Some readers will take a negative view of Kennedy, as the head of the history department, George Wrong, did. In addition to some of the issues just raised, there is also the fact that he had a romantic relationship with a student at St. Francis Xavier College and then at the University of Toronto. But there were no specific prohibitions against such conduct at that time, and it was not uncommon. In addition, some will be concerned about his billing in the *Deeks v. H.G. Wells* case and the extent of his moonlighting for the Rowell-Sirois Commission. Again, there were no rules at the time against such conduct, and many members of the faculty also profited financially from the *Deeks* case and engaged in extensive outside work. Today, at the University of Toronto, full disclosure of such activities to the person to whom the academic reports would be required, and approval of the conduct would be necessary.

One of Kennedy's strengths seen throughout this book is his lack of prejudice. As his son Gilbert stated in an oral interview when asked about the values he learned at home, 'the first and most important that stands out in my mind is tolerance for others.'[5] This outlook included religious tolerance and the promotion of women. One sees it again and again throughout this book.

Kennedy adopted a multidisciplinary and empirical approach to law, which remained somewhat dormant at the University of Toronto law school after Caesar Wright took over in 1949, but is now a dominant part of the philosophy, teaching, and research at this, and many other law schools. How much did Kennedy influence this revival? Perhaps not directly, except – to give one important example – through the *University of Toronto Law Journal*. Moreover, the multidisciplinary approach, supported by American academics, was likely transmitted through Laskin, LaBrie, and other influential graduates to the students in the 1950s and showed new life in the late 1960s and the 1970s. Kennedy also stressed the importance of a strong graduate program, which was not a high priority during Caesar Wright's reign as dean. The present School of Law owes a debt to Kennedy at least as great as it does to Caesar Wright.

Finally, in spite of his faults, it is clear that Presidents Falconer and Cody liked and respected Kennedy, as did his colleagues and students, many of whom went on to important positions. I think that if I had known Kennedy, I would have liked him, just as Father Edmund McCorkell, who taught with him at St. Michael's College told an interviewer: 'I liked him personally a lot, I think we all did.'[6]

Notes

Preface

1 Correspondence between Jennie Rubio and Martin Friedland, 27 March 2013 et seq.
2 W.P.M. Kennedy, *The Constitution of Canada: An Introduction to Its Development and Law* (London: Oxford University Press, 1922, republished by Oxford University Press Canada, 2014).
3 Martin Friedland, *The University of Toronto: A History* (Toronto: University of Toronto Press, 2002; 2nd ed., 2013).
4 Ibid. at 306.
5 C.T. Bissell, 'On Coming Back' (1958) 6 *Varsity Graduate* at 113.
6 Sydney Harris oral interview (Osgoode Society, 1992) at 17. See also Wishart Spence oral interview (Osgoode Society, 1986) at 21.
7 David Vanek, *Fulfilment: Memoirs of a Criminal Court Judge* (Toronto: University of Toronto Press, 1999) at 68. See also Robin Harris, oral interview with Sydney Hermant – a student in the Honour Law course in the mid-1930s – 2 October 1978 at 2: 'great character ... wonderful person – great personality.'
8 Vanek, *Fulfilment* at 68.
9 See chapter 20.
10 See chapter 22.
11 It is not clear how much of the plan was known by Laskin: see chapter 22.
12 See chapter 24.
13 R.B.C. Risk, 'The Many Minds of W.P.M. Kennedy' (1998) 48 *University of Toronto Law Journal* 353.
14 See A.B. McKillop, *The Spinster and the Prophet: Florence Deeks, H.G. Wells, and the Mystery of the Purloined Past* (Toronto: Macfarlane, Walter and Ross, 2000).
15 Friedland, *The University of Toronto* at 285.
16 Martin Friedland, 'Searching for Truth in the Criminal Justice System' (2014) 60 *Criminal Law Quarterly* 487; Martin Friedland, 'Beyond a Reasonable Doubt: Does It Apply to Finding the Law as Well as the Facts?' (2015) 62 *Criminal Law Quarterly* 428.
17 Email from Barbara Laskin to Martin Friedland, 14 November 2015.

18 I have used a personal approach in other books I have written – from my first book, *Detention Before Trial* (Toronto: University of Toronto Press, 1965), where I discuss how I went about finding the source material on the bail system, to *The University of Toronto: A History*, where I conclude the book with a personal walk through the campus.

19 W.M. Kennedy, *Archbishop Parker* (London: Pitman, 1908) at vii.

20 W.P.M. Kennedy, 'Political Biography in Canada' (May 1919) 49 *The Bookman* 297.

21 W.P.M. Kennedy, *Lord Elgin* (Toronto: Oxford University Press, 1926) at v.

22 See Brian Busby, 'Canada's 100 Best Books? 102? 111?' *The Dusty Bookcase* (blog), 20 August 2012, http://brianbusby.blogspot.com/2012/08/canadas-100-best-books-101-111.html.

23 Martin Friedland, *My Life in Crime and Other Academic Adventures* (Toronto: University of Toronto Press, 2007).

24 Martin Friedland, 'R.S. Wright's Model Criminal Code: A Forgotten Chapter in the History of the Criminal Law' (1981) 1 *Oxford Journal of Legal Studies* 307 at 345. A narrative form was also used in my history of the University of Toronto and in my three true crime books, starting with a book on an English murder trial that took place in 1887, *The Trials of Israel Lipski: A True Story of a Victorian Murder in the East End of London* (London: Macmillan London, 1984; New York: Beaufort Books, 1985). See also *The Case of Valentine Shortis: A True Story of Crime and Politics in Canada* (Toronto: University of Toronto Press, 1986); and *The Death of Old Man Rice: A True Story of Criminal Justice in America* (Toronto: University of Toronto Press and New York University Press, 1994). Each is similar to a biography, but, instead of an exploration of a single individual, each looked at the biography of a trial, examining the characters involved and what preceded and followed the trial. Those true crime books, I believe, give us a better understanding of the frailty of the criminal process, just as the present book gives us a fuller understanding of the development of Canadian constitutional law and of legal education in Canada through the exploration of the intriguing life of W.P.M. Kennedy.

1 Coming to America

1 'R.M.S. Caronia Passenger List 30 March 1912' *Gjenvick-Gjønvik Archives*, https://www.gjenvick.com/PassengerLists/CunardLine/Westbound/1912-03-30-PassengerList-Caronia.html.

2 Letter from Hugh P. Darville 12 August 1912. St. Francis Xavier (StFX) Archives. I am grateful for the assistance given by archivist Kathleen MacKenzie of the StFX Archives and archivist Anne Marie MacNeil of the Beaton Institute Archives for providing copies of the correspondence used in this chapter.

3 Alan Scarth, *Titanic and Liverpool* (Liverpool, UK: Liverpool University Press, 2009) at 113; see also 'RMS Titanic – Ship of Dreams' *titanicandco.com*, http://www.titanicandco.com/.

4 'New York, Passenger Lists, 1820–1957' *Ancestry.ca*, https://www.ancestry.ca/search/collections/nypl/.

5 I have been unable to find information about the school.
6 Letter from Hugh P. Darville, 12 August 1912. StFX Archives.
7 Letter from Horace S. Chown, 31 August 1912. StFX Archives.
8 Letter from Joseph Darlington to James Tompkins, 23 March 1913. StFX Archives.
9 George Boyle, *Father Tompkins of Nova Scotia* (New York: P.J. Kennedy & Sons, 1953) at 67–8.
10 James Cameron, *For the People: A History of St Francis Xavier University* (Kingston, ON: McGill-Queen's University Press, 1996) at 151–2; Boyle, *Father Tompkins of Nova Scotia* at 36–7 and 45–6.
11 Cameron, *For the People* at 152.
12 Letter from Edward Dowden, 20 November 1900. StFX Archives. Dowden is now best remembered because James Joyce mentioned him – unfavourably – in his novel *Ulysses*. Unlike his treatment of Kennedy, Dowden had refused to give Joyce a good reference for a position. Helen Sword, *Ghostwriting Modernism* (Ithaca, NY: Cornell University Press, 2002) at 62–3; references to Dowden in James Joyce's *Ulysses* can be found in Random House's 1961 Modern Library Edition at 204 and 214.
13 Cable from W.P.M. Kennedy to James Tompkins, 4 April 1913. StFX Archives.
14 Letter from W.P.M. Kennedy to James Tompkins, 23 April 1913. StFX Archives.
15 Letter from W.P.M. Kennedy to James Tompkins, 18 May 1913. StFX Archives.
16 Cable from W.P.M. Kennedy to James Tompkins, 24 May 1913. StFX Archives.
17 Cameron, *For the People*, at 3–5, 11, and 35.
18 'A Historian for St. Francis Xavier' *Globe*, 14 June 1913 at 6.
19 Interview with W.P.M. Kennedy, *Xaverian* [StFX student paper], October 1913.
20 'Death of the Bishop of Oxford' *Tamworth Herald*, 27 April 1901.
21 Cameron, *For the People* at 390 and 154. I am grateful to Professor Cameron for his assistance in investigating Kennedy's time in Nova Scotia.
22 Letter from James Tompkins to David Allison at Beaton Institute, 29 March 1914. Beaton Institute Archives.
23 Letter from H.P. MacPherson to John Somers, 18 May 1914. StFX Archives.
24 Letter from James Tompkins to J.M.P. Coady, 19 May 1914. Beaton Institute Archives.
25 Father Edmund McCorkell oral interview (interviewed by Richard Alway 1974, St. Michael's College) at 81. St. Michael's Archives.
26 Martin Friedland, *The University of Toronto: A History* (Toronto: University of Toronto Press, 2002) at 217.
27 Calendar of St. Francis Xavier College, 16 and 27 April 1916, at 65.
28 Sara Cameron, 'Catholic Women Educators' *The Memorare*, Mount St. Bernard College, December 1916 at 10–13.
29 'Angus D. Cameron' *Ancestry.ca*.
30 W.P.M. Kennedy, *Parish Life under Queen Elizabeth: An Introductory Study* (London: The Manresa Press, 1914).
31 Gilbert Kennedy oral interview (interviewed by Maryla Waters 1983, Victoria University), introductory pages; Author's interview with Frere Kennedy.

32 'Sara Josephine Cameron' [obituary] *The Casket*, 11 April 1990 [Antigonish weekly newspaper] at 7; Sara Cameron's gravestone, rootsweb.ancestry.com/~cansacem/regina/6094.jpg.

33 I am grateful to Professor Donald Brean, a professor of finance at the Rotman School of Management, for assisting me in contacting these people. I was chatting with him at a lunch at Massey College and telling him about my Kennedy project, and he said he was from the Maritimes and knew the Cameron family. This encounter can be filed in the 'small world' file.

34 'Our Graduates' *The Memorare*, December 1916 at 29–30.

35 *The Memorare*: the newspaper of Mount St. Bernard, a separate women's institution.

36 Sara Cameron, "Conversation" *The Memorare*, various issues in 1915 and 1916.

37 'Our Graduates' *The Memorare*, December 1916 at 29–30.

38 'Sara Josephine Cameron' [obituary] *The Casket*, 11 April 1990 at 7.

39 'Sara Cameron's gravestone,' rootsweb.ancestry.com/~cansacem/regina/6094.jpg.

40 Cameron, *For the People* at 458n95.

41 P.B. Waite, *Lord of Point Grey: Larry MacKenzie of UBC* (Vancouver: UBC Press, 1987) at 58.

42 Letter from W.P.M. Kennedy to St. Francis Xavier College, 6 January 1915. StFX Archives.

43 Letter from H.P. MacPherson to W.P.M. Kennedy, 15 January 1915. StFX Archives. It is not known if Archbishop McNeil put Kennedy up for an honorary degree in the United States, which I assume would have been from the Catholic University of America in Washington.

2 Earlier Years

1 Email from Ellen O'Flaherty to Martin Friedland, 17 May 2013. I am grateful for Ms. O'Flaherty's assistance in obtaining records from Trinity College Dublin (TCD). I am also indebted to Christopher Morash, now a graduate student at Cambridge University, for his help in digging through the TCD records and for commenting on this chapter in draft. Unless stated otherwise, all material pertaining to Kennedy's time at Trinity College Dublin is from the TCD Archives.

2 W.M. Kennedy, *Archbishop Parker* (New York: Sir Isaac Pitman & Sons, 1908).

3 Author's personal copy of Clarence M. Lindsay, *Cavalier Poets* (New York: The Abbey Press, 1901).

4 As cited in Eugene LaBrie, 'William Paul McClure Kennedy: 1879–1963' (1964) 15 *University of Toronto Law Journal* 255 at 256.

5 Alexander Brady, 'William Paul McClure Kennedy: 1879–1963' in *Proceedings and Transactions of the Royal Society of Canada*, 4th series, vol. 2, *Meeting of June 1964* (Ottawa: Royal Society of Canada, 1964) at 109–11.

6 Marriage certificate between Pauline Simpson and W.P.M Kennedy, 14 June 1920, *Ancestry.ca*.

7 R.B.C. Risk, 'The Many Minds of W.P.M. Kennedy' (1998) 48 *University of Toronto Law Journal* 353 at 353.

8 'William (Paul) Waugh McClure Kennedy' *Ancestry.ca*, https://www.ancestry.ca/search/?name=william+paul+mccl ure_kennedy&event=_toronto&birth=1879&birth_x=2-0-0.

9 'R.M.S. Caronia Passenger List 30 March 1912' *Gjenvick-Gjønvik Archives*, https://www.gjenvick.com/PassengerLists/CunardLine/Westbound/1912-03-30-PassengerList-Caronia.html.

10 'Documenting the History of the Lurgan Area,' *Lurgan Ancestry*, http://www.lurganancestry.com/

11 'Lurgan Business Directory 1880, from the Directory of Belfast and Ulster, page 3' *Lurgan Ancestry*, http://lurganancestry.com/lurgand1880p3.htm.

12 'Charles William Kennedy' in Hew Scott, *Fasti Ecclesia Scoticana: The Succession of Ministers in the Church of Scotland from the Reformation* (Edinburgh: Oliver and Boyd, 1928) at 407.

13 'William Waugh McClure' *Ancestry.ca*.

14 Letters from Supervisor John Smith to the Commissioner of Excise at the Excise Office of London, 15 November 1844 and 27 January 1845. UK National Archives.

15 S. Sidlow McFarland, *Presbyterianism in Maghera: A Social and Congregational History* (Maghera: Presbyterian Church, 1985) at 70. A new minister and a new church building were needed because the previous minister, John Glendy, who had preached revolutionary ideas in Maghera following the American and French revolutions, had been required to leave for America. In America, Glendy became a leading churchman and in 1807 was chosen as the chaplain of the US Congress.

16 McFarland, *Presbyterianism in Maghera* at 71–3.

17 Ibid.

18 'January 1814 Report to the Secretary of the Protestant Union' in *The Protestant Advocate: A Review of Publications Relating to the Roman Catholic Question and Repertory of Protestant Intelligence*, vol. 2 (London: J.J. Stockdale, 1814) at 153.

19 Sean Farrell, *Rituals and Riots: Sectarian Violence and Political Culture in Ulster, 1784–1886* (Lexington: The University Press of Kentucky, 2009) at 60.

20 'Riot and Homicide at Maghera' *The Connaught Journal*, 12 April 1824.

21 'Riot at Maghera' *The Connaught Journal*, 3 April 1825.

22 'The Troubles in Lurgan' *Wikipedia.org*, https://en.wikipedia.org/wiki/The_Troubles_in_Lurgan.

23 The fairs continued during Kennedy's father's tenure as a minister in Lurgan. There are letters in the Public Records Office of Northern Ireland, written by W.P.M. Kennedy's father, inviting the Marquis of Dufferin to open a county fair at the Town Hall in Lurgan – a fair to raise money for the Presbyterian Church of which he was the minister. It appears that the Marquis did not attend the bazaar. Letter from Reverend Charles W. Kennedy to the Marquis of Dufferin and Ava, 25 August 1900. Public Record Office of Northern Ireland.

24 *Annual Glasgow Directory, Volume 1904–1905* at 1072, https://digital.nls.uk/directories/browse/archive/85400365.

25 'Deaths' *Aberdeen Press and Journal*, 10 March 1927.

26 The value of his estate was £154. *Scotland, National Probate Index (Calendar of Confirmations and Inventories), 1847–1936* at K10. *Ancestry.ca*.

27 See James Alexander McClure, *The McClure Family* (Petersburg, VA: Presses of Frank A. Owen, 1914) at 7.

28 Alan Grant, 'Dr. W.P.M. Kennedy' (1942) 1 *School of Law Review* 3.

29 See 'Kennedy, William Paul McClure,' *British Who's Who: An Annual Biographical Dictionary* (London: A & C Black Ltd., 1935) at page 1828; and 'Kennedy, William Paul McClure,' *Who's Who in Canada 1951–52* (Toronto: International Press Ltd.) at page 418.

30 Grant, 'Dr. W.P.M. Kennedy' at 3.

31 'Lurgan Business Directory, 1880, from the Directory of Belfast and Ulster, page 2' *Lurgan Ancestry*, http://lurganancestry.com/lurgand1880p2.htm.

32 Ian Wilson, 'Lurgan High School Register 1923' (n.d.) 6, no. 1 *Journal of Craigavon Historical Society*, http://www.craigavonhistoricalsociety.org.uk/rev/wilsonilurganhighschool.html; Ian Wilson, 'Lurgan College Register 1873–99' (n.d.) 6, no. 3 *Journal of Craigavon Historical Society*, http://www.craigavonhistoricalsociety.org.uk/rev/wilsonilurganregister.html. Ian Wilson, a former vice-principal of Lurgan College and now its historian, kindly assisted me with this section on Lurgan College.

33 The historian of Lurgan schools speculated: 'It is possible that Mrs. Graham was a member of Rev. Kennedy's church … Rev. Kennedy may simply have been trying to support Mrs. Graham … It is also possible that there were theological problems between Rev. Kennedy and Mr. Kirkpatrick, the Lurgan College headmaster. Reverend Kennedy was an evangelical, while Kirkpatrick, despite the fact that he had trained for the Presbyterian ministry, was, by the 1890s, an avowed atheist.' Email from Ian Wilson to Martin Friedland, 13 March 2016.

34 Wilson, 'Lurgan College Register 1873–99.'

35 Ian Wilson, '19th Century Schools in Lurgan – Part 2' (n.d.) 5, no. 1 *Journal of Craigavon Historical Society*, http://www.craigavonhistoricalsociety.org.uk/rev/wilsoni19thcenturypt2.html. The brewery, owned by Samuel Watts, is no longer in existence.

36 Wilson, '19th Century Schools in Lurgan – Part 2.'

37 Wilson, '19th Century Schools in Lurgan – Part 2.' Kirkpatrick was the model for a character in one of Lewis's novels.

38 Trinity College Dublin, 'Names of Students Taken Off for Non-Payment December 1885.'

39 Email from Ellen O'Flaherty to Martin Friedland, 18 May 2013.

40 Trinity College Dublin, 'Calendar of Dublin University, 1900–01.'

41 W.B. Yeats, *Reveries Over Childhood and Youth* (Basingstoke, UK: The Macmillan Company, 1916) at 100–1.

42 Trinity College Dublin, 'Bursar's Day Books, Michaelmas 1896.'

43 I have, however, not been able to find documents to prove this conjecture. A later tutor was George Lambert Cuthbert, a scientist or, as they were called at the time, a natural philosopher. He appears to have had a rather undistinguished career and may not have had much influence on Kennedy. Trinity College Dublin, Term Books: Record of Terms and Examinations 1894/1895–1898/1899.

44 John Mahaffy, *The Principles of the Art of Conversation* (New York: Macmillan, 1887).

45 Merlin Holland, *Wilde Album* (New York: Henry Holt, 1998) at 27.

46 Jack Batten, *Robinette: The Dean of Canadian Lawyers* (New York: Macmillan, 1984) at 27.

47 Email from Sydney Robins to Martin Friedland, 19 August 2013.

48 W.B. Stanford and R.B. McDowell, *Mahaffy: A Biography of an Anglo-Irishman* (Abingdon, UK: Routledge & Kegan Paul, 1971) at 185–7.

49 Ibid. at 123.

50 Ibid. at 39 and 156–7.

51 J.B. Mahaffy, *Social Life in Greece from Homer to Menander* (London: Macmillan, 1874).

52 Stanford and McDowell, *Mahaffy: A Biography* at 87.

53 'Doctors in Literature' (1920) *The Dublin Calendar 1919–1920* at 117.

54 'Doctor's Degree for Prof. W.P.M. Kennedy' *Globe*, 25 March 1919.

3 After Trinity College Dublin

1 W.B. Stanford and R.B. McDowell, *Mahaffy: A Biography of an Anglo-Irishman* (Abingdon, UK: Routledge & Kegan Paul, 1971) at 39.

2 'Our New Professors' (October 2013) 28 *Xaverian* at 27. St. Francis Xavier Archives.

3 William Holden Hutton, *William Stubbs: Bishop of Oxford, 1825–1901* (Edinburgh: Archibald Constable, 1906) at 390.

4 'Calendars' *University of Toronto Faculty of* Arts. University of Toronto Archives.

5 Email from Sian Astill, 26 June 2013. I am grateful for the assistance of the Oxford archivists.

6 'A History of Incorporation at Oxford' *Oxford University Archives*, https://www.bodleian.ox.ac.uk/oua/enquiries/incorporation.

7 See, for example, letter from William Kennedy Esq., 25 October 1901; Letter from T.W. Holleston Esq., 26 October 1901. St. Francis Xavier Archives.

8 *Trinity College Dublin: A College Miscellany*, vol. 7, *1901* (Dublin: Dublin University Press, 1902) at 97. Trinity College Dublin Archives.

9 Philosophical Society Registrars' Records, 28 March 1901. Trinity College Dublin Archives.

10 "The PHIL' *Facebook*, https://www.facebook.com/pg/TCDPhil/about/?ref=page_internal.

11 *Torontonensis: The Year Book of the University of Toronto 1926*, vol. 28 at 353; see also the 1928 to 1930 *Torontonensis* volumes. See also the correspondence in the John Willison papers, Library and Archives Canada, where Kennedy, as honorary president of the Historical Club, invited Willison to address the club in February 1926.

12 Letter from Richard A. Hayes, 25 March 1912. St. Francis Xavier Archives.

13 Alan Grant, 'Dr. W.P.M. Kennedy' (1942) 1 *School of Law Review* 3.

14 Gilbert Kennedy oral interview (interviewed by Maryla Waters 1983, Victoria University) at 8.

15 Email from Andrew Lyall to Martin Friedland, 16 September 2016. One of Lyall's students, Siobhan Ni Chulachain, a practising barrister in Dublin, did a dissertation on wardship and agreed about the unlikelihood of records surviving. Email from Siobhan Ni Chulachain to Martin Friedland, 21 September 2016.

16 C.S. Phillips et al., *Walter Howard Frere: Bishop of Truro* (London: Faber & Faber, 1947) at 46.

17 'Welcome to the Home of the Community of the Resurrection,' https://www.mirfield.org.uk/.

18 Email from Brother Steven Hawes, 13 May 2013. I am grateful to Brother Hawes for his assistance in examining the records about Kennedy at Mirfield and in arranging for my wife and me to visit the House of Resurrection in April 2018.

19 Mirfield Register at 82.

20 Phillips et al., *Walter Howard Frere* at 14–15, 24, and 47.

21 W.P.M. Kennedy, *The 'Interpretations' of the Bishops and Their Influence on Elizabethan Episcopal Policy* (London: Longmans, Green, 1908).

22 W.P.M. Kennedy, *Elizabethan Episcopal Administration: An Essay in Sociology and Politics*, 3 vols. (London: A.R. Mowbray, 1924).

23 See 'Prominent Anglican at Convocation Hall' *Varsity*, 31 January 1921.

24 Walter Howard Frere, *The English Church in the Reigns of Elizabeth and James I, 1558–1625* (London: Macmillan, 1904).

25 Phillips et al., *Walter Howard Frere* at 43.

26 Emails from Lydia Dean to Martin Friedland, 13 May 2013 and 13 June 2013.

27 Walter Howard Frere, *Visitation Articles and Injunctions of the Period of the Reformation*, vol. 1 (London: Longmans, Green, 1910); Walter Howard Frere, with the assistance of William McClure Kennedy, *Visitation Articles and Injunctions of the Period of the Reformation*, vol. 2 (London: Longmans, Green, 1910); Walter Howard Frere, ed., *Visitation Articles and Injunctions of the Period of the Reformation*, vol. 3 (London: Longmans, Green, 1910).

28 Frere and Kennedy, preface to *Visitation Articles and Injunctions*, vol. 1 at v.

29 E.W. Watson, 'Reviews of Books: *Visitation Articles and Injunctions of the Period of the Reformation* by W.H. Frere and W. McC. Kennedy' (1911) 26 *English Historical Review* 781–3.

30 Benjamin Gordon-Taylor and Nicholas Stebbing, eds., *Walter Frere: Scholar, Monk, Bishop* (Norwich, UK: Canterbury Press, 2011) at 123.

31 Ibid. at 12–13.

32 W.P.M. Kennedy, *Studies in Tudor History* (London: Constable and Company, 1916) at 282–317.

33 'Reservation in the Anglican Church, 1547–1661' in *Studies in Tudor History* by W.P.M. Kennedy at 282.

34 W.M. Kennedy, *Archbishop Parker* (London: Sir Isaac Pitman and Sons, 1908).

35 Ibid. at ix.

36 Ibid. at v.

37 Ibid. at ix.

38 Kennedy, *The 'Interpretations' of the Bishops* at 3 and 5.

39 F.E.B., 'Short Notices: *The 'Interpretations' of the Bishops and their Influence on Elizabethan Episcopal Policy*' (1910) 25 *English Historical Review* at 199–200.

40 Kennedy, *Archbishop Parker* at vii–viii.

41 This review appears in the *Pitman's Catalogue of General Literature*, found at the back of several books by the publisher, including Paul Janet, *Fénelon: His Life and Works* (London: Pitman and Sons, 1914).

42 A.F. Pollard, 'Reviews of Books: *Archbishop Parker* by W.M. Kennedy' (1909) 24 *English Historical Review* 795–7.

43 One such anachronism involved Queen Anne Boleyn and her daughter Elizabeth, who later became Queen Elizabeth. Parker was Anne Boleyn's priest. Kennedy refers to the 'tender and interesting fact' (*Archbishop Parker* at 38) that Queen Boleyn 'specially recommended to [Parker] care of her daughter Elizabeth, and laid a strict charge on [Elizabeth] to make a grateful return if occasion offered.' A nice story, but, as Pollard pointed out, 'Elizabeth was two years old when her mother was executed.' However, the review by Pollard did not prevent a later friendship. Indeed, Kennedy's later book, *Studies in Tudor History*, was dedicated to Pollard. Kennedy stated in the preface: 'Professor Pollard has kindly added to his friendship by accepting the dedication of the book, and I cannot let it go to press without stating that I am indebted to him in almost every chapter.'

44 S.L. Ollard, 'Reviews of Books: *Studies in Tudor History* by W.P.M. Kennedy' (1917) 32 *English Historical Review* 608.

45 Walter Howard Frere, ed., *Visitation Articles and Injunctions of the Period of the Reformation*, vol. 1 (London: Longmans, Green, 1910) at vi.

46 Perhaps he chose the name as an allusion to the conversion of Apostle Paul on the road to Damascus, but it is also possible that he named himself after Pope Paul IV, the pope in Queen Elizabeth's early years, whom Kennedy speaks well of in the Parker book.

47 W.P.M. Kennedy, *Parish Life under Queen Elizabeth: An Introductory Study* (Roehampton: The Manrisa Press, 1914).

48 Ibid. at viii.

49 'Books of the Day' *Globe*, 22 May 1915.

50 Kennedy, *Archbishop Parker* at vii.

51 John Craig, 'Parish Religion' in *The Elizabethan World*, ed. Susan Doran and Norman Jones (London: Routledge, 2011) at 226.

52 Kennedy, *Parish Life under Queen Elizabeth* at 29.

53 Email from John Craig to Martin Friedland, 14 September 2016. Professor Craig notes that the 'history of the Church of England has been riven along confessional lines from the 1530s to the present although the past 50 years has seen a marked lessening of these divisions.'

54 J. Campbell, 'Review: How Protestantism Prevailed in England' (1914) 42 *The Irish Monthly* 582–4.

55 H.T., 'The Catholic Library' (1914) 155 *The Dublin Review* 198–201.

56 E.W. Watson, 'Short Notices' (1914) 29 *English Historical Review* 791.

57 See, for example, 'Fines under the Elizabethan Act of Uniformity' (1918) 33 *English Historical Review* 517–28; 'A Declaration before the Ecclesiastical Commission, 1562' (1922) 37 *English Historical Review* 256–7; 'Notes on Visitations, 1536–58' (1926) 41 *English Historical Review* 577–9.

58 W.P.M. Kennedy, 'List of Visitation Articles and Injunctions, 1576–1603' (1917) 32 *English Historical Review* 273–6.

59 W.H. Frere and W.P.M. Kennedy, eds., *Visitation Articles and Injunctions of the Period of the Reformation*, vols. 1–3, reprint edition (London: Longmans, Green and Co., 1917).

60 Kennedy, Studies in Tudor History at vii.

61 Kennedy, *Studies in Tudor History*.

62 Letter from Pollard to Kennedy, 29 May 1914. St. Francis Xavier Archives.

63 J.D., '*Studies in Tudor History* by W.P.M. Kennedy' (1916) 5 *Studies: An Irish Quarterly Review* 296–8.

64 An Anglican clergyman, S.L. Ollard, was not as enthusiastic, stating in the *English Historical Review* (1917) 32 at 607–8: '[The] studies are mainly ecclesiastical … and the religious changes are their constant theme. Upon those changes the writer [Kennedy], as a Roman Catholic, holds strong opinions, and though, as he says in his preface, he has "done his utmost to lift the book out of the atmosphere of controversy," yet he is conscious that "he has at times failed in his ideal."'

65 Roger B. Merriman, 'Reviews of Books: *Studies in Tudor History* by W.P.M. Kennedy' (1916) 22 *American Historical Review* 143.

66 'History of the Royal Historical Society' *Royal Historical Society*, https://royalhistsoc.org/about/history.

67 Email from Susan Carr to Martin Friedland, 14 September 2016.

4 St. Michael's College

1 Gilbert Kennedy oral interview (interviewed by Maryla Waters 1983, Victoria University) at 9–10.

2 Letter from W.P.M. Kennedy to Archbishop Neil McNeil, 16 September 1914. Archives of the Roman Catholic Archdiocese of Toronto (ARCAT).

3 It is unclear which journal this letter was referring to as there are many Catholic publications called *The Record* in North America. It is likely Kennedy meant the *Louisville Record*, the Archdiocese of Louisville's weekly newspaper, which has been active since 1879.

4 St. Michael's College, Treasurer ledger cards. St. Michael's Archives.

5 Martin Friedland, *The University of Toronto: A History* (Toronto: University of Toronto Press, 2002) at 567.

6 Ibid. at 39.

7 Ibid. at 106–7.

8 Ibid. at 108.

9 'The Development of St. Michael's' in *The Year Book of St. Michael's College*, vol. 6, *1915* at 38.

10 P. Wallace Platt, *Dictionary of Basilian Biography: Lives of Members of the Congregation of Priests of Saint Basil from Its Origins in 1822 to 2002* (Toronto: University of Toronto Press, 2005) at 394–6.

11 Platt, *Dictionary of Basilian Biography* at 85–6.

12 Friedland, *The University of Toronto* at 218.

13 Ibid. at 295.

14 Letter from Robert Falconer to W.P.M. Kennedy, 3 September 1915. University of Toronto Archives: Falconer papers, replying to a letter from Kennedy to Falconer, not in the file.

15 Letter from W.M. Meredith to W.P.M. Kennedy, 13 August 1915. ARCAT.

16 'Firth, Sir Charles Harding' *Oxford Dictionary of National Biography*, http://www.oxforddnb.com/view/10.1093/ref:odnb/9780198614128.001.0001/odnb-9780198614128-e-33137.

17 Letter from Robert Falconer to W.P.M. Kennedy, 3 September 1915. University of Toronto Archives: Falconer papers.

18 Letter from W.M. Meredith to W.P.M. Kennedy, 13 August 1915. ARCAT.

19 Letter from Joseph A. Wall to Archbishop Neil McNeil, 21 January 1915. ARCAT.

20 Letter from W.P.M. Kennedy to Archbishop Neil McNeil, 28 September 1915. ARCAT.

21 Letter from W.P.M. Kennedy to Archbishop Neil McNeil, 21 July 1918. ARCAT. It is not clear whether the sale went through or whether the material was sold to the University of Toronto Library, which Kennedy said was offering to buy the books.

22 Friedland, *The University of Toronto* at 295.

23 Ibid.

24 A.J.R., 'Reviews: *A Century of Scientific Thought and Other Essays* by Sir Bertram C. A. Windle' (1916) 5 *Studies: An Irish Quarterly Review* 303–4; J.D., '*Studies in Tudor History* by W.P.M. Kennedy' (1916) 5 *Studies: An Irish Quarterly Review* 296–8. Kennedy's book was his *Studies in Tudor History* ('Mr. Kennedy's books should not be neglected by students of Tudor History. May their success encourage the author to give us more of the same workmanship'); Windle's was *A Century of Scientific Thought and Other Essays* ('valuable as there are few Catholics competent

to discuss the difficult problems connected with the specifically human applications of the theory of Evolution').

25 Father Edmund McCorkell oral interview (interviewed by Richard Alway 1974, St. Michaels College) at 1.

26 McCorkell oral interview at 76–9.

27 *The Year Book of St. Michael's College, 1915*; *The Year Book of St. Michael's College, 1916*.

28 'First Intercollege Debate, St. Michael's vs. Osgoode' *The Year Book of St. Michael's College, 1915* at 50.

29 'Music and the Drama' *The Year Book of St. Michael's College, 1916* at 74.

30 Elizabeth M. Smyth, 'Sister-Professors: Roman Catholic Women Religious at Academics in English Canada, 1897–1962' in *Historical Identities: The Professoriate in Canada*, ed. Euthalia Lisa Panayotidis and Paul James Stortz (Toronto: University of Toronto Press, 2006) at 216–17.

31 'Announcements' *Globe*, 14 February 1917.

32 'Prof. Kennedy Will Address "Le Club Politique" Today' *Varsity*, 20 February 1918.

33 'The Canadian Business Women's Club' *Globe*, 8 February 1917.

34 'The Women's Literary Society of University College' *Torontonensis: The Year Book of the Graduates of the University of Toronto*, vol. 20, *1918* at 37.

35 W.P.M. Kennedy, 'The Provincial University' *Globe*, 10 November 1920.

36 'Prof. W.P.M. Kennedy Discusses Respective Values of Lecture and the Group System' *Varsity*, 5 November 1917.

37 G. Oswald Smith, ed., *University of Toronto Roll of Service, 1914–1918* (Toronto: University of Toronto Press, 1921) at xi.

38 Friedland, *The University of Toronto* at 253–5.

39 'A Spirited Address' *The Year Book of St. Michael's College, 1916* at 53–4.

40 W.P.M. Kennedy, 'The War and Character' *The Year Book of St. Michael's College, 1916* at 52–3. Yes.

41 'W.P. Kennedy Invited to Bratislava University' newspaper unknown, 1928. University of Toronto Archives: Friedland papers, 1998 Accession.

42 Robert Craig Brown, *Robert Laird Borden: A Biography*, vol. 2 (Toronto: Macmillan of Canada, 1980) at 161 and 168.

43 W.P.M. Kennedy and Teresa Johnson marriage certificate, 14 December 1915. Found on *Ancestry.ca*.

44 Kennedy and Teresa Johnson marriage certificate, 14 December 1915.

45 Gilbert Kennedy oral interview at 37–8.

46 Author's oral interview with Betty Kennedy, 8 July 2013.

47 Gilbert Kennedy oral interview at 36–7, where further information on the family can be found. See also page 8, which notes that Gilbert corresponded with Jane Johnson, a daughter of Teresa's younger brother. A letter from her is appended to Gilbert's oral interview. A sister, Margaret or Peggy, married a Dr. Clayton, who worked at Columbia University.

48 St. Michael's College, Treasurer ledger cards. St. Michael's Archives.

49 Letter from Robert Falconer to W.P.M. Kennedy, 16 June 1916. University of Toronto Archives: Falconer papers.

50 Letter from W.P.M. Kennedy to Archbishop Neil McNeil, 9 July 1916. ARCAT.

51 Gilbert Kennedy oral interview at 1 and 38.

52 'Mallory, William Henry Jr.', *Biographical Dictionary of Architects in Canada, 1800–1950*, http://dictionaryofarchitectsincanada.org/node/649.

53 St. Michael's College, Treasurer ledger cards. St. Michael's Archives.

54 University of Toronto, *Faculty of Arts and Sciences Calendar, 1914–1922*. University of Toronto Archives: University calendars.

55 Friedland, *The University of Toronto* at 103 and 108–9.

56 Letter from Alexander to Falconer, 14 November 1916. University of Toronto Archives: Falconer papers.

57 Ian Drummond, *Political Economy at the University of Toronto: A History of the Department, 1888–1982* (Toronto: University of Toronto Press, 1983) at 42.

58 University of Toronto, *Faculty of Arts and Sciences Calendar, 1914–1922*. University of Toronto Archives: University calendars. See also Robert Bothwell, *Laying the Foundation: A Century of History at the University of Toronto* (Toronto: University of Toronto Press, 1991) at 58.

59 Letter from Robert Falconer to W.P.M. Kennedy, 28 June 1918. University of Toronto Archives: Falconer papers.

60 Letter from W.P.M. Kennedy to Robert Falconer, 1919. University of Toronto Archives: Falconer papers.

61 Letter from the acting head of history to Robert Falconer, 20 January 1919. University of Toronto Archives: History department papers. If Kennedy did deliver the lectures, it was not likely he gave all of them because his wife died on 13 April 1919.

62 Letter from George Wrong to Robert Falconer, 18 December 1918.

63 Letter from W.P.M. Kennedy to Robert Falconer, 15 November 1918.

64 Teresa Kennedy's death certificate, 14 April 1919. *Ancestry.ca.*

65 See generally, Esyllt W. Jones, *Influenza 1918: Disease, Death, and Struggle in Winnipeg* (Toronto: University of Toronto Press, 2007); and Heather MacDougall, 'Toronto's Health Department in Action: Influenza in 1918 and SARS in 2003' in *Epidemic Encounters: Influenza, Society, and Culture in Canada, 1918–20*, ed. M. Fahrni and E.W. Jones (Vancouver: UBC Press, 2012) at 225 et seq.

66 Teresa Kennedy's death certificate.

67 Letter from W.P.M. Kennedy to James Mavor, 19 April 1919. University of Toronto Archives: Mavor papers.

68 There are no cemetery records of Teresa Kennedy being buried at Mount Pleasant Cemetery (email from Mount Pleasant dated 1 August 2018), but the Ontario death register states that she was buried there. It was likely a common grave

without a headstone: see Mike Filey, *Mount Pleasant Cemetery: An Illustrated Guide* (Toronto: Dundurn Press, 1999) at 181, who mentions such plots.

69 Letter from Ralph Hodder Williams to Robert Falconer, 20 April 1919. University of Toronto Archives: Falconer papers.

70 Letter from Ralph Hodder Williams to Robert Falconer, 7 June 1919. University of Toronto Archives: Falconer papers.

71 Letter from W.P.M. Kennedy to Robert Falconer, 4 August 1919. University of Toronto Archives: Falconer papers.

72 Gilbert Kennedy oral interview at 38–9.

73 Author's oral interview with Betty Kennedy, 8 July 2013.

74 Letter from George Wrong to Robert Falconer, 4 May 1919. University of Toronto Archives: Falconer papers.

75 Letter from W.P.M. Kennedy to Robert Falconer, 4 August 1919. University of Toronto Archives: Falconer papers.

76 Letter from George Brett to Robert Falconer, 15 August 1919. University of Toronto Archives: Falconer papers.

77 George Sidney Brett, *A History of Psychology* (New York: George Allen & Unwin, 1921).

78 Letter from W.P.M. Kennedy to Robert Falconer, n.d. (likely August 1919). University of Toronto Archives: Falconer papers.

5 Turning to the Canadian Constitution

1 Alexander Brady, 'William Paul McClure Kennedy: 1879–1963' in *Proceedings and Transactions of the Royal Society of Canada*, 4th series, vol. 2, *Meeting of June 1964* (Ottawa: Royal Society of Canada, 1964) at 109–11.

2 R.C.B. Risk, 'The Many Minds of W.P.M. Kennedy' (1998) 48 *University of Toronto Law Journal* 353 at 361.

3 University of Toronto, *Faculty of Arts and Sciences Calendar, 1917–1918*. University of Toronto Archives: University calendars.

4 Letter from George Wrong to Robert Falconer, 23 March 1911. University of Toronto Archives: Falconer papers.

5 The other lectures were given by Sir John Willison, the Canadian correspondent for *The Times*, and Z.A. Lash, a leading Canadian lawyer with the Blake-Lash firm who had been deputy minister of justice in Ottawa.

6 George M. Wrong et al., *The Federation of Canada 1867–1917: Four Lectures delivered in the University of Toronto in March, 1917, to Commemorate the Fiftieth Anniversary of the Federation* (Toronto: Oxford University Press, 1917).

7 William Stewart Wallace, *A History of the University of Toronto, 1827–1927* (Toronto: University of Toronto Press, 1927) at 218.

8 Ibid.

9 Martin Friedland, *The University of Toronto: A History* (Toronto: University of Toronto Press, 2002) at 141. See also Robert C. Vipond, 'Mills, David' in *Dictionary*

of Canadian Biography, vol. 13, http://www.biographi.ca/en/bio/mills_david_13E. html; Robert C. Vipond, *Liberty & Community: Canadian Federalism and the Failure of the Constitution* (Albany, NY: State University of New York, 1991).

10 R.C.B. Risk, 'A.H.F. Lefroy: Common Law Thought in Late Nineteenth-Century Canada: On Burying One's Grandfather' (1991) 41 *University of Toronto Law Journal* 307.

11 The Marquis of Ruvigny and Ranieval, *The Plantagenet Roll of the Blood Royal: The Mortimer-Percy Volume* (Bowie, MD: Heritage Books, 2013) at 246.

12 A.H.F. Lefroy, 'Should Canadian Women Have the Parliamentary Vote?' (1913) 21 *Queen's Quarterly* 91–6.

13 A.H.F. Lefroy, *A Short Treatise on Canadian Constitutional Law* (Toronto: Carswell, 1918). The dedication reads: 'To the Memory of My Son ... Who Willingly Gave His Life for Canada and the Empire, and for the Principles of a Christian Civilization, on the Western Front in France ... in his 23rd Year.'

14 'Prof. Lefroy Passes Away' *Globe*, 9 March 1919.

15 Ibid.

16 W.P.M. Kennedy, *The Constitution of Canada: An Introduction to Its Development and Law* (London: Oxford University Press, 1922) at x.

17 W.P.M. Kennedy, 'A.H.F. Lefroy – In Appreciation' *Varsity*, 10 March 1919.

18 W.P.M. Kennedy, 'In Memoriam: A.H.F. Lefroy, M.A., K.C., Late Editor of *The Canadian Law Times*' (1919) 39, no. 4 *Canadian Law Times* 197–200. See also W.P.M. Kennedy, 'Lefroy, Augustus Henry Frazer' in *Encyclopaedia of Social Sciences*, vol. 9 (London: Macmillan, 1933) at 319.

19 Richard C.B. Risk, 'Lefroy, Augustus Henry Frazer' in *Dictionary of Canadian Biography*, http://www.biographi.ca/en/bio/lefroy_augustus_henry_frazer_14E.html.

20 A.H.F. Lefroy, *The Law of Legislative Power in Canada* (Toronto: Toronto Law Book and Publishing Company, 1897).

21 W.P.M. Kennedy, 'In Memoriam: A.H.F. Lefroy' *Varsity*, 10 March 1919.

22 Kennedy, 'Lefroy, Augustus Henry Frazer' in *Encyclopaedia of Social Sciences*, vol. 9 at 319.

23 R.C.B. Risk, 'Constitutional Scholarship in the Late Nineteenth Century: Making Federalism Work' in *A History of Canadian Legal Thought: Collected Essays*, ed. G. Blaine Baker and Jim Phillips (Toronto: University of Toronto Press, 2006) at 59n13.

24 Kennedy, 'Lefroy, Augustus Henry Frazer' in *Encyclopaedia of Social Sciences*, vol. 9 at 319.

25 R.C.B. Risk, 'A.H.F. Lefroy' (1991) 41 *University of Toronto Law Journal* 307 at 316.

26 Lefroy, *A Short Treatise on Canadian Constitutional Law* at v–vi.

27 Ibid.

28 Risk, 'A.H.F. Lefroy' at 320.

29 A.H.F. Lefroy, 'The Alberta and Great Waterways Railway Case' (1913) 29 *Law Quarterly Review* at 288.

30 Lefroy, *A Short Treatise on Canadian Constitutional Law* at vi.

31 W.P.M. Kennedy, 'Historical Introduction' in *A Short Treatise on Canadian Constitutional Law* by A.H.F. Leroy at 1–3.

32 'Minor Notices' (1919) 13 *American Political Science Review* 696–7.

33 H.J.L., 'Book Reviews: *A Short Treatise on Canadian Constitutional Law* by A.H.F. Lefroy' (1919) 32 *Harvard Law Review* at 582.

34 'New Books: *A Short Treatise on Canadian Constitutional Law* by A.H.F. Lefroy with an Historical Introduction by W. P. M. Kennedy' (1919) 39 *Canadian Law Times* 238–329.

35 H.E.E., 'Short Notices' (1919) 34 *English Historical Review* 128.

36 A.H.F. Lefroy, 'A University Training as a Preparation for the Legal Profession' (1901) 1 *University of Toronto Monthly* 263.

37 Ibid. at 265.

38 Risk, 'A.H.F. Lefroy' at 307.

39 Carol Whitfield and Richard Jarrell, 'Lefroy, Sir John Henry' in *Dictionary of Canadian Biography*, http://www.biographi.ca/en/bio/lefroy_john_henry_11E.html.

40 'Records Shattered in Heffel's $10.5 Million Fine Art Auction' (2006) *Heffel Fine Art Auction House*, https://www.heffel.com/links/News/A2006s_Results_dr5-rv.pdf.

41 Jessica Wong, 'The 5 Most Valuable Canadian Artworks Ever Sold at Auction,' *CBC News*, 23 November 2016, http://www.cbc.ca/news/entertainment/auction-canada-top-5-1.3863792.

42 'Lefroy, Thomas Langlois' *Library Ireland*, https://www.libraryireland.com/biography/ThomasLangloisLefroy.php.

43 Conversation with John Honsberger several years ago.

44 Laura Boyle, 'Who Was the Real Tom Lefroy' Jane Austen Centre, https://www.janeausten.co.uk/who-was-the-real-tom-lefroy/.

45 Letter from Jane Austen to Cassandra Austen, 16 January 1796, https://pemberley.com/janeinfo/brablet1.html#letter2. See also 'Austen's very own Mr Darcy" *Independent*, https://www.independent.co.uk/arts-entertainment/books/features/austens-very-own-mr-darcy-843552.html. Whether A.H.F. Lefroy knew about that affair is uncertain. His father, John Henry Lefroy, does not mention Jane Austen in his lengthy detailed autobiography published in 1895 by his widow. See J.H. Lefroy and Lady C.A. Lefroy, *Autobiography of General Sir John Henry Lefroy, Colonel Commandant, Royal Artillery* (London: Pardon & Sons, 1895).

46 Trent University Digital Collections, 'Robinson Family Tree' *Digital Collections*, http://digitalcollections.trentu.ca/exhibits/beverley-robinson/zr2famt.htm.

47 W.P.M. Kennedy, *Documents of the Canadian Constitution, 1759–1915* (London: Oxford University Press, 1918).

48 Kennedy, *Documents of the Canadian Constitution* at vi.

49 A.H.F. Lefroy, *Leading Cases in Canadian Constitutional Law* (Toronto: Carswell, 1914).

50 'Life and Letters' *Globe*, 2 November 1918.

51 'New Books and New Editions: *Documents of the Canadian Constitution, 1759–1915*' (1918) 38 *Canadian Law Times* 729.

52 H.E. Egerton, 'Short Notices' (1919) 34 *English Historical Review* at 276. H.E. Egerton was the author of *Canadian Constitutional Development: Shown by Selected Speeches* (London: J. Murray, 1907).

53 Kennedy, *Documents of the Canadian Constitution* at iii and vii.

54 W.P.M. Kennedy, ed., *Statutes, Treaties and Documents of the Canadian Constitution, 1713–1929*, rev. and enlarged ed. (Toronto: Oxford University Press, 1930) at v, vii, and x.

6 Pauline Simpson

1 'Engagements' *Globe*, 20 May 1920. Pauline Simpson was born on 18 January 1895. See 'Obituary' *Globe and Mail*, 27 April 1966.

2 W.P.M. Kennedy and Pauline Simpson marriage license, 3 May 1920. Found on *Ancestry.ca*.

3 'Marriage Announcement' *Globe*, 22 June 1920.

4 Pauline Simpson's University of Toronto Application for Admission to the Faculty of Household Science (General). University of Toronto Archives: Pauline Simpson file.

5 Gilbert Kennedy oral interview (interviewed by Maryla Waters 1983, Victoria University) at 41.

6 Pauline Simpson's University of Toronto Application for Admission to the Faculty of Arts, 2 October 1919. University of Toronto Archives: Pauline Simpson file.

7 *Torontonensis: The Year Book of the Graduates of the University of Toronto*, vol. 21, *1919* at 24.

8 Martin Friedland, *The University of Toronto: A History* (Toronto: University of Toronto Press, 2002) at 94.

9 *Torontonensis*, vol. 20, *1918* at 42.

10 Gilbert Kennedy oral interview at 39. See also Father Edmund McCorkell oral interview (interviewed by Richard Alway 1974, St. Michaels College) at 18: Pauline was 'one of his senior students.'

11 Gilbert Kennedy oral interview at 39–40.

12 Kennedy and Simpson marriage license, 1920.

13 'Railroad Man Dies a Hero' *Syracuse Post-Standard*, 10 October 1904.

14 'Deadly Gas in Sarnia Tunnel' *The Northern Advance*, 13 October 1904.

15 Author's oral interview with George Simpson, 28 July 2016.

16 Ibid. I also communicated by phone or email with a number of grand nieces and nephews.

17 1921 Canadian census. Found on *Ancestry.ca*.

18 (1921) 21 *University of Toronto Monthly* at 337.

19 Author's oral interview with George Simpson, 28 July 2016.

20 Ibid.

21 Ibid.

22 Ibid.

23 John Ross Simpson and Alice Gray Hogarth marriage certificate, 8 June 1920. Found on *Ancestry.ca*.

24 Kennedy and Simpson marriage license, 1920.

25 Author's oral interview with George Simpson, 28 July 2016.

26 Letter from W.P.M. Kennedy to Berriedale Keith, n.d. Edinburgh Archives.

27 John English, *Shadow of Heaven: The Life of Lester Pearson*, vol. 1, *1897–1948* (London: Random House UK, 1994) at 109.

28 Friedland, *The University of Toronto* at 305.

29 Father Edmund McCorkell oral interview (interviewed by Richard Alway 1974, St. Michaels College) at 80.

30 Vincent Bladen, *Bladen on Bladen: Memoirs of a Political Economist* (Toronto: privately published, 1978) at 37.

31 Letter from George Wrong to Robert Falconer, 18 December 1918. University of Toronto Archives: Falconer papers.

32 Friedland, *The University of Toronto* at 158–74.

33 Ibid. at 163.

34 Letter from Hume Wrong to George Wrong, 8 February 1926. University of Toronto Archives: Wrong papers.

35 Christopher Moore, 'Interpreting History' *The Beaver*, February/March 2000 at 82.

36 Letter from W.P.M. Kennedy to James Mavor, 26 June 1920. University of Toronto Archives: Falconer papers.

37 Letter from W.P.M. Kennedy to Robert Falconer, 29 November 1920. University of Toronto Archives: Falconer papers.

38 Letter from George Wrong to Robert Falconer, 25 November 1920. University of Toronto Archives: Falconer papers.

39 Reference letter by Robert Falconer, 22 March 1921. University of Toronto Archives: Falconer papers.

40 Letter from Sir Arthur Currie to Robert Falconer, 16 May 1921. University of Toronto Archives: Falconer papers.

41 Letter from Robert Falconer to Sir Arthur Currie, 20 May 1921. University of Toronto Archives: Falconer papers.

42 Ian M. Drummond, *Political Economy at the University of Toronto: A History of the Department, 1888–1982* (Toronto: University of Toronto Press, 1983) at 37 and 53.

43 Memo from Robert Falconer, 12 April 1922. University of Toronto Archives: Falconer papers.

44 Letter from Robert Falconer to W.P.M. Kennedy, 5 June 1922. University of Toronto Archives: Falconer papers.

45 Edmund McCorkell oral interview at 77–8.

46 Gilbert Kennedy oral interview at 61–2.

47 Letter from W.P.M. Kennedy to Robert Falconer, 14 March 1922. University of Toronto Archives: Falconer papers.

48 Letter from W.P.M. Kennedy to John Defoe, 26 March 1928. University of Manitoba Archives: Defoe papers.

49 One can see the obvious importance of the consecration ceremony, linking the monarch to God, in the portrayal of the coronation of Elizabeth II in the popular TV series *The Crown*.

50 Bladen, *Bladen on Bladen* at 37.

51 W.P.M. Kennedy, *The Constitution of Canada: An Introduction to Its Development and Law* (London: Oxford University Press, 1922) at v and ix.

52 See R.M. MacIver, *The Modern State* (London: Oxford University Press, 1926), which cites Kennedy's *Constitution of Canada*, but does not mention Kennedy or, indeed, anyone in the preface.

53 Friedland, *The University of Toronto* at 320.

54 Ibid.

55 Robert MacIver, *As a Tale That Is Told* (Chicago: University of Chicago Press, 1968) at 89.

56 W.P.M. Kennedy, *Elizabethan Episcopal Administration: An Essay in Sociology and Politics*, 3 vols. (London: A.R. Mowbray, 1924).

57 W.P.M. Kennedy, 'List of Visitation Articles and Injunctions, 1576–1603' (1917) 32 *English Historical Review* 273–6 at 273.

58 Kennedy, *Elizabethan Episcopal Administration*, vol. 1 at vii.

59 Kennedy also thanked the many persons in the United Kingdom who assisted him in collecting material: 'To the keepers of the national archives, to librarians at the diocesan centres, to enthusiastic helpers in many dioceses and parishes I should like to record my great obligations – not forgetting those happy hours up and down England when collecting the material which are always valued memories.'

60 Kennedy, *Elizabethan Episcopal Administration*, vol. 1 at v.

61 Ibid. at vii.

62 Ibid. at vi.

63 Ibid. at xxxii.

64 Ibid. at vi.

65 Ibid. at v.

66 John Scott and Gordon Marshall, 'Pluralism' in *Oxford Dictionary of Sociology* (London: Oxford University Press, 2009). See also David Schneiderman, 'Harold Laski, Viscount Haldane, and the Law of the Canadian Constitution in the Early Twentieth Century' (1998) 48 *University of Toronto Law Journal* 521.

67 Kennedy, *Elizabethan Episcopal Administration*, vol. 1 at ccxc.

68 Ibid. at cciii. One sees today, as this book is being written, echoes of this desire for greater sovereignty by the English in a possible break with Brussels (rather than Rome) in the Brexit controversy.

69 W.P.M. Kennedy, 'List of Visitation Articles and Injunctions, 1604–1715' (1925) 4 *English Historical Review* 586–92 at 586.

70 W.P.M. Kennedy, 'Notes on Visitations 1536–58' (1926) 41 *English Historical Review* 577–99 at 577.

7 *The Constitution of Canada* and Beyond

1 W.P.M. Kennedy, 'Canada and the Empire' (1919) 12 *New Statesman* 393 at 394.
2 Ibid. at 395.
3 Ibid.
4 W.P.M. Kennedy, 'Canada and the Imperial Conference' (1921) 120 *British Contemporary Review* 61.
5 W.P.M. Kennedy, 'The Nature of Canadian Federalism' (1921) 2 *Canadian Historical Review* 106 at 124. He uses the following definition, which obviously brings about that result. A federation is 'a union of component states, wherein there is a central legislature which has authority to pass laws directly obligatory upon the people, the component states also having legislative power. In confederations, on the other hand, the central body has relations with the component states only, and not directly with individuals, *e.g.*, Austria-Hungary.'
6 W.P.M. Kennedy, *The Nature of Canadian Federalism* (Toronto: University of Toronto Press, 1921). In a short prefatory note, Kennedy thanks historian W. Stewart Wallace, political scientist R.M. MacIver, and Justice C.A. Masten, a High Court judge 'for directing me in difficult constitutional questions and for guiding me to much material.'
7 W.P.M. Kennedy, 'Nationalism and Self-Determination' (1921) 2 *Canadian Historical Review* 6–18.
8 Ibid. at 10.
9 Ibid. at 14–15, 17.
10 W.P.M. Kennedy, *Documents of the Canadian Constitution, 1759–1915* (London: Oxford University Press, 1918).
11 Email from Dr. Martin Maw to Martin Friedland, 8 July 2013. I am grateful for Dr. Maw's assistance in searching for documents relating to the publication.
12 Memorandum between William Stewart Wallace and William Paul McClure Kennedy, and Oxford University Press, 28 October 1918. Oxford University Press Archives.
13 Ibid.
14 Letter from W.S. Wallace to W.P.M. Kennedy, 3 October 1921. Oxford University Press Archives.
15 Martin Friedland, *The University of Toronto: A History* (Toronto: University of Toronto Press, 2002) at 306; W. Stewart Wallace, *A First Book of Canadian History* (Toronto: Macmillan, 1928).
16 W.P.M. Kennedy, *The Constitution of Canada: An Introduction to Its Development and Law* (London: Oxford University Press, 1922) at x.
17 'Wm. Tyrrell & Co. Toronto,' *Vintage Post Cards*, http://www.vintagepostcards.ca/Tyrrell.html.
18 Advertisement for *The Constitution of Canada* by Wm. Tyrrell & Co., Oxford University Press Archives.

19 Ibid.

20 'Canada – a Political Miracle: A Fitting Title for Volume' *Star Weekly*, 20 October 1923.

21 Ibid.

22 Harold Laski, 'Canada's Constitution' *The New Republic*, 4 July 1923 at 159.

23 Alan Cairns, 'The Judicial Committee and Its Critics' (1971) 4 *Canadian Journal of Political Science* 301–45 at 306.

24 Letter from W.P.M. Kennedy to Robert Falconer, 24 August 1923. University of Toronto Archives: Falconer papers.

25 I am grateful for the assistance of researcher Christopher Cook in obtaining this material on Mackenzie King.

26 Letter from W.P.M. Kennedy to William Lyon Mackenzie King, 14 September 1926. Library and Archives Canada: W.L.M. King papers, vol. 207.

27 Friedland, *The University of Toronto* at 159–60.

28 Letter from W.P.M. Kennedy to Robert Falconer, 24 August 1923. University of Toronto Archives: Falconer papers.

29 Letter from W.P.M. Kennedy to Berriedale Keith, 12 July 1923. University of Edinburgh Archives: Keith papers.

30 Kennedy, *The Constitution of Canada* at iii.

31 Letter from Robert Falconer to W.P.M. Kennedy, 25 June 1922. University of Toronto Archives: Falconer papers.

32 Kennedy, *The Constitution of Canada* at vii.

33 Ibid.

34 Ibid. at 6.

35 Ibid. at 300–1.

36 Ibid. at vii.

37 Ibid. at 446, 451–2.

38 Carl Berger, *The Writing of Canadian History: Aspects of English-Canadian Historical Writing: 1900–1970* (Toronto: Oxford University Press, 1976) at 40.

39 Kennedy, *The Constitution of Canada* at 455–6.

40 Ibid. at viii.

41 W.P.M. Kennedy, 'The Conception of the British Commonwealth' [1924] *Edinburgh Review* 227 at 238.

42 R.B.C. Risk, 'The Many Minds of W.P.M. Kennedy' (1998) 48 *University of Toronto Law* 353 at 363–4. The unpublished paper with Kennedy's Convocation Hall speech can be found in the University of Toronto Fisher Rare Book Library, Kennedy papers.

43 Kennedy, *The Constitution of Canada* at 436.

44 Ibid. at 431.

45 *Liquidators of the Maritime Bank of Canada v. Receiver-General of New Brunswick* [1892] A.C. 437 at 441–2.

46 Kennedy, *The Constitution of Canada* at 411.

47 Ibid. at 398.

48 *Re Board of Commerce Act 1919 and the Combines and Fair Prices Act 1919* [1922] 1 A.C. 191.

49 Ibid.

50 *Toronto Electric Commissioners v. Snider* [1925] A.C. 396.

51 Indigenous issues are discussed in chapter 17 of this book.

52 Kennedy, *The Constitution of Canada* at 5.

53 Harold Laski, 'Canada's Constitution' *The New Republic*, 4 July 1923 at 159.

54 Kennedy, *The Constitution of Canada* at 449.

8 *Deeks v. H.G. Wells*

1 A.B. McKillop, *The Spinster & the Prophet: Florence Deeks, H.G. Wells, and the Mystery of the Purloined Past* (Toronto: Osgoode Society; Macfarlane Walter & Ross, 2000) at 174.

2 Ibid. at 21.

3 Ibid. at 102–3.

4 *Florence A. Deeks v. H.G. Wells and Others (Deeks v. Wells)*, [1932] U.K.P.C. 66.

5 McKillop, *The Spinster & the Prophet* at 87.

6 Ibid. at 128, 112–13.

7 For more information on Teresa Kennedy, see chapter 4: St. Michael's College.

8 'Record of Proceedings,' *Deeks v. Wells* at 23.

9 McKillop, *The Spinster & the Prophet* at 127–9.

10 Ibid. at 136–7.

11 'Record of Proceedings,' *Deeks v. Wells* at 453.

12 Robert Fulford, 'Imperial Bedroom (*Deeks v. Wells*)' (April 1993) *Saturday Night* 24–6.

13 McKillop, *The Spinster & the Prophet* at 159.

14 Ibid. at 152.

15 A recent review in the *Times Literary Supplement*, on the occasion of the 100th anniversary of the completion of Wells's book, states: 'Almost miraculously, the writing of the *Outline* took little more than a year.' Yet, the author of the review dismisses the possibility of plagiarism. See Patrick Parrinder, 'The Time Traveller Goes Backwards: H.G Wells and *The Outline of History*,' *Times Literary Supplement*, 24 October 2018 at 18.

16 McKillop, *The Spinster & the Prophet* at 172.

17 Ibid. at 211.

18 Memo from Florence Deeks, n.d. Deeks papers in the Baldwin Room of the Toronto Reference Library.

19 McKillop, *The Spinster & the Prophet* at 183.

20 'Case for the 2nd Respondents,' *Deeks v. Wells* at 2.

21 McKillop, *The Spinster & the Prophet* at 260.

22 Ibid. Most of the evidence was taken by what is called 'commission evidence' from witnesses, such as the defendants' collaborators in England and the heads of Macmillan in London and New York, or was introduced by counsel from depositions or examinations for discovery.

23 Ibid. at 210.

24 Ibid. at 261.

25 Ibid. at 211, 279.

26 Letter from George Brett to Hugh S. Eayrs, 16 September 1927. McMaster University Archives: Macmillan of Canada papers.

27 He received a fee of $750 for his evidence. McKillop, *The Spinster & the Prophet* at 341.

28 'Record of Proceedings,' *Deeks v. Wells* at 376.

29 Ibid.

30 Ibid. at 86.

31 McKillop, *The Spinster & the Prophet* at 217–9.

32 Ibid.

33 Ibid.

34 Memo from Robert MacIver, 27 September 1927. Deeks papers in the Baldwin Room of the Toronto Reference Library.

35 Letter from Robert Falconer to W.P.M. Kennedy, 25 June 1922. University of Toronto Archives: Falconer papers.

36 Letter from George Brett to Hugh S. Eayrs, 28 September 1927. McMaster University Archives: Macmillan of Canada papers.

37 McKillop, *The Spinster & the Prophet* at 219.

38 Ontario Land Registry Office. See also *Might's Greater Toronto City Directory* (Toronto: Might Directories, 1921–5). The yearly Toronto directory, *Might's Directory*, shows Kennedy living at 110 Quebec Avenue from 1921 to 1924 and then living at 77 Spadina Road in 1925.

39 McKillop, *The Spinster & the Prophet* at 267.

40 Robert MacIver, *As a Tale That Is Told* (Chicago: University of Chicago Press, 1968) at 89.

41 McKillop, *The Spinster & the Prophet* at 220. There is no specific reference to this information about the payment in the Falconer papers.

42 Ibid. at 267.

43 See W.P.M. Kennedy, *Some Aspects of the Theories and Workings of Constitutional Law* (New York: Macmillan 1932).

44 Letter from George Wrong to Robert Falconer, 13 July 1926. University of Toronto Archives: Falconer papers.

45 Formally called the Appellate Division of the Supreme Court.

46 McKillop, *The Spinster & the Prophet* at 346–9. There were insufficient funds to pay for a lawyer.

47 Ibid. at 356.

48 Ibid. at 365–6.

49 Ibid. at 374–5.
50 *Deeks v. Wells.*
51 McKillop, *The Spinster & the Prophet* at 374–6.
52 Letter from J.M. Dent and Sons to Florence Deeks, 23 November 1932. Deeks papers in the Baldwin Room of the Toronto Reference Library.
53 'Florence Amelia Deeks' Find a Grave Memorial, https://www.findagrave.com/memorial/28862173/florence-amelia-deeks.
54 McKillop, *The Spinster & the Prophet* at 387–8.
55 Ruth Panofsky, *The Literary Legacy of the Macmillan Company of Canada* (Toronto: University of Toronto Press, 2011) at 83.
56 McKillop had put it this way: The head of Macmillan Canada 'knew a great deal more than he let on.' McKillop, *The Spinster & the Prophet* at 322.
57 'Record of Proceedings,' *Deeks v. Wells* at 271.
58 McKillop, *The Spinster & the Prophet* at 342.

9 The Irish Constitution

1 Personal conversation with Shelagh Lindsey, 2014.
2 W.P.M. Kennedy, 'Review of *The Constitution of the Irish Free State*' (1934) 20 *American Bar Association Journal* 365–6. Leo Kohn's book grew out of a doctoral dissertation submitted to the University of Heidelberg in 1927.
3 'W.P.M. Kennedy Lectures Today: University of Toronto Professor to Speak on British Dominions' Constitution' *Cornell Daily*, 6 January 1927.
4 'Development of Ireland's Laws Told in Lectures' *Cornell Daily*, 8 January 1927.
5 Letter from George Wrong to Robert Falconer, 13 July 1926. University of Toronto Archives: Falconer papers.
6 Leo Kohn, *The Constitution of the Irish Free State* (London: Allen & Unwin, 1933).
7 Honourable Hugh M. Kennedy, 'The Association of Canada with the Constitution of the Irish Free State' (1928) 6 *Canadian Bar Review* 747–58.
8 Donald J. McDougall, 'Canada and Ireland: A Contrast in Constitutional Development' in *Essays in Canadian History: Presented to George Mackinnon Wrong for his Eightieth Birthday*, ed. R. Flenley (Toronto: Macmillan, 1939).
9 D.H. Akenson and J.F. Fallin, 'The Irish Civil War and the Drafting of the Free State Constitution' (1970) 5 *Eire-Ireland* 10–93.
10 Brian Farrell, 'The Drafting of the Irish Free State Constitution' (1970) 5 *Irish Jurist* at 115–60 [part 1]; (1970) 5, no. 2 at 343–56 [part 2]; (1971) 6 at 111–35 [part 3].
11 Justice Gerard Hogan of the Irish Court of Appeal gives a good thumbnail sketch in a 2012 publication of the Royal Irish Academy, which will serve to familiarize readers with the general outline of the story. Hogan writes: 'The Constitution of the Irish Free State entered into force on December 6, 1922 after six turbulent years that saw rebellion against British rule, the success of the Sinn Féin party at the 1918 general election, the War of Independence, the partition of the island of

Ireland and, ultimately, the Anglo-Irish Treaty of December 1921. The 1921 Treaty had provided for the establishment of the Irish Free State, with Dominion status within the emerging British Commonwealth ... Yet, within a space of fifteen years, that Constitution was itself replaced following years of political and constitutional turmoil and debate, a process which accelerated following the accession of de Valera to power in March 1932.' Gerald Hogan, *The Origins of the Irish Constitution: 1928–1941* (Dublin: Royal Irish Academy, 2012) at 1.

12　Thomas Towey, 'Hugh Kennedy and the Constitutional Development of the Irish Free State, 1922–1923' (1977) 12 *Irish Jurist* at 355.

13　Article 2, *Articles of Agreement for a Treaty between Great Britain and Ireland,* 1922. The treaty, which was to take precedence over the constitution, provided, for example, that 'the position of the Irish Free State in relationship to the Imperial Parliament and Government and otherwise shall be that of the Dominion of Canada, and the law, practice and constitutional usage governing the relationship of the Crown or the representative of the Crown and of the Imperial Parliament to the Dominion of Canada shall govern their relationship to the Irish Free State.'

14　'Kennedy, William Paul McClure,' *British Who's Who: An Annual Biographical Dictionary* (London: A & C Black Ltd., 1935) at 1828.

15　'Kennedy, William Paul McClure,' *Who's Who and Who Was Who* (Oxford University Press, 2019). https://www.ukwhoswho.com/search?q=kennedy%2C+william+paul+mcclure.

16　Further, in January 1924, Kennedy told *The Mail and Empire* that he was 'at present collaborating with Mr. Darrell Figgis ... in working out the whole question of judicial appeals in the Irish Free State.' See 'Toronto Professor Enters a Protest: Sees Misrepresentation of Imperial Conference Functions' *The Mail and Empire,* 21 January 1924.

17　There is no evidence that Kennedy supported or sympathized with subversive activity against the British. The two men were, however, about the same age, and both were interested in Shakespeare and literature. For a number of years Figgis had been an editor for Dent and Sons in London, and Kennedy's first wife was a Canadian editor for Dent in Canada. Did this provide a connection between Figgis and Kennedy? Coincidentally, Figgis's first wife, like Kennedy's, died of the Spanish flu just after the war ended. Figgis's second wife committed suicide in 1924.

18　The author is indebted to archivist Seamus Helferty for his assistance in this matter. The finding aid is not online.

19　Laura Cahillane, 'The Genesis, Drafting and Legacy of the Irish Free State Constitution' (PhD diss., University College Cork, 2011).

20　Email from Laura Cahillane, 3 June 2014, who goes on to state: 'Much of my research was based on the archives of the constitution committee (some of these are missing), the notes of the secretary of the committee, the personal papers of those involved and various secondary sources. I don't remember ever coming across references or letters to Kennedy – although some of the personal paper collections are quite substantial and I may have taken no notice.'

21 Thomas Mohr, 'The Irish Free State and the Legal Implications of Dominion Status' (PhD diss., University College Dublin, 2007).

22 Email from Thomas Mohr, 6 June 2014. See also Thomas Mohr, *Guardian of the Treaty: The Privy Council Appeal and Irish Sovereignty* (Dublin: Four Courts Press, 2016), where W.P.M. Kennedy is not mentioned in the text and is cited in one footnote on another matter.

23 Email from Thomas Mohr, 19 August 2016.

24 Charles Murphy was a Liberal politician, who was appointed to the Canadian Senate in 1925, and Charles Doherty was a former minister of justice in the Borden and Meighen administrations. Another Canadian who played a role was Henri Bourassa, the founder and editor of *Le Devoir*, who was in England in June 1922 and met with some members of the committee.

25 *Select Constitutions of the World, prepared for the Irish Constitutions Committee* (published by the Authority of the Provisional Government Ltd, printed by A. Thom Co. Ltd, 1922).

26 Kennedy's preface is dated 18 March 1922, and the text of *Select Constitutions* was completed in September 1922.

27 'In its original form,' Professor Mohr writes, 'Figgis introduced each Constitution with commentary of his own ... The Irish government learned that this commentary was potentially controversial and pulled the plug on all funding and cooperation for this project. The book was eventually published but without any of Figgis' commentary.' It is possible that Figgis communicated with Kennedy to get his ideas for the commentary to the volume that was never published. Email from Thomas Mohr to Martin Friedland 19 August 2016.

28 Ibid.

29 The author is grateful to Thomas Mohr for his assistance in this matter. Additionally, the author wishes to thank Orna Somerville, archivist at University College Dublin.

30 Darrell Figgis, *The Irish Constitution Explained* (Dublin: Millifont Press, 1922).

31 'Note,' *Toronto Telegram*, March 1924.

32 'Canada Is Model for Dail Eireann' *Globe*, 22 February 1922.

33 'Irish Free State Writes for Book' *Varsity*, 24 February 1922.

34 W.P.M. Kennedy, 'Significance of the Irish Free State' (1923) 218 *The North American Review* 316 at 316–18.

35 Ibid. at 319–22. Kennedy also noted that members of the House of Deputies and the Senate are elected by proportional representation. The Senate does not employ the Canadian system of appointment to the senate. 'No one,' he stated, 'wanted a nominated Senate after the manner of the Canadian Senate, which is based on no conceivable political principle and fulfils no conceivable political function ... They aimed only to include in the Senate "citizens who have done honour to the nation."'

36 Ibid. at 323–4.

37 Ibid.

38 'Canadian Development Colors Constitution of Irish State' *Toronto Daily Star*, 5 March 1924.

39 W.P.M. Kennedy, 'The Irish Free State: A Lecture Delivered in the Convocation Hall of the University of Toronto,' 4 March 1924. University of Toronto Fisher Library: Kennedy manuscripts.

40 'The Spotlight: Professor W.P.M. Kennedy' *Toronto Daily Star*, 7 March 1924.

41 Kennedy, 'The Irish Free State.'

42 Ibid.

43 Letter from Desmond Fitzgerald to W.P.M. Kennedy, 9 April 1925. University College Dublin Archives: P80/537(1).

44 Ibid.

45 Letter from W.P.M. Kennedy to W.L. Mackenzie King, 21 February 1924. Library and Archives Canada: W.L. Mackenzie King papers, vol. 113.

46 The *Varsity* of 28 September 1933 refers to a debate between McGill and Toronto on Irish politics and states: 'When questioned concerning the political situation in Ireland, Prof W.P.M. Kennedy of the Department of Law, legal advisor of the Cosgrave Government, declined to make any statement for the Press on account of his professional connection with the government.' Whether Kennedy was involved as an advisor in this later stage in Irish politics, I will leave to others to investigate. His claim was in connection with the 1922 Constitution.

10 Productive Years

1 Martin Friedland, *The University of Toronto: A History* (Toronto: University of Toronto, 2002) at 295–7.

2 Letter from Robert Falconer to W.P.M. Kennedy, 1 May 1926. University of Toronto Archives: Falconer papers.

3 Gilbert Kennedy oral interview (interviewed by Maryla Waters 1983, Victoria University) at 32.

4 W.P.M. Kennedy, ed., 'Social and Economic Conditions in the Dominion of Canada' (1923) 107 Special issue, *The Annals of the American Academy of Political and Social Science*.

5 W.P.M. Kennedy, 'Preface to "Social and Economic Conditions in the Dominion of Canada"' (1923) 107 *Annals* at i.

6 Letter from W.P.M. Kennedy to Sir Edmund Walker, 27 October 1923. University of Toronto Fisher Library: Walker papers.

7 W.P.M. Kennedy (rev. Elizabeth Baigent), 'Walker, Sir Byron Edmund,' *Oxford Dictionary of National Biography*, http://www.oxforddnb.com.

8 R.H. Coats, 'The Growth of Population in Canada' (1923) 107 *Annals* 1–6.

9 Duncan Campbell Scott, 'The Aboriginal Races' (1923) 107 *Annals* 63–6 at 65.

10 Kennedy, 'Preface' (1923) 107 *Annals* at i.

11 Marion Findlay, 'Protection of Workers in Industry' (1923) 107 *Annals* 254–66 at 258.

12 H. Rives Hall, 'Divorce in Canada' (1923) 107 *Annals* at 275–81.

13 'Toronto Professor Given Heavy Task' *Globe*, 25 September 1925.

14 Ibid.

15 W.P.M. Kennedy, ed., *The Cambridge History of the British Empire*, vol. 6, *Canada and Newfoundland* (Cambridge: Cambridge University Press, 1930).

16 John Holland Rose, A.P. Newton, and Ernest Alfred Benians, 'Preface' in *The Cambridge History of the British Empire*, vol. 6 at vii.

17 Falconer had originally promised only one and completed a draft in September 1926. (Letter from Robert Falconer to W.P.M. Kennedy, 14 September 1926. University of Toronto Archives: Falconer papers.) A year later, Kennedy suggested another article, but Falconer declined the invitation in June 1927, stating that he was unable to do it because he was getting ready for the centenary celebration at the University of Toronto, which was taking place in the fall of 1927. (Letter from Robert Falconer to W.P.M. Kennedy, 14 June 1927. University of Toronto Archives: Falconer papers.) Falconer suggested that Kennedy ask Frank Underhill. In the end, because of serious delays in publication, Falconer was able to write the second article.

18 Letter from W.P.M. Kennedy to Robert Falconer, 20 April 1927. University of Toronto Archives: Falconer papers.

19 A.P. Coleman, 'The Geographical and Ethnical Background' in *The Cambridge History of the British Empire* at 1–16.

20 Sir Robert Falconer, 'Cultural Development – English' in *The Cambridge History of the British Empire* at 811.

21 Rose, Newton, and Benians, 'Preface' in *The Cambridge History of the British Empire* at vi.

22 W.P.M. Kennedy, 'The Constitution and Its Working, 1867–1921' in *The Cambridge History of the British Empire* at 686.

23 Ibid. at 703.

24 Ibid. at 688.

25 John Herd Thompson and Allen Seager, *Canada 1922–1939: Decades of Discord* (Toronto: McClelland & Stewart, 2016) at 134.

26 Material drawn from Carl Berger, *The Writing of Canadian History* (Toronto: University of Toronto Press, 1986) at 11; papers of the Historical Club of the University of Toronto 1925–1926, University of Toronto Archives.

27 'Kennedy Goes to England' *Toronto Daily Star*, 19 May 1926.

28 Material drawn from W.G. Leland, 'The Anglo-American Conference of Historians, London, July 12–16, 1926' (1926) 32 *American Historical Review* 56–61.

29 'Prof. Kennedy Ill' *Toronto Daily Star*, 15 July 1926.

30 Letter from W.P.M. Kennedy to Robert Falconer, 2 August 1926. University of Toronto Archives: Falconer papers.

31 Letter from Robert Falconer to W.P.M. Kennedy, 16 June 1916. Falconer papers.
32 Letter from W.P.M. Kennedy to Robert Falconer, 24 August 1923. Falconer papers.
33 Letter from Robert Falconer to W.P.M. Kennedy, 29 April 1924. Falconer papers.
34 Letter from Robert Falconer to W.P.M. Kennedy, 24 October 1927. Falconer papers.
35 Letter from Robert Falconer to W.P.M. Kennedy, 4 February 1930. Falconer papers.
36 Letter from W.P.M. Kennedy to Robert Falconer, 11 February 1930. Falconer papers.
37 Letter from Robert Falconer to W.P.M. Kennedy, n.d. Falconer papers.
38 Email from Betty Kennedy to Martin Friedland, 29 October 2015.
39 'Canadian Professor to Lecture at Cornell,' *The Mail and Empire*, 3 November 1926.
40 Friedland, *The University of Toronto* at 202–9.
41 Report of the University of Toronto Board of Governors for the Year Ending June 30th, 1910. University of Toronto Archives: Board of Governors Collection.
42 Friedland, *The University of Toronto* at 208–9. If invested at 3 per cent interest, that sum in today's value would be worth about a quarter of a billion dollars.
43 'W.P. Kennedy Invited to Bratislava University' newspaper unknown, 1928.
44 'Offer from India Declined by Toronto Professor' *The Canadian Press*, n.d.
45 Material drawn from M.G. Agrawal, *Freedom Fighters of India* (New Delhi: Gyan Publishing House, 2008); Showick Thorpe, ed., *The Pearson General Studies Manual for the UPSC Civil Services Preliminary Examination* (Delhi: Pearson Education India, 2009).
46 Material on Reddy drawn from 'Cattamanchi Ramalinga Reddy' *Wikipedia*, https://en.wikipedia.org/wiki/Cattamanchi_Ramalinga_Reddy.
47 Email from John O'Brien, curator of Post-1858 India Office Records at The British Library, 31 January 2017.
48 Gilbert Kennedy oral interview at 35.
49 Material on Ramaswami drawn from 'C.P. Ramaswami Iyer,' *Wikipedia*. https://en.wikipedia.org/wiki/C._P._Ramaswami_Iyer.
50 Material drawn mainly from James Greenlee, *Sir Robert Falconer: A Biography* (Toronto: University of Toronto Press, 1988) at 252–5.
51 Letter from Robert Falconer to W.P.M. Kennedy, 28 June 1918. University of Toronto Archives: Falconer papers.
52 Vincent Bladen, *Bladen on Bladen: Memoirs of a Political Economist* (Toronto: privately published, 1978) at 32–3.
53 Kennedy lectures, transcribed by H.H. Loosemore, 'Modern Governments and Public Finance,' *Toronto Bankers' Educational Association*, 1926–27 and 1927–28. University of Toronto Archives: Friedland papers.
54 His grandson, John Loosemore, a graduate of the University of Toronto School of Law, provided helpful information: emails from John Loosemore to the author July 2016. See the biographical sketch in (1933) 8 *The Caduceus* (staff magazine of the Canadian Bank of Commerce). H.H. Loosemore was a Boer War veteran, who later served in the 1940s as the treasurer of the Toronto branch of the Occupational Therapists of Ontario.

55 Letter from W.P.M. Kennedy to artist C.W. Jefferys, 27 April 1927. Art Gallery of Ontario Archives. The letter states: 'Irwin and Gordon are publishing, under my editorship, a new National History of Canada in several volumes and we would deem it a great honour if you could arrange to have your portfolio published in the History.' The series was never published. Jefferys published his pictures with Ryerson Press in 1932: *Canada's Past in Pictures*.

56 Appeals to the Privy Council from the High Court of Australia were abolished in constitutional cases in 1903, but could be granted with leave of the High Court. Only one appeal was permitted between then and when the High Court declared such appeals obsolete. Appeals from state courts continued, however.

11 *Lord Elgin* and More

1 See Brian Busby, 'Canada's 100 Best Books? 102? 111?' *The Dusty Bookcase* (blog), 20 August 2012, http://brianbusby.blogspot.com/2012/08/canadas-100-best-books-101-111.html.

2 Letter from Robert Falconer to W.P.M. Kennedy, 27 August 1926. University of Toronto Archives: Falconer papers.

3 W.P.M. Kennedy, 'Lord Haldane – A Personal Note' (1928) 6 *Canadian Bar Review* 567–8.

4 Letter from Viscount Richard Haldane to W.P.M. Kennedy, 24 July 1923. National Library of Scotland: Haldane papers.

5 Kennedy, 'Lord Haldane – A Personal Note' at 568.

6 W.P.M. Kennedy, 'Law as a Social Science' (1934) 3 *South African Law Times* 100.

7 W.P.M. Kennedy, 'Legal Subjects in the Universities of Canada' (1933) 10 *Journal of the Society of Public Teachers of Law* 23 at 26.

8 Memo from W.P.M. Kennedy to Sidney Smith, n.d. University of Toronto Archives: Smith papers.

9 Atkin and Haldane do not appear to have been in Canada in 1925.

10 Letter from W.P.M. Kennedy to Larry MacKenzie, 29 August 1928. University of Toronto Archives: MacKenzie papers.

11 W.P.M. Kennedy, preface to *Lord Elgin*, The Makers of Canada series (Toronto: Oxford University Press, 1926).

12 W.L. Grant, general introduction to *Samuel de Champlain*, The Makers of Canada series (Toronto: Oxford University Press, 1926).

13 Kennedy, preface to *Lord Elgin*.

14 See the favourable review of *Lord Elgin* in the *Globe*: 'How Elgin Helped Canada: Responsible Government a Necessary Prelude to Confederation – Prof. Kennedy's Informing Book' *Globe*, 18 June 1927, which refers to 'the fine Biblical analogy in which he delights.'

15 Kennedy, *Lord Elgin* at 66.

16 'How Elgin Helped Canada,' *Globe*, 18 June 1927.

17 Material in this section drawn mainly from A.B. McKillop's introduction to *William Lyon Mackenzie: A Reinterpretation* by William LeSueur (Kingston: McGill-Queen's University Press, 1979).

18 For an overview of Leacock's works, see Carl Spadoni, *A Bibliography of Stephen Leacock* (Toronto: ECW Press, 1998).

19 W.P.M. Kennedy, preface to *Mackenzie, Baldwin, LaFontaine, and Hincks* by Stephen Leacock, The Makers of Canada series (Toronto: Oxford University Press, 1926).

20 Grant, general introduction to *Samuel de Champlain* (1926).

21 McKillop, introduction to *William Lyon Mackenzie: A Reinterpretation*.

22 Ibid. at vii.

23 Ibid. at ix.

24 William Lyon Mackenzie King Diary, 28 April 1908. Library and Archives Canada: Diaries of William Lyon Mackenzie King, http://www.bac-lac.gc.ca/eng/discover/politics-government/prime-ministers/william-lyon-mackenzie-king/Pages/diaries-william-lyon-mackenzie-king.aspx. King is adopting the words of George Lindsey, with whom he had lunch.

25 LeSueur, *William Lyon Mackenzie: A Reinterpretation* at 389.

26 Clifford Holland, 'William Dawson LeSueur' (1998) *Dictionary of Canadian Biography*, http://www.biographi.ca/en/bio/lesueur_william_dawson_14E.html.

27 'I have no manner of doubt that the publishers are altogether in the wrong, in this case; and more than that, that they are themselves quite well aware of the fact, and are defending this action, if they are really, and not merely in form, defending it at all, at the instance of interested third persons.' *LeSueur v. Morang & Co.* [1910] 20 Ont. L.R. 594.

28 William Lyon Mackenzie King Diary, 27 December 1911. Library and Archives Canada: Diaries of William Lyon Mackenzie King.

29 Kennedy, preface to *Mackenzie, Baldwin, LaFontaine, and Hincks* at 14–15 and 19. Later biographies of Mackenzie have stressed the importance of Mackenzie's contribution to self-government. See William Kilbourn, *The Firebrand William Lyon Mackenzie and the Rebellion in Upper Canada* (Toronto: Clarke, Irwin, 1956); John Sewell, *Mackenzie* (Toronto: Lorimer, 2002); see also Peter Russell, *Canada's Odyssey: A Country Based on Incomplete Conquests* (Toronto: University of Toronto Press, 2017); and F.H. Armstrong and R.J. Stagg, *Dictionary of Canadian Biography*.

30 Leacock, *Mackenzie, Baldwin, LaFontaine, and Hincks* at 62.

31 Bickersteth and King were sufficiently close that King wanted Bickersteth to be the first holder of a new post of executive assistant to the Canadian prime minister. Bickersteth, however, decided to remain at Hart House.

32 Martin Friedland, *The University of Toronto: A History* (Toronto: University of Toronto Press, 2002) at 276.

33 George Wrong had agreed to write the biography of Mackenzie for the earlier series, but withdrew. LeSueur was then asked to undertake the task. One wonders

. whether Wrong withdrew because King forcefully and rightly argued that Wrong had an obvious conflict of interest.

34 Letter from W.P.M. Kennedy to W.L. Mackenzie King, 20 May 1926. Library and Archives Canada: W.L. Mackenzie King papers, vol. 155.

35 Letter from W.L. Mackenzie King to W.P.M. Kennedy, 22 May 1926. Mackenzie King papers, vol. 155.

36 Letter from W.L. Mackenzie King to William B. Munro, 22 May 1926. Mackenzie King papers, vol. 159.

37 Letter from William B. Munro to W.L. Mackenzie King, 28 May 1926. Mackenzie King papers, vol. 159.

38 Letter from Robin Carlaw to Martin Friedland, 18 April 2017.

39 The only other sources I have found that exceed in quantity the Kennedy/King correspondence are the exchanges between Kennedy and President Falconer in the Falconer papers and in the University of Toronto School of Law departmental files, and the letters left in the trunks at the cottage.

40 Letter from W.P.M. Kennedy to W.L. Mackenzie King, 21 February 1924. Library and Archives Canada: Mackenzie King papers, vol. 113.

41 Letter from W.P.M. Kennedy to W.L. Mackenzie King, 13 January 1925. Mackenzie King papers, vol. 132.

42 Letter from W.P.M. Kennedy to W.L. Mackenzie King, 30 January 1925. Mackenzie King papers, vol. 132.

43 Letter from W.L. Mackenzie King to W.P.M. Kennedy, 22 January 1925. Mackenzie King papers, vol. 132.

44 Letter from W.P.M. Kennedy to W.L. Mackenzie King, 14 September 1926. Mackenzie King papers, vol. 155.

45 Letter from W.P.M. Kennedy to Mackenzie King, 15 October 1935. Mackenzie King papers, vol. 207.

46 Gilbert Kennedy oral interview (interviewed by Maryla Waters 1983, Victoria University) at 63.

47 Dedication in *Essays in Constitutional Law* (London: Oxford University Press, 1934).

48 Letter from W.P.M. Kennedy to Robert Falconer, 2 August 1926. University of Toronto Archives: Falconer papers.

49 W.P.M. Kennedy, 'Nationhood in the British Commonwealth' (1926) 130 *Contemporary Review* 555 at 560.

50 Letter from W.P.M. Kennedy to W.L. Mackenzie King, 21 September 1926. Library and Archives Canada: Mackenzie King papers, vol. 155.

51 Letter from W.L. Mackenzie King to W.P.M. Kennedy, 9 October 1926. Mackenzie King papers, vol. 155.

52 Report of the 1926 Imperial Conference at 3. https://www.foundingdocs.gov.au/resources/transcripts/cth11_doc_1926.pdf.

53 Quoted in Norman Hillmer, *O.D. Skelton: The Work of the World, 1923–1941* (Kingston: McGill-Queen's University Press, 2013) at 21.

54 Letter from W.L. Mackenzie King to W.P.M. Kennedy, 17 April 1924. Library and Archives Canada: Mackenzie King papers, vol. 133.

55 RSC 1906, c. 146, s. 207.

56 Letter from W.L. Mackenzie King to W.P.M. Kennedy, 17 April 1924. Mackenzie King papers, vol. 133.

57 See Marianne Valverde, *The Age of Light, Soap and Water: Moral Reform in English Canada, 1885–1925* (Toronto: University of Toronto Press, 2008) at 18 and 56.

58 Letter from W.P.M. Kennedy to W.L. Mackenzie King, 7 May 1924. Mackenzie King papers, vol. 133.

59 *R. v. Palmer* [1937] O.J. No. 82. The words 'public good' had been included in the Criminal Code at s. 207(2) since 1900 (see RSC 1906, c. 146, s. 207).

60 Letter from W.P.M. Kennedy to W.L. Mackenzie King, 7 May 1924. Mackenzie King papers, vol. 133.

61 Quoted in Donald Wright, *The Professionalization of History in English Canada* (Toronto: University of Toronto Press, 2005) at 116.

62 Letter from W.P.M. Kennedy to Professor Mack Eastman, UBC, 9 May 1925. University of Toronto Archives: Law School papers.

12 Starting a Law Program

1 Ian Drummond, *Political Economy at the University of Toronto: A History of the Department, 1888–1982* (Toronto: University of Toronto Press, 1983) at 36–7.

2 Letter from George Wrong to Robert Falconer, 7 January 1926. University of Toronto Archives: Falconer papers.

3 Drummond, *Political Economy at the University of Toronto* at 33, 56.

4 Robert Falconer, 'Banquet of the Ontario Bar Association' (1914) 34 *Canadian Law Times* 149 at 151–2.

5 Letter from Hume Wrong to George Wrong, 8 February 1926. University of Toronto Archives: Wrong papers.

6 William Lyon Mackenzie King Diary, 26 April 1926. Library and Archives Canada: Diaries of William Lyon Mackenzie King.

7 Material on Arthur Doughty is drawn mainly from Ian Wilson, '"A Noble Dream": The Origins of the Public Archives of Canada' (1983) 15 *Archivaria* 16 at 33.

8 Material on J.F. Davison drawn mainly from P.B. Waite, *Lord of Point Grey: Larry MacKenzie of UBC* (Vancouver: UBC Press, 1987); Philip Girard, *Bora Laskin: Bringing Law to Life* (Toronto: University of Toronto Press, 2005); and Ian Kyer and Jerome Bickenbach, *The Fiercest Debate: Cecil A. Wright, the Benchers, and Legal Education in Ontario 1923–1947* (Toronto: University of Toronto Press, 1987).

9 John Willis, *A History of Dalhousie Law School* (Toronto: University of Toronto Press, 1979) at 88–9.

10 Louis D. Brandeis, *Letters of Louis D. Brandeis*, vol. 5, *1921–1941: Elder Statesman*, ed. Melvin Urofsky (Albany, NY: State of New York Press) at 376.

11 Letter from J.F. Davison to Norman ('Larry') MacKenzie, 10 July 1926. University of British Columbia Archives: Norman A.M. MacKenzie papers.

12 Letter from J.F. Davison to Norman ('Larry') MacKenzie, 2 October 1925. Norman A.M. MacKenzie papers.

13 Letter from J.F. Davison to Norman ('Larry') MacKenzie, 10 July 1926. Norman A.M. MacKenzie papers.

14 Letter from J.F. Davison to Norman ('Larry') MacKenzie, 2 October 1925. Norman A.M. MacKenzie papers.

15 Waite, *Lord of Point Grey* at 35.

16 Ibid. at 38.

17 Letter from Robert Falconer to Norman ('Larry') MacKenzie, 14 May 1926. Norman A.M. MacKenzie papers.

18 Ibid.

19 Waite, *Lord of Point Grey* at 58–9.

20 Ibid. at 29.

21 Letter from W.P.M. Kennedy to Norman ('Larry') MacKenzie, 17 August 1940. Norman A.M. MacKenzie papers.

22 Waite, *Lord of Point Grey*.

23 As evidently relayed to Waite by MacKenzie: Waite, *Lord of Point Grey* at 59. Curiously, MacKenzie had not expressed this view in his unpublished draft memoirs, written in 1975. University of British Columbia Archives: Norman A.M. MacKenzie papers.

24 Waite, *Lord of Point Grey* at 69; Letter from W.P.M. Kennedy to Norman ('Larry') MacKenzie, 30 June 1928. Norman A.M. MacKenzie papers.

25 Letter from Robert Falconer to W.P.M. Kennedy, 14 June 1926. University of Toronto Archives: Falconer papers.

26 Martin Friedland, *The University of Toronto: A History* (Toronto: University of Toronto Press, 2002) at 297.

27 Ibid. at 297.

28 Letter from E.J. Urwick to Robert Falconer, 26 October 1927. University of Toronto Archives: Falconer papers.

29 Letter from Harold Innis to Robert Falconer, n.d. Falconer papers.

30 See, for example, 'Kennedy, William Paul McClure,' *Who's Who in Canada, 1951–52* (Toronto: International Press Ltd.) at page 418.

31 In 1929, Kennedy was made a member of the Canadian Bar Association: letter from W.P.M. Kennedy to Robert Falconer, 8 October 1929. University of Toronto Archives: Falconer papers.

32 This section drawn mainly from Friedland, *The University of Toronto* 40–1 and 139–43.

33 Blake was succeeded by George Skeffington Connor, Blake's partner: see 'Connor, George Skeffington,' *Dictionary of Canadian Biography*, http://www.biographi.ca/en/bio/connor_george_skeffington_9E.html.

34 'The necessity for some organized system of legal education in this Province,' the *Varsity* stated in 1886, 'must be apparent to any person who takes the trouble to consider the matter.' 'The most feasible method of establishing an efficient system of legal education in this Province,' it went on to say, 'is to bring about a union of purpose and of forces between the University and the Law Society.' A.H. Marsh, 'The Department of Law' *Varsity*, 6 February 1886.

35 Law Society, *Minutes of Convocation*, vol. 1 at 213.

36 Letter from William Mulock to George Ross, 7 April 1888, Public Archives Ontario RG-2-29-I.

37 *Canada Law Journal*, 16 March 1888 at 132.

38 Law Society, *Minutes of Convocation* at 263; Kyer and Bickenbach, *The Fiercest Debate* at 30.

39 Law Society, *Minutes of Convocation* at 266.

40 'Sir Daniel Wilson's Journal,' University of Toronto Archives B65–0014/004 at 183. University president Daniel Wilson sat beside Proudfoot at a meeting two weeks before his retirement and noted in his diary: 'Justice Proudfoot, our new professor of law, sat next to me, just back from a winter in Italy; so deaf that he hears nothing except what is directly addressed to himself.' Proudfoot taught Roman law and English legal history, but, as the writer of his entry in the *Dictionary of Canadian Biography* states, his interest in Roman law was 'more the result of antiquarianism and pretensions to scholarly elegance' than a 'commitment to constructive cross-pollination between civil law and the common law.' G. Blaine Baker, 'William Proudfoot,' *Dictionary of Canadian Biography*, vol. 13 at 849.

41 Letter from W.P.M. Kennedy to Robert Falconer, 21 December 1928. University of Toronto Archives: Falconer papers.

42 Letter from Robert Falconer to W.P.M. Kennedy, 22 December 1928. Falconer papers.

43 Letter from W.P.M. Kennedy to Robert Falconer, 10 December 1927. Falconer papers. Davison was on leave working with Frankfurter during the 1928–29 academic year, which was the stated reason given that Kennedy could not take up the invitation to be a visiting professor at Bratislava University. See chapter 10: Productive Years.

44 Letter from W.P.M. Kennedy to Robert Falconer, 11 January 1929. Falconer papers.

45 Letter from W.P.M. Kennedy to Robert Falconer, 8 February 1929. Falconer papers.

46 Letter from J.F. Davison to W.P.M. Kennedy, 22 January 1929. University of Toronto Archives: Law School papers.

47 Letter from W.P.M. Kennedy to J.F. Davison, 25 January 1929. Law School papers.

48 Letter from W.P.M. Kennedy to Robert Falconer, 8 February 1929. Falconer papers.

49 Material on Auld drawn mainly from Girard, *Bora Laskin*; and Kyer and Bickenbach, *The Fiercest Debate*.

50 Sydney Hermant oral interview (interviewed by Robin Harris, 2 October 1978) at 4. University of Toronto Archives.

51 Perhaps I am biased by the fact that I took a rather boring and unimaginative course on commercial law from Professor Auld when I was a commerce and finance student in the early 1950s. See Martin Friedland, *My Life in Crime and Other Academic Adventures* (Toronto: University of Toronto Press, 2007) at 7.

52 MacKenzie's unpublished memoirs, 1975. University of British Columbia Archives: Norman A.M. MacKenzie papers, box 129.

53 Letter from W.P.M. Kennedy to Robert Falconer, 10 December 1927. University of Toronto Archives: Falconer papers.

54 Letter from Robert Falconer to W.P.M. Kennedy, 12 December 1927. Falconer papers.

55 'Law, 1929–1930,' *Course Offerings*, University of Toronto Archives 82–0041.

56 University of Toronto Alumni Records.

57 'Former University Student Gains National Prominence' *Varsity*, 5 October 1948.

58 'Adelaide Sinclair, 82, Former UNICEF Official' [obituary] *New York Times* 21 November 1982.

59 Material on Finkelman drawn mainly from Girard, *Bora Laskin*; and Kyer and Bickenbach, *The Fiercest Debate*.

60 Letter from W.P.M. Kennedy to Robert Falconer, 31 January 1930. University of Toronto Archives: Falconer papers.

61 James G. Greenlee, *Sir Robert Falconer: A Biography* (Toronto: University of Toronto Press, 1988).

62 Author's correspondence with Greenlee, August 1999. University of Toronto Archives: Martin Friedland papers: B2002-0022.

63 Finkelman oral interview (interviewed by Christine Kates, 1995, Osgoode Society) at 13–16.

64 Friedland, *The University of Toronto* at 307–8.

65 Letter from W.P.M. Kennedy to Robert Falconer, 31 January 1930. University of Toronto Archives: Falconer papers

66 Finkelman oral interview at 1–3 and 8.

67 Ibid. at 15.

68 Ibid. at 18–19.

13 Creating a Law School

1 The Law Building where Laskin was a student was torn down in the 1960s when the Forestry Building next door was physically moved north on rollers to make room for a new Engineering Building. Martin Friedland, *The University of Toronto: A History* (Toronto: University of Toronto Press, 2002) at 216.

2 Bora Laskin oral interview (interviewed by Robin Harris, 1976, University of Toronto Archives). Material on Laskin is mainly drawn from Philip Girard, *Bora Laskin: Bringing Law to Life* (Toronto: University of Toronto Press, 2005).

3 G. Arthur Martin oral interview (interviewed by Christine Kates, 1983, Osgoode Society).

4 William Howland oral interview (interviewer unknown, 1992, Osgoode Society).

5 Girard, *Bora Laskin* at 47.

6 Ibid.

7 Ibid. at 30.

8 Laskin oral interview (1976) at 2–3.

9 Girard, *Bora Laskin* at 39.

10 Ian Kyer and Jerome Bickenbach, *The Fiercest Debate: Cecil A Wright, the Benchers, and Legal Education in Ontario 1923–1947* (Toronto: University of Toronto Press, 1987) at 116–17.

11 Laskin oral interview (1976) at 16.

12 Ibid. at 7–8.

13 Material on G. Arthur Martin is mainly drawn from Kent Roach, 'G. Arthur Martin and the Rise of the Honourable and Respectable Defence Lawyer,' https://lawsocietyontario.azureedge.net/media/lso/media/legacy/pdf/t/thirteenth_colloquium_roach.pdf.

14 Martin oral interview at 18–19.

15 Ibid. at 19–20.

16 Ibid. at 21.

17 Material on William Howland is mainly drawn from Christopher Moore, *The Court of Appeal for Ontario: Defining the Right of Appeal, 1792–2013* (Toronto: University of Toronto Press, 2014).

18 Howland oral interview at 21.

19 Ibid. at 107.

20 For a comprehensive analysis of the approach to law in the 1930s, see R.C.B. Risk, 'Canadian Law Teachers in the 1930s: When the World Was Turned Upside Down' (2004) 27 *Dalhousie Law Journal* 1.

21 Martin Friedland, 'Harry Arthurs: The Law Student Years' in *The Daunting Enterprise of the Law: Essays in Honour of Harry W. Arthurs*, ed. Simon Archer et al. (Kingston: McGill-Queen's University Press, 2017) at 333.

22 Letter from J.F. Davison to Norman ('Larry') MacKenzie, 22 February 1930. University of British Columbia Archives: Norman A.M. MacKenzie papers.

23 W.P.M. Kennedy, 'Review: Frankfurter and Landis, Business of the Supreme Court' (1929) 44 *English Historical Review* 328.

24 W.P.M. Kennedy, *Some Aspects of the Theories and Workings of Constitutional Law: The Fred Morgan Kirby Lectures Delivered at Lafayette College, 1931* (New York: Macmillan Company, 1932) at 27–8.

25 W.P.M. Kennedy, *Elizabethan Episcopal Administration: An Essay in Sociology and Politics*, 3 vols. (London: A.R. Mowbray & Co., 1924), vol. 1 at vi.

26 W.P.M. Kennedy, 'Preface to "Social and Economic Conditions in the Dominion of Canada"' (1923) 107 Special Issue, *The Annals of the American Academy of Political and Social Science* at vii.

27 Harold Laski, 'Canada's Constitution' *The New Republic* (4 July 1923) at 159.

28 Letter from Harold Laski to Oliver Wendell Holmes, 21 January 1923 in *Holmes-Laski Letters: The Correspondence of Mr. Justice Holmes and Harold J. Laski*, by Oliver Wendell Holmes, Jr. and Harold J. Laski, ed. Mark DeWolfe Howe (Cambridge, MA: Harvard University Press, 1953) at 476. Holmes tried, but could not get Kennedy's book from the Library of Congress: see David Schneiderman, 'Harold Laski, Viscount Haldane, and the Law of the Canadian Constitution in the Early Twentieth Century' (1998) 48 *University of Toronto Law Journal* 521n184.

29 Letter from W.P.M. Kennedy to Norman ('Larry') MacKenzie, 28 May 1928. University of British Columbia Archives: Norman A.M. MacKenzie papers.

30 Letter from W.P.M. Kennedy to Norman ('Larry') MacKenzie, 31 May 1928. MacKenzie papers.

31 W.P.M. Kennedy, 'Legal Subjects in the Universities of Canada' (1933) 23 *Journal of the Society of Public Teachers of Law* 23 at 26.

32 W.P.M. Kennedy, 'Law as a Social Science' (1934) 3 *South African Law Times* 100–1.

33 Kennedy, *Some Aspects of the Theories and Workings of Constitutional Law* at 22–5.

34 W.P.M. Kennedy, 'A Project of Legal Education' (1937) *Scots Law Times* at 1.

35 Cheryl Misak, *The American Pragmatists* (Oxford: Oxford University Press, 2013) at 77–81.

36 Ibid. at 78.

37 Roscoe Pound, 'Mechanical Jurisprudence' (1908) 8 *Columbia Law Review* 605 at 609–10; Girard, *Bora Laskin* at 84.

38 Letter from W.P.M. Kennedy to Norman ('Larry') MacKenzie, 31 May 1928. University of British Columbia Archives: Norman A.M. MacKenzie papers.

39 Material on Caesar Wright is mainly drawn from Kyer and Bickenbach, *The Fiercest Debate*.

40 Girard, *Bora Laskin* at 49.

41 Caesar Wright, 'An Extra-Legal Approach to the Law' (1932) 10 *Canadian Bar Review* 1.

42 Kyer and Bickenbach, *The Fiercest Debate* at 117–18.

43 Ibid. at 116–20. All quotations drawn from Kyer and Bickenbach, *The Fiercest Debate* at 116–20.

44 Girard, *Bora Laskin* at 52.

45 Kyer and Bickenbach, *The Fiercest Debate* at 57.

46 'University of Toronto Board of Governors, Senate, Standing Committees,' 1926–1927. University of Toronto Archives: Board of Governors Collection.

47 John Falconbridge, 'Memorandum of the Chairman of the Board of Legal Studies of the Senate of the University of Toronto,' 28 March 1930. University of Toronto Archives: Law School papers; Letter from John Falconbridge to Robert Falconer, 10 April 1930. University of Toronto Archives: Falconer papers.

48 'Report on the Possible Teaching and Supervision of the Degree of Master of Laws in the School of Graduate Studies' 1930. University of Toronto Archives: Law School papers.

49 W.P.M. Kennedy, 'Legal Subjects in the Universities of Canada' (1933) 23 *Journal of the Society of Public Teachers of Law* 23 at 27.

50 'University of Toronto President's Report for the year ended June 1939.' University of Toronto Archives: Presidents reports.

51 'University of Toronto President's Report for the year ended June 1942.' University of Toronto Archives: Presidents' reports.

52 Kyer and Bickenbach, *The Fiercest Debate* at 113.

53 Ibid. at 121–2.

54 Ibid. at 122.

55 Kyer and Bickenbach, *The Fiercest Debate* at 125.

56 Special Committee on Legal Education, 'Legal Education: Report of the Benchers of the Law Society of Upper Canada' (1935) 13 *Canadian Bar Review* 347 at 351.

57 Ibid.

58 Donald Carrick, 'Education for the Bar: Report of the Special Committee of Students of Osgoode Hall' (1934) 12 *Canadian Bar Review* 144.

59 F.A. Brewin, 'Legal Education in Ontario, 1935'; R.F. Wilson, 'Legal Education in Ontario'; Alfred Z. Reed, 'The Organization of Legal Education in Ontario'; F.C. Cronkite, 'Legal Education – Which Trend?'; Walter S. Johnson, 'The Education of the Lawyer'; R.A. Ritchie, 'Pre-Legal Education – A Nova Scotian View'; Lindley Crease, 'Legal Education'; C.R. Smith, 'Legal Education A Manitoba View' (1935) 13 *Canadian Bar Review* 400.

60 Cecil A. Wright, 'Legal Reform and the Profession' (1937) 15 *Canadian Bar Review* 633.

61 Kyer and Bickenbach, *The Fiercest Debate* at 142.

62 W.P.M. Kennedy, 'A Project of Legal Education' (1937) *Scots Law Times*.

63 Wright quotes Sinclair Shaw, 'Legal Education and Legal Clinics' (1937) 15 *Canadian Bar Review* 361–8.

64 Letter from President Cody to W.P.M. Kennedy, 1 June 1936. University of Toronto Archives: Law School papers.

65 Hilaire Barnett, 'The Province of Jurisprudence Determined – Again' (1995) 15 *Legal Studies* 88 at 110–14.

66 Another reason is the academic and judicial reaction to the much-criticized 1960 decision of the House of Lords in *D.P.P. v. Smith* ([1961] A.C. 290), in which the Lords adopted Holmes's view expressed in his book *The Common Law* that there should be an objective test for the mental element for crime, even in the case of murder. See P.S. Atiyah, 'The Legacy of Holmes through English Eyes' (1983) 63 *Boston University Law Review* at 341 and 343–9.

67 Lon Fuller, 'Positivism and Fidelity to Law – A Reply to Professor Hart' (1958) 71 *Harvard Law Review* 630 at 657.

68 The attack on Holmes has continued in more recent scholarship, such as by my colleague David Dyzenhaus, who compares Holmes with the Nazi sympathizer Carl Schmitt in his essay 'Holmes and Carl Schmitt: An Unlikely Pair' (1997) 63

Brooklyn Law Review 165. See also Albert Alschuler, *Law without Values: The Life, Work, and Legacy of Justice Holmes* (Chicago: University of Chicago Press, 2000).

69 Frederic Kellogg, *Oliver Wendell Holmes, Jr., Legal Theory, and Judicial Restraint* (Cambridge: Cambridge University Press, 2007) at 172.

70 Oliver Wendell Holmes, 'The Path of the Law' (1897) 10 *Harvard Law Review* at 459.

71 Richard Posner, 'Foreword: Holmes' (1997) 63 *Brooklyn Law Review* 7 at 17.

72 Mark DeWolfe Howe, ed., *Holmes-Pollock Letters* (Cambridge, MA: Harvard University Press, 1941).

73 Kennedy, 'Review' (1942) 4 *University of Toronto Law Journal* at 431.

14 More Projects

1 W.P.M. Kennedy and Gustave Lanctôt, eds., *Reports on the Laws of Quebec, 1767–1770* (Ottawa: Printer to the King, 1931).

2 Material on Gustave Lanctôt drawn mainly from Library and Archives Canada, http://www.bac-lac.gc.ca/eng/discover/military-heritage/first-world-war/100-stories/Pages/lanctot.aspx.

3 Lauren La Rose, 'No Order of Canada Medal Sale, eBay Says' *Globe and Mail*, 4 January 2007, https://www.theglobeandmail.com/news/national/no-order-of-canada-medal-sale-ebay-says/article1077550/.

4 Letter from Gustave Lanctôt to W.P.M. Kennedy, 17 March 1930. Library and Archives Canada: Gustave Lanctôt papers, MG30-D95, vol. 6.

5 S. Morley Scott, 'Review of *Reports on the Laws of Quebec*' (1932) 13 *Canadian Historical Review* at 60–2.

6 John Perry Pritchett, 'Review of *Reports on the Laws of Quebec*' (1931) 18 *Mississippi Valley Historical Review* 440.

7 A. Berriedale Keith, 'Review of *Reports on the Laws of Quebec*' (1931) 13 *Journal of Comparative Legislation and International Law* at 278–82.

8 Pritchett, 'Review' (1931) 18 *Mississippi Valley Historical Review* at 440.

9 Kennedy, Preface to *Reports on the Laws of Quebec* at 7.

10 Another report on the topic by the attorney general of Quebec, Francis Maseres, was also printed in the volume, although this report was already known, having been privately printed by Maseres in 1772.

11 Letter from H.P. Biggar to Gustave Lanctôt, 26 October 1932. Library and Archives Canada, Gustave Lanctôt papers, MG30-D95, vol. 6.

12 The Royal Proclamation, 7 October 1763 at 3. https://exhibits.library.utoronto.ca/items/show/2470.

13 Chief Justice William Hey, 'Appendix to the Report upon the Laws and Courts of Judicature in the Province of Quebec by Chief Justice Hey, September 15th, 1769,' in Kennedy and Lanctôt, *Reports on the Laws of Quebec* at 74.

14 Governor Carleton, 'Report upon the Laws and Courts of Judicature in the Province of Quebec by Governor Carleton and Chief Justice Hey, September 15th,

1769' in Kennedy and Lanctôt, *Reports on the Laws of Quebec* at 64–7. See also Philip Girard, Jim Phillips, and R. Blake Brown, *A History of Law in Canada*, vol. 1 (Toronto: University of Toronto Press, 2018) at 332–3, showing that the French Canadian population continued to use French law between 1864 and 1874.

15 Kennedy and Lanctôt, *Reports on the Laws of Quebec* at 67–8.

16 The Quebec Act, 1774 14 George III, c. 83 (U.K.). https://www.solon.org/Constitutions/Canada/English/PreConfederation/qa_1774.html.

17 Quoted in Martin Friedland, *A Century of Criminal Justice* (Toronto: Carswell Legal Publications, 1984) at 48.

18 A.G. Bradley, *Sir Guy Carleton (Lord Dorchester)* (Toronto: Morang, 1909).

19 A.G. Bradley and A.L. Burt, *Lord Dorchester* (Toronto: Oxford University Press, 1926).

20 A.L. Burt, *The Old Province of Quebec* (Minneapolis: University of Minnesota Press, 1933).

21 W.P.M. Kennedy, *Report Submitted to the Honourable the Secretary of State for Canada on Some Problems in the Law of Nationality* (Ottawa: King's Printer, 1930).

22 'Kennedy, William Paul McClure,' *British Who's Who: An Annual Biographical Dictionary* (London: A & C Black Ltd., 1935) at page 1828.

23 R.B. Bennett, *House of Commons Debates*, 15 February 1929, vol. 1 at 184.

24 O.D. Skelton, *Notes on Conference on Operation of Dominion Legislation and Merchant Shipping*, 1929. Library and Archives Canada: O.D. Skelton papers, MG30 D33, vol. 4.

25 I recall struggling with the highly political issue of nationality in the mid-war period – because of the rise of fascism – when I was writing my doctoral dissertation on double jeopardy (Martin Friedland, *Double Jeopardy* [Oxford: Clarendon Press, 1969]) and dealing with the question of whether common law courts should recognize for purposes of double jeopardy convictions and acquittals by foreign courts that take jurisdiction over their 'nationals,' even though the crime had been committed outside the territory of that state.

26 Agnes Macphail, *House of Commons Debates*, 6 April 1927, vol. 2 at 1983.

27 Kennedy, *Report on Some Problems in the Law of Nationality* at 30.

28 Ibid. at 25.

29 Ibid. at 26.

30 Ibid.

31 Letter from W.P.M. Kennedy to W.L. Mackenzie King, 2 February 1930. Library and Archives Canada: W.L. Mackenzie King papers, vol. 213.

32 Draft Bill, *An Act to Define Canadian Nationals and to Provide for Loss or Renunciation of Canadian Nationality* (Ottawa: King's Printer, 1931).

33 Kennedy, *Report on Some Problems in the Law of Nationality* at 8–9.

34 C.H. Cahan, *House of Commons Debates*, 14 April 1931, vol. 1 at 575.

35 Fernand Rinfret, *House of Commons Debates*, 27 May 1931, vol. 2 at 2025.

36 The minister of immigration also privately raised with Prime Minister Bennett some concerns about the proposed legislation with respect to Asian immigration. Letter from the Office of the Minister of Immigration and Colonization to R.B. Bennett, 15 April 1931. Library and Archives Canada: Charles Hazlitt Cahan papers, MG27III B1, vols. 1–5.

37 C.H. Cahan, *House of Commons Debates*, 14 July 1931, vol. 4 at 1931.

38 Thomas Reid, *House of Commons Debates*, 27 May 1931, vol. 2 at 2026.

39 C.H. Cahan, *House of Commons Debates*, 27 May 1931, vol. 2 at 2023.

40 C.H. Cahan, *House of Commons Debates*, 14 July 1931, vol. 4 at 3723.

41 Letter from C.H. Cahan to R.B. Bennett, 11 June 1931. Library and Archives Canada: Charles Hazlitt Cahan papers.

42 Letter from W.P.M. Kennedy to C.H. Cahan, 30 November 1934. Charles Hazlitt Cahan papers.

43 Letter from C.H. Cahan to R.B. Bennett, 3 December 1934. Charles Hazlitt Cahan papers.

44 W.P.M. Kennedy, 'Notes and Documents' (1935–1936) 1 *University of Toronto Law Journal* 137 at 141.

45 Paul Martin, *House of Commons Debates*, 2 April 1946, vol. 1 at 503.

46 Paul Martin, *A Very Public Life* (Ottawa: Deneau, 1983) at 484.

47 Canadian National Committee of the International Congress of Comparative Law, 1931. McGill University Archives: C.S. LeMesurier papers.

48 Material on Lyman Duff drawn mainly from David R. Williams, *Duff: A Life in the Law* (Vancouver: UBC Press, 1984).

49 Ibid. at 156.

50 James G. Snell and Frederick Vaughan, *The Supreme Court of Canada: History of the Institution* (Toronto: University of Toronto Press, 1985) at 146.

51 Letter from W.P.M. Kennedy to Lyman Duff, 8 January 1944. Library and Archives Canada: Lyman Duff papers.

52 Letter from John Wigmore to Faculties of Law in the Association of American Law Schools, 2 January 1932. McGill University Archives: C.S. LeMesurier papers.

53 Letter from O.M. Biggar to C.S. LeMesurier, 17 December 1931. C.S. LeMesurier papers.

54 'International Congress of Comparative Law' (1931) 10 *Canadian Bar Review* 748–9.

55 Letter from John Falconbridge to W.P.M. Kennedy, 16 December 1931. McGill University Archives: C.S. LeMesurier papers.

56 Letter from John Falconbridge to W.P.M. Kennedy, 18 December 1931. C.S. LeMesurier papers. The letter from Falconbridge outlines the concern by Kennedy.

57 Letter from E. Fabre Surveyer to Elemer Balogh, 15 February 15 1932. C.S. LeMesurier papers.

58 Letter from W.P.M. Kennedy to C.S. LeMesurier, 23 January 1932. C.S. LeMesurier papers.

59 Letter from W.P.M. Kennedy to C.S. LeMesurier, 12 January 1932. C.S. LeMesurier papers.

60 Letter from E. Fabre Surveyer to C.S. LeMesurier, 21 January 1932. C.S. LeMesurier papers.
61 Letter from W.P.M. Kennedy to C.S. LeMesurier, 22 January 1932. C.S. LeMesurier papers.
62 Letter from Sidney Smith to C.S. LeMesurier, 26 January 1932. C.S. LeMesurier papers.
63 Letter from John Falconbridge to C.S. LeMesurier, 20 January 1932. C.S. LeMesurier papers.
64 Letter from John Falconbridge to Elemer Balogh, 12 February 1932. C.S. LeMesurier papers.
65 Letter from John Falconbridge to Sidney Smith, 20 January 1932. C.S. LeMesurier papers.
66 Letter from John Falconbridge to Elemer Balogh, 12 February 1932. C.S. LeMesurier papers.
67 H. Milton Colvin, 'Comparative Law: The International Congress of Comparative Law' (1933) 7 *Tulane Law Review* 53.
68 E. Fabre Surveyer, 'The First International Congress of Comparative Law' (15 November 1932) *The Fortnightly Law Journal* at 143.
69 Letter from Elemer Balogh, 16 January 1933. McGill University Archives: C.S. LeMesurier papers.
70 Martin Friedland, *The University of Toronto: A History* (Toronto: University of Toronto Press, 2002) at 343.
71 Letter from Percy Corbett to Arthur Currie, n.d. McGill University Archives: C.S. LeMesurier Papers.
72 Letter from Arthur Currie to Percy Corbett, n.d. C.S. LeMesurier Papers.
73 D.C. Masters, *Henry John Cody: An Outstanding Life* (Toronto: Dundurn Press, 1995) at 192. This professor was Franz Neumann: Letter from Henry Cody to Harold Laski, 11 March 1935. University of Toronto Archives: H.J. Cody papers.
74 Paul Stortz, '"Rescue Our Family from a Living Death:" Refugee Professors and the Canadian Society for the Protection of Science and Learning at the University of Toronto, 1935–1946' (2003) 14 *Journal of the Canadian Historical Association* 231 at 238.
75 Masters, *Henry John Cody* at 217.

15 Running a Law School

1 Material on Henry John Cody drawn mainly from Martin Friedland, *The University of Toronto: A History* (Toronto: University of Toronto Press, 2002); and D.C. Masters, *Henry John Cody: An Outstanding Life* (Toronto: Dundurn Press, 1995).
2 Letter from W.P.M. Kennedy to H.J. Cody, 13 April 1932. University of Toronto Archives: H.J. Cody papers.
3 Letter from W.P.M. Kennedy to H.J. Cody, 10 October 1931. Archives of Ontario: H.J. Cody papers.

4 Friedland, *The University of Toronto* at 321–2.
5 In the early 1980s, professor of higher education Robin Harris surveyed the university community about Cody's appointment, receiving more than a dozen replies. This material was collected for a book on the history of the University of Toronto, which was never completed. University of Toronto Archives A83–0036.
6 Letter from W.P.M. Kennedy to H.J. Cody, 13 January 1931. Archives of Ontario: H.J. Cody papers.
7 Quoted in R. Douglas Francis, *Frank H. Underhill: Intellectual Provocateur* (Toronto: University of Toronto Press, 1986) at 95.
8 Letter from Pauline Kennedy to H.J. Cody, 2 December 1932. Archives of Ontario: H.J. Cody Papers.
9 Letter from W.P.M. Kennedy to H.J. Cody, 17 March 1922. Archives of Ontario: H.J. Cody papers.
10 Letter from W.P.M. Kennedy to H.J. Cody, 2 April 1926. Archives of Ontario: H.J. Cody papers.
11 Material on Maurice Cody drawn from Masters, *Henry John Cody* at 156–8.
12 Material drawn from Friedland, *The University of Toronto*, chapter 26.
13 Letter from W.P.M. Kennedy to H.J. Cody, 9 September 1932. Archives of Ontario: H.J. Cody papers.
14 Ibid.
15 Letter from Pauline Kennedy to H.J. Cody, 2 December 1932. Archives of Ontario: H.J. Cody papers.
16 Letter from W.P.M. Kennedy to H.J. Cody, 19 December 1932. Archives of Ontario: H.J. Cody papers.
17 Letter from Pauline Kennedy to H.J. Cody, 5 March 1936. Archives of Ontario: H.J. Cody papers.
18 Letter from W.P.M. Kennedy to H.J. Cody, 12 January 1937. Archives of Ontario: H.J. Cody papers.
19 Letter from W.P.M. Kennedy to H.J. Cody, 12 March 1926. Archives of Ontario: H.J. Cody papers.
20 Letter from W.P.M. Kennedy to Robert Falconer, 11 February 1930. University of Toronto Archives: Falconer papers.
21 Letter from W.P.M. Kennedy to H.J. Cody, 27 August 1932. Archives of Ontario: H.J. Cody papers.
22 Letter from H.J. Cody to W.P.M. Kennedy, 29 August 1934. Archives of Ontario: H.J. Cody papers.
23 Letter from H.J. Cody to W.P.M. Kennedy, 2 June 1936. Archives of Ontario: H.J. Cody papers. This letter is almost identical to one sent by President Falconer in June 1916 – twenty years earlier: 'We should have been glad to have you take part in the work of the Summer Session, but I hope that though you have been prevented from this by ill-health the rest will soon restore your health.' Letter from Robert Falconer to W.P.M. Kennedy, 16 June 1916. University of Toronto Archives: Falconer papers.

24 Letter from W.P.M. Kennedy to H.J. Cody, 1 October 1929. Archives of Ontario: H.J. Cody papers.

25 Letter from W.P.M. Kennedy to H.J. Cody, 25 November 1936. Archives of Ontario: H.J. Cody papers.

26 The files contain a letter dated 6 March 1935 with a list of detailed instructions from Kennedy to the superintendent of buildings, such as 'place desk and chair and some shelving in each of rooms 202, and 204; but not in 201.' Letter from W.P.M. Kennedy to Colonel LePan, superintendent of buildings, 6 March 1935. University of Toronto Archives: Law School papers.

27 Letter to Robert Falconer (sender unknown), 8 April 1929. University of Toronto Archives: Falconer papers.

28 Letter from W.P.M. Kennedy to John Willison, 12 April 1926. Library and Archives Canada: John Willison papers.

29 Letter from Original Donors to W.P.M. Kennedy, December 1934; Letter from W.P.M. Kennedy to J.J. Gibson, 15 December 1934. University of Toronto Archives: Law School papers.

30 Letter from W.P.M. Kennedy to Robert Falconer, 13 June 1927; and reply to W.P.M. Kennedy 15 June 1927. University of Toronto Archives: Falconer papers.

31 Letter from E.J. Urwick to W.P.M. Kennedy, 13 December 1935. University of Toronto Archives: Law School papers.

32 Letter from W.P.M. Kennedy to E.J. Urwick, 14 December 1935. Law School papers.

33 Letter from C.B. Macpherson to W.P.M. Kennedy, 13 December 1937. Law School papers.

34 Letter from W.P.M. Kennedy to C.B. Macpherson, 16 December 1937. Law School papers.

35 Letter from Kenneth Gray to W.P.M. Kennedy, 28 June 1937. University of Toronto Archives: Law School papers; Letter from W.P.M. Kennedy to Professor C.S. LeMesurier, 3 February 1936. McGill University Archives: Law School papers.

36 Letter from W.P.M. Kennedy to H.J. Cody, 13 April 1932. University of Toronto Archives: H.J. Cody papers.

37 Letter from W.P.M. Kennedy to H.J. Cody, 13 April 1932. University of Toronto Archives: H.J. Cody papers.

38 Ibid.

39 Letter from R.J. Hamilton to W.P.M. Kennedy, 17 May 1932. University of Toronto Archives: Law School papers.

40 Letter from W.P.M. Kennedy to H.J. Cody, 13 April 1932. University of Toronto Archives: H.J. Cody papers.

41 Ibid.

42 Letter from W.P.M. Kennedy to Kenneth Morden, 11 June 1931. University of Toronto Archives: Law School papers.

43 Letter from W.P.M. Kennedy to H.A.L. Fisher, 8 June 1932. Law School papers.

44 Reference Letter for F.A. Vallat, written by W.P.M. Kennedy, 19 March 1932. Law School papers.

45 Letter from W.P.M. Kennedy to F.A. Vallat, 9 May 1934. Law School papers.
46 Letter from W.P.M. Kennedy to H.J. Cody, 16 March 1935. Archives of Ontario: H.J. Cody papers.
47 Letter from E.R. Wade to W.P.M. Kennedy, 7 June 1935. University of Toronto Archives: Law School papers.
48 Letter from W.P.M. Kennedy to E.R. Wade, 23 July 1935. Law School papers.
49 'F.H. Vallat' [obituary] *The Independent*, 26 May 2008.
50 Letter from Francis Vallat to R. St. J. Macdonald, 28 March 1974 in R. St. J. Macdonald, 'An Historical Introduction to the Teaching of International Law in Canada' (1974) 12 *Canadian Yearbook of International Law* 67 at 106.
51 Letter from F.C. Cronkite to W.P.M. Kennedy, 13 July 1936. Archives of Ontario: H.J. Cody papers.
52 Letter from W.P.M. Kennedy to H.J. Cody, 8 August 1936. Archives of Ontario: H.J. Cody papers.
53 Letter from H.J. Cody to W.P.M. Kennedy, 18 August 1936. Archives of Ontario: H.J. Cody papers.
54 Letter from W.P.M. Kennedy to F.C. Cronkite, 25 July 1936. University of Toronto Archives: Law School papers.
55 Letter from Norman ('Larry') MacKenzie to W.P.M. Kennedy, 29 August 1936. Law School papers.
56 Letter from W.P.M. Kennedy to Norman ('Larry') MacKenzie, 4 September 1936. Law School papers.
57 Letter from F.C. Auld to W.P.M. Kennedy, 29 July 1936. Law School papers.
58 Letter from W.P.M. Kennedy to Dean Roscoe Pound, 2 March 1936. Law School papers.
59 Letter from W.P.M. Kennedy to Felix Frankfurter, 27 November 1935. Law School papers.
60 Letter from W.P.M. Kennedy to Jacob Finkelman, 3 August 1936. Law school papers.
61 Letter from F.C. Auld to W.P.M. Kennedy, 29 July 1936. Law School papers. Auld had thought that Gage would not be available and had written to Kennedy: 'If he is, his outstanding academic work plus his practical experience recommend him greatly.'
62 Letter from H.J. Cody to W.P.M. Kennedy, 18 August 1936. Archives of Ontario: H.J. Cody papers.
63 Letter from W.P.M. Kennedy to H.J. Cody, 24 August 1936. University of Toronto Archives: Law School papers.
64 Letter from W.P.M. Kennedy to J.M. Gage, 3 August 1936. Law School papers.
65 Letter from J.M. Gage to W.P.M. Kennedy, 4 January 1937. Law School papers.
66 Letter from W.P.M. Kennedy to Moffat Hancock, 14 December 1936. Law School papers.
67 Letter from W.P.M. Kennedy to Robert Falconer, 14 November 1930. University of Toronto Archives: Falconer papers.

68 Letter from W.P.M. Kennedy to Newton Rowell, 5 January 1937. University of Toronto Archives: Law School papers.

69 Letter from W.P.M. Kennedy to Robert Falconer, 13 February 1929. University of Toronto Archives: Falconer Papers.

70 *Proceedings and Transactions of the Royal Society of Canada*, 3rd series, vol. 36, *Meeting of May 1942* (Ottawa: Royal Society of Canada, 1942) at 115–18. H.J. Cody was the co-author.

71 Letter from R.D. Hume to W.P.M. Kennedy, 9 June 1932. University of Toronto Archives: Law School papers.

72 Letter from W.P.M. Kennedy to Robert Falconer, 29 November 1926. Law School papers.

73 Letter from W.P.M. Kennedy to Arthur Goodhart, 4 January 1929. Law School papers.

74 Letter from W.L. Mackenzie King to W.P.M. Kennedy, 23 November 1937. Law School papers.

75 Letter from R.B. Bennett to W.P.M. Kennedy, 29 November 1937. Law School papers.

76 Letter from R.B. Bennett to W.P.M. Kennedy, 15 February 1934. Law School papers.

77 Letter from the Secretary to the Governor-General to W.P.M. Kennedy, 10 December 1937. Law School papers.

78 Letter from W.P.M. Kennedy to Secretary to the Governor-General, undated. Law School papers.

79 'Professor W.P.M. Kennedy's Speech at the Durham Memorial Banquet, 1838–1938' (March 1938) 38 *University of Toronto Monthly* at 162.

80 See Peter Russell, *Canada's Odyssey: A Country Based on Incomplete Conquests* (Toronto: University of Toronto Press, 2017) at 110–12.

81 'Governor-General Lord Tweedsmuir's Speech at the Durham Memorial Banquet, 1838–1938' (March 1938) 38 *University of Toronto Monthly* at 163.

82 Letter from Sydney Harris to Secretary of the School of Law, 29 October 1975. University of Toronto Archives: Law School papers.

83 Gilbert Kennedy oral interview (interviewed by Maryla Waters 1983, Victoria University) at 33.

16 Encouraging Scholarship

1 See chapter 15.

2 Letter from W.P.M. Kennedy to J.F. Davison, 18 March 1929. University of Toronto Archives: Law School papers.

3 Gilbert Kennedy oral interview (interviewed by Maryla Waters 1983, Victoria University) at 89.

4 See June Fullmer and Melvyn Usselman's discussion about Michael Faraday becoming a member of the Royal Society of London in 1824, even though one

black ball had been deposited by one of the members – the rest were white. June Fullmer and Melvyn Usselman, 'Faraday's Election to the Royal Society: A Reputation in Jeopardy' (1991) 11 *Bulletin for the History of Chemistry* 17. When the Royal Society of London was founded in 1660, a person could be elected with two-thirds of the votes. See Henry Lyons, *The Royal Society 1660–1940* (Cambridge: Cambridge University Press, 1944) at 25, citing the official rule: 'That if two thirds of the present number do consent … that election to be good, and not otherwise.'

5 Letter by Justice Philippe Demers, n.d. Université de Montréal Archives: Law School papers.

6 Letter from W.P.M. Kennedy to Dr. Victor Morin, 5 October 1939. Université de Montréal Archives: Law School papers.

7 Gilbert Kennedy oral interview at 89.

8 A. Berriedale Keith, 'Review of *The Law of the Taxing Power in Canada*' (1931) 13 *Journal of Comparative Legislation and International Law* at 278–82.

9 Charles Morse, 'Review of *The Law of the Taxing Power in Canada*' (1931) 12 *Canadian Historical Review* at 323–5.

10 W.P.M. Kennedy and D.C. Wells, preface to *The Law of the Taxing Power in Canada* (Toronto: University of Toronto Press, 1931) at vii.

11 F.A.V., 'Review of *The Right to Trade*' (1933) 5 *Cambridge Law Journal* at 291–2.

12 A. Berriedale Keith, 'Review of *The Right to Trade*' (1933) 15 *Journal of Comparative Legislation and International Law* at 278–9.

13 See chapter 12; and Jacob Finkelman oral interview (interviewed by Christine Kates, January 1995, Osgoode Society) at 14.

14 Letter from Bora Laskin to Jacob Finkelman, 24 February 1937. Library and Archives Canada: Jacob Finkelman papers, MG31-E27, vol. 10.

15 Letter from Jacob Finkelman to Bora Laskin, 19 March 1937. Library and Archives Canada: Jacob Finkelman papers, MG31-E27, vol. 10.

16 Minutes of the Studies Committee of the University of Toronto Press, 15 June 1938. University of Toronto Archives: University of Toronto Press papers.

17 Minutes of the Studies Committee, 16 March 1939. University of Toronto Press papers.

18 Minutes of the Studies Committee, 12 June 1939. University of Toronto Press papers.

19 Minutes of the Studies Committee, 11 March 1940. University of Toronto Press papers.

20 Minutes of the Studies Committee, 27 April 1942. University of Toronto Press papers.

21 Minutes of the Studies Committee, 11 March 1940. University of Toronto Press papers.

22 *The Lightning Fastener Company, Limited v. The Colonial Company, Limited and others*, [1934] U.K.P.C. 29.

23 Harold Fox, preface to *The Canadian Law of Trade Marks and Industrial Designs* (Toronto: University of Toronto Press, 1940).

24 In Alberta he was known as Robert Vaselanik. His father and his uncle were lawyers in Lethbridge. He became 'Westlake' in Anglo-Saxon Toronto, but then reverted back to Vaselanik when he returned to Alberta to join his father's law firm.

25 Author's telephone discussion with Eugene LaBrie, 11 August 2017.

26 Maxwell Cohen, 'Review of *Deductions under the Income Tax War Act: A Return to Business Principles*' (1949) 15 *Canadian Journal of Economics and Political Science* at 249–51.

27 Letter from Frank Scott to Burroughs, 2 April 1937. McGill University Archives: Law School papers.

28 The next volume did not appear until 1940, with the publication of a book by George Challies entitled *Unjustified Enrichment*. There were three further books in the series, including the final book: Edward Keyserlingk, *The Unborn Child's Right to Prenatal Care*, Quebec Research Centre of Private and Comparative Law, McGill University (Montreal: McGill University Press, 1984).

29 Letter from W.P.M. Kennedy to Dr. James Brebner, university registrar, 21 March 1929. University of Toronto Archives: Law School papers.

30 Letter from Dr. James Brebner to W.P.M. Kennedy, 20 March 1929. Law School papers.

31 'The University of Toronto and Its Colleges, 1827–1906' (Toronto: The University Library, 1906) at 166.

32 Letter from W.P.M. Kennedy to Dr. James Brebner, 3 April 1929. University of Toronto Archives: Law School papers.

33 Regulations for the Degree of Master of Laws, n.d. Law School papers.

34 Wen-Han Chin, 'Administrative Discretion; A Study of Its Nature and Scope in Administrative Law' (LLM thesis, University of Toronto, 1943); Philip Girard, *Bora Laskin: Bringing Law to Life* (Toronto: University of Toronto Press, 2005) at 143–4.

35 This degree was a doctorate, like a PhD. The present JD, which is also referred to as a doctor of jurisprudence, is really the old LLB. The JD, rather than the LLB, was first awarded by the law school in 2001. Persons with an LLB could convert it to a JD. I didn't.

36 Letter from W.P.M. Kennedy to H.J. Cody, 31 January 1936. Archives of Ontario: H.J. Cody papers.

37 Letter from W.P.M. Kennedy to H.J. Cody, 18 April 1935. Archives of Ontario: H.J. Cody papers.

38 W.P.M. Kennedy, 'Foreword' (1935) 1 *University of Toronto Law Journal* 1.

39 R.C.B. Risk, 'Volume 1 of the Journal: A Tribute and Belated Review' (1987) 37 *University of Toronto Law Journal* 193.

40 W.P.M. Kennedy, 'New York Law Revision Commission' (1935) 1 *University of Toronto Law Journal* at 353–5.

41 Letter from G.D. Conant, attorney general of Ontario, 8 November 1941; Letter from W.P.M. Kennedy to G.D. Conant, 10 November 1941. University of Toronto Archives: Law School papers.

42 Jacob Finkelman, 'Industrial Law Research Council' (1935) 1 *University of Toronto Law Journal* at 352–3.

43 Minutes of the Executive Committee of the University of Toronto Press, 5 March 1935. University of Toronto Archives: University of Toronto Press papers.

44 Minutes of the Executive Committee of the University of Toronto Press, 24 January 1938. University of Toronto Press papers.

45 Ibid. In contrast, the *Canadian Historical Review* lost 48 pages.

46 *University of Toronto Law Journal* website, http://www.calj-acrs.ca/journal/university-toronto-law-journal.

17 Rethinking Canadian Constitutional Law

1 E.C.S. Wade, 'Law and Custom in the British Commonwealth' (1935) 5 *University of Toronto Quarterly* 139 at 140.

2 Letter from Newton Rowell to R.A. Mackay, 8 November 1937. Library and Archives Canada: R.A. MacKay papers.

3 Alan Cairns, 'The Judicial Committee and its Critics' (1971) 4 *Canadian Journal of Political Science* 301 at 306. Kennedy also participated in producing a 1937 report (2nd ed., 1938) by the Royal Institute of International Affairs: *The British Empire: A Report on Its Structure and Problems* (London: Oxford University Press). Other Canadians who participated were J.B. Bickersteth, Larry MacKenzie, and Escott Reid. I am grateful for the assistance of Malcolm Madden, Chatham House Library: email to the author, 15 September 2017.

4 J.B. Brebner, 'Harold Adams Innis as Historian' (1953) 32 *Report of the Annual Meeting of the Canadian Historical Association* 14 at 16.

5 W.P.M. Kennedy, *Statutes, Treaties and Documents of the Canadian Constitution 1713–1929*, 2nd ed. (Toronto: Oxford University Press, 1930).

6 R. Flenley, ed., *Essays in Canadian History: Presented to George MacKinnon Wrong for his Eightieth Birthday* (Toronto: Macmillan, 1939).

7 W.P.M. Kennedy, *Some Aspects of the Theories and Workings of Constitutional Law* (New York: Macmillan, 1932).

8 R.A. MacKay, 'Review of *Some Aspects of the Theories and Workings of Constitutional Law*' (1932) 13 *Canadian Historical Review* 201.

9 Kennedy, *Some Aspects of the Theories and Workings of Constitutional Law* at 8.

10 Ibid. at 9.

11 Ibid. at 15.

12 *The Lafayette*, 27 April 1931.

13 Kennedy, *Some Aspects of the Theories and Workings of Constitutional Law* at 93–4.

14 *Toronto Electric Commissioners v. Snider* [1925] A.C. 396.

15 Kennedy, *Some Aspects of the Theories and Workings of Constitutional Law* at 84–7.

16 Letter from W.P.M. Kennedy to H.J. Cody, 9 August 1929. University of Toronto Archives: H.J. Cody papers.

17 Dedication in W.P.M. Kennedy, *Essays in Constitutional Law* (Toronto: Oxford University Press, 1934).

18 E.C.S. Wade, 'Review of *Essays in Constitutional Law*' (1935) *University of Toronto Quarterly* at 142–3.

19 Edward Corwin, 'The Passing of Dual Federalism' (1950) 36 *Virginia Law Review* 1 at 5.

20 William Renwick Riddell, 'Review of *Essays in Constitutional Law*' (1934) 12 *Canadian Bar Review* 678.

21 In addition to these books of essays, we saw in the previous chapter the publication of a number of other books during this period, some of a constitutional nature, such as *The Law of Taxing Power in Canada*, co-authored with Dalton Wells.

22 Donald Creighton, 'Review of *The Encyclopedia of Canada*' (1938) 19 *Canadian Historical Review* 434–5.

23 Letter from W.P.M. Kennedy to William Stewart Wallace, 12 April 1934. University of Toronto Fisher Library: Wallace papers.

24 Letter from W.P.M. Kennedy to Jan Smuts, 3 October 1930. Witwatersrand University Archives. I am grateful to archivist Gabriele Mohale for her assistance.

25 Henry John May, *Red Wine of Youth* (London: Cassell, 1946) at 27–8.

26 W.P.M. Kennedy and H.J. Schlosberg, *The Law and Custom of the South African Constitution* (London: Oxford University Press, 1935).

27 E.C.S. Wade, 'Review of *The Law and Custom of the South African Constitution*' (1935) 5 *University of Toronto Quarterly* at 140.

28 W.P.M. Kennedy, *The Constitution of Canada: An Introduction to Its Development and Law* (London: Oxford University Press, 1922) at 32–3, 37. See, by contrast, Peter Russell, *Canada's Odyssey: A Country Based on Incomplete Conquests* (Toronto: University of Toronto Press, 2017) at 29.

29 Russell, *Canada's Odyssey* at 10.

30 Kennedy and Schlosberg, *The Law and Custom of the South African Constitution* at 451 and 459.

31 Henry John May, *The South African Constitution*, 3rd ed. (Cape Town: Juta and Company, 1955).

32 Kennedy was also invited to be a member of an Ontario attorney general's committee 'appointed in connection with the forthcoming Conference concerning the proposed revision of the B.N.A. Act.' See letter dated 26 October 1934, from W.P.M. Kennedy to Attorney General Arthur Roebuck, accepting the invitation. Found in correspondence between W.P.M. Kennedy and H.J. Cody, dated 29 October 1934. University of Toronto Archives: H.J. Cody papers.

33 Special Committee on British North America Act, *Proceedings and Evidence and Report* (Ottawa: J.O. Patenaude, 1935) at iv.

34 Ibid. at vi.

35 Ibid. at xiii.

36 Ibid. at 75–6.

37 Ibid. at 70.

38 Ibid. at 77.

39 W.P.M. Kennedy, ed., *The Cambridge History of the British Empire*, vol. 6, *Canada and Newfoundland* (Cambridge: Cambridge University Press, 1930) at 689.

40 As discussed in a note 56 in chapter 10, appeals to the Privy Council from the High Court of Australia were abolished in constitutional cases in 1903, but could be granted with leave of the High Court. Only one appeal was permitted between then and when the High Court declared such appeals obsolete. Appeals from state courts continued, however.

41 Special Committee on British North America Act, *Proceedings* at 78.

42 Ibid. at xii.

43 Ibid. at 72.

44 W.P.M. Kennedy, preface to *The Constitution of Canada, 1534–1937: An Introduction to Its Development, Law and Custom*, 2nd ed. (London: Oxford University Press, 1938) at vii.

45 W.P.M. Kennedy, 'Aspects of Administrative Law in Canada' (1934) 46 *Juridical Review*' 203.

46 John Willis, *Parliamentary Powers of English Government Departments* (Cambridge, MA: Harvard University Press, 1933).

47 Edward Corwin, 'Review of *The Constitution of Canada, 1534–1937*' (1938) 19 *Canadian Historical Review* 414.

48 See chapter 14.

49 Kennedy, *The Constitution of Canada* (2nd ed.) at 489.

50 Letter from W.P.M. Kennedy to Arthur Meighen, 13 April 1939. Library and Archives Canada: Arthur Meighen papers.

51 Kennedy, *Aspects of the Theories and Workings of Constitution Law* at 71.

52 Letter from W.P.M. Kennedy to Robert Falconer, 13 February 1929, cited in chapter 15, note 69. University of Toronto Archives: Falconer papers.

53 Robert J. Sharpe and Patricia J. McMahon, *The Persons Case: The Origins and Legacy of the Fight for Legal Personhood* (Toronto: University of Toronto Press, 2007) at 184–5.

54 Kennedy, *The Constitution of Canada* (2nd ed.) at 493–4.

55 Kennedy, *The Constitution of Canada* (1st ed.) at 384n1.

56 Kennedy, *The Constitution of Canada* (2nd ed.) at 494.

57 Ibid.

58 Letter from W.P.M. Kennedy to Jacob Finkelman, 16 June 1937. University of Toronto Archives: Law School papers.

59 Letter from W.P.M. Kennedy to Jacob Finkelman, 27 June 1937. Law School papers. Kennedy's son Gilbert states in his oral interview at 58 that he believes his father was consulted with respect to the abdication.

60 Kennedy, *The Constitution of Canada* (2nd ed.) at 552. See *British Coal Corporation v. The King* [1935] A.C. 500 at 518.

61 Ibid. at 554.
62 Ibid. at 529.
63 Ibid. at 533.
64 Ibid. at 490.
65 Ibid. at 489.
66 Ibid. at 491. See *Toronto Electric Commissioners v. Snider* [1925] AC 396. Haldane had used the following language: 'extraordinary peril to the national life of Canada, as a whole.'
67 Kennedy, *The Constitution of Canada* (2nd ed.) at 492.
68 W.P.M. Kennedy, 'The British North America Act: Past and Future' (1937) 15 *Canadian Bar Review* at 398–9.
69 Letter from Charles Cahan to W.P.M. Kennedy, 29 January 1938. Library and Archives Canada: Charles Cahan papers.
70 Letter from W.P.M. Kennedy to Charles Cahan, 31 January 1938. Charles Cahan papers.
71 Letter from W.P.M. Kennedy to Charles Cahan, 10 March 1938. Charles Cahan papers.
72 Letter from W.P.M. Kennedy to Charles Cahan, 30 April 1938. Charles Cahan papers.
73 Charles Cahan, Speech on the Second Reading of Bill 19. Charles Cahan papers; Letter from W.P.M. Kennedy to Charles Cahan, 13 February 1938. Charles Cahan papers.
74 *Nadan v. The King* [1926] A.C. 482.
75 *British Coal Corporation v. The King* [1935] A.C. 500.
76 *Toronto Daily Star*, Monday, 21 April 1938 at 6; the *Globe and Mail*, Friday, 11 April 1938 at 6.
77 An Act to Amend the Supreme Court Act, s. 1, RS 1937, c. 42.
78 Letter from Charles Cahan to W.P.M. Kennedy, 13 April 1939. Library and Archives Canada: Charles Cahan papers.
79 *Reference as to the Legislative Competence of the Parliament of Canada to Enact Bill No. 9 of the Fourth Session, Eighteenth Parliament of Canada, Entitled 'An Act to Amend the Supreme Court Act'* [1940] S.C.R. 49. Privy Council decision: *Ontario (Attorney General) v. Canada (Attorney General)* [1947] A.C. 127.
80 There was vigorous opposition in the House of Commons from Quebec MPs about the federal government's control of appointments to the Supreme Court of Canada. See Peter Russell, *Canada's Odyssey: A Country Based on Incomplete Conquests* (Toronto: University of Toronto Press, 2017) at 284.
81 *Report of the Royal Commission on Dominion-Provincial Relations*, vol. 1 (Ottawa: King's Printer, 1940) at 14.
82 Ibid. at 18.
83 Alexander Brady, 'Report of the Royal Commission on Dominion-Provincial Relations' (1940) 21, no. 3 *Canadian Historical Review* at 245.
84 Letter from Newton Rowell to W.P.M. Kennedy, 8 November 1937. Library and Archives Canada: Rowell-Sirois Commission papers.

85 Ibid.
86 Letter from Newton Rowell to R.A. MacKay, 8 November 1937. Library and Archives Canada: R.A. MacKay papers.
87 Letter from W.P.M. Kennedy to Newton Rowell, n.d. (accompanying final reports). Library and Archives Canada: Rowell-Sirois Commission papers.
88 Brady, 'Report of the Royal Commission on Dominion-Provincial Relationships' at 245.
89 R.C.B. Risk, 'The Many Minds of W.P.M. Kennedy' (1998) 48 *University of Toronto Law Journal* 385.
90 R.A. MacKay, 'Some Personal Reminiscences of the Rowell-Sirois Commission.' Library and Archives Canada: R.A. MacKay papers.
91 Letter from Newton Rowell to R.A. MacKay, 8 November 1937. R.A. MacKay papers.
92 Letter from Ms. Fowler to Alexander Skelton, 8 November 1937. Library and Archives Canada: Rowell-Sirois Commission papers.
93 Report of Hours Worked, 1 December 1937. Rowell-Sirois Commission papers.
94 Letter from W.P.M. Kennedy to Alex Skelton, 22 December 1937. Rowell-Sirois Commission papers.
95 Ibid.
96 Letter from W.P.M. Kennedy to Miss Rowland, 1 January 1938. Rowell-Sirois Commission papers.
97 Report of Hours Worked, 1 February 1938. Rowell-Sirois Commission papers.
98 Letter from W.P.M. Kennedy to Miss Rowland, 5 May 1938. Rowell-Sirois Commission papers.
99 Letter from W.P.M. Kennedy to Alex Skelton, 4 March 1938. Rowell-Sirois Commission papers. The correspondence would likely have concerned the bill on the abolition of appeals to the Privy Council.
100 Letter from Alex Skelton to W.P.M. Kennedy, 7 March 1938. Rowell-Sirois Commission papers.
101 'Rowell, Newton Wesley,' *Dictionary of Canadian Biography*, vol. 17, http://www.biographi.ca/en/bio/rowell_newton_wesley_17E.html.
102 W.P.M. Kennedy, 'Obituary for Newton Rowell' in *Proceedings and Transactions of the Royal Society of* Canada, 3rd series, vol. 36, *Meeting of May 1942* (Ottawa: Royal Society of Canada, 1942) at 115–18. H.J. Cody was the co-author.
103 Letter from W.P.M. Kennedy to H.J. Cody, 16 February 1942. University of Toronto Archives: Law school papers.
104 W.P.M. Kennedy, 'The Judicial Process and Canadian Legislative Powers' (1940) 25 *Washington University Law Quarterly* 215 at 230.
105 *R v. Wetmore* [1983] 2 S.C.R. 284 at 307.
106 See J.A. Corry, 'Constitutional Trends and Federalism' in *Evolving Canadian Federalism*, ed. A.R.M. Lower et al. (Durham, NC: Duke University Press, 1958) at 103,

cited in Peter Russell, *Canada's Odyssey: A Country Based on Incomplete Conquests* (Toronto: University of Toronto Press, 2017) at 287.

107 Gilbert Kennedy oral interview (interviewed by Maryla Waters 1983, Victoria University) at 99–100.

18 The War Years

1 Michael Kesterton, '1939: When Canada Cheered Loudest,' *Globe and Mail*, 30 March 2002.

2 After what the warden of Hart House described as 'acute' criticism, the government relented somewhat and invited the chairs of the board's standing committees, but no members of the professoriate. Report of the Warden of Hart House, 1939. U of T Archives: Hart House papers.

3 'The King and Queen Come to the University' (1939) 39 *University of Toronto Monthly* at 219.

4 Material drawn from 'The "Voyage of the Damned": The Voyage of the St. Louis,' *Jewish People in Canada: 1867–1945*, https://jewsincanada.weebly.com/objective-conditions.html; Alice Taylor, 'Seeking Refuge from Nazi Persecution, the MS St. Louis Was Turned Away at Every Port,' *University of Toronto Magazine*, 15 December 2015, https://magazine.utoronto.ca/campus/history/seeking-refuge-from-nazi-persecution-the-ms-st-louis-was-turned-away-at-every-port-george-wrong-jewish-refugees; William Rayner, *Canada on the Doorstep: 1939* (Toronto: Dundurn Press, 2011).

5 Judith Robinson, 'Forty-second Signature Is Invisible,' *Globe and Mail*, 8 June 1939.

6 Quoted in Taylor, 'Seeking Refuge from Nazi Persecution.' In 1939, for example, Cody delivered a radio address on 'Canada and the Refugee Problem.' In his talk, he argued that 'those who come to us as strangers and sufferers will help to build a more prosperous Canada,' but said that the issue goes beyond self-interest: 'Christian charity and fundamental humanity unite in demanding an answer to Christ's challenge: "I was a stranger, and ye took me not in."' Quoted in 'Canada and the Refugee Problem' (1939) 39 *University of Toronto Monthly* at 139–41.

7 See chapter 14. Material for this section has been drawn from Taylor, 'Seeking Refuge from Nazi Persecution'; D.C. Masters, *Henry John Cody: An Outstanding Life* (Toronto: Dundurn Press, 1995); and Paul Stortz, 'Refugee Professors and the University of Toronto during the Second World War,' in *Cultures, Communities, and Conflict: Histories of Canadian Universities and War*, ed. Paul Stortz and E. Lisa Panayotidis (Toronto: University of Toronto Press, 2012).

8 Letter from W.P.M. Kennedy to Harold Laski, 13 March 1935. University of Toronto Archives: Law School papers.

9 Letter from W.P.M. Kennedy to Edwin Borchard, 28 May 1935. Law School papers.

10 See Irving Abella and Harold Troper, *None Is Too Many: Canada and the Jews of Europe 1933–1948* (Toronto: Key Porter, 2002).

11 Letter from W.P.M. Kennedy to H.J. Cody, 27 October 1938. University of Toronto Archives: Law School papers.

12 Letter from W.P.M. Kennedy to H.J. Cody, 21 October 1938. Law School papers.

13 Letter from W.P.M. Kennedy to F.C. Blair, 14 December 1938. Law School papers.

14 Letter from F.C. Blair to W.P.M. Kennedy, 20 December 1938. Law School papers.

15 Material in this section drawn primarily from Martin Friedland, *The University of Toronto: A History* (Toronto: University of Toronto Press, 2002) at 335; Masters, *Henry John Cody*; Michiel Horn, *Academic Freedom in Canada: A History* (Toronto: University of Toronto Press, 1999); and R. Douglas Francis, *Frank H. Underhill: Intellectual Provocateur* (Toronto: University of Toronto Press, 1986).

16 Horn, *Academic Freedom* at 119 and 121.

17 The Toronto *Telegram* had earlier published an article (no date) under the headline 'Oust University Professor for "Treacherous" Utterance Demand of I.O.D.E Regent.' Speaking for the Imperial Order of the Daughters of the Empire, the head of the Toronto branch told the *Telegram*: 'It seems to me, and I speak on behalf of four thousand of our members in Toronto, that anyone expressing such sentiments, as this worthy gentleman has dared to voice, should promptly be relieved of his duties and should no longer be permitted to share in the privileges accorded to those of us, who love and respect all that is British.'

18 Memorandum from President Cody, undated. University of Toronto Archives: H.J. Cody papers.

19 In 1928, Premier Howard Ferguson wrote to the chairman of the board, Canon Cody, to object to what he was hearing about Underhill's undergraduate lectures on the First World War, stating that 'the impression left on those who heard him is that the British were as much if not more to blame for the war than the Germans.' Falconer investigated the matter and sent a letter to the premier assuring him that there is 'very little in the reports' and ending with the observation that Underhill 'served throughout the war until he was wounded at Villers-Faucon in the great drive in March, 1918. He thus demonstrated the quality that is within him when the great call was made.' Falconer also said: 'I told Professor Underhill that it would be wise for him to be careful in his casual remarks, and I am sure that he will endeavour to do so.' Letter from Robert Falconer to Howard Ferguson, 23 October 1928. University of Toronto Archives: Falconer papers.

20 Friedland, *University of Toronto* at 219–321; James G. Greenlee, *Sir Robert Falconer: A Biography* (Toronto: University of Toronto Press, 1988) at 289; Horn, *Academic Freedom* at 89; Michiel Horn, '"Free Speech within the Law": The Letter of the Sixty-Eight Toronto Professors, 1931' (March 1980) 72, no. 1 *Ontario History* 27).

21 Greenlee, *Falconer* at 294; Horn, *Academic Freedom* at 90.

22 Letter from Robert Falconer to Frank Underhill, 26 June 1931. University of Toronto Archives: Falconer papers.

23 Letter from Frank Underhill to Robert Falconer, 24 September 1931. Falconer papers.

24 Letter from Robert Falconer to Frank Underhill, 28 September 1931. Falconer papers.

25 Ibid.

26 Letter from W.P.M. Kennedy to Attorney General Arthur Roebuck, 26 October 1934. University of Toronto Archives: Law School papers.

27 Mussolini, Cody said, was 'a very efficient man, who had a plan and the necessary faith in it to carry it out.' In a speech in Convocation Hall several months later, he spoke favourably of the Italian fascists: 'Canadians are inclined to emphasize too strongly the "rights" of the individual and the "duties" of the government.' Quoted in Horn, *Academic Freedom* at 94; and Brian McKillop, *Matters of Mind: The University of Ontario, 1791–1951* (Toronto: University of Toronto Press, 1994) at 390–2.

28 Memorandum written by President Cody, undated. University of Toronto Archives, H.J. Cody papers.

29 These quotes are taken from R. Douglas Francis's version of Cody's rough notes, newspaper reports, and a reconstruction of what he said prepared ten days later: Francis, *Frank H. Underhill* at 115. See Martin Friedland, *The University of Toronto: A History* (Toronto: University of Toronto Press, 2002) chapter 26.

30 Horn, *Academic Freedom* at 154–5.

31 Quoted in Masters, *Henry John Cody* at 258–9.

32 Ibid. at 262–3.

33 Horn, *Academic Freedom* at 160.

34 Philip Girard, *Bora Laskin: Bringing Law to Life* (Toronto: University of Toronto Press, 2005) at 130.

35 Francis, *Frank H. Underhill* at 122.

36 Masters, *Henry John Cody* at 265. I did not specifically mention Kennedy in my history of the University of Toronto with respect to the 7 January meeting, but did say: 'The dean of arts, Sam Beatty, led a delegation of senior professors, who urged Cody not to dismiss Underhill,' implying that Kennedy was part of that group. See Friedland, *The University of Toronto* at 349.

37 Cody's Notes, 7 January 1941. University of Toronto Archives: H.J. Cody papers.

38 Letter from W.P.M. Kennedy to H.J. Cody, 28 March 1926, Archives of Ontario: H.J. Cody papers.

39 Gilbert Kennedy oral interview (interviewed by Maryla Waters 1983, Victoria University) at 31–2.

40 Letter from Frank Underhill to Norman ('Larry') MacKenzie, 18 September 1940. University of British Columbia Archives: Norman A.M. MacKenzie papers.

41 Horn, *Academic Freedom* at 164–5.

42 Telegram from Hugh Keenleyside to H.J. Cody, 9 January 1941. University of
    Toronto Archives: H.J. Cody papers.
43 Keenleyside also prepared a memo for Mackenzie King, which he showed to O.D.
    Skelton, the undersecretary of external affairs. Skelton passed it on to King with the
    following comments: 'Attached is a note from Keenleyside re Frank Underhill ...
    Underhill is, of course, a pretty irritating gadfly but I can imagine nothing more
    stupid or unnecessary than this action at the present time. I do not know whether
    you as a University of Toronto graduate consider you could or should take any
    action.' Memorandum of O.D. Skelton, 7 January 1941, quoted in *O.D. Skelton:
    The World of the World, 1923–1941*, ed. Norman Hillmer and Roger Hall (Toronto:
    Champlain Society, 2013) at 484–5.
44 The next day, Premier Cody prepared a draft letter to Mackenzie King, asking what
    King's position was: 'At the request of the Board of Governors of the University
    of Toronto, I am writing to you direct to ask if it records your own views as the
    head of the department of External Affairs for Canada.' (Letter from H.J. Cody to
    W.L. Mackenzie King, 10 January 1941. University of Toronto Archives: H.J. Cody
    papers.) That letter was never sent. Cody must have found out King's likely position
    from other sources, or perhaps King simply telephoned Cody. Or possibly, it came
    from the Ontario government, because in a follow-up letter from Keenleyside to
    Cody, dated 15 January, Keenleyside wrote: 'When I sent the telegram in question
    I did not know that any "high authority" in this Department had communicated
    with Mr. Hepburn.' (Letter from Hugh Keenleyside to H.J. Cody, 15 January 1941.
    University of Toronto Archives: H.J. Cody papers.) That 'high authority' was likely
    the undersecretary of state, O.D. Skelton, perhaps with the approval of Mackenzie
    King. Or maybe it was the prime minister himself.
45 In 1937, Cody had arranged for Cordell Hull to receive an honorary doctorate
    from the University of Toronto.
46 Hugh Keenleyside, with an introduction by W.P.M. Kennedy, *Canada and the
    United States: Some Aspects of their Historical Relations* (New York: Alfred A.
    Knopf, 1929).
47 A.H.U. Colquhoun, 'Review of *Canada and the United States*' (1929) 10 *Canadian
    Historical Review* at 158–9.
48 Quoted in McKillop, *Matters of Mind* at 522.
49 Quoted in Masters, *Henry John Cody* at 234.
50 Friedland, *The University of Toronto* at 339.
51 Ibid. at 339–40.
52 Ibid. at 350. Major contributions were made by the University of Toronto in a num-
    ber of crucial areas, such as radar, the proximity fuse, the production of penicillin,
    the anti-gravity aviation suit, and biological warfare.
53 Donald Avery, *The Science of War* (Toronto: University of Toronto Press, 1998) at 4.
54 Friedland, *The University of Toronto* at 359–60.

19 The Changing Law School

1 (1944) 3 *School of Law Review*, 16 December 1944.
2 (1945) 3 *School of Law Review*, 28 April 1945.
3 Material in this section is drawn primarily from Martin Friedland, *The University of Toronto: A History* (Toronto: University of Toronto Press: 2002); and Jonathan F. Vance, *Unlikely Soldiers* (Toronto: HarperCollins Publishers, 2008).
4 Letter from W.P.M. Kennedy to the Rhodes Scholarship Committee, n.d. University of Toronto Archives: Law School papers. Kennedy's underlining.
5 Letter from Norman ('Larry') MacKenzie to W.P.M. Kennedy, 16 August 1940. Law School papers.
6 Letter from W.P.M. Kennedy to Norman ('Larry') MacKenzie, 17 August 1940. University of British Columbia Archives: Norman A.M. MacKenzie papers.
7 Letter from W.P.M. Kennedy to H.J. Cody, 11 August 1940. University of Toronto Archives: H.J. Cody papers.
8 Letter from W.P.M. Kennedy to H.J. Cody, 31 August 1940. University of Toronto Archives: H.J. Cody papers.
9 Letter from J.H. MacBrien to W.P.M. Kennedy, 4 April 1935. Archives of Ontario: H.J. Cody papers.
10 Vance, *Unlikely Soldiers* at 43.
11 Philip Girard, *Bora Laskin: Bringing Law to Life* (Toronto: University of Toronto Press, 2005) at 121.
12 Vance, *Unlikely Soldiers* at 119.
13 Letter from J.K. Macalister to Norman ('Larry') MacKenzie, 24 August 1940. University of British Columbia Archives: Norman A.M. MacKenzie papers.
14 Vance, *Unlikely Soldiers* at 88–9.
15 Friedland, *The University of Toronto* at 341.
16 Letter from W.P.M. Kennedy to H.J. Cody, 19 September 1940. University of Toronto Archives: H.J. Cody papers.
17 Letter from W.P.M. Kennedy to H.J. Cody, 21 September 1940. University of Toronto Archives: H.J. Cody papers.
18 Statute Number 1507 *Respecting the School of Law of the University of Toronto*, passed 10 April 1941 by the Senate of the University of Toronto. University of Toronto Archives: Board of Governors Collection.
19 Letter from W.P.M. Kennedy to H.J. Cody, 24 April 1941. University of Toronto Archives: H.J. Cody papers.
20 Letter from W.P.M. Kennedy to H.J. Cody, 22 October. 1941. University of Toronto Archives: H.J. Cody papers.
21 Letter from W.P.M. Kennedy to the Attorney General, 10 November 1941. University of Toronto Archives: Law School papers.
22 Letter from H.J. Cody to W.P.M. Kennedy, 22 January 1941. Law School papers.

23 Letter from Mr. W. Cleveland-Stevens, Council of Legal Education, to W.P.M. Kennedy, 10 June 1942. Law School papers.
24 Letter from W.P.M. Kennedy to Sir Owen Dixon, 4 March 1943. Law School papers.
25 Letter from W.P.M. Kennedy to Bora Laskin, 14 August 1943. Law School papers.
26 Ibid.
27 'Introducing 4T7' (1943) 2 *School of Law Review*, 16 December 1943.
28 Class List, Students in Honour Law, 1941–1942, First Year. University of Toronto Archives: Law School papers.
29 Donald Ruwald, 'The Class of 4T5' (1942) 1 *School of Law Review*, 11 December 1942.
30 Harry B. Parkinson, 'We Went West' (1942) 1 *School of Law Review*, 11 December 1942.
31 Letter from Bora Laskin to the University Registrar, 5 December 1941. University of Toronto Archives: Law School papers.
32 Letter from H.J. Cody to W.P.M. Kennedy, 23 May 1940. Law School papers.
33 Laskin was also seconded in 1942 for part-time work with the Regional War Labour Board. Letter from W.P.M. Kennedy to Peter Heenan, Regional War Labour Board, 28 September 1942. Law School papers.
34 Letter from W.P.M. Kennedy to Major Heathcote, 'A' (Res.) Corps Signals, RCCS, 11 March 1943. Law School papers.
35 Letter from Jacob Finkelman to W.P.M. Kennedy, 2 June 1941. Library and Archives Canada: Jacob Finkelman papers.
36 Letter from Robert Falconer to W.P.M. Kennedy, 17 February 1942. University of Toronto Archives: Law School papers.
37 Undated Report by W.P.M. Kennedy to Sidney Smith. Law School papers.
38 Material drawn from the Law Club files at the University of Toronto Archives: Law School papers.
39 Letter from W.P.M. Kennedy to F.H. Barlow, 8 April 1940. Law School papers.
40 Letter from W.P.M. Kennedy to Sir Gerald Campbell, 3 January 1941. Law School papers.
41 Letter from Sir Gerald Campbell to W.P.M. Kennedy, 16 January 1941. Law School papers.
42 Letter from Samuel Williston to W.P.M. Kennedy, 1 November 1941. Law School papers.
43 Letter from W.P.M. Kennedy to Samuel Williston, 5 February 1942. Law School papers.
44 Letter from W.P.M. Kennedy to Samuel Williston, 9 March 1942. Law School papers.
45 Letter from Samuel Williston to W.P.M. Kennedy, 12 March 1942. Law School papers.
46 Letter from Sir Owen Dixon to W.P.M. Kennedy, 8 March 1943. Law School papers.

47 Letter from W.P.M. Kennedy to Sir Owen Dixon, 22 March 1943. Law School papers.

48 Letter from Sidney Smith to W.P.M. Kennedy, 21 January1946. Law School papers.

49 Letter from Donald Gordon to W.P.M. Kennedy, 7 February 1946. Law School papers.

50 Letter from John Cartwright to W.P.M. Kennedy, 25 January 1946. Law School papers.

51 Letter from R.S. Robertson to W.P.M. Kennedy, 28 February 1946. Law School papers.

52 Letter from W.P.M. Kennedy to H.J. Cody, 3 December 1941. University of Toronto Archives: Cody papers.

53 (1942) 1 *School of Law Review*, 11 December 1942.

54 Sandford World, 'High Light and Low Life of 4T3' (1942) 1 *School of Law Review*, 11 December 1942.

55 (1942) 2 *School of Law Review*, 16 December 1943.

56 Gloria C. Carpenter, 'Professor Auld' (1942) 2 *School of Law Review*, 16 December 1943.

57 *University of Toronto Faculty of Law Review* website, https://www.law.utoronto.ca/scholarship-publications/journals-and-publications/u-t-faculty-law-review.

58 Joan Hodgson oral interview (interviewed by Lesley Bruce, 20 June 2016, Toronto) at 31.

59 Letter from Charles Bourne to W.P.M. Kennedy, 19 March 1941. University of Toronto Archives: Law School papers.

60 Letter from W.P.M. Kennedy to Jacob Finkelman, 29 May 1941. Library and Archives Canada: Jacob Finkelman papers.

61 Letter from Jacob Finkelman to Charles Bourne, 23 July 1941. University of Toronto Archives: Law School Papers.

62 Material on Charles Bourne drawn mainly from R. St. J. Macdonald, 'Charles B. Bourne: Scholar, Teacher, and Editor, Innovator in the Development of the International Law of Water Resources' (1996) 34 *The Canadian Yearbook of International Law* 3.

63 Ibid. at 3.

64 Letter from Jacob Finkelman to W.P.M. Kennedy, 30 June 1942. University of Toronto Archives: Law School papers.

65 N.W. Manley, 'The New Constitution of Jamaica' (1945) 3 *School of Law Review*, 28 April 1945.

66 'Gates Scholar to Speak at Black History Month Event,' *Gates Cambridge*, 18 October 2017, https://www.gatescambridge.org/news/gates-scholar-speak-black-history-month-event. The Girton College archivist would limit the claim to stating that she 'may very well have been one of the first women of Afro-Caribbean heritage to attend Cambridge.' Email from Girton College archivist, 8 December 2017.

67　Chantal Aberdeen, 'Inspiring students: Gloria Claire Carpenter' *The Cambridge Student*, 24 May 2017.

68　Letter from W.P.M. Kennedy to W.J. Dunlop, director of University Extension at the University of Toronto, 23 January 1942. University of Toronto Archives: Law School papers.

69　Gilbert Kennedy oral interview (interviewed by Maryla Waters 1983, Victoria University) at 125.

70　Eric Tomlinson, 'Letter to the Editor' (1942) 1 *School of Law Review*, 11 December 1942.

71　Letter from Bora Laskin to W.P.M. Kennedy, 19 July 1943. University of Toronto Archives: Law School papers.

72　Letter from W.P.M. Kennedy to Bora Laskin, 14 August 1943. Law School papers.

73　'Caribbean Law Students in Toronto' *Law Society of Ontario*, https://lso.ca/about-lso/osgoode-hall-and-ontario-legal-heritage/exhibitions-and-virtual-museum/historical-vignettes/people/caribbean-law-students-in-toronto.

74　'About EDLS,' *Eugene Dupuch Law School*, http://eugenedupuchlaw.edu.bs/about/.

75　Gilbert Kennedy oral interview at 127–8.

76　Letter from Bora Laskin, 26 May 1942. University of Toronto Archives: Law School papers.

77　Letter from Bora Laskin to the University Registrar, 7 April 1943. Law School papers.

78　George Tamaki, 'The Law Relating to Nationality in Canada' (LLM thesis, University of Toronto, 1944).

79　Letter from W.P.M. Kennedy to Professor Angus, 14 August 1943. University of Toronto Archives: Law School papers.

80　Letter from C.E. Higginbottom to the University Registrar, 16 May 1942. Law School Papers; Statute Number 1560 *Respecting the Newton Wesley Rowell Fellowship in Law*, passed 1 June 1942 by the Senate of the University of Toronto. University of Toronto Archives: Board of Governors Collection.

81　Letter from C.E. Higginbottom to J.E. Atkinson, 23 June 1943. University of Toronto Archives: Law School papers.

82　Shumiatcher's biographical sketch, oral examination for the Degree of Doctor Juris. Law School papers.

83　Letter from W.P.M. Kennedy to George Curtis, 5 December 1945. Law School papers.

84　Material drawn from Friedland, *The University of Toronto* at 346–7.

85　Steven Golick, 'The Honourable Mr. Justice Geoffrey B. Morawetz' (2012) 29 *Emory Bankruptcy Developments Journal*, http://law.emory.edu/ebdj/_documents/volumes/29/1/tribute/golick.pdf.

86　Email from Justice Geoffrey B. Morawetz, 1 May 2016. The author is grateful to Chief Justice Morawetz for his assistance in obtaining material about his father.

87　Carl Morawetz, 'The Study of Law at a European University' (1943) 1 *School of Law Review*, 12 March 1943.

88 Council of the Law Society of Prince Edward Island, 'Memo Re; Carl Heinz Morawetz,' n.d. Law Society of Prince Edward Island Archives.

89 Email from Eric Koch, 11 May 2016.

90 Eric Koch, 'The Study of Law at Cambridge and Toronto' (1942) 1 *School of Law Review*, 11 December 1942.

91 Eric Koch, *Deemed Suspect: A Wartime Blunder* (Toronto: Methuen, 1980).

92 While this book was being written, I received an email from Koch – at the age of ninety-eight – stating: 'I am conducting a discussion group in Hazelton [Retirement home] which meets on Wednesday and Friday afternoons at four. Could I persuade you to have a conversation with me in January on a subject to be discussed? It should be a historic event.' I chose the subject: 'The First Dean of the Law School and the Second World War.' (Email from Eric Koch to Friedland, 8 December 2017). I looked forward to the lecture and printed out a copy of a letter to give to Koch that I had come across in the law school files that Kennedy had sent to the United Nations, praising Koch who had applied for a position there. Alas, Koch died just before I gave the talk, which I dedicated to Koch's memory.

93 Material in this section drawn mainly from Charles L. Sanders, 'The Legacy of a Love Affair' *Ebony*, March 1968; and *In the Estate of Fuld, Decd. (No. 3)* [1968] P 675, [1967] 3 W.L.R. 401.

94 Author's oral interview with Joan Hodgson, 26 July 2016.

95 *In the Estate of Fuld* at 687.

96 *In the Estate of Fuld* at 689.

97 *In the Estate of Fuld*.

98 *In the Estate of Fuld* at 703.

99 Randi Chapnik Myers, 'Ivy Maynier Bursary' *University of Toronto Faculty of Law* website, https://www.law.utoronto.ca/alumni/giving-0/gifts-have-made-difference/ivy-maynier-bursary.

20 The Cottage

1 See the preface to this volume.

2 William Knight, 'A Landscape of Science: The Go Home Bay Biological Station' *NICHE*, 20 April 2015; *Madawaska Club, 1898–1923 Go Home Bay* (Privately published, 1923); Philip Girard, 'Cottages, Covenants, and the Cold War: *Galbraith v. Madawaska Club*' in *Property on Trial: Canadian Cases in Context*, ed. Eric Tucker, James Muir, and Bruce Ziff (Toronto: Irwin Law for the Osgoode Society, 2012) at 93.

3 Much of the material pertaining to the Kennedys' life at Narrow Waters is drawn from personal conversations with Frere Kennedy and from the Friedland papers in the University of Toronto Archives, 1998 Accession.

4 The official name of the lake is Bethune Lake – the township was named Bethune Township, probably after a relative of Dr. Norman Bethune, who had been born in Gravenhurst.

5 Frere Kennedy, *The 'Narrow Waters' Log*. University of Toronto Archives: Friedland papers.

6 The author is grateful to Liz Driver of Campbell House Museum for her assistance and for providing information about the Shortreed family.

7 The township had been opened up for settlement by the province in 1878, and Kearney's first bridge over the Magnetawan River had been built in 1880. Material on the history of Kearney and the surrounding area is drawn primarily from *Kearney: One Hundred Years* (Kearney, ON: Kearney Centennial Publications Committee, 2008) at 22–3; and Ralph Bice, *Historical Highlights of the Kearney Area, 1865–1983* (New Liskeard, ON: Temiskaming Printing Company, 1983).

8 Roy MacGregor, *Northern Light: The Enduring Mystery of Tom Thompson and the Woman Who Loved Him* (Toronto: Random House Canada, 2010) at 216.

9 *Kearney: One Hundred Years* at 78.

10 Material on the railway is primarily drawn from *Kearney: One Hundred Years* at 99–102; Niall Mackay, *Over the Hills to Georgian Bay: The Ottawa, Arnprior and Parry Sound Railway* (Toronto: Stoddart Publishing, 1981) at 119.

11 Gertrude White, who grew up in the area in the early 1900s, describes the town she remembers in her memoirs, *The Hills Were Sunny*. She writes: 'By the turn of the century, Kearney was a thriving little town situated by the bright sparkling waters of one of the many bays of the Magnetawan River. With the little homes reflecting in its waters, its scenic beauty surpassed any town in Ontario for summer scenery … Kearney boasted of a bank, hotel, several stores, churches and the Catholic Church which is noted for its fine architectural design work, a blacksmith's shop, chair factory, with chairs still in use today, a post office, a law office, eating places, boarding houses, shoe repairs, and also a tailor shop.' Gertrude White, *The Hills Were Sunny* (self-published, 1984) at 50.

12 Astrid Taim, *Almaguin Chronicles: Memories of the Past* (Toronto: Natural Heritage Books, 2008) at 134.

13 MacGregor, *Northern Light* at 216.

14 After the Friedlands purchased the property, we took advantage of having a Forest Management Agreement with the province, whereby we received a tax break on our municipal taxes if we used the forest responsibly. We still have such an agreement. Because of the agreement, we had to remove some of the very old maple trees – some were over eighty years old – and thin the new pine forest. Every second row of the pine forest had to be cut and then, a number of years later, every second tree had to be removed.

15 David Vanek, *Fulfilment: Memoirs of a Criminal Court Judge* (Toronto: University of Toronto Press, 1999) at 171.

16 Ibid. at 172.

17 Letter from W.P.M. Kennedy to Sam Wilton, 20 April 1947; Letter from W.P.M. Kennedy to James Dwyer, 20 April 1947. University of Toronto Archives: Friedland papers.

21 The Family

1 'Mrs. W.P.M. Kennedy Elected Successor to Mrs. Althouse by Women's Canadian Club' *Globe and Mail*, 28 April 1939.

2 Gilbert Kennedy oral interview (interviewed by Maryla Waters 1983, Victoria University) at 41.

3 Ian Mosby, *Food Will Win the War* (Vancouver: UBC Press, 2014) at 64.

4 'Wartime Prices and Trade Board' *Canadian Encyclopedia*, 17 February 2015, http://www.thecanadianencyclopedia.ca/en/article/wartime-prices-and-trade-board;'Consumers' Association of Canada' *Canadian Encyclopedia*, 15 December 2013, http://www.thecanadianencyclopedia.ca/en/article/consumers-association-of-canada.

5 'The Homemaker' *Globe and Mail*, 9 May 1946.

6 'Consumers to Battle for Ottawa Price-Cut' *Globe and Mail*, 1 October 1947.

7 'Consumers' Association of Canada' *Canadian Encyclopedia*.

8 Canadian Cancer Society, 'Our History,' http://www.cancer.ca/en/about-us/fighting-since-1938/.

9 Canadian Cancer Society, 'Who We Are and What We Do,' http://www.cancer.ca/en/about-us/our-mission/.

10 'Stress Education Need in Fight Against Cancer' *Globe and Mail*, 5 January 1945.

11 'Cancer Sufferers Need Help in Home, Meeting Reminded' *Globe and Mail*, 10 November 1948.

12 Letter from W.P.M. Kennedy to Frere Kennedy, 16 October 1953. University of Toronto Archives: Kennedy correspondence in Friedland papers.

13 Fifty women from Saskatchewan were accommodated in early 1943 in Toronto homes. *Globe and Mail*, 2 February 1943.

14 'Women Taggers' *Varsity*, 20 October 1944.

15 Author's oral interview with Frere Kennedy, 2 April 2015.

16 Letter from Pauline Kennedy to Frere Kennedy, 13 March 1945. University of Toronto Archives: Kennedy correspondence in Friedland papers.

17 Gilbert Kennedy oral interview at 85.

18 Ibid. at 64–7.

19 Ibid. at 83–5. According to Shelagh, Gilbert and Beatrice got a small inheritance from his birth mother, and Gilbert was able to finish his law studies with this money. Author's oral interview with Shelagh Lindsey, 2 May 2014.

20 Gilbert Kennedy oral interview at 38.

21 Author's oral interview with Betty Kennedy, 8 July 2013.

22 Gilbert Kennedy oral interview at 68.

23 Philip Girard's oral interview with Eugene LaBrie, 1 October 2000.

24 Author's oral interview with Frere Kennedy, 25 May 2016.

25 Gilbert Kennedy oral interview at 118.

26 Ibid. at 123.

27 Ibid. at 130.
28 Ibid. at 139.
29 Letter from W.P.M. Kennedy to Vincent MacDonald, 15 December 1947. University of Toronto Archives: Law School papers.
30 Gilbert Kennedy oral interview at 60–2.
31 Ibid. at 56.
32 Gilbert would in the early days purchase mint Canadian stamps, later expanding the countries in which he was interested. Frere would trade with other collectors throughout the world. Gilbert Kennedy oral interview at 69–75.
33 Letter from C.K. Stottmeyer to W.P.M. Kennedy, 23 March 1932. University of Toronto Archives: Law School papers.
34 Author's oral interview with Frere Kennedy, 25 May 2016.
35 Gilbert Kennedy oral interview at 159–60.
36 Email from Betty Kennedy to Martin Friedland, 29 October 2015.
37 'Weddings: Kennedy-Dodwell' *Globe and Mail*, 27 August 1948.
38 Email from Betty Kennedy to Martin Friedland, 29 October 2015.
39 Ibid.
40 Author's oral interview with Shelagh Lindsey, 2 May 2014.
41 Author's oral interview with Betty Kennedy, 8 July 2013.
42 See chapter 6.
43 'Prof Kennedy Gives "Requiescat in Pace" to Le Club Politique' *Varsity*, 22 February 1918.
44 Author's oral interview with Eugene LaBrie, 29 June 2016.
45 Joan Hodgson oral interview (interviewed by Lesley Bruce 20 June 2016, Toronto) at 42–3.
46 Ibid. at 41.
47 Ibid. at 50–1.
48 Email from Betty Kennedy to Martin Friedland, 29 October 2015.
49 Toronto Psychiatric Institute (Toronto, Ontario), 'Clinical Record,' for Beatrice Kennedy, Dr. Jackson entry, 6 May 1940, record no. 36821.
50 Ibid.
51 Ibid.
52 Toronto Psychiatric Institute (Toronto, Ontario), 'Clinical Record,' for Beatrice Kennedy, Dr. Campbell entry, 19 December 1940.
53 'Time Line: Dr. Clarence Bynold Farrar (1874–1970).' University of Toronto Archives: Clarence B. Farrar papers.
54 Edward Shorter, *Partnership for Excellence: Medicine at the University of Toronto and Academic Hospitals* (Toronto: University of Toronto Press, 2013) at 360; Edward Shorter, ed., *TPH: History and Memories of the Toronto Psychiatric Hospital, 1925–1966* (Toronto: Wall and Emerson, 1996). See also James FitzGerald, *What Disturbs Our Blood: A Son's Quest to Redeem the Past* (Toronto: Random House Canada, 2010).

55 Judith H. Gold et al. *Pioneers All: Women Psychiatrists in Canada: A History* (Ottawa: Canadian Psychiatric Association, 1995) at 6.

56 I am grateful for the advice and assistance in finding and interpreting the records used in this section by the archivist of the Centre for Addiction and Mental Health (CAMH), Professor John Court.

57 Letter from Kenneth Gray to W.P.M. Kennedy, 5 October 1944. University of Toronto Archives: Law School papers. See also 'School of Law' (April 1942) *University of Toronto Monthly* at 205.

58 Letter from W.P.M. Kennedy to C.B. Farrar, 5 February 1944. University of Toronto Archives: Law School papers.

59 'Historical Synopsis – The Department of Psychiatry at the University of Toronto' Department of Psychiatry University of Toronto, https://tspace.library.utoronto.ca/handle/1807/90061.

60 Toronto Psychiatric Institute, 'Clinical Record,' for Beatrice Kennedy, Dr. Jackson entry, 12 July 1940.

61 Ibid., 14 December 1940.

62 Shorter, *Partnership for Excellence* at 360.

63 Toronto Psychiatric Institute, 'Clinical Record,' for Beatrice Kennedy, Dr. Jackson entry, 6 May 1940.

64 Letter from W.P.M. Kennedy to H.J. Cody, 17 June 1940. Archives of Ontario: H.J. Cody papers.

65 Letter from W.P.M. Kennedy to H.J. Cody, 11 August 1940. H.J. Cody papers.

66 Toronto Psychiatric Institute, 'Clinical Record,' for Beatrice Kennedy, Dr. Jackson entry, 12 July 1940.

67 Toronto Psychiatric Institute, 'Clinical Record,' for Beatrice Kennedy, Dr. McNeal entry, 26 December 1940.

68 Toronto Psychiatric Institute, 'Social Record,' for Beatrice Kennedy, E.H. Algie entry, 13 February 1941.

69 Ibid., E.H. Algie entry, 24 February 1941.

70 Ibid., E.H. Algie entry, 6 November 1941.

71 Ibid., E.H. Algie entry, 15 June 1941.

72 Toronto Psychiatric Institute, 'Clinical Record,' for Beatrice Kennedy, Dr. Farrar entry, 4 January 1944.

73 Toronto Psychiatric Institute, 'Clinical Record,' for Beatrice Kennedy, Dr. Geoghegan entry, 23 August 1944.

74 Toronto Psychiatric Institute, 'Clinical Record,' for Beatrice Kennedy, Dr. Jackson entry, 4 July 1944.

75 Ibid., Dr. Jackson entry, 8 December 1943.

76 Robert Baskett, 'The Life of the Toronto Psychiatric Hospital' in Shorter, *TPH: History and Memories of the Toronto Psychiatric Hospital, 1925–1966* at 118: 'Electroshock was regarded as an alternative to [the drug] metrazol rather than to insulin because it also produced seizures.'

77   Toronto Psychiatric Institute, 'Clinical Record,' for Beatrice Kennedy, Dr. Jackson entry, 4 July 1944.

78   Toronto Psychiatric Institute, 'Clinical Record,' for Beatrice Kennedy, Dr. Farrar entry, 16 August 1944. There was no discussion of a lobotomy, which was used at TPH from 1941 on, though Farrar was a believer in its effectiveness.

79   Toronto Psychiatric Institute, 'Clinical Record,' for Beatrice Kennedy, Dr. Jackson entry, 6 May 1940.

80   Toronto Psychiatric Institute, 'Clinical Record,' for Beatrice Kennedy, Dr. Farrar entry, 16 August 1944.

81   Toronto Psychiatric Institute, 'Clinical Record,' for Beatrice Kennedy, Dr. Jackson entry, 30 November 1943.

82   Toronto Psychiatric Institute, 'Clinical Record,' for Beatrice Kennedy, Dr. Farrar entry, 16 August 1944.

83   Toronto Psychiatric Institute, 'Clinical Record,' for Beatrice Kennedy, Dr. Farrar entry, 26 July 1940.

84   Toronto Psychiatric Institute, 'Clinical Record,' for Beatrice Kennedy, Dr. Easton entry, 13 August 1940.

85   Toronto Psychiatric Institute, 'Clinical Record,' for Beatrice Kennedy, Dr. McNeal entry, 27 August 1940.

86   Toronto Psychiatric Institute, 'Clinical Record,' for Beatrice Kennedy, Dr. Campbell entry, 18 December 1940.

87   Toronto Psychiatric Institute, 'Clinical Record,' for Beatrice Kennedy, Dr. Campbell entry, 9 December 1940.

88   Toronto Psychiatric Institute, 'Clinical Record,' for Beatrice Kennedy, Dr. Farrar entry, 27 November 1940.

89   Whitby Psychiatric Hospital, 'Clinical Record,' for Beatrice Kennedy, Dr. Fletcher entry, 14 December 1944.

90   Toronto Psychiatric Institute, 'Clinical Record,' for Beatrice Kennedy, Dr. Farrar entry, 27 November 1940.

91   Whitby Psychiatric Hospital, 'Clinical Record,' for Beatrice Kennedy, Dr. Zeman entry, 31 July 1970.

92   Whitby Psychiatric Hospital, 'Medical Practitioner's Certificate for the Admission of a Mentally Ill Patient,' for Beatrice Kennedy, 27 November 1944.

93   Whitby Psychiatric Hospital, 'Clinical Record,' for Beatrice Kennedy, Dr. Fletcher entry, 14 December 1944.

94   Author's oral interview with Betty Kennedy, 8 July 2013.

95   Author's oral interview with Frere Kennedy, 2 April 2015.

96   Author's conversation with John Laskin.

97   Whitby Psychiatric Hospital, 'Clinical Record,' for Beatrice Kennedy, Dr. Zeman entry, 31 July 1970; Letter from W.P.M. Kennedy to Harold G. Fox, 5 December 1944. University of Toronto Archives: Law School papers. 'The financial situation arising from that other matter at home is almost impossible to contemplate. It will mean an expenditure of five or six hundred dollars annually, which we simply cannot get hold of.'

98 Email from Betty Kennedy to Martin Friedland, 29 October 2015.

99 Whitby Psychiatric Hospital, Memorandum from Mabel Gregg to Dr. Sweet, 9 January 1963.

100 Author's oral interview with Frere Kennedy, 2 April 2015.

101 Ibid.

102 Ibid.

103 Letter from W.P.M. Kennedy to H.J. Cody, 19 May 1944. Archives of Ontario: H.J. Cody papers.

104 Letter from W.P.M. Kennedy to Frere Kennedy, 21 October 1944. University of Toronto Archives: Kennedy correspondence in Friedland papers.

105 Letter from W.P.M. Kennedy to Frere Kennedy, 8 July 1945. Kennedy correspondence in Friedland papers.

106 Letter from W.P.M. Kennedy to Frere Kennedy, 4 March 1945. Kennedy correspondence in Friedland papers.

107 Letter from W.P.M. Kennedy to Frere Kennedy, 25 April 1945. Kennedy correspondence in Friedland papers.

108 Letter from W.P.M. Kennedy to Frere Kennedy, 26 June 1945. Kennedy correspondence in Friedland papers.

109 Letter from W.P.M. Kennedy to Frere Kennedy, 27 May 1945. Kennedy correspondence in Friedland papers. W.P.M. also sent a note to the university librarian Stewart Wallace, whose son was in the 48th Highlanders, telling him about Frere's decision, writing: 'I've heard from him a few days ago to the following effect, almost in his own words: He turned matters over and decided that it would be [cowardly] … as Canada had trained him and he had seen or done nothing in return actively in service, if he did not follow his conscience and his duty to volunteer for the Pacific. This he has done and now awaits news if he will be accepted. We are quite proud of him and his letter was manly and patriotic.' Letter from W.P.M. Kennedy to Stewart Wallace, 1 June 1945, University of Toronto Archives: Law School papers.

110 Letter from W.P.M. Kennedy to Frere Kennedy, 17 May 1945. University of Toronto Archives: Kennedy correspondence in the Friedland papers.

111 Letter from Eugene LaBrie to University of Toronto Bursar, 19 February 1946. University of Toronto Archives: Law School papers; 'University College Graduates' (1946) 48 Torontonensis.

112 Letter from Roger L. Vincent, president of CCH, 25 September 1951. University of Toronto Archives: Kennedy correspondence in the Friedland papers.

113 Email from Paul Leatherdale, Law Society Archives, 4 January 2019. I am grateful to Paul Leatherdale and his colleagues at the Law Society of Ontario Archives for their helpful assistance in finding material for me on this project.

114 Email from Bernice Chong, manager of operations, Law Society of British Columbia, to Martin Friedland, 12 June 2018. The dean of law at UBC, George Curtis, had taken the position that an LLB from Kennedy's School of Law should be recognized by the BC Law Society in the same way as a degree from Osgoode:

letter from George Curtis to W.P.M. Kennedy, 16 November 1945. University of Toronto Archives: Law School papers.

115 Author's oral interview with Frere Kennedy, 2 April 2015.

116 Gilbert Kennedy oral interview at 43.

117 'Shelagh Lindsey Obituary' *Vancouver Sun*, 7 March 2015.

118 Author's oral interview with Shelagh Lindsey, 2 May 2014.

119 Author's oral interview with Frere Kennedy, 2 April 2015.

120 *Varsity*, September 1945; 17 October 1945; 17 January 1946; 26 September 1946; 'University College Graduates' (1948) 50 *Torontonensis*.

121 'Marriage Announcement: Lindsey-Kennedy' *Globe and Mail*, 31 May 1948.

122 'Nuclear Physicist George Lindsey Was DND's "Best Mind"' *Globe and Mail*, 25 September 2011.

123 Letter from Cas Lindsey to Martin Friedland, September 2016. See also a letter from Cas Lindsey to Martin Friedland, 4 August 2016 and letters and a telegram from Mackenzie King sent to Shelagh and Cas in 1948, which were passed on to me by Cas in August 2016.

124 Letter from W.P.M. Kennedy to Frere Kennedy, 4 March 1945. University of Toronto Archives: Kennedy correspondence in Friedland papers.

125 Letter from Gilbert Kennedy to Frere Kennedy, 8 March 1945. University of Toronto Archives: Kennedy correspondence in Friedland papers.

126 'Casimir Lindsey,' *Canadian Who's Who*, vol. 96, ed. Lynn Browne and Gwen Peroni (Orillia: Third Sector Publishing, 2011) at 736. www.canadianwhoswho.ca.

22 Sidney Smith Arrives

1 Material on Henry Cody is drawn from Martin Friedland, *The University of Toronto: A History* (Toronto: University of Toronto Press, 2002). The rest of the chapter is primarily drawn from Ian Kyer and Jerome Bickenbach, *The Fiercest Debate: Cecil A. Wright, the Benchers, and Legal Education in Ontario 1923–1947* (Toronto: University of Toronto Press, 1987); and also from Philip Girard, *Bora Laskin: Bringing Law to Life* (Toronto: University of Toronto Press, 2005); and David Vanek, *Fulfilment: Memoirs of a Criminal Court Judge* (Toronto: University of Toronto Press, 1999). Unless otherwise stated, the documents are from the University of Toronto Archives.

2 Referenced in Friedland, *The University of Toronto* at 363.

3 Relations could not have been helped by a 'private and confidential' letter that Cody had sent to a friend, which was passed on to Drew, comparing him to Hitler on the issue of 'enemy aliens.' Quoted in Friedland, *The University of Toronto* at 363.

4 Ibid.

5 Patricia Williams, 'Sidney Earle Smith,' *The Canadian Encyclopedia*, https://thecanadianencyclopedia.ca/en/article/sidney-earle-smith.

6 'Tribute Paid Sir William by Heads of All Faculties' *Varsity*, 18 October 1944.

7 Many people had wanted Vincent Massey to be the chancellor. In 1947, Massey's angry supporters arranged for the passage of an Act limiting a chancellor's term to three years, rather than four, and making it retroactive. Moreover, a representative committee – not the senate – would make the decision, subject to approval by the board and confirmation by the senate. Both Cody and Massey allowed their names to stand. Massey was selected as chancellor by the board. (Letter from F.C. Auld to W.P.M. Kennedy, 5 June 1947. Law School papers.) Cody did not attend Massey's installation in November 1947.

8 Letter from W.P.M. Kennedy to H.J. Cody, 1944. Law School papers.

9 Letter from W.P.M. Kennedy to Sidney Smith, 14 May 1944. Law School papers.

10 Letter from Sidney Smith to W.P.M. Kennedy, 22 May 1944. Law School papers.

11 Kyer and Bickenbach, *The Fiercest Debate* at 163.

12 Letter from H.J. Cody to W.P.M. Kennedy, 17 May 1944. Law School papers.

13 Letter from W.P.M. Kennedy to H.J. Cody, 19 May 1944. Law School papers.

14 Kyer and Bickenbach, *The Fiercest Debate* at 182.

15 Ibid. at 182–3.

16 Ibid. at 41.

17 Ibid. at 44–5.

18 Ibid. at 162.

19 Ibid. at 54–5.

20 Ibid. at 37.

21 Kyer and Bickenbach, *The Fiercest Debate* at 80.

22 Ibid. at 80–1.

23 Ibid. at 94.

24 Ibid. at 97.

25 Ibid. at 102.

26 Ibid. at 100.

27 Ibid. at 108.

28 Ibid. at 108; Cecil Wright, 'An Extra-Legal Approach to Law' (1932) 10 *Canadian Bar Review* 3. Wright was also interested in law reform and published a fine article on the work of the American Law Institute in the first volume of Kennedy's new *University of Toronto Law Journal*. Cecil Wright, 'The American Law Institute's Restatement on Contracts and Agency' (1935) 1 *University of Toronto Law Journal* 17. See generally, on Wright's view of the law: R.C.B. Risk, 'Canadian Law Teachers in the 1930s: When the World Was Turned Upside Down' (2004) 27 *Dalhousie Law Journal* 1.

29 'Editor's Note' (1983) 33 *University of Toronto Law Journal* 147.

30 Kyer and Bickenbach, *The Fiercest Debate* at 135.

31 Ibid.

32 Wright did write a report for the Ontario Law Reform Commission in 1965 on reforming the law of perpetuities.

33 Girard, *Bora Laskin* at 296.

34 He was replaced as a full-time teacher at Osgoode by the great J.J. Robinette, who taught there for several years before going into practice. It seems that Kennedy had tried to hire Robinette at about that time without success. Kyer and Bickenbach, *The Fiercest Debate* at 104–5.

35 Ibid. at 120.

36 Ibid. at 142.

37 Ibid. at 143.

38 Ibid. at 105.

39 Kyer and Bickenbach, *The Fiercest Debate* at 180.

40 Ibid. at 163.

41 Ibid. at 170.

42 Letter from W.P.M. Kennedy to H.J. Cody, 18 August 1943, Law School papers.

43 Letter from W.P.M. Kennedy to H.J. Cody, 24 August 1943. Law School papers.

44 Letter from W.P.M. Kennedy to F.C. Auld, 29 June 1944. Law School papers.

45 Letter from W.P.M. Kennedy to Vincent MacDonald, 13 March 1946. Law School papers.

46 Friedland oral interview with Eugene LaBrie, 28 June 2016.

47 Quoted in Kyer and Bickenbach, *The Fiercest Debate* at 169 and 208n8.

48 Letter from Moffatt Hancock to W.P.M. Kennedy, 28 June 1945. Law School papers.

49 Philip Girard interview with Eugene LaBrie, 1 October 2000. Osgoode Society for Canadian Legal History.

50 Girard, *Bora Laskin* at 158.

51 Ibid. at 146–7.

52 Ibid. at 130.

53 Quoted in Kyer and Bickenbach, *The Fiercest Debate* at 170.

54 Ibid. at 169.

55 Ibid. at 165–6.

56 Ibid. at 166.

57 Ibid. at 164.

58 Kyer and Bickenbach, *The Fiercest Debate* at 166.

59 Ibid. at 167.

60 Ibid. at 169.

61 Ibid. at 169.

62 Ibid. at 168.

63 Interview with Eugene LaBrie, 7 September 2016.

64 Letter from W.P.M. Kennedy to Frere Kennedy, 15 July 1945. Law School papers.

65 Kyer and Bickenbach, *The Fiercest Debate* at 170.

66 The dissertation was later published by the University of Toronto Press in 1953: Francis Eugene LaBrie, *The Meaning of Income in the Law of Income Tax* (Toronto: University of Toronto Press, 1953).

67 Philip Girard's interview with Eugene LaBrie, 1 October 2000.

68 Martin Friedland, *My Life in Crime and Other Academic Adventures* (Toronto: University of Toronto Press, 2007) at 33.
69 Oral interview with Eugene LaBrie, 28 June 2016.
70 Vanek, *Fulfilment* at 68.
71 Ibid. at 158.
72 Quoted in Kyer and Bickenbach, *The Fiercest Debate* at 169.
73 Claude Bissell, *Halfway Up Parnassus: A Personal Account of the University of Toronto 1932–1971* (Toronto: University of Toronto Press, 1974) at 29.
74 Quoted in Friedland, *The University of Toronto* at 370.
75 Quoted in Friedland, *The University of Toronto* at 370–1.
76 Letter from Sidney Smith to W.P.M. Kennedy, 2 October 1945. Law School papers.
77 Letter from W.P.M. Kennedy to Sidney Smith, 16 October 1945. Law School papers.
78 Letter from Sidney Smith to W.P.M. Kennedy, 15 December 1945. Law School papers.
79 Quoted in Kyer and Bickenbach, *The Fiercest Debate* at 178.
80 Ibid. at 172.
81 Ibid.
82 Kyer and Bickenbach, *The Fiercest Debate* at 179.
83 Ibid.
84 Ibid. at 180–2. The committee's membership was drawn from a special committee that had been set up to investigate complaints about legal education in Ontario, including physical facilities and the increase in number of students.
85 Kyer and Bickenbach, *The Fiercest Debate* at 182–3.
86 Ibid. at 185.
87 Letter from Sidney Smith to W.P.M. Kennedy, 5 February 1947. Law School papers.
88 Letter from W.P.M. Kennedy to Leonard Brockington, 3 March 1947. Law School papers.
89 Letter from Sidney Smith to W.P.M. Kennedy, 27 March 1947. Law School papers.
90 Letter from W.P.M. Kennedy to Sidney Smith, 27 March 1947. Law School papers.
91 'Claim Lawyers Scorn Osgoode Hall System' *Globe and Mail*, 20 October 1948.
92 Kyer and Bickenbach, *The Fiercest Debate* at 185.
93 Ibid. at 190.
94 Smith wrote to board chairman Eric Phillips in November, stating: 'I have reason to believe that John Cartwright and Wilson are favourably disposed to the general ideas embodied in the memorandum while, on the other hand, the Chairman of the Joint Committee, the Chief Justice, and perhaps the Treasurer of the Law Society, Mr. Mason, have obvious doubts with respect to any co-operation between the Law Society and the University. Mr. Denison, I understand, is fundamentally opposed to any liaison.' Kyer and Bickenbach, *The Fiercest Debate* at 191.
95 Ibid.

23 Final Years as Dean

1 David Vanek, *Fulfilment: Memoirs of a Criminal Court Judge* (Toronto: University of Toronto Press, 1999) at 168.
2 Letter from Jacob Finkelman to the Registrar of the University of Toronto, 22 September 1945. University of Toronto Archives: Law School papers.
3 Letter from Eugene LaBrie to A.B. Fennell, 5 November 1948. Law School papers.
4 Letter from Eugene LaBrie to A.B. Fennell, 14 May 1946. Law School papers.
5 Letter from Sidney Smith to Charles Dubin, 15 August 1945. Law School papers.
6 Letter from F.C. Auld to W.P.M. Kennedy, 8 July 1946. Law School papers.
7 Letter from Sidney Smith to Samuel Beatty (copy for Kennedy), 3 May 1948; Letter from Sidney Smith to W.P.M. Kennedy, 9 April 1948. Law School papers.
8 Letter from Sidney Smith to W.P.M. Kennedy, 9 April 1946. Law School papers; Ian Radforth and Joan Sangster, 'A Link between Labour and Learning: The Workers Educational Association in Ontario 1917–1951' (1981/1982) 8/9 *Labour / Le Travail* 41 at 65.
9 Letter from Sidney Smith to W.P.M. Kennedy, 5 December 1945. University of Toronto Archives: Law School papers.
10 Letter from T.A. Goudge to Eugene LaBrie, 12 February 1946. Law School papers.
11 Letter from W.P.M. Kennedy to Norman ('Larry') MacKenzie, 28 February 1947. Law School papers.
12 'Faculty of Law Banquet' (1947) 47 *University of Toronto Monthly* at 181.
13 Letter from Leonard Brockington to W.P.M. Kennedy, 18 March 1947. University of Toronto Archives: Law School papers.
14 Letter from W.P.M. Kennedy to Thibaudeau Rinfret, 14 November 1947. Law School papers.
15 Letter from Thibaudeau Rinfret to W.P.M. Kennedy, 12 November 1947. Law School papers.
16 Letter from Thibaudeau Rinfret to W.P.M. Kennedy, 8 December 1947. Law School papers.
17 Letter from W.P.M. Kennedy to Thibaudeau Rinfret, 4 December 1947. Law School papers.
18 Letter from W.P.M. Kennedy to Lester Pearson, 15 January 1948. Law School papers.
19 Letter from Lester Pearson to W.P.M. Kennedy, 19 January 1948. Law School papers.
20 Letter from W.P.M. Kennedy to Vincent Massey, 20 January 1948. Law School papers.
21 Letter from Vincent Massey to W.P.M. Kennedy, 28 January 1948. Law School papers.
22 Letter from J.T. Thorson to W.P.M. Kennedy, 23 March 1948. Law School papers.

23 Letter from Frank Scott to W.P.M. Kennedy, 19 September 1947. Law School papers.

24 Letter from W.P.M. Kennedy to Frank Scott, 22 September 1947. Law School papers.

25 Letter from Cecil Wright to Frank Scott, October 1947. McGill Archives: Law School papers.

26 Vincent MacDonald to W.P.M. Kennedy, 11 December 1947. University of Toronto Archives: Law School papers.

27 Report of the Canadian Law Teachers Meeting, Montreal, 30 August 1948. Library and Archives Canada: CALT papers.

28 See Philip Girard, *Bora Laskin: Bringing Law to Life* (Toronto: University of Toronto Press, 2005) at 185 et seq.

29 Letter from W.P.M. Kennedy to Sidney Smith, 24 April 1946. University of Toronto Archives: Law School papers.

30 Letter from Vincent MacDonald to W.P.M. Kennedy, 11 March 1946. Law School papers.

31 Letter from W.P.M. Kennedy to Vincent MacDonald, 13 March 1946. Law School papers.

32 Oxford University Press Canada has no record of any contract with Kennedy: email from Phyllis Wilson to Martin Friedland, 13 November 2018.

33 Letter from W.P.M. Kennedy to Vincent MacDonald, 13 March 1946. University of Toronto Archives: Law School papers.

34 Letter from Vincent MacDonald to W.P.M. Kennedy, 11 December 1947. Law School papers.

35 Ibid.

36 Letter from W.P.M. Kennedy to Vincent MacDonald, 15 December 1947. Law School papers.

37 Letter from Clerk of the Special Committee to W.P.M. Kennedy, 11 July 1947. Law School papers.

38 Letter from W.P.M. Kennedy to Louis St. Laurent, 29 September 47. Law School papers.

39 Christopher MacLennan, *Toward the Charter: Canadians and the Demand for a National Bill of Rights, 1929–1960* (Kingston: McGill-Queens University Press, 2004) at 86.

40 Letter from W.P.M. Kennedy to Louis St. Laurent, 29 September 1947. University of Toronto Archives: Law School papers.

41 Letter from Escott Reid to W.P.M. Kennedy, 26 November 1947. Law School papers.

42 W.P.M. Kennedy, 'Ave Atque Vale' (1949) 8 *University of Toronto Law Journal* 1.

43 Cecil Wright, 'Stone on Jurisprudence' (1947) 7 *University of Toronto Law Journal* 227.

44 W.P.M. Kennedy, Review of *Interpretations of Modern Legal Philosophies*, ed. Paul Sayre (1947) 14 *University of Chicago Law Review* 519.

24 The Struggle Continues

1 Letter from W.P.M. Kennedy to Cecil Wright, 26 February 1948. University of Toronto Archives: Law School papers.

2 Letter from Cecil Wright to W.P.M. Kennedy, 1 March 1948. Law School papers.

3 Letter from W.P.M. Kennedy to John Falconbridge, 18 December 1947. Law School papers.

4 This chapter is drawn primarily from Ian Kyer and Jerome Bickenbach, *The Fiercest Debate: Cecil A. Wright, the Benchers, and Legal Education in Ontario 1923–1947* (Toronto: University of Toronto Press, 1987); Martin Friedland, *The University of Toronto: A History* (Toronto: University of Toronto Press, 2002); and to a lesser extent from Philip Girard, *Bora Laskin: Bringing Law to Life* (Toronto: University of Toronto Press, 2005); David Vanek, *Fulfilment: Memoirs of a Criminal Court Judge* (Toronto: University of Toronto Press, 1999); Martin Friedland, *My Life in Crime and Other Academic Adventures* (Toronto: University of Toronto Press, 2007); and Christopher Moore, *The Law Society of Upper Canada and Ontario's Lawyers, 1797–1997* (Toronto: University of Toronto Press, 1997).

5 Cassels was also the solicitor for the University of Toronto, whom we met in the earlier discussion of the Underhill affair.

6 Kyer and Bickenbach, *The Fiercest Debate* at 201–2.

7 Ibid. at 204.

8 Ibid. at 203.

9 Kyer and Bickenbach, *The Fiercest Debate* at 206.

10 Ibid. at 207.

11 Ibid. at 209.

12 Bora Laskin said many years later that he had not seen the full report until Professor Robin Harris showed it to him in 1977 when conducting an oral interview of Laskin. Girard, *Bora Laskin* at 164, 568n31; Bora Laskin, 'Cecil A. Wright: A Personal Memoir' (1983) 33 *University of Toronto Law Journal* 148–61 at 154.

13 'More Practical Training Decreed for Lawyers' *Globe and Mail*, 21 January 1949.

14 Quoted in Kyer and Bickenbach, *The Fiercest Debate* at 212.

15 'Hall Pushed Back 25 Years, Osgoode Dean Says, Quits' *Globe and Mail*, 22 January 1949. About a month later, Wright wrote in a legal magazine: 'To insist that the only method of obtaining a legal education in Ontario is to compel students to serve as glorified office boys in Toronto offices seems to us definitely wrong.' Osgoode, he went on, had reverted to an 'outmoded system of what is in reality a poor quality night school run during two hours of the day.' Cecil Wright, 'The Legal Education Controversy in Ontario – The Academic View' (1949) 44 *The Brief* 177–83 at 182.

16 'Law School Dispute to Split Profession Lawyers Prophesy' *Varsity*, 24 January 1949.

17 Moore, *The Law Society of Upper Canada* at 231–2.

18 Friedland, *The University of Toronto* at 439.
19 Bora Laskin, oral interview (interviewed by Robin Harris, 1977). University of Toronto Archives.
20 Girard, *Bora Laskin* at 167.
21 Kyer and Bickenbach, *The Fiercest Debate* at 230.
22 Ibid. at 227–8.
23 Ibid. at 221.
24 Letter from Eugene LaBrie to Cecil Wright, 20 May 1949. University of Toronto Archives: Law School papers.
25 Philip Girard's oral interview with Eugene LaBrie, 1 October 2000 at 64.
26 Kyer and Bickenbach, *The Fiercest Debate* at 227.
27 Letter from W.P.M. Kennedy to Sidney Smith, 25 May 1949. University of Toronto Archives: Law School papers.
28 This section is drawn primarily from Kyer and Bickenbach, *The Fiercest Debate*; Friedland, *The University of Toronto*; and to a lesser extent from Girard, *Bora Laskin*; Vanek, *Fulfilment*; and Moore, *The Law Society of Upper Canada and Ontario's Lawyers*.
29 John Arnup, 'The 1957 Breakthrough' (1982) 16 *The Law Society Gazette* 180–203 at 182.
30 Ibid. at 181.
31 Ibid. at 183–4.
32 Kyer and Bickenbach, *The Fiercest Debate* at 233–4; Moore, *The Law Society of Upper Canada* at 254–5.
33 Moore, *The Law Society of Upper Canada* at 252. The faculty also included practitioner Willard Estey, later a Supreme Court of Canada justice, who had taught at the University of Saskatchewan and had earlier been highly recommended to Kennedy as a full-time law teacher. Letter from F.C. Cronkite to W.P.M. Kennedy, 28 April 1947. University of Toronto Archives: Law School papers.
34 Kyer and Bickenbach, *The Fiercest Debate* at 248–53; Arnup 'The 1957 Breakthrough' 180–203.
35 Kyer and Bickenbach, *The Fiercest Debate* at 249.
36 Ibid. at 258.
37 Arnup, 'The 1957 Breakthrough' at 198.
38 Ibid. at 180.
39 In the course of my research for this book, I happened to come across the little-known fact that Rand had been offered and turned down the deanship of the University of Alberta over thirty years earlier. Letter from Ivan Rand to H.M. Tory, 7 June 1921; Letter from Roscoe Pound to H.M. Tory, 17 June 1921. University of Alberta Archives.
40 H.W. Arthurs, 'The Affiliation of Osgoode Hall Law School with York University' (1967) 17 *University of Toronto Law Journal* 194–204.
41 Ibid. at 198.

42 Caesar Wright obtained a clarification from the University of Toronto Senate that it was, indeed, a faculty, not a school.

43 Kyer and Bickenbach, *The Fiercest Debate* at 223–4.

44 Accommodating these students created problems. Students who had entered the four-year Honour Law program at the University of Toronto in 1947 – sixty students had entered that year – were given no credit by Osgoode, but Wright allowed them to enter second year of his new program. All but one did so. But those who entered the Honour Law course the following year, 1948, were given two year's credit by Osgoode, thus – strangely – getting their call to the bar a year before the students who had entered the Honour Law program the year before them. University of Toronto, Faculty of Law, 'Brief History of the Law School: Class of 1951,' https://www.law.utoronto.ca/about/brief-history/class-1951.

45 'Proposed changes in the courses in the School of Law leading to the Degree of Bachelor of Laws, and in the Combined Course in the Faculty of Arts and the School of Law leading to the Degrees of B.A. in law and of the LL.B.' Memo, 1949. University of Toronto Archives: Law School papers.

46 Girard, *Bora Laskin* at 171, 569n1.

47 Kyer and Bickenbach, *The Fiercest Debate* at 222–3.

48 Letter from Frank Rust to W.P.M. Kennedy, 31 December 1948. University of Toronto Archives: Law School papers.

49 Girard, *Bora Laskin* at 171–2.

50 Letter from Cecil Wright to David Vanek, 15 June 1949. University of Toronto Archives: Law School papers.

51 Girard, *Bora Laskin* at 173.

52 'Proposed changes in the courses in the School of Law leading to the Degree of Bachelor of Laws, and in the Combined Course in the Faculty of Arts and the School of Law leading to the Degrees of B.A. in law and of the LL.B.' Memo, 1949. University of Toronto Archives: Law School papers. See also Girard, *Bora Laskin* at 177.

53 Meeting of Convocation Minutes, 29 June 1949 at 124. Law Society of Ontario Archives. Christopher Moore describes this request for recognition from the university as a 'critical misstep' by the university. Moore, *The Law Society of Upper Canada* at 253.

54 Kyer and Bickenbach, *The Fiercest Debate* at 227–8.

55 Martin Friedland, *My Life in Crime and Other Academic Adventures* (Toronto: University of Toronto Press, 2007) at 30–3.

56 Vanek, *Fulfilment* at 175.

57 Philip Girard's oral interview with Eugene LaBrie, 1 October 2000 at 65.

58 'School of Law Graduates' (1952) 54 *Torontonensis*.

59 'School of Law Graduates' (1953) 55 *Torontonensis*; 'School of Law Graduates' (1954) 56 *Torontonensis*.

60 Friedland, *The University of Toronto* at 440.

61 Letter from W.P.M. Kennedy to Frere Kennedy, 16 October 1953; Letter from W.P.M. Kennedy to Frere Kennedy, 21 March 1952. University of Toronto Archives: Friedland papers.

62 Girard, *Bora Laskin* at 177–8.

63 Quoted in Friedland, *The University of Toronto* at 441.

64 Ibid.

65 'Students Picket Benchers for Varsity Recognition' *Varsity*, 28 February 1952.

66 Friedland, *The University of Toronto* at 441.

67 Friedland, *My Life in Crime and Other Academic Adventures* at 27.

68 Kyer and Bickenbach, *The Fiercest Debate* at 226; Friedland, *The University of Toronto* at 441.

69 Friedland, *The University of Toronto* at 438.

70 'Lord Devlin, Dean Griswold, Chief Justice McRuer and Principal Corry Join Lieutenant-Governor in Opening Ceremonies for Law Building' *The Bulletin*, 1 November 1962.

71 Author's oral interview with Eugene LaBrie, 28 June 2016.

72 Friedland, *The University of Toronto* at 441.

73 Friedland, *The University of Toronto* at 442, citing Bissell Diary, 30 January 1967.

74 'Dean of U of T Law School, Scholar, Cecil A. Wright Dies' *Globe and Mail*, 25 April 1967.

75 Kyer and Bickenbach, *The Fiercest Debate* at 270.

76 Quoted in Friedland, *My Life in Crime and Other Academic Adventures* at 194–5.

77 Ibid. at 196.

78 In *My Life in Crime and Other Academic Adventures*, I set out in some detail some of the things I tried to do with respect to teaching, scholarship, student life, and funded programs.

79 Friedland, *The University of Toronto* at 442.

25 Retirement

1 'They Should Get Together' *Globe and Mail*, 12 March 1949.

2 Letter from J.D. MacDonald to Harold Innis, 23 February 1949. University of Toronto Archives: Law School papers.

3 'Dean Kennedy Bows Out' *Globe and Mail*, 18 March 1949.

4 Philip Girard's oral interview with Eugene LaBrie, 1 October 2000 at 90.

5 'To Study at Cambridge' *Globe and Mail*, 31 October 1947.

6 Letter from W.P.M. Kennedy to Charles Bourne, 7 November 1947. University of Toronto Archives: Law School papers.

7 Letter from W.P.M. Kennedy to Vincent MacDonald, 15 November 1947. Law School papers.

8 Letter from C.E. Higginbottom to W.P.M. Kennedy, 19 May 1949. Law School papers.

9 Letter from W.P.M. Kennedy to Sidney Smith, 17 May 1949. Law School papers.

10 College Council Minutes, 5 May 1949. St John's College Archives: 5 May 1949, CM1909/4:(CM1863/3). I am grateful to Fiona Colbert, biographical librarian of St. John's, for her assistance.

11 Letter from W.P.M. Kennedy to Mrs. N.W. Rowell, 16 February 1948. University of Toronto Archives: Law School papers.

12 Gilbert Kennedy oral interview (interviewed by Maryla Waters 1983, Victoria University) at 15.

13 See chapter 19, 'The Changing Law School.'

14 Philip Girard, *Bora Laskin: Bringing Law to Life* (Toronto: University of Toronto Press, 2005) at 173. Letter from W.P.M. Kennedy to Frere Kennedy, 16 October 1953. University of Toronto Archives: Kennedy correspondence in Friedland papers.

15 Letter from C.E. Higginbottom to Cecil Wright, 27 March 1953. University of Toronto Archives: Law School papers.

16 Letter from W.P.M. Kennedy to Frere Kennedy, 19 January 1952. University of Toronto Archives: Kennedy correspondence in Friedland papers.

17 Girard, *Bora Laskin* at 173.

18 Wright's personal notes, September 1955. University of Toronto Archives: Cecil Wright papers.

19 Letter from Irwin Cass to H.J. Cody, 20 February 1950. University of Toronto Archives: Law School papers.

20 'Law Club – Annual Dinner.' University of Toronto Archives: Cecil Wright papers, 23 March 1953.

21 'Law Club – Annual Dinner.' Cecil Wright papers, 15 March 1956; 'Law Club – Annual Dinner.' Cecil Wright papers, 15 March 1957.

22 Leslie Frost to W.P.M. Kennedy, 19 January 1950. Archives of Ontario: Frost papers.

23 R.C.B. Risk, *A History of Canadian Legal Thought: Collected Essays* (Toronto: University of Toronto Press, 2006) at 214.

24 Girard, *Bora Laskin* at 153.

25 Ian Kyer and Jerome Bickenbach, *The Fiercest Debate: Cecil A. Wright, the Benchers, and Legal Education in Ontario 1923–1947* (Toronto: University of Toronto Press, 1987) at 276.

26 Bora Laskin, 'Law Teachers and Law Teaching in Canada' (1953) 2 *Journal of the Society of Public Teachers of Law* 115.

27 University of Toronto Convocation program, 5 June 1953. University of Toronto Archives: Friedland papers.

28 Letter from Sidney Smith to W.P.M. Kennedy, 11 June 1953. University of Toronto Archives: Sidney Smith papers.

29 Letter from Sidney Smith to W.P.M. Kennedy, 11 June 1953. Sidney Smith papers.

30 Letter from William Ebenstein to W.P.M. Kennedy, 11 May 1948. University of Toronto Archives: Law School papers.

31 Letter from W.P.M. Kennedy to William Ebenstein, 19 May 1948. Law School papers.

32 Girard, *Bora Laskin* at 173, 569n8.

33 'Speech Made on the Opening of the New Law School – Flavelle House 1962.' University of Toronto Archives: Cecil Wright papers.

34 'Opening – 1962.' Cecil Wright papers.

35 Letter from Eugene LaBrie to Martin Friedland, 4 March 1993. University of Toronto Archives: Friedland papers.

36 Author's personal knowledge. The Weir Foundation presently funds an Art Museum. See 'New Incorporation of Riverbrink Art Museum,' http://riverbrink.org/new-incorporation/.

37 See generally, Roger Graham, *Old Man Ontario: Leslie M. Frost* (Toronto: University of Toronto Press, 1990), chapters 9 and 10.

38 Letter from Leslie Frost to W.P.M. Kennedy, 20 November 1950; Agenda for Dominion Provincial Conference, 25 September 1950. Archives of Ontario: Frost papers, RG 75–40; Letter from W.P.M. Kennedy to Frere Kennedy, 25 November 1950. University of Toronto Archives: Kennedy correspondence in Friedland papers.

39 *Proceedings of the Constitutional Conference of Federal and Provincial Governments, January 10–12, 1950* (Ottawa: King's Printer, 1950) at 6–7. See also page 18 in Canadian Intergovernmental Secretariat, *First Ministers' Conferences 1906–2004*, http://publications.gc.ca/collections/collection_2015/scic-cics/CE34-2-2004-eng.pdf.

40 W.P.M Kennedy, *The Constitution of Canada: An Introduction to Its Development, Law and Custom*, 2nd ed. (London: Oxford University Press, 1938) at 529–30.

41 *Proceedings of the Constitutional Conference of Federal and Provincial Governments, January 10–12, 1950* at 7–11.

42 Ibid. at 13.

43 Letter from Leslie Frost to W.P.M. Kennedy, 19 January 1950. Archives of Ontario: Frost papers RG75–40.

44 *Proceedings of the Constitutional Conference of Federal and Provincial Governments, (Second Session) September 25–28, 1950* (Ottawa: King's Printer, 1950). See also pages 19–20 in Canadian Intergovernmental Secretariat, *First Ministers' Conferences 1906–2004*, http://publications.gc.ca/collections/collection_2015/scic-cics/CE34-2-2004-eng.pdf.

45 'Talks on Constitution Ended with an Agreement on Many Phases: PM' *Globe and Mail*, 29 September 1950.

46 Ibid.

47 *Proceedings of the Constitutional Conference of Federal and Provincial Governments, December 4–7, 1950* (Ottawa: King's Printer, 1951) at 66. See also page 21 in Canadian Intergovernmental Secretariat, *First Ministers' Conferences 1906–2004*, http://publications.gc.ca/collections/collection_2015/scic-cics/CE34-2-2004-eng.pdf. See generally, J.H. Perry, *Taxation in Canada* (Toronto: University of Toronto Press, 1953); J.H. Perry, *Taxes, Tariffs and Subsidies: A History of Canadian Fiscal*

Development, 2 vols. (Toronto: University of Toronto Press, 1957) at 555 et seq.; and J.H. Perry, *A Fiscal History of Canada – The Postwar Years* (Toronto: Canadian Tax Foundation, 1989).

48 *Proceedings of the Constitutional Conference of Federal and Provincial Governments, December 4–7, 1950* at 3.

49 E.J. Young to W.P.M. Kennedy, 10 November 1950. Ontario Archives: Frost papers.

50 See page 21 in Canadian Intergovernmental Conference Secretariat, *First Ministers' Conferences: 1906–2004*, http://publications.gc.ca/collections/collection_2015/scic-cics/CE34-2-2004-eng.pdf.

51 Letter from W.P.M. Kennedy to Frere Kennedy, 25 November 1950. University of Toronto Archives: Kennedy correspondence in Friedland papers.

52 'Frost Favors Joint Occupancy Pact for Income, Corporation Tax Fields' *Globe and Mail*, 5 December 1950.

53 Section 91(3) of the BNA Act provides for federal jurisdiction over 'the raising of Money by any Mode or System of Taxation.' And section 92(2) of the BNA Act provides for provincial jurisdiction over 'Direct Taxation within the Province in order to the raising of a Revenue for Provincial Purposes.'

54 It is a complicated story: see Claude Bélanger, 'Canadian Federalism, the Tax Rental Agreements of the Period of 1941–1962 and Fiscal Federalism from 1962 to 1977,' http://faculty.marianopolis.edu/c.belanger/quebechistory/federal/taxrent.htm. See also Peter Russell, *Canada's Odyssey: A Country Based on Incomplete Conquests* (Toronto: University of Toronto Press, 2017) at 286–7.

55 'Ontario First Province to Agree to Federal Old-Age Pension Plan' *Globe and Mail*, 8 December 1950.

56 'New Age Pension Plan May Operate in 1952' *Globe and Mail*, 9 December 1950.

57 Unlike in the United States, as political scientist Andrew Stark recently wrote, 'in the 1950s, Canadian politicians recognized that if its federation was to survive, it would have to include a system for redistributing resources to the country's poorer regions. Only then could [workers in marginal industries] continue to earn a livelihood while staying in the far-flung regions where their families had for generations been rooted, instead of flooding to cities to look for work and incurring harsh psychological and economic costs.' Andrew Stark, 'Oh, Canada,' *New York Review of Books*, 19 July 2018, reviewing, among other books, Michael Adams, *Could It Happen Here? Canada in the Age of Trump and Brexit* (Toronto: Simon and Schuster, 2017). See also J.H. Perry, *Taxes, Tariffs and Subsidies: A History of Canadian Fiscal Development*, 2 vols. (Toronto: University of Toronto Press, 1955 and 1957); and Richard Bird, 'Policy Forum: Equalization and Canada's Fiscal Constitution: The Tie that Binds?' (2018) 66 *Canadian Tax Journal*, https://papers.ssrn.com/sol3/papers.cfm?abstract_id=3309707.

58 Letter from W.P.M. Kennedy to Frere Kennedy, 9 December 1950. University of Toronto Archives: Kennedy correspondence in Friedland papers.

59 Letter from Leslie Frost to W.P.M. Kennedy, 9 October 1951. Ontario Archives: Frost papers.

60 Gilbert Kennedy oral interview at 15.
61 W.P.M. Kennedy, 'The Office of Governor General in Canada' (1953) 31 *Canadian Bar Review* 994 at 999.
62 Former governor general Adrienne Clarkson states in her memoir *Heart Matters*: 'Even many politicians don't seem to know that the final authority of the state was transferred from the monarch to the Governor General in the Letters Patent of 1947, thereby making Canada's government independent of Great Britain.' *Heart Matters* (Toronto: Penguin Canada, 2007).
63 (1949) 8 *University of Toronto Law Journal*.
64 (1951) 9 *University of Toronto Law Journal* at v–vi, 304.
65 (1953) 10 *University of Toronto Law Journal* at 248–54.
66 Marshall Jeanneret, *God and Mammon: Universities as Publishers* (Toronto: Macmillan of Canada, 1989) at 177–8.
67 Ibid. at 178.
68 Ibid. at 178–9.
69 Martin Friedland, *The University of Toronto: A History* (Toronto: University of Toronto Press, 2002) at 497–8.

26 Final Days

1 Letter to Pauline Kennedy, 2 November 1954. University of Toronto Archives: Law School papers.
2 *Globe and Mail*, 11 April 1956.
3 Letter from W.P.M. Kennedy to Frere Kennedy, 2 May 1956. University of Toronto Archives: Kennedy correspondence in Friedland papers.
4 'Deaths' *Globe and Mail*, 27 April 1966. Her address was 321 Bloor St. West.
5 'Deaths' *Globe and Mail*, 27, 28, and 29 April 1966. The Rev. Canon R.P. Dann and The Rev. E.G. Bull officiated.
6 Letter from W.P.M. Kennedy to Frere Kennedy, 8 August 1954. University of Toronto Archives: Kennedy correspondence in Friedland papers.
7 Letter from W.P.M. Kennedy to Frere Kennedy, 6 August 1956. Kennedy correspondence in Friedland papers.
8 All information concerning Pauline Kennedy's will was found in Pauline Kennedy, Last Will and Testament of Pauline Kennedy, 24 June 1954. MS 869, reel 13, grant 22646, folio 2896. Archives of Ontario, York County Surrogate Court Records.
9 'School of Law Diamond Jubilee, 1887–1947' (1947) 47 *University of Toronto Monthly* at 126.
10 Email from Barbara Laskin to Martin Friedland, 28 March 2018.
11 Email from Betty Kennedy to Martin Friedland, 29 October 2015.
12 In a *Canadian Bar Review* comment in 1951 on a constitutional law case that had been decided by the Supreme Court of Canada after appeals to the Privy Council had been abolished, Gilbert wrote that he wondered 'whether we shall ever be more than children of the old country, taking all-over leads, except for occasional

pranks, from mother's apron strings.' Gilbert Kennedy, 'Case and Comment' (1951) 10 *Canadian Bar Review* at 93.

13 These publications include 'The Legal Effects of Adoption' (1955) 33 *Canadian Bar Review* 751; and 'Adoption in the Conflict of Laws' (1956) 34 *Canadian Bar Review* 507.

14 Gilbert Kennedy oral interview (interviewed by Maryla Waters 1983, Victoria University) at 168–9.

15 Author's oral interview with Betty Kennedy.

16 Gilbert Kennedy oral interview at 170; 'Honorary Degree Recipients,' *University of Victoria*, https://www.uvic.ca/universitysecretary/senate/honorary/recipients/index.php.

17 'The Best Premier B.C. Never Had' *Globe and Mail*, 17 November 2009.

18 Gilbert Kennedy oral interview (interviewed by Richard Vogel 1983, Victoria University) at 240.

19 Ibid. at 288.

20 Email from Maryla Waters to Martin Friedland 7 July 2013.

21 'Doreen Elizabeth Kennedy' [obituary] *Victoria Times Colonist*, 26 April 2019. https://www.legacy.com/obituaries/timescolonist/obituary.aspx?n=doreen-elizabeth-kennedy&pid=192712102.

22 Letter from Gilbert Kennedy to Martin Friedland, 13 September 1972. University of Toronto Archives: Friedland papers.

23 Whitby Psychiatric Hospital, 'Clinical Record,' for Beatrice Kennedy, Dr. Zeman entry, 19 June 1970.

24 Whitby Psychiatric Hospital (Whitby, Ontario), 'Clinical Record,' for Beatrice Kennedy, Dr. Zeman entry, 5 August 1970.

25 Whitby Psychiatric Hospital, 'Outpatient Information Form,' for Beatrice Kennedy, Dr. Zeman entry, 25 February 1976.

26 Author's oral interview with Frere Kennedy, 2 April 2015.

27 Letter from Frere Kennedy to Martin Friedland, 31 December 2014.

28 St. Mark's Anglican Church, Emsdale. Burial records obtained from Perry Township municipal office.

29 Author's oral interview with Shelagh Lindsey, 2 May 2014.

30 Gilbert Kennedy oral interview (interviewed by Maryla Waters 1983, Victoria University)at 62.

31 Letter from W.P.M. Kennedy to Frere Kennedy, 13 May 1954. University of Toronto Archives: Kennedy correspondence in Friedland papers.

32 Letter from W.P.M. Kennedy to Frere Kennedy, 15 September 1955. University of Toronto Archives: Kennedy correspondence in Friedland papers.

33 'Walter Howard Frere Kennedy' [obituary] *Globe and Mail*, 17 April 2019.

34 'C.C. (Cas) Lindsey' *Canadian Society of Zoologists*, n.d. https://cars.fisheries.org/legends-of-canadian-fisheries-science-and-management/#Casimir%20Lindsey.

35 'Bio for Cas Lindsey, "Altered Territories" Exhibition' *Prince of Wales Northern Heritage Centre*, Yellowknife, and *Norman Wells Historic Centre*, Norman Wells, 1995.

36 Letter from Shelagh Kennedy to Marshall McLuhan, 18 September 1966. Library and Archives Canada: Marshall McLuhan papers.

37 'Shelagh Lindsey' *University of British Colombia*, 16 March 2015, https://ceremonies.ubc.ca/2015/03/16/shelagh-lindsey/.

38 Thomas W. Cooper, 'McLuhan and Innis: The Canadian Theme of Boundless Exploration' (1987) 37 *Journal of Communication* 153–61 at 153.

39 Correspondence from Peter Russell with the author, 15 November 2018.

40 'Upsizing and Downsizing' *The Bulletin*, April 2007 at 7.

41 Author's oral interview with Shelagh Lindsey, 2 May 2014.

42 Author's oral interview with Cas Lindsey, 3 November 2014.

43 Letter from Cas Lindsey to Martin Friedland, 4 August 2016.

44 'Shelagh Lindsey Obituary' *Vancouver Sun*, 7 March 2015.

45 'Deaths' *Globe and Mail*, 13 August 1963.

46 Author's oral interview with Eugene LaBrie, 28 June 2016.

47 Author's oral interview with Frere Kennedy, 25 May 2016.

48 Author's oral interview with Eugene LaBrie, 28 June 2016.

49 Author's oral interview with Frere Kennedy, 2 April 2015.

50 Letter from W.P.M. Kennedy to Frere Kennedy, 5 January 1952. University of Toronto Archives: Kennedy correspondence in Friedland papers.

51 Letter from W.P.M. Kennedy to Frere Kennedy, 24 March 1953. Kennedy correspondence in Friedland papers.

52 Marshall Jeanneret, *God and Mammon: Universities as Publishers* (Toronto: Macmillan of Canada, 1989) at 177–8.

53 Letter from W.P.M. Kennedy to Frere Kennedy, 13 May 1954. University of Toronto Archives: Kennedy correspondence in Friedland papers.

54 Letter from W.P.M. Kennedy to Frere Kennedy, 25 July 1954. Kennedy correspondence in Friedland papers.

55 Letter from W.P.M. Kennedy to Frere Kennedy, 8 August 1954. Kennedy correspondence in Friedland papers.

56 Letter from W.P.M. Kennedy to Frere Kennedy, 25 July 1954. Kennedy correspondence in Friedland papers.

57 Letter from W.P.M. Kennedy to Frere Kennedy, 2 May 1956. Kennedy correspondence in Friedland papers.

58 Letter from W.P.M. Kennedy to Frere Kennedy, 24 July 1957. Kennedy correspondence in Friedland papers.

59 Author's oral interview with Shelagh Lindsey, 2 May 2014.

60 Letter from W.P.M. Kennedy to Frere Kennedy, 4 March 1953. University of Toronto Archives: Kennedy correspondence in Friedland papers.

61 Letter from W.P.M. Kennedy to Frere Kennedy, 6 August 1956. Kennedy correspondence in Friedland papers.

62 Philip Girard's oral interview with Eugene LaBrie, 1 October 2000 at 128.

63 Letter from W.P.M. Kennedy to Frere Kennedy, 14 January 1951. University of Toronto Archives: Kennedy correspondence in Friedland papers.

64 Letter from W.P.M. Kennedy to Frere Kennedy, 24 February 1956. Kennedy correspondence in Friedland papers.
65 Letter from W.P.M. Kennedy to Frere Kennedy, 8 August 1954. Kennedy correspondence in Friedland papers.
66 Letter from W.P.M. Kennedy to Frere Kennedy, 24 July 1957. Kennedy correspondence in Friedland papers.
67 'Deaths' *Globe and Mail*, 13 August 1963.
68 Girard's oral interview with Eugene LaBrie, 1 October 2000 at 67.
69 Author's oral interview with Frere Kennedy, 2 April 2015. The year was likely 1970
because the St. Mark's records in the Perry Township municipal office say simply
that his 'year of death' was 1970, which is not correct.
70 'Deaths' *Globe and Mail*, 13 August 1963.

27 Summing Up

1 'College Dean Taught Law, Church History' *Globe and Mail*, 13 August 1963.
2 Eugene LaBrie, 'William Paul McClure Kennedy: 1879–1963' (1964) 15 *University
of Toronto Journal* 255–8 at 255.
3 Ibid. at 257.
4 Emails to and from Mary Seeman, December 2018. I am, of course, grateful for her
assistance.
5 Gilbert Kennedy oral interview (interviewed by Maryla Waters 1983, Victoria
University) at 56.
6 Father Edmund McCorkell oral interview (interviewed by Richard Alway 1974, St.
Michael's College) at 76–9. St. Michael's Archives. See chapter 4.

Photo Credits

Pictures of the pages of books and reports where the source is obvious have not been included in the photo credits below.

1 **Coming to America** – St. Francis Xavier College: St. Francis Xavier College Archives; Sara Josephine Cameron's gravestone: http://sites.rootsweb. com/~cansacem/regina/6094.jpg.

2 **Earlier Years** – Charles William Kennedy, W.P.M. Kennedy's father: Nigel McCullough, Northern Ireland; Second Presbyterian Church, Lurgan: ©Sinton Family Trees; Great Library, Trinity College Dublin: Google Images; John Pentland Mahaffy: W.B. Stanford and R.B. McDowell, *Mahaffy: A Biography of an Anglo-Irishman* (1971).

3 **After Trinity College Dublin** – House of the Resurrection, Mirfield, England: Wikimedia Commons, https://commons.wikimedia.org/wiki/ File:House_of_the_Resurrection,_Mirfield.jpg; Bishop Walter Howard Frere: C.S. Phillips et al., *Walter Howard Frere: Bishop of Truro* (1947).

4 **St. Michael's College** – St. Michael's College and St. Basil's Church: St. Michael's College Archives, photo 1870, no. 6; Father Henry Carr: St. Michael's College Archives, photo 1905, no. 2; Robert Falconer: J.G. Greenlee, *Sir Robert Falconer: A Biography* (1988); George Wrong: U of T Archives, B91-0010 (neg. 2001-31.).21; Yonge Street Gate, Mount Pleasant Cemetery: Mount Pleasant Cemetery website.

5 **Turning to the Canadian Constitution** – A.H.F. Lefroy: Law Society of Ontario Archives; Sopwith Camel aircraft: U of T Archives, A65-0004/0.221.

6 **Pauline Simpson** – Pauline Simpson's yearbook entry: *Torontonensis*, vol. 21, *1919* at 24; Simpson family: Simpson family photos; George Wrong: Robert Bothwell, *Laying the Foundation: A Century of History at the University of Toronto* (1991); Robert MacIver: Ian Drummond, *Political Economy at the University of Toronto: A History of the Department, 1888–1982* (1983).

7 *The Constitution of Canada* **and Beyond** – Wm Tyrell advertisement: Oxford University Press Archives; Canon Henry Cody: William C. White, *Canon Cody of St. Paul's Church* (1953).

8 *Deeks v. H.G. Wells* – Florence Deeks and her sister: Brian McKillop, *The Spinster and the Prophet: Florence Deeks, H.G. Wells, and the Mystery of the Purloined Past* (2000); H.G. Wells: National Portrait Gallery, London; University College Cloisters: U of T Archives, A65-00041.177; 77 Spadina Road: Keith Garrett photo; Lord J.R. Atkin: G. Lewis, *Lord Atkin* (1983).

9 **The Irish Constitution** – Hugh Kennedy: ©The Honourable Society of King's Inns; Irish Constitutional Committee: Internet Archive, *The Irish Constitution Explained*; Darrell Figgis: Internet Archive, *Recollections of the Irish War*; University of Toronto Convocation Hall: Toronto Public Library; W.P.M. Kennedy: *Toronto Daily Star*, 7 March 1924.

10 **Productive Years** – Kennedy on hammock: University of Toronto Archives, Friedland papers; Edmund Walker: Victor Ross, *A History of the Canadian Bank of Commerce* (1920); Alexander Brady: Drummond, *Political Economy at the University of Toronto* (1983).

11 *Lord Elgin* **and More** – Viscount Richard Haldane: *Richard Burdon Haldane: An Autobiography* (1929); Lord Elgin: W.P.M. Kennedy, *Lord Elgin* (1926); Mackenzie King: Library and Archives Canada, c75053; William Lyon Mackenzie: www.uppercanadahistory.ca.

12 **Starting a Law Program** – Robert Falconer: U of T Archives, A65-0004/135.28; Norman ('Larry') MacKenzie: P.B. Waite, *Lord of Point Grey: Larry MacKenzie of U.B.C.* (1987); E.J. Urwick: Drummond, *Political Economy at the University of Toronto* (1983); Lyman Duff: Law Society of Upper Canada Archives, P291; Clara Brett Martin: Law Society of Upper Canada Archives, P291; Frederick Auld: Philip Girard, *Bora Laskin: Bringing Law to Life* (2000); A.H.G. Sinclair: BiblioArchives/LibraryArchives, www.flickr.com/photos/lac-bac/4678560711; Jacob Finkelman: U of T Archives, A78-0041/0007(08).

13 **Creating a Law School** – 45 St. George Street: Girard, *Bora Laskin* (2000); Bora Laskin: Law Society of Ontario Archives; G. Arthur Martin: Law Society of Ontario Archives; William Howland: Law Society of Ontario Archives; Oliver Wendell Holmes: Library of Congress Prints and Photography Division; C.A. Wright: Ian Kyer and Jerome Bickenbach, *The Fiercest Debate: Cecil A. Wright, the Benchers, and Legal Education in Ontario, 1923–1957* (1987); John Falconbridge: Osgoode Hall Law School Archives.

15 **Running a Law School** – Canon Henry Cody and Premier George Henry: Ontario Archives, AO 1929 F980; C.B. Macpherson: Drummond, *Political Economy at the University of Toronto* (1983); Honour Law class of 1936: Law Society of Ontario Archives; Moffatt Hancock: Faculty of Law composite; Newton Rowell: Margaret Prang, *N.W. Rowell: Ontario Nationalist* (1975).

16 **Encouraging Scholarship** – W.P.M. Kennedy: Kennedy family photos; Harold Fox: Harold G. Fox Education Fund.

17 **Rethinking Canadian Constitutional Law** – W.P.M. Kennedy: Lafayette College Archives.

18 **The War Years** – King George VI and Queen Elizabeth: U of T Archives, A73-0050/002P; Frank Underhill: R.D. Francis, *Frank Underhill: Intellectual Provocateur* (1986); W.P.M. Kennedy: Kennedy family photos; Hart House library, 1942: U of T Archives, A73-0050/002.

19 **The Changing Law School** – J.K. Macalister: Douglas LePan, *Macalister, or Dying in the Dark* (1995); Bora Laskin: Girard, *Bora Laskin* (2000); First-year Honour Law class 1942: Law Society of Ontario Archives; Carl Morawetz: Morawetz family photos; Peter Fuld: Faculty of Law photos; Ivy Lawrence: Faculty of Law photos.

20 **The Cottage** – W.P.M. and Pauline Kennedy, Kennedy at cottage gate, and the Kennedy cottage: Kennedy family photos; Kennedy in front of cottage: U of T Archives, Friedland papers.

21 **The Family** – Pauline Kennedy: Kennedy family photos; Gilbert and W.P.M. Kennedy: Law Society of Ontario Archives; Beatrice Kennedy and Judy Friedland: U of T Archives, Friedland papers; Frere Kennedy: Kennedy family photos; Shelagh Lindsey and W.P.M. Kennedy: Kennedy family photos.

22 **Sidney Smith Arrives** – Henry Cody and Sidney Smith: Ontario Archives, AO 1929 F980; Cecil Wright and Sidney Smith: Kyer and Bickenbach, *The Fiercest Debate* (1987); Eugene LaBrie: Faculty of Law composite picture, 1952; David Vanek: David Vanek, *Fulfillment: Memoirs of a Criminal Court Judge* (1999); Benchers: Kyer and Bickenbach, *The Fiercest Debate*.

23 **Final Years as Dean** – W.P.M. Kennedy: Kennedy family photos; Frank Scott: Library and Archives Canada PA -1162815; Vincent MacDonald: Dalhousie University Archives.

24 **The Struggle Continues** – John Willis, Bora Laskin, and Cecil Wright: U of T Faculty of Law Archives; Cumberland House: U of T Archives, A78-0041/018(20); Law student demonstration: Faculty of Law website; Flavelle House: City of Toronto Archives, SC 568, item 340; Official opening of Flavelle House: Kyer and Bickenbach, *The Fiercest Debate* (1987).

25 **Retirement** – Convocation procession, 1953: U of T Archives, Friedland papers; Pauline and W.P.M. Kennedy at cottage: U of T Archives, Friedland papers; Dominion-Provincial Conference: *Toronto Daily Star* 5 December 1950.

26 **Final Days** – Frere, Beatrice, and Shelagh at cottage with the Friedlands: U of T Archives, Friedland papers; Frere at age ninety: U of T Archives, Friedland papers; St. Paul's Anglican Church (website): http://www.stpaulsbloor.org/st-pauls-bloor-street-history; St. Mark's Cemetery: U of T Archives, Friedland papers.

Index

Page numbers in *italics* refer to illustrations.